NINTH EDITION
MODERN HUMAN RELATIONS AT WORK

RICHARD M. HODGETTS

Florida International University

KATHRYN W. HEGAR

Mountain View College

THOMSON

SOUTH-WESTERN

Australia · Canada · Mexico · Singapore · Spain · United Kingdom · United States

Modern Human Relations at Work, 9e

Richard M. Hodgetts and Kathryn W. Hegar

VP/Editorial Director:
Jack W. Calhoun

VP/Editor-in-Chief:
Michael P. Roche

Senior Publisher:
Melissa S. Acuña

Acquisitions Editor:
John Szilagyi

Developmental Editor:
Emma F. Guttler

Marketing Manager:
Jacquelyn Carrillo

Production Editor:
Chris Sears

Manufacturing Coordinator:
Rhonda Utley

Technology Project Editor:
Kristen Meere

Media Editor:
Karen L. Schaffer

Senior Designer:
Chris Miller

Production House:
The GTS Companies/York, PA
Campus

Book Designer:
Chris Miller

Cover Images:
© Corbis

Printer:
Thomson-West
Eagan, MN

For more information
contact South-Western,
5191 Natorp Boulevard,
Mason, Ohio, 45040.
Or you can visit our Internet site
at: http://www.swlearning.com

SPECIAL DEDICATION FOR THE 9th EDITION

Dr. Richard M. Hodgetts (1942–2001)

Distinguished Professor, Prolific Author, Renowned Consultant, and Inspiring Teacher

Your scholarship touched our minds; your teaching touched our souls; and your contributions touched the very fabric of Management. Your impact will be felt forever!

Dr. Kathryn W. Hegar

To my husband, Henry W. Hegar, for your strength, faith and encouragement through out this project and many others over the years. I am truly blessed to have you in my life. You are my foundation and inspiration.

To my daughters, Sonya and Jill, who over the years have been both my best critics and supporters in all of my professional projects. I am proud to have watched you grow into beautiful, talented, and successful women. Your support will always be treasured and my love for you will always be present.

Brief Contents

Contents

Part Three
The Technical System   159

Preface

As always, the original intent of the book remains paramount: to provide an up-to-date textbook for readers who are novices in the area of human relations or for practitioners with little formal training in the subject. For the ninth edition of *Modern Human Relations at Work,* approximately 20 percent new material was added, representing both new trends and additional information on important concepts previously discussed.

Key Changes

This edition examines the most interesting human relations developments of the early millennium. Many of these issues, although not found in other human relations textbooks, relate to current topics discussed in today's newspapers and magazines. Examples include the impact of technology in the workplace, the development of knowledge-based organizations, the use of total quality management tools and techniques for developing and maintaining organizational efficiency and effectiveness, the use of charismatic and transformational leadership in managing a diverse workforce, ways of dealing effectively with cultural diversity, and steps that firms must take to become world-class organizations. The purpose of examining these topics is to merge the concepts of human relations theory and human relations practice. *Theory* explains why things are done the way that they are; *practice* describes what is being done. No study of human relations can be effective without considering both areas.

How This Book Will Help You

The primary objective of the book is to familiarize you with the field of human relations, pointing out ways this information can be of personal value. For the most part, the text is written from the standpoint of human relations in organizations, as this is the setting in which most adults have the greatest need for such information. However, much of the material is also applicable to your own life. In particular, this book will provide you with four major benefits:

1. *Fact—not intuition.* The information in this book is based on fact. In gathering the material for each chapter, information was drawn from research studies and reports from industry, government, and other major organizations. Although the art of human relations is not overlooked, it is not allowed to interfere with proven, scientific findings.

2. *Comprehensiveness.* This book is thorough in its coverage of the field of human relations. All the major areas of concern to the modern manager, as well as many minor ones, are addressed. The ninth edition has also been thoroughly updated and revised to include the very latest available human relations material.

3. *Applicability.* Information that is too theoretical has limited value for practicing managers and others who are interested in learning about human relations. In this book, every effort has been made to show how the information can be applied.

4. *Personal insights.* Each chapter contains short quizzes and exercises to provide feedback on your own personal human relations style or philosophy. The purpose of these exercises is to supplement the text material and involve you in further analysis of the concepts under discussion, thereby increasing your insights.

Some of the information presented here will be of value almost immediately, as in the case of material related to communication effectiveness. Some of the material may be of more value a little later in your career, as in the case of the material related to performance evaluation and appraisal. Yet, regardless of where your career path takes you, the material in this book is designed to help you meet the human relations challenges you will face in the world around you.

Organization and Features

Human relations is a broad field composed of many practices and concepts. *Modern Human Relations at Work* focuses on the most important of these. The organization of the book flows from the human element to the work environment and then considers methods by which to achieve an effective fit between people and organizational systems. The last section of the book addresses ways in which readers can apply these ideas to help manage their careers, now and in the future. In accordance with this flow, the book is divided into six parts as follows:

- Part i examines the foundation of human relations.
- Part ii focuses on social systems involving individuals, groups, and informal organizations.
- Part iii addresses technical systems, including technology, productivity, and quality improvement.
- Part iv discusses the administrative system and topics such as leadership, appraisal, and rewards.
- Part v focuses on behavioral effectiveness, including communication and management of conflict and change.
- Part vi addresses future human relations challenges and the value of this information to the reader.

IN ACTION

In each chapter, a "Human Relations in Action" box illustrates the practical application of chapter concepts. Subjects include how to increase achievement drive, network for effectiveness, become a whole-brain thinker, deal with technology, lead effectively, conduct an effective performance appraisal, become a more active listener, and manage more effectively with fewer resources. Each chapter further addresses in a practical manner key issues facing organizations through another type of "In Action" box: "Cultural Diversity in Action" or "Ethics and Social Responsibility in Action." Each of these boxes examines human relations issues that are emerging challenges in today's business world.

SELF-EXAMINATION EXERCISES

A "Time Out" exercise is included in each chapter. "Time Out" exercises encourage the reader to participate, gain personal insights, and consider key concepts in a more in-depth manner.

EXAMPLES AND CASES

In-depth examples and cases are included in every chapter to illustrate the practical and realistic application of its concepts. Each chapter opens with several in-depth examples that relate to the main topics of the chapter. At the end of each chapter, you will find two cases. One is a short case and another is a consulting case, "You Be the Consultant," which provide opportunities for readers to apply the information from the chapter to resolve human relations problems. These cases add weight to the relevancy of the topics covered in the chapter.

EXPERIENTIAL EXERCISES

One or more experiential exercises are included in each chapter. These exercises are designed to be performed in a group setting. They present a forum in which students can discuss concepts, resolve problems, and consider results in real-life situations.

NEW WORLD WIDE WEB EXERCISES

Several *Visit the Web* exercises are included in each chapter. Web exercises encourage students to explore company Web sites and perform analyses. Research skills are used to answer human relations questions about actual companies.

Instructor Ancillary

South-Western will provide complimentary supplements or supplement packages to those adopters qualified under our adoption policy. Please contact your sales representative for more information.

INSTRUCTOR'S MANUAL WITH TEST BANK AND TRANSPARENCY MASTERS (ISBN: 0-324-23652-2)

A comprehensive Instructor's Manual and Test Bank is available to assist in lecture preparation. Included are suggestions for class schedules, research papers, research sources, and chapter outlines. The Test Bank includes approximately 100 questions per chapter to assist in writing examinations. Types of questions include true/false, multiple choice, essay, and matching questions. Fifty Transparency Masters, which contain prominent figures from the text also are included in the Instructor's Manual.

EXAMVIEW

Available on the Instructor's Resource CD-ROM, ExamView contains all of the questions in the printed test bank. This program is an easy-to-use test creation software compatible with Microsoft Windows. Instructors can add or edit questions, instructions, and answers, and select questions (randomly or numerically) by previewing them on the screen. Instructors can also create and administer quizzes online, whether over the Internet, a local area network (LAN), or a wide area network (WAN).

POWERPOINT LECTURE PRESENTATION SOFTWARE

An asset to any instructor, the lectures provide outlines for every chapter, graphics of the illustrations from the text, and additional examples providing instructors with a number of learning opportunities for students. The PowerPoint Lecture Presentations are available as downloadable files on the text support site and on the Instructor's Resource CD-ROM.

INSTRUCTOR'S RESOURCE CD-ROM (ISBN: 0-324-23655-7)

Key instructor ancillaries (Instructor's Manual, Test Bank, ExamView and PowerPoint slides) are provided on CD-ROM, giving instructors the ultimate tool for customizing lectures and presentations.

COMPANION WEB SITE

Modern Human Relations at Work's web site at http://hodgetts.swlearning.com/ provides a multitude of student resources. Additional supplementary materials are included on a password-protected site for instructors. Student Resources include downloadable PowerPoint files slides from the web site for note taking, and links to news articles and hot marketing topics are provided for extra student research.

Instructor Resources include downloadable Instructor's Manual and Test Bank files available in Microsoft Word 2000 format and Adobe Acrobat format. Also, downloadable PowerPoint presentation files are available in Microsoft PowerPoint 2000 format.

TEXTCHOICE: MANAGEMENT EXERCISES AND CASES

TextChoice is the home of Thomson Learning's online digital content. TextChoice provides the fastest, easiest way for you to create your own learning materials. South-Western's Management

Exercises and Cases database includes a variety of experiential exercises, classroom activities, management in film exercises, and cases to enhance any management course. Choose as many exercises as you like and even add your own material to create a supplement tailor fitted to your course. Contact your South-Western/Thomson Learning sales representative for more information.

eCOURSEPACKS

Create a tailor fit, easy to use and online companion for any course with eCoursepacks, from Thomson companies South-Western and Gale. eCoursepacks gives educators access to content from thousands of current popular, professional, and academic periodicals, as well as NACRA and Darden cases, and business and industry information from Gale. In addition, instructors can easily add their own material with the option of even collecting a royalty. Permissions for all eCoursepack content are already secured, saving instructors the time and worry with securing rights.

eCoursepacks online publishing tools also save time and energy by allowing instructors to quickly search the databases to make selections, organize all the content, and publish the final online product in a clean, uniform, and full color format. eCoursepacks is the best way to provide current information quickly and inexpensively. To learn more visit: http://ecoursepacks.swlearning.com

ACKNOWLEDGEMENTS

Many thanks go to those who offered insights and assistance in writing this book. I would especially like to thank Dr. Fred Luthans of the University of Nebraska, Lincoln; Dr. Jane Gibson of Nova Southeastern University; Dr. Gary Dessler and Dr. Karl Magnusen of Florida International University; Dr. Regina Greenwood of Kettering University; and Dr. Julia Teahen of Baker College, who provided continuous encouragement in this effort.

I would like to thank those who read, reviewed, and commented on portions of this text and the previous incarnations, including:

John Adamski II, Indiana College
Joy D. Andrews, Indiana Vocational Technical College
Stephen C. Branz, Triton College
Kathleen A. Bigelow, Cambridge College
J. E. Cantrell, De Anza College
Delores Cauthen, Webster University
Renee L. Cohen, Southwestern Community College
Ronald M. Gordon, Florida Metropolitan University
Carol P. Harvey, Assumption College
Lorene B. Holmes, Jarvis Christian College
Marilyn A. Hommertzheim, Seward County Community College
Jeffrey S. Hornsby, Ball State University
James R. Hostetter, Illinois Valley Community College
Steven Jennings, Highland Community College
Deborah Jones, Hi-Tech Institute
Howard J. Klein, Ohio State University

William M. Lally, Webster University
Miles LaRowe, Laramie County Community College
Gary D. Law, Cayahoga Community College
David Lydick, Paul D. Camp Community College
Edward Miller, Kean University
Peter J. Moustatson, Montcalm Community College
David Murphy, Madisonville Community College
Jim Murtha, Hartford Community College
Robert O. Nixon, Pima Community College
William S. Pangle, Metro Community College
Gary W. Piggrem, DeVry-Columbus
Bob Redick, Lincoln Land Community College
Robert E. Seyfarth, Lock Haven University
Susan Thompson, Palm Beach Community College
Ronald C. Young, Kalamazoo Valley Community College
Edward Valsi, Oakland Community College

To the publishing staff who provided assistance and guidance—Mike Roche, Editor in Chief; Melissa Acuña, Senior Publisher; John Szilagyi, Executive Editor; Jacquelyn Carrillo, Marketing Manager; Emma Guttler, Developmental Editor; Chris Sears, Production Editor and Chris Miller, Senior Designer—thank you for your hard work.

About the Authors

Richard M. Hodgetts, Ph.D., (1942–2001) was the Suntrust Professor of Strategic Management at Florida International University (FIU). He had earned a Ph.D. from the University of Oklahoma, an M.B.A. from Indiana University, and a B.S. from New York University. Dr. Hodgetts published more than 125 articles and papers on a variety of topics ranging from entrepreneurship to strategic management to total quality management. His articles appeared in a host of journals, including the Academy of Management Journal, Academy of Management Executive, Organizational Dynamics, Business Horizons, Personnel, Personnel Journal, and the Journal of Small Business Management. He was also the author or coauthor of 49 books. Some of the most recent include International Business, International Management, Modern Human Relations at Work, Measures of Quality and High Performance, and Effective Small Business Management, Seventh Edition, which he wrote with Dr. Kuratko.

Dr. Hodgetts consulted for a number of Fortune 500 firms and provided training for a wide variety of companies, including AT&T Technologies, Delco Electronics, Eastman Kodak, General Electric, IBM, Motorola, Texas Instruments, and Wal-Mart. He also lectured in Mexico, Venezuela, Peru, Chile, Jamaica, Trinidad, Denmark, Kuwait, and at a host of U.S. colleges and universities.

Professor Hodgetts was a Fellow of the Academy of Management and a past member of the Academy's Board of Governors. He served on three academic review boards and wrote a biweekly column on small business and entrepreneurship in the Ft. Lauderdale Sun Sentinel.

Kathryn W. Hegar, Ph.D., Professor of Management, has taught courses in management since 1970. She has received recognition and awards for her innate ability to teach and create an environment for learning. Dr. Hegar also has been recognized for her innovation in developing nontraditional courses in management that fit the lifestyle of today's students who live a busy hectic life. Several of her other accomplishments include, authoring 30 programs for the initial telecourse in business, It's Everybody's Business, that was used for over 10 years by colleges across the country and in the military services; initiating the development of self-paced courses in management at Mountain View College at a time when traditional methods were being promoted; piloting the first online course in organizational behavior for the Dallas County Community College District, which ultimately resulted in the District offering a degree online; and instructing management courses online, including organizational behavior, from distant locations. For over twenty-five years, Dr. Hegar has helped students learn and progress in their courses by authoring a number of pedagogical materials.

Dr. Hegar has been the recipient of many distinguished awards, including "Collegiate Teacher of the Year," Post-Secondary Teacher of the Year," "Minnie Stevens Piper Professorship Award nomination," and "Innovator of the Year." She is listed in Who's Who in the South and Southwest, 17th Edition; World's Who's Who in Women, 6th Edition; Personalities of the South; International Register of Profiles, 6th Edition; and The International Who's Who of Contemporary Achievement.

For several years, Dr. Hegar worked outside the academic world. In addition she conducted workshops and training seminars in supervision and management for major companies. She has participated in and held offices in professional organizations at all levels. Dr. Hegar has served as the president of the United States Chapter of the International Society for Business Education, which meets in a different country each year. Her travels include Austria, Scotland, Germany, Canada, England, Spain and Mexico. Other interests include photography, arts, crafts, quilting, and spending time with her husband and family on their farm in Central Texas.

In Remembrance

Dr. Richard M. Hodgetts (1942–2001)

On November 17, 2001, Richard M. Hodgetts passed away after a $3^1/_2$ year battle with bone marrow cancer. The field of Management lost one of its most significant contributors.

Dr. Hodgetts was a prolific author. He authored or co-authored over 45 college texts in numerous languages and published over 125 articles in some of the world's most highly regarded research journals. He was also the editor of *Journal of Leadership Studies* and served on a number of editorial boards.

Dr. Hodgetts was an active Academy of Management member his whole career, serving as program chair in 1991, chair of the Management History Division, editor of the New York Times special issue of *Academy of Management Executive*, and served on the Board of Governors from 1993–1996. Dr. Hodgetts received the prestigious Distinguished Educator Award from the Academy of Management.

Besides his tremendous contributions to the knowledge base of Management, Dr. Hodgetts was a truly outstanding teacher. He won every Distinguished Teaching Award offered at both his first job for 10 years at the University of Nebraska and his home school for the past 25 years at Florida International University, including Faculty Member of the Year by the Executive MBA students the year of his passing. He literally developed thousands of students at all levels –undergraduate, MBA, executive development and doctoral—and millions across the world were influenced by his texts and innovative distance education materials and courses. Simply put, he was the ultimate educator!

Dr. Hodgetts distinguished career as a scholar and educator, was exemplified in his humor, his dedication to research, his genuine interest in his students, his compassion, and his true courage. Millions of students and practicing leaders have been and will continue to be influenced by his teaching and publications. His legacy will live forever!

Introduction

part **i**

The purpose for this part of the book is to introduce you to the area of human relations and its impact on the organization. Effective human relations give employees a sense of usefulness and a sense of pride. Human relations also helps managers meet company goals.

Why do people act the way they do on the job? Understanding motivation is fundamental to understanding why people behave the way they do. Motivation is at the heart of human relations and is how managers get people to do their job. Life on the job can be more enjoyable by making work more meaningful, thus improving performance.

THE GOALS OF THIS SECTION ARE TO:

- *Examine the nature of human relations, trace its evolution from industrialism through scientific management up to the present, examine some of the important human relations studies conducted during the last five decades, identify the steps in the scientific method, and discuss the role of behavioral science in human relations.*

- *Study the fundamentals of motivation—movement and motive, identify the basic needs that all people have, explain each of these needs and their importance in the motivation process, study the two-factor theory of motivation and its relevance for the practicing manager, deal with the expectancy theory and its application to motivation, and discuss the practical side of rewards and their relevance to motivation.*

After reading this part of the book, you should have a solid understanding of the nature of human relations, who the people are who study and investigate human relations problems, and how they go about conducting their investigations. You also should know a great deal about motivation and its role in directing, influencing, and channeling behavior at work.

1

The Nature Of Human Relations

Getting work accomplished in a business environment is a complex process that requires understanding human behavior and the context within which the work is to be done. Human relations is at the heart of that process. Therefore, it is important for managers, as well as for workers, to understand the key role human relations plays in the workplace.

AFTER STUDYING THIS CHAPTER, YOU SHOULD BE ABLE TO:

1. Explain human relations and its implications for management.
2. Trace the evolution of human relations thinking from industrialism through scientific management to the present.
3. Compare and contrast the traditional model of the worker with the modern human resources model.
4. Discuss the role of behavioral science in human relations.
5. Describe some of the emerging challenges in the human relations area.

LEARNING OBJECTIVES

①

Explain human relations and its implications for management

②

Trace the evolution of human relations thinking from industrialism through scientific management to the present

③

Compare and contrast the traditional model of the worker with the modern human resources model

④

Discuss the role of behavioral science in human relations

⑤

Describe some of the emerging challenges in the human relations area

Tapping Human Potential

Many organizations today are finding themselves locked in a highly competitive battle for market share, sales revenue, profits, and other bottom-line performance measures. How can they win this battle? The most successful are discovering that they need to implement one critical strategy: Hire the right people with the right talent and then give them the opportunity to unlock their full creative potential. There are three ways in which organizations are doing this.

First, they are providing everyone with a chance to succeed. For example, Pitney-Bowes, the multibillion-dollar global provider of informed mail and messaging management, is a strong advocate of diversity and equal opportunity. Almost 40 percent of its workforce is female, as are nearly 30 percent of its managers. Additionally, 40 percent of those who report directly to the chief executive officer (CEO) are women, and 38 percent of the corporate officers are female. This effort to be inclusive rather than exclusive began back in the 1940s, when the chairman of the board made the decision that the makeup of the employees in the manufacturing plant would mirror that of the population in Stamford, Connecticut, where it was located. This policy has continued over the years. For the years 1999–2001, Pitney Bowes ranked among *Fortune* magazine's "American Best Companies for Minorities" and also ranked among "The Top 100 Companies for Hispanics by *Hispanic* magazine. In 2001 and 2002, it ranked among DiversityInc.com's "Top 50 Companies for Diversity." Even though, according to *Fortune* magazine, women are moving up in manufacturing, the United States still has a long way to go in making the fullest use of women. Young women who head Fortune 500 companies include Cindy B. Slater, Maytag Corporation; Marissa Peterson, Sun Microsystems; and Carole C. Rich, Hershey Chocolate USA.

The complexion of the workforce is becoming more culturally diverse. For example, at Motorola's annual International Day Celebration in 2001, employees representing nineteen cultures attended; whereas, a year later, employees attending represented thirty-four cultures. Building and sustaining an inclusive work culture is one of Motorola's highest priorities and is the reason for bringing them together to celebrate their differences, as well as their similarities. Companies that appreciate differences and capitalize on each worker's potential will enjoy a competitive advantage in a global market. In 2001 and 2002 it ranked among DiversityInc.com's "Top 50 Companies for Diversity."

Pitney-Bowes is not alone in its effort to ensure equal opportunity. Xerox, MasterCard, Goldman Sachs, IBM, AT&T, and Kraft Foods, to name but a half-dozen, all have programs in place to ensure that their workforces are diverse and that women and people of color are given the same opportunities as are white men. Of course, there is still a long way to go. Recent research reveals that women still account for only 10 percent of senior managers in Fortune 500 firms, hold fewer than 4 percent of the top jobs from executive vice president through CEO, and represent fewer than 3 percent of the biggest corporate earners. Women of color fare far worse. According to a recent study of female managers, only 6.6 percent are African Americans, 5 percent are Hispanic, and a mere 2.5 percent are Asian. On the other hand, a growing number of companies are coming to realize that diversity is a critical issue, and those firms that hire and tap the abilities of women and people of color are more likely to prosper, whereas those who fail to do so are going to be left behind.

A second way in which organizations are winning the competitiveness challenge is by hanging on to their aging workforce. Rather than offering attractive early retirement programs, they are allowing workers to stay as long as they can do the job. Research shows that older workers tend to be highly productive. One reason is that they learn how to do their jobs well and then develop shortcuts and other time-saving features that allow them to produce even more output. A second reason is that they tend to be more careful and thus are involved in fewer accidents and take fewer sick days. When using machinery, they follow the operating rules carefully, so they make fewer mistakes and experience fewer accidents. When the weather turns bad, they bundle up and protect themselves from the elements, so they suffer fewer colds and other maladies. As a result, they tend to be in good health. In fact, research by the Andrus Gerontology Center at the University of Southern California reports that people older than fifty tend to use fewer health care benefits than do workers with school-age children. Still another advantage of older employees is that they are less likely to change jobs or move from their communities, so the company can count on them for the future. Most important, major companies such as Motorola appreciate older workers because "they add a dimension that younger people can't: They have experience, and they understand business." A recent study in California revealed that the number of people age fifty to sixty-four will increase 10 percent by 2010 and 47 percent by 2020. The life expectancies of all groups of people will rise to 82.2 years by 2040. Based on these findings, there will be a large pool of older people from which to select workers. This older pool of people will be a dominant force that will change our notions about work, retirement, and pensions.

A third way in which organizations are winning the competitiveness challenge is by continuing to invest in employee training and knowledge acquisition. Peter Drucker predicts that knowledge will be the key resource of the Next Society—the era that lies ahead. In fact, American firms spend more on training and education than does the entire U.S. educational system (from kindergarten to postdoctoral studies). Such companies as Motorola require that all their employees have at least forty hours of training per year, and many smaller firms report that they spend as much as 5 percent of their gross revenues on training and development programs. Recently Motorola implemented a Web-based technical training program for engineers. Online training is growing and will play an important role in how workers learn about their jobs in the next decade. Older people in the workforce will need their skills continually updated. New work patterns will emerge. This helps to explain why America is now the most competitive nation in the world. Notes one U.S. Nobel Prize-winning economist in *Business Week*:

> The U.S. tends to spend more than other nations on knowledge and high-level skills because its economy is the most advanced in the world. For example, a much larger fraction of American teenagers receive some college education than youths in most European countries. This is why international comparisons of investment that focus only on physical capital understate the efforts of the U.S. and other nations that spend a lot on knowledge—and overstate those of nations that emphasize plant and equipment at the expense of people.

These three approaches to tapping human potential—giving everyone a chance to succeed, keeping older employees, and training and developing the workforce so that it is on the cutting edge of knowledge—are key human relations strategies. They are also proving to be critical factors in today's competitiveness battle.

Sources: Stephanie N. Mehta, "What Minority Employees Really Want," Fortune, July 10, 2000, pp. 181–186; Joseph B. White and Carol Hymowitz, "Watershed Generation of Women Executives Is Rising to the Top," Wall Street Journal, February 10, 1997, pp. A1, A8; Anne Fisher, "Wanted: Aging Baby-Boomers," Fortune, September 30, 1996, p. 204; and Gary S. Becker, "Human Capital: One Investment Where America Is Way Ahead," Business Week, March 11, 1996, p. 18. Gene Bylinsky and Alicia Hills Moore, "Women Move Up in Manufacturing," Fortune, May 15, 2000; Hans P. Johnson, Ph.D., "Here's Looking at 50: Past, Present, and Future Demographic Structure of California," Paper, Employment and Health Policies for Californians Over 50 Conference, University of California, January, 2000. http://www.pb.com (diversity, awards & recognition); "The Great Peter Drucker Talks About the Next Society and What's Ahead for Each of Us," Bottom Line, Volume 24, Number 3, February 1, 2003. 1–3.

LEARNING OBJECTIVE

① Explain Human relations and its implications for management

Human relations *is the process by which management and workers interact and attain their objectives.*

What Is Human Relations?

The process by which management brings workers into contact with the organization in such a way that the objectives of both groups are achieved is **human relations.** The organization is concerned with such objectives as survival, growth, and profit. The worker is concerned with such objectives as good pay, adequate working conditions, a chance to interact with other personnel, and the opportunity to do interesting and meaningful work. Human relations, then, is concerned with four major areas: the individual worker, the group, the environment in which

HUMAN RELATIONS IN ORGANIZATIONS

The following true-false questions are designed to give you some initial insights regarding your current knowledge of human relations in modern organizations. Read each statement carefully and then choose the correct answer. The key, along with explanations, is provided at the end of the chapter.

T/F 1. When asked what motivates them, most workers put money at the top of their list.

T/F 2. In the long run, a work group with high morale and a basic understanding of job requirements will always outperform a work group with moderate morale and a basic understanding of its job requirements.

T/F 3. While in physics it is true that opposites attract, in human relations just the reverse occurs—that is, people tend to associate with others who do the same jobs, have the same training, or work in the same unit.

T/F 4. The most efficient employees report that they do their best work when placed under high stress.

T/F 5. When it comes to getting and giving information along informal lines, managers tend to use the grapevine more than workers do.

T/F 6. Most top managers are not very intelligent, but they have terrific personalities.

T/F 7. Many managers do not get all their daily work done because the boss overloads them with assignments.

T/F 8. The higher up the organization you go, the greater the amount of job-related stress you will encounter.

T/F 9. The major reason why workers do not have high productivity is that they are lazy.

T/F 10. Most managers say they are very effective two-way communicators, but their subordinates report that the managers seldom listen and are usually interested in only one form of communication—downward.

the work is performed, and the leader responsible for seeing that everything is done properly. In this book, we study human relations from the standpoint of the leader or manager who must influence, direct, and respond to both the people and the work environment. Before we begin our study of human relations, however, two points merit attention.

First, human relations implies a concern for the people, but the effective manager never loses sight of the organization's overall objectives. He or she must be interested in the people, the work, *and* the achievement of assigned objectives. Some managers are so interested in pleasing their people that they never get the work done. Others are overly concerned with the work and spend very little time trying to understand the psychological and sociological aspects of the job. The effective manager balances concerns for people and work. In addition, he or she draws on experience and training in deciding how to use many of the ideas presented in this book.

Second, the effective manager realizes that human relations is important at all levels of the organization, but the way the ideas are applied is *not* always the same. The situation dictates the right way to use human relations ideas.

Much of what we know about people in organizations is a result of careful study. If we were to trace the development of human relations in industry, we would see that two hundred years ago managers knew very little about how to manage their human assets. The next section of the chapter examines the evolution of modern human relations and sets the stage for our study of this area. Before going on, however, take the true-false quiz in the following "Time Out" box and see how much you already know about human relations.

LEARNING OBJECTIVE

*Trace the evolution
of human relations
thinking from industri-
alism through scientific
management to the
present*

②

The Evolution of Human Relations

In industry today, it is common to hear a great deal of talk about human relations and its importance to management. However, a concern for human relations is largely a modern development. This should become clearer as we discuss the three major stages through which business has progressed on its way to developing a philosophy for managing human assets:

1. **The emergence of industrialism.**
2. **The scientific management movement.**
3. **The behavioral management movement.**

The Emergence of Industrialism

Industrialism emerged in England in the latter half of the eighteenth century. New inventions enabled wealthy proprietors of this period to invest their money in efficient machinery that could far outpace people doing similar work by hand. For example, no weaver could hope to match the speed and accuracy of the power loom. The age of machine-made goods had begun. These machines were placed in factories, and a workforce was hired to run the equipment. The same pattern emerged as industrialism spread to the United States.

The primary concern of the factory owners was increased output (see Figure 1.1). However, there was a great deal the owner-managers did not understand about this new work environment. For example, they knew very little about machine feed and speed, plant layout, and inventory control. Nor were they very knowledgeable about the management of people. Some tended to use a paternalistic style, in which they told the workers what was expected of them and rewarded those who "toed the line" by giving them more money than their less cooperative counterparts. Others simply exploited their people in the name of efficiency and profit.

FIGURE 1.1

*Rules Posted in 1872 by the Owner
of a Carriage and Wagon Works*

Starting the New Year Right

1. Office employees will sweep the floors and dust the furniture, shelves, and showcases every day.
2. Each clerk will bring a bucket of water and a scuttle of coal for the day's business.
3. Clerks will fill the lamps, clean the chimneys, and trim the wicks every day and wash the windows once a week.
4. Make your pens carefully. You may whittle the nibs to your own individual taste.
5. This office will open at 7 A.M. and close at 8 P.M. daily, except on the Sabbath, when it will remain closed.
6. Male employees will be given an evening off each week for courting purposes, or two evenings a week if they attend church regularly.
7. Every employee should put aside some of his pay so as to provide for himself in later years and prevent becoming a burden on others.
8. Any employee who smokes Spanish cigars, uses liquor, gets shaved at a barber shop, or frequents pool or public halls will give the employer good reason to suspect his worth, integrity, and honesty.
9. Any employee who has performed his labors faithfully for a period of five years, has been thrifty, attentive to religious duties, and is looked upon by his fellow workers as a substantial and law-abiding citizen, will be given an increase of 5¢ per day in his pay, providing profits allow it.

In the United States, the people who helped the factories and industrial establishments develop more efficient work measures for increasing output brought about what is known as the scientific management movement. Today, of course, we can fault them as being shortsighted. However, they simply did not understand how to manage a factory, so they sought to solve the technical (work) problems facing them, which are simpler to resolve than are the human (people) problems.

Scientific Management Movement

The **scientific management** movement in America had its genesis in the post-Civil War era. The scientific managers were, for the most part, mechanical engineers. Applying their technical expertise in factories and industrial settings, they tried to merge people and the work environment *scientifically* so as to achieve the greatest amount of productivity.

Scientific management *sought to merge the people and the work.*

The interest of these managers in people involved identifying the "one best man" for each job. For example, in a task requiring heavy lifting, they would select the person who had the best combination of strength and endurance. If a machinist was needed to feed parts into a machine, a scientific manager would choose the person with the best hand–eye coordination and the fastest reflexes. If someone lacked the requisite physical skills for a job, he would be scientifically screened out.

The scientific managers sought to increase work efficiency by employing such measures as plant design, plant layout, time study, and motion study. By placing the machinery and materials at strategically determined points on the shop floor, they sought to reduce the amount of time needed to move goods from the raw materials stage to the finished products stage. By studying the rate at which the machines were run and the way in which material was fed, they attempted to achieve optimum machine speeds while eliminating excessive time taken and motion used by the machinists.

Yet scientific management had its problems. Primarily, these problems stemmed from the tendency to view all workers as factors of production rather than as human beings. Many of the scientific managers saw the hired help as mere adjuncts of the machinery, who were to be carefully instructed in how to do the job and then offered more money for productivity increases. Quite obviously, this behavioral philosophy is shallow. Although these early scientific managers may have known a lot about machinery and equipment, they knew very little about human relations in a work setting.

Behavioral Management Movement

If business and industrial organizations were to continue expanding, investigations of individual and group behavior were imperative. It was obvious that management knew a great deal more about its production facilities than it did about the people staffing them. By the 1920s, breakthroughs began to occur. As scientific management moved into its heyday, an interest in the behavioral side of management began to grow. It was becoming obvious that concern for production brought about people-related problems and that the effective manager had to be interested in *both* personnel and work.

Many people believe that modern behavioral management had its genesis in the Hawthorne studies. These studies were started as scientific management experiments designed to measure the effect of illumination on output and wound up lighting the way for much of the behavioral research that was to follow.

THE HAWTHORNE STUDIES

The **Hawthorne studies** were begun late in 1924 at the Hawthorne plant of Western Electric, located near Cicero, Illinois. In all, there were four phases to these studies.

The **Hawthorne studies** *started the modern behavioral management movement.*

Phase 1   The researchers first sought to examine the relationship between illumination and output. Was there an ideal amount of lighting under which workers would maximize their productivity? The researchers sought to answer this question by subjecting some employees to varying amounts of illumination (the test group), while others kept on working under the original level of illumination (the control group). To the surprise of the researchers, the results of these experiments were inconclusive, because output increased in *both* the test group and the control group. They concluded that variables other than illumination were responsible for the increases. At this point, Elton Mayo and a number of other Harvard University researchers took an interest in the problem.

Phase 2   To obtain more control over the factors affecting work performance, the researchers isolated a small group of female workers from the regular workforce and began to study them. The women were told to keep working at their regular pace because the purpose of the experiment was not to boost production but to study various types of working conditions to identify the most suitable environment. During this period, the researchers placed an observer in the test room. This observer was chiefly concerned with creating a friendly atmosphere with the operators so as to ensure their cooperation. He also took over some of the supervision, conversed informally with the women each day, and tried to dispel any apprehensions they might have about the experiment. In turn, the women began to talk more freely among themselves and formed much closer relationships with one another than they had in the regular factory setting. The researchers then began introducing rest breaks to see what effect these would have on output. As productivity increased, the researchers believed that these work pauses were reducing fatigue and thereby improving output. Shorter workdays and workweeks were instituted, and output again went up. However, when the original conditions were restored, output still remained high. This proved that the change in physical conditions could not have been the only reason for the increases in output. After analyzing the possible cause of the results, the researchers decided that the changes in the method of supervision might have brought about improved attitudes and increased output.

Phase 3   At this point, the investigators began to focus on human relations. More than twenty thousand interviews were conducted in which the interviewers were primarily interested in gathering information about the effect of supervision on the work environment. Although the interviewers told their subjects that everything would be kept in strict confidence, the workers often gave guarded, stereotypical responses. This led the interviewers to change from direct to *indirect* questioning, allowing the employee to choose his or her own topic. The result was a wealth of information about employee attitudes. The researchers started to realize that both the person and the group members influenced an individual's performance, position, and status in the organization. To study this impact more systematically, another test group was chosen.

Phase 4   In the fourth phase of the studies, the investigators decided to examine a small group engaged in one type of work. They chose the bank wiring room, in which the workers were wiring and soldering bank terminals. No changes in their working conditions were made, although an observer was stationed in the test room to record employee interactions and conversations. During these observations, several behaviors were noted.

- **The group had an informal production norm that restricted output.**
- **There were two informal groups or cliques in the room, and individual behavior was partially dictated by the norms of the groups.**
- **To be accepted by the group, one had to observe informal rules, such as not doing too much work, not doing too little work, and never telling a superior anything that might be detrimental to an associate.**

RESULTS OF THE HAWTHORNE STUDIES

From their work, the researchers arrived at some conclusions about human behavior in organizations. However, it should be noted that some of their findings were not developed until years later, because more information was needed, whereas other conclusions were only partially accurate. Some of the major conclusions follow.

- Organizations were not just formal structures in which subordinates reported to superiors; they were **social networks** in which people interacted, sought acceptance from and gave approval to fellow workers, and found enjoyment in the work and in the social exchange that occurred while doing the work.
- People will act differently when they know they are being observed.
- Quality of supervision has an effect on the quality and quantity of work.

REFINEMENT OF HUMAN RELATIONS THEORY

The Hawthorne research generated a great deal of interest in human relations. However, some misunderstandings also arose from the findings of both these studies and subsequent research.

Happiness and Productivity Many behaviorists have attacked some of the Hawthorne findings, calling them naive and, in certain cases, erroneous. One of the most vigorous attacks has been made against the supposedly Hawthorne-generated finding that happy workers will be productive workers. This stinging attack has so stigmatized human relations that the term *human relations* is no longer used in many colleges of business, because it carries the connotation that "happiness automatically leads to productivity." The term *organizational behavior* is used instead.

The Role of Participation A second misunderstanding revolved around the role of participation. For many of the post-Hawthorne human relationists, participation was viewed as a lubricant that would reduce resistance to company directives and would ensure greater cooperation.

Over the last fifty years, this view has changed. Human relationists realize that it is important to allow people to participate, feel important, "belong" as members of a group, be informed, be listened to, and exercise some self-direction and self-control. However, this is not enough. All these things ensure that the workers will be treated well, but modern human relationists now realize that personnel want not only to be treated well but also to be *used well*. A good example is found in the currently popular use of job autonomy, in which people are given a task and then allowed to do it without interference or unnecessary direction on the part of the manager. The very subtle yet important difference between these two philosophies is that the latter views people as vital human resources who *want* to contribute to organizational goals and, under the proper conditions, will do so. This is why it has been said that human relations is in a "human resources" era. (See the "Human Relations in Action" box.)

Human Resources Era

The scientific managers had a philosophy of management. Its basic ideas constitute a **traditional model.** Today, this philosophy has given way to a **human resources model** that, in essence, sees personnel as untapped resources containing unlimited potential. Through the effective application of human relations ideas, these resources can be released and used for the overall good of both the organization and the personnel. Table 1.1 provides a summary of the points of contrast between the traditional (scientific management) and the human resources models.

How can modern managers use the human resources model? An answer can be found through an analysis of Rensis Likert's four systems of management, which extend from exploitive autocratic (System 1) to participative democratic (System 4). A brief description of each follows.

System 1: *Exploitive autocratic.* Management has little confidence in subordinates, as demonstrated by the fact that subordinates seldom are involved in decision making. Management makes most of the decisions and passes them down the line, using threats and coercion, when necessary, to get things done. Superiors and subordinates deal with one another in an environment of distrust. If an informal organization develops, it usually opposes the goals of the formal organization.

HUMAN RELATIONS IN ACTION

Commitment Is Everything

One way in which highly successful organizations are now developing their human resources is by helping personnel cope with both their work demands and family responsibilities. In turn, the firms are finding that these efforts are leading to greater employee commitment— and this is true for both small and large organizations. In fact, a recent survey in Business Week found that 42 percent of the respondents said that work had a negative impact on their home life. Yet, at the same time, 51 percent of these individuals reported that their company had high-quality programs for helping them care for their children and elder family members, and this was very important to the workers.

At the DuPont Corporation, for example, an employee's elderly aunt had a stroke and was unable to care for herself. A company-contracted referral agency helped the employee place the woman in a nursing home and, during the time it took to find the facility, the individual worked only half-days. After that, he and his supervisor developed a flexible work shift that allowed the individual to start work at 6:30 A.M., thus letting him visit his aunt as she awoke, put in a full day of work, and then return to the nursing home to feed her dinner and put her to bed. Commenting on all the help the company gave him, the individual recently noted, "I feel like I owe something back." As a result, he is deeply committed to the firm.

Hewlett-Packard is another company that has developed special programs for helping its people deal with personal issues. In every business unit, an action plan has been designed to identify specific work and family issues of employees. If the unit suddenly faces higher consumer demand and must increase the number of work hours or work shifts, it examines how these new work demands will affect the personnel, then reschedules and rearranges the plan so that it will not negatively affect the personal lives of the workers. The company believes that this type of planning leads to more effective work output, less employee burnout, and stronger personnel commitment.

Another example is provided by First Tennessee National Corporation. A few years ago, the company started taking family issues seriously, treating them as strategic business questions. As a result, the bank eliminated many of its old rules and gave employees the authority to determine which work schedules would best suit them. The company also started introducing programs to help employees meet their personal and family demands, including on-site child care, job sharing, and fitness centers. As a result, employee retention at the bank is twice the industry average, retention of customer business is 7 percent higher than that in the industry, and profits have increased 55 percent over the last two years.

At Aetna Life & Casualty, the company has extended unpaid parental leave to six months. As a result, the firm cut the rate of resignations among new mothers by more than 50 percent, thus saving it $1 million annually in hiring and training expenses. At a number of Xerox locations, work responsibility for scheduling shifts has been turned over to the employees, resulting in a sharp decrease in absenteeism coupled with higher productivity. Commenting in Business Week on these recent developments, one observer has noted:

Slowly, employers are beginning to grasp the importance of examples such as Xerox, Hewlett-Packard, and First Tennessee. They had better. Poll after poll indicates that U.S. workers feel a loss of control over their lives. "Companies are seeing they have all these programs, but people are still really stressed out," says Ellen Galinsky, the Families & Work Institute's director. Certainly, employees bear some responsibility for determining their own family balance, but they need help. Companies that recognize the need and adapt work to peoples' lives will win workers' loyalty—and, with that, a competitive edge.

Sources: Karen Springen, "Who'll Care For Dad?" Newsweek, November 6, 2000, pp. 85–86; Joseph B. White and Carol Hymowitz, "Watershed Generation of Women Executives Is Rising to the Top," Wall Street Journal, February 10, 1997, pp. A1, A8; Anne Fisher, "Wanted: Aging Baby-Boomers," Fortune, September 30, 1996, p. 204; and Keith H. Hammonds, "Balancing Work and Family," Business Week, September 16, 1996, pp. 74–80.

TABLE 1.1   *Traditional and Human Resources Models*

Traditional Model	Human Resources Model
Assumptions	**Assumptions**
1. Work is inherently distasteful to most people.	1. Work is not inherently distasteful. People want to contribute to meaningful goals that they helped to establish.
2. What workers do is less important than what they earn for doing it.	2. Most people can exercise far more creative, responsible self-direction and self-control than their present jobs demand.
3. Few want or can handle work that requires creativity, self-direction, or self-control.	
Policies	**Policies**
1. The manager's basic task is to supervise closely and control his or her subordinates.	1. The manager's basic task is to make use of his or her untapped human resources.
2. He or she must break tasks down into simple, repetitive, easily learned operations.	2. He or she must create an environment in which all members may contribute to the limits of their ability.
3. He or she must establish detailed work routines and procedures and enforce these firmly but fairly.	3. He or she must encourage full participation on important matters, continually broadening subordinate self-direction and control.
Expectations	**Expectations**
1. People can tolerate work if the pay is decent and the boss is fair.	1. Expanding subordinate influence, self-direction, and self-control will lead to direct improvements in operating efficiency.
2. If tasks are simple enough and people are closely controlled, they will produce up to standard.	2. Work satisfaction may improve as a byproduct of subordinates making full use of their resources.

System 2: *Benevolent autocratic.* Management acts in a condescending manner toward subordinates. Although there is some decision making at the low levels, it occurs within a prescribed framework. Rewards and some actual punishment are used to motivate personnel. In superior–subordinate interaction, the management is condescending, and the subordinates appear cautious and fearful. Although an informal organization usually develops, it does not always oppose the goals of the formal organization.

System 3: *Consultative democratic.* Management has quite a bit of confidence and trust in subordinates. Although important decisions are made at the top of the organization, subordinates make specific decisions at the lower levels. Two-way communication is evident, and there is some confidence and trust between superiors and subordinates. If an informal organization develops, it either gives support or offers only slight resistance to the goals of the formal organization.

System 4: *Participative democratic.* Management has complete confidence and trust in subordinates. Decision making is highly decentralized. Communication flows not only up and down the organization but also among peers. Superior–subordinate interaction takes place in a friendly environment and is characterized by mutual confidence and trust. The formal and the informal organization often are one and the same.[1]

Workers from each system display different behaviors as illustrated in Figure 1.2. For example, workers in System 4 have complete confidence and trust in the superior, whereas the workers in System 1 have no confidence and trust in the superior.

Likert has found that the most effective organizations have System 4 characteristics and the least effective organizations have System 1 and System 2 characteristics. A number of organizations have converted to System 4 with very good results. For example, a comprehensive organizational

System 2
managers are benevolent autocrats.

System 3
managers are consultative and democratic.

System 4
managers are participative and democratic.

FIGURE 1.2

The System 4 Approach

Characteristic	System 1	System 2	System 3	System 4
Extent to which subordinates have confidence and trust in the superior	Have no confidence and trust in the superior	Have subservient confidence and trust, such as a servant has to a master	Have substantial but incomplete confidence	Have complete confidence and trust
Extent to which superiors behave so that subordinates feel free to discuss important things about their jobs with their immediate superior	Subordinates do not feel free at all to discuss things about the job with their superior	Subordinates do not feel free to discuss things about the job with their superior	Subordinates feel rather free to discuss things about the job with their superior	Subordinates feel completely free to discuss things about the job with their superior
Attitudes toward other members of the organization	Subservient attitudes toward superiors coupled with hostility; hostility toward peers and contempt for subordinates; widespread distrust	Subservient attitudes toward superiors; competition for status resulting in hostility toward peers; condescension toward subordinates	Cooperative, reasonably favorable attitudes toward others in the organization; possibly some competition between peers, resulting in hostility and some condescension toward subordinates	Favorable, cooperative attitudes throughout the organization, with mutual trust and confidence
Satisfaction derived	Usually dissatisfaction with regard to membership in the organization, with supervision, and with one's own achievements	Dissatisfaction to moderate satisfaction with regard to membership in the organization, supervision, and one's own achievements	Some dissatisfaction to moderately high satisfaction with regard to membership in the organization, supervision, and one's own achievements	Relatively high satisfaction throughout the organization with regard to membership in the organization, supervision, and one's own achievements
Amount of cooperative teamwork that is present	None	Relatively little	A moderate amount	Very substantial amount throughout the entire organization
Extent to which forces are present by which to accept, resist, or reject goals	Goals are overtly accepted but covertly resisted strongly	Goals are overtly accepted but often covertly resisted to at least some degree	Goals are overtly accepted but, at times, with some covert resistance	Goals are fully accepted both overtly and covertly
Extent to which there is an informal organization present and supporting or opposing goals of the formal organization	Informal organization is present and opposing the goals of the formal organization	Informal organization usually is present and partially resisting formal goals	Informal organization may be present and may either support or partially resist the goals of the formal organization	Informal and formal organizations are one and the same; all social forces support efforts to achieve organization's goals

change project involving the Weldon Company, a sleepwear manufacturing firm, has been well documented.[2] In this project, substantial changes were made in the organization's work flow, training programs, leadership styles, incentive and reward systems, and use of employees as a source of expertise. The results were impressive. Improvements in all aspects of the organization's functioning occurred and were maintained over an extended period.

System 4 management has been used in a General Motors assembly plant. William F. Dowling, a researcher, reported that the results were improved operating efficiency and decreases in grievances and waste.[3] The program involved:

- **Training sessions on Likert's theory.**
- **Team-building sessions starting at the top of the organization and moving to lower levels.**
- **Improved information and communication flows to the hourly employees.**
- **Changes in the job of first-line supervisors.**
- **Increased participation of hourly employees in job changes.**
- **New approaches to goal setting.**

Quite obviously, System 1 represents the traditional model and System 4 represents the human resources model. At present, there appears to be a decided swing toward the use of Systems 3 and 4. Astute managers know that people provide organizations with their competitive edge. If the enterprise cannot keep its people motivated, these individuals will go elsewhere. As a result, modern managers must be keenly aware of the changing attitudes and values of their personnel.

Behavioral Science and Human Relations

④ LEARNING OBJECTIVE
Discuss the role of behavioral science in human relations

A great deal of what people know about human relations is a direct outgrowth of what they have heard, read, or experienced. Many try to classify this information into the form of rules or principles of behavior.[4] For example, just about everyone knows Murphy's first law: "If anything can go wrong, it will." Another commonly cited behavioral adage comes from Parkinson, who holds, "The time spent on the discussion of any agenda item is in inverse proportion to the sum involved."[5]

Are these laws scientific or are they generalizations that make for an interesting discussion but little else? Human relations experts opt for the latter view, noting that such rules are too broad in coverage to provide much operational assistance. Furthermore, because nothing is more dangerous than generalizing behavioral findings from one situation to another without systematically studying the facts, modern human relationists prefer to use the scientific method in developing their theories and rules about human relations.

The Scientific Method

The greatest barrier to our understanding of human relations can be found within ourselves. Biases, personal opinions, inaccurate perceptions, and errors of judgment all combine to give us our own views of the world. Sometimes these factors lead us to see things as we would like them to be rather than as they really are. For example, a manager who dislikes the union may easily regard the shop steward as a mouthpiece for union dissension and may discount anything the steward says as mere "union rhetoric." Practitioners of modern human relations know that they must step outside themselves and study human behavior in the workplace from an *objective* standpoint. In analyzing behavioral problems, for example, they must rely on the scientific method, because, as Kerlinger has noted:

> The **scientific method** [bolded term mine] has one characteristic that no other method of attaining knowledge has: self-direction. There are built-in checks all along the way to scientific knowledge. These checks are so conceived and used that they control and verify the scientist's activities and conclusions to the end of attaining dependable knowledge outside himself.[6]

The following are generally regarded as the basic steps in the scientific method:

- **Identify the problem.** What exactly is the objective of the entire investigation?
- **Obtain background information.** Gather as much data as possible about the problem under study.

The **scientific method** *is an objective approach to gaining knowledge.*

- **Pose a tentative solution to the problem.** State a hypothesis that can be proved to be either right or wrong and that is most likely to solve the problem.
- **Investigate the problem area.** Using available data—as well as any information gathered through experimentation—examine the problem in its entirety.
- **Classify the information.** Take all the data and classify them in a way that expedites their use and helps to establish a relationship with the hypothesis.
- **State a tentative answer to the problem.** Draw a conclusion regarding the correct answer to the problem.
- **Test the answer.** Implement the solution. If it works, the problem is solved. If not, develop another hypothesis and repeat the process.

Behavioral Research in Human Relations

Behavioral
scientists
*are individuals who
apply their training to
the study of behavior in
organizations.*

A test group
*is a group that is
given some form of
treatment.*

A control group
*is a group that is not
given any treatment.*

Obviously, practitioners of human relations do not have time to make a systematic study of human behavior at work. They are too busy being operating managers. However, there are people in academia and industry who do have time for scientific, behavioral research, including psychologists (who are interested in individual behavior) and sociologists (who are most concerned with group behavior). These highly skilled people are known as **behavioral scientists** and are responsible for a great deal of what we know about human relations in industry.

How is the scientific method applied in the study of human relations? There are numerous ways. One way is to set up **test** and **control groups.** A test group is a group that is given some form of "treatment," such as a training course; whereas a control group is a group that is not given any treatment. For example, a company is considering the value of customer service training for store personnel. Will this training be useful? One way to answer this question is by training some of the personnel and then evaluating the results. The group to be trained would be randomly selected. This means that each of the personnel would have an equal chance of being picked for the training; the company would not send the best or poorest workers, even if it believed that these individuals would profit most from the training. If those with the training were found to be more effective in providing customer service, the behavioral scientist would conclude that the training accounted for these results. If the group members were no more effective than the other personnel in providing customer service, the behavioral scientist would conclude that the training was of no substantive value.

Behavioral scientists also use their knowledge to help managers motivate and lead people. For example, in recent years many managers have been taught how to use effective reinforcement to encourage desired behaviors and to discourage undesired behaviors. Through the effective use of rewards, personnel are motivated to perform their duties quickly and efficiently. Conversely, by withholding rewards, managers motivate personnel to modify their behaviors and to stop doing things (coming in late, filing incomplete reports, failing to complete work on time) that are nonproductive.[7] Behavioral scientists also obtain important human relations information through the use of formal questionnaires: In **structured interviews,** specific questions are asked in a predetermined order, whereas in **unstructured interviews,** the interviewer has questions to be asked but follows no set format, allowing the interview to develop on its own. All these approaches are designed to gather data about workers and working conditions. Through analysis of this information and study of the environment in which the subjects work, it is often possible to draw conclusions about factors that affect communication, attitudes, and work habits.

Structured
interviews
*use specific questions
asked in a predeter-
mined manner.*

Unstructured
interviews
*follow a general direc-
tion but no rigidly set
format.*

Empirical Data and Pop Psychology

The science of modern human relations is based not on generalizations, hunches, opinions, and "gut feelings" but on empirical information that is systematically gathered and analyzed by trained scientists. Much of what you will study in this book is a direct result of such scientists' investigations. At the same time, some behavioral findings seem to combine research with pop psychology, and it can be difficult to know exactly where to draw the line regarding what is accurate and what sounds good but is incorrect. For example, Frank Sulloway conducted research on how birth order affects personality. His concept holds that the order in which someone is born helps to determine how this person will behave. As a result, the oldest brother of three brothers, according to birth-order rank advocates, will be distinctly different from his youngest brother. Here is a sample birth-order rank profile:

Oldest Brother of Brothers   The oldest brother of brothers is considered to be a good worker when he wants to be. He can inspire and lead others competently, and he often takes the greatest hardship upon himself. He can accept the authority of a male supervisor, however, only if he identifies with that authority. Otherwise, he is likely to look for loopholes in the boss's position and to try to undermine the latter's power. Ultimately, the oldest brother of brothers wants the power for himself.

Youngest Brother of Brothers   The youngest brother of brothers is seen as an irregular worker, sometimes excellent in his achievements and at other times highly unproductive. He is at his best in scientific or artistic endeavors, where his environment is taken care of by others. He not only accepts authority but also loves it. However, he tends to be careless with his money and often squanders it.

Are these descriptions accurate? A recent book by a Massachusetts Institute of Technology research scholar argues that later-born children are indeed more innovative and adventurous than are first-born children. In support of his statement, the researcher has identified some well-known business executives and compared their birth-order rank and business behavior. Here are three examples. These people have served as chief executives in one or more companies.

- **Lou Gerstner: A later-born child, Gerstner makes an effort to learn about his customers rather than dictate to them from a position of technological superiority. Like many later-borns, he identifies with his peer group. He also likes to work with people and, when he was in charge of RJR Nabisco, before coming to IBM, he was able to rein in a free-wheeling corporate culture and pay down a stupendous debt load without selling off many assets. Simply put, he is an adaptable individual and uses a leadership style that best fits the situation.**
- **Gerald M. Levin: A later-born child, Levin is soft-spoken and combines an easygoing, personal style with a surprising tenacity and a marked penchant for risk taking. For example, Levin went to work on purchasing Turner Broadcasting even though things at Time Warner still needed to be straightened out and made to run more smoothly. Simply put, he does not hesitate to take risks.**
- **Albert J. Dunlap: A first-born child, Dunlap likes to dominate, is willing to take charge, and does not hesitate to make difficult decisions. When he ran Scott Paper, he sharply cut the workforce and then proceeded to sell away the company, making a fortune for himself in the process. At Sunbeam, he downsized the workforce and focused on productivity measures. Simply put, he is a take-charge person.**

Of the three, Dunlap is the only first-born, and his career has been marked by a willingness to cut the workforce, sell off unprofitable divisions, and make unpopular decisions. The other two executives are more human relations oriented. Is this because they are not first-born children? Answering this question is not easy, because many critics of birth-order rank theory argue that personality and behavior cannot be predicted simply by identifying where one falls in terms of sibling birth order. On the other hand, the theory is interesting if only because it has intuitive appeal—It seems to be accurate, and many people can relate to the general descriptions associated with birth-order rank.

This information may be useful to marketers. For example, "A Dell or a 3M should probably pitch its latest innovations differently to potential first-born buyers than to later-borns.

Any innovation-oriented company not testing this first-born/later-born hypothesis in its own marketing initiatives is doing itself a disservice. Sulloway's Darwin-driven insight gives marketers a powerful way to segment and capture customers."[8]

LEARNING OBJECTIVE

Describe some of the emerging challenges in the human relations area

⑤ Emerging Challenges

Over the last decade, human relations concerns have not remained static. New challenges have emerged, increasing the importance of understanding human relations at work. Four major issues now in the forefront are managing knowledge workers, managing diversity, addressing ethics and social responsibility concerns, and adapting to international and cultural challenges. These areas are interdependent, but each warrants individual consideration because of its major effect on human relations.

Managing Knowledge Workers

Many of the most profitable companies in recent years have been those that have successfully managed what are now being called *knowledge workers.* Focusing their recruiting and development efforts on highly creative and talented employees, these enterprises have been able to develop new products and services that have helped to change the way millions of people live. Dell Corporation, for example, has revolutionized the way companies and individuals buy computers. Now customers can go online, customize their order so that their new computer has exactly what they want (and nothing more), and have delivery within a matter of days. At the same time, Dell has significantly increased its sales while sharply reducing its inventory. Yet none of this would have been possible had the company not been able to attract and retain innovative personnel who brought new ideas to the company and were willing to share this knowledge with their associates.

Another example is General Electric. It is a world-class organization in which all divisions are the best (or among the best) in their respective categories. As a world-class organization, the culture of the company changed. Today, its aircraft engine, appliance, GE Capitol, and industrial systems, among others, are leaders in their field. The acquisition of Honeywell made GE the largest supplier in the aerospace industry, capable of providing aircraft manufacturers with one-stop shopping for everything from engines to complex cockpit software systems.

The company has also shifted away from manufacturing and toward providing higher margin services.[9] In the process, GE has placed a strong emphasis on training, education, and development of managers. Today, its knowledge-based workers are among the best in the world. One reason is because the unions agreed that personnel must be continually trained and kept on the cutting edge of technology. In this way, if a GE business does not perform well and ends up being closed or sold to another firm, the workers can take their knowledge base and go somewhere else. They are marketable. GE needs them more than the workers need the firm, because they are knowledge workers who are in demand.

Siemens is another company using knowledge management to pool the expertise of its workers. At the heart of the operations is a Web site called ShareNet. "So far the payoff has been a dandy: Since its inception in April, 1999, ShareNet has been put to the test by nearly 12,000 salespeople in Siemens' $10.5 billion Information & Communications Networks Group, which provides telecom equipment and services. The tool which cost $7.8 million has added $122 million in sales." The toughest obstacle to overcome is getting employees to change their ways and share. "You have to go in and change processes around. It takes a lot of time," says Greg Dyer, a senior research analyst of knowledge management services at IDC. "While only 6% of global corporations now have company-wide, knowledge-management programs, that will surge to 60% in five years, according to a 2000 survey by the Conference Board. Among the early birds: Chevron, Johnson & Johnson, Royal Dutch/Shell, Ford Motor, and Whirlpool."[10]

Another example is provided by Skandia, a financial services and insurance group based in Stockholm. In a recent survey conducted among industry analysts, the company was ranked as having the strongest brand in Europe and received top marks in the global savings and life insurance area as well as for increasing shareholder value. One reason why the firm is so well ranked is because of its emphasis on developing knowledge workers. In fact, the firm measures the intellectual capital within its organization by looking at how well the company in general, and its people in particular, are performing. In a recent three-year period, Skandia's return on capital increased from 12.2 percent to 21.9 percent, value added per employee rose by 40 percent, and the increase in net premiums almost doubled.

Hewlett-Packard, another example, found the amount of product knowledge required to support complex computer products effectively was exploding. As a result, customers with problems had to be talked through a solution that often involved interactions among hardware, software, and communications products. In meeting this challenge, the firm implemented a knowledge management tool called **case-based reasoning** to capture technical support knowledge and make it available to personnel worldwide. This change resulted in a 67 percent reduction of average call times and a 50 percent reduction in the cost per call, and the company has been able to hire fewer technical support agents because of the help received from the system.[11]

How are companies sustaining a base of knowledge workers? One way is by developing a knowledge-sharing culture. The importance of this strategy has been noted by the Organization for Economic Cooperation and Development, which reports that more than 50 percent of the gross domestic product in major industrial countries is a result of production, distribution, and use of knowledge and information. Commenting on this, one writer recently noted that:

Today's businesses must position themselves within these new economic realities, and leveraging brainpower through knowledge management is one way to jump-start that process. Intel Corp., the Santa Clara, California-based computer chip maker, for example, has designed its knowledge management initiative to propel the company into a leadership position in the new knowledge era. The program initially facilitated the reuse of knowledge in-house and then expanded the knowledge sharing to business partners. Intel's final goal is to start revolutionary new businesses worldwide to become a leader in its field.[12]

Once a company has established its direction, it must create an environment that encourages employees continuously to share what they know. This is done through interactive learning. For example, at Buckman Laboratories International, a manufacturer of specialty chemicals for aqueous industrial systems, top management has built a knowledge-sharing, interactive-learning culture. The firm connects all its associates worldwide via the Internet and allows them to take courses from an electronic learning center. As a result of this global knowledge-sharing system, Buckman has significantly increased its "time to market" so that new goods now account for more than one third of its total revenue, and operating profit per associate has increased by 93 percent in a recent ten-year period.

Similarly, Sun Microsystems in Palo Alto, California, initiated a program to share employees' practical knowledge. Work teams at Sun can use technology-aided, knowledge-sharing tools to work more efficiently. The key to this interactive learning is the give and take that occurs when employees share knowledge.

Hiring highly knowledgeable people and facilitating their sharing of information is going to be critical to organizational success in the twenty-first century. So too will be the challenge of getting these workers to remain on the cutting edge so their knowledge can be used in creating a highly competitive enterprise. Yet the greatest challenge may well be that of retaining these personnel. Unless organizations know what their knowledge workers want, and are willing to provide it, they can end up hiring and training outstanding talent and then seeing these people leave for jobs with competitive firms. For example, recent research shows that many black employees feel that they are not being paid as much as white employees and that their pay increases are not as likely to be tied to performance.[13] Companies will have to ensure that they are treating all their employees equitably. Firms will also have to realize that when personnel are disgruntled, unlike the old days when they would simply quit, they are likely to make things difficult for the company. Some of the most recent approaches that have been reported include:

- **Quitting, but offering to come back as a consultant at three times their former salary.**
- **Telling the human resources department, during the exit interview, negative things about their boss.**
- **Sending an e-mail to senior executives about how bad their boss has treated them.**
- **Asking for an incentive bonus to stay the typically required two weeks and, if they do not get it, leaving immediately.**
- **Recruiting members of their old department to quit and come with them to the new firm.**
- **Going on a break—and never coming back.[14]**

Obviously, effective human relations are going to be of paramount importance to these firms in managing their knowledge-based workers.

Managing Diversity

Workforces are becoming more multiethnic and diverse. Figure 1.3 provides government forecasts on the ethnic breakdown of the U.S. labor force between 1995 and 2050. These data reveal that minorities will account for an increasing percentage of the nation's workforce.

These changes are compelling organizations to review their old human relations philosophies in order to answer the following question: How can we prepare ourselves to manage effectively the workforce of the twenty-first century? The days of managing large groups of white men are

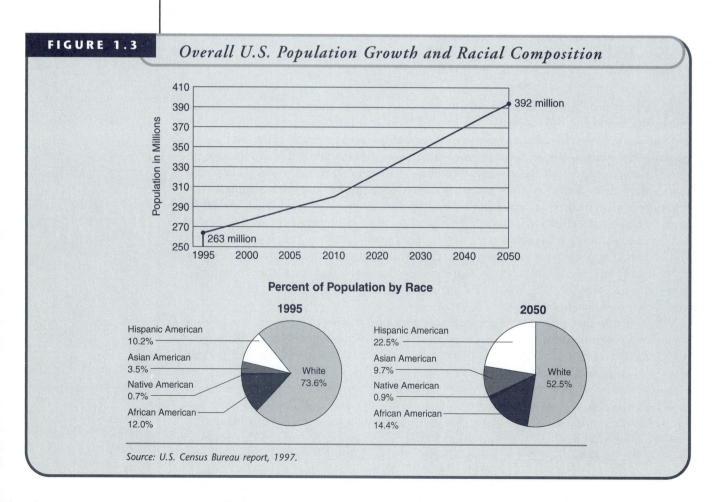

FIGURE 1.3 *Overall U.S. Population Growth and Racial Composition*

Percent of Population by Race

1995

- Hispanic American 10.2%
- Asian American 3.5%
- Native American 0.7%
- African American 12.0%
- White 73.6%

2050

- Hispanic American 22.5%
- Asian American 9.7%
- Native American 0.9%
- African American 14.4%
- White 52.5%

Source: U.S. Census Bureau report, 1997.

a thing of the past. Tomorrow's managers must motivate and lead work groups in which women, Hispanics, African Americans, and Asian Americans are being employed in increasing numbers.

Managers also will manage older workers, because many employees are remaining in the workplace well past their sixty-fifth birthday. A survey by the Society of Human Resource Management and the Commerce Clearing House shows that many companies are aware of this need to manage diversity effectively and are taking steps in this direction. Sixty-one percent of the survey respondents said that the management of diversity was a major obligation of their company, and many of the respondents reported that their firms were hiring women, Hispanics, African Americans, and Asians in record numbers.[15] In turn, this has led companies to consider the following questions: What will our workforce look like in the future? What do we do now to deal effectively with these changes?[16] In some cases, firms are finding that a diversity consultant can be extremely useful in providing advice and guidance.[17] In any event, organizations are discovering that they need to develop policies and guidelines for ensuring equality for their people in the workplace.[18]

Another area in which organizations must examine their human relations practices is that of compensation. The Equal Pay Act was enacted in the United States in 1963 to ensure that women and men were paid the same salary for doing the same job; however, a woman, on average, still earns only seventy-seven cents for every dollar earned by a man. Minority women fare even worse: African-American women earn approximately 64 percent of what white men earn, and Hispanic women earn approximately 55 percent of what white men are paid.[19]

Another diversity issue is the **glass ceiling,** a term used to describe artificial barriers that prevent women from being promoted into the upper ranks of management. No matter how well women perform, in some companies there seems to be an organizational level beyond which they are unable to progress. Recent research reveals that at some of the largest firms in America, women hold only a small percentage of managerial positions. Women in CEO positions are increasing in number. Recently *Fortune* magazine listed fifty of the most powerful women in business. The top ten women in business are listed in Table 1.2.

At Hewlett-Packard "23% of all department and division heads are women and two women are among the company's top five earners." The number of women in corporate-officer positions

A **glass ceiling** *is an artificial barrier preventing women from being promoted.*

TABLE 1.2	*Top Ten Women in Business*		
Rank	**Name**	**Company**	**Title**
1	Carly Fiorina	Hewlett-Packard	Chairman and CEO
2	Betsy Holden	Kraft Foods	Co-CEO
3	Meg Whitman	EBay	President and CEO
4	Indra Nooyi	PepsiCo	President and CFO
5	Andrea Jung	Avon Products	Chairman and CEO
6	Anne Mulcahy	Xerox	Chairman and CEO
7	Karen Katen	Pfizer	EVP; President Pharmaceuticals Group
8	Pat Woertz	ChevronTexaco	EVP, Downstream
9	Abigail Johnson	Fidelity Management & Research	President
10	Oprah Winfrey	Harpo Entertainment Group	Chairman

Source: Adapted from "Most Powerful Women in Business," Fortune, October 14, 2002.

FIGURE 1.4 — Top 20 Best Companies for Minorities

2002 Rank	Company Name	Revenues in Millions
1	Fannie Mae	$50,803
2	Sempra Energy	8,029
3	Advantica	1,391
4	SBC Communications	45,908
5	McDonald's	14,870
6	PNM Resources	2,352
7	Southern California Energy	12,184
8	U.S. Postal Service	65,834
9	Freddie Mac	35,523
10	BellSouth	24,130
11	Union BanCal	2,912
12	Lucent Technologies	25,132
13	Consolidated Edison	9,634
14	Xerox	16,502
15	PepsiCo	26,935
16	Colgate-Palmolive	9,428
17	Wyndham International	2,105
18	Silicon Graphics	1,854
19	Hyatt	3,950
20	Proctor & Gamble	39,244

Source: Adapted from "Best Companies for Minorities," Fortune, July 8, 2002)

in 2000 was still low, only 12.5 percent. And in 2001, women held only 12.4 percent of the board seats in five hundred of the largest companies. Just because a handful of corporate women have made it to the top does not mean the battle for equal opportunity is over. Women must take an active role in breaking down barriers impeding their advancement. One of these barriers is the good old boys' network. Many business deals are made in this network, and women typically are not part of the inner circles of male executives. Women leaders must recognize that businesses still have a long way to go before women can play by the same rules and be judged by the same standards as men.[20]

Another reason for the glass ceiling's existence is the belief that women tend to place family responsibilities ahead of work; this perception reduces women's chances of being promoted. However, there is evidence that cracks are beginning to appear in the glass ceiling and that things are beginning to improve for some women.[21] Figure 1.4 provides examples of some of the companies that are leading the way in managing diversity. These companies are committed to hiring, promoting, and retaining talented employees of all races. Others that have implemented such strategies are discussed next.

AVON PRODUCTS, INC.

Avon Products, Inc., has initiated awareness training at all levels of its hierarchy and uses affirmative action to ensure that doors are opened to talented individuals. The company has helped three minority groups—African Americans, Hispanics, and Asians—to form networks that crisscross the company in all 50 states. Each network elects its own leaders, has an adviser from senior management, and has representatives on the company's Multicultural Participation Council, through which management feedback is provided about employee views on diversity issues. The company's efforts have not gone unnoticed. Avon was named among the top ten companies listed by Minneapolis-based *Business Ethics* magazine's "100 Best Corporate Citizen." Avon also was recognized by *Fortune* as one of American's most admired companies.[22]

Business Week magazine voted Andrea Jung, CEO, and Susan Kropf, COO, two top women managers of Avon products, among the best managers for 2002. Andrea Jung, age 44, updated the Avon product line launching new ads, which resulted in improving gross margins. Susan Kropf, age 34, was instrumental in conducting an internal overhaul. She "cut 10 days off its inventory turns, reduced product development cycles by more than 40%, and should trim total costs by $230 million during the next three years."

JC PENNEY

When the giant retailer JC Penney relocated from New York City to Dallas, it lost a number of female managers, including the highest ranking woman in the firm. Since then, the company has set up a Diversity Steering Committee of top executives and has launched a formal mentoring program and other efforts designed to identify promising female and minority management candidates and to promote them up the management ranks. Also, JC Penney is committed to providing assistance to minority- and women-owned businesses to make their products or services more attractive to JC Penney. In 1972 a Supplier Diversity Program was established and in 1983 a Supplier Diversity Awards Program was implemented. The program further evolved in 1993, when women-owned businesses were made an integral part of the Supplier Diversity Program, increasing purchases from $5 million in its first year to $613 million in 2001.[23]

MOTOROLA

Motorola began its initiative toward hiring and promoting women in 1989, after management took a look at census data and predicted future demographics for workers in such fields as electrical engineering and computer science. The firm then set targets for the year 2000 that reflected the increases it wanted to achieve for women, Blacks, Asians, and other minorities. The firm also revamped its succession planning program by focusing first on its senior-level management. Top managers must now supply the names of three people most likely to replace them. The first is the manager who would take their job in the case of an emergency. The second is the individual who could be groomed for the job in three to five years. The third is reserved for the woman or minority closest to being qualified for the position. Today at Motorola, managers are expected to give this third person the opportunities to obtain the experience needed to secure the promotion. As a result, women have now moved into the first or second slots for approximately three-fourths of the company's three hundred most prized jobs![24]

Ethics and Social Responsibility Concerns

Ethics is the study of standards and moral judgment. **Social responsibility** is the obligations that a business has to society. In today's workplace, managers are continually confronted with ethical and social responsibility issues. For example, suppose a purchasing manager lies to a supplier, telling her, "We cannot pay $6 per unit any longer. If you can't provide it for $5.75, we'll have to do business elsewhere." Is the manager guilty of unethical behavior? If the supplier cuts the price, thereby saving the company $27,000, or if the purchasing manager tells the boss, "I saved you $27,000 on these units. I think that entitles me to a raise," has the manager acted unethically? Consider a company president who tells a news reporter that her company is not interested in acquiring Company X, when all the while she is meeting with her investment bankers to plan a takeover bid. And what about the stockbroker who learns that Company X

Ethics
is the study of standards and moral judgment.

Social responsibility
is the obligations of a business to society.

is about to be taken over and quietly buys stock for himself before the news hits the market and the shares rise dramatically?

These are all ethical and social responsibility dilemmas. Day after day during 2002, headlines in newspapers and news on television were filled with stories of executives employing a slew of scams to siphon big money out of companies and investors, off-the-book partnerships that concealed millions of dollars, aggressive accounting practices that hid losses and revealed a financially healthy company, and dishonest behavior of CEOs and executives who borrowed millions of dollars they never intended to repay. These activities resulted in a succession of bankruptcy filings, which ultimately made history. For example, as a result of unethical behavior and practices, Enron, WorldCom, Adelphia, Global Crossing, and Conseco Inc. were forced to file for Chapter 11 bankruptcy, impacting both employees and investors. Many employees lost their jobs, benefits, and retirement plans. Company stock in employees' retirement plans became worthless. In another example, Martha Stewart was accused of profiting by trading ImClone stocks based on insider information. It was a year of scandal and mistrust that attenuated investor's belief in the integrity of markets and management. Investors were outraged that many execs accused of dishonest activities faced no charges.

Many of these bankruptcies were a direct result of the actions of a whistle blower, an employee who worked in the company. It was a time in history, like no other, when whistle blowers raised the alarm about misdeeds at their employers and made history in the process. Three whistle blowers were named as "Persons of the Year" on the cover of *Time Magazine* for December 30, 2002/January 6, 2003: Cynthia Cooper of WorldCom Inc., Coleen Rowley of the FBI, and Sherron Watkins of Enron. They took huge professional and personal risks to come forth and tell their story. Cynthia Cooper and two other internal auditors took it upon themselves to dig into the accounting practices at WorldCom Inc., which led to the discovery of artificially boosted profits, and SEC charged WorldCom with civil fraud and the company declared bankruptcy. Ms. Cooper provided a "wake-up call for this country. There's a responsibility for all Americans—teachers, mothers, fathers, college professors, corporate people—to help and make sure the moral and ethical fabric of the country is strong."[25]

Coleen Rowley testified before the House and Senate Intelligence Committee about failed operations in the FBI, and Sherron Watkins uncovered a wave of accounting scandals in the Houston-based energy giant, Enron Corporation. Another whistle blower, Barron Stone, an accountant, warned his bosses at the utility company they were overcharging ratepayers. Duke Power agreed to credit twenty-five million dollars to utility customers in North Carolina and South Carolina and change the company's accounting practices.[26]

During these challenging times, trust in corporate America changed. A Gallup poll found that just 17 percent of Americans gave execs high marks for honesty and ethics, a 32 percent decline from the previous year. That is still better than stockbrokers, whom only 12 percent of Americans find highly honest and ethical.[27]

A survey conducted in 2000 by the Ethics Resource Center found that 43 percent of respondents believed their supervisors did not set good examples of integrity. "The same percentage felt pressured to compromise their organization's ethics on the job. That's a startling number, two years before Enron imploded."[28]

What set the stage for the rapid outbreak of fraud and unethical behavior? In President Bush's speech to the nation, he said "the 1990s was a decade of tremendous economic growth. As we're now learning, it was also a decade when the promise of rapid profits allowed the seeds of scandal to spring up. A lot of money was made, but too often standards were tossed aside." People lived the good life and believed it would continue. Corporate boards became overly cozy with management and insufficient controls were in place. After the September 11, 2001, disaster, things changed. The economy began to weaken and pressure mounted for executives to meet unrealistic goals, which made it easy for some executives to rationalize putting ethics aside. "And then there was greed. The opportunity to take money to meet your simplest needs or to meet your most extravagant needs is always present, says Carl Pergola, national director of the litigation and fraud investigation practices for accounting firm BDO Seidman in New York."[29]

Unfortunately, fraud and scandals have been around forever and will continue to occur. Over time they take different form and shape. What can a company do to protect itself? Carl Pergola outlines what companies can do to reduce the temptation to commit fraud.[30]

1. *Set realistic goals.* Unrealistic goals and overt pressures to achieve those goals often lead otherwise conscientious and ethical employees to do unethical things. For example, if meeting unrealistic budgets is expected, people will become innovative. Sometimes they believe it is the right thing to do.

2. *Hire competent managers.* Managers must set realistic goals and communicate those goals, agreed to listen to their employees and understand the challenges of their employees. Managers must help employees overcome those challenges as opposed to simply developing unachievable goals and putting undue pressure on them.

3. *Create a positive work environment.* Within the right environment, it is possible to manage a very effective and profitable business by setting realistic goals and giving the people the tools to achieve those goals. Also, management must review what the organization considers to be fraudulent behavior and what the implications are if caught. It might be cheating on an expense report or taking gifts from vendors. Standards of behavior must be clear and employees serve as role models for one another. Ethics can be taught and should be taught and talked about. Communication is key to building trust between employees and management. Whereas, for example, an environment or culture where management's view is "do it, or you're out of here" can lead to fraud.

To help executives manage company ethics, William D. Hall has outlined a series of steps.[31]

- Establish compliance standards and procedures to be followed by all company employees and their agents.
- Assign specific individuals at a high level within the organization to oversee standards and procedures compliance.
- Ensure that substantial discretion and authority have not been delegated to known individuals with a propensity to engage in illegal activities.
- Communicate the standards and procedures to all employees and other agents through training programs and printed materials.
- Develop systems to achieve compliance with company requirements such as monitoring and auditing systems.
- Reinforce standards consistently through appropriate disciplinary mechanisms.
- Respond appropriately to reported offenses and take action to prevent recurrence.

Practicing good business ethics creates dividends that go beyond avoiding legal disaster. A host of studies have shown that employees who perceive their companies to have a conscience possess a higher level of job satisfaction and feel more valued as workers. The 2000 Ethics Resource Center study canvassed corporations and nonprofits across the country. Among it's findings: Managers' efforts to instill good business ethics were welcomed overwhelmingly by workers. "We found a strong connection between employees' perception of their leaders and their own ethical behavior," says Josh Joseph, top researcher in the ethics center. Workers also said their own behavior was influenced by the perceived ethics of direct supervisors and coworkers.[32]

"Ethics is a matter of developing good habits, and it doesn't happen overnight," says W. Michael Hoffman, executive director for the Center for Business Ethics at Bentley College. "It happens through repetition and a long process of development." Commitment to ethics must start at the top of a company. Most CEOs and executives are ethical and diligent in overseeing major issues. Many, however, have too many things on their plates and are too preoccupied to focus on the ethical consequences of results. Enron was an eye opener for many execs causing them to reevaluate their policies and procedures.

On July 9, 2002, by executive order, President George Bush created a new corporate fraud task force headed by the deputy attorney general. Its purpose is to target major accounting fraud and other criminal activity in corporate finance. The task force will function as a financial crimes SWAT team overseeing the investigation of corporate abusers and bringing them to account. President Bush challenged leaders in business to set high standards and clear expectations of conduct, demonstrated by their own behavior. Everyone in a company should live up to high standards, but the burden of leadership rightly belongs to the chief executive officer. CEOs set the ethical direction for their companies. They set a moral tone by the decisions they make, the respect they show their employees, and their willingness to be held accountable for their actions. They set a moral tone by showing their disapproval of other executives who bring discredit to the business world.[33]

The composition of board members of many companies has since changed. The board now takes accountability serious and "lousy performance won't be tolerated," says Barbara Franklin, who sits on five corporate boards. "Now we're trying to get ahead of the curve and make changes before you have an absolute crisis." For example, the CEO of Dow Chemical was canned after just two years on the job due to disappointing financial performance.[34]

CODE OF CONDUCT

Code of conduct
A guide summarizing the ethical principles and standards for individual behavior.

A **Code of Conduct** outlines the values of the company and the expected behavior of all employees, and in some cases, the consequences for unethical behavior. If it is to promote ethics, the Code of Conduct must, however, be meaningful and be communicated to all employees through a planned training program. Before the Code can be followed vigilantly, everyone must understand its contents, including the CEOs and executives. For example, Coca-Cola's Code of Business Conduct includes a set of procedural guidelines, which uses a question/answer format covering topics such as reporting the violations, the investigation processes, discipline, and record-keeping process.[35]

Code of Business Conduct for The Coca-Cola Company: Our Code of Business Conduct serves to guide the actions of our employees, officers, and directors in ways that are consistent with our core values: honesty, integrity, diversity, quality, respect, responsibility, and accountability. The Code helps our people play by the rules wherever we operate around the world. And, we have well-defined procedures for times when concerns arise, in the Code of Business Conduct Procedural Guidelines.

Another way to address the issue of improving ethics would be to take a course in business school. In a survey conducted by *Business Week* magazine, "the readers thought the teaching of ethics should be rooted in practical discussions of actual business situations; 46% thought that alone would be sufficient, while 47% advocated combining practical discussions with instruction on the philosophical underpinnings of ethics. Incidentally, "75% of the readers said that best values are taught at home by parents."[36] The questions posed in the "in Action" box can serve as guidelines in determining ethical behavior.

Why not pass laws and more regulations? "History demonstrates that enacting more laws and posting more regulations do not solve the problem. Laws can help on the margin. . ., but no set of principles by themselves will eliminate wrongdoing. Even monitoring systems with their checks and balances, while useful, do not make good people; it is the other way around, good people produce good organizations."[37]

Ervin Hosak, VP of Manufacturing, Superior Uniform Group, responded to the editor of *Industry Week* by saying, "we are becoming a greedy nation that is driven by the almighty. It is sad that as smart as certain individuals are, we have to stoop to train them in basic ethics." CEOs and executives must be accountable to the company and its investors, not just to themselves.

This requires implementing practices that reflect ethical decisions. Rick Wagoner, GM President and CEO, states "no single action is enough to restore investor confidence in this current climate of concern over corporate accountability. We have to earn investor confidence day in and day out by running our business with integrity and honesty."[38]

Current Ethical Dilemmas

An interesting human relations-oriented dilemma is how to handle critical problems such as downsizing. In recent years, many companies have cut their workforces and laid off thousands of employees. How should these people be handled? How much assistance should management provide? What responsibility does the company have to help these people locate new jobs? What is the company's responsibility to those who remain and must take on the extra work? How does a company recover, regroup, and forge ahead successfully? Forcing people to take jobs you do not like is not the way to go. Management must find ways to key in on the remaining employee's motivations and adapt management strategies employee by employee. Conducting an employee survey, using The Predictive IndexR instrument, can be helpful in learning employee motivations. Another way is to "hold employees accountable for achieving difficult new goals and reward them accordingly."[39]

Trust must be rebuilt. More recently, some firms have been striving to avoid downsizing because they are now convinced that it results in only short-term benefits and that the long-term impact is very costly.

Companies such as State Farm Insurance agree, and whenever the giant insurer must downsize because of new technology, it tries to shift the affected individuals to other jobs. As a result of such concern, State Farm's sales agents stay with the company two to three times longer than the industry average. They also achieve far higher sales per agent than the competition. One reason is that customers like doing business with agents whom they know and with whom they have worked before.[40]

According to the EEOC, employers cannot use downsizing as a means for eliminating older employees from their workforce. Recently, Gulfstream Aerospace paid $2.1 million to sixty-one former employees who lost their jobs during layoffs.[41]

Another challenge is *treating people fairly* in the workplace and not discriminating against them on the basis of gender, race, religion, age, or physical appearance. In recent years, the Supreme Court has made it easier for employees to sue because of discrimination on the job,[42] and a growing number of women have filed lawsuits, citing bias by employers[43] or sexual harassment by employees. In those cases in which sexual harassment has been found, the plaintiffs have been accorded restitution and, in some cases, juries have awarded substantial damages. Moreover, in recent years, some plaintiffs have been trying to extend the coverage they are accorded by the Civil Rights Act to include protection from bullying tactics and obscene remarks by managers and other members of their workforce. However, the courts appear reluctant to extend coverage to these areas, and a number of jury awards have been set aside by appellate courts that feel that the use of workplace vulgarity or bad manners does not, in and of itself, constitute sexual harassment.[44] The area of sexual harassment will continue to be one of ongoing debate. However, one thing is certain. Management in effective firms does not tolerate either harassment or bad conduct and will take action against those who engage in such behavior.

The EEOC has recently settled several discrimination cases brought against well-known companies for violations involving religious beliefs, multiple sclerosis disability, same-sex harassment, and blindness. For example, Brink's, Inc. paid $30,000 to a woman in Peoria, Illinois, for failure to accommodate her religious beliefs. Her religious beliefs precluded her form wearing pants. She requested to wear culottes of uniform material, instead of pants, purchased at her own expense. Brink's refused her request and terminated her employment. Religious bias charged filings with the EEOC have risen 40 percent from 1994. In another case, the Target Corporation paid $95,000 to a qualified employee with multiple sclerosis, when it refused to transfer her to a vacant position after her disability interfered with her ability to perform her current job. A Target supervisor also had disclosed information regarding her disability to another prospective employer. Target denied liability. ADA (American Disability Act) cases comprise about 20 percent of EEOC's annual case load.[45]

Sexual harassment cases include same-sex harassment, cases filed by women and cases filed by men, which have increased to 15 percent in 2002 of all sexual harassment cases filed. Recently, EEOC settled a lawsuit between Babies R US and a male employee for $205,000. The employee alleged he was subjected to a sexually hostile work environment because of his sex. The Sears, Roebuck and Company settled a disability discrimination suit for $125,000. Sears failed to provide a reasonable accommodation to an employee who was blind.[46]

Companies must also be careful not to discriminate against older employees who are protected by the Age Discrimination Act, despite the fact that some firms find that these workers make more money than do younger employees. Some recent age-bias lawsuits have awarded thousands of dollars to older employees who were fired because of their age. In one recent case, a television station was found guilty of discriminating against a news anchor person because of his age. The company was ordered to pay more than a year's back wages and to desist from practices that might violate the civil rights of other employees in the firm.[47]

The Equal Employment Opportunity Commission recently declared obesity a protected category under federal disability law. This means that individuals who have been obese for a long period now qualify for federal protection and cannot be fired because of their weight.[48] Another area that is becoming a focal point is personal appearance. Do attractive people perform their jobs better than unattractive people? Recent evidence reveals that attractive people earn approximately 10 percent more annually than do those with below-average looks; these findings carry over to jobs in which personal appearance has no link to job performance.[49]

Another dilemma facing more and more companies each day is how to deal with ethical and moral issues involving the Internet and e-commerce operations. Decisions must be made about how to handle privacy issues with employees, suppliers, and customers. To what extent will employees' e-mails be monitored and what will be the consequences for engaging in Internet activities not related to company business. For example, recently the news reported firing an employee who failed to follow the company guidelines for using the Internet. The debate goes on about invading individual's privacy when companies place cookies on an individual's hard drive to identify each subsequent time the individual visits the company's Web site. There are also ethical issues about using spam e-mails. As more and more personal information becomes publicly available and is stored and analyzed more easily, managers must establish systems for protecting this information in order to retain not only employee trust but also that of the customers. As technology changes and the use of the Internet increases, managers also must keep pace by developing systems to protect information and sustain the integrity of the company.

Ethical dilemmas run paramount in the medical field. They impact decisions in research firms, hospitals, and clinics. For example, recently a woman was diagnosed with breast cancer. Her doctors performed a double mastectomy. Within a few days, she learned she did not have cancer. What ethical responsibility does the hospital have in this case? In another situation, ethical issues are being debated over whether—and how—to ban human cloning technology after it was recently reported that a 31-year-old American woman had given birth to a seven-pound girl who is her own clone. No evidence of the birth has been provided.[50]

Knowledge is fast becoming the single most important resource any company can own. In the next decade—next society—knowledge will be the central fiber of business operations. How can all the widespread knowledge, which exists in so many forms and in so many places, be integrated into a single, accessible resource that adds value to the business? Managers must create systems for knowledge sharing. These systems must allow all people access to the information they need. It cannot discriminate against certain individuals in any way. Xerox was one of the first global companies to get involved in knowledge management (KM) when the movement emerged in 1996. For helping CIOs and IT execs, Xerox has created a Web site called Global IT Knowledge Forum (**http://www.it-globalforum.org**). It gives free access to a collection of resources that can make work life easier. Xerox's Knowledge Perspectives Web site covers insight into knowledge management.[51]

Organizations today are finding that they must develop effective strategies for dealing with these ethical and social responsibility challenges. Good intentions are no longer a defense against poor human relations practices. Business firms must formulate codes of conduct and implement well-designed training programs to build an internal response system that identifies biased or unethical behavior and deals with it quickly and firmly.

Adapting to International and Cultural Challenges

Concerns about diversity, ethics, and social responsibility are not confined to workplaces in the United States. These are international human relations challenges as well, a fact that has been made particularly evident by the changing makeup of the global workforce. Research shows that the world's workforce will become more mobile and that employers will increasingly reach across borders to find the needed human skills. Hiring personnel from nearby countries is a practice that has been used for decades. However, in the future, it will result in workers being hired from around the globe as the world's supply of labor seeks better salaries and working conditions. Today, much of the world's skilled and unskilled human resources are produced in the developing world (China, India, Indonesia, and Brazil),[52] whereas the best paid jobs are generated in the cities of the industrialized world (United States, Japan, Germany, and Great Britain). This "mismatch" has several important implications for the future:

1. **The triggering of massive relocations of people, such as immigrants, temporary workers, retirees, and visitors. The greatest relocations will involve young, well-educated workers who are flocking to the cities of the developed world.**
2. **The reevaluation of protectionist immigration policies by some industrialized economic growth.**
3. **Economic improvement for countries that are well educated but economically underdeveloped. Examples include Egypt, Poland, Hungary, and the Philippines.**
4. **A gradual standardization of labor practices among industrialized countries.**[53]

Another reason why internationalization will be important is that many multinational corporations will continue to increase their overseas expansion. This means that management must be prepared to deal with people from other cultures and learn to adjust to the way business is conducted in those cultures. The belief that there is one universal method of managing that can be exported to other countries is unfounded. People have different values and beliefs, and the way things are done in the United States is not necessarily the way they are done elsewhere. This is particularly clear if countries are examined on the basis of common traits. One researcher recently conducted statistical analyses on the cultures of various countries and found that there is a series of "cultural allies," the cultures being similar within groups and different among them. For example, Australia, Canada, Great Britain, New Zealand, Singapore, and the United States tend to be culturally similar. Argentina, Brazil, Italy, Mexico, Spain, and Venezuela constitute a second group. Austria, Belgium, Finland, France, Germany, the Netherlands, and Sweden make up a third.

The ability to deal with these cultural groups is a major challenge. One primary reason is the values each society places on lifestyles. For example, the Japanese work longer hours than do Americans, and they view work as more important to their life than do people in the United States. In contrast, Americans place stronger value on family life and leisure, whereas Scandinavian countries place an even greater value on quality of life. A multinational company doing business around the world must adjust to local concerns. Expatriate managers must be trained properly to fit into overseas assignments.

An area of special challenge is how business is conducted internationally. What are the ethical and social responsibility issues? The way business is conducted in the United States often is sharply different from the way it is done overseas. For example, in such economic powers as Japan and Germany, women are not prominent in the workplace. In most cases, the best they can hope for is an upper-middle-management position, and this usually is not achieved. As one writer described the situation in Japanese firms:

> *While men are hired with the general assumption that they will build careers with their companies, women are still typically separated into one of the categories—ippan shoku (miscellaneous workers or often simply office ladies) and sogo shoku (a career track).*
>
> *The miscellaneous workers, still legion in every Japanese ministry and large company . . . are typically women in their 20s who dress in company uniforms or in smart clothing of their own. They smilingly direct visitors to their appointments and serve tea to guests. Some may do clerical work, sales work, or accounting work, but what they generally do not do . . . is rise above this lowly status and enter career tracks largely reserved for men.*[54]

In a recent lawsuit brought by a Japanese worker against her employer, the woman charged the firm with sex discrimination. She had worked for her company for six years before getting her first small promotion and twenty-one more years before getting another pay raise. Despite the fact that she earned a college degree during these years and continued to perform well, she never advanced in the company. So she brought legal action and the courts awarded her $55,000 in the largest sex discrimination judgment ever rendered in Japan. However, critics point out that such action is unlikely to change the fact that Japanese corporations have a separate-track

ETHICS AND SOCIAL RESPONSIBILITY IN ACTION

Gifts and Kickbacks

In Japan, it is common practice for individuals who are doing business with one another to exchange gifts. Often, these gifts are of low value and are merely a way of complying with a social custom. Sometimes, however, large sums of money change hands as a way of ensuring that a business deal goes through without hitches, an illegal practice in the United States. Foreign firms operating in the United States are careful not to engage in such behavior. These firms know that most American companies not only believe in ethical practices but that many of them have codes of ethical conduct that strictly guide their business behaviors. Given this background, Honda Motors of Japan recently was surprised to learn that some of its American managers were involved in taking kickbacks and bribes.

The illegal activity began in the 1980s when Honda automobiles, particularly Acuras, were in great demand, and dealers found that they could sell these cars at window price or higher. Because of the strong demand, all the company's dealers wanted a steady supply of these cars, but they were unavailable. Consequently, some of the people who were responsible for managing Honda's U.S. sales operations began to accept money from dealers in exchange for ensuring that they were given a steady supply of these cars. Those interested in obtaining Honda dealerships also found that payments were necessary to ensure the success of the deal.

Eventually, the kickback scheme was uncovered. Honda dealers who did not pay money and were not given a steady supply of popular models complained that other dealers were being favored over them. One individual, whose dealership failed, filed a lawsuit claiming that the cause of his failure was an illegal scheme that limited his dealership's ability to compete. An investigation by federal authorities found that many of these charges were accurate. This, in turn, led to the arrest of more than a dozen executives, including a retired senior vice-president of the American Honda Motor Company.

Honda expressed its dismay and anger toward the unethical behavior of these executives. The company cooperated fully with the government and announced that it would carefully review its operating procedures and practices to ensure that nothing like this occurred again. In particular, the firm learned that the management of personnel often requires direct, close contact to ensure that company rules and regulations are not being broken.

Sources: Doron P. Levin, "Wide Fraud Linked to U.S. Executives with Honda Motor," The New York Times, March 15, 1994, pp. A1, C8; Andrew Stark, "What's the Matter with Business Ethics?" Harvard Business Review, May–June 1993, pp. 38–48; "Ethics: A New Profession in American Business," HR Focus, May 1993, p. 22; and Richard M. Hodgetts and Fred Luthans, International Management, 4th ed. (Burr Ridge, IL: Irwin/McGraw, 2000), chapter 14.

personnel management system for men and women. Men are often put on the fast track, whereas women are denied such opportunities, even though in 1985 a landmark antidiscrimination law was passed and, in 1999, amendments were adopted to strengthen the law, including sanctions for sexual harassment. Simply put, most women in Japan do not have equal opportunity in the workplace.[55]

Another area of ethical concern is piracy and counterfeiting. In China, for example, it is common to find small firms copying computer software, books, records, and other proprietary materials. Dealing with these issues is not easy for American firms because many Chinese businesspeople accept copyright piracy as a way of doing business.[56] They do not see what is wrong with these practices. Moreover, the government sometimes turns its back and ignores what is going on. The international firm, then, is left to deal with the problem, which can be complicated because it involves proprietary rights and human relations challenges. Another example is provided in the "Ethics and Social Responsibility in Action" Box.

① LEARNING OBJECTIVE
Explain human relations and its implications for management

Human relations is a process by which management brings workers into contact with the organization in such a way that the objectives of both groups are achieved. Human relations is people oriented, work oriented, effectiveness oriented, based on empirical experience as opposed to relying solely on intuition and common sense, and useful at all levels of the work hierarchy.

② LEARNING OBJECTIVE
Trace the evolution of human relations thinking from industrialism through scientific management to the present

The modern manager must be concerned with human relations if he or she hopes to be effective. When industrialism emerged in the latter half of the eighteenth century, however, the owner-managers were more interested in efficient production than they were in their employees. This concern for efficiency continued through the nineteenth century and was vigorously promoted by scientific managers. Employing their engineering skills in a work setting, these managers studied plant design, plant layout, machine feed and speed, and a host of other factors that could bring about increased productivity. The greatest weakness of the scientific managers, however, was that they knew very little about the management of people.

③ LEARNING OBJECTIVE
Compare and contrast the traditional model of the worker with the modern human resources model

As the scientific management movement progressed, an interest in the behavioral side of management began to grow. It was becoming obvious that concern for production brought about people-related problems and that the effective manager had to be interested in both personnel and the work. The Hawthorne studies revealed the work organization to be a social system and pointed to the need for consideration of psychological and sociological aspects of organizational behavior. The Hawthorne studies helped to light the way for much behavioral research. Since then, the behavioral movement has made great progress.

④ LEARNING OBJECTIVE
Discuss the role of behavioral science in human relations

Even though today, the human relations model of management has replaced the traditional model of management, there is still need to use scientific methods. By using scientific methods, behavioral scientists help unravel many of the mysteries of human behavior at work. Scientists can gather data from using tests and control groups. Questionnaires, surveys, and interviews also provide data that can affect communication, attitudes, and work habits. By learning what motivates employees, managers can use effective reinforcement and rewards to modify employee behavior.

⑤ LEARNING OBJECTIVE
Describe some of the emerging challenges in the human relations area

Over the last decade, human relations concerns have not remained static. New challenges have emerged, making it even more important for managers to understand human relations at work.

Four major issues now in the forefront are managing knowledge workers, dealing with diversity, addressing ethics and social responsibility concerns, and adapting to international and cultural challenges. These areas are interdependent, but each merits individual consideration because of its growing impact on the field of human relations. One topic that directly affects these challenges is that of motivation. This subject will be the focus of attention in the next chapter.

KEY TERMS IN THE CHAPTER

Human relations	Scientific method
Scientific management	Behavioral scientists
Hawthorne studies	Test group
Social networks	Control group
Traditional model	Structured interviews
Human resources model	Unstructured interviews
System 1	Glass ceiling
System 2	Ethics
System 3	Social responsibility
System 4	Code of Conduct

REVIEW AND STUDY QUESTIONS

1. What is *human relations?* Define this term in your own words.

2. How much did the owner-managers of factories in the latter half of the eighteenth century know about human relations? Describe the model used by management.

3. What did scientific managers know about human relations? What were their shortcomings in this area?

4. What were some of the principal findings of the Hawthorne studies? Why were these findings important?

5. Are happy workers also productive workers? Explain.

6. How does the traditional model differ from the human resources model? Compare and contrast the two models.

7. How does a System 1 manager differ from a System 2 manager? How does a System 3 manager differ from a System 4 manager? Which of these systems is most reflective of the human resources philosophy? Why?

8. In analyzing behavioral problems, practitioners of modern human relations rely on the scientific method. What is the logic behind this statement?

9. What do managers need to know about managing knowledge workers?

10. Why is the management of diversity so important to the study of human relations? Why is the management of diversity likely to become more important in the next decade?

11. What are two of the major ethical problems with which managers must deal? In what way is training of value in helping managers do this?

12. How can a Code of Conduct help build an ethical environment?

13. Why are more and more organizations interested in preparing their managers to deal with international and cultural challenges?

VISIT THE WEB

The Company That Brings Good Things to Life

In this chapter, you examined the nature of human relations, an area of concern to every organization. One of the most successful is General Electric, which has a worldwide workforce the size of St. Paul, Minnesota. To run this company efficiently, management must know a great deal about effective human relations. Visit their Web site at **www.ge.com** and then answer the following questions.

1. What is General Electric's "Statement of Integrity?"

2. Describe General Electric's position on "Diversity."

3. From your assessment of the information found on the Web site, what do you feel are two human relations challenges of the twenty-first century that managers in this company will have to meet?

What Are The Rules of Conduct?

A Code of Conduct or Code of Business Conduct is a guideline for outlining the company's values and expected behavior of a company's personnel. Two companies used as examples in this chapter are General Electric and Motorola, both large global companies with many employees working in many countries around the world. Is there a difference between the Codes of these two companies? If so, what? Go to their Web sites, find their Codes, review them, and identify any differences between the Codes of the two companies.

1. Go to (**http://www.ge.com** and **http://www.motorola.com**

2. Review the Codes for each company.

3. Identify the key points in each Code.

4. List the major differences between the two Codes. Tell why you believe these differences exist.

5. Discuss the significance of the Code for each company.

TIME OUT ANSWERS

1. **False** Although money is certainly an important motivator, most workers place it in fourth or fifth position. The most commonly cited factors include recognition for a job well done, a chance to succeed, a feeling that the work is important, and an opportunity to contribute to the accomplishment of worthwhile objectives.

2. **False** The work group with high morale will outperform the work group with moderate morale only if the first group's objectives or goals call for higher output than the second group's. If the first group sets low output goals because it is in conflict with the management, the group's output will be low.

3. **True** Workers who do the same job, belong to the same union, or are members of the same unit are more likely to associate with one another than they are to associate with individuals who do none of these things.

4. **False** The most efficient workers perform best when placed under moderate stress. Under high stress, their output slows because they have to adjust to job-related tension and anxiety.

5. **True** Managers tend to use the grapevine far more than workers do in sending *and* receiving information.

6. **False** Top managers tend to be more intelligent than the average intelligence of their subordinates. Additionally, although personality is important, it is no substitute for intelligent problem solving and decision making.

7. **False** Many managers do not get all their work done, because they fail to establish priorities and do not delegate enough minor work to subordinates.

8. **False** Although job-related stress increases as one goes up the hierarchy, it is greatest at the middle to upper-middle ranks. After this, it tends to decrease because the executive can delegate to subordinates many stress-creating tasks.

9. **False** The major reason is that the organization's machinery is inefficient, the workers are not trained as well as they should be, and the rewards associated with high output are not sufficiently motivational to encourage personnel to maximize their output.

10. **True** Research reveals that eight of ten managerial communications are downward, whereas only one of ten involves an upward flow of information.

Scoring

9–10	Excellent. Your score is in the top 4 percent of all individuals taking this quiz.
8	Good. Your score is in the top 26 percent of all individuals taking this quiz.
7	Average. Your score is just about in the middle. Thirty-seven percent of all individuals taking this quiz received this score.
6 or less	Below average. Thirty-seven percent of all individuals taking this quiz received this score.

Regardless of your score, you should use this quiz only as an indication of the amount of general human relations knowledge you now have. You will be learning a great deal more as you read this book.

case: DON'T MESS WITH CARLY

Carly Fiorina has changed the way management operates at Hewlett-Packard (HP). She has done what HP's Board of Directors hired her to do—turn the sluggish company into a top world-wide competitive company. At first her ideas, did not always fit well with all members of the board—After all she was a young woman, age 44, who was using too much power to make changes too fast. Although it was not easy, she managed to successfully complete the controversial $19 billion dollar merger with Compaq Computer within three years after being hired.

Carly's own management style has penetrated the entire company. She is direct, articulate, driven, decisive, customer-focused, and successful. She is a market-focused executive skilled in major organizational change. She has been described as everything from brilliant and visionary to arrogant and self-serving; but one thing is certain: She expects the very best from her 141,000 employees. Fiorina believes that HP's culture should be based on performance, self-motivation, and high achievement. When she arrived, HP was a flat, decentralized company, with individual departments having a great deal of autonomy. Consensus was how decisions were made. Today, most of the important decisions come from the top. It's a top-down, do-as-I-say company.

The consensus-driven style had its problems. Because power was concentrated at the lower levels in the organization, it took too much time to get things done. Now decisions are made more quickly. Before Carly, people were reluctant to make decisions until they had all the facts. Now it's okay to take risks and go with just 80 percent of the data. Of course, not everyone is happy with HP's new culture. "It's a culture of fear right now," says a former director-level employee. "Nobody believes their job is secure, and it's become habitual to wonder when your number is going to come up."

Morale also is suffering in parts of the company where managers who were used to their own empires now have to coordinate their activities.

In the pre-Carly days, HP concentrated on innovation and product development. Today, the market reigns supreme with all employees focused on customer needs. It is an environment of finding out what the customer needs, so HP knows what to make next. The new mindset is "people first, technology second." Research and analysis are still important, but so is speed. Employees are held accountable for increasing customer loyalty and having fewer at-risk customers. As well as serving customers more effectively, employees are being asked to perform at a higher level. If employees perform poorly, they are given a specific time to improve their performance. The company tries to deal with unacceptable performance in a positive way. During the economic slowdown after September 11, 2001, employees were ranked and were told that people without competitive skills would be terminated. Carly believes that employees should be rewarded and promoted based on results, not on longevity or who they know. All of these changes and standards have had an impact on the workplace at HP, making it a very different workplace from that before Carly Fiorina was hired.

Questions

1. Does Carly Fiorina subscribe to the traditional model or the human resources model? Defend your answer.

2. How would you describe Carly in terms of Systems 1 through 4? Which one best fits her approach to managing people? Tell why.

3. What problems do you foresee for Carly as the workplace becomes more diversified?

Source: Shari Caudron, "Don't Mess With Carly," Workforce, July 2003, p. 15.

The Space Shuttle Accidents

On February 1, 2003, Space Shuttle Columbia exploded during its return to earth. All seven astronauts lost their lives as debris was scattered over East Texas with most of it landing around and near the city of Nacogdoches. While the investigators determined that broken tiles caused by foam hitting them during launch was at fault, they sited poor management being just as responsible. They blamed the problem at least in part on so-called tribalism. It is a particular culture that has its own rules and its own behavior patterns. It is a competitive environment where the chain of command controls operations. Space shuttle engineers were too uncomfortable and too afraid to speak up at key meetings and never told the managers in charge of the flight their concerns about safety issues. Engineers were concerned about losing their jobs and about their careers. After the Columbia disaster, NASA chief Sean O'Keefe promised dramatic change. For starters, employees can go to the NASA Web site and file their concerns.

James Oberg, a noted author and former shuttle flight controller doubts that things will change. He has heard it before—seventeen years ago on January 25, 1986, when the Space Shuttle Challenger exploded only seconds after launch. The Rogers Commission Report cited the failure of the O-ring, the faulty design of the solid rocket boosters—Evidence of this surfaced as far back as 1984, inadequate low-temperatures testing of the O-ring material and the joints the O-rings sealed, and the lack of proper communications among different levels of NASA management. The Rogers Report was critical of the entire NASA management process. The management process prevented serious concerns about flight safety from being aired to the highest levels of the agency.

The single chain of command management structure at NASA means that engineers could report only to their group managers, who would in turn report to their project managers. The chain of command structure helped keep important information from those who were in charge of the launch. A major problem in the system was that information often was distorted on the way up or silenced and sometimes completely lost. The chain of command dictated the only path which information could travel at NASA leaving the engineers with no other route to communicate their concerns without the fear of losing their jobs. In both disasters the managers did not feel the problem was as serious as the engineers stated. In some meetings managers simply failed to speak up. Managers also were operating under schedule pressures to achieve planned flight rates. These pressures contributed to an increase in unsafe practices and influenced the degree of risk a manager would take concerning a launch.

Your Advice

1. What do you recommend that the management of NASA do to divert future space shuttle disasters?

   _____a. Continue with the present management system. This system works in the space program. After all, many more flights have been successful than have been lost.

   _____b. Change the culture and environment of NASA to reflect a team effort.

   _____c. Replace top personnel with people who understand the worth and contributions of employees, as well as meet launch deadlines.

2. What are the major behavior issues that impact the present culture of NASA?

3. How would you approach changing an established bureaucratic system that has been in place for years?

4. What impact will your changes have on the safety of the space program? Be specific in your ideas.

Source: "Administrative Causes of the Challenger Accident" **http://www.nasa.gov.** and "NASA Promises to Break Silence on Shuttle," Temple Daily Telegram, July 27, 2003.

Purpose

- To enrich your understanding of the traditional and human resources models.
- To observe supervisor–employee relations in the traditional and human resources models.

Procedure

1. Two students are chosen to role-play the situation described in the following. One is assigned the traditional management model role and the other, the human resources model role (see Table 1.1).

2. After the role-playing exercise is completed, discuss the following:

   a. How well did each person represent his or her role?

   b. Which model provides the best answer for the situation?

Situation

You and another student are store managers of a national retail chain. Your stores sell a wide variety of consumer merchandise, including appliances, auto supplies, clothing, electronic goods, garden equipment, household fixtures, and pharmaceuticals. Employee tardiness during recent months has been excessive and is affecting sales. A regional meeting has been called to discuss the problem. Each of you is to present briefly your approach to handling the situation. The person recommending a traditional approach should speak first and set forth his or her recommendations in three to four minutes. Then the person recommending a human resources management approach should speak for three to four minutes. Finally, each should ask the other to elaborate on any points that were unclear. No more than five minutes should be used for this question-and-answer process.

2

Fundamentals Of Motivation

One of the most important questions in human relations today is: How do you get people to do things? The answer rests on an understanding of what motivation is all about, for it is motivated workers who ultimately get things done and, without such people, no organization can hope to be effective. In this chapter, the fundamentals of motivation are examined.

AFTER STUDYING THIS CHAPTER, YOU SHOULD BE ABLE TO:

1. Describe the two sides of motivation: movement and motive.
2. Identify the five basic needs in Maslow's need hierarchy.
3. Describe the two-factor theory of motivation and explain its relevance to the practicing manager.
4. Discuss expectancy theory, noting how both valence and expectancy influence motivational force.
5. Explain the value of money, employee satisfaction, incentives, and recognition in the motivation process.

Maintaining Motivation

The U.S. economy has changed substantially during the last decade, especially since the tragic events of September 11, 2001. Large firms have downsized and begun focusing on increasing their efficiency; small firms have begun springing up in record numbers, with women, in particular, accounting for a large number of these new, entrepreneur-driven companies. In the midst of this turmoil, however, one question has remained the same: How can managers more effectively motivate their people? One answer is: Not the way they have been doing so in the past.

A good example is provided by the Lincoln Electric Company of Cleveland, Ohio, which has been cited as one of the best firms in America by many people. For many years, Lincoln has been known for its bonus system. Employees earn large annual bonuses (sometimes as much as 100 percent of their base pay) based on a carefully formulated plan that encourages high individual productivity while working under minimal supervision. There is no sick or holiday pay, and benefit programs, such as health care, are paid out of the employee bonus pool prior to distribution.

The incentive program for those who have been with Lincoln for a long time and who have the best paying production jobs has resulted in annual salaries of more than $100,000 after bonuses. And although the average bonus in a recent year was only slightly more than 50 percent—the lowest in a long time—employees have continually taken home larger paychecks than have competitive workers in other firms.

However, Lincoln is now looking into revising its incentive program and putting less focus on bonuses and more on base salary. The company believes that workers are more interested in their overall earnings than strictly in the opportunity to earn large bonuses. And the firm has begun changing the pay rate for new employees, who now earn less when they join the company than did their predecessors just a few years ago. These changes are causing some concerns within the workforce, but Lincoln believes that it needs to review and revise the compensation system so that it remains competitive both in the United States and in its worldwide operations. If this means less emphasis on bonuses and more on base salary, then that is the direction in which the company intends to go in motivating its personnel.

Weyerhaeuser, a giant forest and paper products company, employs what it calls *goalsharing* in its container board packaging and recycling plants. The company's objective is to enlist the workforce in a major performance improvement initiative designed to achieve world-class performance by reducing waste and controllable costs and increasing plant safety and product quality. The work-systems improvement and employee involvement are treated as a key business strategy.

Still another common form of financial motivation is bonuses that are tied to both recruitment and performance. For example, in June 2000, Conseco Inc., the giant insurance company, paid Gary Wendt, a former executive at General Electric, a $45 million bonus for agreeing to join the company and to stay for at least five years as its chairman and chief executive officer. Additionally, Conseco agreed to pay Wendt a bonus of between $8 million and $50 million at the end of his second year, depending on performance, and a minimum bonus of $2.8 million at the end of the fifth year. Although this bonus package is extremely large, successful managers and individuals who can generate large accounts for a firm can also expect sizable bonuses. Although Wendt received the $45 million sign on bonus and $8 million at the end of the second year, he was forced to step down from CEO to Chairman in October 2002 and his salary was reduced to $50,000 a year. He is due to receive a pension upon turning age 65—$1.5 million for the rest of his life. The events following September 11, 2001, had a tremendous impact on operations at Conseco Inc., causing Conseco, except for its insurance operations, to file for bankruptcy-court protection.[1] In another example, the Paine-Webber Group recruited a top-producing brokerage team from its rival, Merrill Lynch, by offering the group a signing bonus of $5.25 million and an additional $2 million if they could bring more customers to Paine-Webber.

Another strategy to attractive top executives is the split-dollar life insurance policies, whose purpose is to provide tax-free pay and loans to top executives, not life insurance protection. The executive pays only a small portion of the premiums, whereas the company pays the balance of the premiums, in millions of dollars, into a tax-sheltered investment account. The executive can borrow from this account and is not required to repay the loan. Companies providing split-dollar arrangements include Equifax Inc., General Motors Corporation, H.J. Heinz Company, and Unifi Inc.

Yet not all motivation efforts are based on monetary rewards. In more cases than not, companies try to motivate their personnel with nonmonetary rewards such as praise and recognition for a job well done. For example, at Tricon, the world's largest restaurant company in units and second behind McDonald's in sales, the chief executive officer recently gave a Pizza Hut general manager a foam cheesehead for achieving a crew turnover rate of 56 percent in an industry where 200 percent is the norm. Commenting on the event, the CEO noted, "I wondered why anyone would be moved by getting a cheesehead, but I've seen people cry. People love recognition."

Sources: "Lincoln Electric Reports Third-Quarter Financial Results in Line with Revised Expectations; Ends Charter Acquisition," October 20, 2000, Public Relations Newswire; Calmetta Y. Coleman, "Conseco Package Has $45 Million for CEO Wendt," Wall Street Journal, July 11, 2000, p. A4; Charles Gasparino and Pui-Wing Tam, "Hot Broker Market Fuels Questions About Pay," Wall Street Journal, March 28, 2000, pp. C1, C4; Theo Francis and Ellen E. Schultz, "Insurers Move to Protect Executive Policy, Wall Street Journal, December 30, 2002 p. C1; Patricia K. Zingheim and Jay R. Schuster, "Value Is the Goal," Workforce, February 2000, pp. 57–59; Shirley Fung, "How Should We Pay Them?" Across the Board, June 1999, pp. 37–41; K. Barron, "Praise and Poodles in that Order," Forbes, September 20, 1999, p. 153; and Richard M. Hodgetts, "A Conversation with Donald F. Hastings of the Lincoln Electric Company," Organizational Dynamics, Winter 1997, pp. 68–74. **http://www.weyerhaeuser.com**

What Is Motivation?

LEARNING OBJECTIVE
1
Describe the two sides of motivation movement and motive

The psychological drive that directs a person toward an objective is **motivation.** The word comes from the Latin word *movere,* "to move." When we see people working hard, we say that they are motivated because we can see them moving. This is as true for a secretary typing 100 words a minute as it is for an executive slowly reading a complex legal document. Yet motivation involves more than just movement. A student staring at some notes on a piece of paper may be memorizing this information, but we see virtually no movement occurring. Thus, motivation involves both physical *and* mental movement. "Motivation is a set of processes that moves a person toward a goal." Interviewed.[2]

In addition, any systematic analysis of motivation must be concerned with both *how* and *why* people act as they do. The former may be easy to pinpoint, but the latter often is not easy to identify. For example, Ralph has been offered time-and-a-half pay to work on Saturdays, and he has agreed to do so. We can, therefore, respond to the question "How do you get Ralph to work on Saturday?" by answering "Money." However, we cannot say with certainty *why* he is willing to work on Saturday. It may be because he wants to buy a boat, go on a vacation, put aside some money for a rainy day, or help pay some hospital bills for an elderly aunt. The "why" is currently unclear and, if we want to know the reason, we must investigate his motives. Motivation, therefore, has two sides: *movement* and *motive.* The former can be seen, whereas the latter can only be inferred. Before reading on, take the quiz "What Motivates You?" in the "Time Out" box and then read the interpretation of the results at the end of the chapter. This quiz should provide some insights to your own job-related motivation.

The "whys" of behavior are the **motives.** Often, they are defined as needs, drives, wants, or impulses within the individual. Regardless of how they are defined, however, motives arouse and maintain activity as well as determine the general direction of an individual's behavior. Many psychologists believe that there are two types of motives: primary and secondary. Primary

Motivation
is a psychological drive that directs a person toward an objective.

Motives
are the "whys" of behavior.

WHAT MOTIVATES YOU?

Many things motivate people. The following list contains 10 work-motivating factors. Read the list carefully and place a 10 next to the factor that has the greatest work-motivating potential for you. Place a 9 next to the second most important work-motivating factor. Continue until you have rank-ordered all 10. If you do not currently work, mentally choose a job for yourself and use it in completing the list.

_____ 1. Interesting work

_____ 2. Job security

_____ 3. Up-to-date equipment

_____ 4. A feeling of doing something important

_____ 5. Good wages

_____ 6. Challenging work

_____ 7. Effective supervision by the boss

_____ 8. A chance for advancement

_____ 9. Pleasant working conditions

_____ 10. The opportunity to succeed at what you are doing

The interpretation of your answers can be found in the back of the chapter under "Time Out Answers."

motives are unlearned. The needs for food and shelter are examples. In contrast, secondary needs are learned. The needs for power, achievement, and affiliation are examples.

In studying how motives prompt people to action, we must first examine two related topics: motive strength and goals. Motives are *directed toward goals.* For example, a person who needs money (motive) will opt for overtime (goal). An individual who desires recognition (motive) will strive for promotion to the top ranks of the organization (goal).

Of course, an individual often has many motives or needs and cannot actively pursue all of them simultaneously. To determine which motives a person will attempt to satisfy through activity, it is necessary to examine *motive strength.* In Figure 2.1, a diagram of relative motive strengths, Motive 7 has the greatest strength and will receive the most activity. An individual will work hardest to satisfy this motive. On the other hand, Motive 2 has a very low strength and will be given the lowest priority. Finally, once a motive or need is satisfied, it will no longer

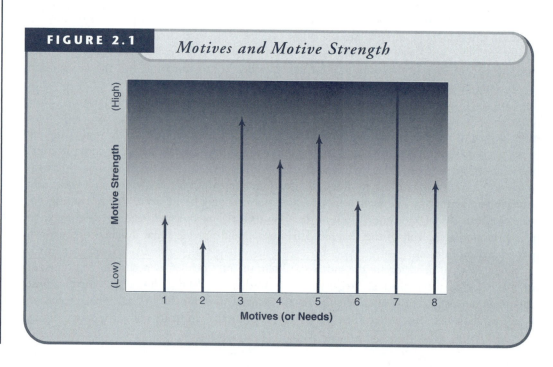

FIGURE 2.1 *Motives and Motive Strength*

January 9, 2003

MORALE STINKS!

But before you can improve it, you must first understand the key elements that foster—or ruin—morale

by Benson Smith and Tony Rutigliano

Authors of Discover Your Sales Strengths: How the World's Greatest Salespeople Develop Winning Careers *(Warner Books, February 2003)*

For many companies, 2002 will prove to have been a lackluster year financially. Even historically low interest rates couldn't produce the much-heralded second-half recovery. To make matters worse, most business news seems focused on threats rather than opportunities. Competitive threats, economic threats, terrorist threats, the potential impact of war, and a prolonged occupation of Iraq are all contributing to a malaise among businesses. Is it any wonder that so many managers are concerned about their sales forces' morale?

So, how is morale among your salespeople? Perhaps more importantly, how do you know, and what can you do to improve it? Let's look at a scenario that may seem very familiar to you.

Shortly before an upcoming annual sales meeting, the company president asked the vice president of sales a pointed question: "How is morale?" The V.P. hemmed and hawed before admitting that morale wasn't so great.

"I'm afraid our troops are a little down," the V.P. said. "Competition is getting tougher. And with the economy still in the doldrums, many of our customers are feeling the pinch. Orders aren't as robust as they should be. All this has a negative effect on our commission structure, so people aren't as pumped up as I would like them to be."

"So what the heck are you doing about it?" the president barked.

"Well," the V.P. answered, "we're throwing a few extra dollars into the commission pot. We're planning a big first-quarter promotion. And we're going to give away a BMW to the first salesperson who breaks the $2 million mark this year. That should get our troops juiced up and give us something positive to talk about at the upcoming sales meeting."

After the sales meeting, the V.P. came back to the home office and was happy to report that the sales force

responded enthusiastically to those changes. "They're all primed and ready to go," he told the president. "You should have seen the looks on their faces when we announced the car contest," he said. "They couldn't wait to get back home and start selling!"

"Really?" the president asked, unconvinced.

Wouldn't you be skeptical, too? Did the V.P. really solve the problem? Or was he deluded? Do these types of programs and gestures actually improve morale?

Defining morale

Before we can answer that, we have to ask an even more basic question: What exactly is "morale" anyway? Sales managers agree that morale is important, but they seem to interpret it in very different ways. Is morale something we can clearly define? Is it something we can measure? Is it something we can improve? Is it even important?

Based on The Gallup Organization's substantial research, we can tell you that the answer to each of these questions is an emphatic yes. But our research also reveals some very disturbing facts about morale in most sales forces — facts that every sales manager must understand.

First, let's start with a meaningful definition. Morale is best thought of as the emotional attachment or sense of engagement a salesperson has for his or her job. We know that engagement has a direct and meaningful relationship to the results every sales manager gets paid to deliver. Sales teams with high engagement levels are more productive, more profitable, and develop far more sustainable customer relationships.

So, sales managers and presidents alike are quite right to be concerned about morale. It is too important to leave to guesstimates.

In fact, engagement is so important that sales managers must pay constant attention to improving it within their ranks. But our extensive studies show this is often far from the case. In most sales forces Gallup has studied, we find that as many as two-thirds to three-quarters of individuals in the sales force are operating at engagement levels that substantially inhibit the workgroup's performance.

Research also suggests that short-term fixes, like tweaks in commission plans, new contests, or even giving away BMWs, have very short-lived effects on improving the engagement or morale of sales forces.

Sure, your sales force might act excited at the sales meeting when these tweaks are announced. But most sales forces have been conditioned to react positively at such

in action box cont.

gatherings. They have been explicitly or implicitly coached to hoot and holler at just the right moments, and they can deliver standing ovations precisely on cue. These outward signs of "good morale" are as credible as the Pavlovian laughter of a sitcom's live studio audience.

In most instances, your sales force's morale is driven much more by local management than by home office policies. Front-line managers improve morale by setting clear expectations, providing needed resources, focusing sales reps' attention on what they do best, showing frequent appreciation for their efforts, and providing a culture in which they can learn and grow. Those are the key ingredients that create emotional attachment to a company.

When front-line managers pay attention to these fundamentals, engagement improves dramatically and quickly. And improved engagement levels relate to key business outcomes.

Too often, we think that if we simply wait until business gets better, then morale will improve accordingly. A more effective strategy is to focus on improving employee engagement, which can lead to improved business outcomes. This is especially true in tough times when improved engagement levels can be a conspicuous competitive advantage.

Every manager, from the president on down, should rightfully be concerned about the morale or engagement of his or her employees. Our research suggests that it's much too important to leave to guesswork or quick fixes.

Benson Smith is a consultant, speaker, and author for The Gallup Organization and an expert in the area of sales force effectiveness.

Tony Rutigliano is a Senior Managing Consultant, speaker, and author for The Gallup Organization and an expert in sales force effectiveness, organizational effectiveness, and talent assessment.

motivate an individual to seek goal-directed behavior. Therefore, after Motive 7 is satisfied, an individual will direct behavior toward activities to fulfill Motive 3. Once that motive is satisfied, an individual will proceed to seek satisfaction for Motives 5, 4, 8, 6, 1, and 2, in that order.

When an individual is given the opportunity to attain a desired goal, he or she is positively motivated and will pursue that objective. Sometimes, however, an organization will use negative motivation because an individual has done something wrong, such as committing a major violation of company policy. In this case, the person may be turned down for promotion or be suspended from work without pay for a predetermined period, such as three weeks. Negative motivation is used to enforce rules and to shape employee behavior. If used incorrectly negative motivation can result in low morale. Morale impacts motivation, which in turn affects production and how things get done. To build a motivated workforce, research suggests that management pay more attention to creating and fostering an environment that promotes good morale. Read "Morale Stinks!" in the In Action Box and think of things your employer could do to increase morale where you work.

LEARNING OBJECTIVE

Identify the five basic needs in Maslow's need hierarchy

② The Need Hierarchy

We have examined motives or needs in very general terms. What kinds of needs do people have that, in turn, result in goal-directed behavior? Abraham Maslow, the noted psychologist, has set forth five needs that he believes are universal: *physiological, safety, social, esteem,* and *self-actualization* (see Figure 2.2).

Physiological Needs

Physiological needs

are basic requirements, such as food, clothing, and shelter.

The most fundamental of all needs, according to Maslow, are **physiological needs.** Some common examples are food, clothing, and shelter. A person deprived of everything would want to satisfy these basic needs first. Safety, social, esteem, and self-actualization needs would be of secondary importance.

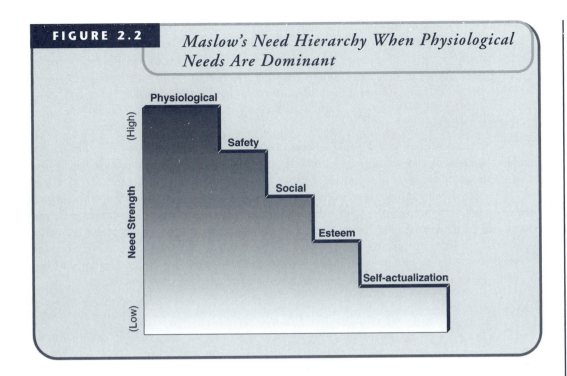

FIGURE 2.2 — *Maslow's Need Hierarchy When Physiological Needs Are Dominant*

In the workplace, many organizations try to satisfy physiological needs by providing cafeterias, vending machines, adequate ventilation, lighting, heating, and other physical facilities. In addition, the firms pay workers a salary with which they can meet these needs by purchasing food and clothing for themselves and for their families. Although many physiological needs exist, the most basic would get prime attention until satisfied and then would be replaced by other physiological demands with greater need strength.

Safety Needs

Once physiological needs are basically satisfied, **safety needs** replace them. These are of two types. First, there is the need for *survival;* this need is so great that many of the laws in our society are designed to protect lives. Second, there is the need for *security;* this need has physical and psychological dimensions. On the physical side, businesses often provide safety equipment and safety rules for protecting workers on the job. They also provide accident, health, and life insurance to help meet safety needs. The psychological aspect of safety is evident in workers' desire for secure jobs in a predictable environment. Individuals who work in government bureaucracies often fall into this category. They want guaranteed employment. Their pay may not be very high, but they are assured of a steady job. Other people find such safety in business bureaucracies where, although a firm may not pay well, it just about guarantees continued employment to anyone who performs even minimally.

Safety needs *provide for survival and security.*

Social Needs

When physiological and safety needs are basically satisfied, **social needs** become important motivators. These needs involve interaction with others for the purpose of meaningful relationships. On the job, interaction often occurs among people who work near one another and come into frequent daily contact. Over time, they build up friendships and look forward to the interaction. In their personal lives, people fulfill social needs when they meet their neighbors and socialize with them and other friends regularly.

Business firms try to meet this need by allowing workers to interact and talk with one another. On assembly lines, workers know they can do their routine jobs and interact at the same time. In retail and banking firms, there is an increased opportunity for interaction because the workers carry out their jobs by socializing to some degree with the customers.

Social needs *are satisfied through meaningful interaction with others.*

It is important to note that social affiliation helps to make boring, routine work more bearable. When such interaction occurs, morale is higher and productivity tends to remain at least within tolerable ranges. However, when social interaction is denied, workers tend to fight the system by restricting work output or by doing no more than is required by their job descriptions. Allowing personnel to fulfill social needs on the job often helps to prevent these negative behaviors.

Esteem Needs

When social needs are basically satisfied, **esteem needs** come into play. People need to feel important, and self-esteem and self-respect are vital in this process. Esteem is much more *psychological* in nature than the other three needs we have discussed. We can give a person food, clothing, shelter, protection, and social interaction. However, the esteem with which individuals regard themselves is mostly a function of what they allow themselves to believe. For example, a person who is told by his boss that he does an excellent job will be motivated by this praise only if he accepts the laudatory comments. If the individual believes that the manager is complimenting his work only as a matter of course and is insincere, the praise has no motivational effect. Research reveals that two motives closely related to esteem are prestige and power.[3]

Prestige

For many people, **prestige** means "keeping up with the Joneses," or perhaps getting ahead of them. In any event, prestige carries with it respect and status and influences the way people talk and act around an individual. A company president has considerable prestige and is treated with great respect by organizational members. Out on the golf course, however, the company president may have limited prestige among the players, and the country club's golf pro is given the greatest amount of respect. Thus, one's prestige depends on the situation.

Power

The ability to influence or induce behavior in others is **power.** Power can be of two kinds: positional and personal. *Positional* power is derived from an individual's position in the company. The president has a great deal more positional power than does a middle manager in the same organization, for instance. *Personal* power derives from an individual's personality and behavior. Anne may have a pleasing personality and an easygoing manner, which results in her being able to cut across departmental lines and gain support for her proposals; Andy, however, is considered hard-nosed and bossy and is unable to secure such cooperation. Within bounds, people like power because it provides them with feelings of self-esteem.[4]

Self-Actualization Needs

When all the other needs are basically satisfied, **self-actualization needs** manifest themselves. Because people satisfy these needs in so many different ways, behavioral scientists know less about them than about the other needs. However, research reveals that two motives are related to self-actualization: competence and achievement.

Competence

Competence is similar to power in that it implies control over environmental factors. At a very early age, children begin illustrating their need for competence by touching and handling objects to become familiar with them. Later on, they begin trying to take things apart and put them back together again. As a result, children learn tasks at which they are competent.

On the job, the competence motive reveals itself in the form of a desire for job mastery and professional growth. An individual begins matching his or her abilities and skills against the environment in a contest that is challenging but that can be won. Organizations that provide meaningful, challenging work help their people meet the need for competence. In some companies, such as those using assembly lines, such jobs are not in abundance, and the competence motive often goes unsatisfied.

Achievement

Over the last fifty years, a great deal of research has been conducted on people's desire for **achievement.** One of the leading researchers, David C. McClelland of Harvard University, has been particularly interested in this urge.[5] On the basis of his research, he has set forth the following characteristics of **high achievers:** They

- Like situations in which they can take personal responsibility for finding solutions to problems.
- Tend to be moderate risk takers.
- Like concrete feedback on their performance so that they know how well they are doing.

Although only about 10 to 15 percent of the population in the United States has the desire to achieve, high achievement can be encouraged and developed. McClelland has recommended several methods for individuals who want to become high achievers:

- Strive to obtain feedback so your successes can be noted and you can make them serve as reinforcement for strengthening your desire to achieve even more.
- Pick out people you know who have performed well and use them as models to emulate.
- Modify your self-image by imagining yourself as someone who needs to succeed and to be challenged.
- Control your daydreaming by thinking and talking to yourself in positive terms.[6]

How can you use these ideas? The "Human Relations in Action" box offers some specific steps.

Achievement *is the desire to attain objectives.*

High achievers *are moderate risk takers who like specific feedback on their performance.*

---

in action

HUMAN RELATIONS IN ACTION

Increasing Your Achievement Drive

There are many things you can do to increase your achievement drive. The following are the most helpful.

1. *Put your goals in writing.* This serves two useful purposes. First, it forces you to think through your objectives. Exactly what are you trying to accomplish? Second, it serves as a basis for comparing desired and actual progress.

2. *Make the goals challenging yet attainable.* If the goals are easy to attain, you really are not achieving much. If the goals are too difficult, you will not be able to reach them. Choose objectives that stretch you but are within your grasp. In this way, the goals become learning devices that help you grow.

3. *Be sure your goals are compatible.* If your goals are not compatible, you are working at cross-purposes with yourself. For example, if one of your objectives is to double your sales this quarter, it is unrealistic to have a second objective of cutting travel

and entertainment by 30 percent. If anything, this budget will probably go up because you will have to do more traveling and entertaining.

4. *Have specific goals.* Where possible, quantify your goals; for example, you might wish to reduce production costs by 7 percent, increase sales by 9 percent, and increase the number of salespeople by twenty-two. If this is not possible or desirable, write the objective in such a way that progress can be measured.

5. *Establish timetables.* Tie your goals to a timetable, noting when progress will be achieved. This will help you to keep track of how well you are doing. If you start to fall behind, you will be able to identify when and where things are going wrong.

6. *Establish priorities.* Determine which goals must be attained first and which ones can wait. If sales have to be increased as quickly as possible, put this goal high on your list of things to do. If trips to the field to check on your salespeople can wait until next month, schedule them for next month

in action box contd.

and get back to work on those things that must be done now.

7. *Review and revise your goals.* Look over your list of goals every ninety days and see how well you are doing. Have any of the goals been attained? If so, remove them from the list. Do any of the current objectives need to be changed? If so, change them. Do any new ones need to be added? Put them on the list. This process keeps your goal-directed behavior properly focused.

8. *Reward yourself.* Every time you accomplish one of your objectives, reward yourself. When you close that big sale, treat yourself to dinner or buy that suit you have had your eye on. This work-reward approach will encourage you to keep up your efforts. Remember that successful people are good to themselves. If one of your subordinates did something well, you would reward the individual as a way of encouraging a repeat performance. Be no less kind to yourself.

On the job, organizations help create the proper climate for developing high achievement by giving people jobs that provide feedback, increase personal initiative, and allow individuals to take moderate risks. However, although the enterprise can encourage its personnel toward high achievement, to a large degree this drive is something that develops in early childhood. Also, high achievers get things done themselves but often are ineffective in managing others, so organizations do not want all their employees to possess high achievement drive.

Need mix

An important premise of the need hierarchy is that as one need is basically fulfilled, the next most important need becomes dominant and dictates individual behavior. Note that we say "basically fulfilled." This is because most people in our society are *partially satisfied* and *partially dissatisfied* at each level. Greatest satisfaction tends to occur at the physiological level and least satisfaction at the self-actualization level. Maslow put it this way:

> *In actual fact, most members of our society who are normal are partially satisfied in all their basic needs and partially unsatisfied in all their basic needs at the same time. A more realistic description of the hierarchy would be in terms of decreasing percentage of satisfaction as we go up the hierarchy of prepotency. For instance, if I may assign arbitrary figures, . . . it is as if the average citizen is satisfied perhaps 85 percent in his physiological needs, 70 percent in his safety needs, 50 percent in his [social] needs, 40 percent in his self-esteem needs, and 10 percent in his self-actualization needs.*[7]

Need mix
is an individual's need strength at each level of the need hierarchy.

As a result, the Maslow need hierarchy cannot be viewed as an all-or-nothing framework. Rather, to understand the fundamentals of human behavior, we should regard the hierarchy as useful in predicting behavior on a high- or low-probability basis. For example, among people who come from abject poverty, the **need mix** pictured in Figure 2.3 probably is highly representative. However, most people in American society are characterized by strong social or affiliation needs, relatively strong esteem and safety needs, and somewhat less important physiological and self-actualization needs; this need mix is illustrated in Figure 2.4. For individuals whose physiological, safety, and social needs are greatly satisfied, esteem and self-actualization are most important. A person born to great wealth would fit into this category, as would a top management executive. The need mix for these people is pictured in Figure 2.5. Of course, these configurations are intended only as examples. Different configurations would be appropriate for different people because, in reality, the need mix changes from one individual to another. Maslow's theory is interesting, but its practical value is limited. To see its application to the motivation of personnel, we must turn to Frederick Herzberg's two-factor theory.

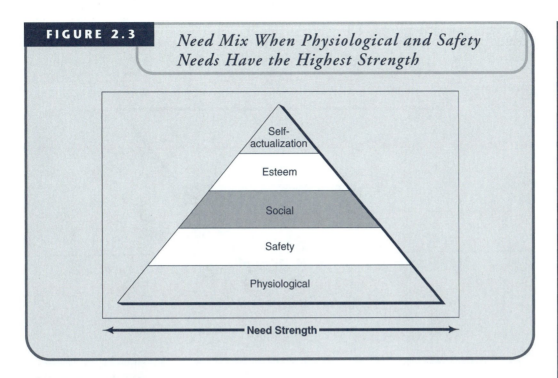

FIGURE 2.3   *Need Mix When Physiological and Safety Needs Have the Highest Strength*

Self-actualization

Esteem

Social

Safety

Physiological

← **Need Strength** →

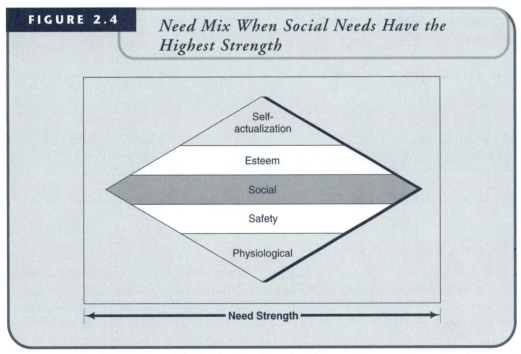

FIGURE 2.4   *Need Mix When Social Needs Have the Highest Strength*

Self-actualization

Esteem

Social

Safety

Physiological

← **Need Strength** →

The Two-Factor Theory

The two-factor theory of motivation is a direct result of research conducted by Frederick Herzberg and his associates on job satisfaction and productivity among two hundred accountants and engineers.[8] Each subject was asked to think of a time when he or she felt especially good about his or her job and a time when he or she felt particularly bad about the job and to describe the conditions that led to these feelings. The researchers found that the employees named different types of conditions for good and bad feelings. This led Herzberg to conclude that motivation consists of two factors: hygiene and motivators (Table 2.1).

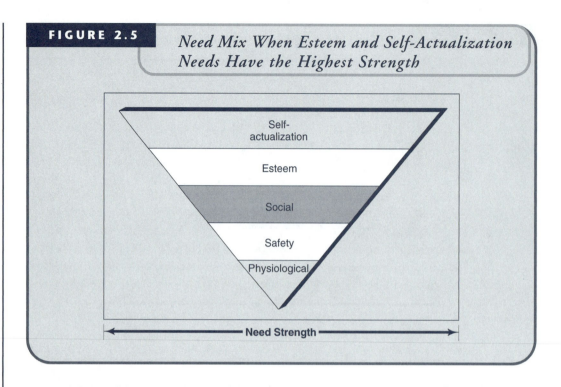

FIGURE 2.5 *Need Mix When Esteem and Self-Actualization Needs Have the Highest Strength*

Self-actualization
Esteem
Social
Safety
Physiological

Need Strength

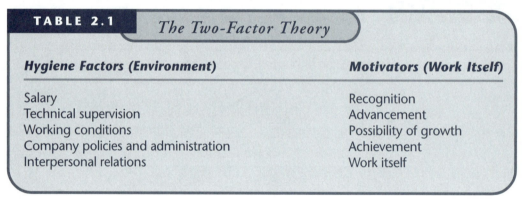

TABLE 2.1 *The Two-Factor Theory*

Hygiene Factors (Environment)	Motivators (Work Itself)
Salary	Recognition
Technical supervision	Advancement
Working conditions	Possibility of growth
Company policies and administration	Achievement
Interpersonal relations	Work itself

Hygiene Factors

Hygiene factors are environmentally related.

The factors associated with negative feelings Herzberg called **hygiene factors.** Illustrations included salary, technical supervision, working conditions, company policies and administration, and interpersonal relations. When the subjects of Herzberg's study were asked what made them feel exceptionally bad about their jobs, typical answers included: "I'm really not satisfied with the salary I'm being paid; it's much too low." "My boss is always too busy to offer me any technical supervision." "The working conditions around here are really poor." All the responses have one thing in common: They relate to the environment in which the work is performed.

Herzberg called these environment-related factors *hygiene* because, like physical hygiene, they prevent deterioration but do not lead to growth. For example, if you brush your teeth (a hygiene step) you can prevent cavities, but your teeth will not become stronger nor will a chipped tooth grow back to its original size. Thus, you have two alternatives: Brush your teeth and prevent further damage, or do not brush your teeth and end up losing them. Analogously, Herzberg felt that if you provide for hygiene factors, you will not give individuals motivation but you will prevent dissatisfaction.[9] Using our own percentages as examples, Figure 2.6 illustrates how Herzberg believes hygiene can affect performance. Note that when hygiene factors are satisfied, workers perform at less than their full ability. When these factors are not satisfied, performance drops. Thus, hygiene will not bring about an increase in productivity, but it will prevent a decline.

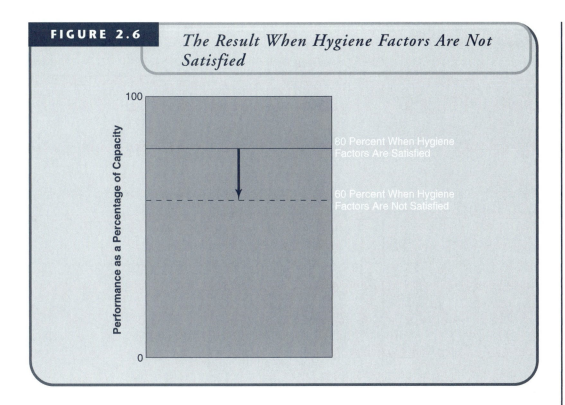

FIGURE 2.6

The Result When Hygiene Factors Are Not Satisfied

100

Performance as a Percentage of Capacity

80 Percent When Hygiene Factors Are Satisfied

60 Percent When Hygiene Factors Are Not Satisfied

0

Motivators

The factors associated with positive feelings Herzberg called **motivators.** Examples are recognition, advancement, growth, achievement, and the work itself. When subjects were asked what made them feel exceptionally good about their jobs, typical answers included: "My job gives me a feeling of achievement." "I like the recognition I get for doing my job well." "The work is just plain interesting." All these responses have one thing in common: They relate to the work itself. Additionally, they are psychological in nature and relate to upper-level need satisfaction. Herzberg termed these factors *motivators* because he believed that they caused increases in performance. Using our own percentages as examples, Figure 2.7 shows the ways in which Herzberg believes motivators can affect performance. Note that the employees represented are performing at 80 percent of their ability. When they are given motivators such as recognition, advancement, and the possibility of growth, their performance increases, measuring closer to their potential. In short, as performance potential increases, output goes up.

Motivation–Hygiene Theory and Managers

One major reason that Herzberg's two-factor theory has been so well accepted by managers is that it applies Maslow's need concept to the job. For example, Herzberg suggests using hygiene factors to help people attain their lower-level needs. Conversely, he recommends motivators to meet upper-level needs. Figure 2.8 integrates these two concepts. As you can see, Herzberg suggests that physiological, safety, social, and, to some degree, esteem needs can be satisfied with hygiene factors. The remainder of the esteem needs and all the self-actualization needs can be satisfied with motivators.

A second reason for the popularity of Herzberg's theory is that practicing managers agree with it. In a study designed to learn more about work motivations of men and women, 128 managers were asked to rank eight motives for pursuing a managerial career. The results showed that the two top choices—a sense of achievement and challenge—correspond to Herzberg's motivators, illustrating the value of his theory.

A third reason for the popularity of the theory has been revealed by recent research: The most powerful rewards are psychological in nature, a finding that corresponds with Herzberg's

Motivators
are associated with positive feelings.

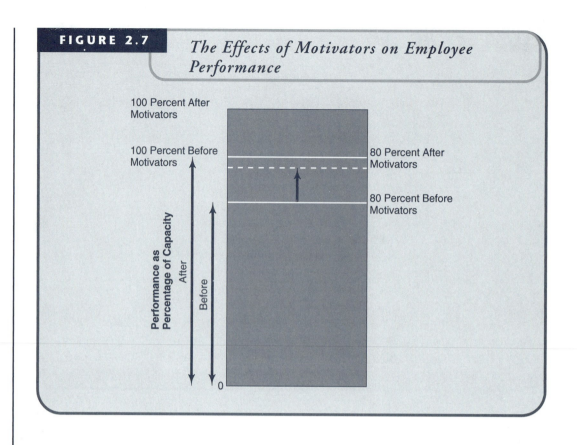

FIGURE 2.7

The Effects of Motivators on Employee Performance

100 Percent After Motivators

100 Percent Before Motivators

80 Percent After Motivators

80 Percent Before Motivators

Performance as Percentage of Capacity

After

Before

0

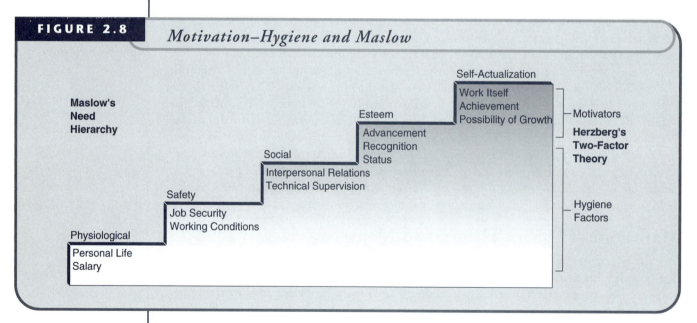

FIGURE 2.8

Motivation–Hygiene and Maslow

Maslow's Need Hierarchy

Self-Actualization

Work Itself
Achievement
Possibility of Growth

Esteem

Advancement
Recognition
Status

Social

Interpersonal Relations
Technical Supervision

Safety

Job Security
Working Conditions

Physiological

Personal Life
Salary

Motivators

Herzberg's Two-Factor Theory

Hygiene Factors

research. Hence, organizations are now using approaches such as recognition in a variety of ways to build and sustain motivation.

When employees in a small manufacturing company attained a major safety milestone—100 days without a single accident, the company made them feel like heroes.

On the morning of day 100, it was announced that a catered lunch would be served the next day, if they made it to the 5:30 shift without an accident. At 5:15, anticipation was building. Managers took confetti streamers to the balcony overlooking the shop floor. When the 5:30 whistle blew, there were congratulations all around, confetti flew through the air, and banners were unfurled. It was a great moment for everyone—and one that was not soon forgotten. The recognition value of this celebration was extremely high, while the monetary cost was relatively low.

Highly motivating organizations even celebrate small successes. A health-conscious company distributes fruit bowls to employees' work areas when key personal milestones are attained. Another company uses a more fattening approach: fresh-baked chocolate-chip cookies to say thank you.[10]

Motivation–Hygiene Theory in Perspective

Many businesspeople who read about the motivation–hygiene theory are likely to accept it as totally accurate. Certainly, to the extent that it encourages the manager to provide upper-level need satisfaction, the theory is relevant to our study of motivation. However, the theory has several serious shortcomings that merit attention.

First, Herzberg contends that something is *either* a hygiene factor *or* a motivator—the two are independent of each other. Additionally, a lack of hygiene will lead to dissatisfaction, but its presence will not lead to satisfaction. Satisfaction results only from the presence of motivators. We can diagram the relationship as in Figure 2.9. If you give people hygiene factors, you will not motivate them, but you will prevent dissatisfaction. Thus, hygiene, according to Herzberg, creates a zero level of motivation. Research, however, reveals that some people are indeed motivated by hygiene factors. For example, many individuals say that money is a motivator for them. Some people report that recognition and the chance for advancement lead to dissatisfaction; for them, these are not motivators. Researchers have found that some factors are satisfiers some of the time and dissatisfiers the rest of the time. For example, many people want a chance to achieve but not every minute of every workday. If achievement opportunities are offered too often, workers will be unhappy, believing that too much is expected of them. On the basis of findings such as these, Herzberg's critics claim that his initial theory has not been supported well by further investigation.

A second major criticism centers on the way in which the original data were gathered. The researchers asked accountants and engineers what they particularly liked and disliked about their jobs. Critics say the answers are biased because people tend to give socially acceptable responses when asked such questions. What would you expect people to say they disliked about their jobs? Stereotypical answers would include salary, supervision, and working conditions. Similarly, people could be expected to say that they liked recognition, advancement, and achievement. A close analysis of these two groups of answers shows that things people dislike about their jobs are related to the work environment, a factor the employee cannot control. The aspects of their jobs that people like are related to their own achievements and accomplishments and are factors that they can control. It is therefore possible that Herzberg's methodology may have encouraged stereotypical answers.

Despite such problems, however, Herzberg's theory sheds some important light on the subject of motivation. In particular, it stresses the importance of helping people fulfill *all* their needs, not just basic needs. The theory also helps to explain what motivates people in international cultures. The "Cultural Diversity in Action" box provides some examples.

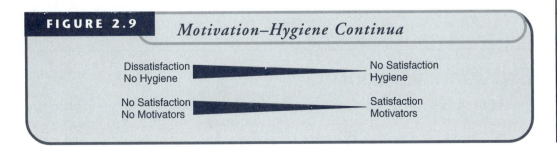

FIGURE 2.9 *Motivation–Hygiene Continua*

Dissatisfaction
No Hygiene ⟶ No Satisfaction
Hygiene

No Satisfaction
No Motivators ⟶ Satisfaction
Motivators

CULTURAL DIVERSITY IN ACTION

View From Abroad

Everyone can be motivated, but are the factors that are important in the United States the same as those in other countries? Research shows that there is a considerable cultural impact on achievement, and those motivational factors that are high on the list of workers in one country may be low on the list of workers in another country. This is particularly true when comparing nations that have different political systems. For example, four Far Eastern countries were examined by researchers who wanted to find out the importance of certain motivational variables. The higher the score, the more important the variable. Here is what they learned:

Motivational Variable	People's Republic of China	Hong Kong	Taiwan	Singapore
Cooperative coworkers	635	579	571	624
Need for autonomy	603	512	480	532
Job challenge	515	548	548	571
Good working relations with the manager	483	522	524	551
Salary	454	567	442	552
Job security	450	452	506	437
Work benefits	439	323	363	439
Good working conditions	433	436	407	432
Opportunity for promotion	364	640	630	593
Job recognition	446	487	487	442

The results show there is considerable cultural impact on the importance of these variables. For example, in China, where the government guarantees everyone a job and the economy is state-run, earnings are not as important as they are in Singapore, which has a free-enterprise system. Similarly, the opportunity for promotion is not very important in China because there are few rewards that accompany the job. In contrast, workers in Hong Kong and Taiwan are highly motivated by such opportunities.

At the same time, however, it is important to realize the many similarities among the four countries examined here. For example, job recognition is of approximately equal importance for all these workers, and they all place similar value on the importance of favorable working conditions.

What, then, can be concluded about motivation in the international arena? The answer is that it varies from country to country, and any generalization about workers in a particular geographical region is likely to be erroneous. Motivation is greatly affected by culture, which helps to create both similarities and differences in work values. The only way to determine precisely how to motivate workers in a specific country is by studying that culture and then fashioning a motivational package that addresses those particular employees.

Sources: Geert Hofstede, Culture's Consequences: International Differences in Work-Related Values (Beverly Hills: Sage Publications, 1980); Oded Shenkar and Simcha Ronen, "Structure and Importance of Work Goals Among Managers in the People's Republic of China," Academy of Management Journal, September 1987, p. 571; and Richard M. Hodgetts and Fred Luthans, International Management, 4th ed. (Burr Ridge, IL: Irwin/McGraw, 2000), pp. 364–366.

LEARNING OBJECTIVE (4)

Discuss expectancy theory, noting how both valence and expectancy influence motivation force

Expectancy Theory

Although a study of the need hierarchy and blocked need satisfaction is one way of examining motivation, there is now a great deal of interest in **expectancy theory.**[11] Developed by Victor Vroom,[12] and based on earlier work by others, expectancy theory has been expanded and refined by such individuals as Lyman Porter and Edward Lawler.[13] Vroom's motivation formula is a simple yet powerful one that can be expressed as follows:

Motivation = Valence × Expectancy.

To understand the theory, we must examine the concepts of valence and expectancy.

Expectancy theory
holds that motivation is equal to valence times expectancy.

Valence

A person's preference for a particular outcome or objective can be expressed as a **valence.** A valence describes how much someone likes or dislikes something. This preference can range from +1 (highest preference) to −1 (lowest preference). For example, Bob wants a promotion to the New York office. On a scale from −1 to +1, his valence is +1. Suzy, meanwhile, is indifferent to the idea of promotion to the New York office. Her valence is 0. Tom, however, will not take a promotion to the New York office under any conditions. His valence is −1. Figure 2.10 illustrates the valence range.

Note that expectancy theory forces the manager to answer the question: What motivates the individual? By examining the preference of workers for various outcomes, ranging from increased salary to a feeling of accomplishment, the manager is in a good position to offer workers what they want. However, it is important to realize that most managers do *not* know what motivates their workers. Table 2.2 is a list of job qualities for which workers would have varying degrees of preference. This list was given to workers and managers all around the country. The workers were asked to rank the factors from most important to least important. The

Valence
is a person's preference for a particular outcome.

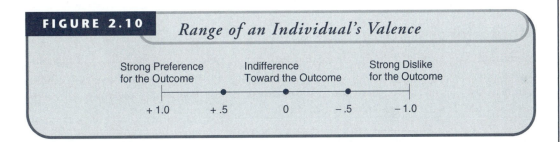

FIGURE 2.10 *Range of an Individual's Valence*

Strong Preference for the Outcome	Indifference Toward the Outcome	Strong Dislike for the Outcome
+ 1.0 + .5	0	− .5 − 1.0

TABLE 2.2 *What Do Workers Want From Their Jobs?*

Job Qualities	Rank (1–10)
Job security	_____
Full appreciation for work done	_____
Promotion and growth with the company	_____
Tactful disciplining	_____
Good wages	_____
Feeling in on things	_____
Interesting work	_____
Management loyalty to the workers	_____
Good working conditions	_____
Sympathetic understanding of personal problems	_____

Source: Reported in Paul Hersey and Kenneth H. Blanchard, Management of Organizational Behavior: Utilizing Human Resources, *3d ed. (Englewood Cliffs, NJ: Prentice Hall, 1977), p. 47.*

managers were asked to rank the factors the way they thought the workers would. Before reading further, take time to rank the items on this list by placing a 1 after the item you think workers said was most important to them, a 2 after the item you think they ranked second, down to a 10 after the item you think the workers ranked last. Then compare your answers to those given at the end of the chapter. You may find that your list was closer to that of supervisors in industry than to that of the workers themselves. Most readers' lists are, because like many managers, they do not know the valences that workers actually have for various qualities of the work environment.

Expectancy

Expectancy
is the perceived probability that a specific outcome will follow a specific act.

The probability that a specific outcome will follow from a specific act is termed **expectancy.** People at work are motivated to perform because of expectations. Their perception of the value and probability of an outcome will affect the degree of motivation. For example, what is the likelihood that Bob will get a promotion to the New York office if he receives the highest efficiency rating in his department? If Bob thinks that the chances are very good, he will assign to this a very high probability, such as .99. If Bob believes the likelihood of the promotion is fair (that efficiency ratings help, but getting the job depends most heavily on how well the boss likes him personally), he may assign it a probability of .50. Finally, if Bob believes the high efficiency rating will knock him out of consideration for the New York position (that if he is a good worker, the firm will keep him here rather than let him go away to New York), he will assign it a very low rating, such as 0.01.

Do not confuse valence and expectancy. Although Bob may have a high valence (+1) for a promotion to New York City, he also may believe that the manager does not like him. So, no matter how high his sales, he assigns the probability of his being promoted to New York City (expectancy) as very low, for example, 0.10.

Motivational Force

Motivational force
is equal to valence times expectancy.

Motivation is a function of both valence and expectancy. One without the other will not produce motivation. This becomes clearer if we apply some illustrations to the expectancy theory formula. Also, let us use the term **motivational force** rather than simply motivation, because force or effort is what we are interested in measuring. The formula then is:

Motivational Force = Valence × Expectancy.

If either expectancy or valence is 0, the motivational force will be 0. Likewise, if one is high and the other is low, the motivational force will be low. Let us take an example. The vice president of sales has just announced that the salesperson with the best sales record for next month will get an all-expenses-paid trip for two to Hawaii at Christmas. The three top salespeople are Charles, Fred, and Maureen. To determine each one's motivational force, we look at the valence and expectancy each has regarding the free trip.

Charles has a very high valence for this trip (valence = 1.0). He has never been to Hawaii, and he knows his wife would love to go. However, the last time the vice president made a promise like this he was overridden by the company comptroller, who said the firm could not afford to send two people to Paris for a week. Instead, the winner was given a check for $250. Charles remembers this incident vividly, as he was the winner. As a result, he believes that the possibility of the winner's going to Hawaii is good but not certain (expectancy = 0.5). We can determine Charles's motivational force as follows:

Motivational Force = $V(1.0) \times E(0.5) = 0.5$.

Fred would also like to win the free trip to Hawaii. However, as luck would have it, Fred took his wife and family there four months ago for their vacation. Nevertheless, his valence for this trip is still quite high (valence = 0.7). Furthermore, although he also remembers that the vice president was prevented from awarding an all-expenses-paid trip last time, Fred believes that this time the contest probably was cleared with the company comptroller and that the winner will indeed travel to Hawaii (expectancy = 0.9). Fred's motivational force can be calculated as follows:

Motivational Force = $V(0.7) \times E(0.9) = 0.63$.

Maureen is the only one who is not delighted with the prospect of the trip. Last week, she and her fiancé decided the date for their wedding would be December 22. They plan to spend the next two weeks honeymooning in Switzerland. The bridegroom's father has a chalet there, right near one of the finest ski resorts in the country. Maureen knows that there is simply no way she can take the trip. As a result, she is indifferent about the prize (valence = 0), although she does believe that the winner will be sent to Hawaii (expectancy = 1.0). Her motivational force can be computed this way:

Motivational Force = $V(0) \times E(1.0) = 0$.

Of the three, Fred is the most motivated to attain the highest sales record. A close look at the motivational force computations shows that he had neither the highest valence for the Hawaiian trip (Charles did) nor the highest expectancy (Maureen did). However, the *combination* of the two produced a greater motivational force than that for the others.

Expectancy Theory in Perspective

Obviously, no manager is going to spend time trying to determine the motivational force of each worker for each objective. However, for many reasons, expectancy theory is helpful in understanding motivation.

First, the expectancy model urges us to look at motivation as a *force* or strength of drive directed toward some objective. As a result, we no longer consider *whether* a person is motivated toward doing something but *how great* the motivation may be. Just about every worker is motivated by money, but some workers are more highly motivated by it than are others.

Second, although Maslow's need hierarchy can be applied to everyone in general, it does not address *individual motivation* and its specific aspects. Expectancy theory does.

Third, the model suggests that people learn what kinds of rewards they like and dislike through *experience*. They also learn to determine the probabilities of their attaining these rewards. Thus, both valence and expectancy are a result of individual experiences, and what highly motivates one person may create no motivational force in another.

Fourth, to a large extent, motivation is determined not only by rewards available but by their degree of *equity* or fairness. **Equity theory** holds that workers compare their work-reward ratio to that of others in determining how fairly they are being treated. If Tony and Barbara are both receiving the same salary, but Tony feels that she works harder than Barbara, Tony will also feel that she is being treated inequitably. If the organization does not raise her salary above Barbara's, Tony is likely to be dissatisfied and may start doing less work or look for a job elsewhere. Remember that this dissatisfaction is a result of perceived inequity. As long as Tony believes that a lack of equity exists, her dissatisfaction will remain.

Fifth, if we accept the expectancy model, it follows that to motivate an individual to work we can do only two things:

1. **increase the positive value of outcomes by increasing rewards,**
2. **strengthen the connection between the work and the outcomes.**

One way of achieving these steps is through effective goal setting, which involves both setting goals and establishing objectives. Goals provide general directions, whereas objectives provide specific directions for achieving the goals. Without goals, there is no reason for existence. For example, a goal of a successful business is to provide quality products; another goal is to make a profit. Until clear, specific, attainable objectives are established for each goal, nothing will happen. A goal is a vague statement that fails to provide specific guidance for accomplishing results; whereas an objective identifies the strategy, the process, the timetable, and a means of measuring the

Equity theory
holds that people use a work-reward ratio in determining how fairly they are being treated.

results of the goal. Through objectives, goals are accomplished. It also is important to provide people with frequent feedback so they know how well they are doing and can make any necessary changes.

LEARNING OBJECTIVE

Explain the value of money, employee satisfaction, incentives, and recognition in the motivation process

⑤ The Practical Side of Rewards

Much of what has been discussed thus far has been theoretical in nature. However, motivation also has a practical side, and financial rewards and employee satisfaction play big roles here. There are three reasons for this.

1. **Everyone needs lower-level satisfaction, and money often plays a major role in fulfilling this need**
2. **Money also can help people attain upper-level need satisfaction. A person who is making 10 percent more than anyone else doing the same job can look in the mirror and say, "Wow, I must be good. Otherwise, I wouldn't be making so much money."[14]**
3. **Employee satisfaction is important, and rewards, monetary and nonmonetary alike, can influence the extent to which this is present.[15]**

When rewards are discussed, most people immediately think of money—and there is certainly good reason for this.[16] Especially at the upper levels of the hierarchy, financial packages are important in attracting and retaining the services of successful managers.[17] Table 2.3 reports the recent total compensation for some of the best-paid executives in America. Over the last couple of years, however, other approaches have become increasingly important.

- **Stock options, which are tied directly to company performance and, in some cases, not restricted to only senior-level managers.**
- **Broad banding, which allows managers greater freedom in giving raises to their personnel.**
- **Cafeteria incentive programs, which allow employees to choose the types of rewards that will be most motivational for them.**
- **The use of different types of recognition programs.**

Stock Options

In recent years, employee salaries in the workforce at large have been increasing by approximately 3 percent annually. However, executive compensation packages have been going up at a much faster rate. One reason is that these managers have been given stock options that allow them to buy company stock at very attractive prices and exercise these options when the stock price is high. So the stock market boom of the 1990s resulted in some executives making millions of dollars by exercising their options, and some senior-level managers currently hold unexercised options that are worth hundreds of millions of dollars.[18] One of the problems with some of these stock option plans was that they allowed the option to be exercised even if the company's performance was poor. As a result, the current trend in executive options is now moving toward "pay for performance" plans. The Incentive Performance System at Lincoln Electric is one of the oldest "pay-for-performance" systems in the country. It was implemented by James F. Lincoln in the early twentieth century and is frequently used for benchmarking by other businesses. Several features of the system include:

- **Open communication with senior management.**
- **Piecework incentive rewards for all production work.**
- **A profit-sharing bonus plan.**
- **Guaranteed employment after three years of service.[19]**

TABLE 2.3 — Some of America's Highest Paid Executives

Company	Name	Total Compensation (in millions)
Oracle	L. J. Ellison	706,077
Forest Laboratories	H. Soloman	148,476
IBM	L. V. Gerstner, Jr.	127,404
Apple Computer	S. P. Jobs	83,996
Applied Micro Circuits	D. M. Rickey	59,587
Coca-Cola	D. N. Draft	55,004
Philip Morris	G. C. Bible	49,907
Citigroup	S. I. Weill	42,613
Electronic Data Systems	R. H. Brown	37,287
Cendant	H. R. Silverman	36,352
MBNA	A. Lerner	27,881
Broadcom	H. T. Nicholas, III	25,617
American Express	K. I. Chenault	23,728
Pfizer	H. A. McKinnell	23,642
BLACK & DECKER	N. D. Archibald	23,553
Home Depot	R. L. Nardelli	22,830
United Technologies	G. David	22,636
J. P. Morgan	W. B. Harrison, Jr.	22,141
Verizon Communications	C.R. Lee	21,389
Best Buy	R. M. Schulze	20,294
Bed, Bath & Beyond	W. Eisenberg	19,888
Lockheed Martin	V. D. Coffman	16,556
Analog Devices	J. G. Fishman	16,403
General Electric	J. F. Welch	16,247
Kimberly Clark	W. R. Sanders	14,763
Citizens Communications	L. Tow	13,345
Harley-Davidson	J. L. Bleustein	13,078
Alcoa	A. J. Belda	12,569
Bank One	J. Demon	12,430
Colgate-Palmolive	R. Mark	11,115
Abbott Laboratories	M. D. White	10,563

Reference: "Executive Compensation Scoreboard," Business Week, April 15, 2002, pp. 86–100. Refer to this article for a more comprehensive listing of companies.

WorldCom Inc. provides a good example of "pay for performance." WorldCom Inc. filed for bankruptcy protection in July 2002 for one of the largest accounting frauds ever. A new chief executive, Michael Capellas, was appointed to take the company out of bankruptcy and turn it into a model of what a company should be. He was given a three-year pay package valued at $20 million. Under the contract Michael Capellas will receive an annual salary of $1.5 million, a signing bonus of $2 million and a further $1.5 million bonus if he meets certain performance targets, $12 million in restricted shares, with an additional $6 million in restricted stock only if he meets performance targets. In addition, the guaranteed $12 million in restricted stock has a vested period of three years, and if Mr. Capellas exercises any stock options, he can-not sell the WorldCom stock for a twelve-month period. Companies are forcing their executives to assume financial risks if they want to exercise stock options.

The restricted shares will not become the property of Mr. Capellas until he meets performance targets. Therefore, executives are more highly motivated to improve company productivity and profits.

A few companies have already put their CEOs to the test. Level 3 Communications, a network company, "grants options that reward top officers only when Level 3's stock outperforms the S&P 500. But there's little sign that variable options will become the norm. CEOs don't like them because they have to be expensed. And for most execs, the payout would be much less than the riches that fixed options deliver."[20]

Synygy, Inc., a large provider of incentive management software and services, implemented what company spokesman Oliver Picher describes at a "bonus program that ranges in amount from 5 to 100 percent of an employee's base salary and is paid quarterly."[21]

MetLife credits its company's upswing to a pay-for-performance program. Lisa Weber, the executive vicepresident, says, "one of the most essential aspects of developing a good plan is to be clear about expectations."[22]

In response to efforts to push companies to treat stock options as expenses, the Dell Computer Corporation recently announced a cutback on stock options to its senior executives; instead it plans to pay cash bonuses. Because the executives are still eligible to receive stock options, the new plan is intended to help retain senior executives and to ease Dell's bottom line. The issuing of stock options can expand the company's cash flow and reduce its taxes, but expensing the stock options would reduce Dell's earnings, their bottom line.

With the range of options in pay-for-performance plans, do these plans really work? "The range of opinion about pay-for-performance is broad and deep. Its *proponents* say that rigorous, long-term pay-for-performance systems offer effective methods of helping companies continually improve the workforce while getting and keeping the best people. *Opponents* argue that incentive pay plans tend to pit employees against one another, erode trust and teamwork, and create what critics call dressed-up sweatshops."[23]

Broad Banding

One of the easiest ways for a manager to reward a subordinate who continues to perform well is to recommend the person for a salary raise. However, in many companies, this is not always possible because the individual currently is being paid the highest rate established for the job. For example, an assistant warehouse manager who holds a job with a salary range of $35,000 to $50,000 cannot earn more than $50,000 unless the manager can facilitate the promotion of the assistant manager to a position that commands a higher salary or can convince higher-level management to raise the cap for assistant warehouse managers. Both of these efforts can take a great deal of time and energy.

Broad banding
replaces the number of
salary grades with
fewer, wider bands.

To overcome this problem, a growing number of firms are turning to **broad banding,** which replaces the number of salary grades with fewer, wider bands. Under broad banding, the assistant warehouse manager's job might now be grouped with a host of other midlevel management positions and have a salary range of $35,000 to $70,000. In this case, it would be much easier for the manager to give the assistant warehouse manager a raise to $55,000.

More and more firms are turning to broad banding.[24] Why has this approach been gaining popularity in recent years? One reviewer gave this answer:

Blame part of it on global competition and the changing nature of work.
Companies have cut back their staffs and set up new structures that give them more flexibility to respond quickly to competition. But highly vertical traditional pay systems, with their vast numbers of grades, are out of sync with the new, flatter, team-oriented structures.
The solution is broad banding, which makes it much easier to assign workers to different jobs without having to worry about exactly what grade they're moving to. It also allows companies to put workers in traditionally lower-level jobs to learn different skills without demoting them or decreasing their pay.[25] *The Effective Compensation, Incorporated, an independent consulting firm, in Lakewood, Colorado, summarizes the features that attract firms to broad banding.*[26]

1. **Efficiency**—Less time is spent on evaluating jobs and defending grade placement decisions.
2. **Flexibility**—It is easier to transfer employees between jobs.
3. **Decentratization**—Local managers can make and defend pay decisions, which is consistent with many quality-oriented firms.
4. **Performance focus**—Supervisors can more easily provide significant rewards within a broad salary range for those who consistently do an outstanding job.

A number of prominent firms have turned to broad banding. At Sears, managers found that when they tried to recruit a potential employee, the individual's first question was "What is the pay grade?" Applicants did not want to accept a position in which they would soon reach the maximum pay level and, in order to get a salary raise, would have to change jobs again. General Electric has also introduced broad banding because it reduces the bureaucratic red tape associated with salary increases for those who have reached the top of their pay grade, and it allows the company more easily to tie pay to performance. In April 2002, BBC Worldwide introduced its broad banding pay structure. Its major features include:

1. **A reduction in the number of job grades.**
2. **The introduction of job family target salaries.**
3. **A new job evaluation system.**[27]

Cafeteria Incentives

Cafeteria incentives provide employees with a host of choices and allow each individual to select those that best meet his or her needs. The term *cafeteria* is used because choices are similar to those in a cafeteria, in which a diner proceeds down the line and chooses those foods that he or she would like and leaves the others. Cafeteria incentives take a variety of forms. In many cases, the company will put aside a pool of money that each individual can spend on these options, such as $3,000 annually. Then, if one person has a family with two small children and wants to use some of this money for a child-care program, the costs are automatically deducted from that employee's pool of money. Another individual might purchase additional life insurance or medical coverage to meet his or her specific needs. At Lincoln Electric, for example, all payments for worker medical insurance come from the bonus pool. The employees decide what type of coverage they want and the cost is deducted from their bonus.

In some cases, companies also give their lower-level personnel a choice between a guaranteed weekly wage and an incentive program that is tied directly to work output. For example, an individual might be given a choice between $600 a week or $6 per unit produced each week. If the person is in good health, feels capable of producing more than 100 units per week, and wants the opportunity to make more money, she or he will opt for the incentive plan rather than the guaranteed weekly wage.

Another example of cafeteria incentives is the rewards that are offered to individuals and groups that do outstanding work. For example, some firms offer a weekly award to the group that produces the greatest output. Each person in the group can then choose from the available rewards. Examples include a day off with pay, a portable television set, a dinner for two, two tickets to a play, and a week of reserved parking near the main door to the company. Research reveals that many individuals like this cafeteria approach because it allows them to match the reward with their personal needs. As a result, they find the programs to be highly motivational.

In each of these cases, the objective is the same: Motivate individuals to achieve higher performance. At the heart of this process, of course, are the ideas that were discussed earlier in the chapter: needs, achievement drive, expectancy, and valence. Indeed, there is a link between motivation theory and motivation practice.

Recognition Programs

Money is an important form of reward but, for a number of reasons, recognition is much more widely used. One reason is that organizations typically have pay systems that are designed to review performance and give financial rewards only once or twice annually. Therefore, if some-one does an outstandingly fine job in July, the manager may be unable to give the person a financial reward until after the annual performance review in December. Nonfinancial rewards such as recognition, on the other hand, can be given at any time. Additionally, these rewards can take many different forms, can be given in small or large amounts, and, in many instances, are controllable by the manager. For example, the individual can give an employee increased responsibility, which the latter finds motivational and which results in greater productivity. As a follow-up, the manager can then give the individual even greater responsibility. Unlike many financial forms of reward, there is no limit to the number of people who can receive this type of reward. One expert on rewards put it this way:

> *You can, if you choose, make all your employees . . . eligible for nonfinancial rewards. You can also make these rewards visible if you like, and performance-contingent, and you needn't wait for high level sign-offs and anniversary dates, because nonfinancial rewards don't derive from the budget or the boss and are seldom mentioned in employment contracts and collective bargaining agreements. Furthermore . . . if you inadvertently give someone more freedom or challenge than he can handle, you can take it back. Therefore, organizations can be bold and innovative in their use of nonmonetary rewards because they don't have to live with their mistakes.*[28]

Research reveals many types of recognition that can be given to inspire performance and loyalty. One of these that is receiving increased attention is recognition of the fact that many employees have work and family responsibilities and, when the organization helps them to deal with these obligations, loyalty increases. This finding is particularly important in light of the fact that a recent survey reports that 25 percent of the most sought-after workers (highly edu-cated, high-income professionals) would change jobs for a 10 percent increase in salary and 50 percent would move for a 20 percent raise. This research is not an isolated example. The Walker Information and Hudson Institute recently conducted a survey of the attitudes and experiences of workers in business, government, and nonprofit organizations around the United States. The organization mailed 3,075 questionnaires to a cross-sample of organizations and received usable responses from 75 percent of them. The data from the survey revealed the following:

1. **Only 30 percent of employees feel an obligation to stay with their current employer.**
2. **Individuals who are highly committed to their organization tend to do the best work.**
3. **Workers who are discontented with their jobs are least likely to be productive.**
4. **Employees in large organizations (100 or more people) tend to be less satisfied than are their peers in small enterprises.**
5. **Lower-level employees are less satisfied than those in higher-level positions.**
6. **The things that the respondents would like their companies to focus more on include being fair to employees, caring about them, and exhibiting trust in them.**[29]

Although the last point will come as a surprise to few organizational managers, groups such as the National Association for Employee Recognition have concluded that employee recognition is often misunderstood by businesses as a frill—or saved for only monumental events. A simple thank you to a coworker can greatly impact the bottom line of a business." That was the mes-sage concluded from the two companies that received the Best Practices Award in June 2002. They were CalPERS, a Sacramento-based organization that manages employee benefit and retire-ment programs and TELUS, one of Canada's leading communications firms based in Vancouver.

Even in the tough economic times following September 11, 2001, employee recognition pro-grams increased. A survey by the WorldatWork and the National Association for Employee Recog-nition (NAER) shows that companies used employee recognition programs extensively to retain their best and brightest employees. According to the NAER, recognition is one of the most effec-tive ways to reinforce an organization's culture, support its objectives, and retain top performers.

Michael Abrashoff, author of *It's Your Ship,* former USN Commanding Officer, was a recent keynote speaker at NAER's 2002 Regional Seminar in Seattle. He recited five reasons why employees quit a position. Pay and benefits were number five. The other four reasons are:

- Employees want to be treated with respect and dignity—not be treated like a child.
- Employees want to be allowed to have influence on their situation—being allowed to improve their environment.
- Employees want to be listened to (managers do not know their own people, their goals, needs, or aspirations) and have their suggestions taken seriously.
- Employees want to be rewarded with greater responsibility and leadership positions.[30]

Implementing a meaningful recognition program can satisfy these employee wants and needs. Companies also will save money by retaining good employees, because it is expensive to hire and train new employees.

Creating a recognition process need not be sophisticated or time consuming. In fact, many firms that are now working to improve their recognition systems use fairly basic and easy-to-implement programs. One expert in the area has recommended the following steps in setting up and managing a reward and recognition program:

1. When introducing new recognition procedures and programs, take advantage of all communication tools including Intranet and other knowledge-sharing networks—Let everyone know what is going on.
2. Educate the managers so that they use recognition as part of the total compensation package.
3. Make recognition part of the performance management process, so that everyone begins to use it.
4. Have site-specific recognition ceremonies that are featured in the company's communication outlets such as the weekly newsletter and the bimonthly magazine.
5. Publicize the best practices of employees, so that everyone knows some of the things they can do in order to earn recognition.
6. Let everyone know the steps that the best managers are taking to use recognition effectively.[31]
7. Continually review the recognition process in order to introduce new procedures and programs and scrap those that are not working well.
8. Solicit recognition ideas from both employees and managers, as they are the ones who are most likely to know what works well and what does not.

Today, a wide number of recognition systems are being used by organizations nationwide. Many of these are the result of continual modification, as the enterprises have altered and tweaked their systems to meet the changing needs of their workforce. However, all these programs have two things in common.

First, they are designed to maintain worker satisfaction and thus reduce the likelihood that people will leave the firm.

Second, they are designed to meet the specific needs of the employees. Simply put, what works in one enterprise may have little value in another. This explains why many firms have used a trial-and-error approach to honing their recognition programs. Moreover, the ultimate programs often vary widely from company to company, and many of them are highly creative. For example, one expert on the subject has offered the following creative suggestions for recognizing and motivating worker performance:

1. Select a pad of Post-it notes in a color that nobody uses and make it your "praising pad." Acknowledge your employees for work well done by writing your kudos on your praising pad.

2. Hire a caterer to bring in lunch once weekly. Besides showing your respect and appreciation, this encourages mingling and the sharing of information, ideas, and solutions.
3. To get your team motivated during an important project, design a simple logo for the assignment. This will give the team a sense not only of camaraderie but of group identification.[32]

In addition to these types of recognition, there are many others. Beverly Kaye, Chief Executive of Scranton, PA-based Career Systems International and co-author of Love `Em or Lose `Em: Getting Good People to Stay practices what she preaches. "Every year she asks her key staff members what she can do to keep them for one more year." For example, one employee wanted a job title change, another wanted part of her work delegated so she could work on another company project. Kaye believes that in a small company, it is easier to tailor rewards to individual employees. If something is expected, it is not a reward. Kaye has found evidence that modest tokens of appreciation make a more powerful statement. Ken Siegel, a managerial psychologist and president of The Impact Group in Beverly Hill, California, suggests that "The smaller the item is, and the more consistently it's applied, the more it's viewed as a significant motivator." An example of a simple, but powerful motivator is a small business rewarding employees by hiring a financial adviser to come into the company for a few days to provide financial planning advice to employees on an individual and confidential basis. Employees interviewed later stated that it was one of the things that made the company the most special place they'd ever worked.[33]

Another type of recognition focuses on pampering and destressing employees. "According to the results of a workplace survey released in October by Riverwoods-based business publisher CCH Inc., nearly half of unscheduled absences from work are due to family issues or personal needs, not illness." For example, Jan Goldman, a senior vice president with Mesirow Financial, often takes her team to a Day Spa for manicures and pedicures.[34]

summary

① LEARNING OBJECTIVE
Describe the two sides of motivation: movement and motive

In this chapter, we examined the fundamentals of motivation. It was noted that motivation has two sides: movement and motive. Movement can be seen, whereas motive can only be inferred. Yet motives are important, for they constitute the "whys" of behavior. Motives also are directed toward goals. The goal that has the highest motive strength is the one a person will attempt to satisfy through goal-directed behavior. Having satisfied that goal, an individual then will proceed to the goal with the next highest motive strength.

② LEARNING OBJECTIVE
Identify the five basic needs in Maslow's need hierarchy

In examining motives or needs in greater depth, we focused attention on Maslow's need hierarchy. The most fundamental of all needs, according to Maslow, are physiological needs, such as food, clothing, and shelter. When these are basically satisfied, safety needs replace them. Safety needs are of two types: survival and security. Next in the hierarchy are social needs, such as the desire for friendship, affection, and acceptance. The fourth level of the hierarchy comprises esteem needs, such as the need to feel important and respected. Research shows that prestige and power are two motives closely related to esteem needs and, to the degree that these motives can be satisfied, esteem needs can be met. At the top of the hierarchy are self-actualization needs. Because people satisfy these needs in so many different ways, behavioral scientists know less about them than the other four types of needs. However, research does reveal that there are two motives related to self-actualization: competence and achievement. If individuals can satisfy these motives, they can fulfill their drive for self-actualization.

③ **LEARNING OBJECTIVE**
Describe the two-factor theory of motivation and explain its relevance to the practicing manager

Frederick Herzberg has also found that people desire upper-level need satisfaction. In his famous two-factor theory of motivation, he divided all job factors into two categories: hygiene factors and motivators. Into hygiene factors he placed those things that he found do not motivate people but stop them from becoming unmotivated: salary, technical supervision, working conditions, and interpersonal relations. Motivators include all the factors that motivate people to increase their contribution to the organization: recognition, advancement, the possibility of growth, and achievement. Herzberg contends that hygiene factors do not produce motivation but do prevent dissatisfaction. Conversely, motivators can give satisfaction but not dissatisfaction. Today, the two-factor theory is criticized as incomplete and erroneous. For example, some researchers report that money is a motivator for many people, despite Herzberg's claim that it is a hygiene factor. Similarly, some researchers report that workers regard recognition and the chance for advancement as dissatisfiers. At best, then, the two-factor theory is a controversial approach.

④ **LEARNING OBJECTIVE**
Discuss expectancy theory, noting how both valence and expectancy influence motivation force

The last part of the chapter examined expectancy theory, which holds that motivation can be expressed as the product of valence and expectancy. Valence is the measure of a person's preference for a particular outcome. Expectancy is the perceived probability that a specific outcome will follow from a specific act. By multiplying the values of valence and expectancy, one can arrive at a motivational force number; the higher the number, the greater is the motivation.

Expectancy theory is very helpful in understanding motivation for several reasons. The expectancy model urges us to look at motivation as a force greater in some people than in others. It also suggests that valence and expectancy are a result of individual experiences, and what will highly motivate one person may create no motivational force in another. Expectancy theory makes it possible to study the issue of equity in motivation among specific individuals as opposed to examining the general motivation of groups.

⑤ **LEARNING OBJECTIVE**
Explain the value of money, employee satisfaction, incentives, and recognition in the motivation process

Money is a motivator. It helps fulfill both lower- and upper-level needs. Money can take numerous forms, including salary and benefits. In recent years, organizations have begun adapting financial incentives to individual needs through the use of cafeteria-style plans. This allows people to choose those rewards that are best for them.

However, organizations also realize that nonfinancial rewards such as recognition are important motivators. These can take a wide number of forms including thank you notes, recognition parties, and publication of achievements in the company newspaper.

KEY TERMS IN THE CHAPTER

motivation	power
motives	self-actualization needs
physiological needs	competence

safety needs

social needs

esteem needs

prestige

motivators

expectancy theory

valence

expectancy

achievement

high achievers

need mix

hygiene factors

motivational force

equity theory

broad banding

REVIEW AND STUDY QUESTIONS

1. Motives are the "whys" of behavior. What does this statement mean?

2. What are physiological needs? Give some examples of how your job (company) can satisfy your physiological needs.

3. How important are safety needs to people just starting their business careers? How important are they to top executives in large organizations? If your answers differ, what accounts for the difference? Give examples.

4. How do people attempt to meet their social needs? Cite some examples of how a business can meet the social needs of its employees.

5. Research shows that two motives related to esteem are prestige and power. Define these two motives, and explain how people try to satisfy them.

6. One of the ways in which individuals try to satisfy the self-actualization need is through the development of competence. How do they go about doing this? Give an example of how a business can improve an employee's competence.

7. What are the characteristics of high achievers? How can a high achievement drive be developed?

8. In Herzberg's terms, what are hygiene factors? In Herzberg's terms, what are motivators? Give some examples of each.

9. According to the two-factor theory, if you give people hygiene factors, you will not motivate them, but you will prevent dissatisfaction. Conversely, if you give people motivators, you may get satisfaction, but you will never get dissatisfaction. Explain the meaning of these two statements.

10. The two major terms in expectancy theory are *valence* and *expectancy.* What is meant by each of these terms?

11. Using the expectancy theory formula, compute the motivational force for Mr. A, whose valence (V) is 0.8 and expectancy (E) is 0.7. Compute the motivational force for three other individuals who had the following respective valences and expectancies: Ms. B, $V = 0.7$, $E = 0.4$; Mr. C, $V = 1$, $E = 0.5$; Ms. D, $V = 0.9$, $E = 0.5$. Which of the four has the greatest motivational force?

12. Is money a motivator or does it simply prevent dissatisfaction? Explain.

13. How are companies now trying to use "pay for performance" to motivate their personnel? Give an example.

14. Why is broad banding gaining popularity as a way to motivate employees? Give an example.

15. How does a cafeteria incentive plan work? Describe two of its advantages.

16. Identify two factors that are common to well designed recognition programs used to motivate employees?

Everyday Low Prices—And a Lot More

In this chapter, you studied the complex nature of motivation. No organization can survive if it does not motivate its personnel—and its customers, for that matter. One company that has been very successful in doing this is Wal-Mart, the world's largest retailer. So Wal-Mart managers must know a great deal about the process of motivation.

Visit the company's Web site at **http://www.wal-mart.com** and then answer these questions:

1. What are some things the company is doing to motivate its associates (employees)?

2. What is it doing to motivate its customers?

What Motivates Employees?

How did the Mary Kay Company become one of the largest direct sellers of skin care products in the United States? Visit its Web site at **http://www.marykay.com** and learn its secrets.

1. Visit the company's "Headquarters," "Career Path," and "Job" sections.

2. Review Mary Kay's "Business Basics" and "Profiles."

3. Under "profiles," click on several people and read their stories. What did you find fascinating?

4. After assessing the information viewed in the Web site, identify practices and techniques Mary Kay uses to motivate its personnel. Make a list. It may be helpful to divide your suggestions into groups.

5. Discuss how the Mary Kay motivation process is similar or different from the one used at another business, or at the one where you currently work.

TIME OUT ANSWERS

Interpretation of What Motivates You

Remember that you gave a 10 to the most important factor and a 1 to the least important factor, so high scores indicate greater motivating potential than do low scores. With this in mind, fill in the number you assigned to each of the 10 factors and then add both columns.

Column A		Column B	
_____	1	_____	2
_____	4	_____	3
_____	6	_____	5
_____	8	_____	7
_____	10	_____	9
_____	Total	_____	Total

If your total in column A is higher than that in column B, you derive more satisfaction from the psychological side of your job than from the physical side. Notice that the five factors in column A are designed to measure how you feel about the job. These factors are internal motivators. If your score in column A is higher than 30, you are highly motivated to succeed and achieve at your current job. Individuals who are most successful in their careers have jobs with higher psychological value than physical value.

If your total in column B is higher than that in column A, you derive more satisfaction from the physical side of your job than from the psychological side. Notice that the five factors in column B all relate to the environment in which you work or the pay you receive for doing this work. These factors are external, and you have limited control over them. A score of 30 or more indicates that you do not particularly care for the job, but you do like the benefits the company is giving you. Most people who have a higher total in column B than in column A rank good wages as one of their top two choices. If you are younger than 40, it is likely that you will either be promoted to a job with greater psychological value or you will leave the organization. If you are older than 40, you may find that your job mobility is reduced, the money is too good to pass up, and you will stay with the organization because of these financial rewards.

ANSWERS TO TABLE 2.2

	As Ranked by	
	Workers	Supervisors
Job security	4	2
Full appreciation for work done	1	8
Promotion and growth with the company	7	3
Tactful disciplining	10	7
Good wages	5	1
Feeling in on things	2	10
Interesting work	6	5
Management loyalty to the workers	8	6
Good working conditions	9	4
Sympathetic understanding of personal problems	3	9

case: WHY DO PEOPLE WORK?

Harry Barrett, department manager of a well-known retail chain, has been with his store for 23 years, but he has been passed over for promotion and will probably remain a department manager for the rest of his career. This does not greatly concern Harry. He believes that he does the best job he can, and not being promoted is all right with him. Some of Harry's friends, however, believe that Harry killed his chances of moving up by failing to understand human relations. They think that Harry does not know how to manage his people very well. One of their complaints is that Harry misunderstands why people work. He believes that salary, working conditions, and security are the three most important objectives. One day Harry remarked that people work only to make a living and then go home to enjoy their lives. The other manager claimed that this simply was not so. "People want more out of a job than just an opportunity to satisfy their physiological and safety needs," he told Harry. "They want to interact with other workers on the job, feel that what they are doing is important, and contribute to the overall good of the organization."

Harry disagreed with this point of view, claiming that his friend had been to too many management courses. "You know, ever since you started working on your master's degree in business, you've come out with some really wild ideas. I'll tell you this: I've been a department manager here for over 10 years and I certainly don't let people socialize on the job. When they are not selling, I want them standing around the counters, alert to the needs of any passing customer. If they get into conversations, they'll lose half their business. And as far as the rest of your ideas about doing important work and contributing to the organization's overall good, that's all philosophical nonsense. People work to make a living and that's all."

Having finished their coffee, the two men stood up to leave. "Harry," said his friend, "you've had the poorest performance record now for almost two years, and evaluations among your personnel reveal that you are considered below average. I've heard some of your workers say you don't care anything about human relations."

"Oh, I've heard that stuff, too," Harry said. "It's all just sour grapes because I won't buckle under and let them get away with breaking the rules the way some other department managers do." The two men then returned to their jobs.

Questions

1. What types of needs does Harry think that people satisfy on the job?

2. What did the other manager mean when he said that people want more from a job than the opportunity to satisfy their physiological and safety needs? Give examples.

3. In what way do Harry's beliefs account for his department's performance? How could an understanding of Maslow's need hierarchy be of value to Harry? Explain.

case: YOU BE THE CONSULTANT

Trying to Motivate Everyone

Three years ago, the Waidley Company, a food distribution warehouse, set a sales objective of 20 percent annual growth over the next five years. Since then, the company has done extremely well. Sales are up an average of 27 percent per year, and the company's workforce has increased from 126 to more than 500.

The company sells a wide variety of food (sugar, coffee, tea, flour, butter) to wholesalers and institutional buyers (schools and governmental agencies). Orders are typically placed the day before they are needed, and it is the responsibility of Justin Brown, head of warehouse operations, to see that the food is loaded on the trucks for delivery. Each order is entered in the computer and then sent to the warehouse where it is assigned to a team of workers. This team gathers all the items and loads them on to the assigned truck. Most of this work is fairly simple, as the computer automatically matches up trucks and food orders in the most efficient way possible. The biggest problems are incomplete or slow deliveries. An incomplete delivery occurs whenever an order is filled improperly and the desired merchandise is not loaded. A slow delivery occurs when the driver fails to arrive at the customer's location before the assigned time.

Justin's major problem is keeping the 250 warehouse workers motivated so that they load the trucks quickly and accurately. Because the work is fairly boring, he has instituted a motivational program designed to encourage both accuracy and speed. Every month an award is given to the 15 work teams that have the best loading record. The 5 members of each team are allowed to decide whether they each want a $100 bonus or 1 day off with pay. The program has been in effect for 90 days, and 225 individuals have received awards. Justin has broken down the teams' choices on the basis of gender and age. Here are his findings:

	Chose a Day Off	Chose a $100 Bonus
Men		
18–35	8	32
36–55	29	23
56+	38	2
Women		
18–35	4	25
36–55	19	14
56+	25	6

Justin feels that the motivational program is working well and believes that the company would benefit by using it in other departments also.

Your Advice

1. What do you recommend that the company do regarding the motivation program?

    ____ a. Scrap the program because it is not working.

    ____ b. Continue the program, but deemphasize the $100 bonus and focus on giving more days off.

    ____ c. Continue the program with both options.

2. How important is money in motivating the employees in Justin's department?

3. Of what value are "days off" in motivating the people in Justin's department?

4. What overall conclusion can you draw regarding the value of the motivation program among the warehouse personnel?

EXPERIENCING MOTIVATIONAL VARIABLES

Purpose

- To realize that different people are motivated by different things.
- To investigate our own motivational needs.

Procedure

1. Individually rank the following variables (in decreasing order) according to how important they are to you at this stage of your life.

    ____ a. Good relationship with coworkers

    ____ b. Private, nicely furnished office

    ____ c. Personal secretary

    ____ d. Satisfying work

    ____ e. Individual responsibility

    ____ f. Creative work

    ____ g. Decision-making authority

    ____ h. Company car

    ____ i. Good rapport with your supervisor

    ____ j. Company expense account

2. As a class or small group, discuss the list of variables according to the Herzberg model. Is each a hygiene factor or a motivator?

3. Individually assess your answers. Look at those you ranked 1 to 5. Were they mainly hygiene factors or motivators? How would you interpret these findings?

4. As a class, discuss:

    a. Each of the variables in reference to achievement theory. Which ones are high achievers most likely to pick? How about people with high affiliation needs? High power needs?

    b. Is money a motivator? Do you expect this answer to change as your career develops?

The Social System

The reason for studying the *social system* of organizations is to learn why people act as they do. In this section, three major areas will be explored: individual behavior, group behavior, and the informal organization.

THE GOALS FOR THIS SECTION ARE TO:

- *Review the nature of individual behavior, study some of its components—values, perceptions, attitudes, and personality—and examine ways for managers to improve their understanding of interpersonal behavior.*

- *Examine common types of groups, study their major characteristics—roles, norms, status, and cohesiveness—look at decision making within groups with a focus on ways groups gain power over other groups, and explore how managers can resolve intergroup conflict and improve performance.*

- *Compare and contrast formal and informal organizations, explore grapevine communication patterns within informal organizations, examine the benefits and drawbacks associated with informal organizations, and look at ways managers can deal with and use the informal organization to increase employee productivity.*

After reading this part of the book, you should have a solid understanding of human behavior at work. In particular, you should know a great deal about individual and group behavior in organizations and be aware of how both individuals and groups use the informal organization to accomplish their objectives.

3

Individual Behavior

LEARNING OBJECTIVES

①

Identify and describe some of the common values held by all Individuals

②

Describe perception and explain why it is a determinant of individual behavior

③

Explain how stereotyping can influence a person's view of another's behavior

④

Define attitude and describe its impact on worker output

⑤

Define personality and discuss the major forces affecting personality development

⑥

Describe how assertiveness training can help managers and subordinates improve their understanding of interpersonal behavior

At the very heart of human relations is the need for an understanding of human behavior. Managers need to have an understanding of how and why people act as they do to be effective. In this chapter, individual behavior is explored.

AFTER STUDYING THIS CHAPTER, YOU SHOULD BE ABLE TO:

1. Identify and describe some of the common values held by all individuals.
2. Describe perception and explain why it is a determinant of individual behavior.
3. Explain how stereotyping can influence a person's view of another's behavior.
4. Define attitude and describe its impact on worker output.
5. Define personality and discuss the major forces affecting personality development.
6. Describe how assertiveness training can help managers and subordinates improve their understanding of interpersonal behavior.

Individual Opinions Really Count

Not only do effective organizations believe that their employees are their most important asset, but also they go out of their way to ensure that these individuals feel they are being treated fairly and their talents are being effectively used. A good example is AT&T's Universal Card Services (UCS) business. When this organization was first founded, management wanted to create a climate that emphasized entrepreneurial traits and allowed the personnel not merely to meet—but to exceed—customer expectations. If this goal were to be achieved, UCS management knew that one other objective would also have to be attained: associate delight. The employees would have to love what they were doing and be totally committed to it. If this happened, the associates then would carry this attitude over to the way in which they dealt with the customer.

In pursuing this objective, UCS management did a number of things. One was to give the associates control over their jobs and let them decide how things should be done. This empowerment increased the entrepreneurial spirit of the personnel and freed them from petty bureaucratic controls, allowing them to devote themselves to creating highly satisfied customers. Another approach was to give associates the opportunity to learn about other jobs in the company. Under a program known as "Associate of the Day," anyone can sign up to observe what others do in their jobs by following the individual around for a day or by attending presentations about the job by subject-matter experts. This program has helped associates to make career decisions and has given them a better understanding of how they can coordinate their work with that of others. As a result, employee attitudes have remained positive, and customers have reported that they are delighted with the service.

In fact, UCS was so successful in its overall efforts that the firm won the Baldrige National Quality Award within five years of its inception. A large degree of this success is directly attributable to the company's ability to understand individual behavior and extract outstanding personal performance from people throughout the organization.

This idea of giving more authority to individuals is also being pursued by multinational firms such as Coca-Cola, which has recently begun replacing American managers with locals in its overseas operations. The reason is that local managers better understand the needs of the local market, and this focus on individual markets is important to Coke, given that it owns 51 percent of the world market for carbonated soft drinks and that 80 percent of its profits come from overseas. In fact, the new head of Coca-Cola, Douglas Daft, has replaced almost all of Coke's senior management with local executives.

Some of this recent effort is designed to convince regulators in the European Union (EU) that Coca-Cola is not trying to violate European competition laws and drive other firms from the marketplace. Coke wants to convince EU regulators that it is prepared to work with regulators and to build good personal relationships with them. The company also wants to strengthen its relations with its personnel in Europe, many of whom feel the company has neglected them. In particular, Coke wants to build the company as a host of international markets that are allowed to respond to the needs of their collective niches and not have to take orders from the home office regarding how to run local operations. Simply put, the firm is pushing a new philosophy of "think globally, act locally." This means working more closely with local authorities, local managers, and local customers and giving more authority to local operations. This was particularly clear when the head of the company's Eurasia division recently proposed two new brands, Apple and Pear Fresca, for sale in Kazakhstan. It used to take three months to get approval for new brands, but the division head received an okay in 13 days. In the past, Coke succeeded because it understood and appealed to global commonalties. In the future, it hopes to succeed by better understanding and appealing to local differences.

Coca-Cola continues to use new and innovative ways to seek input from its consumers. For the first time in January 2003, Coca-Cola Fountain and the ICEE Company conducted a nationwide Internet vote to determine the newest flavor, from among ten flavors, to be promoted in 2004. Everyone casting a vote took part in the "Which Flavor Do You Favor?" sweepstakes. The Grand Prize was a four-day, three-night trip for four to Universal Orlando, including round-trip coach air transportation for the winner and three guests, hotel accommodations, rental car, and theme park admission passes.

Coca-Cola also is involved in bridging the growing "digital divide" between the information and communications technology "haves" and "have-nots." Recently, Coca-Cola and the United Nations Development Programme created a partnership to pilot a project to bridge the "digital divide" in Malaysia. In this first endeavor for Coke, the goal was to bring e-learning opportunities and ICT training resources to students, teachers, and local communities. For Coca-Cola bridging the information and knowledge gap is an extremely important priority as they move into the new global knowledge economy. Coca-Cola is built on a deep and abiding relationship and trust between it and all its constituents: bottlers, customers, consumers, shareowners, employees, suppliers, and the varying communities of which it is an integral part.

Sources: "Coke Settles Racial Suit for Record $192 Million," Miami Herald, November 17, 2000, Section A, pp. 1–2; Betsy McKay, "To Fix Coca-Cola, Daft Sets Out to Get the Relationship Right," Wall Street Journal, June 22, 2000, pp. A1, A12; Richard M. Hodgetts, Measures of Quality and High Performance (New York: American Management Association, 1998); and Jac Fitz-Enz, The 8 Practices of Exceptional Companies (New York: American Management Association, 1997). Doug Daft, Chairman and CEO, "Viewpoints," October 2, 2002, **http://www.cocacola.com**, News Release, "Coca-Cola and United Nations Development Programme (UNDP) launch partnership to help bridge digital divide in Malasia", March 6, 2002, **http://www.cocacola.com**, News Release, "ICEE and Coca-Cola Fountain to Conduct First Nationwide "Which Flavor Do You Favor?" Vote to Determine the People's Choice for the Newest ICEE Flavor," January 27, 2003, **http://www.cocacola.com**

LEARNING OBJECTIVE

Identify and describe some of the common values held by all individuals

① The Nature of the Individual

The individual is a complex being, but this complexity does not stop most people from trying to generalize about human behavior by summing up individuals with a descriptive cliché such as, "People are basically good," or "Everybody has his or her price; it's just a matter of how much." Some clichés are totally accurate, some partially accurate, and the rest erroneous. In human relations, however, we need to be much more scientific in our analysis of individuals and to realize that people are a *blend of many different types of behavior*. For example, sometimes people are very rational, and at other times they are highly emotional; sometimes they are controlled by their environment, and at other times they control their environment; sometimes they are interested in economic objectives, and at other times they are more concerned with self-actualizing.

However, in any examination of individual behavior, we must look at the *total person*. This requires an examination of the major components of individual behavior. The four major components that merit our attention are values, perceptions, attitudes, and personality.

Values

*A **value** is something of worth or importance to an individual.*

*A **terminal value** is one that is expressed in terms of a desired goal or end.*

*An **instrumental value** is the means for achieving desired goals.*

A **value** is something that has worth or importance to an individual. Values are influenced in many ways. Parents, friends, and teachers all play a role; so do coworkers, business associates, and others with whom we come in contact. In fact, learning and experience are the two greatest forces in shaping an individual's values.

One way of examining values is in terms of terminal and instrumental values. A **terminal value** is expressed in terms of a desired goal or end. An **instrumental value** is the means for achieving the desired goals.[1] Here are some examples:

Terminal Values (Ends)	Instrumental Values (Means)
Self-respect	Honesty
A comfortable life	Independence
Family security	Ambition
Wisdom	Courage
A sense of accomplishment	Helpfulness

FIGURE 3.1

Spraunger's Value Types

Theoretical

The overriding interest of the theoretical person is the discovery of truth. In pursuing this goal, the person often looks for identities and differences, trying to divest himself or herself of judgments regarding the beauty or utility of objects. The chief aim in life of this person is to systematize and order knowledge.

Economic

The economic person is basically interested in what is *useful*. In addition to self-preservation, the person is concerned with the production of goods and services and the accumulation of wealth. The individual is thoroughly practical and conforms well to the prevailing stereotype of the American businessperson.

Aesthetic

The aesthetic person sees highest value in *form* and *harmony*. Although the person might not necessarily be an artist, the individual's chief interest is in the artistic episodes of life. For example, aesthetic people often like the beautiful insignia of pomp and power but oppose political activity that represses individual thought.

Social

The highest value for the social person is *love* of people. This individual prizes other people as ends and, as a result, is kind, sympathetic, and unselfish. The social person regards love itself as the only suitable form of human relationship. This person's interests are very close to those of the religious person.

Political

The political person is interested primarily in *power*. This individual need not be a politician. Because competition and struggle play a large part in life, he or she will do well in any career or job in which a high power value is necessary for success, whether this be power over people (as in the case of a top manager) or over the environment (as in the case of an engineer who makes the final decision on how to build something).

Religious

The highest value for the religious person is *unity*. This individual seeks to relate himself or herself to the embracing totality of the cosmos. For some, there is an attempt to withdraw from active association with the outside world (as in the case of monks in a monastery); for others there is some self-denial and meditation coupled with a life of work among local people who attend their church or subscribe to the same religious beliefs.

Another way to examine values is in terms of a predetermined list and the preferences people have for these values. Edward Spraunger has identified six values common to everyone: theoretical, economic, aesthetic, social, political, and religious (see Figure 3.1).

Different occupational groups tend to have different value profiles. For example, professors of biology tend to be highest in theoretical interests, businesspeople have very high economic values, artists place great significance on aesthetic values, social workers have high social values, politicians have strong political values, and members of the clergy hold high religious values. However, to some degree, each of these values is present within and important to each of us. We must remember that what may be important to management is *not* necessarily important to the "rank and file." For this reason, values are of major importance in the study of human relations.

Study of Values

The most popular test designed to provide information and insight on individual values is the Allport-Vernon-Lindzey *Study of Values.*[2] This test is designed to measure one's preference for

TABLE 3.1	Value Profiles for Different Groups			
Spraunger Value	Average Male College Student[a]	Average Female College Student[a]	Successful Male Manager[b]	Successful Female Manager[c]
Theoretical	43	36	44	39
Economic	42	37	45	47
Aesthetic	37	44	35	42
Social	37	42	33	31
Political	43	38	44	46
Religious	38	43	39	35

[a]Study of Values Manual (Boston: Houghton Mifflin Company, 1970), p. 11.

[b]William D. Guth and Renato Tagiuri, "Personal Values and Corporate Strategy," Harvard Business Review, September–October 1965, p. 126.

[c]Richard M. Hodgetts, Mildred G. Pryor, Harry N. Mills, and Karen Brinkman, "A Profile of the Successful Executive," Academy of Management Proceedings, August 1978, p. 378.

each of Spraunger's values. From the responses, a value profile can be constructed for the individual. In fact, the test has been given a sufficient number of times so as to establish value profiles for different groups. Table 3.1 provides such profiles for the average male college student, average female college student, successful male business manager, and successful female business manager. Figure 3.2 is a graph of these four profiles. Note that the profile of the successful female manager is similar to that of the successful male manager and distinctly different

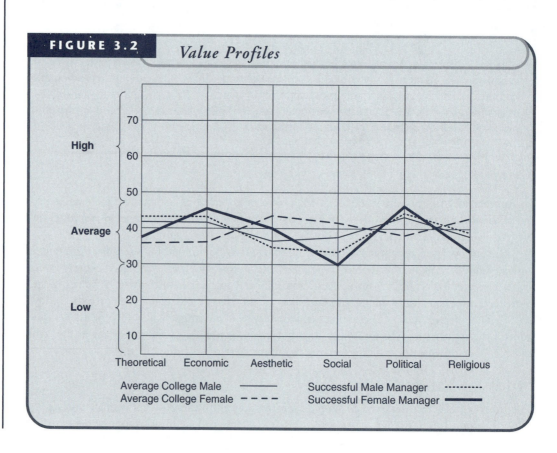

FIGURE 3.2 Value Profiles

WHAT IS IMPORTANT TO YOU?

The following quiz is designed to measure how you value certain lifestyles and rewards. Read and then rank each statement using the following scale:

5 = Strongly agree or definitely true

4 = Generally agree or mostly true

3 = Neither agree nor disagree

2 = Generally disagree or mostly false

1 = Strongly disagree or definitely false

_____ a. You often take the lead and direct others.

_____ b. You believe people should be paid based on how hard they work and what they accomplish.

_____ c. You would like to be rewarded in direct proportion to your performance.

_____ d. You believe that in the long run, good people win and bad people lose.

_____ e. You would be more motivated by financial rewards than by praise.

_____ f. You enjoy being in charge.

_____ g. Dishonesty should not be tolerated.

_____ h. It makes you angry when you know how to do something but no one wants to listen to you.

_____ i. One of your life's goals is to be financially independent.

_____ j. Getting ahead should be based on performance and not politics.

_____ k. You would enjoy working on a sales commission rather than a straight salary.

_____ l. You would like a job that requires hard selling.

_____ m. Owning your own business has strong appeal for you.

_____ n. Everyone should be treated equally, and favoritism should be discouraged.

_____ o. You would enjoy managing a business.

Enter your answers in the appropriate spaces below. Then total each group and divide by five to obtain your average response for each group.

The interpretation of your answers can be found at the end of the chapter.

Group 1	Group 2	Group 3
a. _____	b. _____	c. _____
f. _____	d. _____	e. _____
h. _____	g. _____	i. _____
l. _____	j. _____	k. _____
o. _____	n. _____	m. _____
Total _____	Total _____	Total _____
Average _____	Average _____	Average _____

from that of the average female college student. Apparently, successful managers have the same basic value profiles regardless of their gender.

Value tests such as the one described here are useful to understanding human behavior because they identify what is important to an individual. Unless we know what a person holds in high regard, there is little hope that we can motivate or manage the person effectively. (The "Time Out" box provides some insights regarding your own values.) The great problem for today's managers, however, is that values appear to be changing. The values of their fathers and grandfathers are different from those of the modern generation. Raised in a period of affluence and reared on television in a hightechnology society, young people have different ideas about what is important. When they enter the workforce, they bring these new values with them. As a result, modern employees' values are an important focal point of human relations study.

Modern Employee Values

Over the last three decades, employee values have changed, and they are still in a state of flux. In particular, during this period, employee loyalty in many companies has declined. This is particularly true in large and medium-sized firms, where workers report lower levels of job satisfaction, opportunity for advancement, and challenging work than do their counterparts in smaller companies. Additionally, women report that their opportunities for advancement are fewer than those for men; and African-American employees feel that they are underpaid and given limited access to higher level jobs. They are not alone. Recent government economic findings reveal that increasing salary and upward mobility are becoming a thing of the past for many people.

> . . . a spate of new research on U.S. income mobility suggests that America is shutting out more people. . . . A dozen or so academic studies have examined data that follow the same individuals for many years. This allows them to go beyond research showing rising income inequality to reveal a more unsettling trend: As the economy stratified in the 1980s, workers at the bottom became less likely to move up in their lifetimes. At the same time, upward mobility is increasing for some higher-end professionals and college-educated workers whose skills remain in high demand.

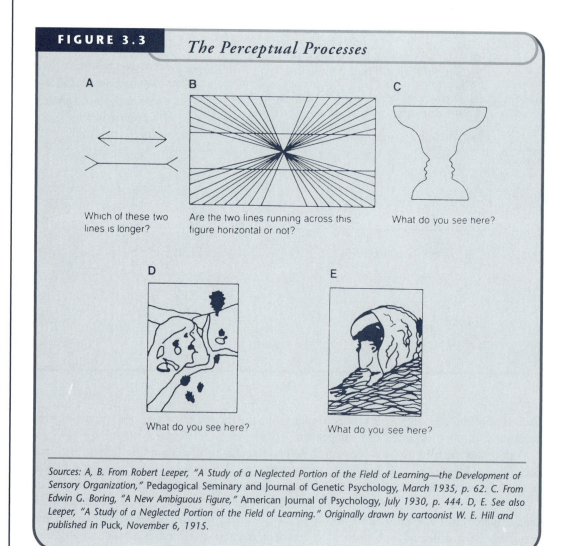

FIGURE 3.3 *The Perceptual Processes*

A

Which of these two lines is longer?

B

Are the two lines running across this figure horizontal or not?

C

What do you see here?

D

What do you see here?

E

What do you see here?

Sources: A, B. From Robert Leeper, "A Study of a Neglected Portion of the Field of Learning—the Development of Sensory Organization," Pedagogical Seminary and Journal of Genetic Psychology, March 1935, p. 62. C. From Edwin G. Boring, "A New Ambiguous Figure," American Journal of Psychology, July 1930, p. 444. D, E. See also Leeper, "A Study of a Neglected Portion of the Field of Learning." Originally drawn by cartoonist W. E. Hill and published in Puck, November 6, 1915.

The splintering is something new in America, suggesting that our economy is becoming more rigid and class-bound. Unlike past decades, when opportunities for advancement existed at all levels, America today is cleaving into economic camps divided largely by education. Those born in families and neighborhoods that provide the money and motivation to help them complete college are more likely to get ahead. Those who lack the access or the ability to achieve high skills are increasingly likely to sink, no matter how much they hustle.[3]

There are also problems among young workers who have different values from those of their bosses and expect different things in the workplace. These Generation Xers, who were born between 1965 and 1981, grew up during the computer revolution, the advent of MTV sound bites, and a business world in which downsizing, layoffs, and continual change resulted in their parents often having to switch jobs or take early retirement. These developments helped to shape the values of today's young employees, who have attitudes sharply different from those of their bosses, many of whom are baby boomers who were born between 1946 and 1964. Commenting on the two groups, one business executive noted:

While much of today's younger workforce is drawn to small, entrepreneurial start-ups (where fortunes can be made overnight), many are working their way up the corporate ladder and proving to be just as cynical as their entrepreneurial counterparts. According to the experts, the Fortune 100 are acutely aware that Gen Xers expect and need a different kind of work environment than that of the Baby Boomer generation that came before them. Yesterday it was: "Thank you for the job opportunity, I'll try to please you." Today, it's "Here's what I want to stay with the company, and if I am not happy and if I am not having fun, I'll take my skills elsewhere."[4]

As the population in the United States becomes older, a greying workforce is emerging. An untapped labor pool of qualified employees is among the older talent and companies are just beginning to recruit from this mature group (see table). The needs and wants of the Generation Xers differ from those of more mature employees in the workplace. For example, see Figure 3.3.

Workplace Needs

Generation Xers Workforce	Greying Workforce
Ongoing training, especially in cutting-edge technologies	Pay, benefits, and incentives (long-term care and health insurance, Eldercare programs
Innovative career paths	Avenues for profession development
Floating assignments	Decreased and/or flexible hours
Flex schedules, part-time work, telecommuting and job-shares that won't affect career growth	Short commutes of 5–10 miles to the job
Performance-based monetary incentives	Computer education classes
Competitive pay	
Increased freedom in the workplace, prefer mentoring rather than a traditional supervisory style.	

Source: **http://www.reidlondonhouse.com** "Today's Hiring Needs Call for Creative Strategies."

These values clearly indicate that there is a generation gap between managers and employees. Even more disturbing is research that shows that the values of many managers have not changed over the last two decades. This means there is a "values gap" between the way managers run their organizations and the way lower level employees want the organizations run, and this is likely to create major human relations problems in the future. For this reason, many organizations are now developing new approaches to managing their people. For example, Amoco gives its employees generous leave and flexible work arrangements—a strategy designed to promote product quality and to address employees' desires for more control of their lives in the workplace.[5] Planters Life Savers Company of Fort Smith, Arkansas, has done away with time clocks, installed basketball courts and workout facilities, and given the employees an active voice in layoff decisions.[6]

Another recent trend is a move toward reducing meetings and eliminating busy work, so that people have more time to sit back, relax, and unleash their creative potential. At Nestle USA, for example, meetings after 10 A.M. on Friday are prohibited. At Hewlett Packard, backup people are used to fill in so personnel can take extended vacations. These efforts are all part of a growing trend toward helping employees "unplug" from the office and "get a life."[7] These strategies are also designed to create a stronger employer–employee partnership and to show workers that management's values and their own are similar.[8] Of course, to a large degree, these strategies are successful only if employees perceive them as valuable, because perception is a key element in individual behavior.[9]

LEARNING OBJECTIVE

Describe perception and explain why it is a determinant of individual behavior

②

Perception
is a person's view of reality.

Perception

Perception is a person's view of reality and is affected by, among other things, the individual's values. For example, if a person is a member of a union, he or she may discount much of what management says about declining sales, decreased profit margins, and the need for the union and management to work as a team. Most of this talk may be regarded as an attempt by management to exploit the workforce for its own gain. Conversely, many people in management admit they have a hard time understanding the union's point of view, because they believe it is more interested in "ripping off" the company than in working for the overall good of both groups. This is an example of a common situation in which each person agrees with his or her own group's point of view but regards the other group's point of view as incorrect or biased. Human relationists call this *selective perception,* and sometimes this perception is incorrect. For example, many people believe that the Internal Revenue Service (IRS) is most likely to audit those who make large amounts of money, because the chance of finding errors in their income tax returns is more likely than is finding errors in the returns of those who make small incomes. However, since 1988, the percentage of audits of taxpayers making $200,000 or more annually has fallen by 90 percent, whereas the percentage of audits of taxpayers making less than $25,000 annually has increased by 30 percent.[10] Similarly, many people believe that the U.S. Post Office provides very poor service, but recent satisfaction surveys report that most respondents are pleased with the service, and they rank the post office ahead of all major airlines and most hotel chains.[11] So selective perception is sometimes incorrect. To understand why individuals perceive things differently, it is helpful to compare sensory reality and normative reality.

Sensory Reality and Normative Reality

Sensory reality
is physical reality.

Physical reality is **sensory reality.** A typewriter, an automobile, and a house are all physical objects that people tend to perceive accurately. However, sometimes physical items present perception problems. Before you read further, examine the pictures in Figure 3.3 and answer the question accompanying each.

In Figure 3.3A, the two lines are the same length, although most people think that the lower line is longer than the upper one. The two diagonal lines at the ends of each horizontal line create this perceptual illusion, which make those lines seem stretched or compressed. In Figure 3.3B, the two lines running across the picture are horizontal, although most people think the

FIGURE 3.4 — *The Pirate and the Rabbit*

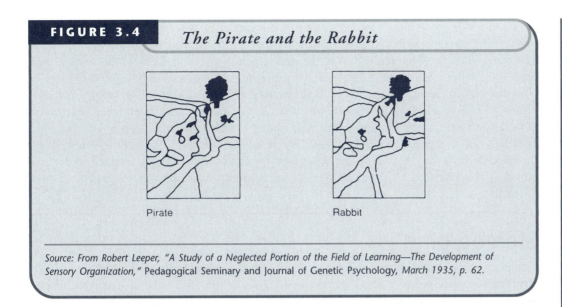

Pirate   Rabbit

Source: From Robert Leeper, "A Study of a Neglected Portion of the Field of Learning—The Development of Sensory Organization," Pedagogical Seminary and Journal of Genetic Psychology, March 1935, p. 62.

lines bend in at the end. This illusion is a result of the diagonal background lines, which appear to be bowing the center parts of the horizontal lines outward.

In Figure 3.3C we are moving away from sensory reality and toward **normative reality,** which is best defined as interpretive reality. In the first two pictures in Figure 3.3, there was a right answer, whether or not you saw it there. You can verify the answers by simply using a ruler to measure the lines or the distance between them. There is *more* than one right answer in Figure 3.3C, however, and what one person sees, another may not. This is why we call it *interpretive reality.* Some people see a goblet in this picture; others see the facial profiles of twins facing each other.

The picture in Figure 3.3D is deliberately ambiguous. Some people see a road, a rock, a tree, and some surrounding terrain. Others see the face of a pirate. Still others see a rabbit. Look at Figure 3.4, in which the clear pictures of the pirate and the rabbit can be seen. Note that the ambiguity is reduced if the artist puts more detail in one part of the picture than in the other.

Figure 3.3E is also a deliberately ambiguous picture. Some people see an old woman; some see a young woman. Figure 3.5 is a clear picture of both. Once again, the artist has reduced the ambiguity by putting in the necessary detail.

Normative reality *is interpretive reality.*

FIGURE 3.5 — *The Old Woman and the Young Woman*

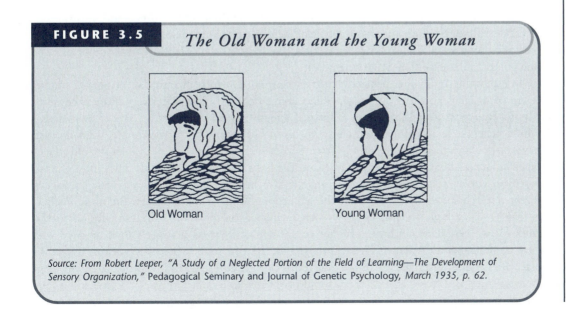

Old Woman   Young Woman

Source: From Robert Leeper, "A Study of a Neglected Portion of the Field of Learning—The Development of Sensory Organization," Pedagogical Seminary and Journal of Genetic Psychology, March 1935, p. 62.

When we examine individual behavior and the impact of perception on that behavior, it is important to remember that people see what they either *want* to see or *are trained* to see. Therefore, in terms of human relations, the manager must try to understand the worker's perception of reality. Employees willingly accept management's methods only when they perceive those methods to be in the employees' best interests. Otherwise, they will resort to such perceptual pitfalls as selective perception, which we just examined, and stereotyping. For example, Harvey Lester, a new employee, has been having trouble mastering his new job. His boss, Lois, tells him that if he does not improve, she will have to let him go. Feeling that he is on the verge of being fired, Harvey quits. What Lois saw as a mild reprimand designed to improve output is interpreted as a threat resulting in a resignation. Each party interpreted the action differently.

LEARNING OBJECTIVE

Explain how stereotyping can influence a person's view of another's behavior

③ # Stereotyping

Stereotyping
is generalizing a particular trait to all members of a given group.

One of the most common perception problems is that of **stereotyping,** which is generalizing a particular trait or behavior to all members of a given group. Too often a stereotype is based on an oversimplified or mistaken attitude, opinion, or judgment. The manager who believes that no union can be trusted has a stereotyped view of unions. The worker who believes that management is always out to exploit employees also has a stereotyped belief. So, too, does the male manager who believes that women are unsuitable for top management positions because they are too emotional and lack aggressiveness.

Every one of us tries to stereotype people, whether it is in the job environment or in a social setting. We even have standard stereotypes for classes or nationalities. Read the following descriptions and try to identify the nationality described.

- **These people are loyal to family ties and always look after their younger brothers and sisters.**
- **These people believe in fair play, are conservative, and keep a stiff upper lip.**
- **These people are very scientific, industrious, and hard working.**
- **These people love caviar, Bolshoi dancing, and music by Tchaikovsky.**
- **These people love pasta, wine, and—most of all—great opera.**

Most people say that the first description is that of the Chinese and the second is that of the English. The remaining three are German, Russian, and Italian. To some degree, all these stereotypes are both accurate and inaccurate. For example, in regard to the first description, are not most people loyal to family ties? In regard to the second description, is Britain the *only* country in which fair play is important? And is Germany the *most* scientific and industrious of all nations? Research shows that most people of the world attribute these traits not to the Germans but to the Americans! The last two descriptions are also stereotypes because they do not describe one group to the exclusion of all others.

In examining individual behavior, then, it is important to realize that most people employ stereotyping. It is an easy way to generalize about behavior. The effective manager, however, tries to evaluate each person as an individual and to remain aware of his or her own stereotypical beliefs so as to reduce their effect on his or her judgments. For example, what do men have to say about their female counterparts? Successful male managers do not let the old stereotypes influence them. They judge women on the basis of how well they do their jobs. In fact, based on survey responses from more than 6,500 middle- and upper-level male managers, recent research shows that the higher the educational level of the manager, the more likely it is that he has a high acceptance of women in managerial positions. Additionally, men who work for women generally have a higher acceptance of them as managers than do men who have not had such experience. These findings indicate that stereotypes of women in the workplace are beginning to fade. As more and more women enter the ranks of management, negative attitudes and biases against them should continue to lessen. However, there is still a long way to go.

Attitudes

A person's feelings about objects, activities, events, and other people are termed **attitudes.** These feelings usually are learned over time and are a major factor in determining individual behavior.

LEARNING OBJECTIVE

④ *Define attitude and describe its impact on worker output*

Components of Attitudes

There are three basic components of attitudes: cognitive, affective, and behavioral. Each plays a major role in attitude formation.

- The **cognitive component** is the set of values and beliefs that a person has toward a person, an object, or an event. For example, a coworker tells us, "I don't like the boss. He's out to get me." The cognitive component of this attitude is the belief that the boss is unfair or punitive. The cognitive component creates the basis or reason for the negative attitude. If the worker were to change his mind and believe that the boss was fair, the basis for the attitude would change and the worker would now have a positive attitude toward the boss.

- The **affective component** is the emotional feeling that is attached to an attitude. It is the emotion that is felt with regard to a person, an object, or an event. When we feel happiness or anger or disappointment, this is the affective component. When our favorite baseball team loses an important game and we feel sad, this too is a result of the affective component. The affective component is a result of our feelings toward someone or something. The cognitive component influences the affective component. The person who dislikes the boss may feel happy when he learns that the manager has been transferred to another office.

- The **behavioral component** is the tendency to act in a particular way toward a person, an object, or an event. For example, when the employee learns that the boss is to be transferred, the employee smiles. When your favorite team comes from behind to win a game in the bottom of the ninth, you cheer. If you enjoy your human relations course, you are likely to show up on time for all classes and participate when asked to do so.

One way to remember the three components of attitude is to think of them in the order they have been presented. This order moves from the cause of attitudes to the results. The cognitive component is the belief that is the reason for the attitude, the affective component is the emotional feeling that results from this belief, and the behavioral component is the tendency to act in a particular way in response to this feeling. A good example of how attitudes affect behavior is found by comparing baby boomers (or *boomers* for short) and Gen Xers (also called *busters* because they are trying to break into the workplace and begin moving up the ranks). Here is a comparison of the attitudes that each holds about the other:

Attitudes
are a person's feelings about objects, events, and people.

The **cognitive component**
is the set of values and beliefs a person has toward a person, an object, or an event.

The **affective component**
is the emotional feeling attached to an attitude.

The **behavioral component**
is the tendency to act in a particular way toward a person, an object, or an event.

How Boomers Feel About Busters	How Busters Feel About Boomers
They are too cocky and unwilling to pay their dues.	They spend too much office time politicking and not enough time working.
They lack loyalty and commitment to their work.	They lack technical know-how.
They will not go the extra mile.	They have coasted through life by arriving on the scene during the golden age of American business.
They are naive and whine too much.	They are holding down jobs for which younger employees are better qualified.
They have no respect for authority.	They want to control things and not share power.

Obviously, the two groups have different attitudes regarding each other, and the challenge rests in the lap of the boomers because today they are the managers. What can these individuals do to manage the Gen Xers effectively? One of the first steps is to realize that Gen Xers have grown up in an environment vastly different from that of the boomers. During the years 1946–1964, the boomers saw both economic growth and recession a number of times. For example, recessions marked the late 1950s, the late 1960s, and the mid-1970s, and the last one was both strong and prolonged. At one point, interest rates on loans approached 20 percent and hundreds of thousands of businesses went bankrupt. Growing up and working in this environment, many boomers were happy to have a job, and they were loyal to their company. Beginning in the mid-1980s, however, the economy began to regain strength and, except for a downturn in the early 1990s, America enjoyed two decades of economic prosperity. The Gen Xers who grew up in this period saw unemployment drop dramatically, while the importance of knowledge workers increased sharply and traditional work arrangements gave way to new approaches such as flexible work hours.[12] Additionally, many of the Gen Xers' working parents who were thrown out of work because of company cutbacks often found other jobs in smaller, more entrepreneurial firms. This experience led many Gen Xers to believe that company loyalty was a thing of the past, which engendered their willingness to make demands on the company and to switch to other firms if these demands were not met.

How, then, can the young, aggressive workforce be managed? One expert on the subject has recommended that managers understand the needs that Gen Xers have and what they are looking for in their jobs. These include the following:

1. **They do not want to do the same thing day after day; they like variety.**
2. **They are not motivated by money alone; they also want to grow and learn by facing new challenges and opportunities.**
3. **They are looking for jobs that are cool, fun, and fulfilling.**
4. **They believe that if they keep growing and learning, that's all the security they are going to need; advancing their skill set is their top priority.**
5. **They have a tremendous thirst for knowledge.**
6. **They like to work in a team environment, in contrast to their bosses, who typically like to work independently.**
7. **They like to learn by doing—and by making mistakes as they go along.**
8. **They tend to challenge the established way of doing things because they believe there is always a better way.**
9. **They want regular and frequent feedback on their performance.**
10. **They are looking to blend their careers with their personal lives.[13]**

A comparison of these two groups clearly illustrates why many firms have found attitude to be a major productivity challenge.

Civil Behavior Human behavior is a reflection of attitude. Managers must make every effort to create a workplace that inspires civil behavior among its workers. According to various studies, people are deeply concerned about behavior toward one another. *U.S. News & World Report* found 89 percent of the respondents described incivility as a serious problem; 78 percent said it had worsened in the past 10 years. Another research group, Public Agenda, found that four out of five Americans think that the "lack of respect and courtesy" has become "a serious problem and we should try to address it." For example, airlines have dealt with uncivil passengers on flights across the nation, unhappy employees have shot their bosses, irate parents have harmed coaches, and children have shot their teachers and classmates. These behaviors stem from attitude. Other examples of incivility behavior in the workplace include verbal harassing someone on a regular basis, withholding resources to guarantee failure, and spreading stories to undermine a person's reputation in the workplace. Incivility behavior in the workplace affects productivity, as shown in a study by Christine

Pearson, a management professor at the University of North Carolina's graduate business school. Her results indicated:[14]

28 percent lost work time tying to avoid the instigator.

53 percent lost work time worrying about the incident or future interactions.

37 percent reported a weakened sense of commitment to their organization.

46 percent thought about changing jobs to get away from the instigator.

12 percent did change jobs—to avoid the instigator.

A question every manager must ask, "Are my actions creating a kinder workplace, an environment where all people are treated with deep respect day after day?"

Impact of 9/11 on Employees' Attitude   The attitudes of many people were forever changed on 9/11. Dr. Richard Chaifetz, Chairman and CEO of ComPsych, is seeing a renewed emphasis on overall relationship building in the workplace. Employees are concentrating on ways to excel at their current jobs instead of looking for new employment. Employees are realizing that a key ingredient to maximizing their present job is to build strong bonds with their peers and supervisors."[15]

Family Friendly Workplace   "Employees also want a workplace that helps them balance the demand of their work and family lives, rather than forces them to choose one over the other. People quit when rigid workplace rules cause unbearable family stress. Employees want a family-friendly workplace. For example, a manager can promote a family-friendly workplace by allowing employees to change work hours whenever a family crisis arises, such as taking a sick child to the doctor or attending important events at school. Other ideas include:

- **Visiting an employee following a death in the family.**
- **Accompanying employees to their children's ball games and recitals.**
- **Allowing employees' children to come to work with them occasionally.**
- **Allowing well-behaved pets into the workplace.**
- **Researching elder-care alternatives for an employee's parents.**
- **Sending birthday cards or cakes to employees' family members.**
- **Getting the company lawyer to help an employee with health insurance problems.**
- **Allowing family members to accompany employees during weekend travel time.**
- **Exploring the possibility of employees working from home.**
- **Giving employees a floating day off.[16]**

Attitude About Generation Os   Each year Americans, especially children, are growing fatter and more obese. It is predicted the next generation of workers will be known as Generation Os. These workers will bring a new set of attitudes, issues, and challenges to the workplace. For example these workers will require changes in workplace structure and new benefits. The results of a survey conducted by the NPD Group showed that three-quarters of those surveyed felt it's OK to be overweight, which is a 45 percent increase over 1985.[17]

Attitudes are changing and reflecting a positive view. It is the responsibility of managers and supervisors to work effectively with all groups of workers and not discriminate among groups of workers.

Ways to Improve Employee Attitudes   SCORE, Counselors to American's Small Business, suggests that improving employee attitudes should begin with an examination of the manager's attitude. Managers must:

- **Be genuinely interested in their employees, customers, and suppliers.**
- **Respect their employees' dignity.**

- **Be patient, understanding, and helpful to employees.**
- **Let employees know that they are important to them and to the company.**
- **Let employees know that performance will be rewarded.**
- **Help employees identify what makes them feel fulfilled and happy within the job.**
- **Include employees as team members; ask for suggestions and respect their ideas.**
- **Give employees credit for their ideas, which are used.**
- **Listen to their employees.**[18]

Attitudes are changing and one way of dealing with this challenge is to measure it carefully.

Attitude Measurement

*An **attitude questionnaire** is an instrument for measuring attitudes.*

One way of measuring attitudes is through the use of an **attitude questionnaire** (see Figure 3.6). Attitude questionnaires are important for several reasons. First, they reflect current attitudes in an organization. Second, they provide a baseline against which to compare future attitude surveys. (Are attitudes improving or declining?) Third, they serve as a source of information about those areas or issues to which the organization needs to pay greater attention and those areas that are all right.

*An **intervening variable** is one that is influenced by a causal variable and that affects an end-result variable.*

An organization must realize that attitudes are an **intervening variable.** They are influenced by causal variables and, in turn, affect end-result variables (see Figure 3.7). An individual's attitude will not decline without some cause, such as a change in leadership style, a failure to get a merit raise, or the submission of a poor performance appraisal. This cause brings about a change in attitude—the intervening variable—which then results in a decline in output—the end-result variable.

Conversely, if attitudes improve because a person is given a merit raise or is told how to obtain a merit raise in the future, his or her output increases. The raise (a causal variable) will improve attitudes (the intervening variable) and result in more output (the end-result variable).

Attitudes are internal. They cannot be seen; they can only be inferred through such end-result variables as output and can be measured by means of attitude surveys. Attention to attitudes, therefore, can be one of the keys to increasing productivity, because how a person feels about the organization will affect his or her output. For example, research shows that those who think positively tend to be more productive than those who do not. Seligman, a university psychologist, found that individuals with positive attitudes tend to do better jobs than the average worker. Working with the Metropolitan Life Insurance Company, Seligman gave twenty-minute written tests to new salespeople to determine their attitudes. Within months, the new recruits with positive attitudes were dramatically outselling the new recruits who did not have positive attitudes. The company then used the test to screen prospective employees. During the first year of the program, this new hiring practice increased revenues by $10 million. Seligman's research shows the power of positive thinking. Those who believed that they would succeed were more successful than those who did not. Their attitudes resulted in a number of important behaviors, including:

1. **The ability to shrug off bad news.**
2. **A willingness to take risks.**
3. **A desire to assume personal control of events rather than just allowing things to happen.**
4. **A willingness to set ambitious goals and to pursue them.**[19]

In recent years, a growing number of firms have found that attitude surveys are extremely useful in helping to measure morale and in improving performance. The Springfield Manufacturing Group of Springfield, Missouri recently discovered that responses from its heavy-duty division personnel were sharply different from what management expected. In particular, 62 percent

FIGURE 3.6 · *Wild Oats Staff Survey (Partial Form)*

This survey has been created so that you can anonymously relate your experiences as a staff member of Wild Oats. We will be using the numerical portion to come up with a store "Happiness Index," which will tell us whether morale is giddy or suicidal. This feedback will help us to create a better working environment for everyone. Please do your best to complete this survey in an honest and open manner and with as much detail and explanation as possible.

Please rate your responses by circling the number that most closely describes your experience. Feel free to use the back of these sheets for additional comments.

1. How happy are you with your job overall?
   Not happy at all . . . . Ecstatic
   1   2   3   4   5   6   7   8   9   10
   Any comments or suggestions?

2. How do you feel about your benefits at Wild Oats?
   Terrible . . . . Great
   1   2   3   4   5   6   7   8   9   10
   Any comments or suggestions?

3. How do you feel about the pay levels at Wild Oats as compared to similar employers?
   Worse than most . . . . Ecstatic
   1   2   3   4   5   6   7   8   9   10
   Any comments or suggestions?

4. How do you feel about the employee review system at Wild Oats?
   Hate it . . . . Love it
   1   2   3   4   5   6   7   8   9   10
   Any comments or suggestions?

5. How is overall morale in your store?
   Awful . . . . Wonderful
   1   2   3   4   5   6   7   8   9   10
   Any comments or suggestions?

6. How do you feel about the responsibilities of your job?
   Too little . . . . Too much
   1   2   3   4   5   6   7   8   9   10
   Any comments or suggestions?

7. How effectively is your store managed?
   Very poorly . . . . Very well
   1   2   3   4   5   6   7   8   9   10
   Any comments or suggestions?

8. How effective is your department manager?
   Remarkably bad . . . . Terrific
   1   2   3   4   5   6   7   8   9   10
   Any comments or suggestions?

9. Why do you come to work every day?
   Have to . . . . Want to
   1   2   3   4   5   6   7   8   9   10
   Any comments or suggestions?

10. How does Wild Oats compare to your previous employers?
    Worse. Same . . . . Much better
    1   2   3   4   5   6   7   8   9   10
    Any comments or suggestions?

Source: Reproduced with permission of Wild Oats.

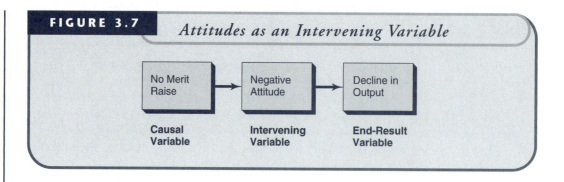

FIGURE 3.7 · *Attitudes as an Intervening Variable*

No Merit Raise → Negative Attitude → Decline in Output

Causal Variable · **Intervening Variable** · **End-Result Variable**

of the workers said that no one had talked to them about personal development within the last six months; 48 percent said that they did not feel that they had the opportunity to become a leader in the firm; and 43 percent said that their work-related opinions did not count. These responses were particularly surprising to management, since the heavy-duty plant was the firm's most successful operation.

Management decided to find out what was wrong. A worker committee was formed from departments throughout the division and began investigating how to improve employee attitudes. The group quickly found that many workers had been asking for a variety of efficiency-related changes for more than two years, and nothing had been done. The group also discovered that most of the complaints and concerns were a result of small problems that had been allowed to go uncorrected. Using this feedback as the basis for action, the company then began making all the necessary changes. Additionally, the firm now uses attitude measurement surveys every six months to ensure that worker concerns are quickly identified and addressed.[20]

LEARNING OBJECTIVE ⑤

Define personality and discuss the major forces affecting personality development

Personality
is a relatively stable set of characteristics and tendencies that help to describe individual behavior.

Personality

The relatively stable set of characteristics and tendencies that determine similarities and differences between people is termed **personality.** For example, some people are very outgoing, whereas others tend to be introverted. Some are assertive; others are passive. Every individual has a personality different from the next individual, which we can think of as a composite of all the person's behavioral components as reflected in how he or she acts.

Sometimes we try to generalize about an individual's overall personality by calling him or her aggressive, hostile, kind, easygoing, or warm. These adjectives are all designed to categorize the person in a word or two; although this may be an incomplete way of describing someone, we all tend to do it. Likewise, most of us look at the way a person walks, talks, and dresses in seeking clues to his or her personality. Obviously, personality consists of *many* factors, making it very difficult to define the term. Psychologists, however, tend to accept certain ideas about personality:

1. **Personality is an organized whole; otherwise, the individual would have no meaning.**
2. **Personality appears to be organized into patterns. These are, to some degree, observable and measurable.**
3. **Although there is a biological basis to personality, the specific development is a product of social and cultural environments.**
4. **Personality has superficial aspects, such as attitudes toward a team leader, and a deeper core, such as sentiments about authority or the Protestant work ethic.**
5. **Personality involves both common and unique characteristics. Each person is different from every other person in some respects while similar in other respects.**

FIGURE 3.8

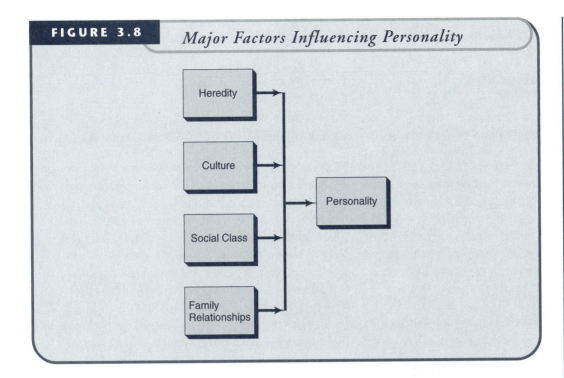

FIGURE 3.8 — Major Factors Influencing Personality

What accounts for differences in personality? Four major forces can be cited as directly affecting personality development: heredity, culture, social class, and family relationships (Figure 3.8).

- *Heredity* affects personality because people are born with certain physical characteristics. Intelligence, height, and facial features all are inherited. The person who is highly intelligent may be arrogant toward fellow students; the tall girl may be quiet because she feels awkward; the short boy may compensate for his size by being aggressive in his dealings with others.
- *Culture* is important because the values and beliefs of the society in which one is raised help to determine how a person will act. A society that puts great value on money will be different from one in which leisure is emphasized over work. A society in which education is believed to be important will be substantially different from one in which education is not highly regarded. Culture also affects the way managers and subordinates act. The "Cultural Diversity in Action" box provides an example.
- *Social class* helps to shape personality because an individual's mores are heavily influenced by his or her neighborhood and community life. This social class also affects the individual's self-image; perception of others; and assumptions about authority, work, and money. A manager who wants to understand how people adjust to the demands of organizational life must consider these social class factors.
- *Family relationships* influence personality by rewarding a person for certain behaviors and by not rewarding him or her for others. These actions help to shape a pattern of behavior and serve as a basis for interpersonal relations outside the home.

Each of these four factors influences behavior, and managers have little control over them. This is not to say that managers cannot direct, channel, or reorient an individual's behavior, which can be done by using the motivational concepts discussed in Chapter 2. However, unless managers understand the bases for individual behavior, they will have great difficulty managing it. One of the most recent approaches for helping managers to do this has been training in the area of emotional intelligence.[21]

CULTURAL DIVERSITY IN ACTION

Working for the Japanese

Japanese firms in America now employ more than 300,000 people, and the number is likely to double by the year 2000. This trend raises an important question for many Americans: Should you work for a Japanese company? The answer is a result of two interdependent factors: culture and personality. The Japanese tend to bring their culture to the United States and try to get Americans to adapt to it. If an individual has the "right" personality, this is no problem; otherwise, working for the Japanese can be a cultural nightmare. This is particularly true for high achievers and women.

One problem for high achievers is that the Japanese culture promotes group relatedness and activity. This means that when someone does something well, he or she is not individually recognized for it. Instead, the work group gets the praise. A Japanese employee would say, "We are all equal members of the group. So while I may have suggested the idea, it was a product of group interaction." Americans, in general, want to be recognized for their own individual achievements. Conclusion: Individuals who are unwilling or unable to be subsumed into the group are unlikely to do well in Japanese-owned firms.

A second, related problem is that of slow promotion. Japanese firms do not advance their people quickly through the hierarchy as do American companies. Promotions are slow, and those who are in a hurry often find themselves stymied. Conclusion: Individuals who are accustomed to rapid rewards for their efforts will be extremely frustrated in Japanese-managed firms.

Many American women who work for Japanese companies report a great deal of frustration with the way they are treated. Most Japanese have never learned how to cope with high-achieving women. In fact, many Japanese managers believe that women will soon quit the firm to raise a family, so there is little need to be concerned with them as human resources. Conclusion: Women who are looking for a business career with a Japanese firm should first talk to other women in that company about how they have been treated.

Another problem is the time demands that are made on employees. A great deal of business is conducted after hours when Japanese managers go to a bar and drink and discuss decisions that must be made. American managers are accustomed to going home to their families at the end of a workday, not hanging out in bars until the wee hours of the morning. Conclusion: Individuals who want to draw a line between their business life and their family life may find working for a Japanese firm to be highly unrewarding.

However, there is some good news. Many Japanese managers are now becoming aware that their international employees do not work the same way that they do. Hence, a slow change process is taking place as Japanese firms become more westernized.

Sources: John E. Rehfeld, "What Working for a Japanese Company Taught Me," Harvard Business Review, November–December 1990, pp. 167–176; Susan Moffat, "Should You Work for the Japanese?" Fortune, December 3, 1990, pp. 107–120; and Richard M. Hodgetts and Fred Luthans, International Management, 4th ed. (Burr Ridge, Il; Irwin/McGraw, 2000), chapter 5.

Emotional intelligence
is the capacity for recognizing one's own feelings and those of others.

Emotional intelligence is the capacity for recognizing one's own feelings and those of others, for motivating oneself, and for managing emotions well in both oneself and one's relationships.[22] Recent research shows that many individuals with very high IQs do not have high emotional intelligence (EI). As a result, they do not do well in the workplace, especially at the higher levels. Daniel Goleman, one of the leading authorities on EI, puts it this way:

> . . . IQ has the least power in predicting success among that pool of people smart enough to handle the most cognitively demanding fields, and the value of emotional intelligence for success grows more powerful the higher the intelligence barriers for entry into a field. In MBA programs or in careers like engineering, law, or medicine, where professional selection focuses almost exclusively on intellectual abilities, emotional intelligence carries much more weight than IQ in determining who emerges as a leader.[23]

Similar findings have been recognized at the lower levels of the hierarchy, where businesses report that a knowledge of technical skills (IQ) is important, but social skills (EI), such as the ability to listen and speak well, adapt to setbacks, generate creative responses to problems, cooperate with others, and exude confidence are even more important. Simply put, the ability to interact well with others, manage work relationships effectively, and contribute to overall group effort are much more important than the ability to know the technical aspects of one's job. For example, the results of a recent study of 358 managers across the Johnson & Johnson Consumer & Personal Care Group showed that the highest performing managers have significantly more "emotional competence" than other managers.[24]

Why do many people lack high EI? One answer is that their personality has been shaped by a focus on values that are not critical to success in the workplace. They put highest emphasis on the tools and techniques needed to do their jobs, but they overlook the importance of building strong social skills. In a growing number of successful firms, managers now are being trained to help their people develop these basic emotional and social (EI) competencies.[25] In particular, these include:

- *Self-awareness*—being able to assess realistically one's own abilities and self-confidence.
- *Self-regulation*—being able to handle one's emotions so that they help rather than interfere with the task at hand.
- *Motivation*—learning how to use one's deepest preferences to move toward desired goals, to improve performance, and to persevere in the face of setbacks and frustrations.
- *Empathy*—learning to sense what others are feeling and to use that information to cultivate rapport with broadly diverse people.
- *Social skills*—learning to handle emotions in relationships; to read social situations accurately; to interact smoothly; and to apply these skills to persuading, leading, negotiating, and settling disputes, thereby increasing cooperation and teamwork.[26]

Since Daniel Goleman published his book, *Emotional Intelligence*, in 1995, many businesses, the U.S. government and institutions have adopted EQ development programs with great success. "Organizations like American Express, Prudential, Johnson and Johnson and even the U.S. Air Force have reported improvement in performance with EQ and the evidence continues to mount."[27]

Interpersonal Behavior

Values, perceptions, attitudes, and personality all are important components of individual behavior. However, no one lives in a vacuum. People interact with other people. In fact, this is how we develop values, perceptions, attitudes, and, to a large degree, personality. Before finishing our discussion of individual behavior, therefore, we should examine interpersonal behavior. We will do so by first looking at the importance of gender differences in interpersonal behavior. We then will examine the value of assertiveness training and the ways in which motivational profiles can help to improve interpersonal behavior.

Gender Differences

The number of women in the U.S. workplace has increased sharply over the last two decades. As a result, managers need to know how to interact effectively with both genders. One way is by understanding some of the differences in the way each group behaves. For example, Helen

Fisher, an anthropologist, has studied the differences between the genders and found that certain qualities that women have help them to succeed in the workplace by being more effective in terms of interpersonal behavior.[28] For example, women tend to be better than men at articulating their ideas. They are particularly adept at finding the right words to convey what they want to say. They also tend to be better at reading emotions in faces and in deciphering postures, gestures, and vocal inflections. As a result, many women are very effective in reading problem situations and figuring out how to deal with them.

Another area where women tend to excel is in processing information. Fisher has found that men tend to address a problem by formulating a simple, basic solution, whereas women often gather more information and look at a variety of approaches to solving the problem. Here is an example.

> An employer who couldn't decide whether to give a raise to a young man or a young woman called both into his office. He said, "Here's a business problem. Which solution would you choose: A, B, or C?" Both went home and thought about it. The following morning the young man walked in and said, "I'd choose solution B." The young woman said she would choose solution A if she wanted to solve problems X and Y; solution B if she wanted to solve problems W and Z; and so on.[29]

LEARNING OBJECTIVE

⑥

Describe how assertiveness training can help managers and subordinates improve their understanding of interpersonal behavior

As the world of business becomes more complex and problems must be looked at from a variety of perspectives, this type of thinking will be particularly helpful in terms of complementing the linear approach that is used by many men. Women are also very effective in trying to build consensus and getting everyone to work together as a team. Many men in group situations try to win at the expense of others. Women, on the other hand, tend to be more focused on win-win approaches, in which everyone goes away with a positive feeling.

Assertiveness Training

Assertiveness training teaches people how to assert themselves in work and social situations.

Another way to develop improved interpersonal relations is with **assertiveness training.** The purpose of such training is to teach people how to tactfully and effectively express their preferences, needs, opinions, and feelings in work and social situations. The goals of the training are threefold:

1. **The individual is taught how to determine personal feelings.**
2. **The individual learns how to say what he or she wants.**
3. **The individual learns how to get what he or she wants.**

Assertiveness training can be particularly helpful for those employees who are bottling up too much inside themselves; they become so uptight that, psychologically, they are ready to explode. Often these people do not recognize that their rights are being denied; they simply want to be "nice" and "not cause trouble," and instead they "suffer in silence" and assume nothing can be done to change the situation. Assertiveness training can help these people recognize that their rights are being denied.[30]

Passive, Aggressive, and Assertive Behavior

Assertiveness training is something of a misnomer because the word *assertive* often conjures up thoughts of pushiness or belligerence. However, this is not what the term means. Actually, in assertiveness training the objective is to teach an individual how to make a clear statement of personal desires without being obnoxious or abusive. Consider the case of Mary Harrison, who has been asked to meet an incoming job applicant at the airport first thing in the morning, show the individual around the organization, be sure the person gets to all of his scheduled interviews, and see that he gets back to the airport on time for his departure flight. Mary does not want to take on this assignment because she is snowed under with work. There are three types of behavior available to her in responding to the situation: passive, aggressive, and assertive. Here is how Mary can use each response:

Passive.   Mary is angry and really wants to tell her boss off. However, she grits her teeth, puts her work aside, and makes plans to get to the airport on time.

Aggressive.   Mary tells her boss, "Hell, I'm not going to do that. I'm up to my nose in work. Get someone else who is not that important. I'm not going to be treated like this, so don't ask me to do it again."

Assertive.   Mary says to her boss, "I appreciate your thinking of me, but I'm really snowed under with work. I don't have the time to do this. However, I don't think you'll have any trouble getting someone else. There are a number of people in the department who have light workloads this week."

Notice that when using assertive behavior, Mary stood her ground without being rude or discourteous.

Becoming More Assertive

How can an individual increase his or her assertiveness? Over the last decade, many assertiveness-training programs have been offered by organizations (for their own personnel) and by professional consultants and trainers (for organizational personnel and the general public). Although these various workshops employ different techniques for improving individual assertiveness, knowledge of a series of basic steps is essential for every participant. Phrased in the form of questions, the list includes the following:

1. **What is my goal? What exactly do I want to accomplish? (Clarify the situation and focus on the issue.)**
2. **How will assertive behavior help me accomplish my goal?**
3. **What would I usually do to avoid asserting myself in this situation?**
4. **Why would I want to give that up and assert myself instead?**
5. **What might be stopping me from asserting myself?**
   a. **Am I holding on to irrational beliefs? If so, what are they?**
   b. **How can I replace these irrational beliefs with rational ones?**
   c. **Have I (as a woman or a man) been taught to behave in ways that make it difficult for me to act assertively in the present situation? If so, what ways? How can I overcome this?**
   d. **What are my rights in this situation? (State them clearly.) Do these rights justify turning my back on my conditioning?**
6. **Am I anxious about asserting myself? What techniques can I use to reduce my anxiety?**
7. **Have I done my homework? Do I have the information I need to go ahead and act?**
8. **Can I do the following:**
   a. **Let the other person know I hear and understand him or her?**
   b. **Let the other person know how I feel?**
   c. **Tell him or her what I want?**[31]

Assertiveness training is an excellent complement to effective behaviors such as those spelled out in the "Human Relations in Action" box.

HUMAN RELATIONS IN ACTION

What Your Boss Wants You to Know

One of the biggest reasons why some people in organizations succeed is that they know what their boss wants them to know. Whether it is explicitly spelled out or learned through experience or intuition, successful people know what the boss is looking for. For example:

1. *Do more than what is expected.* Your boss expects everyone to do his or her job. If you do more, however, you will stand out as a superior performer.

2. *Forget about making up excuses.* The boss expects you to do things right. When you do not, it may cause problems, but it will do you no good to blame someone else. Even if you are right, the boss does not want to hear about it. He or she has more important things to do than trying to assign blame. It is your job to get the work done right the first time. If you did not, work harder to do so the next time.

3. *Anticipate things going wrong.* If you do, you will seldom be disappointed. However, you will be prepared to deal with them before they become too serious. If part of your job calls for getting information from other people and processing it before passing it on to others, anticipate getting the information late or finding that some of it is erroneous. Allow yourself time to check and correct the information.

4. *Remember that punctuality and attendance count.* Do not be late for work or meetings. Even if nothing important happens, you are expected to be on time. If you are continually tardy or absent, your boss will see this as an attitude problem, and it will count against you later.

5. *Get along with your coworkers.* Bosses like to think that everyone in their unit is a team player. If there is internal dissension, the boss will not want to know who is right or wrong. The boss is not there to referee employee squabbles. Everyone involved will have a black mark against him or her. Make it a point to stay on good terms with everyone in the unit.

6. *Be protective of the organization.* Do not say anything that will reflect negatively on the enterprise or anyone who works there. Keep organizational politics and problems within the enterprise and, if you must do anything that reflects on another, go out of your way to minimize its negative effect.

7. *Learn to read your boss.* Listen closely to what your boss tells you and learn to interpret its meaning. If your boss says, "This really warrants our looking into," it may mean that you should drop everything you are doing and start working on the matter he or she has been talking about. On the other hand, if the individual says, "This sounds very interesting," it may mean the matter is a minor one and should be ignored. Every boss has a specific way of communicating. Figure out what your boss is really talking about.

8. *Never lie.* The biggest problem with lying is that it calls your integrity into question. What other lies have you told? What exactly are you up to? Your boss may suspect that you are not as reliable as he or she thought. When this happens, your credibility comes into question and your future with the organization may be affected. If you cannot tell the truth, limit what you say.

Motivational Profiles

Another way to improve interpersonal behavioral skills is to understand what is important to a person. For example, some companies give bonuses such as $1,000 to individuals who do outstanding work, whereas others reward excellent performance by allowing their people to choose from a group of rewards such as a $1,000 bonus, three days off with pay, or reserved parking next to the main entrance for the next twelve months. Although many people choose the bonus, research shows that the other two rewards tend to be more popular, especially among employees with young families and managers who have been with the company for more than ten years. The latter groups are more motivated by nonfinancial rewards because these best fit their lifestyle.

Research also shows that because people are different, the way in which one person is motivated may vary sharply from that of another.[32] In fact, by understanding personal profiles, it is possible more effectively to motivate, lead, and retain individuals. New employees, for example, tend to fit into one of six profiles (although there is overlap between these in terms of shared characteristics) and, when managers understand these profiles, they are better able to deal effectively with these people.

Independent Thinkers   **Independent thinkers** are very entrepreneurial in their approach. These individuals want to be free to choose what they are going to do and how they are going to do it. They tend to be impatient with rules, policies, and procedures and have low loyalty to the organization. They like to create their own way of doing things and are prepared to take full responsibility for their successes and failures. In motivating and leading these people, managers need to focus on individual rewards such as pay-for-performance plans, bonuses, and commissions.

Lifestylers   **Lifestylers** are particularly interested in their quality of life. The job is important to them, but it is a means to an end. They want to enjoy their work, but the job is not the most important thing in their life. People with young children who want to balance work and family responsibilities often fit into this category. So, too, do young professionals who value their freedom and want to pursue personal priorities and midcareer people who have responsibilities for older relatives who need their help. Lifestylers are prepared to work hard to get the job done, but they also expect the organization to give them flexible work schedules and additional vacation days so that they can meet their personal responsibilities.

Personal Developers   **Personal developers** are interested in jobs that give them the opportunity to keep on learning and becoming more proficient. Individuals who fall into this category include young people who are interested in building a skill base and people who frequently change jobs and need to be on the cutting edge of their field so that they are attractive to new employers. Personal developers evaluate their work in terms of whether they are being challenged and whether they are acquiring new skills. Their primary interest is their career and not the company for which they are working, so if better opportunities come along, they will change jobs. One way that companies are able to retain these people is by continually offering them training that focuses on building skills or updating their skills.

Careerists   **Careerists** are individuals who want to get ahead and are prepared to make the necessary sacrifices to do so. These people have a lot in common with baby boomers who are loyal to their company and willing to make a career with the firm. These individuals are ambitious, motivated by prestige and status, and want to advance continually and finish their careers in the upper ranks of the hierarchy.

Authenticity Seekers   **Authenticity seekers** are interested in self-expression. They are best represented by the cliché, "I gotta be me." These individuals will not sacrifice their personal expressiveness to play a corporate role nor will they repress their personal values in favor of what is good for the company. At the same time, authenticity seekers can be creative (albeit difficult to manage), and managers must carefully direct their efforts so they contribute to company goals while not losing their personal identification.

Collegiality Seekers   **Collegiality seekers** like to work with others. They are very social in orientation and are excellent team players. In fact, they identify with their work group and are extremely loyal to these people. When asked what is important to them, they typically say that it is working with people.[33]

These motivational profiles are useful in helping to explain what is important to individuals. When managers know what motivates their people, they are in a better position to lead them. They also know how and why these people interact with other group members and can use this information to increase group morale and productivity.

Independent thinkers
are very entrepreneurial and want freedom.

Lifestylers
are most interested in their quality of life.

Personal developers
are interested in jobs that give them the opportunity to continue learning.

Careerists
want to get ahead and are prepared to make the necessary sacrifices to do so.

Authenticity seekers
are interested in self-expression.

Collegiality seekers
like to work with others and are excellent team players.

① LEARNING OBJECTIVE
Identify and describe some of the common values held by all individuals

Individuals are complex beings. Nevertheless, many descriptive clichés have been used in trying to sum them up in a word or two. In human relations, we need to be much more scientific in our analysis of individuals and to realize that people are a blend of many different types of behavior. For example, sometimes they are rational and at other times they are emotional; sometimes they are motivated by economic considerations and at other times they are self-actualizing. To understand individual behavior more fully, we examined four of the major components: values, perceptions, attitudes, and personality.

A value is something that has worth or importance to an individual. People have, in overall terms, six values: theoretical, economic, aesthetic, social, political, and religious. When examined in a job context, values can be studied in terms of worker satisfaction. The most recent research shows that many employees are dissatisfied with their jobs, feel they do not have equitable promotion opportunities, and are underpaid.

② LEARNING OBJECTIVE
Describe perception and explain why it is a determinant of individual behavior

Perception is a person's view of reality. There are two types of perception: sensory (physical) and normative (interpretive). Normative perception is particularly important in the study of human relations, because people's interpretations of reality will influence their behavior. In particular, it can result in selective perception and stereotyping, perceptual problems the effective manager tries to avoid.

③ LEARNING OBJECTIVE
Explain how stereotyping can influence a person's view of another's behavior

Stereotyping forms an instant or fixed picture of a person or group, which is then generalized to all members of a given group. These impressions may or may not be accurate. It is important to understand most people employ stereotyping because it is an easy way to generalize about human behavior. Effective managers, however, evaluate each person as an individual. As the workplace becomes more diversified ethically and more women, minorities, and special needs people are hired, managers must be aware of their negative attitudes and biases and not let stereotyped images influence decisions.

④ LEARNING OBJECTIVE
Define attitude and describe its impact on worker output

Attitudes are a person's feelings about objects, activities, events, and other people. Attitudes have three basic components: cognitive, affective, and behavioral. It is common to find organizations using instruments such as questionnaires to measure these feelings in their employees, because attitudes often are key variables affecting output.

⑤ LEARNING OBJECTIVE
Define personality and discuss the major forces affecting personality development

Personality consists of a relatively stable set of characteristics and tendencies that determine both similarities and differences between one person and another. Some of the major forces affecting personality are heredity, culture, social class, and family relationships.

The manager should also be aware of the available approaches to understanding interpersonal behavior. After all, values, perceptions, attitudes and, to a large degree, personality are developed through interpersonal relations. An understanding of gender differences helps to explain the challenges managers often have in managing diverse work groups.

---

⑥ LEARNING OBJECTIVE
Describe how assertiveness training can help managers and subordinates improve their understanding of interpersonal behavior

Assertiveness training teaches people how to determine personal feelings, verbalize them, and get what they want without being abusive or obnoxious. Motivational profiles help explain individual needs and desires and offer suggestions regarding how to manage people on a one-to-one basis.

KEY TERMS IN THE CHAPTER

Value

Terminal value

Instrumental value

Perception

Sensory reality

Normative reality

Stereotyping

Attitudes

Cognitive component

Affective component

Behavioral component

Attitude questionnaire

Intervening variable

Personality

Emotional intelligence

Independent thinkers

Lifestylers

Personal developers

Careerists

Authenticity seekers

Collegiality seekers

REVIEW AND STUDY QUESTIONS

1. What is meant by *value*? Distinguish between terminal values and instrumental values and give examples of each.

2. How are work values changing in America? Support your answer with examples.

3. What are some characteristics of the baby boomers, the generation Xers, and the greying workforce? What do managers need to know to manage each group?

4. How can perception impact a manager's decisions?

5. How does sensory reality differ from normative reality?

6. What is stereotyping? How effective is it in generalizing about behavior?

7. What is attitude? Describe the cognitive component, the affective component, and the behavior component of attitude.

8. How can attitude measurement be of value to an organization? Explain.

9. What is meant by *personality*? What are some ideas that psychologists tend to accept about personality?

10. How do heredity, culture, social class, and family relationships affect personality development?

11. What is meant by *emotional intelligence* (EI), and how can people develop their EI competencies?

12. What are some gender differences that help to make women more effective in interpersonal relations? Describe three.

13. Of what value is assertiveness training to the modern manager? Of what value is assertiveness training for subordinates? Explain.

14. How do independent thinkers differ from lifestylers? What do managers need to know about managing each?

15. How do personal developers differ from careerists? What do managers need to know about managing each?

16. How do authenticity seekers differ from collegiality seekers? What do managers need to know about managing each?

VISIT THE WEB

What Do Corporations Value?

In this chapter, you studied the nature and process of individual behavior. One of the most important topics is that of values, both individual values and organizational values. The results of the Time Out exercise that you completed in this chapter identified what is important to you. How do your values match with corporation values? How important is it to consider corporate values when seeking employment?

Using the Internet, research the values of a pharmaceutical company, a manufacturing firm, a fast food service company, and a major hotel chain and answer the following questions.

1. What are the values of each company? (The company values may be found in the company vision statement, in the company core values statement, or in information about the company.) Prepare a list or a table of your findings.

    • **http://www.pfizer.com**

    • **http://www.johndeere.com**

    • **http://www.mcdonalds.com**

    • **http://www.marriott.com**

2. What is the common thread that runs among the values of all companies? Why do you believe it is the common thread?

3. Which company fits best with your personal values? Of the four companies researched, which one would be more compatible with your values? Tell why.

4. How important are company values to you in seeking employment? Discuss.

What is Your Emotional Intelligence?

Understanding one's emotions is important to managing one's self, as well as managing others. Goleman found in his research that EI is more important than IQ for people holding higher positions in a company, and also EI is a determining factor in who emerges as a leader. How well do you measure up?

Directions. Go to http://www.queendom.com Take the Emotional Intelligence test, which is free. Click on "tests" and scroll down until you see the free tests. Click on

"Emotional Intelligence" and follow the directions. (For some tests, there is a small charge for receiving a more complete analysis of the results. This is not an endorsement for their products, nor is it a requirement for this assignment.) Answer the following questions:

1.   What is your score? Where does it fall along the scale?

2.   What does your score mean? Summarize the results of your assessment.

3.   How satisfied are you with the results? What do you need to do to change?

Optional. For a more complete analysis of your skills, select and complete several of the free tests that focus on specific skills, such as ethics, self-esteem, assertiveness, honesty, anger, etc. The Values Profile is an interesting test and is based on Spraunger's six values discussed in the chapter. A complete analysis of your results, however, will cost a small fee.

TIME OUT ANSWERS

What Is Important to You?

Enter your average scores on the designated lines below.

Average Score	Interpretation
Group 1	*Importance of control.* This score measures your desire to take charge and control situations.
Group 2	*Importance of fairness.* This score measures the importance you assign to equity and fairness.
Group 3	*Importance of material rewards.* This score measures the extent to which you value money and other tangible rewards.

case: A MATTER OF PERSONALITY

Frank Payne is the manager for a chain store located in the southwestern part of the United States that handles electronic products. He has been with the organization for five years, and his store's sales have been rated "low average" in comparison with sales of similar stores in locales with the same general population and per capita income. Frank's boss, Lisa Sutter, has been with the organization for twelve years. For five of those years, Lisa was a store manager, during which time her sales were the highest in the region, and her employees rated her "excellent."

Lisa believes that one of the most important characteristics of an effective store manager is a good personality. The individual must like people, be willing to listen to customer complaints without taking the matter personally, and express a sincere interest in the well-being of the workers. To Lisa, Frank seems to lack all these traits. He acts as if he has a chip on his shoulder, and Lisa is afraid that this type of personality is likely to lead to the loss of customer goodwill.

During her recent visit to Frank's store, Lisa watched him talk to a customer who wanted to return some merchandise. The woman insisted the merchandise was damaged when she opened the package, and she wanted to exchange it for an undamaged item.

Frank refused to accept the return. "We don't sell damaged goods," he told the woman. "It must have been damaged after you took it from the store."

The customer was furious and, in a loud voice, began telling Frank what she thought of the store and its personnel. Many of the other customers in the store at the time heard the ruckus, and Lisa noticed that most of them left without buying anything.

When Frank resumed his discussion with Lisa, he explained that the woman had been wrong in saying that the merchandise was damaged and that the store should not be expected to take the loss. Lisa tried to help Frank to see the customer's point of view, but she was unable to do so. She dropped the subject and turned to other business matters, including the decline in sales.

"Things haven't been going too well since you took over," she told Frank. "What seems to be wrong?"

Frank talked about some of the areas in which he felt there were problems that needed to be straightened out. All the problems related to inventory control and the need for more motivated personnel. At no point during the conversation did Frank indicate that he might be causing any of the problems because of his personality or his leadership style.

Before leaving, Lisa walked around the store and talked to some of the employees. From her brief conversations with them, she learned they did not care much for Frank as a store manager. One of the workers referred to him as "uncaring," while another said he had "the personality of an army drill sergeant." Lisa decided she would let Frank run the store for another three months but, if sales kept slipping, she would have to replace him.

Questions

1. What type of personality would you expect to find in a successful store manager?

2. How is Frank's personality affecting the attitudes of the workers? Explain.

3. Using what you know about emotional intelligence, describe how you would advise Frank about being more effective. Do you think you would succeed? Explain.

case: YOU BE THE CONSULTANT

Strike While the Iron Is Hot

Over the last six years, Rita Shrewsman's optical company has invested $14 million in research and development (R&D) to improve optics for eyewear. Last week, the company concluded a sixteen-month experiment with a new colored contact lens to correct severe astigmatism that is also bifocal and progressive. The lenses are made from a new product just released into the marketplace. This is a new breakthrough in the development of contact lenses, which puts her firm at least a year ahead of the competition. "I want to make my mark as a researcher who improved the vision of millions," she recently told her husband.

The latest R&D breakthrough is good news for the company because it means the firm will start manufacturing and selling a new line of lenses.

Rita's firm has a contract with a large optics firm that handles all its distribution needs. However, this latest breakthrough may catapult the firm to new financial heights. Rita's vice president of operations has suggested that she increase the size of the production facility and begin producing at full capacity. Rita is hesitant about doing this because she believes it will be possible to improve the quality of the contact lens over the next year. "Why mass produce a product that will be outmoded within 12 months?" she asked. "Wouldn't it make more sense to produce a smaller amount while we are developing a better quality lens? In this way, those who buy next year will be getting an even better product than those who buy tomorrow. And since contact lenses last only about a year before being replaced, what's the hurry to produce so many today?"

The vice president of operations disagrees, as does Rita's banker, who has suggested she consider a public stock offering to raise money and ensure the company a secure financial future. He explained his reasoning to Rita and concluded by noting, "You'll never be in a better position to sell stock and raise money than you are now. You've got to strike while the iron is hot."

Your Advice

1. What do you recommend that Rita do?

    a. Manufacture and sell the new contact lenses while continuing to work on improving the quality of the product.

    b. Dramatically increase the size of the production facilities, sell as many of the current product as possible, and continue working on improving the quality of the lenses.

    c. Dramatically increase the size of the production facilities and sell stock in the company, while continuing to work on improving the quality of the lenses.

2. Which one of Spraunger's six values is most important to Rita? Defend your answer.

3. Which one of Spraunger's six values is most important to the vicepresident of operations? Give an example.

4. How does Rita's perception vary from that of the vice president of operations? Is this a result of sensory or normative reality?

EXPERIENCING VALUE ORIENTATIONS

Purpose

- To understand Spraunger's value model.
- To examine value profiles and identify them on the basis of occupation or career.
- To demonstrate why people in different occupational groups will have different value profiles.

Procedure

1. Review the Spraunger model and be sure you understand the basic differences among the six values: economic, theoretical, aesthetic, social, political, and religious.

2. Examine the six value profiles provided in the situation and match them with one of the six individuals identified according to occupation.

3. Discuss the reasons for the differences in value profiles and how these can affect the way that individuals behave.

Situation

The following six value profiles are from these individuals: (A) clergyman, (B) industrial engineer, (C) chief executive officer, (D) aerospace engineer, (E) salesperson, (F) drug counselor.

Value	A	B	C	D	E	F
Theoretical	62	46	49	26	43	25
Economic	51	66	42	44	55	40
Aesthetic	29	27	64	22	34	23
Social	33	30	24	59	23	50
Political	47	49	41	41	66	41
Religious	18	22	20	48	20	61

4

Group Behavior

Individuals may act on their own, but the perceptions, values, and attitudes that cause their behavior are often a result of group interaction. People influence those around them. Therefore, we cannot adequately study human relations without considering group behavior. To accomplish objectives, managers use several types of groups, which, even though they all have common characteristics, have their own roles, norms, status, and cohesiveness. It is imperative for managers to understand how decisions are made and how power functions within each group and its effect between groups. Managers from time to time will need to resolve conflict within groups. In this chapter, we examine how people act within groups as well as how groups interact with one another.

AFTER READING THIS CHAPTER, YOU SHOULD BE ABLE TO:

1. Describe a group and distinguish among organizational groups—functional, cross-functional, project, virtual, and interest-friendship.
2. Explain the stages of group development.
3. Discuss the importance of roles, norms, status, cohesiveness, and group size to group behavior.
4. Describe how communication and decision-making styles, risk taking, and creativity affect group decisions.
5. List ways in which groups try to gain power over other groups.
6. Identify ways to resolve intergroup conflict.

Innovative Teams in Action

In recent years, more and more organizations have been creating teams for the purpose of generating creative solutions to business-related problems. In many cases, these teams have a great deal of autonomy and often do things their own way regardless of management's rules and regulations. For example, at Corning Inc.'s glass and glass ceramics research and development (R&D) laboratory, scientists work to understand glass chemistries better and to develop both better and new kinds of glass. In this innovative environment, the personnel often do exactly as they please. Noted one scientist recently, "I don't really report to anybody. I don't care who my boss is. I can't be managed. I can just be suppressed and frustrated." Another noted that he began working on a new kind of glass that he thought would be valuable in Corning's booming fiber-optic business. He proposed the idea to management, but it was shot down. They wanted him to work on a different project. However, he ignored them and ended up creating a special type of optical fiber that holds the potential for earning millions of dollars for the firm.

In other cases, innovation is generated by people in a particular area being investigated and not by people who are the experts. For example, British Airways recently brought together a group of experts to help them with their baggage handling operations. None of these individuals was connected to airline baggage handling, but all knew a lot about moving and reclaiming merchandise. The company established five criteria that were critical to baggage handling:

1. **Passengers had to be able to reclaim their baggage within 20 minutes of arrival time.**
2. **More than 99 percent of all bags at Heathrow, in London, had to be routed properly.**
3. **Dependence on the "human element" in baggage handling was to be decreased.**
4. **The company had to show a progressive, measurable improvement in baggage handling.**
5. **Customer confidence and satisfaction in the firm's baggage handling had to be increased.**

The expert group was told that the baggage facilities had not yet been built, so they were free to be as innovative as they wanted. The group then generated sixty-two actions that the company could take. The company eventually rejected some of the suggestions because their implementation was too costly or difficult. One was the use of a voice-recognition system. The firm found that the system was unable to distinguish between the cockney accents of East Enders and the Scottish brogue of Glaswegians. So bags that were bound for Birmingham would sometimes end up being sent to Bremen. However, the company did accept the bar-code baggage system recommendation, and today British Airways has one of the world's most efficient baggage handling systems.

In fact, the results were so successful that the firm has begun using innovative teams to help it attack other productivity-related problems in such areas as cargo handling, the cleaning of aircraft, and catering operations. In the latter case, the team proposed forty-seven recommendations, of which six were selected for further study and development. One of these dealt with the movement of food from the catering center to the aircraft. This activity is highly labor-intensive and time-consuming. Loads must be assembled on the loading dock and then reloaded into high-lift transport vehicles. The company now is in the process of eliminating an entire section of this routine by introducing demountable swap bodies that can be parked within the catering center marshaling area and then connected to the drive unit for the journey to the plane.

These approaches have resulted in a 67 percent increase in productivity, thus helping British Airways to maintain its reputation as the best international airline in the world. As a result, the company is continuing to use expert innovation teams to help it find new ways of increasing productivity and customer service. The key is the effective use of group effort.

Sources: Gwen Ortmeyer, "Making Better Decisions Faster," Management Review, *June 1996, pp. 53–55; Frederick D. Buggie, "Expert Innovation Teams: A New Way to Increase Productivity Dramatically," Planning Review, August 1995, pp. 26–31; and Charles Fishman, "Creative Tension," Fast Company, November 2000, pp. 361–388.*

LEARNING OBJECTIVE

Describe three common characteristics of groups and distinguish among the major organizational groups—functional, cross-functional, project, virtual, and interest-friendship

① Definition of a Group

Unfortunately, there is no universally accepted definition of the term *group*. However, all groups do seem to have three characteristics in common.

1. **A group is a social unit of two or more members, all of whom engage, at some time or other, in *interaction* with each other. In work groups, this interaction often occurs on a face-to-face basis, although some groups are geographically dispersed and interact through letters and telephone conversations.**
2. **Members all are *dependent* on one another. In the pursuit of their objectives, each member realizes the need for the others. In a work setting, an individual is aware that the overall job cannot be done without assistance from other people.**
3. **The members of the group receive some *satisfaction* from their mutual association. Otherwise, they will drop out of the group. In a work setting, for example, they will ask for a transfer to another department or locale or will simply resign.**

Now that we have examined the three major characteristics of a group, let us incorporate them into a meaningful definition. A **group** is a social unit consisting of two or more interdependent, interactive individuals who are striving to attain common goals.

Before examining the nature and activities of groups, it is important to dispel some of the common myths that have sprung up about them:[1]

A group *is a social unit of two or more interdependent, interactive people striving for common goals.*

Myth	Reality
The importance of working together has replaced that of individual contributions.	Individual contributions are critical to the overall success of groups.
If a group consists of high-performing individuals, the team will automatically become a high-performing group.	Sometimes the talents and egos of high-performing individuals will reduce the overall effectiveness of a group because of the internal strife that is created.
It takes a long time for a group to be up and running.	Many groups can very quickly work out their agendas and interpersonal relationships and be up and running in record time.
Decision making by consensus is the best way to make a group work effectively.	Sometimes group consensus works best, but often one or two members take the lead and everyone follows.
Group accountability means that everyone is collectively responsible for everything.	Although the group is accountable in theory, in practice everyone has individual responsibilities and is evaluated on her or his ability to meet those obligations.
There are no leaders or followers on teams; everyone is equal.	Everyone on a team is equal, but some are more equal than others, as determined by such factors as ability, contribution, and personality.

Many types of groups can be found in organizations. Most of them, however, can be classified as one of the following: functional group, cross-functional group, project group, virtual group, or interest-friendship group.

Functional Group

Individuals in **functional groups** *perform the same tasks.*

A **functional group** is composed of individuals performing the same tasks. In a manufacturing firm, for example, it is common to find major functional groups or departments, such as marketing, production, and finance, and further divisions of the personnel within each group. In the marketing department, for example, there is often an advertising group and a personal selling group. In a personal selling group, there are sales forces for product lines or geographical territories. In all these divisions, functional groups are formed to promote internal efficiency.

Cross-Functional Group

A **cross-functional group** is composed of individuals from two or more different functional areas. For example, in designing and bringing a new product to the market and ensuring its continued, long-run success, companies commonly use the talents of a cross-functional group whose members come from a variety of different areas, including design, development, production, marketing, and finance.[2] In hospitals, cross-functional groups often include people from such areas as radiology, hematology, nursing services, surgical support, and administration. If members of the cross-functional team are chosen carefully and their roles and responsibilities are spelled out clearly, the group can produce extremely effective results.[3]

*A **cross-functional group** is a group composed of individuals from two or more functional areas.*

Project Group

A **project group** consists of individuals from many different areas or backgrounds. The group's purpose is to attain its objective within predetermined time, cost, and quality limits, after which the group is disbanded and everyone goes back to his or her regular department. Project groups are used often in building spacecraft, skyscrapers, bridges, and ships. They have also been employed in designing new products and solving particularly complex problems. Whatever the objective, however, a project group draws personnel from many different areas of expertise and combines their talents in the hope of attaining the project goal.

*A **project group** includes members from many different backgrounds.*

Virtual Group

A **virtual group** is a task-focused group that meets without all the members being present in the same locale or at the same time. Virtual groups use videoconferences, e-mail, and conference calls to exchange ideas and discuss problems. Virtual groups, sometimes called virtual teams, are becoming increasingly common thanks to advances in communication technology. For example, companies with worldwide R&D groups have found that they can have these teams working around the clock. At the end of its workday, the design group in Germany will forward its daily work progress to the one in the United States, which will pick up where the other group left off. In turn, the American R&D team will forward its work to the company's Japanese R&D group. In this way, groups worldwide are working on the design. Additionally, thanks to e-mail, the groups do not have to communicate with one another in real time. As a result of these benefits, a growing number of firms are relying increasingly on the use of virtual groups.[4]

*A **virtual group** is a task-focused group that meets without all the members being present in the same locale or at the same time.*

"Companies that use virtual teams say they save money, result in more productive and effective use of workers' time, and ultimately generate better products because of the collaborative nature of the teams. Virtual teams allow employees to be fast and competitive in disseminating information."[5] Virtual groups reduce travel expenses. "There's a phenomenal cost savings for people not having to meet face-to-face," says HR director Pratt at Nortel Networks.

Interest-Friendship Group

An **interest-friendship group** is formed on the basis of common beliefs, concerns, or activities. On the job, interest-friendship groups sometimes are found within departments, whereas in other instances they cut across departmental lines. For example, people who have been in an organization for a long time tend to have many contacts, and they often find it possible to ask friends in other departments to expedite a process or to put a high priority on a particular job. Or they may simply enjoy having lunch together, and sometimes these people exercise together during the lunch hour.

Interest-friendship groups also function away from the job, as in the case of three members of the accounting department and three members from production who are on the company

Interest-friendship groups are formed on the basis of common beliefs, concerns, or activities.

bowling team. Their primary interest is to win the bowling league title. However, such friendships carry back to the job, and it is not uncommon to find people using their friendships to help attain job-related objectives. Thus, it should be obvious that people are often members of two or more groups.

LEARNING OBJECTIVE
Explain the stages of group development

② Stages of Group Development

When a group is first formed, initially there is a "feeling out" stage during which the members get to know one another and learn how to interact effectively. As the members become comfortable working together and learn what each can contribute to the group effort, performance begins to improve and may eventually result in a highly effective work team. During this process, the group goes through four stages: forming, storming, norming, and performing.

Forming

*The **forming stage** is characterized by efforts to determine initial direction.*

The **forming stage** of group development is characterized by efforts to identify carefully what the group should do and how it can get started in this direction. During this stage, group members develop initial interaction; gain insights into one another's values, beliefs, and attitudes; and begin working on role definitions and expectations of each member. Examples of group behavior in this stage include the following:

1. Everyone is extremely polite to everyone else.
2. Many individuals remain quiet and make minimal contributions to group discussions while trying to determine where they want to fit in the scheme of things.
3. Some initial efforts are made by members to establish bonds and to disclose personal insights.
4. Early efforts are made toward gaining power and building influence in the group.

These behaviors help to create the climate within which the team will function during this early stage. They also help the group to clarify its vision and find common ground for understanding one another.[6]

Storming

*The **storming stage** is characterized by confrontation, questioning, and resistance.*

The **storming stage** of group development is characterized by confrontation, questioning of the group's direction and progress, and resistance to task assignments. During this stage, group members believe it is necessary to gain control, and there is often concern that the group has been drifting and lacks a clear sense of focus or direction. Examples of group behavior in this stage include the following:

1. Some members question the group's progress and want the group leader to use a more direct approach to get things done.
2. Some members question the group's goals, assignments, and procedures and want to see changes made.
3. Some participants show frustration because the group's task now appears more difficult than before, and members begin to doubt the group's ability for success.

These behaviors help the group to rethink its approach, make necessary changes, and get on with the job. In carrying out these tasks, the group leader often spends a great deal of time listening to challenges and complaints and calmly responding, renegotiating expectations, and reassigning work based on member interests and skills.

Also common during this phase is the weeding out of ineffective group leaders who are replaced by more effective members. A group leader may be ineffective because he or she is unwilling to communicate with group members. Alternatively, the leader may be unable to be a team player. Commenting on these types of group leaders, one team of researchers offered the following explanations for the replacement of certain individuals:

> *He was not interested in communicating with his team, coworkers, or peers; not committed to sharing and transferring experience, information, knowledge, or process. He tended to be a block in the flow of information, a bottleneck within the company. He was too individualistic. He was not a team player and unable to work with others. A one-man show. He did not accept belonging to a big company.*[7]

Norming

The **norming stage** of group development is characterized by agreement regarding the responsibilities of each member, a new sense of cooperation, and a desire to accomplish group goals. The group has now reached the stage at which it knows how to work as a team and the focus is on getting things done effectively and efficiently. Examples of group behavior in this stage include:

1. Effective conflict management by the group leader as well as the members.
2. Clear identification and prioritizing of problems and action plans for resolving them.
3. A willingness of members to accept responsibility and carry out their tasks as agreed.
4. Effective member interaction resulting in highly effective meetings.

During this phase, group members begin developing negotiation skills, mentoring skills, and the ability to balance differences and similarities. They also learn how to deal with ambiguity and establish common ground for understanding.[8]

Performing

The **performing stage** of group development is characterized by openness and collaboration among group members and the willingness of individual members to monitor their own performance and make necessary changes. In this stage, the group functions effectively on both an individual and a team level. Examples of behavior include:

1. The open sharing of problems and solutions.
2. Cooperation on the part of all members.
3. Wide use of recognition and praise by team members.
4. Integration of personal and team goals.

As a result, a sense of unconditional trust exists among the members, and everyone's attitude is positive and productive. This is particularly important, because researchers are finding that tomorrow's successful enterprises are more likely to be led not by visionary individuals but by "smart teams." These teams value learning as a core group capability, which allows them to imagine continuously and to give shape to future objectives and the approaches that must be taken to reach them.[9]

Not all groups reach the fourth stage of development. Those that do, however, learn how to achieve the necessary balance between group and individual approaches and become adept at tolerating creative tension that allows them to reach higher levels of productivity.[10] And regardless of a group's progress, some characteristics are common to all groups. Refer to the Time Out Exercise and continue the assignment.

Characteristics of Groups

All groups have certain characteristics. Some of the most important are roles, norms, status, cohesiveness, and size.

*The **norming stage** is characterized by cooperation and teamwork.*

*The **performing stage** is characterized by openness and collaboration.*

③ LEARNING OBJECTIVE
Discuss the importance of roles, norms, status, cohesiveness and group size to group behavior

Roles

A role is an expected behavior.

A **role** is an expected behavior. In many organizations, job descriptions provide the initial basis for determining one's role. The individual can read this description and obtain a general idea of what he or she is supposed to be doing. Of course, the description does not cover everything, but it will give the person enough general information to begin doing the job.

Role ambiguity *occurs when the job description is vague.*

One of the most serious and most common role-related problems occurs when job duties are unclear either because the job description is vague or because no description has ever been written for the work. We call this **role ambiguity,** because what the individual is supposed to do is uncertain or vague. For example, many workers find that when they are promoted to the rank of supervisor, they are told to "Get out there, manage those people, and get the work done." This statement is too general. They do not understand the specific roles they are supposed to assume. One of the most effective ways of preventing role ambiguity is to have job descriptions that are clear and describe in detail the responsibilities and tasks of the position.

In **role conflict,** *two roles are mutually incompatible.*

A second major role-related problem is **role conflict.** This occurs when an individual faces a situation in which he or she must assume *two* roles, and the performance of one *precludes* the performance of the other. For example, a manager is told to do everything she can to build morale in the department. At the same time, she is instructed to reprimand anyone who comes late to work. In this case, the manager may face a role conflict problem because she feels she cannot perform both of these tasks. If she is to build morale, she will have to be lenient with those who are tardy while working to change their behavior. If she reprimands anyone, she may feel this action will affect morale negatively. Clearly, this represents a role conflict problem.

Norms

Norms *are rules of conduct adopted by group members.*

The rules of conduct adopted by group members are **norms.** These norms indicate how each group member *ought* to act. Usually, norms are few and relate only to those areas that have *significance* for the group. For example, a work group will often have norms related to output (how much you ought to do), participation (whether you should help slower workers), and communication with management (what you should and should not say to the boss). It will not have norms related to where you should live, how you ought to raise your children, or what church you should attend.

Additionally, there are *degrees* of conformity. For example, you ought to turn out 480 pieces per day, plus or minus twenty. There is, thus, an *acceptable range,* and those individuals who want to remain in good standing with the group will conform to it.

Overall, we can draw some conclusions about individuals and their conformity to group norms.

1. **Adults tend to conform less than do children.**
2. **Women, because of our cultural values, tend to conform more than do men.**
3. **Highly intelligent people tend to conform less than do people of low intelligence.**
4. **If all other members agree on something, the remaining person is likely to go along with them.**
5. **If a person in the group disagrees with the others but receives support from one of them, the person is much less likely to conform. The individual will take heart from the fact that some support has been forthcoming and will often cling tenaciously to his or her original position.**
6. **If a person does not understand what is going on, he or she is more likely to follow the direction of a group member who does seem to have a grasp of the situation.**

Any individual who does not conform to at least the major norms of the group is denied membership. That person is not permitted to participate in group activities and, in some cases, is ostracized or subjected to various forms of harassment by the members.

The manager must be aware of group norms because they play a key role in determining what a group will and will not do. If the group's informal work norm, for example, is much lower than the quota set by the company, the group is likely to have low productivity. The manager's awareness of such informal norms, however, can serve as the basis for developing a change strategy, by which the manager can influence the group to increase its informal work norms. (Such change strategies are explored further in Chapter 12).

Status

The relative ranking of an individual in an organization or a group is **status.** Status can be achieved in a number of ways.

Status

is the relative ranking of an individual in a group.

- In our society, a Rockefeller has status merely through being *born* into a rich, influential family.
- On the job, people can achieve status through the *position* they hold. For example, the president of the organization has more status than a vice president.
- Other people achieve such status by the *job* they do. For example, in some firms, the advertising manager has greater status than the purchasing manager.
- Another way to achieve job status is through *personality.* An individual who gets along with others, is easy to work with, and is always ready to say a kind word is more likely to be given status by the other members of the organization than is an individual with whom no one can work because he or she is unpleasant to others.
- A work status determinant is *job competence.* The better a person knows his or her job, the more likely it is that the person will be accorded status by members of the peer group. For example, in a group that values high productivity, those individuals who are the highest producers will be afforded the highest status.

Of course, to determine exactly how group status will be accorded, we must examine the specific situation. In some groups, competence (what the person can do) is very important but, in other groups, job title (what position the person holds) is of greatest value in obtaining status. Additionally, if we were to move from one organization to another, we might well find different status determinants. This would be particularly obvious if we were to put six people—two professors, two bank executives, and two students—into three different group settings. As seen in Figure 4.1, the status of these individuals will vary from one situation to the next. Yet if one were to give them scores—one point for first place through five points for fifth place—in all three group settings, one would find that the overall score per person is about the same. In short, they all have about the same average status across the three groups, but this status varies dramatically within the group. For example, in a university setting, the full professor has the highest status, followed by other faculty, and then students and, finally, members of the group whose occupations are not academic. In a bank, the president has the highest status, followed

---

FIGURE 4.1	*Changing Status*		
	Academia	**Bank**	**Bowling Alley**
High Status	Professor of finance	Bank president	Graduating senior in zoology (195 average)
	Assistant professor of biology	Professor of finance	MBA student (180 average)
	MBA student	MBA student	Assistant professor of biology (170 average)
	Graduating senior in zoology	Assistant professor of biology	Bank president (150 average)
Low Status	Bank president	Graduating senior in zoology	Professor of finance (135 average)

by individuals knowledgeable in finance, students working toward a master's degree in business administration (MBAs), and then members of the group whose occupations do not relate to finance in any way. Finally, in a bowling alley, the status of each is accorded strictly on the basis of bowling skill.

To understand fully the importance of status within groups, it is necessary to realize there can be status problems. The most serious is **status incongruence,** which occurs when there is a discrepancy between a person's supposed status and the way he or she is treated. For example, if all the senior-level managers except one are given new desks, there is a discrepancy between the way this last person is being treated and the way this person's peers are being treated. Unless there is reason for this discrepancy, such as the fact that the manager does not want a new desk and prefers to continue using the old one, the manager's status may be in jeopardy. People will begin to wonder why the manager is not being treated as well as the other senior-level managers. In fact, in some organizations, this is the way managers are told they are "on the way out": They are not given things that are provided to other managers at their organizational level.

A second status-related problem is **status discrepancy,** which occurs when people do things that do not fit with their status in their group. For example, in an organization where there are bitter feelings between management and the union, members of these two groups do not associate with one another. Anyone who is seen being friendly to a member of the other group is considered a traitor, and his or her status will decline. Members of the management team who act friendly toward union representatives may soon find such actions negatively affecting promotion potential. Union representatives who are friendly with management personnel may soon be voted out of office. We can sum it up this way: Status is accorded to people for behaving according to the expectations of those assigning the status rank, and any time people do things that do not fit into this category, they threaten their own status.

Cohesiveness

The closeness or interpersonal attractions that exist among group members are referred to as **cohesiveness.** If cohesion is high, member satisfaction tends to be high, and there is increased cooperation within the group.[11] Conversely, if cohesion is low, there is often dissatisfaction and members will seek to leave the group.[12]

However, cohesiveness does *not* guarantee high productivity. Individuals may all like one another very much and may also have an informal norm of low output; they have all agreed to do as little work as possible. Figure 4.2 provides an illustration. Note that Group X has the highest productivity. Everyone in this group is turning out more work than is required by the organization norm. In fact, all the high producers are in this group. Conversely, all the low producers are in Group Z. Their average is far below that of the other two groups. However, cohesiveness is very high; everyone in the group is conforming to an informal work norm. Note how little each person's productivity deviates from this norm; this is why we can conclude that it is indeed an informal norm. Otherwise, there would be several high and low producers. For example, in Group X there is a greater variation between high and low producers, indicating less acceptance of a group norm. In Group Y, the variation is even more significant. We can conclude that Group Z has the greatest cohesion and that Group Y has the least.

Group cohesiveness presents two major challenges to the manager. First, the manager needs to work closely with low-producing groups to motivate them to increase their productivity norms to the level established by the organization. Many of the ideas presented in Chapter 2 can be used to accomplish this.

Second, the manager must protect the cohesiveness of the high-producing groups. Changes in the work or transfer of people into or out of the group can negatively affect cohesion. One of the most famous cases of this has been provided by the coal-mining industry in Great Britain, which introduced new technology and procedures into the mines after World War II. Before the change, the miners had worked together in teams, and there was high cohesion within these groups. However, the new technology disrupted these arrangements. Many of the small, cohesive groups were reorganized into larger teams, and some of the work previously done by the

Status incongruence *is a discrepancy between a person's supposed status and the way the individual is treated.*

Status discrepancy *occurs when people do things that do not fit in with their status in the group.*

Cohesiveness *refers to the closeness among group members.*

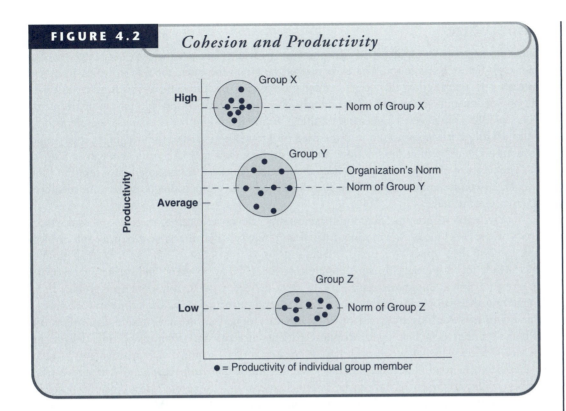

FIGURE 4.2 *Cohesion and Productivity*

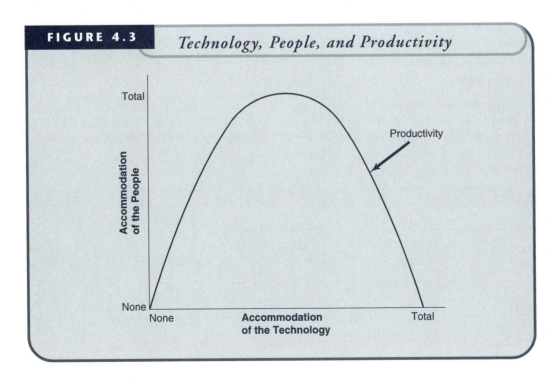

FIGURE 4.3 *Technology, People, and Productivity*

miners was now done by machine. The restructuring destroyed group cohesiveness, and the coal miners began to slow their production. It became necessary for the companies again to reorganize some of their operations, this time, however, to accommodate the miners better.

Obviously, every organization needs to consider both technology and people. If technology is overemphasized, cohesiveness declines and productivity falls. Conversely, if people are accommodated at the expense of technology, the firm suffers in comparison with other companies that have adopted the latest technological breakthroughs. A balance is needed, as illustrated in Figure 4.3.

Group Size

Some work groups are quite small (three or four people), whereas others are very large (twenty or more). Research has found that as the size of the group increases, the way in which members interact with one another changes. As group size expands, the time and attention given to creating and maintaining group harmony diminish. This is in contrast to small groups, in which members typically exhibit greater agreement on things and seek one another's opinions more frequently. In large groups, it is common to find the need for group approval also diminishing; people begin focusing more on getting the job done and less on how their coworkers feel about their actions.

The secret to effective teams is to keep them small, ideally, a team should have seven to nine people. "If you have more than 15 or 20, you're dead: The connections between team members are too hard to make."[13]

Research also reports that as groups become larger, turnover tends to increase and satisfaction tends to decline. One explanation that has been offered is that in a large group, people are less able to fulfill their upper-level needs, which leads to dissatisfaction. Conversely, in small groups, there tends to be greater cohesion, more concern for fellow workers, and greater satisfaction, resulting in lower employee turnover.[14] In fact, in recent years, some enterprises have been organizing their people into groups of three and using these triads as the primary work group. For example, some hospitals and other health care organizations have found that triads are extremely effective in helping to diagnose patient ailments and recommend and deliver the needed services. One large company has assigned each of its regional vice presidents to serve as a member of a triad. The other members are an individual from corporate staff and a field manager. This arrangement has proven extremely useful in helping the firm to identify problem areas that cut across functional lines and require coordinated effort. Moreover, to ensure that the three managers use their triad to help reduce bureaucratic red tape and promote efficiency, 20 percent of their overall compensation is tied to triad responsibilities.[15] Take a few minutes to apply the information you have just read. Complete the following Time Out Exercise.

time out

IN WHAT TYPE OF GROUPS DO YOU HOLD MEMBERSHIP OR PARTICIPATE?

You have just learned about different types of groups, stages of group development, and characteristics of groups. Now, let's see if you can apply this information? Complete each step, using the form provided.

Step 1—Make a list of several groups of which you are a member, or regularly attend, or participate in. For example, it might be a sports group, musical group, church group, work group, family group, chat group, friends, and so forth.

Step 2—For each group listed, identify its type, such as functional, cross-functional, project, virtual, interest-friendship.

Step 3—Decide the stage of development for each group, such as forming, storming, norming or performing.

Step 4—Identify your role in each group and your status.

Step 5—Describe the norm, cohesiveness, and size of each group.

Group Name	Type of Group	Stage of Development	Your Role	Your Status	Group Norm	Group Cohesiveness	Group Size

Intragroup Behavior

Communication and decision making are two major activities that impact intragroup behavior.

LEARNING OBJECTIVE **4** *Describe how communication and decision-making styles, risk taking, and creativity affect group decisions*

Communication

The social system within a group helps dictate the way information is communicated internally, as well as externally. Several common roles function within each social system. The role played by each individual member typically is a result of that individual's knowledge and personality and the needs of the group.

Depending on the size of the group, a varying number of roles may be assumed by the members. In a small group, an individual may assume more than one communication role. In large groups, two or more people may assume the same role, whereas others have no specific role. Five of the most common roles are the following:

1. The **opinion leader** is often the informal leader of the group. This person typically receives more communiqués than anyone else in the group and is most responsible for determining group goals and actions.

2. The **gatekeeper** regulates the flow of information to other members of the group. If this individual chooses not to tell something to someone, the latter is deprived of the information because the gatekeeper is the only one in a position to provide this information.

3. The **liaison** links the group to other groups. He or she is the contact person who communicates with the other groups and gets information from them.

4. The **isolate** is a person who generally is ignored by the group and receives very little communication. He or she is treated as an outsider, even though the person is a member of the group.

5. The **follower** goes along with whatever the opinion leader or the group at large wants done. He or she is a loyal group member who can be counted on to "stay in line."

*The **opinion leader** is typically the informal leader.*
*The **gatekeeper** controls the flow of information to the group members.*
*The **liaison** links the group to other groups.*
*The **isolate** is a person who is generally ignored.*
*The **follower** goes along with the opinion leader or group at large.*

Decision Making

How are decisions made within groups? Answering this question is difficult because it is multifaceted. However, we know some things about group decision making that are related to styles, risk taking, and creativity.

DECISION-MAKING STYLES

When making decisions, individuals often display a personal style that reflects how they perceive what is happening around them and how they process information.[16] These decision-making styles are determined by two dimensions: a *value orientation* and a *tolerance for ambiguity*. The value orientation focuses on the individual's concern for task and technical matters as opposed to people and social concerns. The tolerance for ambiguity orientation measures how much the person needs structure and control (a desire for low ambiguity) as opposed to being able to thrive in uncertain situations (a desire for high ambiguity). These two orientations, with their low and high dimensions, result in four styles of decision making—directive, analytical, conceptual, and behavioral—and are illustrated in Figure 4.4.

Directive Style Individuals with a directive style have a low tolerance for ambiguity and are oriented toward task and technical concerns in their decision making. These people tend to be efficient, logical, pragmatic, and systematic in their approach to problem solving. They also like to focus on facts and to get things done quickly. In short, they are action oriented. In addition, they tend to have a very short-run focus, like to exercise power, want to be in control, and display an autocratic type of leadership style.

FIGURE 4.4   *Decision-Making Styles*

	Task and technical concerns	People and social concerns
High Tolerance for ambiguity **Low**	Analytical	Conceptual
	Directive	Behavioral

Value Orientation

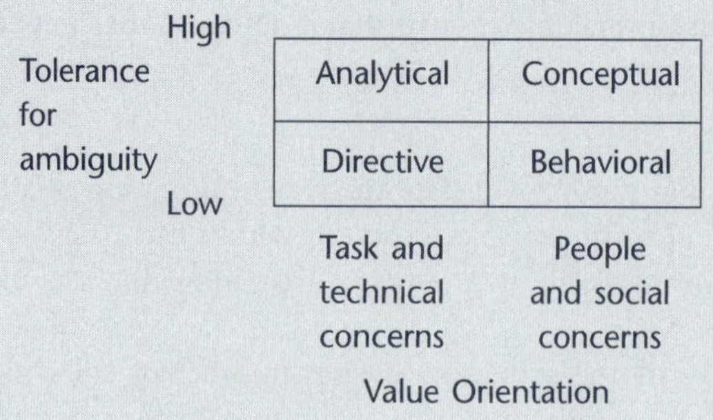

Analytical Style   Analytical decision makers have a high tolerance for ambiguity and a strong task and technical orientation. These people like to analyze situations; in fact, they often tend to overanalyze things. They evaluate more information and alternatives than do directive decision makers. They also take a long time to make decisions, but they do respond well to new or uncertain situations. They tend to be autocratic.

Conceptual Style   Decision makers with a conceptual style have a high tolerance for ambiguity and for strong people and social concerns. They take a broad perspective in solving problems, and they like to consider many options and future possibilities. These decision makers discuss things with many people in order to gather a great deal of information, and they also rely on intuition. Additionally, they are willing to take risks, and they tend to be good at discovering creative solutions to problems. At the same time, however, they can foster an idealistic and indecisive approach to decision making.

Behavioral Style   The behavioral-style decision maker is characterized by a low tolerance for ambiguity and for strong people and social concerns. These decision makers tend to work well with others and like situations in which opinions are openly exchanged. They tend to be receptive to suggestions, supportive, and warm and prefer verbal to written information. They also tend to avoid conflict and be overly concerned with keeping everyone happy. As a result, these decision makers often have a difficult time saying no to people, and they do not like making tough decisions, especially when it will result in someone being upset with the outcome.

Style Implications   Research reveals that decision makers typically rely on two or three styles, and these will vary by occupation, job level, and culture. For example, *analytical* decision makers make decisions rapidly, but they also tend to be autocratic in their approach to doing things. *Conceptual* decision makers are innovative and willing to take risks, but they often are indecisive. These styles also help to explain why different managers will arrive at different decisions after evaluating the same information. In particular, the decision-making styles model is useful in providing insights regarding how and why people make decisions, as well as offering guidelines regarding how to deal with these decisions.

RISK TAKING

A number of important findings have been uncovered about risk taking within groups. First, groups are often more effective than individuals in decision making. For example, when faced with the task of evaluating ambiguous situations, groups appear to be superior to individuals. They also are more effective in generating unique ideas or accurately recalling information. However, they are not as effective as individuals in solving problems that require long chains of decisions.[17]

Second, individuals tend to take greater risks when they are in groups than when they are acting alone. This is known as the **risky-shift phenomenon.**[18] Behavioral scientists studying this phenomenon have used measures similar to the questionnaire you will find in the end-of-chapter section, "Experiencing Risk Taking." The individual is asked questions and then is placed in a group, which is asked the same questions. The people in groups tend to be greater risk takers. Why is this so? Some explanations for this phenomenon follow:

The **risky-shift phenomenon** *is the tendency to take greater risks in a group than when acting alone.*

- If the decision proves to be wrong, the individual feels less guilt or concern because other people were involved and responsibility is diffused among everybody.

- In group discussions, risk-taking people tend to be more influential than their conservative counterparts. As a result, their viewpoints tend to win out.

- Risk is a function of knowledge. The less someone knows about a given area or problem, the greater the risk he or she assumes in trying to remedy the situation. Because group thinking often leads to deeper consideration of, and greater familiarity with, the possible pros and cons of a particular course of action, the risk tends to be reduced. Thus, a high-risk decision for an individual can be a moderate risk for a group.

- Risk taking is socially desirable in our culture. As a result, individuals in groups often choose a risk level that is equal to or greater than that risk which is acceptable to the average person.[19]

We should note, however, that groups do not always encourage higher risk taking. Sometimes they motivate a manager to be even more moderate in setting goals. For example, in many organizations, it is common to find the head of the sales department encouraging the managers to strive for 20 percent higher sales. However, sometimes the individual manager's sales force reports that the market is not increasing and that, at best, a 10 percent rise in sales can be expected; the manager may then be influenced by the sales force to set a more realistic objective for the group. In short, group pressure—toward risky or more moderate goals—influences management behavior. Culture also affects decision making. (See the "Uncertainty Versus Risk Taking" box.)

CREATIVITY

Sometimes decisions require creative thinking. This process has four phases: preparation, incubation, illumination, and verification.

1. During the *preparation* stage, the group members prepare themselves mentally to make the decision. This phase is characterized by information gathering.

2. During the *incubation* stage, the group often will sit back and let the subconscious mind work on the problem. Often, the result will be a better decision than one that is forced or made hurriedly. On the other hand, if group members are unable to come up with an effective approach after, say, one week, they will go back to the preparation stage and start the process anew by gathering additional data or reviewing what is there.

3. The *illumination* phase is characterized by the group's realization of the best decision to make. Sometimes the decision will suddenly hit them; other times it will slowly dawn on them. In any event, they now know what to do.

4. The final stage is *verification,* during which the group modifies or makes final changes to the solution. Often, the decision will need some fine-tuning because of minor problems. Once this is done, the decision can be implemented. For example, when Art Fry invented Post-It notes, no one understood their value. As he put it, "People had never heard of a 'repositionable note,' and they couldn't conceive of such a phenomenon."[20] However, once they began using the notes, they realized their value and then, as Fry put it, "they became addicted to them."

CULTURAL DIVERSITY IN ACTION

Uncertainty Versus Risk Taking

Managers in the United States encourage their people to take risks. This is socially acceptable behavior. However, in many countries of the world, risk taking is avoided. The term given to this cultural dimension is uncertainty avoidance, *and it refers to the extent to which people feel threatened by situations that have unclear outcomes or over which they have little control.*

In the United States, workers are characterized as having weak uncertainty avoidance. Managers are encouraged to make decisions and learn to live with the consequences. Other countries with weak uncertainty avoidance are Canada, Australia, Hong Kong, Singapore, and Jamaica. At the opposite extreme are those countries whose workers exhibit strong uncertainty avoidance—for example, Portugal, Guatemala, Uruguay, Japan, Korea, and Spain.

Cultures characterized by strong uncertainty avoidance tend to favor group decision making over individual decision making. In this way, the group members are given support by their colleagues, and no one need fear that he or she will be responsible for a major mistake. Companies operating in these cultures also tend to have bureaucratic structures, so that everyone knows exactly what is expected of him or her and there is no uncertainty regarding work assignments. Employees of such companies have a high need for security, and it is likely that the companies will offer guaranteed employment and provide good health and retirement benefits. Likewise, employees tend to have a high degree of anxiety and stress, and they often exhibit aggressive behavior.

In contrast, companies operating in countries with low uncertainty avoidance are more permissive of mistakes and errors and try to keep job anxiety and stress to a minimum. These companies also shun bureaucratic structures, frown on excessively aggressive behavior, and believe that effective employees have to balance a concern for family and personal life with the demands of the job.

The cultural dimensions of uncertainty help to explain why risk-taking propensity varies from country to country. They also help to explain why multinational corporations often find that the way they do business at home does not work overseas. Willingness to accept or reject risk is heavily influenced by culture, and what is acceptable behavior in one country often is frowned on in another.

Sources: Jane Whitney Gibson and Richard M. Hodgetts, Organizational Communication: A Managerial Perspective, 2d ed. (New York: HarperCollins, 1991), pp. 427–428; and Richard M. Hodgetts and Fred Luthans, International Management, 4th ed. (Burr Ridge, IL: Irwin/McGraw, 2000), p. 117.

Recent research suggests that a number of factors influence group creativity. For example, although group size seems to have no effect on the overall levels of team innovation, larger groups tend to produce more radically innovative solutions to problems than do smaller groups. In addition, groups that have a higher proportion of innovative members tend to generate more creative ideas. Two other critical factors are organizational support for innovation and the willingness of group members to participate in the creative process. It is also important to remember that innovation tends to vary depending on the phase of creative thinking in which the team is operating. One group of researchers put it this way:

> *Individual innovativeness may be most important at the initial stage in determining the quality of ideas available from the pool of individual innovativeness. At the second stage—the proposal, development, and implementation of ideas—group processes may become important in either hindering or facilitating the expression and development of ideas via articulated and enacted support from team members, as well as through participation (interaction, information sharing, and decision making) and constructive conflict processes (task orientation). Finally, perhaps one can speculate that the longer a management team is in position (at least for the relatively short duration enjoyed by the teams . . .), the more the team is constrained to consider the needs of staff when introducing organizational change.*[21]

How can individuals increase their own creativity and generate more interesting and profitable solutions? A number of useful ideas have been offered by successful managers and researchers.[22] Michael Eisner, chief executive officer and chairman of the Walt Disney Company, has long contended that creativity is not a "bolt out of the blue" but rather the result of careful thought and examination. In fact, early in his career, one of his bosses wanted to have him fired because every time the boss suggested a new idea, Eisner would ask the manager if he could "think about it and get back to you." The boss was convinced that creativity was based on rapid responses, while Eisner believes that creativity is typically a result of careful, deliberate thought, an idea that often is echoed by many successful managers.[23] In fact, Eisner has often said, in contrast to stereotypical views of the creative process, that creativity is a disciplined process. In a recent interview, he explained his thinking this way:

> *Discipline is good for the creative process, and time limits are good. An infinite amount of time to do a project does not always make it creatively better. The image of an artist being temperamental and acting like a 16-month-old child is usually false. It's a cliché that we've helped perpetuate in the movie business. Artists are always depicted as crazies. But in reality, insane artists are rare. In fact, some of the most creative people I've ever met—Steven Spielberg, George Lucas, I. M. Pei, Frank Stella, and Frank Gehry, just to name a few—are the most organized, mature individuals you'll ever meet. Not many creative people have the urge to cut off an ear.[24]*

Brainstorming   The average group member will find it difficult, if not impossible, to be creative on the spur of the moment. However, techniques exist that can help stimulate creative thinking. The most popular is **brainstorming.** A typical brainstorming session begins with the group leader, often the manager, telling the participants the problem under analysis and urging them to be as creative and imaginative as they can. Initial emphasis is placed on generating as many ideas as possible without too much consideration of their realism. As people call out ideas, the others are encouraged to build on them or use them as a basis for developing their own ideas. This approach eventually results in consensus among the group members regarding the best solution(s) to use. Sometimes, however, the general consensus approach is supplemented by **dialectic inquiry,** which involves the use of structured discussion and debate in arriving at a final decision. In dialectic inquiry, the brainstorming group is broken into two teams. One develops assumptions and recommendations for action; the other is given this information and asked to develop assumptions and recommendations that are counter to those of the first group. The two teams then meet and hammer out a consensus approach to the problem. Researchers have found that the use of dialectic inquiry results in greater individual acceptance of the final decision and higher member satisfaction with behavior within the group.[25] For this reason, some organizations are now using dialectic inquiry in their brainstorming processes.

Brainstorming is particularly popular when seeking creative solutions to nontechnical problems, such as effective advertising campaigns. Consumer product firms, such as Campbell Soup, which is continually developing new foods based on consumer research and creative packaging concepts, widely use brainstorming. Xerox employs the idea to develop new technology-driven products, such as circuit boards and battery-operated copiers.[26] Moreover, brainstorming has become so critical in the development of automobile products that firms such as Nissan actually use examples of brainstorming sessions in their advertisements to help viewers understand how the firm determines the final design and production of its cars.

In recent years, researchers have been experimenting with electronic brainstorming, in which individuals use computers to communicate and share their ideas.[27] This approach has been found to produce more creative ideas than those generated during typical brainstorming sessions. In addition, firms such as Boeing have found that electronic brainstorming eliminates socializing, thus reducing meeting time by as much as 70 percent.

Creative brainstorming techniques go beyond the traditional process for generating new ideas to solve problems. Creative brainstorming techniques can take many forms, such a random word, random picture, false rules, and role-playing. A discussion of these and many more forms is found on the Internet at **http://www.brainstorming.co.uk.** This Web site is an excellent source for learning about brainstorming and how to use it effectively with groups.

Brainstorming
is a freewheeling approach for generating creative ideas.

Dialectic inquiry
involves the use of structured discussion and debate.

Sue Barrett has outlined some suggestions for traditional brainstorming.[28]

FOLLOW BASIC RULES

1. **Realize everyone can be creative. Creative people take chances; others don't.**
2. **Avoid judgment and think outside the real world.**
3. **Let go of your defenses—Anything is possible.**
4. **No idea is bad—Accept all ideas.**
5. **Ask provoking questions—How can things be modified, minimized, substituted, rearranged, reversed, combined, or put to other uses?**

USE A PROCESS FOR GENERATING IDEAS

1. **Break down the problem—Be concise.**
2. **Set a time limit—twenty to thirty minutes**
3. **Write down all idea—Don't worry about how they might work.**
4. **Select the five to ten ideas you like best.**
5. **Decide on five to six different criteria for judging the ideas.**
6. **Score the idea on a scale of 1 to 10 using the criteria.**
7. **Select the idea with the highest score—It should solve the problem.**

Empathic Design Approach

Other firms use similar creative approaches. One of these is empathic design, which relies heavily on visual information.[29] The empathic design approach is particularly useful in creating new products because it sidesteps the built-in problem associated with customer feedback. Most customers, when asked what new products they would like, typically respond in terms of the company's current products and suggest that they be made smaller or lighter or less expensive. Customers are notoriously poor in providing useful ideas for new products, because their thinking is too closely linked to current products and their everyday uses.[30] Empathic design focuses on observing how people respond to products and services and on drawing creative conclusions from the results. For example, when Nissan developed the Infinity J-30, it tested more than ninety samples of leather before selecting three samples preferred by U.S. car buyers. When Harley Davidson builds a motorcycle, it adjusts the motor so that it is pleasing to the customer's ears—That is, it sounds like a Harley (and it has sued competitors that have tried to imitate this sound).

By watching how people respond, companies can generate more creative and consumer-pleasing offerings. This can be accomplished in a number of ways. One way is by taking pictures of people using the products. For example, when the Thermos Company had pictures taken of people using their charcoal grills, they saw that their units were much easier to use by men than by women, although women were the ones most likely to be doing the cooking. They then proceeded to redesign their grills so that they were appealing to women. Envirosell, an international research group, takes millions of photos every year of shoppers in retail stores for the purpose of helping answer the question: Who shops here and what do they like? Among other things, the research group has found that shoppers want wide aisles (they do not like to be bumped), good lighting (they like to see the merchandise clearly), and good signage (they want to know where things are located). Companies pay Envirosell large annual fees to provide them with marketing information regarding how to improve their retail sales. And Envirosell gets these ideas from analyzing the pictures of shoppers in their stores.[31] Instead of asking people questions about their decision-making habits, the empathic design approach relies on observation to generate creative ideas and solutions. Table 4.1 provides some contrasts between these two types of approaches.

LEFT-BRAIN, RIGHT-BRAIN THINKING

In recent years, attention has been focused on creativity and brain function. Most people are either left-brain dominant or right side of the brain dominant. The right side of the body is controlled

TABLE 4.1	Inquiry Survey/Focus Group Approach Versus Innovative Observation Empathic Design Approach

Inquiry	Innovative Observation
People often are unreliable when it comes to explaining the types of goods and services that they would be interested in purchasing.	Observers can rely on how people act in drawing conclusions regarding the types of products and services they would be willing to buy in the future.
People often give answers that they feel are acceptable to the questioner.	People give nonverbal clues through body language and spontaneous, unsolicited comments.
People often are unable to recall how they felt about a particular product or service that they received.	Observers can see how well people like a product or service based on the person's reactions.
The questions that are asked can bias the responses.	No questions are asked; all data are based on open-ended observation.
People's routines often are interrupted by someone stopping them to ask questions.	People continue doing whatever they are doing, oblivious to the fact that they are being observed.
When comparing two similar products, respondents often have difficulty explaining why they like one product better than the other.	By giving people an opportunity to use two similar products, observers can determine which is better liked or easier to use by simply watching how people behave.

Source: Adapted from Dorothy Leonard and Jeffrey F. Rayport, "Spark Innovation Through Empathic Design," Harvard Business Review, November–December 1997, p. 111.

by the left side of the brain, and the left side of the body is controlled by the right side of the brain. This dominance also dictates the way people do things. For example, **left-brain people** tend to be very logical, rational, detailed, active, and objectives-oriented. In contrast, **right-brain people** are more spontaneous, emotional, holistic, nonverbal, and visual in their approach to things. Left-brain people have a preference for routine tasks or jobs that require precision, detail, or repetition. Right-brain people like jobs that are nonroutine or call for idea generation. Left-brain people like to solve problems by breaking them into parts and approaching the problems sequentially and logically. Right-brain people like to solve problems by looking at the entire matter and approaching the solution through hunches and insights.

Most people are left-brain dominant. They tend to be less creative and imaginative than people who are right-brain dominant. In an effort to encourage individuals to use both sides of the brain, some organizations now are providing their employees with "whole-brain" training, in which the participants learn how to use each side of the brain (see the "Different Types of Thinkers" in Action box). The focus is on making highly rational thinkers more creative and on getting highly intuitive types to supplement their approach with greater emphasis on detail, logic, and procedure. The approach is proving to be an excellent supplement to standard creative-thinking approaches such as brainstorming. (Before continuing, take the Time Out quiz to find out whether you are more right-brain or left-brain dominant.) A good example

Left-brain people
are logical, rational, and detailed.
Right-brain people
are spontaneous, emotional, and visual.

HUMAN RELATIONS IN ACTION

Different Types of Thinkers

Most people are left-brain thinkers. They are analytical, rational, goal-oriented, explicit, and sequential in their approach to decision making. They have been encouraged to think and act this way and, in the process, have failed to develop right-brain approaches characterized by thinking that is spontaneous, emotional, nonverbal, artistic, and holistic. Today there is a major effort to get people to use both sides of their brain—whole-brain thinking. There are a number of ways of developing this thinking; some are simple and can be used on a day-to-day basis, including the following ways.

Right-Brain Thinking	Left-Brain Thinking
Doodle, draw, or print on a piece of paper.	Outline things, solve math problems, or do a crossword puzzle.
Shift the phone to your left ear, allowing empathic listening.	Shift the phone to your right ear, allowing for analytical listening.
Carry a clipboard, notes, or other comfortable symbols.	Use a dictating machine, a pointer, or some symbol of authority.
Be aware of the colors, space, and sounds around you.	Estimate the value of your net worth.
Hum, joke, chuckle with others.	Ask questions; make puns.
While sitting at your desk, take a minute to lean back, close your eyes, and daydream.	Go off alone and write a memo related to a major problem you are facing.

These approaches may seem a little silly, depending on which list you are using; however, this is because you are more accustomed to doing one set of activities than the other. By switching from left to right or vice versa, you enter a mental world that is somewhat strange to you. Yet that is what whole-brain thinking is all about—getting yourself to use the part of your brain that usually lies dormant.

is provided in the case of the Hawaii Telephone Company (HTC). Industry deregulation greatly affected this firm by creating both problems and opportunities. In an effort to deal with these, HTC decided to tap the intuitive skills of its personnel. First, HTC administered a diagnostic test to identify left-brain and right-brain managers. Left-brain managers then were introduced to other left-brain managers, whereas right-brain managers were grouped with other right-brained managers. The firm set forth its objectives for the future. Some of these objectives were best pursued by right-brain managers, some were best pursued by left-brain managers, and some were best approached by having right-brain managers provide initial suggestions and then having left-brain managers critique and complement these ideas. This "dual" approach to dealing with uncertainty and competitive problems has proven very effective for HTC.

Intergroup Behavior

Intergroup behavior is interactions between or among *two* or more groups. Sometimes these groups are in the same department; sometimes they are in different departments. In any event, the groups, for some reason, must coordinate their efforts to attain organizational goals. The purpose of intergroup behavior is to achieve high performance. However, sometimes power struggles develop between the groups, and conflict resolution is required.

Achieving High Intergroup Performance

High intergroup performance depends on a number of factors.

- Each group has to know what it is supposed to be doing. *Goals* must be clear.[32] If Group A is charged with building part A, Group B is responsible for constructing part B, and Group C is supposed to assemble the two parts into a finished product, any delay by the first two groups will slow up Group C. Groups A and B must understand how to build the parts and know how much output is required of them.
- There must be *cooperation* among all three groups, because a slowup or bottleneck in any of them will result in a drop in production.[33] Each group is a vital link in the production process.
- There must be *careful planning* of all interfaces between the groups, so that if one group falls behind, the manager knows about it and can start correcting the problem before the situation gets out of control.[34] One way this can be done is through daily monitoring of output. Another way is to designate a liaison or coordination manager, who works out any bottlenecks. For example, if Group A is falling behind because it has run out of raw materials, the coordinating manager checks with the purchasing department to see that the materials are rushed to the group.

Such planning and liaison work can do much to ensure high intergroup performance. However, this is not always enough. Sometimes the problem is that groups are squabbling with each other, a common occurrence when power struggles develop.

Power Struggles

LEARNING OBJECTIVE
⑤ *List ways in which groups try to gain power over other groups*

Power is influence over others and, although struggles for power can be detrimental to organizational efficiency, they are an inevitable part of intergroup behavior. Sooner or later, one group will try to gain power over others by means of several behaviors.

Providing Services

One of the most common ways to gain power over other groups is to provide services for them that they either cannot or will not provide for themselves. For example, many large and medium-sized businesses in industrial states are unionized. To deal with the union members, each company usually has an industrial relations department, which negotiates a contract with the union and works out the finer points of management-union prerogatives. What type of seniority system will there be to protect the rights of union members who have worked for the company for a long time? If some union people are laid off, in what order must they be rehired? What right of appeal does a member have if he or she is threatened with demotion or dismissal? Most department managers look to the industrial relations department for help in resolving any problem related to these issues. As a result, in the area of labor-management issues, the industrial relations department holds power over the others.

Integrative Importance

A second power struggle is directly related to the degree of integrative importance. If a group has an important integrative role in a process involving many groups, the other groups depend on it.

Consider the case of the manufacturing firm that produces a specialized power tool for industrial use. Figure 4.5 is a representation of the production process. The process entails five steps: manufacture, assembly, painting, quality inspection, and packing. Six major components are manufactured. These then are sent to one of four assembly groups, each of which assembles an identical product. From here, the products are forwarded to the painting groups, each of which is charged with painting 100 units per day. The products then are sent to the quality inspection group, which has a special machine that checks each for paint quality and determines that the product works properly. If there is some failure in the product, the inspector identifies

FIGURE 4.5

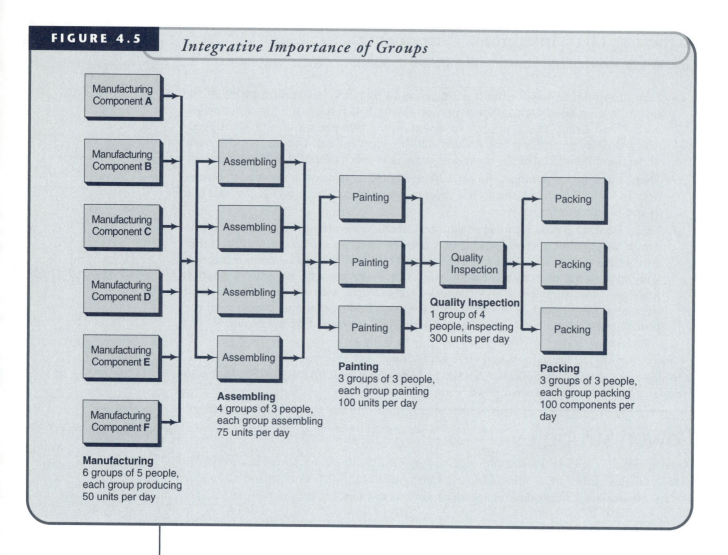

FIGURE 4.5 Integrative Importance of Groups

Manufacturing Component **A**

Manufacturing Component **B**

Manufacturing Component **C**

Manufacturing Component **D**

Manufacturing Component **E**

Manufacturing Component **F**

Assembling

Assembling

Assembling

Assembling

Painting

Painting

Painting

Quality Inspection

Packing

Packing

Packing

Manufacturing
6 groups of 5 people, each group producing 50 units per day

Assembling
4 groups of 3 people, each group assembling 75 units per day

Painting
3 groups of 3 people, each group painting 100 units per day

Quality Inspection
1 group of 4 people, inspecting 300 units per day

Packing
3 groups of 3 people, each group packing 100 components per day

the problem, writes a ticket on it and, depending on what is wrong, sends it back to the assembly or painting group. If the product passes inspection, it is sent to the packing group, where it is carefully boxed and made ready for shipment. A close study of Figure 4.5 reveals that, of all the groups, quality inspection has the greatest integrative importance. There is only one such group, and it performs a very important role: The group can either accept or reject the work of the other groups. Additionally, the other groups are larger, and several groups perform identical tasks. If one of these groups, such as assembly, is short of personnel because of illness, the other assembly groups can take up the slack. However, if the quality inspection people slow down, no one is available to help them catch up, and the whole organization can be adversely affected. Therefore, because of its integrative importance, the quality inspection group has a degree of power over the others.

Budget Allocation

A third common power struggle between groups is related to budget allocation. Most organizational groups, especially at the departmental level, would like to increase their budgets. Under favorable economic conditions, when the average annual increase is 10 percent, they will fight for a 15 to 20 percent increase. If sales or revenues have not been good and budgets are being reduced by 10 percent, departmental groups will strive to maintain their original allocation.

One of the most effective ways of succeeding in budget battles is to show top management that the department is doing a better job than most of the other departments. For example, the manufacturing group argues that its production costs have dropped and it is turning out more goods than ever before; if the group is given an increase in budget, more machines can be purchased and efficiency can be further improved. The marketing department produces statistics showing that sales per dollar of advertising are way up so its budget should be increased. Meanwhile, the finance department opposes the manufacturing and marketing groups, arguing that the company is spending too much too fast and that it would be wiser to pay off some of the long-term debt, maintain a more liquid financial position, and add more finance personnel for control and evaluation purposes.

Obviously, each group has its own ax to grind, and a big increase in one group's budget can come only at the expense of the others. If the manufacturing group is given a 20 percent increase, the marketing and finance groups will feel slighted. If the large increase is given to marketing, the production and finance departments will be unhappy. If the finance department's argument convinces top management to withhold increases, the other groups will be angry.

This group power struggle arises because of **goal conflict.** Each group must learn that its goal may not benefit other groups and that decisions must sometimes be made that appear to be detrimental to that group's welfare.

Goal conflict
is conflict that arises when one group can achieve its aims only at the expense of others.

Conflict Resolution

LEARNING OBJECTIVE

⑥

Identify ways to resolve intergroup conflict

The astute manager is aware of these intergroup power struggles but also realizes that there are ways of eliminating or diminishing their negative effects. The individual works to accomplish this through what is called *conflict resolution.* A number of ways exist to resolve intergroup conflict. Four of the most common are confrontation, collaboration, compromise, and altering the organizational structure (Figure 4.6).

| FIGURE 4.6 | *Conflict Resolution Methods* |

Conflict Resolution Method	Characteristics of Resolution Method
Confrontation	Face-to-face meeting between groups
	All parties discuss the problem
	All parties agreed on a solution
	Create steps to monitor compliance
	Problem is solved
Collaboration	All parties understand the situation
	All parties fully cooperate in resolving the problem
Compromise	Each party reluctantly gives up something
	Problem is temporarily solved
	Problem may reoccur
Altering the Organizational Structure	Transfer workers to new locations
	Change work assignments
	Change the flow of work or supervision
	Rearrange the furniture to separate people
	Move wall petitions to regroup people

Confrontation

Confrontation
involves face-to-face problem solving.

Problem solving on a face-to-face basis is **confrontation.** If the manager finds that several groups in the department are unable to get along and decides to use confrontation, the groups or their leaders are asked to meet to discuss their differences. Sometimes they are able to express their dissatisfaction with one another quickly and easily; sometimes it is a long process. In any event, there are some common complaints: "Those guys don't want to work with us. They're always doing something to slow up the flow of operations." "Whenever we're slow with our end of the work, those guys gripe, but if they're slow, they get angry if we say anything." "We don't know what the problem is with that group, but we just don't feel we can trust them, so we don't like working with them."

These standard responses are often the result of misunderstanding among the groups. By encouraging each group to express its objections, the manager usually can cultivate a feeling of harmony among them. Each group begins to see how the other groups view it and obtains a better understanding of its own behavior. Then the groups are asked how they are going to increase their interaction with one another and what steps should be taken to ensure that they do not slip back into their old habits.

This confrontation method is one of the most successful approaches to conflict resolution because it concentrates on solving the problem directly rather then trying to avoid it or to smooth over the issues.

Collaboration

Collaboration
requires full cooperation of everyone.

Sometimes goals desired by two or more parties cannot be reached without the cooperation of those involved; this is when collaboration can be effective. **Collaboration** calls for all parties to work out their differences and to realize that without full cooperation, all of them will fail. A common illustration is the case of the powerful union that wants a lucrative contract from a company on the verge of bankruptcy. It is obvious that if the union insists on its demands, the firm will go out of business. The only way to resolve the situation is for the union to take less money and to cooperate with the company in working to attain a more profitable position. When the company is stable, the union can resubmit demands for a lucrative contract. In this method both parties understand the causes of the problem and both parties are willingly to give up something to solve the problem.

Compromise

In **compromise**
each party gives up something.

When each party gives up something and no group is the clear winner, **compromise** occurs. It is a give-and-take situation. Consider the case of the foreman who fires a worker for being late four days in a row. During the ensuing labor-management meeting required by the contract, the union argues that the offense has not justified such a harsh penalty. Both sides, the company and the union, then compromise on the situation: They agree that laying the worker off for five days (without pay) is sufficient punishment. Thus, the worker has not been fired, but he has not escaped punishment for blatant infringement of the rules.

Altering the Organizational Structure

If the manager finds that a particular group cannot get along with some of the other groups, he or she may decide to resolve the conflict by reorganizing the department structure. For example, using Figure 4.5 again, the manager finds that some of the members of the quality control group cannot get along with members of the other groups. He or she may simply remove the people by transferring them to other departments or work assignments and replacing them with more congenial workers. Alternatively, if the manager finds that the assembling and painting departments resent the fact that their work can be sent back to them by quality control people, a supervisor may be appointed to make the final decision regarding what is to be returned as unacceptable. In this way, the manager interposes someone between the antagonist (quality control) and the antagonized (assembly and painting groups). This type of organizational rearrangement has been found to be very effective in cases in which workers object to taking orders from other workers.

summary

① **LEARNING OBJECTIVE**
Describe a group and distinguish among organizational groups—functional, cross-functional, project, virtual, and interest-friendship

A group is a social unit consisting of two or more interdependent, interactive individuals who are striving to attain common goals. There are five types of groups: functional groups, cross-functional groups, project groups, virtual groups, and interest-friendship groups. Functional groups are composed of individuals performing the same tasks. Cross-functional groups are composed of individuals from two or more functional areas. Project groups consist of individuals from many different areas or backgrounds who are gathered together to carry out some task; when its task is completed, the group is disbanded and its members return to their original departments. Virtual groups are task-focused groups that meet without all the members being present in the same locale or at the same time. Interest-friendship groups are formed on the basis of common beliefs, concerns, or activities.

② **LEARNING OBJECTIVE**
Explain the stages of group development

A productive work group is created through a process, which involves four stages of development. The purpose of the group is identified in the *forming stage*. Group members get to know each other and learn how they may contribute. The *storming stage* occurs when group members begin to question the direction of the group, certain members take control, and there is resistance to task assignments. When group members take responsibility, have a sense of cooperation, and work to accomplish the group's objectives, the group is in the *norming stage*. A group is in the *performing stage* when its members openly share problems and solutions, cooperate with each other, recognize and praise team members, and have an integration of personal and team goals.

③ **LEARNING OBJECTIVE**
Discuss the importance of roles, norms, status, cohesiveness, and group size to group behavior

All groups have certain characteristics. These include roles, norms, status, and cohesiveness. A *role* is an expected behavior; it indicates what a person is supposed to do. Some of the most serious role-related problems include role ambiguity and role conflict. A *norm* is a behavioral rule of conduct that is adopted by group members. Norms dictate how each group member ought to act. The manager must be aware of group norms because they play a key role in determining what a group will and will not do. *Status* is the relative ranking of an individual in an organization or group. There are many ways of achieving job status, including position, the nature of the job, personality, and job competence. Two of the greatest job status-related problems with which the manager must be familiar are status incongruence and status discrepancy. *Cohesiveness* is the closeness of interpersonal attractions among group members. However, cohesiveness does not guarantee high productivity; a group can have high cohesion and low output. *Group size* influences member interaction and satisfaction. Small groups tend to be more satisfied than large groups.

④ **LEARNING OBJECTIVE**
Describe how communication and decision-making styles, risk taking, and creativity affect group decisions

The manager must also understand intragroup and intergroup behavior. Intragroup behavior consists of behavioral interactions within the group. Of primary interest in this chapter were communication and decision making among group members. Five common communication roles played in businesses include the opinion leader, gatekeeper, liaison, isolate, and follower. The *opinion leader* is responsible for determining group goals and actions. The *gatekeeper* regulates the flow of information to other members in the group. The *liaison* is the contact person who links the group with other groups. An *isolate* is treated as an outsider by group members and is generally ignored by other group members. A *follower* is a loyal group member who goes along with whatever members want. Each group member plays at least one of these roles, and some may play more than one. Groups are often more effective than individuals in decision making, particularly when faced with estimating or evaluating ambiguous situations, generating unique ideas, or accurately recalling information. Creative-thinking techniques such as brainstorming can also help. Additionally, when making decisions in a group, individuals tend to be greater risk takers, a phenomenon known as the *risky-shift phenomenon.*

---

⑤ LEARNING OBJECTIVE
List ways in which groups try to gain power over other groups

Intergroup behavior consists of behavioral interactions between or among groups. Managers can achieve high intergroup performance by making group goals clear, obtaining cooperation, and carefully planning all interfaces between the various groups. When such performance drops off, it is often a result of power struggles in which one group achieves or strives for some influence over the others. Some of the most common ways of gaining power are providing services for other groups that they either cannot or will not provide for themselves, playing an important integrative role among the other groups, and defeating other groups in budgetary allocation battles.

---

⑥ LEARNING OBJECTIVE
Identify ways to resolve intergroup conflict

Some ways for resolving conflicts include confrontation, collaboration, compromise, and altering the organizational structure. *Confrontation* involves solving problems using a face-to-face approach, whereas, *collaboration* calls for all parties to work out their differences. This approach requires full cooperation of everyone. The *compromise* approach asks each party to give up something to reach a solution. The manager can always *alter the organizational structure* to separate individuals and groups.

KEY TERMS IN THE CHAPTER

Group	Cohesiveness
Functional group	Opinion leader
Cross-functional group	Gatekeeper
Project group	Liaison
Virtual group	Isolate
Interest-friendship group	Follower
Forming stage	Risky-shift phenomenon
Storming stage	Brainstorming
Norming stage	Dialectic inquiry
Performing stage	Empathic design
Role	Left-brain people
Role ambiguity	Right-brain people
Role conflict	Goal conflict
Norms	Confrontation
Status	Collaboration
Status incongruence	Compromise
Status discrepancy	

1. Define a group. Identify three characteristics that all groups have in common?

2. What is the difference between a functional and a cross-functional group?

3. What is the purpose of a project group? How does it work?

4. By what means do virtual groups communicate? How are virtual groups used?

5. Describe an interest-friendship group and give an example.

6. What are the four stages of group development? Give a description of what happens in each stage.

7. What conclusions can be drawn about individuals and their conformity to group norms? Cite at least four.

8. Describe the difference between role ambiguity and role conflict.

9. Identify four ways status can occur in groups.

10. Discuss the difference between status incongruence and status discrepancy.

11. What is meant by *cohesiveness?* Are all high-producing groups highly cohesive? Do all low-producing groups have low cohesiveness?

12. Describe the role of an opinion leader, a gatekeeper, a liaison, an isolate, and a follower.

13. What impact does group size have on member satisfaction and employee turnover? Explain.

14. Identify four decision-making styles.

    Which style makes decisions quickly, is innovative, takes risks, and tends to be indecisive?
    Which style uses an open exchange of ideas, works well with others, and is receptive to suggestions?
    Which style evaluates information, takes a long time to make decisions, and tends to be autocratic?
    Which style is task oriented, and uses a logical, pragmatic, and systematic approach to decision making?

15. What is the risky-shift phenomenon? How does it work in groups?

16. What are the four phases of creative thinking? Describe them.

17. How can brainstorming be used effectively in companies?

18. Why would an organization be interested in knowing which of its managers are right-brain dominant and which are left-brain dominant? Explain.

19. What are some of the ways in which groups try to gain power over other groups? Cite and explain at least two.

20. How can a manager go about resolving intergroup conflict? Identify four methods and distinguish among them.

VISIT THE WEB

How Well Do You Measure Up Socially?

Management is about getting things done through people. Managers are responsible for working with and through people to accomplish result, which requires an ability to interact successfully with people. To assess your social skills, complete several assessment tests found at **http://www.queendom.com.**

Select tests that are free. (Some tests require a fee to receive an analysis of the results. This is not required for this assignment, nor is it an endorsement for their products.)

1. Complete each of the following tests:

- Ethics test
- Self-esteem test
- Assertiveness test
- Honesty test
- Anger test
- Communications test

2. Write a summary for each test completed.

3. Prepare a statement to answer the questions: What did I learn about myself from the tests results? How might the information be useful in my career?

Use Brainstorming and Be Creative

By using brainstorming techniques, a manager can develop creative solutions to problems that seem overwhelming and impossible to solve. There are many brainstorming techniques from which to choose, but most often the traditional technique is used because it is the most familiar. To learn about new techniques, go to the Web site **http://www.brainstorming.co.uk.** Answer the following questions.

1. Study the eleven "creative techniques." Which one did you like the best? If you were in charge of finding a solution to a big problem, which technique would you most likely use? Why?

2. How would you start creating a creative environment for brainstorming? Make a list of suggestions.

3. Click on "puzzles" found on the menu page. Complete a couple of puzzles, which are fun and challenging. What did the exercises teach you about creativity?

4. Click on the "creative quotations for brainstorming" found on the menu page. Review them and determine which one you like the best. Why would you use it?

TIME OUT ANSWERS

What Type of Thinker Are You?

Circle your answers on the answer sheet. For example, if your first answer was an *a* and your second was a *b,* put a circle in column I for answer 1 and in column II for answer 2. Continue this for all 16 answers and then total the number of circles you have in each column.

Answer	Column I	Column II
1.	a	b
2.	a	b
3.	b	a
4.	b	a
5.	a	b
6.	b	a

7.	a	b
8.	b	a
9.	b	a
10.	a	b
11.	a	b
12.	a	b
13.	b	a
14.	b	a
15.	b	a
16.	b	a
Total	_____	_____

Your answers in column I indicate your preference for left-brain thinking. Your answers in column II indicate your preference for right-brain thinking. Highly analytical people have higher scores in column I; highly creative people have higher scores in column II. Of course, these 16 questions are not sufficient to determine whether you are left-brain or right-brain dominant. However, they should provide you with insights regarding your preference. Most people's scores indicate they are more left-brain than right-brain dominant.

case: THE NEW SUPERVISOR

When Gary Paterson was put in charge of the small-products assembly department, out-put was at an all-time low. Bob Willard, the retiring supervisor, had been in charge of the department for the last 10 years, during which time the output had slowly declined. When Bob had first taken over the department, the average worker was assembling 200 units per day, but the company norm was 225. During his decade as supervisor, the firm introduced some technological advances, and the norm was raised to 250 units per day. However, the average output declined to 193.

The management's time-and-motion studies showed that 250 units were well within the ability of the average worker, and the manual dexterity tests given to members of the department revealed that each was physically capable of attaining this objective. Bob, however, explained the situation in terms of changing values. "People are different today," he said. "They no longer want to work hard. They've lost the old work ethic, especially our young people, and that's who works in the assembly department. The average age there has declined from 29 to 23 in the last eight years. I guess lower

output is just something we're going to have to learn to live with."

These remarks had Gary worried. He wondered how he might keep the output from declining even more. After serious thought, he decided to call the department together and talk to everyone as soon as he took over. During this talk, he emphasized three points to the assembled workers.

- First, *he told them he wanted them to continue working in their present groups. Because the members of all eight groups knew one another well, he said, there was no sense breaking up satisfied work teams. However, if someone did want to change to another work group, he promised to help him or her do so, although it would require a mutual exchange of personnel with the other group.*

- Second, *he urged them all to come talk with him if they had any problems.*

- Third, *he asked their assistance in boosting output to 225 units per person per day.*

During the next three months, Gary was asked to make a few changes in group composition. He also resolved several job-related technical problems. Overall, however, he found the groups to be congenial and fun to supervise. In addition, output began to move up slowly. At the end of 90 days, the average daily output was 219 units.

One of the women in the department, when asked why production was up, said, "We like this new supervisor. He's a good guy. He talks to us, helps us solve problems, and doesn't keep emphasizing output. He lets us work at our own pace. It's such a change from when Bob Willard was here."

QUESTIONS

1. Is group cohesion in the small-products assembly department high or low? Has cohesion changed since Gary took over? What factors support your answer?

2. Have group production norms changed since Gary took over? Explain your answer.

3. What role do the workers want the supervisor to assume? How did Bob err in this regard? What is Gary doing right?

YOU BE THE CONSULTANT

Creativity to the Rescue

Perry Pailwaite is head of new-product development for a large insurance company. In the insurance business, many product offerings are similar, and companies compete on the basis of price. For example, most firms sell life insurance policies that, for all intents and purposes, provide the same amount of coverage and other benefits. As a result, customers typically shop around and buy the policy that offers them the best price.

At the same time, the insurance industry continues to develop new products that provide a variety of different benefits to customers. For example, in the 1990s, the industry developed universal life policies that offer both protection and savings. These policies have become very popular. Another innovation that has proved profitable was credit life insurance, which covers outstanding credit bills in case the insured is killed or injured and unable to work.

The most profitable insurance policies are those for which there is little competition. This often occurs when a company develops a new type of policy that commands a high premium and proves highly popular in the marketplace. Of course, the minute the competition learns the policy is doing well, it will offer a similar version of the insurance and the price will be driven down.

Perry's job is to develop new products that will have strong initial market appeal. He does this by working closely with his new-product development team and with salespeople who can provide him with information on the new types of insurance that people are seeking.

Later this week, Perry is going to have a two-day meeting with his product team and ten salespeople drawn from around the country. The goal is to identify five areas of insurance coverage in which new policies could be developed. The group is going to work together to come up with as many new ideas as possible, and then the list will be trimmed down to the best five. In the past, this approach helped the company develop a very profitable policy for providing kidnap and ransom insurance for managers who are working in dangerous international locations (a policy of particular interest to companies with key employees in South America and the Middle East) and liability protection for members of boards of directors who can be sued by stockholders for poor decision making (a type of coverage on which many board members have insisted, making the policy one of Perry's biggest financial successes). Right now, Perry is trying to decide how to create the best environment for generating new, profitable ideas from the product team and salespeople.

Your Advice

1. What do you recommend that Perry do?

    _____ a. Put the participants together in a large room and have them brainstorm new ideas.

    _____ b. Have the participants exchange ideas via electronic brainstorming.

    _____ c. Have the participants simply make high-risk decisions.

2. If Perry knows that some of the individuals in the group are left-brain thinkers and others are right-brain thinkers, how can he use this information profitably?

3. If Perry would like to get some of the left-brain thinkers to be more creative and some of the right-brain thinkers to be more logical and sequential, how could he accomplish this?

4. How can Perry ensure that the participants will continue to challenge one another's ideas and generate highly creative recommendations?

EXPERIENCING RISK TAKING

Purpose

- To determine your personal willingness to take risks.
- To evaluate your score and those of other students.
- To examine how your willingness to take risks changes when you are in a group.

Procedure

1. Complete the risk-taking questionnaire provided here. When you are finished, enter your scores on the answer sheet that is provided and then total them.

2. Work with a group of two to four students and collectively complete the same questionnaire. For each statement, there must be agreement among the group members on which alternative to choose. When you are finished, total the scores for the group.

3. Compare your individual scores to the group scores and explain the reasons for the differences.

Situation

Ten situations are presented here. In each case, read the situation and then choose the lowest probability or odds that you would accept.

1. You have just learned you have a serious heart ailment. If you choose not to have an operation, you can live only another ten years. If you choose to have the operation, there is a chance that you will not survive the operation. Should you survive, however, you will have a normal life expectancy. Check the lowest probability of survival you would consider to be acceptable.

    _____ 1 of 10   _____ 3 of 10   _____ 5 of 10

    _____ 7 of 10   _____ 9 of 10

    _____ You would not take the chance.

2. You are playing chess against a much better player. Early in the game, you notice that you have a chance for a quick win, provided your opponent does not see through your strategy. If he does, you are finished. Check the lowest probability you would consider acceptable for the risky play.

_____ 1 out of 10   _____ 3 out of 10   _____ 5 out of 10

_____ 7 out of 10   _____ 9 out of 10

_____ You would not take the chance.

3. You have $5,000 in conservative stock holdings returning 9 percent annually. You have learned from your cousin that she is in the process of selling stock in her new firm. If her company survives the next five years, your stock will quadruple in value. Check the lowest probability of survival you would consider acceptable for investing the $5,000.

_____ 1 of 10   _____ 3 of 10   _____ 5 of 10

_____ 7 of 10   _____ 9 of 10

_____ You would not take the chance.

4. You are thinking about applying to two colleges for admission. College A has a national reputation but also flunks out more than 50 percent of all those admitted. College B has only a local reputation, but the flunk-out rate is less than 2 percent. Check the lowest survival probability you would accept in opting for College A.

_____ 1 of 10   _____ 3 of 10   _____ 5 of 10

_____ 7 of 10   _____ 9 of 10

_____ You would not take the chance.

5. You have a good, steady job at a moderate rate of pay. Your best friend has offered you a job in his firm at a much higher rate of pay. However, his company is small and may not survive the next two years. Check the lowest probability of survival you would look for in this new firm.

_____ 1 of 10   _____ 3 of 10   _____ 5 of 10

_____ 7 of 10   _____ 9 of 10

_____ You would not take the chance.

6. You are thinking about getting married. Your intended is a wonderful person but is also emotional and sometimes very hard to get along with. On the other hand, this individual makes you happier than anyone you have ever met. Check the lowest probability of your marriage surviving that you would accept before going ahead with the wedding.

_____ 1 of 10   _____ 3 of 10   _____ 5 of 10

_____ 7 of 10   _____ 9 of 10

_____ You would not take the chance.

7. You are the coach of a football team. Your team is attempting to win the state title and is a point behind, having scored a touchdown just as the final gun went off. If you allow the team to kick the extra point, you will have a tie. If you try a trick play, you can go for two points. What is the lowest probability of success with the trick play that you would accept?

_____ 1 of 10   _____ 3 of 10   _____ 5 of 10

_____ 7 of 10   _____ 9 of 10

_____ You would not take the chance.

8. You have saved $3,500 over the last two years and are considering buying a bond paying 13.5 percent annually. Your brother, an oil wildcatter, wants you to invest the money with him. If he is successful, you will double your money

in one year. If he is not, you will lose it all. What is the lowest probability of success that you would accept for investing with your brother?

____ 1 of 10   ____ 3 of 10   ____ 5 of 10
____ 7 of 10   ____ 9 of 10
____ You would not take the chance.

9. You have the option of taking a steady job in the human resources department, where your future with the firm is just about guaranteed. Another option is to go with the advertising department. It will take five years of hard work before you know whether you will succeed in this department but, if you do, your salary will be almost double that in the human resources department. If you fail, you will have to find another job elsewhere. What is the lowest probability of success in the advertising department that you would be willing to accept?

____ 1 of 10   ____ 3 of 10   ____ 5 of 10
____ 7 of 10   ____ 9 of 10
____ You would not take the chance.

10. You can keep your current stateside job or take one in the Far East. If you stay here, you will receive moderate pay increases and promotions for the indefinite future. If you opt for the overseas assignment and do well, you will be a vice-president within five years and will be one of the highest-paid people in the firm. If you do not do well, you will be fired. What is the lowest probability of success in the overseas assignment that you would be willing to accept?

____ 1 of 10   ____ 3 of 10   ____ 5 of 10
____ 7 of 10   ____ 9 of 10
____ You would not take the chance.

Scoring Instructions: Fill in your answers by transferring the numbers you chose in each case. For example, if you chose "1 of 10," put in a 1. If you chose "5 of 10," put in a 5. If you opted not to take the chance, put in an answer of 10. Then total your scores for both the individual and group assignments.

Answer Sheet

Situation	Individual Score	Group Score
1.	_____	_____
2.	_____	_____
3.	_____	_____
4.	_____	_____
5.	_____	_____
6.	_____	_____
7.	_____	_____
8.	_____	_____
9.	_____	_____
10.	_____	_____
Total	_____	_____

5

The Informal Organization

In the last two chapters, individual behavior and group behavior were examined. To complete the discussion of the social system, we now study the informal organization, which engages in both individual and group behavior. The informal organization operates through the grapevine and is an integral part of the formal organization. The informal organization has its benefits and disadvantages for management. Effective managers learn to deal with and use the informal organization to get things done.

AFTER READING THIS CHAPTER, YOU SHOULD BE ABLE TO:

1. Compare and contrast the formal and informal organizations.
2. Discuss some of the behavioral controls used by members of the informal organization to ensure compliance with its norms.
3. Explain how the informal communication network functions.
4. Identify the primary benefits associated with the informal organization.
5. List some of the disadvantages associated with the informal organization.
6. Cite some of the ways in which a manager can deal with the informal organization.

Teamwork, Teamwork, Teamwork

Over the last decade, many small banks have folded or have been taken over by larger banks. Competition in the industry is keen, and only the best are surviving. Phelps County Bank (PCB) in Rolla, Missouri, is not a big bank but, thanks to the teamwork of its personnel, the bank is growing rapidly. To compete effectively in this environment, PCB has built a reputation for outstanding service, and this service depends heavily on support from the informal as well as the formal organizations within the bank.

The original idea for a high-service bank began with the bank's chief executive officer, Emma Lou Brent, who visualized what a community bank of the future should look like: customer-driven and staffed by knowledgeable, intelligent bankers who enjoy working with people. Once Emma began recruiting the people she needed, her attention turned to creating an environment in which the goals of formal and informal organizations were the same. She did this in a number of ways. One way was to train everyone in effective banking procedures and human relations strategies, so that they knew what they were doing and could interact effectively with customers. Another way was to create an employee stock ownership program in which the workers eventually took ownership of the bank, and their retirement program was tied to the bank's stock value.

Today, everyone at PCB works as a team. Teller lines are short, service is prompt, and the relationship between the bank and the customers is excellent. And, although everyone carries her or his share of the workload, this does not mean there is no time for relaxation. In addition to picnics and periodic parties, some of the employees recently purchased a charades game: When they feel the pressure or tension is too great, they schedule a thirty-minute break to play the game and relax, while senior-level staff fills in for them. Does all of this really pay off? It certainly seems to: PCB's stock over the last decade increased from $35 a share to $135.

The Granite Rock Company of Watsonville, California, is another good example of how teamwork pays off. The company produces and sells crushed stone from a nearby quarry, as well as cement, asphalt, and similar construction-related materials. These offerings are not unique, and the competition is intense. However, the firm manages to stay far ahead by getting everyone in the company to pitch in on a formal and an informal basis.

One way in which Granite maintains its competitive edge is by having state-of-the-art equipment that is both efficient and effective. Every year the firm creates teams of individuals to investigate such things as the types of cement trucks to buy. The group then begins identifying what the ideal truck should be. What make of engine should it have? What type of mixer? What kind of transmission? Then the team begins visiting companies that use trucks with these key components and finds out how well the units work. Armed with this information, the group then puts together a report regarding the benefits of buying trucks with these features. After all the trade-offs are weighed and compared to price, a recommendation is sent to the company's executive committee.

Granite's management believes that this formal and informal worker participation results in greater productivity and profit. The company realizes that it is expensive to pull people out of work to analyze problems and study solutions, but the benefits outweigh the costs. Commenting on the importance of this approach, the president of the firm has noted:

Our competitors are investing in many of the same ways we are. They have engineering departments working to build the best plants, offering the highest reliability and lowest maintenance costs. We have no monopoly on smart people.

But I hope by having everyone involved, we're doing more things sooner. We may be, in certain areas, just weeks or months ahead of somebody. Not years. The industry doesn't work that way. These are powerful companies, multibillion-dollar companies, doing business all over the world.

We can't stand still.

On the other hand, given the company's high profitability and rapid growth rate, there is no doubt that teamwork is helping Granite Rock stay two steps ahead of the competition.

Sources: Richard M. Hodgetts, Measures of Quality and High Performance: Simple Tools and Lessons from America's Most Successful Companies (New York: American Management Association, 1998); Richard M. Hodgetts, Implementing TQM in Small and Medium-Sized Organizations (New York: American Management Association, 1996); John Case, "Total Customer Service," Inc., January 1994, pp. 52–61; and David Krackhardt and Jeffrey R. Hanson, "Informal Networks: The Company Behind the Chart," Harvard Business Review, July–August 1993, pp. 104–111.

LEARNING OBJECTIVE

Compare and contrast the formal and informal organizations

(1)

Nature of the Informal Organization

The informal organization plays a significant role in the dynamics of human behavior at work. As a result, no discussion of human relations would be complete without consideration of this area. In this part of the chapter, we examine the nature of the informal organization by pointing out how it differs from the formal organization. In particular, we direct our attention to four major areas:

1. **interpersonal relations,**
2. **informal leadership,**
3. **behavioral control**
4. **dependency**

Before reading on, however, take the informal organization quiz in the Time Out box and obtain a preliminary evaluation of your use and understanding of an informal organization.

Interpersonal Relations

In the formal organization, relationships among people are clearly defined. For example, all the members of an assembly group are charged with assembling 30 units per hour and placing the

---

time out

THE INFORMAL ORGANIZATION: AN INITIAL APPRAISAL

The following fifteen statements are designed to measure your understanding and use of the informal organization. Assume you are a manager and determine, from that viewpoint, whether each statement is true or false. An interpretation of your answers is provided at the end of the chapter.

T/F 1. I always work through formal channels.

T/F 2. I don't care how my people get things done as long as they get them done.

T/F 3. Everyone should have a job description and stick to it exclusively.

T/F 4. If I can get things done faster, I cut across formal channels and use whatever means necessary.

T/F 5. All rules and procedures are made to be obeyed.

T/F 6. I use the informal organization to give and get information.

T/F 7. I discourage grapevine activity.

T/F 8. Almost all the grapevine communications are inaccurate.

T/F 9. The grapevine can be influenced by management.

T/F 10. The grapevine is inevitable.

T/F 11. Workers will form into informal groups regardless of what the organization does.

T/F 12. The grapevine's basic objective is to undermine management's efforts.

T/F 13. Most informal communiqués are passed to others on a purely random basis.

T/F 14. The goals of the informal organization almost always conflict with those of the formal organization.

T/F 15. Just about all grapevine messages are started by individuals with an ax to grind.

FIGURE 5.1

Who Helps Whom?

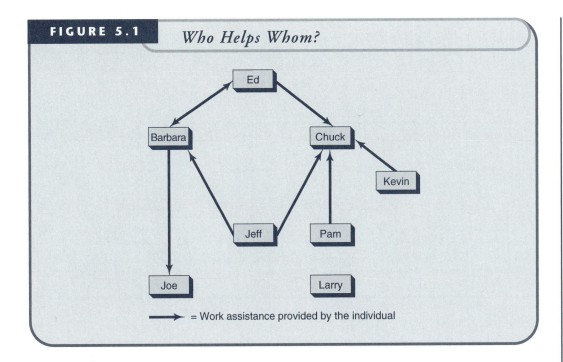

= Work assistance provided by the individual

completed items on a large table. Everyone is supposed to be doing the same job and turning out an identical number of items. Most organizations, however, do not work this way.

Over time, workers begin to form friendships with one another. This, in turn, results in workers going beyond their job descriptions and helping the workers they like to complete their jobs. Consider the case of the assembly group we mentioned previously. Although each person is supposed to be working independently of the others, we know that in every group there are slow workers and fast workers. Additionally, some of these workers are so well liked that their peers help them with their work. Conversely, some will be disliked and will be ignored by their fellow workers.

Figure 5.1 is an illustration of the degree of assistance that some members of a work group give to others. Note that Jeff is helping two of his coworkers but is not receiving any help in return. This indicates that Jeff is probably a very fast worker. Chuck receives assistance from four of his fellow workers, so Chuck is not a fast worker. However, the other members of the group like him and are therefore willing to assist him in assembling the units. Barbara and Ed help each other. Joe receives help from Barbara but does not reciprocate. Finally, Larry neither receives help from anyone nor does he give any.

Figure 5.1 depicts a **sociogram,** a schematic drawing that shows the social relationships that exist among members of a group. In this case, the relationship is being measured in terms of who helps whom. Sociograms provide interesting insights to informal group behavior because they help to pinpoint those members who are most popular, those who do all the work, those who get help from others, and those with whom no one interacts.

Recent research reveals that three types of relationships help to provide insights to informal networks: advice, trust, and communication.

1. The **advice network** shows the prominent players in an organization on whom others depend to solve problems and provide technical information.
2. The **trust network** tells which employees share delicate political information and back one another in a crisis.
3. The **communication network** reveals the employees who talk about work-related matters on a regular basis.[1]

Informal Leadership

In a formal organization, management designates the leader, whereas in an informal organization, members of the group choose the leader. If the formal leader does a good job, he or she

*A **sociogram**
shows intragroup social
relationships.*

*The **advice
network**
shows who provides
helpful information to
whom.*
*The **trust network**
shows who shares
delicate information
with whom.*
*The **communica-
tion network**
shows who regularly
talks with whom about
work-related matters.*

FIGURE 5.2

Formal Authority

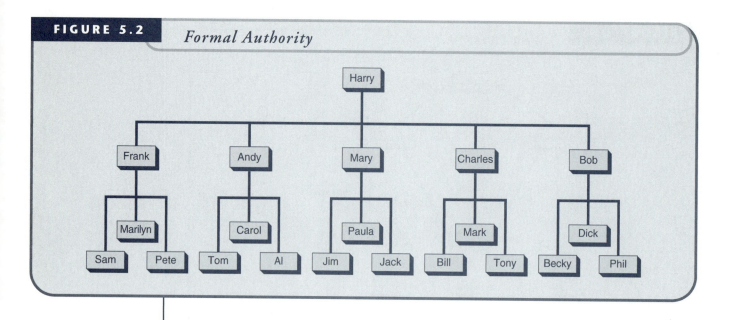

is often promoted away from the department. If the informal leader does a good job, he or she maintains that position, but if he or she does a poor job, someone else will be chosen who can help the group meet its objectives.

When we compare formal and informal leaders, therefore, we can see that the formal leader has authority and the informal leader has power. **Authority** is the right to command, and flows from the superior to the subordinate. **Power** is the ability to influence, persuade, or move another person to one's own point of view. The informal leader uses his or her power in two ways:

1. **to achieve informal group objectives (such as persuading the supervisor that because the workers are doing the best they can, there is no need to crack down any harder).**
2. **to maintain his or her position of leadership in the group.**

AUTHORITY AND POWER

What makes these concepts of authority and power in the formal and informal organizations so interesting is that the person who has the authority may *not* always have the power.[2] We can illustrate this with Figures 5.2 and 5.3, which represent the organization of a fictional department. In both illustrations, the closer a name is to the top of the figure, the more power the individual has in the department. Figure 5.2 shows the formal organization chart. Note that Harry is in charge of five subordinates, and each of them has three subordinates. Figure 5.3 shows the informal organization. Here we see quite a difference. For example, although Harry is the designated leader, Andy is the person with the real power. For some reason, Harry listens to Andy and goes along with whatever he says. One common explanation for such an arrangement is that Harry is new on the job, and Andy has been around for a long time and is the informal group leader. Realizing he must rely heavily on Andy's help, Harry defers to him on most matters.

The informal organization chart also reveals some other interesting facts. For example, Andy's three subordinates have more power than the other twelve subordinates. (Look how high up in the informal power structure they are located.) Also, although Mary and Bob are equal in authority (see Figure 5.2), Bob has more power than Mary. Moreover, Charles is supposed to be in charge of Bill, Mark, and Tony, but a close look at Figure 5.3 shows that Bill is giving the orders in the group and Charles has the *least* amount of power. Finally, although all the subordinates are supposed to be equal, some are more equal than others. A look at Bob's three subordinates—Becky, Dick, and Phil—shows that Dick has the greatest power and Phil has the least.

Authority
is the right to command.
Power
is the ability to influence.

FIGURE 5.3 — Informal Power

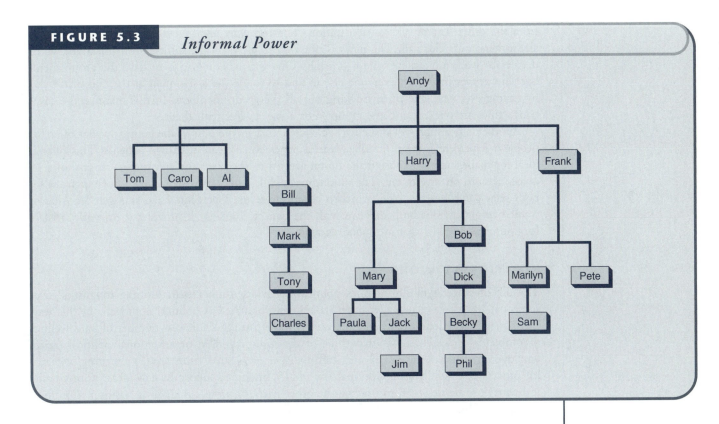

Some people like to define the formal organization as the one the company creates and the informal organization as the one the people themselves re-create. Certainly, there is give-and-take between the needs of the organization and those of its personnel. A company, for example, is most interested in attaining economic goals, such as profit and return on investment. The employees in the business are most concerned with getting good pay, adequate fringe benefits, and doing satisfying work. The company (organization) must strive to make the workers see its point of view, and the workers must persuade top management to understand theirs. Figure 5.4 lists examples of company/organizational goals and individual/group goals. As the lists reveal, the goals of the two groups are very different, thus, setting up a combination of cooperation and competition forces.

Who usually wins this conflict between organizational goals and individual group goals? Usually, neither side emerges totally victorious. Each side takes less than it deems ideal, but neither accepts anything less than it regards as minimal. In human relations terms, we say that each side engages in **satisficing behavior** by agreeing to accept adequate or satisfactory payoffs

Satisficing behavior
leads to satisfactory payoffs.

FIGURE 5.4 — Organizational Goals and Individual–Group Goals

The Organization Goals	The Individual–Group Goals
Good profit	Good pay
High return on investment	Job security
Adequate worker efficiency	Adequate fringe benefits
High-quality goods and services	Challenging work
Strong competitive posture	A chance to achieve
Low tardiness and absenteeism	Work satisfaction
Low turnover	

from the other. Let us take an illustration. The company announces that beginning Monday all workers must clock in. The news is not well received by the informal organization, which decides to work around the rule if possible. One way of doing so is to have the group member who arrives first clock everyone else in and to rotate the assignment at the end of the day by having everyone take turns clocking out all the group members. In this manner, the company's rules are obeyed, and the group finds a way to live with them.

Another illustration of satisficing behavior occurs in the case of the company that offers its people a 3 percent increase in salary and a 3 percent increase in fringe benefits. This offer is ideal for management because if the union accepts it, the company will surpass its goal of a 15 percent return on investment. The union, meanwhile, counters with a demand of 9 percent for both salary and benefits. The two then compromise on 5 percent. Each side gets less than it wanted originally, but both can live with the contract because it provides them with satisfactory output or results that are "good enough."

POLITICS AT WORK

The use of power typically requires political behavior.[3] Rather than running roughshod over someone, the effective manager often uses a well-thought-out political approach. In this way, the manager gets done what he or she wants, while causing the fewest number of hard feelings or problems. Research shows that three of the most common organizational political tactics employed by chief executive officers, staff managers, and supervisors are (1) attacking or blaming others, (2) carefully using information, and (3) building support for new ideas.[4] Other political behaviors are designed to upstage the other party or protect one's own position. Common examples include:

Purse snatching—stealing other people's ideas and presenting them as one's own.

Trapshooting—shooting down ideas, requests, and proposals from others and claiming that these efforts are not worth the trouble of implementation.

Gatekeeping—refusing to share useful ideas with others who could profit from this information.

Perimeter guarding—protecting one's organizational turf at the expense of company teamwork and overall efficiency.

Fox holing—digging in and protecting one's position by not contributing or by doing anything that can result in problems; this is the typical "protect yourself at all times" strategy.

Fashion modeling—getting caught up in the latest management fads and using them to find quick answers to complex problems rather than sticking to well-planned, longer-term solutions.[5]

In addition, some defensive behaviors can be used to minimize the effects of these political actions. Examples include playing it safe, passing the buck, playing dumb, stalling, and over conforming. For example, when the market research people at Ford Motor investigated the demand for minivans, they found a very large, untapped market. However, the company's finance executives felt that building a minivan was too risky and could endanger the firm's financial status. So, to play it safe and avoid getting in trouble, the finance people rejected the proposed minivan, a market that Chrysler then dominated and which netted that company billions of dollars of profit.[6] Overall, these proactive and defensive behaviors help to create and sustain a political climate in the workplace.

Politics is also employed widely in the appraisal process, as managers use these evaluations to control their subordinates. Following are some of the latest research findings:

- **The higher one rises in the organization, the more political the appraisal process becomes.**
- **Because of the dynamic, ambiguous nature of managerial work, appraisals are susceptible to political manipulation.**

- Performance is not necessarily the bottom line in the executive appraisal process. Ratings are affected by the:
  - boss's agenda
  - "reputation" factor
  - organization's current political climate
- Senior executives have extraordinary latitude in evaluating subordinate executives' performance; the pitfalls associated with this latitude include:
  - a failure on the part of superiors to specify meaningful performance goals and standards
  - a lack of communication between supervisors and executives about the desired style and means of goal accomplishment
  - the "good-but-not-good-enough syndrome"
- Executive appraisal is a political tool used to control people and resources.[7]

In dealing with these issues, it is important to know how to play the game. The In Action box provides some insights regarding how women have worked effectively within the political environment.

in action

CULTURAL DIVERSITY IN ACTION

Knowing How to Play the Game

An increasing number of women now head large organizations. They attained these positions by learning the informal, as well as formal, rules regarding how to get ahead—and, in many cases, the strategies that they have used were more a reflection of their own personalities than of organizational rules. However, in four areas many of these women have followed similar approaches: work experience, personal relationship building, vision, and creativity.

Almost all the women who have risen to the upper ranks of large organizations have had a wealth of experience that provided them important insights regarding how the organization operates, or should operate. A good example is Shirley DeLibero, executive director of New Jersey Transit. In addition to 19 years in the electronics industry, she spent 12 years as production manager for the reconstruction of trolley cars for the Massachusetts Bay Transit Authority in Boston. By 1990, she had learned all sides of the transportation business and was offered the helm at New Jersey Transit. Her previous experience has helped her to cut almost $1 million annually from the company's energy bill, increase annual revenues by more than $50 million, and create an organization in which empowered employees make critical decisions. During this same period, ridership has increased by 14 percent, customer complaints

are down 40 percent, and the system's overall favorable ratings from customers have increased by 18 percent.

Personal relationship building is another key success factor. Linda Marcelli is the only woman among Merrill Lynch's 29 district directors. Her bailiwick is New York City, which generates annual revenues of $300 million for the firm. Based on a number of key measures, including total revenues, business growth, and recruitment of new brokers, she ranks first in the Merrill system. How does she do it? In her words, "In order to lead in a man's world, you can't be plain vanilla." And she never has been. She wears loud suits and jewelry that make her stand out from the crowd. At the same time, she also knows how to build personal relationships in a business where this is the key to success. During her early days with the firm, everyone sold stocks by cold calling. She preferred personal meetings. It paid off. People liked her approach to doing business and invested with her.

Vision consists of knowing where one wants to go and then convincing others that they want the same objective. Beverly Harvard, police chief of Atlanta and the first African-American to lead a police department in a major city, is a good example of how successful women use vision to get ahead. Harvard routinely works around the clock at least six days per week and controls a budget of more than $100 million. Commenting on her success, she recently noted, "The primary job of chief is to provide direction for the department. I think you have to be a visionary. Once you define that vision, you have to show leadership in

in action box cont.

order to have people follow you to where you want to go." Harvard has been able to do this and to get the department behind her. In addition, her initiatives to install microcomputers in patrol cars to give officers instant access to police reports, and to combine the department's school detectives and curfew enforcement units in response to concerns about teen crime have helped to reduce robberies, aggravated assaults, and burglaries.

Successful women also tend to be highly creative and know how to swim against the tide. Roberta Williams is a good example. One evening her husband brought home a computer game. After playing it for a while, she was hooked and began thinking about creating games of her own. The first game she developed was packaged in Ziploc bags by her husband and her in their kitchen. That was more than two decades ago. Today their company, Sierra On-Line, is the world's number 1 seller of computer games, and she is the firm's chief game designer. In a field dominated by men, she creates games "guys wouldn't think to do." She designs fairy tales instead of Doom-like shoot-'em-ups. She does this by first concocting a story and its characters. She then turns it over to a team of engineers, programmers, and artists to create the technical package, working closely with them to ensure that everything is done correctly. As a result, she has become a legend in the industry. Her creativity led to the first game that blended graphics and text, the first three-dimensional animated adventure, and the first adventure involving a female antagonist. Williams and her husband recently were offered $1 billion in stock for the ownership of the company while being given the right to continue running the operation. The acquiring firm has no intention of doing anything to disrupt Williams's creative talents.

Sources: Stephanie N. Mehta, "What Minority Employees Really Want," Fortune, July 10, 2000, pp. 181–186; Paula M. White, "Wonder Women," Black Enterprise, April 1997, pp. 114–120; Patricia Sellers, "Women, Sex, & Power," Fortune, August 5, 1996, pp. 42–56; and David Krackhardt and Jeffrey R. Hanson, "Informal Networks: The Company Behind the Chart," Harvard Business Review, July–August 1993, pp. 104–111.

THE VALUE OF NETWORKING

Networking
is the process of socializing, politicking, and interacting with people throughout the enterprise.

In informal organizations one of the most important activities that occurs is **networking,** the process of socializing, politicking, and interacting with people throughout the enterprise. Researchers have found that successful managers are promoted much more often than average managers, and these successful individuals also spend a great deal more of their time networking throughout the organization. Table 5.1 provides a percentage breakdown of how successful managers in one large organization spent their time. A close look at the table quickly shows the importance of networking.

How people network, however, tends to vary based on such factors as gender and ethnicity. For example, research shows that many women tend to be conservative in their networking activities, whereas men tend to be bolder. One reason is that in some organizations women who are aggressive in their networking are seen as being too pushy, whereas men who behave similarly are regarded as forceful and confident. Successful women tend to use networks selectively. They quickly learn the organization's norms of behavior and operate within these parameters.

Researchers have also found networking differences between managers in general and minority managers in particular. For example, one researcher studied the networking activities of sixty-three managers: twenty-six white men, twenty white women, and seventeen minorities consisting of twelve African Americans, three Hispanics, and two Asian Americans. She discovered a number of major differences in the way in which minority managers networked. Among these differences were the following:

1. Minority managers tended to have a much more diverse group of individuals in their network, including men, women, Blacks, Latinos, and Whites.
2. These managers had fewer close, personal relationships with members in the network.

TABLE 5.1	Average Versus Successful Managers: How They Spend Their Time	
Management Activity	Average Manager (percentage of time)	Successful Manager (percentage of time)
Networking (politicking, socializing, interacting with others throughout the organization)	19	48
Routine communication (exchanging information, handling information)	29	28
Traditional management (planning, organizing, and controlling activities)	32	13
Human resource management (motivating, managing conflict, training, developing)	20	11
Total	100	100

Source: Fred Luthans, Richard M. Hodgetts, and Stuart A. Rosenkrantz, Real Managers (Cambridge, MA: Ballinger Publishing, 1988).

3. **Some high-potential minority individuals tended to balance their network contacts between people from the same ethnic group and those from other ethnic groups, whereas other high-potential minority managers had networks that were dominated by ties to whites.**

4. **High-potential minority individuals tended to have more contacts with outside groups and less overlap between their social and network circles.**

5. **In contrast to whites, minority managers saw networks as less useful in providing them career benefits.[8]**

Networking can be very useful to managers, but the specific ways in which they carry out this activity will vary. However, one thing does seem to be true for most successful managers: They are very active at networking, typically extending this activity far beyond just their own unit or department. Many of them spend a great deal of their time networking inside and outside the organization, getting to know a wide array of people, and often socializing throughout the community. In fact, one group of researchers recently analyzed data from more than six hundred managers nationwide and found that there are major differences between the ways in which managers and nonmanagers go about networking. In particular, they discovered that:

Managers belong to more clubs and societies than non-managers; they are also more likely to be members of professional/academic societies and service clubs. In terms of core discussion networks, managers have more network members who are colleagues or coworkers, have more network members who are total strangers to one another, have large networks, and also have a greater number of close ties with network members. Furthermore, coworkers represent a large proportion of managers' discussion networks, and close ties make up a greater proportion of managers' relationships with their network members.[9]

Simply put, managers not only spend more of their time networking than do non-managers, but they carry out these activities in a very systematic way. They also tend to develop a host of different groups on whom they rely. Successful managers know the value of networking, and they carry it out very effectively.[10]

Moreover, in recent years networking activity has become increasingly electronic, particularly in dealing with virtual groups, as seen by the tremendous growth of e-mail and on-line meetings.

General Electric, for example, uses the Internet to conduct all business with its suppliers, a strategy that it estimates will save the company $10 billion annually.[11] The drawback to this electronic networking approach is that there is a loss of informal communication. Team members do not have the opportunity to meet face-to-face, and they often miss this ability to chat informally with one another. As a result, it is common to find managers bringing the team members together periodically, so that they can share information personally and interact socially. Commenting on this, Leigh Thompson, an expert on team productivity, has written:

> Probably the most-felt impact is the inability to chat informally in the hall, inside offices, and so on. The impromptu and casual conversations that employees have by the water cooler and the coffee machine are often where the most difficult problems are solved, and the most important interpersonal issues are addressed . . . Remote group members feel cut off from key conversations that occur over lunch and in the hall. Vince Anderson, director of environmental programs for Whirlpool Corp.'s North American Appliance Group in Evansville, Indiana, oversaw a 2-year project using a virtual team that developed a . . . refrigerator, involving the United States, Brazil, and Italy. The team met approximately every 4 months to discuss the project, and it was these informal meetings—a backyard cookout and a volleyball game—that were the most valuable for the project.[12]

② Behavorial Control

When people in the formal organization do something right, they are given rewards; when they do something wrong, they are punished. If Barry reduces overhead in his department by 5 percent, he may be placed on a list of "up and coming" young executives. On the other hand, if departmental overhead increases dramatically and Barry is unable to control it, he may be labeled as incompetent and lose the chance of ever being promoted or may even lose this job.

In the informal organization, rewards and punishments are also dispensed to members. These, however, usually take the form of giving or denying need fulfillment. If Paula conforms to group norms, she is included in group activities and provided with social interaction. If she violates group norms or refuses to act "properly," she is ostracized and may even be subjected to pressure and ridicule and made to look foolish in the eyes of the other members. The sociogram depicted in Figure 5.1 illustrated who was helping whom in a department; Larry neither helped anyone else nor was helped by them. From this, we can conclude that he is not a member of the informal group, as one of the most common informal norms is that of assisting one's peers.

Dependency

Despite the strength of the informal group leader, the formal leader has a greater capacity for rewarding and punishing personnel. The formal leader can give both physical and psychological rewards to those who obey organizational directives and do things well. Because the informal leader can give only psychological rewards, not everyone conforms to informal group norms. Some people resist because they believe there is more to be gained by *not* joining the informal group, and not even the most extreme form of ostracism budges them. This was seen clearly a number of years ago in the case of the West Point cadet who was accused of cheating, judged guilty by his peer review board (made up of other cadets), and told to resign his commission. However, the man was found not guilty by those in authority and was allowed to stay at the academy. Because he refused to abide by the decision of his peers, none of them talked to or interacted with him for the remainder of his stay at West Point. Despite such pressures, the cadet remained at the academy and graduated with his class.

Those individuals who agree with the informal group's norms, however, strive for membership and depend on the group for social interaction and support. As a result, we have three subgroups in an informal organization structure.

- First is the **nucleus group,** which consists of full-fledged members of the informal organization who interact with one another.

- Second is the **fringe group**, consisting of those seeking admission to the informal organization. These people are often new members of the workforce who are being screened for membership by the nucleus group.
- Finally, there is the **outer group**, consisting of individuals who have been rejected for membership. These people have failed to measure up to the requirements set for admission to the group. Numerous reasons can be cited for this failure: doing too much work, doing too little work, having an unpleasant personality, and "squealing" to a supervisor about a member of the nucleus group.

The **fringe group** members are seeking admission.
The **outer group** members have been rejected.

LEARNING OBJECTIVE
③ Explain how the informal communication network functions

Informal Communication

The **grapevine** is the informal communication network.

One of the most interesting behavioral aspects of the informal organization is its communication pattern. Commonly referred to as the **grapevine,** this communication network is used to carry information among members of the informal organization. In this section, we examine the pattern of grapevine communication and four of the most likely causes of this activity.

The grapevine arises from social interaction and tends to be an oral, as opposed to written, form of communication. Bud, in engineering, could send a message through the interdepartmental mail asking Doris, in accounting, whether she is going to the party on Friday. However, it is more likely that Bud will either call and ask Doris or wait until they meet later in the day.

Much of the information carried by the grapevine deals with matters that are of current interest to employees. For example, the introduction of new work procedures in the metals department, the details of an accident in Plant 2, and the installation of a new computerized accounting system in the comptroller's offices are the kinds of topics commonly discussed via the grapevine. As you can see, these topics are sometimes of interest to people in many departments, so the number of individuals on a grapevine can be extremely large. This is particularly true when the message is viewed with concern or fear. For example, when employees throughout the firm learn about the introduction of new work procedures in the metals department, they may see this as the beginning of an efficiency move by management. If this proves to be the case, the various departments have been forewarned, and each will already have taken action to ensure that its efficiency is already as high as can be expected. Meanwhile, if the message proves to be a total fabrication and no new work procedures have been introduced, grapevine activity related to this topic will cease. Because grapevine members begin checking on the truth of a rumor almost immediately, one of these two actions will be initiated very shortly.

Grapevine Networks

The **single-strand** network passes information along a chain from one person to another.
The **gossip chain** involves one person telling all the others the information.
The **probability chain** involves the passing of information on a random basis.
The **cluster chain** involves information being passed on a selective basis.

Many people believe the grapevine consists of a long chain of people, with each individual passing the message to the next person in the chain. This type of communication network, known as the **single strand** (illustrated in Figure 5.5), is the least frequently used.

Another way in which informal messages can be communicated is by one person telling all the others. This is called the **gossip chain** (see Figure 5.5). Although more commonly used than the single strand, the gossip chain also is one of the less frequently used grapevine networks.

A third way in which information is passed through the grapevine is on a random basis: One person arbitrarily tells another, who goes on and tells one or two others (see Figure 5.5). This is known as the **probability chain** and, of the three chains we have discussed, it is the most widely used.

However, the most common grapevine network is the **cluster chain.** Using this network, one person tells two or three people who, in turn, either keep the information to themselves or pass it on to two or three other people. As a result, we have one individual passing the message to a cluster of people, and those who pass it on tell it to another cluster. In Figure 5.5, for example, Al tells the message to Wayne and Nancy. Wayne keeps it to himself, but Nancy passes it on to Don, Lois, and Ken. Al and Nancy are the links with their respective clusters.

Carrying this idea one step further, we can conclude that if 100 people learn of a particular happening, such as the firing of a top manager, it is very likely that only 15 or 20 people

FIGURE 5.5

Informal Communication Networks

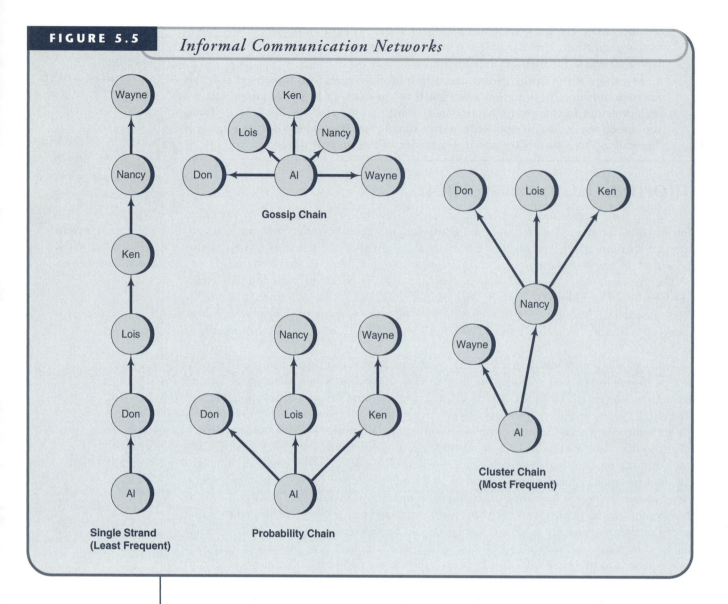

Single Strand
(Least Frequent)

Gossip Chain

Probability Chain

Cluster Chain
(Most Frequent)

have spread the word. These individuals are known as *liaison* people because they serve as the links between those who have the information and those who do not. Commenting on the predominance of the cluster chain, Keith Davis has reported that in one company he investigated, a quality control problem had occurred, and 68 percent of the executives knew about it. However, only 20 percent of them had spread the information. In another firm he studied, 81 percent of the executives knew that a top manager planned to resign, but only 11 percent had passed the news to the others.[13]

Liaison people are very *selective* in the way they communicate. There are some people to whom they pass information and others whom they bypass. For example, Ed Anderson has just learned that he is to be promoted to vice-president of international operations. However, the formal announcement will not be made for 10 days. Ed is very eager to tell someone, but he must be selective in leaking the news, for he does not want to tell anyone who will circulate the story back to top management for fear that they might reverse the promotion decision. Ed chooses his best friend, Bob James, to tell about the impending promotion. Bob is delighted and, realizing the confidential nature of the communiqué, passes the information to other people whom he trusts to treat the matter confidentially. Ten days later, the formal announcement is made and, to most people in the organization, it comes as a surprise. Furthermore, even those who knew of the promotion through the grapevine are careful not to let on. If any one of them does indicate prior knowledge, he or she will be bypassed by future grapevine messages. Bypassing people, however, is not always a sign of distrust or unreliability. The grapevine bypasses those who are not supposed to get a particular message. For example, in one company the president planned a party for twenty-five top executives. The grapevine learned about the party but did not know for sure which executives were on the list. As a result, only those who they thought would be invited were told about the party by informal communicators. As it turned out, twenty-three executives learned of the upcoming announcement and, of these, twenty-two were actually on the list. The cluster chain is indeed a selective communication network.

Grapevine Activity

Some people tend to be very active on the grapevine, and others are fairly inactive. However, given the proper situation and motivation, just about anyone will be grapevine-active. In fact, research reveals that there is little difference between the activities of men and women on the grapevine. If people feel they have cause to be grapevine-active, they will be. Let us discuss four of the most likely causes of grapevine activity.

First, if people lack information about a situation, they try to fill in these gaps via informal channels. Sometimes these efforts lead to distortion of facts or fabrication of rumors. For example, not long ago, the company president informed a senior executive that his office was to be refurbished. He was to be given a new desk, bookcases, furniture, and a very expensive rug. This was a reward for the successful advertising program he had developed for one of the firm's new product lines. As soon as the man's office was torn up, the grapevine began to hum. Before the afternoon was over, rumor had it that the executive had been fired and that his office was being made ready for a new advertising manager. Also, the personnel associated with the manufacture and sale of the new product line all became very concerned, fearing that the next step would be a reduction in their own workforce.

Second, people are active on the grapevine when there is insecurity in a situation. Continuing our illustration, people associated with the new product were quick to contact the sales manager to ask whether there were any truth to the rumor. The manager informed them that sales for the product were running 37 percent ahead of projections. After putting these facts together with those about the work being done in the senior executive's office, the workers realized that the executive was being rewarded for the product's success. They then passed this information back through the grapevine, and informal communications related to this development ceased. There was nothing more to talk about.

Third, there is grapevine activity whenever people have a personal interest in a situation. For example, if Mary and her boss get into an argument over the monthly cost control report, Mary's friends will tend to be grapevine-active. Likewise, if management decides to lay off 15 salespeople, the rest of the sales force will be interested in the situation because they have a stake in what is going on. People want to share among themselves any information about what is happening in the part of the world that is important to them.

Fourth, people are most active on the grapevine when they have information that is recent rather than stale. Research shows that the greatest spread of information occurs immediately after it is known. When most people learn the news, grapevine activity slows down. Figure 5.6 summarizes the causes for grapevine activity.

FIGURE 5.6   *Causes for Grapevine Activity*

Causes for Grapevine Activity

Information is lacking

Insecurity in a situation

Personal interest is involved

Possession of new information

FIGURE 5.7	*Informal Versus Formal Groups*

Informal Groups	Formal Groups
Roles and norms are flexible	Roles and norms are rigid
Membership is voluntary	Positions are chosen
Organizational structure is loose	Organizational structure is formal
Size is smaller	Size is larger
Sentimental and traditional	Utilitarian and functional

As discussed in this chapter, the informal organization differs from the formal organization in several ways. Some of the differences listed in Figure 5.7 were discussed in Chapters 3 and 4.

LEARNING OBJECTIVE

Identify the primary benefits associatead with the informal organization

④

Benefits of the Informal Organization

Every organization has an informal structure. By definition, then, there must be some very important benefits to be derived from its existence; otherwise it would cease to function. One of the most obvious reasons for an informal organization is that most of the personnel—both workers and managers—like it, want it, use it, and benefit from it! In this section, we examine five major benefits to be derived from the informal organization:

1. **Getting things done.**
2. **Lightening managerial workloads.**
3. **Providing job satisfaction.**
4. **Serving as a safety valve for employees' emotions.**
5. **Providing feedback to the manager.**

Getting Things Done

One of the primary benefits of the informal organization is that it supplements the formal organization in getting things done. Howard, a supervisor in the components assembly department, needs some help in securing parts from an outside supplier. The company's purchasing department is dragging its feet on the matter. Howard's friend Claire is the comptroller's secretary and a cousin of Greg, who is in charge of purchasing. Howard calls Claire and tells her his problem. Claire contacts Greg, who calls in Eddie, one of his assistants. Their discussion might go something like this:

> **Greg:** How come Howard down in the manufacturing section is having trouble getting parts from outside suppliers?
>
> **Eddie:** Is he calling to complain again?
>
> **Greg:** No, I got the message from someone else in the firm. Apparently this order is jeopardizing the production schedule. What is its current status?
>
> **Eddie:** Well, it's sitting on my desk, but I wanted to get some of my other paperwork cleared up before sending the order to the supplier.
>
> **Greg:** Forget about sending it. Call it in this afternoon and tell them we need those parts by tomorrow.
>
> **Eddie:** Okay, I'll get on it right now.

Later in the afternoon, Howard gets a call from Eddie telling him the parts are on the way, and they arrive the next morning.

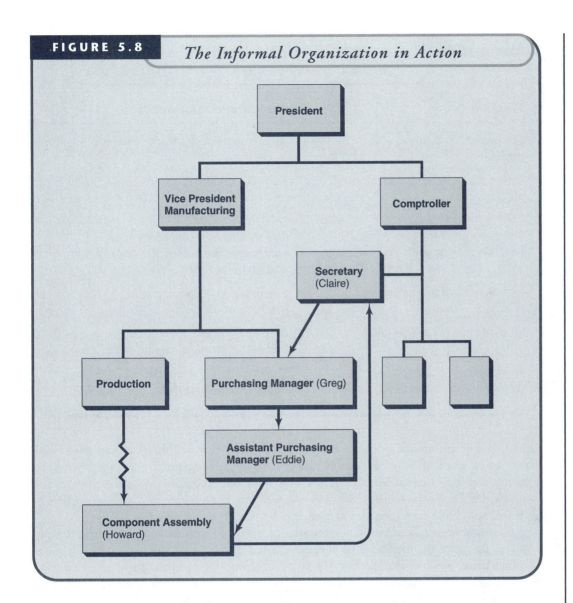

FIGURE 5.8 *The Informal Organization in Action*

This flow of communication is diagrammed in Figure 5.8. Note that Howard used the authority of the purchasing manager to help him get the needed parts. However, he worked through the informal organization in contacting Claire, and she used the network in reaching Greg. Without the informal organization, everyone would go through established channels, and it would take a lot longer to accomplish anything. Many of the organization's best workers would leave, and those who remained would simply stop putting out extra effort. After all, who wants to spend all his or her time fighting organizational red tape?

Lightening Managerial Workloads

Another benefit of the informal organization is to lighten managerial workloads. When managers realize the informal organization is on their side, they are more likely to delegate authority and rely on their subordinates to get things done. This results in looser, more generalized control and often creates a feeling of trust among the workers who respond by showing the manager they are indeed reliable. The outcome is higher productivity.

Providing Job Satisfaction

An accompanying benefit is job satisfaction, a term that relates to the favorableness or unfavorableness with which employees view their work. This topic is discussed in greater depth later, but let us briefly examine a few of its aspects here. Satisfaction is a relative matter in that

TABLE 5.2	*Formal Working Groups Versus Formal and Informal Teams*

Working Group	**Formal and Informal Team**
The group has a strong, clearly focused leader.	All members of the team share in providing leadership.
Each person in the group is individually accountable.	Each person in the group is individually and collectively responsible for the success of the group's efforts.
The purpose of the group is in total sync with the organization's mission.	The specific purpose for the team's existence is defined by the organization and team members.
Each individual produces work products or outputs.	The group collectively produces work products or outputs.
Meetings are run efficiently.	Meetings involve open-ended discussions and active problem-solving decisions.
The members discuss, decide, and delegate work to be done.	The members discuss, decide, and carry out the work to be done.

whether people are satisfied or dissatisfied is determined by how well their expectations fit with what they are given. If Tony has been led to believe that the company stresses imagination and creativity and finds himself instead saddled with rules and procedures, he will be dissatisfied. Conversely, if Dick expects his new job to pay well but to be boring and, to his surprise, he finds the work both interesting and challenging, he will be very satisfied.

Job satisfaction is also related to absenteeism, turnover, and productivity. The higher the satisfaction, the lower the likelihood of absenteeism and turnover and the higher the likelihood of productivity. When employees find the work satisfying, they derive a sense of meaningfulness and tend to remain on the job. Much of this satisfaction is related to the social environment in which the work is done. Thus, the informal organization helps to create a climate conducive to high productivity. As a result, the participants are not merely members of a working group but are team members in the true sense of the word. Table 5.2 illustrates this idea.

Serving as a Safety Valve

The grapevine also functions as a safety valve for employees' emotions. It lets the workers blow off steam and release some of their job pressures. When people are angry over something, they need some release for their frustration and resentment. The informal organization plays a role in this release. For example, if Don and his boss had an argument and Don told his boss where to get off, Don could be fired. Instead, Don complains to his fellow workers. By sharing his problem with other employees, Don is able to release much of his pent-up anger in a way that does not threaten his job. Also, after he talks about the issue for a while, it is likely to appear minor and he can turn his attention back to doing his job.

Providing Feedback

Perhaps the greatest overall benefit of the informal organization is that of providing the manager with feedback. The grapevine reflects how the workers feel about the company, the managers, and the work. By tapping the communication flow, the manager can learn what is going on. If a manager makes a bad decision or does not know how to supervise the subordinates properly, this information will eventually be carried back to the boss. What better way to protect one's job than by learning of problems through the grapevine and working to correct them before the boss asks, "What's this I hear about you having trouble with . . . ?" Wise managers use the grapevine to receive and to send information.

Disadvantages of the Informal Organization

LEARNING OBJECTIVE
5 Identify the disadvantages associated with the informal organization

Despite its potential benefits, the informal organization has disadvantages. The most common include:

1. Resistance to change
2. Goal conflict
3. Conformity problems
4. Rumor

Resistance to Change

One of the greatest disadvantages of the informal organization is its resistance to change. Often, the organization systematically ignores or only partially carries out directives related to such changes as new work procedures or rules. The overriding philosophy of many informal organizations is "Live and let live." They do not want the status quo changed. This behavior often is labeled *homeostasis,* which is the tendency of a group to maintain things as they are.

Of course, change is inevitable.[14] Technological innovations, plant redesign, and competitive developments in the external environment all require the organization to adapt operations to meet these conditions. If an innovative press is developed that will reduce current operating costs by 33 percent, a company must buy it. However, part of this cost savings may be a result of personnel reduction, which explains why the informal organization will fight the change. It does not want any of its members to be fired nor, as noted about group cohesion in Chapter 4, does the informal organization approve of any people being reassigned. If the company breaks up a cohesive group, productivity may drop decrease.

Another reason that the informal organization resists change is that work standards or quotas often are increased. In many cases, change generates new job demands; in *all* cases, it brings about higher efficiency (or at least attempts to achieve efficiency). For example, if a company establishes new work procedures, it is usually because a faster way of doing the job has been discovered. If work assignments are changed, it is because the firm has found a way to get more output with the same number of people. The informal organization resists such efficiency moves for three reasons.

1. First, as mentioned, the people like the status quo and believe that any change will disrupt their work environment. DaimlerChrysler is a good example. Daimler controls the company and wants all of its divisions to be profitable. Chrysler, however, has been having problems recently and, in order to deal with its financial losses, the German management has put one of its own managers in charge of U.S. operations and has begun a massive restructuring program.[15] It is still too early to know whether the program will generate the desired results, but one thing is certain: The informal organizations at Chrysler will work to minimize the effects of these actions because they upset the status quo.

2. Second, if employees conform and do more work, management may believe it can introduce change any time it wants, and it may begin regarding employees as mere factors of production who need not be consulted in advance about changes. By resisting, the informal organization ensures that management keeps the human element in mind when introducing change.

3. Third, many members of the informal organization believe it is unfair for management to introduce efficiency measures and keep all the profit for the company. If employees are going to do more work, they should be paid more money. Keep in mind, however, that this is not always a fair argument. If the firm buys a new machine for $500,000, the cost savings may allow it to pay for the machine and

keep costs at a competitive level but may not increase profit. Of course, not being privy to such financial data, the informal organization may simply assume that changes in the work environment always increase profit.

Goal Conflict

Goal conflict *arises when a person pursues two incompatible objectives.*

Whenever someone is asked to pursue two objectives that work against each other, **goal conflict** occurs. For example, Joe wants to be a member of the informal organization but also wants to meet the work quota assigned by management. The informal organization quota is only 80 percent of the company quota. Clearly, Joe cannot be totally loyal to both.

As we discover later in this chapter, management must carefully cultivate mutual interests with informal groups so as to integrate the goals of both. This is particularly true for young members of the informal group who, according to recent research, often have very high monetary expectations, a goal that often conflicts with management's desire to control costs closely. A survey by JobTrak.com found that 25 percent of today's college graduates expect to make their first million before they are thirty years old, and another 27 percent believe they will achieve this goal before they reach the age of forty. Only 29 percent of the 2,500 people who were surveyed believed they would never make a million dollars in their lifetime.[16] This is not an area where the firm will ever achieve perfect harmony, as there will always be some differences between the formal and informal organizations, but management must strive to reduce the differences to an acceptable level.

Conformity

Conformity *is the willingness to go along with the other members of the group.*

Closely related to goal conflict is the problem of **conformity.** Group norms and sanctions are used in persuading members to accept informal goals. Sometimes these norms and sanctions are so strong that individuals feel compelled to go along with the group despite their own inclinations. More likely, however, the informal organization becomes so much a part of the employees' work lives that they are unaware of its presence. As a result, they conform without consciously weighing the pros and cons of such action; even if their conformity were pointed out to them, they would be unwilling to deviate from these informal norms.

Rumor

Rumor *is a product of interest and ambiguity.*

The most undesirable feature of the informal organization is **rumor.** Many people believe the word is synonymous with the total product of the grapevine, but this is not so. Rumor is the unverified or untrue part of grapevine information. Communication theorists often define *rumor* as a product of interest and ambiguity.[17]

Rumor = Interest × Ambiguity

The logic behind this equation is simple. First, rumor can exist only if the issue is of interest to someone. You undoubtedly have never heard a rumor about the impact of the Ice Age on the existence of the penguin. However, you may have passed on a rumor about the type of examination given by a math professor in whose class you were currently registered. Second, rumor is unnecessary if all the facts about a situation are known. If the professor told you the final examination would come from the last 10 chapters of the book, ambiguity would be much less than if the questions were to be drawn from all 20 chapters and all class discussion. Ambiguity would be further reduced if the professor gave out a list of 50 equations from which the 25 examination problems would be drawn exclusively. Ambiguity could never be totally eliminated (which 25 equations?), but it would be reduced.

Selective filtering *is the screening and modifying of rumor.*
Elaboration *is the expansion and modification of rumor.*

Rumor is both maintained and magnified through the use of selective filtering and elaboration. **Selective filtering** involves the screening of rumor so that part of the story is maintained and the rest is discarded. Usually, the part that is kept is of greatest interest to the person repeating the rumor. This then is elaborated on: Details are added and are rearranged to fit the individual's point of view. **Elaboration** thus contributes to the further modification of a rumor.

Dealing with the Informal Organization

LEARNING OBJECTIVE

6 *Cite some of the ways in which a manager can deal with the informal organization*

In dealing with the informal organization, the manager must undertake two major tasks: recognize the inevitability of the informal network and attempt to influence its direction so that the goals of the formal and informal organizations are in harmony. The manager must also stay abreast of changes within the informal organization[18] and work to create an environment of trust with the members.[19] This is particularly important given that in recent years it has become more difficult to retain highly talented employees because there is such a demand for their services by other organizations.[20]

Recognize Its Inevitability

Some managers believe the disadvantages of the informal organization more than outweigh the benefits. As a result, they try to develop means of stamping it out. However, this approach is never completely successful. Using the grapevine as a representative segment of the informal organization, Keith Davis has offered the following explanation of its inevitability:

> *In a sense, the grapevine is a human birthright, because whenever people congregate into groups, the grapevine is sure to develop. It may use smoke signals, jungle tom-toms, taps on the prison wall, ordinary conversation, or some other method, but it will always be there. Organizations cannot "fire" the grapevine, because they did not hire it. It is simply there.*[21]

Because the informal organization is inevitable, the manager must develop methods for influencing it.[22]

Influence Its Direction

One of the most direct ways for a manager to influence the informal organization is by tapping its grapevine, learning what is being communicated, and countering any negative rumors by getting the formal organization's message into the channel. This can be done by learning who the liaison people in the informal network are and using them as a point of entry. The manager must also work closely with these personnel and show them that the company is interested in them and views them as important resources. One observer put it this way:

> *The American workplace has evolved to a kinder, gentler state. With unemployment at a 30-year low, bosses realize that they have to do more than pay good salaries and lavish perks on their employees if they want to keep them. They also have to be nice to them.*
>
> *And now comes a Gallup Organization study that shows that most workers rate having a caring boss even higher than they value money or fringe benefits. In interviews with two million employees at 700 companies, Gallup found that how long an employee stays at a company and how productive he or she is there is determined by the relationship with the immediate supervisor. "People join companies and leave managers," said . . . a senior managing consultant at Gallup and the primary analyst for the study.*[23]

Of course, if the manager begins feeding rumors or half-truths back into the grapevine, the liaison people will either modify the message or simply refuse to carry another organization's message. The manager cannot fight rumor with rumor. He or she must determine whether the information in the grapevine is accurate and, when it is inaccurate, must substitute correct information.

Do managers really use the grapevine to influence the informal organization? Research shows they do. Jay Knippen studied the grapevine in a large grocery store and found that although employees knew only 42 percent of the grapevine information, managers knew about 70 percent. Furthermore, while the managers accounted for only a small percentage of the 170 employees, they initiated almost 50 percent of the grapevine information. On average, each manager told eight other people, while the typical employee told four. The managers were not waiting to see what information the employees were passing through the grapevine. Rather, they were using this informal channel to get their own messages across.[24] Other research supports these conclusions. For example, the American Productivity & Quality Center recently conducted a study to determine how the best organizations create an environment that promotes teamwork. They found that one of the most important things that management has to do is to share knowledge and keep everyone apprised of what is going on.[25]

The purpose of these management-initiated messages should be to smooth the way for more cooperation between formal and informal organizations. The manager's objective should be to create conditions that help align the goals of both groups (see the Human Relations in Action box). When this is accomplished, the manager will find that resistance to change is minimized, rumors are reduced, and overall organizational cooperation is achieved.

Stay Abreast of Changes

The informal organization is continually undergoing change. Some people are dropping out of its ranks, while others are becoming members. Sometimes this is a result of the membership

HUMAN RELATIONS IN ACTION

Influencing the Informal Organization

There are a number of ways to influence the informal organization. Most of them relate to how you interact with members of this group. In particular, you have to keep in mind four guidelines.

First, when you communicate with the informal organization, always convey the fact that the message you are providing has importance. *Do not wait too long or your listener will begin to wander off mentally and you will have trouble getting him or her back.* For example, if you want to tell Jack something of importance, say it right up front. "Jack, this is something that you'll be interested in. It directly relates to the type of problem you've been investigating in the shipping department." Notice how quickly you have zeroed in on your main point.

Second, speak authoritatively and with conviction. *Do not end your sentences with a question mark. Phrase them so that they are factual and accurately represent your point of view. If you can make them sound like the other party should also accept them as such, so much the better. Also remember to maintain eye contact as you speak.*

Third, do not give the other person much chance to disagree or attempt to prove you wrong. *This undermines your efforts.* For example, if you need to have something done, do not say, "Tim, I think this is a good time for you to handle that cost control report." This sounds too wishy-washy, and Tim may say, "No, I don't think it is." If this happens, you are going to be engaged in an argument regarding whether the time is right. A better way to handle the situation is to say, "Tim, now is the time for you to han-

dle that cost control report." He may still disagree, but you have reduced the chances of this happening. Remember that if you narrow the options, you improve your chances of dealing effectively with the informal organization. For example, instead of asking someone when she would like her vacation, figure out what weeks are available and offer only those weeks: "Mary, would you like your vacation during the first two weeks of August or the first two weeks of September?" This approach saves you time because it eliminates all the other weeks of the year, which have already been taken by people in the unit who have more seniority.

Fourth, know when to listen. *Sometimes you can influence the informal organization by listening to others.* For example, if you are interested in finding out why so many people throughout the organization are coming late to work, you might ask, "Frank, why is everyone showing up late all the time?" Frank may know the answer, and this information will be useful to you. One company vice-president recently found out why so many people were leaving work early. It was a reaction to his example. Every day, the senior vice-president would leave at 4:30 P.M., and the rest of the personnel would begin leaving within five minutes. They reasoned that if the senior vice-president did not think it was important to stay until 5 P.M., why should they? During one of his informal chats with some of the employees, the vice-president indirectly learned of the effect that his behavior was having. From that day on, he made it a point to stay until 5 P.M. or later. He listened and learned.

In dealing with the informal organization, one must know when to take the initiative and when to hold back and listen. Both can be important strategies in influencing people.

itself, which accepts and rejects members and thus keeps membership in a state of flux. Often, it is a result of people leaving the company or being transferred to other units or departments. Because transferred people are no longer in the nearby vicinity, they will drop out of the local informal organization and, in all likelihood, be replaced by others. Managers who want to deal effectively with the informal organization have to keep abreast of the changing membership.

Managers also must remember that different problems will bring different informal leaders to the fore. If a university is having a problem with its part-time employees and they are unionized, the shop steward or union spokesperson will probably be the informal leader. This individual is chosen because he or she is perceived as someone who can help the group achieve its goals. This person is seen as able to wield power. If a hospital is having a salary dispute with its nursing staff, the nurse who informally represents the group may be chosen because of her job experience and tenure. She is chosen on the basis of work-related expertise. If a work team on a loading dock sets a goal of loading 10 percent more trucks than any other team, the individual who is the fastest worker may be chosen as the informal leader. This person's informal authority is based on his or her job expertise.

Because informal organizational membership is continually in a state of flux, the manager must continually ask the question: Who is in charge of the informal group and why? The answer will help the manager decide how to influence or deal most effectively with the informal group.

summary

① LEARNING OBJECTIVE
Compare and contrast the formal and informal organizations

The informal organization plays a significant role in the dynamics of behavior at work. Comparison with the formal organization shows that the two organizations differ in terms of interpersonal relations, leadership, behavioral control, and dependency. In formal organizations relationships are clearly defined, whereas in the informal organization relationships evolve and change continually; so do authority and power. The use of power typically requires political behavior and works various ways throughout the formal and informal organization. It is important to learn how to use power. One of the most important activities that takes place in the informal organization is networking, the process of socializing, politicking, and interacting with people throughout the company. Gender and ethnicity are important factors in how people network.

② LEARNING OBJECTIVE
Discuss some of the behavioral controls used by members of the informal organization to ensure compliance with its norms

In formal organizations, people are rewarded for doing things right and punished when doing things wrong. Also in the informal organization, rewards and punishments are dispensed to members. A member will be included in the group for following group norms, but may be ostracized, subjected to pressure, ridiculed and made to look foolish in the eyes of the other members for not properly acting within the group norms. The formal leader has greater power to reward and punish than the informal leader. Some workers simply resist because they believe they have nothing to gain by not joining the group.

③ LEARNING OBJECTIVE
Explain how the informal communication network functions

One of the informal organization's most interesting behavioral aspects, however, is its communication network. Commonly known as the *grapevine,* this communication network is used to carry information between members of the informal organization. Four common types of grapevine network are the single strand, gossip chain, probability chain, and cluster chain. The cluster chain, which involves the selective transmission of messages, is the most common. Some people tend to be very active on the grapevine, but others are fairly inactive. However, given the proper situation and motivation, just about everyone will be grapevine-active. Research reveals that some of the most likely causes for such activity are lack of knowledge about a situation, insecurity, personal interest in a situation, and the possession of recent information.

④ LEARNING OBJECTIVE
Identify the primary benefits associated with the informal organization

Some of the commonly cited benefits of the informal organization are getting things done, lightening managerial workloads, providing job satisfaction, serving as a safety valve for employee emotions, and providing feedback to the manager.

⑤ LEARNING OBJECTIVE
Identify the primary disadvantages associated with the informal organization

Despite its benefits, however, some major disadvantages are associated with the informal organization: resistance to change, goal conflict, conformity, and rumor. Most people do not want the status quo to change. The informal organization can be instrumental in determining the rate at which change occurs in a company. Resistance involves concerns about standards, quotas, unfair management treatment and profits. Often the goals of the formal and informal groups are different, which causes conflict. A rumor is the unverified or untrue part of grapevine information.

⑥ LEARNING OBJECTIVE
Cite some of the ways in which a manager can deal with the informal organization

In any event, the informal organization is inevitable. It cannot be stamped out, so the manager will do well to understand its presence and, if possible, to influence its direction so that the goals of both the formal and informal organizations are brought into harmony. Some of the most effective ways of doing this include tapping the grapevine to learn what is going on, countering rumor with fact, and creating conditions that help align the goals of both groups. If this can be accomplished, the manager will find that resistance to change is minimized, rumors are reduced, and overall organizational cooperation is achieved.

KEY TERMS IN THE CHAPTER

Sociogram	Grapevine
Advice network	Single strand
Trust network	Gossip chain
Communication network	Probability chain
Authority	Cluster chain
Power	Goal conflict
Satisficing behavior	Conformity
Networking	Rumor
Nucleus group	Selective filtering
Fringe group	Elaboration
Outer group	

REVIEW AND STUDY QUESTIONS

1. One of the ways in which the informal organization differs from the formal organization is that of interpersonal relations. What does this statement mean?

2. How does the formal leader differ from the informal leader?

3. How is authority different from power? Which is of greater importance in the informal organization?

4. What kinds of political tactics do managers use? Explain

5. What is networking? How is networking used in the informal organization?

6. Identify some ways minority managers network differently than managers in general.

7. What are some of the behavioral controls used by members of the informal organization to ensure compliance with its norms? Give examples

8. What is a grapevine? How does a grapevine work?

9. How does each of the following grapevine networks function: single strand, gossip chain, probability chain, cluster chain? Explain

10. When are people most likely to be grapevine-active? Give at least three illustrations.

11. In what way does the informal organization help in getting things done?

12. How does the informal organization lighten managerial workloads?

13. Job satisfaction is a benefit of informal organizations. How does it work?

14. How can the informal organization serve as a safety valve?

15. What type of feedback does the informal organization provide to managers?

16. One of the biggest complaints about the informal organization is that it tends to resist change. Is this true? Defend your answer.

17. How does goal conflict differ from goal conformity?

18. What is a rumor? How are rumors and grapevines associated?

19. What are two ways managers can effectively deal with the informal organization?

20. Why must managers stay abreast of changes in the informal organization?

VISIT THE WEB

What Is Your Work Orientation?

Do you prefer to work alone or do you prefer to work in teams (groups)? To gain insight about your work preferences, take the assessment test, Teams vs. Individual, posted on the web site, **http://www.queendom.com.** This is a free test. On the home page click on "tests" listed on the left side of the screen, then on the "tests tests tests" page, click on Test No. 9, "Teams vs. Individual." Evaluate your individual orientation toward work by completing the test. After reviewing the analysis of your results, answer the following questions.

1. How did you measure up? What was your score? What does it mean?

2. What are some of the characteristics of your work orientation?

3. How can this information help you in your job and in your career?

4. Why is it important to understand your work orientation?

How can the informal organization help Proctor & Gamble?

The informal organization is alive in every company. It plays a significant role in the dynamics of employee behavior, which directly affects the accomplishments of company goals and objectives. How does the informal organization impact the success at Proctor & Gamble? Go to Proctor & Gamble's web site **http://www.pg.com.** On the home page, read about the company under "About Our Company." Then go to "Careers" and then Corporate Information click on "Corporate Structure" and read

"First Impressions." On the right side of the screen, click on and read "Four Pillars—Overview," "Think Globally, Act Locally," "Minimize Costs—Be Smart," "How the Structure Works," and "Your Role."

1. Review the corporate structure of Proctor & Gamble and learn how teams are used throughout the company.

2. Based on your analysis of P&G's corporate structure and the information you learned about informal organization in this chapter, identify some ways the informal organization can benefit the teams at P&G. Be creative with your suggestions.

3. What is the most interesting thing you learned about P&G's corporate structure? Would you like to work for P&G? Why?

TIME OUT ANSWERS

Interpretation of the Informal Organization Initial Appraisal

This quiz consists of two parts. Questions 1–7 measure your use of the informal organization. Questions 8–15 measure how much you really know about the informal organization.

Do you use the informal organization? The following key is for scoring your answers to Questions 1–7. For each answer you have that agrees with this key, give yourself a point.

1. False   5. False

2. True   6. True

3. False   7. False

4. True

The higher your score, the greater is the likelihood that you use the informal organization. However, if you have a score of 6 or 7, you must be careful that you are not simply ignoring the formal structure. A high score can indicate total disregard for organizational policies and procedures, but only you can determine this. Most effective managers have a score of at least 5 on this part of the quiz.

What do you know about the grapevine? Questions 8–15 are designed to measure your knowledge of the informal organization. For each answer you have that agrees with this key, give yourself a point.

8. False   12. False

9. True   13. False

10. True   14. False

11. True   15. False

If you currently know a great deal about the informal organization, your score here will be in the 6–8 range. In any event, as you read the material in this chapter, you will learn the logic behind each of the answers.

case: A CASE OF LAYOFFS

The rumor mill in Betty Harrigan's department has been in full operation this week. It seems everyone's mind is on the new equipment being installed. The machinery was approved by a management committee more than six months ago and is the result of company efforts to modernize the facilities. The machines are state-of-the-art but, despite their sophistication, still require just as many people to run them as did the old machines. Nevertheless, this has not stopped the rumors about impending layoffs.

In an effort to deal with the situation, Betty called a meeting of her staff and explained to them that three months before she became department manager, a committee had approved the purchase of this new machinery. She was unable to explain why no one in the unit knew about the impending purchase, but she assured everyone there would be no layoffs or cutbacks in the number of hours worked. "These machines are going to help us increase the quality of work, but they will not increase the quantity. We are going to need everyone in the department and will probably have to hire two more people." The group listened quietly as Betty spoke. When she was finished, she asked if there were any questions. One of the young men in the back said, "Are we the only department getting new equipment?" Betty explained that two other units also were having new machinery installed. She then hastened to add, "And like us, neither of them is going to have any layoffs either." With this, the meeting broke up.

As soon as she returned to her office, Betty had a call from her boss. "Look, I don't want to panic you," he said, "but I've just had a call from the vice-president of administration. The other departments that got new equipment are going to have some layoffs because they were overstaffed to start. However, you will not have any. You are understaffed and, as we agreed, you will be getting two new people within the month. Unfortunately, none of the people being laid off has the qualifications you need, or we would simply transfer them to your department. The reason I wanted to call was to let you know that you have nothing to worry about." Betty thanked him and hung up. Just then there was a knock at her door. The young man from the meeting came in and said, "I just heard that people in those other two departments are to be laid off. I was wondering what effect this would have on the new hires in our department. If I'm going to get laid off, I'd like to start looking for a new job as soon as possible." Betty asked the man to sit down.

QUESTIONS

1. How did the young man find out about the layoffs in the other departments? Explain.

2. Will Betty's comment about no layoffs in her department now be regarded with skepticism? Why?

3. What would you advise Betty to say to the young man? Explain.

4. What should Betty do to maintain her credibility? Tell why.

YOU BE THE CONSULTANT

The Value of Networking

In recent months, things have not been going well at the county manager's office. Last week, they seemed to have reached a head when the county commission held a public hearing, during which the county manager was asked to explain why it cost so much money to maintain the county bus line. The manager explained that the lack of new equipment in the maintenance department and the difficulty of hiring qualified mechanics were the two main reasons. After the county manager had spoken, members of the public were allowed to come forward and speak to the commission members. Everyone who spoke complained about the bus system and how poorly it was run. They all, directly or indirectly, blamed the county manager for not controlling the system more efficiently.

This morning's paper had an editorial that soundly criticized the county manager and supported the citizens who spoke out at the meeting. It appears that the county manager's job may well be on the line. However, before any drastic action is taken, the commission will first talk to several of the major department heads in the county to find out what they think about the situation. Earlier today, the heads of three major county departments met. Fred Cox is in charge of all transportation services; the head of bus maintenance is under his direction. Paul Whitney is in charge of the municipal airport. Randi Schulman is head of county roads and maintenance. All are connected in some way with transportation, and they believe that if the county manager is let go, they too might be fired. They have therefore decided to formulate a plan for stopping the situation before it gets out of control. Here is what they plan to do to gain support for the county manager and themselves:

1. Blame the bus problem on the fact that the county does not have enough equipment for providing first-class maintenance of the buses and point out that this is the result of decisions made by the old commission five years ago.

2. Support the county manager and get five other major department heads to do the same.

3. Call in all the favors they are owed by other influential county personnel to ride out this storm.

Your Advice

1. To which of the three strategies should the department heads give first priority?

    ____ a. Blame the problem on the county.
    ____ b. Support the county manager and get others to do the same.
    ____ c. Call in favors owed by influential county personnel and ride out the storm.

2. What tactics are the managers using? Tell why?

3. What is the logic in their blaming the old county commission?

4. How effectively are the commission members resolving the citizen's complains?

5. How are politics impacting the decision of the commission? Give several examples.

6. How realistic is the situation presented in this case?

EXPERIENCING GRAPEVINE COMMUNICATIONS

Purpose

- To understand how the grapevine works.
- To use each of the four basic grapevine networks to convey information.
- To evaluate the grapevine networks in terms of speed and accuracy.

Procedure

1. The instructor will assist the class in forming teams of six people. The instructor then will give each team a set of four messages. These messages are labeled *1*, *2*, *3*, and *4*, respectively.

2. Each team should form a single-strand informal communication network and pass message 1 from one team member to the next. The last person to receive the message will write it down.

3. Each team then should form a gossip chain. The individual in the center will convey message 2 to everyone in the group. Everyone then will write down his or her interpretation of the message.

4. Each team next should form a probability chain to pass message 3 and then a cluster chain to pass message 4. In each case, the last person to receive the message will write it down.

5. Individually, review each of the four informal networks. Which was easiest to use? Which resulted in the fastest conveyance of information? Which was slowest? Which was most accurate? Which was least accurate? Finally, when choosing an informal network, when would each of the four be the first choice? When would each be the last choice?

The Technical
System

The focus of this section of the book is to study the technical system of organizations. The three major components of the technical system are (1) the impact of technology on people at work, (2) a focus on productivity and quality improvement, and (3) job redesign and job enrichment.

THE GOALS OF THIS SECTION ARE TO:

- *Trace the evolution of technology, describe the major characteristics of a postindustrial society, explain the effect of technology on work values, and discuss industrial democracy and the ways in which organizations now are dealing with workplace violence.*

- *Study the nature of productivity and quality improvement, examine total quality management, explain how participative management approaches are improving productivity and quality, and discuss how intrapreneurship attitudes can make a difference in productivity and quality.*

- *Discuss how modern organizations deal with the challenge of technology and its dysfunctional effects; explain what job design is; explore job rotation, job enlargement, and job enrichment; describe core job dimensions and illustrate how selected enrichment principles can be used to fulfill these dimensions; and discuss current challenges in job design.*

When you have finished reading this part of the book, you should have a solid understanding of the technical system. Additionally, you should know what is meant by *job redesign,* and you should understand the job core dimensions and job enrichment principles that play a key role in job redesign. Most important, you should have gained an awareness of the all-important personnel–organizational structure interface and how modern human relations managers try to integrate the needs of both groups in attaining overall efficiency.

6

Technology and People at Work

The organization must respond to many factors, one of which is technology. As technology advances, the organization finds itself bombarded with change. The relationship between technology and people at work is known as *sociotechnical systems,* and modern managers are finding that they must pay increased attention to this technology–human interface.

AFTER READING THIS CHAPTER, YOU SHOULD BE ABLE TO:

1. Trace the evolution of technology from the handicraft era to the cybernated technology stage.
2. Identify and describe the four major characteristics of a postindustrial society.
3. Discuss the effect of technology on organizational culture.
4. Identify and describe four ways employees feel alienated by technology.
5. Explain how technology can cause workers to fear their replacement by machines.
6. Discuss how knowledge-based organizations, industrial democracy, and participative management can aid in integrating technology and the organization's personnel.
7. Discuss workplace violence and how managers are dealing with it.

People and Machines: Working as One

Technology is increasing at mind-boggling rates. Jobs that used to take weeks to complete can now be finished in minutes, thanks to high-speed computers. World-class companies are finding that by blending the abilities of their personnel with the high-tech capabilities of their machines, they can offer new products and services to a growing number of customers. A good example is Andersen Windows.

For many years, Andersen was basically a mass-producing firm that made a range of standard windows in large batches. However, the company found that more and more customers wanted unique offerings. They did not want their windows to look just like their neighbors'. In fact, they wanted their windows to be totally different from anyone else's. The firm attempted to meet these demands by offering various embellishments that could make a window appear as prairie-style or Gothic-style or whatever other style the customer wanted. However, as it began accommodating the individual tastes of its customers, Andersen found that it was making more and more mistakes in meeting orders. At this point, the company decided to blend technology all the way down the line to the customer level.

The firm has now created an interactive, computerized version of its catalog so that salespeople can help customers to determine the design of their ideal windows. Working as a team, salespeople and customers can add, modify, and strip away features until they have designed the desired window. Then this information can be sent electronically from the showroom to the factory, where it is assigned a unique "license plate number" that can be tracked in real time, using bar-code technology, from the assembly line through the warehouse.

Today Andersen Windows is a mass customizer, capable of turning out hundreds of thousands of products, all specially designed to meet the unique requirements of the customer. At the same time, error rates have been driven down sharply. Recently, the company offered 188,000 different products and fewer than 1 in 2,000 van loads contained an order discrepancy.

The firm has been so successful in its efforts to bring technology and people together that it is expanding its offerings and pursuing the window replacement market. Many homeowners would like to replace their current windows with new ones. Using a newly patented product called *Fibrex* (a composite of wood and vinyl), Andersen can easily design a new window to replace an old one. Because *Fibrex* is tougher than vinyl and does not age as does wood, the firm now is making big inroads in the $15 billion U.S. window replacement market. At the same time, it is running its factories on a 'round-the-clock basis and offering bonuses to its employees to work overtime. Obviously, Andersen has learned the secret of getting people and machines to work in harmony.

DaimlerChrysler provides another good example of blending people and technology. This company purchases a total of 60,000 different items from more than 1,100 suppliers. The entire process is coordinated efficiently by a combination of high technology with supplier assistance. As a result of involving suppliers in the design process, DaimlerChrysler often learns about new materials, parts, and other technologies before other automobile makers are in the know.

Sometimes these ideas are quite small. One supplier, for example, reduced the thickness of the splash shield (a sheet of plastic that covers the wheel well) for a savings of $72,500. However, these savings can really add up. To ensure that the suppliers work synchronously with one another, DaimlerChrysler assigns a particular supplier to act as a team leader. The team leader's job is to oversee other suppliers in the design and manufacture of a component, such as a seat. As a result, DaimlerChrysler is able to save money by letting the suppliers handle production of products for the car and delivery of these products to the assembly plant just in time for installation. Through these efforts, the company has saved $2.5 billion. It's all a matter of learning how to merge technology and people effectively.

Sources: Neil Gross, "New Tricks for Help Lines," Business Week, *April 29, 1996, pp. 97–98; J. William Semich,* "Manage Factory Production with CA-Unicenter," Datamation, *April 15, 1996, pp. 34–38; and Justin Martin, "Are You as Good as You Think You Are?"* Fortune, *September 30, 1996, pp. 142–146.*

① The Evolution of Technology

One of the most dramatic events of the twentieth century has been the dynamic development of technology. Today, people are traveling faster than ever before, residing in houses made of material that was unavailable twenty-five years ago, using home appliances and tools that make their lives more enjoyable and, thanks to medical technology, living longer. However, technology has had its price. Many people are now living at a very fast rate, being subjected to what Alvin Toffler called **future shock**—the effect of enduring too much change in too short a time.[1] How has our society arrived at this advanced state of technology? We attempt to answer this question by examining the eras of technological development through which humankind in general and the United States in particular have progressed.

The first phase of technological development was the **handicraft era.** During this period, people made things by hand. They built their own houses, made their own clothes, and developed their own medicines and herbs to combat illness. In short, they were self-sufficient. Examples of specialists during this era were carpenters, cobblers, and tailors, who provided the local population with their services and, in turn, received goods or money with which to buy food, clothing, and shelter. However, these craftsmen were to be found only in larger towns where their services were required. In outlying areas such as farm communities, there was little need for a tailor or a cobbler, although a blacksmith might be able to eke out a living. In any event, specialization was minimal at this time; almost everyone was a jack-of-all-trades.

Next came the **mechanization era,** in which machine labor replaced human labor. One of the most significant developments of this era was job specialization, by which workers were assigned a limited number of tasks that were to be repeated. During this period, humankind began to harness energy and use it to drive machinery; the spinning jenny and the power loom are examples. Hence, mechanization increased on two fronts: the workers and the machines. Each was seen as a complement to the other. Humans and machines, together, increased productivity dramatically. The age of mechanization was upon us.

A further increase in the use of machines and job simplification was represented by the era of **mechanistic technology.** Eli Whitney, best known for his invention of the cotton gin, introduced standardized interchangeable parts in his production plant and soon was turning out muskets and clocks in greater quantities and at a lower cost than ever before. A century later, this basic idea was extended further through the development of the modern assembly line, such as that used by Henry Ford in building his Model T. By this time, the pace of technology was increasing and the role of the worker was diminishing. The number of tasks a person had to perform was decreasing, as was the amount of skill required.

In many organizations, **automated technology** has replaced mechanistic technology. Automated technology involves linking together and integrating assembly-line machines in such a fashion that many functions are performed automatically without human involvement. Some people have contended that this development represents the beginning of a second industrial revolution. Modern auto assembly lines are an excellent example, as well as, office computer systems that are linked to one another, thereby allowing managers using a microcomputer to interface with a giant mainframe. And technology is not confined to office or manufacturing environments. For example, oil companies now use undersea robots for deep-water dives to repair oil platforms or perform other hazardous tasks that used to be carried out by human divers.[2] And Honda is presently developing Asimo, a 4-foot robot, designed to help older people live a better life at home.

At present, a fifth era, **cybernated technology,** is emerging. *Cybernetics* refers to automatic control; today, by means of cybernated technology, machines are running and controlling other machines. A classic example is provided when computers monitor the temperature throughout a plant or building and order the heating and air conditioning units to turn off or on as needed. This form of environmental control is helping to reduce costs throughout industry. Computers also are being programmed to operate machines and to handle jobs automatically that once had

Future shock is the effect of enduring too much change in too short a time.

The **handicraft era** was characterized by self-sufficiency.

The **mechanization era** saw the use of machine labor.

Mechanistic technology brought the assembly line.

Automated technology modernized the assembly line.

With **cybernated technology,** machines run other machines.

to be performed by humans. As a result, robotics is gaining a foothold in many enterprises. Computers not only are a major component in manufacturing operations and in operating businesses, they also serve a major role in marketing—the way products and services are bought and sold. Research shows that more and more people are depending on the Internet for purchasing products and services. E-commerce is emerging as a way to do business. As the twenty-first century progresses, technology will change, but it will continue to be a vital part of business operations and will make the difference between success and failure for many business owners.

Research and Development, Knowledge, and Technology

How has humankind been able to accomplish such tremendous breakthroughs in technology? One way is through the billions of dollars annually invested in research and development (R&D). These expenditures are bringing about the development of all sorts of new products. The results can be seen in any large retail store, where one can find more goods than ever before. But it does not stop there. Thanks to research breakthroughs, we have supersonic transports, telecommunication satellites, and computers for medical research. In short, at work or at home, the employee is surrounded by technological innovation. Furthermore, there is no going back. Technology is speeding up, and the modern organization is being forced to accommodate many breakthroughs. For example, the large drug companies are reinventing their labs to boost productivity. In the past three years, Pfizer, Merck & Co., Abbott Laboratories, and Wyeth have hired new people with strong biotechnology and genomics expertise to find answers to complex conditions such as cancer, diabetes, and Alzheimer's disease. "The trade group Pharmaceutical Research & Manufacturers of America says the R&D spending it tracks for its big drug company members soared from $21 billion in 1998 to an estimated $32 billion in 2002."[3] What is the basic cause of this accelerated technological thrust? The answer is found in *knowledge,* technology's fuel.

The rate at which information has been gathered has been spiraling upward for 10,000 years. The first great breakthrough occurred with the invention of writing. The next great leap forward did not occur until the invention of movable type by Gutenberg in the fifteenth century. Prior to this event, Europe was producing approximately 1,000 book titles annually, and a library of 100,000 titles was taking nearly 100 years to turn out. In the years after Gutenberg's accomplishment, a tremendous acceleration occurred such that, by 1950, Europe was producing 120,000 titles per year. What had once taken a century now required only 10 months. Today, the world's output of books is more than 5,000 titles per day.

Naturally, not every book will lead to a technological breakthrough, but the accelerated curve in book publication crudely parallels the rate at which humankind discovers new knowledge. Advances in science support this statement. For example, before the invention of the movable-type press, only eleven chemical elements were known, and it had been two hundred years since the last one—arsenic—had been discovered. The twelfth element was discovered while Gutenberg was working on his invention. Subsequently, more than seventy additional elements were discovered and, since 1900, scientists have been isolating new elements at the rate of one every three years.

Much of this advance must be attributed to the fact that 90 percent of all the scientists who ever lived are alive now, and new discoveries are being made every day. This is evident from reading local newspapers and magazines. For example, some of the latest technological developments and research breakthroughs include the following:

- **To help junior high school students improve their math skills, Casio Inc. has developed a calculator called ALGEFX 2.0PLS, which doubles as a math tutor. A large, eight-line display and icon-based menu lets students call up and solve problems** such as linear and quadratic equations, as well as samples drawn from geometry, trigonometry, and calculus.[4] Casio's EXILIM EX-S2 and EXILIM ZOOM EX-Z3 are among the thinnest, smallest, and lightest digital cameras with a LCD screen available anywhere in the world. At the 2003 Consumer Electronics Show, four of Casio's new products were elected as honorees in its "Innovations 2003 Design and Engineering Showcase."[5]

- One problem with chemotherapy is that it floods the body with poison, killing healthy cells along with cancerous ones. Now Wyeth-Ayerst Research has developed a technique that allows antibodies to be attached only to leukemia cells, thus attacking the cancer but leaving the good cells untouched.[6]

- Researchers at the University of Wisconsin, Madison, have developed new satellite tools that are helping forecasters track hurricanes and monitor their intensity. The new technologies are based on a technique that merges the images taken by a string of satellites, each of which has its own view of the earth, into a high-resolution composite graphic. The information can then be used to provide more accurate information regarding hurricanes.[7]

- Researchers currently are working on stem cell transplants to determine whether they can help individuals suffering from spinal-cord injury, stroke, and multiple sclerosis. Scientists at Johns Hopkins Medical Institute recently injected stem cells into the spinal fluid of mice and rats that were paralyzed by a virus that attacked the nerve controlling movement. Within eight weeks, 50 percent of the rodents began to show some improvement. Trial tests for humans are scheduled for the future.[8] By the end of 2002, no human disease had been cured with stem cells. Research indicates that some conditions could be treated with embryonic stem cells, for example, Parkinson disease, spinal cord disorders, diabetes, liver disease, organ transplants, skin grafts, and bone disorders. Some researchers hope to combine stem cell research with gene therapy.[9]

- The spectrometer aboard the Mars Odyssey spacecraft has successfully detected the presence of hydrogen in soil in the area of the Martian South Pole. "Researchers believe the hydrogen signaled the presence of significant amounts of water in the form of ice beneath the planet's surface.[10] Technology is what sustains the space exploration program.

New Products Are Continually Emerging

Scientific discoveries are being brought to fruition at a faster rate than ever before. For example, in 1836, a machine was invented that mowed, threshed, and tied straw into sheaves and poured grain into sacks. The machine was based on technology that even then was 20 years old, but it was not until 1930 that such a combine actually was marketed. The first English patent for a typewriter was issued in 1714, but another 150 years passed before typewriters were commercially available. Today, such delays between ideas and application are almost unthinkable. It is not that we are more eager or more ambitious than our ancestors but that we have, over time, invented all sorts of social devices to hasten the process. Thus, we find that the time between the first and second stages of the innovative cycle—between idea and application—has been cut radically. For example, hybrid auto engines developed in the last few years now provide a combination of gas and electric power, thus allowing autos such as the Honda Insight to travel seventy-five miles per gallon and the Toyota Prius to achieve fifty-eight miles per gallon.[11] The Honda Insight was rated the most fuel-efficient care in American for three straight years. In 1970 it introduced its first lightweight, fuel-efficient car, Honda N600, in America. Since then, Honda has continued to be an innovator of new vehicle technology. In fact, Honda just introduced its first fuel cell car, Honda FCX, which is government-certified for everyday use. Honda is currently working with the city of Los Angeles under a two-year lease agreement, where the City of LA pays $500 a month to lease the first of five Honda FCX models, with the other four vehicles scheduled for delivery in

2003. City employees will use these vehicles on a day-to-day basis and provide Honda with valuable, real-world knowledge on the use and operation of fuel cells. Toyota, also, has introduced its fuel cell hybrid vehicle, FC HV-4. "Hydrogen-powered fuel vehicles hold great promise for future clean air vehicles, while at the same time reducing our global dependence on oil," said Tom Elliott, executive vice president, American Honda Motor Com., Inc."[12] Honda believes it is their responsibility to advance technology that moves toward a cleaner environment.

Ceramic technology is critical to American troops, who carry heavy loads of equipment and armor. "Elite American units such as the Delta Force have been wearing ceramic armor—about half as heavy as the metal variety—since the mid-1990s. Now more U.S. ground forces will get it." Not only is it lightweight, it also provides protection in close-up combat. Ceramic technology is used to shield Patriot missiles, used in helicopters, and used in tracked vehicles that glide across water and climb over rough terrain. Through the development of ceramics technology, General Dynamics, Japan's Kyocera Corp. and Lockheed Martin Corp. are helping transform the U.S. Military into a quick, lighter, and more lethal force.[13]

Jim Keyes, CEO of 7-Eleven, has not only spent lavishly on training, technology upgrades, and setting up a distribution system for fresh foods, but also has spend heavily on the development of 7-Eleven's prepaid Vcom cards, developed by Alliance Data Systems. The prepaid everything card "will let customers make ATM transactions as well as buy money orders, transfer funds, cash checks, and eventually pay bills." Keyes thinks the Vcom cards could take off the way credit-card readers at the gas pump did. Convenience needs have changed, requiring a more convenient alternative method of payment. With Vcom cards, there is no interchange fee. By 2004, 7-Eleven expects to see advantages to its system.[14]

Computerized engineering and materials science have become an integral part of sports. For example, space-age technology was applied to Lance Armstrong equipment used in mastering the Tour de France title for the fourth time. His altimeter built into a titanium-coated wristwatch was engineered by Nike and Seiko and his eyes were protected by sunglasses from Oakley, precision molded to thousandths of an inch for aerodynamic efficiency and equipped with optical lenses so clear a laser beam can pass through them without noticeable defraction. Armstrong's superstrong carbon fiber-epoxy bicycle frame was built to cut the wind with tear-drop-shaped tubing and weighted in at a pixiesque 2.27 pounds.[15]

Even the U.S. Post Office is getting involved in the high-tech revolution, as evidenced by its recent plan to provide to each person in the country who does not have electronic mail an e-mail address of his or her own. If someone wants to send an e-mail message to one of these people, the local post office will make a paper printout of the message and deliver it with the snail mail.[16]

In addition, the number of consumer goods is increasing so rapidly that the time between introduction and decline is diminishing. Cheaper, better quality, or more useful goods are being produced. This is true, in part, because a growing number of firms now are spending more and more money on R&D to develop new-age products. One good example is the Polaroid Company, which developed a low-technology offering, the pocket camera that was brought to market in late 1999 and proved to be the biggest seller the firm had in more than two decades. The camera found a strong market particularly among young people who were impressed with pictures that could be peeled off and stuck to another surface.[17] Another example is the Gentex Corporation, which has invented a car rearview electrochromic mirror that turns on the headlights at dusk and turns off the lights at dawn, in addition to adjusting the air conditioning, detecting the presence of rain and automatically turning on the wipers, and providing a button to summon emergency assistance.[18] Spurred on by recent tire recalls and the belief that underinflated tires can lead to accidents, Gentex developed a tire pressure monitoring mirror that warns the driver when one or more of the vehicle's tires becomes underinflated. Sensors located in each tire or from the vehicle's ABS system send information to the mirror, which alerts the driver. Gentex also has developed a microphone located in the rearview mirror that is specifically designed for the harsh, noisy automotive environment. Gentex prides itself in being a technology company.[19] Simply put, technology is changing the way we live. For example, recent research shows that:

- **79 percent of Americans have cable or satellite television.**
- **59 percent have home computers.**
- **53 percent have cell phones.**
- **29 percent log on to the Internet on a typical day.**
- **16 percent have digital videodisc players.**
- **12 percent have personalized Web pages for their investment portfolios.**
- **7 percent get financial news from wireless devices.[20]**

This trend is certain to continue. For example, it is forecast that by the year 2008, 99 percent of all American households will have color televisions, 91 percent will have videocassette recorders, 77 percent will have personal computers, and 30 percent will have a high-speed Internet connection.[21] Moreover, the current emphasis on R&D is unlikely to decline, given that recent research shows that companies with in-house R&D programs are achieving faster growth and better gross margins than are those that either outsource R&D or do not have such a program.[22]

Wi-Fi (Wireless Fidelity) technology is beginning to penetrate the corporate world. It is a radio signal that beams Internet connections out three hundred feet. These are called hot spots. "Its super fast connections to the Web cost only a quarter as much as the gaggle of wires companies use today."[23] "In the last 18 months, KT Corp, South Korea's former phone monopoly and its biggest broadband and a Wi-Fi player, has set up 8,500 wireless commercial local-area networks, or hot spots. That's more than half the world's total."[24] In the U.S. Intel, IBM, and AT&T recently formed Cometa Networks to build a nationwide network of twenty thousand hot spots over the next three years.

Wi-Fi is being used for mission-critical jobs in factories, trucks, stores, and even hospitals. For example, UPS is equipping its worldwide distribution centers with wireless networks at a cost of $120 million. "As loaders and packers scan packages, the information zips instantly to the UPS network, leading to a 35 percent productivity gain." IBM is developing Wi-Fi powered systems to monitor potato fryers at restaurants to air conditioners in computer labs. By 2004 Boeing is scheduled to equip one hundred of its jets with speedy wireless technology. General Motors Corp. has developed Wi-Fi in ninety manufacturing plants. Although Wi-Fi technology is growing and is being used by more companies worldwide, security is still a problem. Until improved security techniques are developed, many companies are reluctant to use Wi-Fi in sensitive areas of the company where privacy is crucial.[25]

Hence, the United States has found itself entering a postindustrial society in which changes in the external environment are bringing about an entirely different set of internal values. In short, technology is changing America in general and employees in particular.

Postindustrial Society

In the last 50 years, the United States has progressed from an industrial society to a **postindustrial society.** This transition has involved four major changes:

1. **A service-oriented workforce.**
2. **A dynamic increase in the number of professional and technical workers.**
3. **An increase in the importance of theoretical knowledge.**
4. **The planning and controlling of technological growth.**

Service-Oriented Workforce

Unlike the workforce in other countries, the majority of the U.S. workforce is no longer engaged in manufacturing or agriculture; it is engaged in services. Workers in transportation, utilities, trade, finance, insurance, real estate, and government now constitute approximately two-thirds of the total workforce. The remaining one-third is in agriculture, forestry, fisheries, mining, construction, and manufacturing. To release such a large number of people from manufacturing and yet maintain our production output, we had to have made great technological advances. The result has been a dramatic change in the work environment.

Dynamic Increase in Number of Professional and Technical Workers

Another characteristic of postindustrialism is the dynamic growth in the number of workers in professional and technical occupations. In particular, the number of white-collar and service workers is increasing, whereas the number of blue-collar workers and farm workers is declining. Currently, white-collar workers constitute approximately 73.7 percent of the labor force and blue-collar workers approximately 26.3 percent (based on 2002 BLS statistics).

Increase in Importance of Theoretical Knowledge

A third characteristic of a postindustrial society is an increase in the importance of theoretical knowledge. Industrial societies are interested in the practical side of things. They concentrate on what works and ignore the rest. A postindustrial society, however, is concerned with more than just this short-run, heavily pragmatic view. For example, in hospitals today, a great deal of research is being conducted. Medical institutions are collecting all sorts of data on their patients: What is the patient's height, weight, age, gender, and religion? From what ailment is the person suffering? Can the patient's condition be traced to any variable and, if so, can we make any generalization about how people with this condition might be cured? In many cases, though the data are analyzed, no answer is found. Nevertheless, medical personnel retain this information in a computer; they do not need to find a short-run value for it. Possibly, in the future, researchers will have collected sufficient data from which to postulate a theory regarding the causes of and cures for a given ailment. This theoretical knowledge is accumulated to serve as a foundation for projecting and planning for the future. A postindustrial society is more future-oriented than were its predecessors.

Planning and Controlling Technological Growth

The fourth characteristic of a postindustrial society is an attempt to plan and control technological growth. When we examine the first three characteristics of a postindustrial society, we realize that it is an environment totally different from anything we have seen. It is a society in which highly educated people work in "think jobs" and in which a tremendous amount of money is spent each year on R&D, with much of the new knowledge being stored for future use. What will the year 2010 look like? The prospect scares many people and helps account for the fact that planning and control have now become important considerations. After all, if we fail to attend to monitoring our technological environment and deciding how we want it to grow, humankind will face a truly uncertain future.

Technology at Work

LEARNING OBJECTIVE

③ *Discuss the effect of technology on organizational culture*

As the external environment changes, the environment within organizations alters as well. Technology permeates the organization's boundaries, affecting not only the structure but also the personnel. It has an effect on people at work for two reasons.

- **Technology is causing a change in people's values, which workers bring with them to the workplace.**
- **Technology is leading to changes in the work environment, from the machines people use in creating output and making decisions to the way in which workers' offices and workstations are designed.**

YOUR JOB AND YOU

This quiz is designed to examine the relationship you have with your job. How comfortable do you feel doing your work? What role is played by technology? After you read each statement, try to be as candid as possible in your answer. Interpretations are provided at the end of the chapter.

	Highly Disagree	Disagree	Indifferent	Agree	Highly Agree
1. Although you have certain things you have to do every workday or workweek, you set the pace at which you work; management simply judges you on whether you have reached your overall objectives.	___	___	___	___	___
2. Basically, you do the same thing day after day, and the work is downright dull.	___	___	___	___	___
3. Your job is mentally challenging; it requires rigorous thought.	___	___	___	___	___
4. Your job is meaningless; anyone could do it and, to be quite frank, you are embarrassed when someone asks what you do for a living.	___	___	___	___	___
5. On your job, you feel extremely tense and anxious, even though you may not know why.	___	___	___	___	___
6. There is virtually no chance for you to socialize on your job.	___	___	___	___	___
7. No matter how fast you work, there is always more to do; you can never finish.	___	___	___	___	___
8. Your work environment is a very comfortable, enjoyable place; it is relaxing and encourages high productivity.	___	___	___	___	___
9. Your job requires a variety of skills, and people in the organization admit that it takes real talent to do what you do.	___	___	___	___	___
10. Face it, on your job you are a small cog in a big machine; if you cannot master the latest technology, the organization will find someone who can.	___	___	___	___	___

In analyzing this people–work environment–technology interface, we will consider five areas:

1. Changing organizational cultures.
2. Alienation in the workplace.
3. Workers' fear of replacement by machines.
4. How workers feel about their jobs.
5. The quality of one's work life.

Before reading further, however, take the quiz in the Time Out box.

Organizational culture *is the environment in which people work.*

Changing Organizational Cultures

When new technology is introduced to an enterprise, some change in the organization's culture often occurs. **Organizational culture** is the environment in which people work. When this environment changes, people must learn to adapt. For example, a decision by a manufacturing firm to bring in robots and streamline production will have an effect on employees. Even if no one is let go, some people will have to learn new jobs, and the overall manufacturing process will change the way that many workers interact. Technological change often affects the cultural match.

Cultural match is the similarity between individual and organizational culture. **Individual culture** is the norms, attitudes, values, and beliefs that a person brings to the job. These can vary from the type of work philosophy to which one adheres (how hard people should work) to their willingness to take risks (high, moderate, or low) to their desire for power and control (high or low). Effective enterprises exhibit a cultural match between the organization and the individual culture. Simply put, people fit into the enterprise. However, when new technology is introduced, a mismatch between the organizational and individual cultures can occur.

A good way of explaining this problem is by first examining typical organizational culture profiles. Table 6.1 describes the four most common cultures. Notice that organizational culture

Cultural match *is the similarity between individual and organizational culture.* **Individual culture** *is the norms, attitudes, values, and beliefs that a person brings to the job.*

TABLE 6.1 *Organizational Culture Profiles*				
	Tough-Guy, Macho	**Work Hard–Play Hard**	**Bet-Your-Company**	**Process**
Risk assumed	High	Low	High	Low
Feedback from decision	Fast	Fast	Slow	Slow
Organizations that often have this kind of culture	Construction, TV, radio, management consulting	Retail sales, auto distribution, real estate	Capital goods, aerospace, investment banks, military	Banks, insurance companies, many government agencies
How successful people in this culture behave	Have a tough attitude, are individualistic, can live with all-or-nothing decisions	Are friendly, supersales types, work well in groups	Can stand long-term ambiguity, are technically competent, check and recheck their decisions	Are very cautious, always follow accepted procedures, are good at taking care of details
Strengths of successful people in this culture	Can get a lot done in a short period	Are able to produce a great deal of work quickly	Can generate high-quality inventions and major scientific breakthroughs	Bring order and system to the workplace
Weaknesses of successful people in this culture	Are short-run in orientation, ignore the benefits of cooperation	Look for quick-fix solutions, are more interested in action than in problem solving	Are slow in getting things done, cannot adjust well to short-term changes	Initiative is discouraged, lots of red tape, work is often boring
Habits of successful people in this culture	Dress in fashion, live in "in" places, enjoy one-to-one sports such as tennis	Avoid extremes in dress, prefer team sports such as softball	Dress according to hierarchical rank, enjoy sports such as golf in which outcome is unclear until the end of the game	Dress according to hierarchical rank, enjoy process sports such as swimming and jogging

Source: Terrence E. Deal and Allan A. Kennedy, Corporate Cultures *(Reading, MA: Addison-Wesley Publishing Co., 1982), chapter 6.*

can be described in terms of two characteristics: risk taking and feedback. In some organizations, success depends on the ability to take risks, whereas in others, success is achieved with low risks. In some successful organizations, feedback on results is very rapid, whereas in others it is very slow. Individuals who work in an organization for an extended period learn to adjust to its culture.

Technological modifications that cause a change in the need to assume risk or obtain feedback can cause problems for employees. For example, many banks and insurance companies have faced increased competition in recent years. As a result, they have been forced to assume increased risks. Those individuals who do not like increased risk have been compelled to leave the enterprise. Similarly, technology in these organizations has increased the amount of feedback regarding the outcome of decisions and thus changed the culture. The old way of doing business is becoming outdated, and personnel must adjust to a new culture.

Providing information to the appropriate people, when needed is vital in many companies. For example Oregon Health & Sciences University in Portland, a leading teaching hospital and dental clinic, is converting data from two hundred different software application packages, many of which where unable to communicate with each other, into Oracle's simplified, streamline software program. The Oracle system will provide more timely patient information where needed within OHSU. The job of John Kenagy, the hospital's chief information officer, is to keep tract of the patient's records from time of admittance through billing. With the new system, the patient's records are available in the department where the patient is being examined. Streamlining business software for OHSU has been a complex process, costing $25 million, $10 million more than originally planned. Data integration and software simplification are changing the environment and culture in businesses.[26]

The way products are developed and the way business is conducted have changed dramatically at Oracle. The company has reduced its products from one hundred fifty to one. A team's success is now measured in terms of how well integrated its product is with what the customer wants, not on how many different products the team can develop. "According to the latest CIO survey from Morgan Stanley, every CIO is looking to reduce the number of vendors they work with." Oracle feels this message plays to their strength. Oracle willingly changes it culture to meet market needs.[27]

Another good example is provided by Ford Motor Company, which has been working to change its culture and become more productive. In doing so, the firm is trying to influence its managers to act more like owners and entrepreneurs and to make decisions that will cut costs and increase output. As a result, it has created "100-day projects" that are designed to produce rapid results. One of these projects involved cutting the costs for sending engineers from headquarters on extended assignments at factory startups. The group ended up renting apartments for the engineers, thus saving the cost of hotels, and giving the engineers company pool cars rather than rental vehicles. The net result was a savings of almost $500,000 annually.[28]

Although Ford is cutting costs, the company is learning how difficult it can be to change "old ways" to "new ways" and operate in an ever-changing environment to satisfy customers' wants and needs. After four years, it still ranks forty-three out of sixty companies in a Harris Interactive Inc. ranking of the best and worst reputations among American corporations. Karen Yvonne Hardin, a Ford truck owner, says after experiencing problems that, "Quality must be job one. Saying it isn't enough."[29]

The biggest challenge for most firms is being able to alter their culture and thus deal with environmental changes. Researchers have found that companies that are able to do this often achieve significant bottom-line results. For example, one group of researchers reported that over an eleven-year period, firms with cultures that accommodated change performed significantly better than did their counterparts who did not accommodate change, including the following accomplishments:

1. **Increasing revenues by an average of 682 percent, as compared with 166 percent for other firms.**
2. **Expanding their workforces by 282 percent, versus 36 percent for the others.**
3. **Achieving stock price increases of 901 percent, versus 74 percent for the others.**
4. **Improving net income by 756 percent, versus 1 percent for the others.[30]**

Enterprises that introduce technology to stay competitive must also ensure that the organizational culture will accommodate these changes. Otherwise, the personnel are likely to feel alienated by what is happening around them.

LEARNING OBJECTIVE

④ Identify and describe four ways employees feel alienated by technology

Technology and Alienation

Of all the behavioral implications of technology, the most important seems to be that of alienation. This concept incorporates (1) powerlessness, (2) meaninglessness, (3) isolation, and (4) self-estrangement.

Powerlessness

Many workers feel they are at the mercy of technology. Their sense of **powerlessness** can lead to alienation. Workers on the assembly line, for example, remain at their stations and the work comes to them. If the line is moving very fast, they must work faster to accommodate it. At the Westinghouse Air Brake Company's factory, a shrill buzzer erupts every two minutes and twenty-six seconds, a signal that the conveyor that carries parts down the line is about to move and everyone must hurry to keep up. Commenting on the activities of one worker, a reporter wrote:

> Gliding between machines, the [worker] is a blur of motion, snapping up a finished part and plopping it on the conveyor as it lurches forward. If he doesn't feed the conveyor each time it moves, he risks hindering the next worker down the line.
> Speed is just part of it. In traditional factories, workers often are assigned to run single machines, churning out huge batches of parts. But this is no traditional plant. [This worker's] job requires him to juggle the operation of three different machines simultaneously while also checking regularly for defects in finished items. The idea is to fill every moment of his 10-hour workday with only the most effective motion. The result is a hyper-productive workday.[31]

Moreover, every worker at the plant is motivated to hustle, because there is $1.50-per-hour bonus if the plant makes its daily production quota. Therefore, although the workers may feel they are powerless, they are willing to accept this condition because the bonus can mean an additional $3,750 annually.

Meaninglessness

Many employees are unable to determine what they are doing or why they are doing it. Individuals who put a bolt on a widget, assemble two minor parts of a major system, or test a component that will be placed in a giant machine feel no relationship with the finished product. Technology helps to create this **meaninglessness** through its emphasis on job specialization, as in assembly-line work. How do workers adapt to these conditions? Some simply fail to show up for work. It is not uncommon to find assembly plants with staff shortages when the hunting season opens. Those who do show up for work often spend a large percentage of their workday playing mental games (doing multiplication tables in their mind) or daydreaming.

Isolation

On the job, people cannot run away from technology. If only to keep up with the competition, it is a part of their work life. Here, then, the individual is locked in, forced to cope with technology. However, **isolation** still occurs in many cases, for the person is often confined to one locale, as in the case of a worker on an automobile assembly line who must remain at a particular place on the line for the entire workday; a computer operator who must stay near the machine, checking on jobs being run and remaining alert for any machine malfunctions; a press operator who is confined to the general area of the printing press, constantly observing the speed and feed of the paper, prepared to adjust or stop the machine should something go awry; or an individual

Powerlessness *is a feeling of being at the mercy of technology.*

Meaninglessness *is the feeling of doing work that has no personal value.*

Isolation *occurs when people are confined to one particular work locale.*

working at home who has no opportunity for face-to-face contact with coworkers or customers. All these people are isolated within a given area and, depending on the specific situation, isolated from other workers. At best, the technology allows them to interact only with those in their immediate vicinity; at worst, the demands of the job sometimes prevent them from associating with anyone for extended periods of the workday. This is particularly true for those workers who are continually on the road. These "mobile workers" report that it is difficult to balance work demands and home demands. Two of them discussed the disadvantages of this work form as follows:

> "[When I was mobile, I was] always away from my family. Lots of travel. I put on 20,000 miles on my car [in less than one year]. Just trying to communicate with . . . many people is very difficult. Just the fact that I was always traveling I think was frustrating . . . being away from my family, [and always] in hotels."
>
> "Well, I don't know that I personally derive any benefit. I gain freeway time. I gain less face time with individuals. My travel time goes up. I have the ability to access information anywhere I'm at. Personally, the only way that it affects me is that I have to spend more time driving and I have less time to see people face to face."[32]

Self-Estrangement

Self-estrangement occurs when the worker can no longer find intrinsic satisfaction in what he or she is doing: The work becomes merely a means to earn a living. No fun or challenge is associated with it. If another job offered more money, the worker would quit. Technology creates self-estrangement by reducing the scope and importance of the work itself. As we saw in chapter 2 when we discussed Herzberg's two-factor theory, the things people liked best about their jobs were related to the work itself: Intrinsic motivators, such as achievement, responsibility, and the possibility of growth, were part of the job. Technology eliminates many of these.

(5) Fear of Replacement by Machines

The workers' fear that machines will replace them is another problem created by technology. This fear is typical among people who are not highly skilled or who are performing paperwork functions, such as checking forms, filling out structured reports, or entering data in accounting ledgers.

Consider, for example, Inco. Ltd., a nickel producer, turned to high technology to cut the cost of its mining operations. Today the firm uses remote-controlled tractors to extract nickel and copper ore at twenty-six hundred feet below ground. The thirty-ton machines are controlled from a ground-level office where an operator directs the machine in scooping, transporting, and depositing the ore. At present, only 2 percent of the company's mining operations are handled via remote control, but soon most of these operations will be computer-operated. In the process, mining jobs at the firm will be cut by more than 20 percent. Other firms in the industry hope to cut even more workers, thanks to modern technology. For example, Noranda Inc. has an automatic guiding system similar to Inco's but that uses tractors guided by sensors placed on each machine's scoop. These sensors tell the scoop what to pick up and where to move it. As a result, a computer operator is not needed to direct the tractor's operations. Someday, perhaps, underground miners will be totally replaced by machines.[33]

Although technology is inevitable, methods exist for dealing with it from a human relations standpoint. The Human Relations in Action box describes some of these methods.

How Workers Feel About Their Jobs

Despite the feelings of alienation that workers have in their jobs, the effect of technology can be effectively addressed, and many employees now report that they like their work better than they have at any point in the recent past. In fact, a recent national survey conducted by *Inc.*

in action

HUMAN RELATIONS IN ACTION

Dealing with Technology

Technology is making many jobs easier. At the same time, it may cause concern among personnel who are convinced that computers, robots, or some other form of advanced technology will replace them. Nothing can be done to prevent the advance of technology. However, some human relations steps can be followed to help with the personnel challenge. Five of the most useful steps follow:

1. *Become familiar with the jobs your people are doing.* This has two benefits. First, if new technology is to be introduced, you will have a fairly good idea of what it can do. Second, most workers object to any changes that are likely to lead to their being displaced. If you understand how their jobs work, you are in a better position to help them confront this problem.

2. *Be aware of the negative impact technology can have.* When people become adjuncts of the machines they operate, their self-esteem and job satisfaction often drop. You cannot help your people deal with this problem until you realize it is a common response to technology. It does no good to tell a person that his or her job is interesting if he or she does not see it that way. Try to empathize with those who are most affected by the impact of technology. Then you will be better able to help them to adjust.

3. *Get worker input regarding how to use technology.* This is one of the most effective ways of introducing work changes. The personnel often have good ideas for using new machinery and equipment; after all, they are the ones who do the job. If any shortcuts can be worked out or any problems will arise in making the machine do what it is supposed to, the workers will find them. There is no better source for evaluating job technology than the workers themselves.

4. *Keep your people apprised of what is going on.* If you and your boss have been talking about putting in new automated machinery, tell this to the workers as soon as the decision is made. If you wait until the machines are delivered, the impact of the change will cause panic. You need to introduce change slowly. Sure, some of the workers may accuse you of trying to undermine their jobs and may threaten to quit. However, most of the workers know that it is your job to maintain high productivity and, if new machines are needed, they will have to be purchased.

5. *Be honest with your people.* Some workers will be displaced by new technology. This is particularly true of those who do simple jobs or those who are unable to learn new work procedures. In many cases, these people will be able to obtain work elsewhere in the organization. If this is not possible, be open with them and tell them they are going to be laid off. No one likes to give people this kind of news, but it is better to be honest with them so that they can make plans than to keep them in the dark until the last minute. The way you treat workers who are being let go will influence the morale and trust of those who remain in the department. Honesty is always the best policy.

---

magazine found new levels of job satisfaction among American employees. Some of these findings include the following:

1. More than 70 percent of the respondents said that they were either satisfied or extremely satisfied with their place of employment, and this satisfaction was highest in small firms.

2. When asked whether they have the opportunity every day to do what they do best, 82 percent said yes; and a similar percentage reported that their supervisor or someone at work seemed to care about them as a person.

3. Eighty-six percent reported that their fellow workers were committed to doing quality work, and 84 percent said that they, themselves, had opportunities at work to learn and to grow.

4. Ninety-seven percent said they knew what was expected of them on the job, and 87 percent reported that they had the materials and equipment needed to do their work properly.

5. Seventy-four percent said that they had been recognized by their employer for their contributions; 69 percent reported that they had been compensated fairly in the past year; and 55 percent said that they intended to stay with their current employer until they retired.[34]

These statistics clearly show that many people in the workplace are satisfied with their jobs and are committed to doing good work. However, this does not mean that all workplace issues related to technology have been resolved. In fact, quality of work life (QWL) continues to be a major challenge facing organizations.

The Issue of Quality of Work Life

A major sociotechnical issue is the quality of work life. QWL is concerned with the overall work climate, with specific emphasis on the effect of the work environment on organizational effectiveness, health, and worker satisfaction. The concern for reducing ergonomic-related injuries and illnesses in the workplace has generated attention at the Occupational Safety and Health Administration. As a result, the National Advisory Committee on Ergonomics (NACE) was established and chartered for a two-year term to focus on ergonomic issues. Its purpose is to develop ergonomic guidelines and presentations on enforcement, outreach, and research issues. Its first committee met on January 22, 2003.[35]

Ergonomics
is concerned with redesigning the physical environment to meet the needs of personnel.

One of the primary areas of attention is **ergonomics,** which is concerned with designing and shaping the physical work environment to fit the physical abilities and characteristics of individuals. A good example is the way in which organizations now redesign the work office so that accomplishing tasks is easier. For example, one ergonomics expert has noted that office chairs should be tested carefully to ensure that they are comfortable and do not detract from productivity. In choosing the best chair, she suggests this procedure:

1. Sit down. Does the chair welcome you? Does it support your legs and back comfortably?
2. Check the height. Your feet should be flat on the floor or on a footrest. Tilt the seat back. Are your feet still flat?
3. Lean back. A good chair gives your lower back a solid hug.
4. Check your hands. As you rest them at keyboard level, they should be in a straight line with your forearm, and your elbow should be bent at a right angle.
5. Test the seat cushion. It should be well padded to prevent fatigue.
6. Wiggle around. Lean forward as if composing a letter. Lean back and think. Sit upright, as though facing a computer. Put your feet up, if that's a position you prefer. Is the chair still comfortable?
7. Stay a while. Are you still at ease? That's your chair.[36]

Another ergonomics-related issue relates to the amount of time people spend in front of video display terminals (VDTs) in the workplace. Some municipalities now have guidelines that regulate the workplace and are designed to prevent such problems as VDT-attributable diseases and injuries associated with continuously striking computer keyboards. Until recently, San Francisco companies with more than fifteen employees were required to make the workplace more ergonomically correct. Employees using VDTs were to be given a fifteen-minute break or transferred to another job after working at their terminals for two hours. The San Francisco law, which also mandated that certain kinds of furniture and equipment be supplied to workers to aid them with ergonomically related problems, was struck down in court. Nonetheless, ergonomics continues to be a QWL issue.

Still other areas of concern include lighting, heating, and ventilation, as well as office layout. In each case, the focus is on designing the workplace so that it is comfortable and conducive to productivity. Some companies now allow their personnel to wear a personal audiotape or compact disk device so that they can listen to music while they work. Especially for workers whose jobs entail repetitive tasks, such as mail sorting or simple assembly, the music provides employees with a way of dealing with the boredom.[37]

Another QWL issue is the amount of authority and participation workers have in the decision-making process. For example, employees who work with large-batch or mass-production technology have the highest reported levels of alienation. However, these workers also seem to be at a loss in determining what can be done.

When managers and workers have formed QWL committees, employees have not been very actively supportive of the committees' work. Many workers distrust these types of joint committees, believing that, in the long run, the only change will be to speed up the assembly line. A number of managers also believe that these committees are of no real value.

What, then, is the answer in dealing with sociotechnical problems? One part of the solution is the use of job enrichment and other redesign techniques, which are discussed in the next chapter. Another part of the answer must be found in the industrial environment itself. In many European countries, industrial democracy is used. In the United States, participative management is more prevalent. Both offer possibilities for meeting the sociotechnical challenge.

Meeting the Sociotechnical Challenge

The dysfunctional effects of technology can be traced, in large part, to the fears it creates among employees. Human relations management requires that the employees' interests be considered and protected by management. (See the Ethics and Social Responsibility in Action box.) Workers need

in action

ETHICS AND SOCIAL RESPONSIBILITY IN ACTION

Selling Them on It

Technology can have negative as well as positive effects on employees. For this reason, management has a social responsibility to employees to ensure technology-based changes are introduced properly. Although a wide variety of steps can be taken, five of the most important are the following:

1. *Let everyone know about the new technological changes that will be taking place.* If new machinery is going to be introduced, explain why these machines are important and stress the fact that employees will be trained to use these units. This step involves "telling and selling.

2. *Introduce the system to the right people first.* Many organizations start off by introducing computerized word-processing systems at the secretarial level. However, it often is more effective first to acquaint middle management with the technology, because this will help win their support for the change. Then, with middle management solidly behind the new system, the machines can be introduced to the secretarial staff. If there is any friction regarding the change, middle management will voice its support and work to sell its people on the need for the new technology.

3. *Be sure the new technology works as promised before introducing it.* If a computer manufacturer says the new personal computers can all be linked to the company's mainframe and used for analysis of centralized records, be sure these claims are backed up. If something goes wrong after the system is installed, convincing people to accept the technology after the corrections have been made will be much more difficult.

4. *Once the new system is up and working, get rid of the old system.* Some companies that have introduced computers started out by making them available for use while leaving the old systems in place. However, they have also given everyone computer training and set a deadline for scrapping the old system. As they begin to master the new technology, employees voluntarily abandon the old system, although it is there in the beginning should the workers encounter problems and need to fall back on a system they understand. Once the old system is scrapped, there is no going back. From that point, only the new system is used.

5. *Be sure the training is hands-on and useful.* Sometimes training involves the teaching of theory, but this should not be given precedence over teaching employees how to use the machines for day-to-day operations. Once the workers master the new technology, they will use it. It's all a matter of getting them to see the value of the new system.

to feel confident that ultimately they will gain from technology. In other words, a supportive climate must exist between employees and management. If this climate can be created, workers will be more receptive to the changes being thrust on them by technology. This is now leading to the development of knowledge-based organizations and the use of industrial democracy and participative management, as well as the creation of programs designed to deal with workplace violence.

LEARNING OBJECTIVE

Explain how knowledge-based organizations, industrial democracy, and participative management can aid in integrating technology and the organization's personnel

⑥ Development of Knowledge-Based Organizations

Technology is radically changing the way organizations are managed. In the past, organizations provided the tools and equipment and some on-the-job training, and the workers were expected to do the rest. Today, technology is making far greater demands on both groups, and each must be prepared to change. Many employees have limited skills and training for meeting current job demands. In management, resource-based organizations are now being replaced by knowledge-based organizations, requiring managers to change their approach to leading the personnel.

One way in which organizations are meeting the sociotechnical challenge that faces employees is by retooling these workers. Some of this training is technical in nature and includes such subjects as just-in-time production, reliability engineering, and statistical sampling. Some of it is behavioral in content and focuses on ways of dealing more effectively with others. In both cases, the training is heavily practical and hands-on and is designed to equip the worker with tools and techniques that can be used for dealing with day-to-day problems.

In the past, colleges and universities provided a great deal of this training. A production worker would be sent to a local community college to study basic electronics; a middle manager would attend a nearby university and learn some of the latest techniques of just-in-time inventory control; a senior-level manager would be sent to Harvard University's thirteen-week Advanced Management Program to learn about new management developments. Today, however, many firms are bringing their training in-house and creating their own colleges and universities. For example, General Electric has a corporate university at Crotonville, New York, where managers from throughout the firm attend specially designed courses taught by in-house personnel and outside consultants. Motorola University in Schaumberg, Illinois, annually trains thousands of corporate personnel, suppliers, and vendors in a wide variety of technical and managerial subjects. And, in some cases, people do not go to a training site; rather, the training comes to them.

> *Federal Express provides a dramatic illustration of education that is not restricted by place. The company spent almost $70 million to create an automated education system. Annually, it spends almost 5 percent of payroll to enhance learning among its 40,000 couriers and customer service agents through the use of interactive video disks (IVDs). Federal Express owns 1,225 IVD units in 700 locations. At each location, the curriculum is housed on 20 to 25 video disks (the equivalent of 37,500 floppy disks) and is updated monthly. Each employee receives four hours of company-paid study and preparation in addition to two hours of self-administered tests every six months.*[38]

A **resource-based organization** *focuses on providing needed physical assets.* A **knowledge-based organization** *relies on information sharing, teamwork, trust, and empowerment.*

Recently, Federal Express and Motorola united to develop the FedEx PowerPad designed to enhance customer service by providing forty thousand FedEx Express couriers with online, near real-time, wireless access to the FedEx network. The FedEx PowerPad enhanced and accelerated "package information available to customers by enabling couriers to wirelessly send and receive near real-time information and updates from any location." This replaced the handheld courier FedEx Supertracker.[39]

Such developments are helping to ensure that workers are able to adjust to the new high-tech environment. At the same time, managers are adapting their approach to meet emerging changes. Whereas managers once functioned in a **resource-based organization,** in which the company provided the necessary tools, equipment, and direction and the employees used these resources to pursue predetermined goals, today managers are operating in a **knowledge-based organization,**

TABLE 6.2	Resource-Based Organizations and Knowledge-Based Organizations	
Job	**Resource-Based Organization**	**Knowledge-Based Organization**
Overall direction	Set by top management	Set by top management but shared by all employees
Planning and decision making	Top management sets the plan and everyone else works on implementing it	Planning and decision making take place at all levels in a well-coordinated, teamwork fashion
Problem solving	Employees analyze the situation, formulate a solution, and then convince others to accept their approach	Through the use of collaboration, cooperation, and the integration of diverse points of view, a solution is formulated that is acceptable to all involved parties
Conflict resolution	The person with the most power bends the others to his or her way of thinking	There is a dialogue and integration of many points of view in deciding how to resolve the conflict
Motivation	Managers get things done by offering rewards that are desired by employees	Managers get things done by offering challenges that are personally acceptable to the employees
Leadership	Top leadership creates a vision for the organization and sells it to the employees	Top leadership creates a vision for the organization that incorporates employee values and beliefs, and the personnel willingly accept and follow this vision
Organizing	Management designs a structure that ensures that everyone knows his or her job and has the necessary authority for carrying out these tasks	Management empowers employees with sufficient resources and knowledge so that they fulfill their jobs with the least amount of bureaucracy or red tape
Controlling	Management sets up checkpoints to monitor employee performance and prevent problems from getting out of hand	Management trains the employees to use self-control to monitor their performance and ensure that work output meets all quality standards

in which information sharing, teamwork, trust, and empowerment are key characteristics. Table 6.2 contrasts these two organizations and helps to illustrate why a new management orientation is necessary. In this emerging environment, industrial democracy and participative management are playing increasingly important roles.

Use of Industrial Democracy and Participative Management

Two major trends in management-worker relations over the last twenty-five years are those of industrial democracy and participative management. Both involve shared decision making between workers and management. However, despite their similarity of intent, fundamental differences exist between the methods of each of these trends. **Industrial democracy** is a formal and usually legally sanctioned arrangement of worker representation in the form of committees, councils, and boards at various levels of decision making. **Participative management,** on the other hand, is an informal style of face-to-face leadership in which management and workers share decision making in the workplace. It is sometimes called *shop-floor democracy.* Some countries of the world make more use of one method than the other.

GERMANY

In Germany, for example, companies with more than five hundred workers have supervisory boards that set company policy. These boards are made up of two-thirds shareholder representatives and one-third worker representatives. Firms with more than two thousand employees have 50 percent worker representation on these boards. By law, industrial democracy is a way

Industrial democracy
is a formal sanctioning of worker representation in the decision-making process.
Participative management
is an informal style of face-to-face leadership in which the workers share decision-making authority.

of life in Germany. German workers also have much more operating authority than do American workers. For example, the workers are allowed to rotate jobs to prevent the work from becoming boring. Some firms even allow their workers to vary the number of hours they work throughout the year. They can work less during some months as long as they work more during other months.

One of the primary reasons for the high degree of participative management in Germany is that the unions and management have a much more cooperative relationship than in the United States. The two sides try to work out their differences in a way that is beneficial to both.[40]

SCANDINAVIA

In the Scandinavian countries—Norway, Sweden, and Denmark—statutory requirements are established for worker representation on governing boards. For example, for almost forty years, Sweden has required that companies with more than fifty employees maintain work councils made up of representatives of both management and labor who meet regularly to solve problems and exchange information.

However, Scandinavians also lead the way in terms of shop-floor democracy. In some of their factories, autonomous work groups have been introduced. These groups have decision-making discretion that allows them to determine for themselves how to do their jobs. Their range of authority often extends from the receipt of orders to final inspection. These groups consist of councils and committees that have been formed to encourage employee involvement in identifying and implementing changes that will improve workplace ambience and help sustain high morale and positive employee attitudes.

BRITAIN

The United Kingdom and Ireland are the only countries in the European community that do not have statutory requirements for information dissemination, consultation, or worker representation on boards. However, this appears to be changing. Current legislative efforts are likely to require that firms with more than five hundred people discuss with their trade union representatives all major proposals affecting workers. The government also believes that employees should have a right to representation on the boards of their companies. Some organizations already are moving to meet these recommendations. For example, the post office has expanded its board of directors from seven to nineteen. Seven of the representatives are from management, seven are trade union members, two are independents chosen from a list submitted by the government minister responsible for the post office, two are members who represent the consumers' interests, and the last is a chief executive from the management side.

UNITED STATES

In the United States, both participative management and industrial democracy have developed. Participative management—if only because of the American traditions of individualism and democracy—has always been very popular. However, industrial democracy is also gaining in importance.

One of the primary reasons for these developments is that they help organizations tap the brainpower of their employees by getting people involved in planning and implementing new ideas. Here are some examples:

- **At Motorola's engineering, manufacturing, and marketing departments, people work together to design and build new products and deliver them to market. As a result, the total time needed for bringing many products to fruition has been reduced from seventy-two months to eighteen months.**
- **At Pioneer Hi-Bred International, scientists breed special strains of corn for disease resistance, high yield, or specific attributes such as oil content. A decade ago, such work ate up hundreds of acres of farmland and consumed untold numbers of worker hours. These days, the plant's DNA is manipulated in a petri dish. Apart from the cost savings, the company expects to knock two years off the seven to ten years that it takes to develop a new hybrid.**

At the heart of participative management and industrial democracy is the concept of **empowerment,** the process of giving employees control over decisions and policies that directly affect them. One reason empowerment tends to work is because it increases motivation. Even if people have power, they must feel they have the power or there is no gain. "People must feel they control their own destiny if they are to be part of a change effort, provide excellent service, or take risks."[41] Over the last ten years, this idea has become very popular. The basic ideas of empowerment include:

- **Giving employees greater authority to make decisions.**
- **Maintaining an open and decentralized communication system.**
- **Drawing on people from many different departments to solve complex organizational problems.**
- **Rewarding and recognizing those who assume responsibility and perform well.**

A survey conducted by the Gallup Organization for the American Society for Quality Control found that workers in small businesses feel they have more authority to take action than those at large companies, and are more likely to believe management would approve. One finding shows that 90 percent of the workers in small businesses versus 80 percent of workers in large businesses say they can stop work in progress to correct a problem.[42]

Dealing with Workplace Violence

Workplace violence is any physical assault, threatening behavior, or verbal abuse occurring in the work setting.[43] In recent years, an upsurge of such violence has occurred, some of which is directly attributable to technology. Moreover, workplace violence is much more common than many people realize. A recent study by the Northwestern National Life Insurance Company found that workplace violence affects one in four employees.[44] Sometimes this violence results in homicide and, as seen in Table 6.3, public transportation and retail establishments are high

TABLE 6.3	Homicide Rates in the Workplace	
Workplace	**Number**	**Rate***
Taxicab establishments	287	26.9
Liquor stores	115	8.0
Gas stations	304	5.6
Detective and protective services	152	5.0
Justice and public-order establishments	640	3.4
Grocery stores	806	3.2
Jewelry stores	56	3.2
Hotels and motels	153	1.5
Eating and drinking establishments	734	1.5

*Per 100,000 workers per year.
Source: National Institute for Occupational Safety and Health, 1999.

on the list of businesses that face this risk. Commenting on this, the Occupational Safety and Health Administration recently reported that:

> Workplace violence has emerged as an important safety and health issue in today's workplace. Its most extreme form, homicide, is the third leading cause of fatal occupational injury in the United States. According to the BLS [Bureau of Labor Statistics] Census of Fatal Occupational Injuries . . . there were 674 workplace homicides in 2000, accounting for 11% of the total 5,915 fatal work injuries in the United States. [45, 46]

Most common were simple assaults—1.5 million a year, followed by aggravated assaults, rapes and sexual assaults, robberies and homicides.

Examples of workplace violence include: [47]

- **Verbal threats to inflict bodily harm; including vague of covert threats.**
- **Attempting to cause physical harm; striking, pushing, and other aggressive physical acts against another person.**
- **Verbal harassment; abusive or offensive language, gestures, or other discourteous conduct toward supervisors, fellow employees, or the public.**
- **Disorderly conduct, such as shouting, throwing or pushing objects, punching walls, and slamming doors.**
- **Making false, malicious, or unfounded statements against coworkers, supervisors, or subordinates which tend to damage their reputations or undermine their authority.**
- **Inappropriate remarks, such as making delusional statements.**
- **Fascination with guns or other weapons, bring weapons into the workplace.**

These acts can be extremely upsetting to those who feel that their rights in the workplace are being violated. Fortunately, many organizations are now taking proactive steps to reduce and, it is hoped, eliminate this problem. Work practice controls affect the way jobs or tasks are performed. OSHA has recommended some engineering and administrative controls to help prevent and mitigate the effects of workplace violence. They include: [48]

- **Physical barriers such as bullet-resistant enclosures or shields, pass-through windows, or deep service counters.**
- **Alarm systems, panic buttons, global positioning systems (GPS), and radios ("open mike switch").**
- **Convex mirrors, elevated vantage points, clear visibility of service and cash register areas.**
- **Bright and effective lighting.**
- **Adequate staffing.**
- **Arrange furniture to prevent entrapment.**
- **Cash-handling controls, use of drop safes.**
- **Height markers on exit doors.**
- **Emergency procedures to use in case of robbery.**
- **Training in identifying hazardous situations and appropriate responses in emergencies.**
- **Video surveillance equipment, in-car surveillance cameras, and closed-circuit TV.**
- **Establish liaison with local police.**

An effective violence prevention program should include postincident response and evaluation. All workplace violence programs should provide treatment for victimized and traumatized employees and witnesses. The types of assistance may include: traumacrisis counseling, critical incident stress debriefing, or employee assistance programs to assist victims.[49]

BEHAVIOR OF THE INDIVIDUALS

One way in which enterprises are trying to reduce workplace violence is by screening people during the job selection process or the probationary period that follows. Although identifying the behavior of those who are prone to violence is sometimes difficult, many such people tend to exhibit specific types of behavior. Among these are:

- *Belligerence*—walking around with a chip on one's shoulder, ready to argue or quarrel with others at the slightest excuse.
- *Excessive moodiness*—spells of the blues, or feeling down in the dumps a great deal of the time.
- *Exaggerated worry*—continuous anxiety about small matters that are blown entirely out of proportion.
- *Suspiciousness and mistrust*—a persistent feeling that the world is full of dishonest, conniving people who are trying to take advantage of them.
- *Helplessness and dependency*—a tendency to let others carry the burden, while exhibiting problems with making decisions.
- *Poor emotional control*—exaggerated emotional outbursts that are inappropriate or out of proportion to the cause.
- *Daydreaming and fantasy*—spending a good part of the day imagining how things could be rather than dealing with them the way they are.
- *Hypochondria*—worrying a great deal of the time about minor physical ailments or experiencing imaginary symptoms of illness.[50]

These behaviors often are very costly to employers. They can result in substandard production, poor morale, excessive labor problems, unnecessarily high labor turnover, and excessive absenteeism. The behaviors can also affect other employees, who do not want to be around these individuals and who find that they cannot get their work done efficiently because of the environment that is created by the emotional problems of these individuals.

DEALING WITH THE ISSUE

Companies are now developing a variety of programs to help them deal with workplace violence.

- One such initiative is to place all workers in positions that best employ their skills. In this way, the individuals feel that they are doing meaningful work and are an important asset.
- A second program calls for providing clear job descriptions and supportive supervision, so that everyone knows what she or he is supposed to be doing and receives any help and guidance required. This approach is particularly beneficial in reducing the anger and hostility that result when people find themselves frustrated or stymied on the job.
- A third initiative is to recognize and value cultural diversity among employees at all levels of the enterprise so that each person feels that he or she is a part of the group rather than an outsider.
- A fourth approach is to conduct periodic reviews of job performance and to recognize and reward work output, thereby assuring all employees that when they do a good job, the organization will show its appreciation.
- A fifth program calls for providing reasonable job security, which affords workers the peace of mind of knowing that they will not be arbitrarily terminated and, if a cutback is needed, they will be given ample advance notice.[51]

In addition, organizations that experience high incidents of workplace violence often provide training to their people regarding how to handle various situations. For example, today's businesses commonly train supervisors to identify workers who seem to be getting out of control and to learn how to diffuse the situation before it escalates. High-risk companies often develop a series of checklist procedures that employees are to follow when confronted with an impending problem.[52]

In most cases, workplace violence is not life-threatening and, if managers or coworkers know how to handle the situation, it can be diffused without incident. The following are some steps that managers can take when dealing with an angry person:

1. **Avoid an audience. This makes the individual feel special and will avoid agitating others who may be angry.**
2. **If possible, have a second employee in the room. This gives you a witness to what occurs, and it may deter an attack.**
3. **Establish the dispute boundaries. Initially, ignore any comments that are not related to the problem. Reduce anxiety by keeping to the subject.**
4. **Listen patiently, attentively, and actively to all parties to the conflict.**
5. **Speak slowly, softly, and clearly. Slow your speech to reduce anxiety. The other person usually will mirror your pace.**
6. **Focus on behaviors, not personalities.**
7. **Make eye contact and give the angry person your full attention.**
8. **Specify acceptable behaviors and, if possible, involve the conflicting parties in the problem resolution.[53]**

An area closely related to workplace violence is stress, which has been found to promote violence, and recent research demonstrates that a growing number of workers suffer from stress. For example, a survey by Northwestern National Life found that 40 percent of the workers report their job is "very or extremely stressful." A survey by the Families and Work Institute found that 26 percent of workers report that they are "often or very often burned out or stressed by their work," and a survey by Yale University reports that approximately 30 percent of workers feel "quite a bit or extremely stressed at work.[54]

Job stress is defined by the National Institute for Occupational Safety and Health (NIOSH) as the harmful physical and emotional responses that occur when the requirements of the job do not match the capabilities, resources, or needs of the worker. Job stress can lead to poor health and even injury. The concept of job stress should not be confused with challenge. They are different. Challenge motivates workers to learn new skills and master new jobs, makes workers feel good when jobs are completed, and is an important ingredient for healthy and productive work.

NIOSH suggests that job stress results from the interaction of the worker and the conditions of work, but views differ on the importance of worker characteristics versus working conditions as the primary cause of job stress. Some believe individual characteristics such as personality and coping style are most important, while others suggest that certain working conditions, such as excessive workload demands and conflicting expectations are stressful to most people, and job redesign as a primary prevention strategy. More on job redesign will be covered in chapter 8.

"St. Paul Fire and Marine Insurance Company conducted several studies on the effects of stress prevention programs in hospital settings. In one study the frequency of medication errors declined by 50% after prevention activities were implemented in a 700-bed hospital. In a second study, there was a 70 percent reduction in malpractice claims in twenty two hospitals that implemented stress prevention activities. In contract, there was no reduction in claims in a matched group of 22 hospitals that did not implement stress prevention activities." The Bureau of Labor Statistics reports that workers who must take time off work because of stress, anxiety, or a related disorder will be off the job for about twenty days. Stress management training can help workers deal with job stress. It is reported that approximately "one-half of the large companies in the U.S. provide some type of stress management training for their workforces."

Low morale, health and job complaints, and employee turnover often provide the first signs of job stress. Although at times, there are no signs, particularly if workers are fearful of losing their jobs. The National Institute for Occupational Safety and Health (NIOSH) suggests ways to change an organization to prevent job stress.[55]

- Ensure that the workload is in line with worker's capabilities and resources.
- Design jobs to provide meaning, stimulation, and opportunities for workers to use their skills.
- Clearly define worker's roles and responsibilities.
- Give workers opportunities to participate in decisions and actions affecting their jobs.
- Improve future employment prospects.
- Provide opportunities for social interaction among workers.
- Establish work schedules that are compatible with demands and responsibilities outside the job.

A number of specific causes have been cited for this stress, including:

1. Heavy workload, infrequent rest breaks, long work hours, and shift work; hectic and routine tasks that have little inherent meaning, do not use workers' skills, and provide little sense of control.
2. Lack of participation by workers in decision making, poor communication in the organization, lack of family-friendly policies.
3. Poor social environment and lack of support or help from coworkers and supervisors.
4. Conflicting or uncertain job expectations, too much responsibility, too many "hats to wear."
5. Job insecurity and lack of opportunity for growth, advancement, or promotion; rapid changes for which workers are unprepared.
6. Unpleasant or dangerous physical conditions such as crowding, noise, air pollution, or ergonomic problems.[56]

In dealing with these problems, companies now are formulating a number of different approaches. For example, at Hewlett-Packard, personnel are encouraged to incorporate "mini-vacations" into their workday by scheduling an aerobics class at 3 P.M. or a brisk, daily walk capped off with a cappuccino. Managers help in this process by examining the amount of work their people are doing and shifting workloads when they find an imbalance. They also try to match tasks to those most capable of doing the work and communicate regularly with their people to ensure that workloads do not become onerous.[57]

summary

① **LEARNING OBJECTIVE**
Trace the evolution of technology from the handicraft era to the cybernated technology state

Technology has gone through five stages. The first was the handicraft era, in which people made things by hand. Next came the mechanization era, characterized by machine labor replacing human labor. This was followed by the mechanistic technology stage, as seen in the case of the early automobile assembly lines. Next came automated technology, in which assembly line machines were linked together in such a way that many functions were performed automatically. Currently a fifth stage, cybernated technology, is expanding, in which machines are running and controlling other machines.

These technological breakthroughs have been possible because large amounts of money are being spent annually on R&D and because more and more members of society are attaining higher levels of education. When these R&D funds and highly educated people are brought together, the result is an accelerated thrust from which more and more goods and services can be produced at an ever-increasing rate.

② LEARNING OBJECTIVE
Identify and describe the four major characteristics of a postindustrial society

The United States has entered the stage of postindustrialism, which is characterized by (1) a service-oriented workforce, which makes up approximately two-thirds of the labor force; (2) a dynamic increase in the number of professional and technical workers; (3) an increase in the importance of theoretical knowledge, not just the practical side of things; and (4) the planning and controlling of technological growth.

③ LEARNING OBJECTIVE
Discuss the effect of technology on organizational culture

In the workplace, technology has some specific effects on employees, which explains why it is important to have a cultural match between the organization and the people. Culture match finds similarity between an organization's culture—shared beliefs, customs, traditions, philosophies and norms of behavior of the organization, and an individual's culture—norms, attitudes, values, and beliefs that a person brings to the job. Technological modifications that cause a change in the need to assume risk can cause problems for employees. Companies that introduce technology to stay competitive must also ensure that the organizational culture will accommodate these changes. Otherwise, employees are likely to feel alienated by what is happening.

④ LEARNING OBJECTIVE
Identify and describe four ways employees feel alienated by technology

Technology can cause alienation in the workplace in the form of powerlessness, meaninglessness, isolation, and self-estrangement. When workers feel they are at the mercy of technology, they feel powerless. Offering incentives can help workers gain a sense of worth. Individuals have a need to know what they are doing and why they are doing it. Technology can take that away from workers and make the work seem meaningless. Unless a company strives to inform employees about their work, the employee may simply fail to show up for work or not strive to do their best on the job. Technology can isolate people. Individuals are social beings and have a need to interact with other people. It is important for companies to prove ways for employees to interact at work. This is especially true of people who are continually on the road. Technology can cause an employee to feel estranged from work. Self-estrangement occurs when the employee can no longer find intrinsic satisfaction in what he or she is doing. The work itself should provide a means for employee achievement, responsibility, and the possibility of growth.

⑤ LEARNING OBJECTIVE
Explain how technology can cause workers to fear their replacement by machines

Additionally, technology is causing some workers to fear that machines will replace them. This is particularly true among those who are not highly skilled or who are performing paperwork functions that can be handled by computers.

Despite these feelings, many workers find life in a modern factory quite livable. In particular, they like the pay and benefits and, to a large extent, seem unclear as to how the quality of work life could be improved.

LEARNING OBJECTIVE
(6) *Explain how knowledge-based organizations, industrial democracy, and participative management can aid in integrating technology and the organization's personnel*

The sociotechnical problem is being addressed through the development of knowledge-based organizations, the use of industrial democracy and the implementation of participative management practices. Technology is drastically changing the way organizations are managed. Knowledge-based organizations are retraining workers to use technology, as well as work in teams, share knowledge, trust, and use empowerment. Much of this training is being done in-house using technology driven educational program. Some companies are establishing their own colleges and universities. In this emerging environment, industrial democracy and participative management are important. In industrial democracy there is a formal sanctioning of worker representation in the decision-making process, and in participative management there is an informal style of face-to-face leadership in which workers share decision-making authority.

LEARNING OBJECTIVE
(7) *Discuss workplace violence behavior and how managers are dealing with it*

Unfortunately, violence in the workplace is growing. Workplace violence creates a safety and health issue, which, sometimes results in homicide. Organizations try to reduce workplace violence by screening people during the job selection process or the probationary period that follows. Behaviors that lead to violence can be costly to employers. To deal with workplace violence, companies are now developing a variety of programs, including training on how to handle various situations. Not only is technology a cause for workplace violence, but also stress has been identified as a cause. To help companies with workplace violence issues, NIOSH (National Institute for Occupational Safety and Health) created a list of ways organizations can reduce stress in the workplace. Effective managers strive to match tasks to those most capable of doing the work and communicate regularly with their people to ensure appropriate workloads.

KEY TERMS IN THE CHAPTER

Future shock	Meaninglessness
Handicraft era	Isolation
Mechanization era	Self-estrangement
Mechanistic technology	Ergonomics
Automated technology	Resource-based organization
Cybernated technology	Knowledge-based organization
Postindustrial society	Industrial democracy
Organizational culture	Participative management
Cultural match	Empowerment
Individual culture	Workplace violence
Powerlessness	

REVIEW AND STUDY QUESTIONS

1. How does the handicraft era differ from the mechanization era?

2. Differentiate between the mechanization era and the mechanistic technology era?

3. Compare the mechanistic technology era with the automated technology era.

4. Contrast the automated technology era with the cybernated technology era.

5. Describe the impact that research and development has had on technology.

6. What are the four characteristics of a postindustrial society? Describe each.

7. How does a tough-guy, macho culture differ from a work hard-play hard culture? Compare and contrast the two.

8. How does a bet-your-company culture differ from a process culture? Compare and contrast the two.

9. What do individuals need to understand about cultural match? How can the basic idea be used effectively? Explain.

10. How can technology cause powerlessness, meaninglessness, isolation, and self-estrangement? Discuss each condition separately.

11. How does technology lead employees to fear replacement by machines? Explain.

12. What is ergonomics? How does ergonomics affect quality of work life? Identify several examples and tell how you, as a manager, would deal with each issue.

13. The major step that the modern organization must take in integrating technology and people is to determine the effects that technology is likely to have and to develop a plan for reducing its dysfunctional effects. What does this statement mean?

14. In managing the sociotechnical challenge, what role can be played by the knowledge-based organization? Explain.

15. What roles can industrial democracy and participative management play? Explain.

16. What is empowerment all about? Why is it important in managing the sociotechnical challenge?

17. Identify workplace violence behaviors.

18. How can organizations deal more effectively with workplace violence? Offer two suggestions.

19. What is job stress? Identify several workplace causes of job stress.

20. Discuss ways to change an organization to prevent job stress.

VISIT THE WEB

Customer-Driven and Custom-Made

Computers are what make the Dell Computer Corporation successful. The company has been growing by leaps and bounds. One reason for its growth is that the firm offers competitive prices on desktop and laptop computers that are purchased over the phone. All the customer has to do is call the firm, tell the salesperson the type of computer she or he wants, and provide a credit card or other form of payment. Dell handles the rest of the process. The computer is built to the customer's specifications and shipped to the buyer. Does this system work well? A recent poll of computer purchasers indicates that Dell is ranked number one in customer service and product reliability. Recently Dell announced it is expanding its marketing strategies to include selling computers in retail stores.

Did you know that Dell does more than make and sell desktop and laptop computers? What else does Dell do with its technology? Visit the company's Web site at **http://www.dell.com** and learn more about the firm.

1. Review several case studies.

2. Identify different ways that Dell is helping businesses.

3. Summarize the most surprising thing you learned about Dell.

Products for Everyone

In this chapter, you examined the ways in which organizations attempt to blend technology and people at work. One company that continues to face this challenge is Sony, well known for its myriad consumer products. Visit the firm's Web site at **http://www.sony.com** and learn about some of the new products that the company is now offering. Then answer these questions:

1. What human relations challenges will Sony face in creating and building these products for the worldwide market?

2. Discuss how Sony has integrated human relations into its Web site.

3. After visiting Sony's Web site, what is your initial react as a potential consumer and as a potential employee of Sony. If you were responsible for changing the site, what would you do and why?

Violence in Your Workplace

It is no secret that incidents of violence in the workplace are increasing. Routinely, there are stories of violent acts reported on the news and in the newspaper. There are many causes, but one in particular is job stress. Assume you have the responsibility for reducing stress and violent behaviors at your workplace. Your goal is to make the workplace safe for all employees. Prepare a plan to present to your manager. Research the topics on the Internet by visiting **http://www.osha.gov.** Use the following questions as a guide in preparing your plan.

1. What are the behaviors associated with violent behavior? Assess what is happening in your workplace and identify which behaviors and actions are present in your workplace?

2. How do you plan to change these behaviors? Prepare a list of suggestions for reducing stress and violent behavior in your workplace.

3. Who will make the changes? Assign someone the responsibility.

4. What will be the result of your plan? Summarize what you believe will be the results of your plan.

TIME OUT ANSWERS

Interpretation of Your Job and You

This quiz is designed to measure the effect that the technological surroundings of your job have on you. Keeping in mind the five possible responses to each statement, here is the way to score each:

	Highly Disagree	Disagree	Indifferent	Agree	Highly Agree
1.	−2	−1	0	1	2
2.	2	1	0	−1	−2
3.	−2	−1	0	1	2
4.	2	1	0	−1	−2

5.	2	1	0	−1	−2
6.	2	1	0	−1	−2
7.	2	1	0	−1	−2
8.	−2	−1	0	1	2
9.	−2	−1	0	1	2
10.	2	1	0	−1	−2

If you have a positive score, the impact of technology and stress on your job is not at all negative. In fact, you are doing well in beating the dysfunctional effects of technology and stress. A score of 4 or better is a very good sign. Conversely, a score of −4 or less indicates that technology and job-created stress are getting to you. A score of −7 or less is a sign that you should consider switching jobs.

case: THE OLD VERSUS THE NEW

Sue Ryan was a secretary at Wilshire Community College for three years. During this time, she received three salary raises and was now at the top of her salary range.

Sue enjoyed working at Wilshire because the work was not extremely demanding, and she liked the interaction with both the faculty and her fellow workers. However, one day she realized that if she remained at the college, she would never increase her salary more than 3 or 4 percent per year. This dismayed Sue, because she had just bought a new car and had been hoping to vacation in Europe with some school friends next year. On her current salary, she could afford the car but not the trip.

Then she learned that a new factory had opened in town. The plant was owned and managed by a national corporation that had decided to assemble some of its consumer products in the area. According to a newspaper ad she read, the starting salary for assemblers was 25 percent higher than her current salary, and there was a guaranteed cost-of-living raise.

Sue decided to find out more about the job. She went to the company's personnel office, talked to someone about the job qualifications, and learned that in addition to what she knew already, there was also a very good medical and pension plan—far better than what was in effect at the community college. After giving the matter serious thought, Sue decided to quit her secretary's job and go to work for the assembly plant.

For the first four weeks, things went very well. Sue was so busy trying to master her job and keep up with the speed of the line that she had little time to think about anything else. At night, she was so tired that she went right home and fell into bed. However, as she began to gain control of the job and to learn some of the shortcuts, Sue realized her job was very different from the one she had held at the college. For one thing, no one was working in close proximity to her. The nearest person was 35 feet away and, because of the machine noise, Sue had to almost shout if she wanted to talk to the woman. In addition, the line was moving so fast that Sue did not have time for any extended talking; it was all she could do to keep up.

As the next few months passed, Sue began to reevaluate her decision. She realized that although the assembly-line job certainly paid well, it was not very enjoyable work. In fact, she disliked it. As a result, at the end of the fourth month, she called her former boss at Wilshire and asked if she could return to the community college. He told her she could and, two weeks later, Sue resigned from her job at the assembly plant. As she went into the personnel department to pick up her paycheck and sign some termination papers, she noticed she was not alone. Seven other women were also terminating their employment that day. On the way out, she heard one of the personnel people saying into the phone, "I don't know what the problem is over here, but we've got a turnover rate of almost 40 percent and we haven't been operating six months yet."

YOU BE THE CONSULTANT

The Silence Was Deafening

The county manager's office used to be a hub of noisy activity. One reason was that a secretarial pool of five typists used to be located in an area to the right of the manager's desk. Anyone entering the large office would be greeted with the clacking of typewriters and the typically loud conversations going on among the group members. Often, the typists knew the person who had entered the office, and a friendly exchange of greetings would ensue. The pool of typists generally was regarded as below-average in performance but an extremely friendly, highly cohesive group.

Six months ago, the county manager resigned. The new manager, José Gonzalez, was hired from outside. José had been an assistant city manager in a large metropolitan area. He had five years' experience in this position and was, in the view of the county commissioners who hired him, just the individual to whip the county into sound financial shape. José's expertise is in the finance area, and he quickly set about axing what he felt were costly and inefficient programs. The county zoo's budget was cut by 15 percent, the bus system's budget was reduced by 12.5 percent, and an all-county hiring freeze was enacted. These efficiency measures even extended into the county manager's office.

Under a new organizational arrangement, José had all the typists placed in a separate room away from the main office. The typists then were given word-processing training, and their work assignments were changed. Instead of typing only material associated with the county manager's office, they were assigned work from many different departments. "With their new word-processing skills," José explained, "they'll be able to do a lot more work than before and, now that they are out of the limelight of the central office, they will have fewer distractions."

Since these changes went into effect, there has been a dramatic turnover in the typing pool. Two of the typists have quit, and one of the others has transferred to another department. The office manager, Sara Fonetella, was asked by José to find out what the problem is in keeping word-processing people. Sara decided that the easiest way to handle this assignment without getting personally involved in the conflict would be to interview the current word-processing personnel. She did so and then wrote a two-page memo to José. Here is an extract from that memo:

The word-processing people do not like the new office arrangement. They are located in a very small room that they find confining. The work is boring, and their opportunities to talk to one another are limited because there is a never-ending flow of work. The word-processing individuals who have been here the longest feel that it was unfair to move the typing pool from the outer office without consulting them and giving them some voice in the decision. They also feel that the only reason the typists were trained in word processing was to increase their work output. No consideration was given to how these changes would affect them psychologically.

My overall impression of the word-processing group is that the turnover will continue to be high. The work is boring, the personnel have no personal power over their jobs, and most of them feel isolated. When they were in the outer office, there was a feeling of togetherness; this no longer exists. If we do not reorganize the work, this situation is going to continue.

Your Advice

1. What should José do to correct the situation?

    _____ a. Empower the employees and give them more authority over their work.
    _____ b. Give the employees increased training in word processing.
    _____ c. Put the workers in a larger room.

2. What are some of the problems the workers are encountering as a result of the new technology and work arrangement? Identify and discuss three of these problems.

3. Could a participative management approach have helped to prevent these problems? Explain.

4. What would you recommend doing to correct the problem? What human relations steps would you suggest? Explain.

EXPERIENCING TECHNOLOGY EVOLUTION

Purpose

- To understand the evolution of technology from the handicraft era to the cybernated technology stage.
- To examine the work ethic underlying each stage of technology.

Procedure

1. The class is divided into five groups, each representing one of the eras of technology: handicraft, mechanization, mechanistic, automated, and cybernated.

    a. Discuss the nature of work in your era.
    b. Describe the work ethic of the times.
    c. What values would be most appropriate for the era?
    d. What type of employee would you want to hire?

2. In turn, each group, starting with the handicraft era and proceeding onward, should describe its findings before the class.

7

Productivity and Quality Improvement

LEARNING
OBJECTIVES

Describe the current status and future directions of management efforts to improve productivity and quality

Discuss how total quality management programs are increasing productivity and quality

Identify the steps in TQM programs and briefly describe each step

Explain how Pareto chart analysis, cause-and-effect diagrams, customer-value-added programs, and benchmarking reduce errors and increase quality

Relate the value of alternative work arrangements and empowerment to increased productivity and quality

Define the term intrapreneurship *and relate its value to improved organization productivity and quality*

⑦

Explain the importance for developing intrapreneurship strategies

Two major objectives of modern organizations are to increase productivity and to improve quality. Today these are important challenges facing businesses in America, especially in a time when economic growth is slow. Increasing productivity and improving quality also are issues facing many competing companies located in other countries. Finding methods and ways of attacking these problems require a commitment from top management. Some participative management approaches can improve productivity and quality. In many businesses, philosophical approaches such as empowerment and intrapreneurship are being considered in management's overall effort to achieve productivity and quality improvement.

AFTER READING THIS CHAPTER, YOU SHOULD BE ABLE TO:

1. Describe the current status and future directions of management efforts to improve productivity and quality.
2. Discuss how total quality management programs are increasing productivity and quality.
3. Identify the steps in TQM programs and briefly describe each step.
4. Explain how Pareto chart analysis, cause-and-effect diagrams, customer-value-added programs, and benchmarking reduce errors and increase quality.
5. Relate the value of alternative work arrangements and empowerment to increased productivity and quality.
6. Define the term *intrapreneurship* and relate its value to improved organizational productivity and quality.
7. Explain the importance for developing intrapreneurship strategies.

Merging Technology and People

Many companies have found that the easiest way to increase their productivity is to downsize. This helps them to reduce their payrolls so that, if they can maintain their sales revenue, they have more profit at the end of the year. More effective organizations, however, realize that downsizing can be fraught with problems, including loss of personnel morale and failure of the remaining employees to keep up with work demands. These enterprises are taking a different approach. They are developing methods to reduce the time needed to do the work by effectively merging technology and people.

A good example is the Yamaha Corporation of America. Just a few years ago, the firm found that its customer hot line was so congested that one-third of all callers hung up before getting through. This was when Yamaha turned to a specialized software company to develop a package that would automate and monitor customer service calls. Now, when a person calls the hot line, the computer-telephony system not only logs in the individual's name but keeps track of the problem and how long it takes to resolve the situation. As a result, Yamaha now is able to identify those problems that occur most often and focus on ways of resolving them quickly and effectively.

One of the keys to the success of these "smart" programs is a well-trained workforce that knows how to follow the primary rule of total quality management: Do things right the first time. By empowering personnel to make the decisions that are needed to ensure that things are done right, companies such as Yamaha are finding that customers are more willing to buy their products. In addition, customers know that if they have a problem, they can always get through on the hot line and receive the assistance they need.

Another good example is provided by Wendy's, the third largest hamburger chain in the country. One of the keys to success in this industry is rapid drive-in service and, according to the latest statistics, Wendy's is the fastest. The average time from the menu board to departure is 2 minutes and 30 seconds, which is 17 seconds faster than McDonald's and 19 seconds faster than Burger King. Given that two-thirds of the sales of most of these fast-food units come from drive-in business and projections show that, over the next decade, drive-through sales are likely to increase three times faster than in-unit sales, rapid service is the key to profitability. In fact, a 10 percent increase in drive-through efficiency will bolster sales by more than $50,000 annually.

Realizing that whatever it does will be copied by the competition, Wendy's is now launching a new efficiency program. This effort involves a combination of new timers to keep track of how long it takes to deliver the food, kitchen choreography that is designed to eliminate unnecessary movement, and wireless headsets that let all workers hear customer orders as they come in. The first units to implement this new program were able to achieve sales increases of 3–4 percent more than units that had not yet introduced the program. Wendy's objective is to reduce the time from menu board to departure to 100 seconds because, at this rate, customers are able to perceive the rapid service and are more likely to return. Simply put, the company's success will depend on how well they can merge technology and people.

Opening more new restaurants and becoming bigger each year does not always bring in more sales. For the first time in its history, McDonald's has recently experienced losses in sales. Mr. Cantalupo of McDonald's states "we tried to get bigger while we should have gotten better." To address these concerns, the company announced an ambitious agenda of changes projected into 2005 that will focus on regaining customers by improving the speed of service, packaging premium sandwiches in boxes rather than foil wraps, installing automated beverage dispensers at drive-through windows and reducing the number of keystrokes crew members make on cash registers to transact a sale. Success comes through constant improvement in the quality of product and service.

Sources: Jennifer Ordonez, *"An Efficiency Drive: Fast-Food Lanes Are Getting Even Faster,"* Wall Street Journal, *May 18, 2000, pp. A1, A10; Otis Porter, "Speed Gets a Whole New Meaning,"* Business Week, *April 29, 1996, pp. 90–91; and Neil Gross, "New Tricks for Helping Lines,"* Business Week, *April 29, 1996, pp. 97–98. (Richard Gibson, "McDonald's Plans Campaign to Woo Customers, Investors,"* Wall Street Journal, *April 8, 2003)*

The Productivity and Quality Challenges

LEARNING OBJECTIVE

1 Describe the current status and future directions of management efforts to improve productivity and quality

Productivity is typically measured by the equation: output/input. Beginning in the mid-1970s, the United States began to feel the effects of growing productivity from foreign competition. The Japanese and Germans, in particular, began making more effective use of their labor and other resources and thus produced output at a lower cost per unit than could many American firms. Japanese manufacturing companies, for example, were able to produce autos at $2,000–$3,000 per car below the cost of their American competitors. In the international services arena, increased productivity was evident in the form of lower prices and better service in the airline, hotel, and restaurant industries. Obviously, the United States was falling behind in terms of productivity growth. America needed to focus more attention on increasing output (goods and services) or lowering input (salaries, wages, benefits, materials, machinery, and equipment).

Productivity
is equal to output and input.

At the same time, quality became a major issue. Auto firms found quality was more important than price in consumer purchase decisions, and American companies were having problems. In manufacturing at large, executives were admitting their firms were losing their place as world-class manufacturers. Airlines were developing an awareness that equipment safety and on-time arrivals, two major quality issues, were critical factors for customers deciding which airline to fly. Hospitals found high-quality service was becoming critical in meeting patient expectations and competitive pressures from other health care outlets. Similarly, restaurants were discovering that service often was more important than price. During this same period, one major research study found that businesses that increased their quality over the competition gained both market share and profitability.[1] Obviously, something had to be done.

Current Status

Currently, the United States is working hard to increase productivity growth and quality. However, because the competition is doing the same, this means the United States must continue its efforts. To date, America has made some significant progress. For example, beginning in the mid-1990s, the economies of Japan and Germany encountered recessions, whereas that of the United States began to grow significantly. In the recent past, U.S. productivity had increased, at best, by around 2 percent annually and is expected to remain at 2 percent. Today with as much as 50 percent reduction in the prices of microprocessors and the increase in spending on information processing equipment and software, it is likely that productivity could grow to 3–5 percent annually in seven to nine years. Economist J. Bradford Delong of the University of California contends that the long-term trend in productivity growth is 3 percent. Economist James K. Glassman of J.P. Morgan Securities says that spending on information processing equipment and software has reached its highest level in two years.[2] At the same time, inflation remained low, unemployment continued to decline, and the stock market reached new heights until the disaster of September 11, 2001. American quality also started to catch up to, and in many cases surpass, that of foreign competitors. And this was true not only in the production of goods but also in the delivery of services. For example, United States Parcel Service (UPS) and Federal Express are two of the most productive shipping companies in the world.[3] Meanwhile, in retailing, Wal-Mart continues to cut costs and increase sales annually. As a result, its sales are growing at a faster rate than that of most competitors. In fact, productivity in the United States in the recent past has been so strong that in 2000 the World Competitiveness Council reported that for the seventh consecutive year the United States was the most competitive nation in the world.

This productivity has manifested itself in a number of ways, including auto production. In recent years the reliability of American vehicles has improved, but still lags behind that of Japanese vehicles. Consumer Reports compared 2003 vehicles with the average of all 2000, 2001, and 2002 vehicles. The results revealed that, "overall, the Japanese nameplates still lead in reliability." Several GM vehicles showed improved liability, namely, the Chevrolet Avalanche, Silverado, Suburban, and Tahoe, and the GMC Sierra, Yukon, and Yukon XL.[4] Brian Walters, Director of Product Research at J.D. Power & Associates, says the quality of new cars is improving. "Reports by consumers 90 days after they bought or leased new 2002 vehicles show a 10% increase in initial quality—measured by 135 problem symptoms from the consumer's perspective—over 2001 models. This continues the trend of 24% improvement over the past five years." Still the quality of completely redesigned vehicles is down 2 percent the first year, but improves an average of 12% the second year.[5]

Additionally, U.S. manufacturers are finding themselves under scrutiny by the National Highway Transportation Safety Agency, which is investigating the likelihood that vehicles will roll over and injure the occupants.[6] Hence, Detroit continues to be plagued by quality issues.

How has the United States managed to increase its productivity so sharply? One way is by introducing quality-related tools and techniques that effectively link technology and worker effort.[7] For example, a growing number of manufacturing firms now are using a form of strategic flexibility that allows them to identify the skills and knowledge needed for specific jobs and then to bring them together with the manufacturing facilities in a way that allows the companies to generate mass customized products.[8] Another way is by carefully creating and focusing the direction of research and development (R&D) departments, thus ensuring that these groups are able to use their energies more effectively. Two researchers who studied American R&D in the computer industry recently reported:

> *The U.S. companies that prevailed in the computer industry in the 1990s abandoned the traditional R&D model and created a radically different one. They did not stop conducting basic research, but they did shift much of the focus of their research efforts to applied science, and they turned to an increasingly diverse base of suppliers and partners—universities, consortia, and other companies—to help generate technological possibilities. In addition, they formed tightly knit teams of expert integrators—people with extensive backgrounds in research, development, and manufacturing—to develop these new generations of major products and processes. . . . Companies charged the integration teams to take a broad, system wide outlook and gave them considerable freedom in conceptualizing the new generation and choosing its technologies. . . . The result was an approach to technology integration that excelled in finding important new technologies that provide extremely successful solutions and finding them very quickly and efficiently.[9]*

Future Directions

Despite these successes, however, research shows that, in many areas, U.S. management must do a better job if productivity is to continue growing. A recent study of more than ten thousand American workers has found a large gap between what workers believe they need to be productive and what managers are providing. In particular, workers say that conditions for collaboration, commitment, and creativity must be improved. They want the chance to work more closely with others, including management, and to break down the barriers that reduce productivity. They also want to feel that the work they are doing is important and that management appreciates their efforts. Finally, the workers want the opportunity to do interesting, creative work in a friendly environment.

Specifically, they feel that management must:

1. Value people as human beings and develop policies and procedures that treat employees better.
2. Develop a support system for recognizing and rewarding good performance.
3. Create an atmosphere of trust and show that management has confidence in the workers.
4. Give employees an opportunity to influence events in the workplace.
5. Provide employees an opportunity to carry out relevant, meaningful work.
6. Develop a shared sense of purpose and commitment among all employees.
7. Create a work environment in which people learn to rely on one another and develop and share creative work ideas.

8. **Create a spontaneous, fun, collaborative social environment in which innovation is recognized.**
9. **Develop a dynamic problem-solving process, the goal of which is to achieve high-quality, productive, relevant output.[10]**

The remainder of this chapter examines some of the major human relations approaches that are proving to be effective in handling the productivity–quality challenge.

Total Quality Management

LEARNING OBJECTIVE
2
Discuss how total quality management programs are increasing productivity and quality

A number of steps can be taken to attack the productivity–quality problem directly. One of the most popular is total quality management (TQM), which is proving extremely useful in increasing both productivity and quality.

Total quality management is a people-focused management system that aims at continual increases in customer service at continually lower cost. TQM is a structured system whose objective is to meet and exceed customer demands while keeping costs as low as possible and at the same time improve quality, delivery, and morale.

In the past, many firms argued that it was impossible to increase quality without also increasing cost. As an example, they contended that if a company made ten thousand television sets and one thousand were defective, the cost of eliminating all these defects would significantly run up the products' overall cost. As a result, they argued firms should learn to live with these mistakes to keep down the price and, where possible, try to eliminate some of the most glaring production mistakes. Over the last few years, however, more and more organizations have learned that the cost of eliminating defects often more than pays for itself. It usually is less expensive to produce things properly the first time than to correct mistakes later.

For example, consider the company that must spend $50,000 to eliminate all mistakes in order to produce defect-free televisions. Consider also that each defective TV costs the firm a total of $200 in reworking costs and another $200 in shipping and customer service costs. If the firm is producing 10,000 television sets each year and 10 percent are defective, the cost of correcting these mistakes is $400,000 ($400 × 1,000). Clearly, it is better for the firm to produce the sets correctly the first time than to remedy the mistakes later. In fact, by dividing the $50,000 that the firm must invest in correcting its production facilities by the $400 average cost to repair and replace each TV, we can see that once the firm produces 125 defective sets ($50,000/$400), it is paying more for repairing these units than it would cost to prevent these mistakes in the first place. This is the **first principle of TQM:** Do it right the first time.

One reason that many firms are now able to do this is that they have changed their beliefs about the nature of quality and have come to accept new ideas. The following are four of these ideas:

1. **The quality output of goods and services is everyone's job.**
2. **The thinking that quality is "good enough" must be replaced by the belief that quality must be continually improved.**
3. **Work can often be done faster without any loss in quality.**
4. **Everybody associated with the organization needs to be part of the quality effort, including top managers, low-level workers, outside suppliers, and customers.[11]**

Table 7.1 provides a contrast between the old way of viewing quality and the way in which highly productive organizations now do so.

Today, thousands of U.S. firms are implementing TQM programs designed to provide better products and services at lower prices than ever. In carrying out this strategy, they are relying on a host of critical steps, including:

1. **Formulation of strategic intent.**
2. **Careful design of organization structure and training efforts.**

Total quality management
seeks to increase customer service and reduce cost.

*The **first principle of TQM**
is: Do it right the first time.*

TABLE 7.1

The Emergence of New Beliefs Regarding the Nature and Role of Quality

Old Myth	New Truth
Quality is the responsibility of the people in the quality control department.	Quality is everyone's job.
Training is costly.	Training does not cost; it saves.
New quality programs have high initial costs.	The best quality programs do not have up-front costs.
Better quality will cost the company a lot of money.	As quality goes up, costs come down.
It is human to make mistakes.	Perfection—total customer satisfaction—is a standard that should be vigorously pursued.
Some defects are major and should be addressed, but many are minor and can be ignored.	No defects are acceptable, regardless of whether they are major or minor.
Quality improvements are made in small, continuous steps.	In improving quality, both small and large improvements are necessary.
Quality improvement takes time.	Quality does not take time; it saves time.
Haste makes waste.	Thoughtful speed improves quality.
Quality programs are best oriented toward such areas as products and manufacturing.	Quality is important in all areas, including administration and service.
After a number of quality improvements, customers are no longer able to see additional improvements.	Customers are able to see all improvements, including those in price, delivery, and performance.
Good ideas can be found throughout the organization.	Good ideas can be found everywhere, including in the operations of competitors and organizations providing similar goods and services.
Suppliers need to be price-competitive.	Suppliers need to be quality-competitive.

Source: Richard M. Hodgetts, Measures of Quality and High Performance: Simple Tools and Lessons from America's Most Successful Companies (New York: American Management Association, 1998), p. 15.

3. Use of common tools and techniques.
4. Emphasis on use of customer value added.
5. Use of benchmarking and continuous improvement.
6. Careful measurement of performance results.

LEARNING OBJECTIVE
Identify the steps in TQM programs and briefly describe each step

③

The following sections examine each of these steps.

Strategic intent *is the company's vision.*

Formulation of Strategic Intent

Strategic intent is the company's vision. Basically, strategic intent sets forth an enterprise's over-riding ambitions or desires that, in turn, create the basis for the organization's mission and help to drive its strategy. Organizations state their strategic intent in a variety of ways. Here are three examples:

Eastman Chemical: to be the world's preferred chemical company and to be the leader in quality and value of products and service.

Xerox: to help people find better ways to do great work by consistently leading in document technologies, products, and services that improve work processes and business results.

Ames Rubber: to focus on developing and producing engineered rubber products that meet the unique technical requirements of our customers' most demanding applications and to embrace the continuous change necessary to deliver value to both customers and the Ames Rubber Corporation.

Strategic intent provides an overriding picture of what the organization wants to accomplish. In the process, it also helps to identify those changes that must occur. When Motorola decided in the late 1970s that it needed to increase its quality to world-class levels, the firm asked itself: What do we have to do to correct the current situation? Table 7.2 shows some of the changes the firm introduced that ultimately made it a world-class organization.

In an effort to increase its market share in Asia, Hewlett-Packard's (H-P's) decision to move away from its traditional approach of selling through stores to selling directly to its customers provides another example of strategic intent. The direct-sales method "is definitely a key element to our strategy if we are going to grow our share in the market," according to Adrian Koch, the senior vice president of H-P's personal systems group for the region.[12]

Another example is Chrysler. It has embarked on a new strategy of outsourcing that is intended to reduce the cost of producing cars. "Instead of developing cars from scratch, as it has done for 75 years, it is leaning on partners like Mercedes and Mitsubishi, as well as on outside suppliers, to provide everything from intellectual capital to assembly-plant paint shops." It's a whole new way of doing business. The first product, a Crossfire sports car, recently drove off an assembly line in Germany. It went from design to market in twenty-four months at a budget price of $280 million.[13]

TABLE 7.2	Motorola's Changing Quality Culture

Decade	Changes
1970s	Acknowledgment that quality needs to be sharply improved
1980s	Naming of a corporate quality officer
	Establishment of the Motorola Training Center
	Setting of a 5-year, 10× quality improvement goal
	Beginning of total-defect-per-unit measurement in the communications sector
	Adoption of the six-sigma goal (3.5 defects per million)
	Setting of a 2-year, 10× quality improvement objective and a 4-year, 100× quality improvement objective
1990s	Setting of a 10× defect reduction every 2 years
	Development of customer satisfaction metrics
	Setting of a 10× improvement of cycle time in 5 years
	Changing of defect measurement base from parts per million to parts per billion

Source: Reported in Richard M. Hodgetts, Measures of Quality and High Performance: Simple Tools and Lessons from America's Most Successful Companies *(New York: American Management Association, 1998), p. 46.*

After making a thorough analysis of its environment, Xerox recently concluded that to remain a leader in the global market, it had to focus on providing document services that enhanced business productivity. In the process, the company identified five areas that are critical to its success:

1. Increasing customer satisfaction and loyalty.
2. Increasing motivation and satisfaction of company personnel.
3. Building market share.
4. Increasing the return on assets.
5. Increasing productivity.

Xerox then began pursuing these concepts by identifying specific goals that had to be achieved:

- *Swifter:* Be more productive by doing things simpler, making quicker decisions, and bringing products to market in a shorter time.
- *Higher:* Increase the growth rate by creating new markets, capturing larger market shares, and generating double-digit growth rates.
- *Stronger:* Develop a better customer focus by achieving a deeper understanding of customer needs, creating value, and continually doing what is right for the customer.
- *Smarter:* Find additional ways to do good work by creating enthusiastic, empowered people, who are able to add value at the right time and in the right way for customers and shareholders.[14]

These goals are helping Xerox to create an agenda for becoming both a leader in the global document market and one of the most productive companies in the world. At present, its two major targets are to become more market-driven and to maintain leadership in digital technology. In the past year, Xerox received fourteen top industry awards, which indicates it has stayed on target. The awards recognize Xerox's superior quality, affordability, and reliability in its color and black-and-white network printers, fax machines, and digital multifunction systems.[15] At the same time, the firm is focusing on ways to increase its productivity, including empowering the workforce and developing more efficient processes. These developments are designed to help Xerox attain new levels of productivity, market share, and sustainable, profitable growth. The company is doing this by using strategic intent to drive the process forward. The tragedy of the space shuttle, Columbia, on February 1, 2003, has raised some painful questions about the space program and its strategic intent. Rick N. Tumlinson, president of Space Frontier Foundation, states "the talents of these incredible people are being wasted. I want to see them going to Mars." The Columbia tragedy could be a brave beginning for NASA as it determines its strategic intent for entering the second Space Age.[16]

Careful Design of Organization Structure and Training Efforts

*A **quality council** is a group of individuals who oversee the quality initiative.*

Companies organize their TQM efforts in a number of ways. It is common to create a **quality council,** a group of individuals who oversee the quality initiative and make decisions regarding the projects to be undertaken and the funding to be provided. This group often is assisted by one individual who is placed in charge of quality and given the authority for coordinating these projects and serving as the full-time quality person in the organization.

Initial quality efforts are directed toward identifying problem areas and creating quality improvement teams to deal with them. These problem areas typically are identified through an analysis of feedback from customers and from attitude surveys of employees. In this way, the organization knows the types of changes its clients and workers would like. Armed with this information, quality improvement teams of five to ten individuals then are formed and assigned projects. Typical examples of project goals include:

- **Reducing the time needed to produce cellular phones from one and a half hours to fifty-five minutes.**
- **Reducing delivery time from twenty-four hours to twelve hours.**
- **Reviewing and making recommendations regarding how service in the employee cafeteria can be improved.**

Sometimes these quality improvement teams consist of members from just one department, but in many cases they are cross-functional teams with members from many different departments.

After the team analyzes the problem assigned to it, the group will reach conclusions regarding what needs to be done and will present its findings to the quality council. The quality council then will decide whether the members agree and, if so, the type of follow-up action that should be taken. In most cases, the council will agree with the quality team and vote to implement the recommendations. For example, at Eastman Chemical Company a network of "interlocking" teams, led by managers and supervisors, and involving virtually all employees is viewed as the most effective means to execute the company's quality strategy.[17]

To help reduce costs for developing or improving a major component, some companies are signing agreements to work together and share the costs. These agreements have many potential benefits not only for the companies themselves but also for their shareholders and customers. For example, Ford Motor Company and General Motors Corporation, the world's two largest automakers, recently signed a contract to develop a high-volume, front-wheel, 6-speed automatic transmission with improved fuel economy.[18]

Research reveals that quality improvement teams cannot function effectively unless they are trained in how to gather and analyze data and how to work together as an effective team. This typically is provided by offering training in both quantitative and behavioral techniques. At Eastman all employees are trained to gather complaint information and enter it into a company-wide database. In addition, many firms now are establishing the necessary budgets to support these efforts. Some do this by setting aside a percentage of overall sales, such as 3 percent, that is to be spent exclusively for training, whereas others establish a specific amount, such as $2.5 million for the year. A supplemental approach is to express training requirements in terms of hours per year. Since the disaster of 9/11 and the weakening of the economy, many companies have changed this approach. For example, recently Motorola renewed its former learning policy by replacing prior emphasis on hours of training per employee, with a new learning policy that emphasizes maximizing learning investments by aligning employee development with Motorola's business strategies.[19]

At IBM the new CEO, Sam Palmisano, wants "to bring back the days when IBM was revered as a great company." He plans to turn the company inside out in pursuit of "e-business on demand," a grand scheme to sell information processing. To do that he will spend "$100 million to teach 30,000 employees to lead, not control their staff, so workers won't feel like cogs in a machine."[20]

Granite Rock Company of Watsonville, California, is a good example. This small construction materials company won the national Baldrige quality award for its outstanding quality, thanks in no small part to its outstanding TQM training. In recent years, employees have averaged around forty hours of training annually, which is thirteen times more than the construction industry average. As part of the firm's effort to reduce process variability and increase product reliability, employees are trained in statistical process control, root-cause analysis, and other quality-assurance and problem-solving methods.

At Solectron, an electronics firm and another Baldrige winner, all employees receive a minimum of 160 hours of training each year. This training is broad in scope and encompasses a wide variety of general training, as well as operations-focused offerings. To identify and address training needs, an advisory committee reviews the firm's strategy and business plan and then conducts a needs analysis among employees. In the process, the committee examines current worker skills and analyzes the company's technology requirements. After this, training needs are prioritized, and the required programs and seminars are developed.

LEARNING OBJECTIVE

Explain how Pareto chart analysis, cause-and-effect diagrams, customer-value-added programs, and bench-marking reduce errors and increase quality

④ Common Tools and Techniques

Organizations use a wide variety of TQM tools and techniques to increase productivity and quality. One of the most common types of training is to teach the participants how to collect information by answering such questions as:

- **What do you want to know?**
- **How can the necessary information be collected?**
- **When and where do the data need to be gathered?**
- **How can the information be displayed so it can be easily totaled and evaluated? (Often, this last question is answered by teaching the participants to construct a Pareto chart.)**

*A **Pareto chart** is a vertical bar graph used to identify and rank-order problems.*

A **Pareto chart** is a special vertical bar graph that helps to identify problems and the order in which they are to be addressed. Figure 7.1 provides an example of a Pareto chart that was constructed based on customer complaints. A close look at the chart shows that 60 percent of all customer complaints relate to delivery time, so the quality improvement team would want

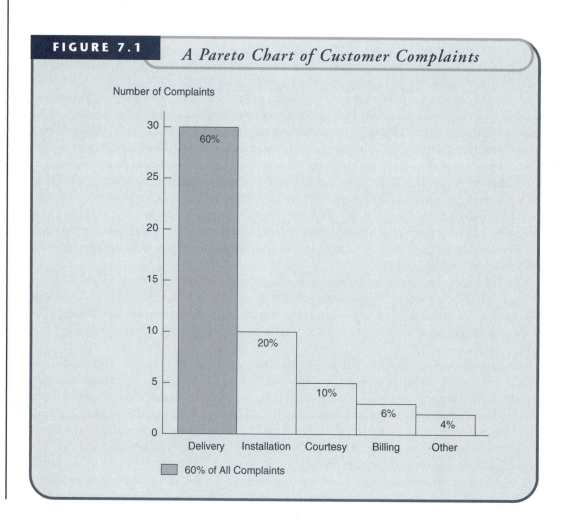

FIGURE 7.1   *A Pareto Chart of Customer Complaints*

to analyze why delivery time is a problem for customers. Another common TQM approach that often is taught is the cause-and-effect diagram.

Cause-and-effect diagrams, often used as a follow-up to Pareto charts, are designed to help identify reasons for the problem. The approach consists of four specific steps:

1. **The quality team will conduct a brainstorming session and identify the most likely causes for the problem.**
2. **These causes will be broken down by category.**
3. **The team will vote for the most likely group of causes.**
4. **Based on this decision, an action plan will be created and implemented.**

Figure 7.2 provides an example of a cause-and-effect diagram for dealing with the problem of cleaning up the work area more quickly. Four major causes have been identified—materials, methods, machinery, and workforce—and the reasons for each cause have been listed. Now the team will decide which of these is the major cause of the problem and will begin working to resolve the issue.

A number of other commonly used TQM tools are available, and they all function in the same way: They help the team to identify and deal with quality-related problems. In addition, teams commonly receive training in how to be an effective group member,

A cause-and-effect diagram is designed to help identify reasons for a problem.

FIGURE 7.2 — *A Cause-and-Effect Diagram*

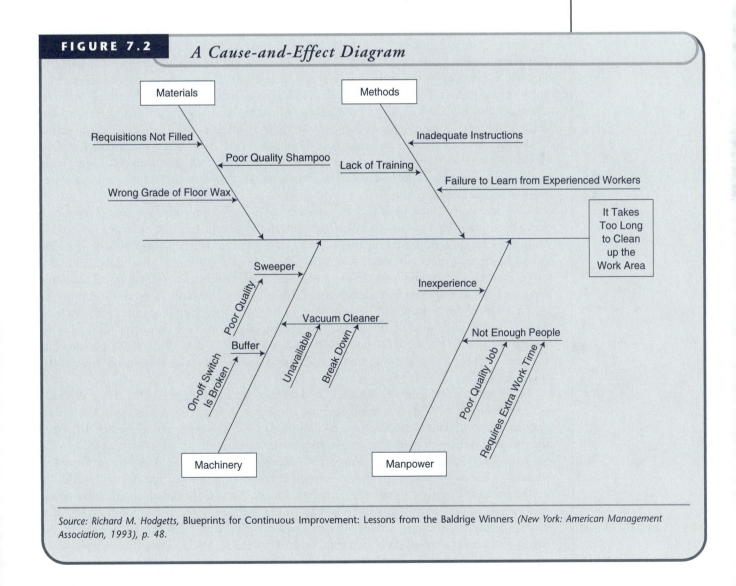

Source: Richard M. Hodgetts, Blueprints for Continuous Improvement: Lessons from the Baldrige Winners *(New York: American Management Association, 1993), p. 48.*

how to lead a TQM team, and how to facilitate team analysis. As a result, team members learn how to work well together and how collectively to identify and solve quality-related problems.

Emphasis on Customer Value Added

Another way in which organizations are improving their quality and productivity is by finding out what the customer wants and giving this to the individual. This approach is known as *customer value added*. Briefly defined, **customer value added** (CVA) is the providing of products and services that offer greater value than is available from the competition. There are copious examples of firms offering CVA. Sony, for example, created the Sony Walkman because it realized that people wanted to listen to the radio while they exercised. In response to this demand, the company designed and built a small unit with earphones that allowed a person to walk or jog while listening to his or her favorite radio station. The technology was not new, but its application was, because it focused on adding value for the customer. The same is true for services. When customers ask for directions in the Ritz-Carlton Hotels, the staff member will stop whatever he or she is doing and walk the individual to the location. This ensures that the guest does not get lost. Again, the emphasis is on customer service

Another example is provided by General Electric (GE), which has an arrangement with Home Depot. Customers who buy a GE appliance at Home Depot have their purchase delivered by GE. In an effort to add value to this purchase, GE began looking at ways that it could better serve the customer and, to its surprise, the firm learned that many of its ideas regarding CVA were incorrect. For example, GE believed that if it delivered the appliance to the customer's home within 24 hours, the buyer would be impressed and more likely to buy a GE product in the future. However, this perception turned out to be incorrect. A survey of customers revealed that they were indifferent about twenty-four-hour delivery. The company also learned that if the product was delivered late or was damaged in transit, customers did not become upset as long as the delivery people had a professional, soothing demeanor. As a result, GE now contacts buyers and tells them when the product will be delivered and then works to meet this target. At the same time, the firm has been giving people-skills training to its installers and deliverers, so that they are able to interact effectively with customers.[21]

GM and Ford Motor provide examples of CVA. Both companies are trying to reduce radically the amount of time needed to build and deliver a car that is "made to order." Unlike the computer industry, in which Dell Computer can deliver a custom-made machine to the buyer in a matter of days, GM currently requires forty-five to sixty days to build a car to buyer specifications and deliver it to the buyer. Few buyers are willing to wait this long, and so auto makers lose these sales. GM and Ford, however, now are beginning to look closely at the process and to develop a strategy for attracting customers who want to have their cars built specially for them. The current plan is to take the order, fill it, ship it, and have the car in the buyer's possession within 14 days.[22] If GM and Ford can do this, they are likely to find a growing number of customers for whom custom-made cars constitute a CVA.[23]

In design improvements, the new CEO Rick Wagoner and Robert A. Lutz, Head of Product Development of GM, decreased the time it takes to develop a new car from nearly four years to twenty months. Lutz uses one committee to cover the entire process rather than have the design pass through marketing, engineering, then manufacturing. Wagoner has pushed GM to get its plants more efficient and improve the quality of its cars.[24] No American or European automaker has come close to the twelve months it takes Toyota to go from the design table to building a new Corolla-class car. Other automakers are reportedly aiming to cut their development cycle to less than thirty months, but Toyota is shooting for a ten-month cycle. Most of the improvement comes through the increase in digital design. About 80 percent of the design development is now done with computers. Advances in production technology allow the automakers to produce on a greater scale.[25]

In providing CVA, organizations now realize that perceived value is often the key to success. Lucent Technologies, for example, has created a quality-driven strategy based on four basic beliefs:

1. **People buy on perceived value.**
2. **Value is a function of quality relative to price.**
3. **Quality includes all non-price attributes.**
4. **Quality, price, and value are all relative measures.**

Research by the company has revealed some interesting links among perception, quality, price, and profit. For example, Lucent has found that customers who see themselves as receiving higher quality also are more willing to pay higher prices. Hence, perceived superior quality earns price premiums. Moreover, higher quality does not always mean higher costs. In fact, Lucent has found that as quality increases, costs tend to decline and then slowly increase and, overall, the cost of the increased quality remains significantly less than the price paid by the customer. Thus, superior quality drives up both profitability and market share.

Use of Benchmarking and Continuous Improvement

In ensuring that they maintain their quality and productivity gains, many firms now rely on benchmarking and continuous-improvement strategies. These two approaches complement each other.

Benchmarking is an ongoing process of measuring products, services, and practices against those of competitors or organizations that are recognized as industry leaders.[26] The general process does not vary much from organization to organization. The steps presented in Figure 7.3 are fairly universal. However, four different types of benchmarking can be used: internal, competitive, functional, and generic. Each of these contributes to improvement but some are more important than others, as can be seen in the table:

Type of Benchmarking	Activity Performed	Amount of Improvement (%)
Internal	Compare similar processes within the company	10
Competitive	Specific competitor-to-competitor comparisons	20
Functional	Compare similar functions to industry leaders	35
Generic	Compare unrelated practices or processes	>35

Benchmarking has been particularly useful in helping organizations to reduce their error rate and drive up quality-related factors, such as customer satisfaction and "time to market." For example, Ames Rubber has used the process to reduce the defect rate for its largest customer, Xerox, from more than thirty thousand to eleven parts per million. As a result, Ames is now the "benchmark" producer of fuser rollers for the very highest-speed copiers. At the same time, delivery performance for Ames's top customers is well above the industry average, and productivity, as measured by sales per teammate, has increased sharply.

Another example of benchmarking is provided by GTE Directories, which uses a host of different information sources to help it carry out benchmarking activities. These include industry comparison data, customer satisfaction feedback, internal and external competitive analysis of both products and services, information from other GTE business units for business and support service as well as employee and supplier performance data, and industry studies for operation and support services benchmarks. The company employs these efforts

Benchmarking
is an ongoing process of measuring products, services, and practices against those of competitors and industry leaders.

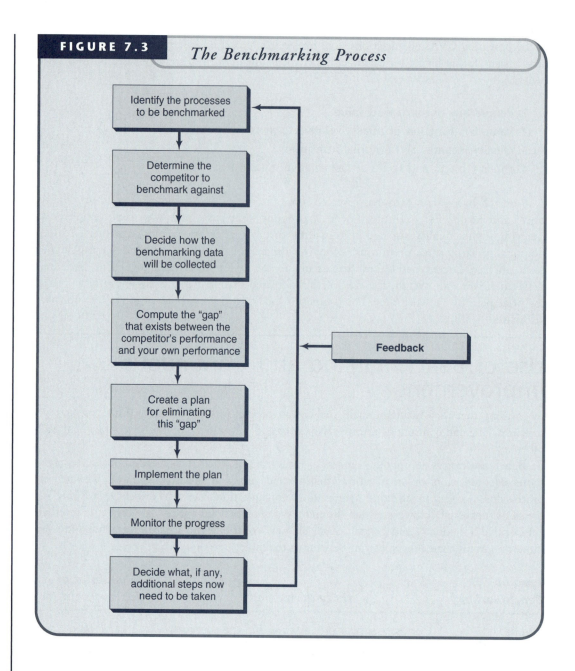

FIGURE 7.3   *The Benchmarking Process*

Identify the processes
to be benchmarked

Determine the
competitor to
benchmark against

Decide how the
benchmarking data
will be collected

Compute the "gap"
that exists between the
competitor's performance
and your own performance

Feedback

Create a plan
for eliminating
this "gap"

Implement the plan

Monitor the progress

Decide what, if any,
additional steps now
need to be taken

to compare current processes to those of other world-class companies and then sets and validates world-class targets of its own. Using these processes, the firm's leadership council then determines gaps and identifies the quality improvement opportunities that can have the greatest impact on customer satisfaction. In addition, the firm continually provides process management tools and training to its people, empowering them to make ongoing assessment of opportunities for quality improvement and to take appropriate action. In fact, benchmarking is the primary vehicle used for information gathering and analysis and, in refining these efforts, GTE Directories has reduced the number of steps in its own benchmarking process from eleven to six.

Closely tied to benchmarking is continuous improvement, which helps organizations to maintain their productivity and quality improvement success. Continuous improvement relies on two developments: consistent, incremental gains and occasional innovation. This approach is critical to TQM because it puts strong emphasis on the value of small improvements that are achieved on a continual basis. When this happens, employees continue to focus on productivity improvements every day rather than devote all their time to making major breakthroughs. Table 7.3 provides a comparison of constant improvement (small gains) to innovation (large gains).

	Constant Improvement	**Innovation**
TABLE 7.3 — *A Comparison of Constant Improvement and Innovation*		
Results	Long-term and long-lasting but fairly undramatic	Short-term but very dramatic
Progress	Many small steps	A few large steps
Time frame	Continuous and incremental	Stop-and-go and nonincremental
Rate of change	Gradual and constant	Abrupt and volatile
Personnel involvement	Everyone in the organization	A few people who are involved in bringing about the major breakthrough
Organizational approach	Group efforts	Individual efforts
Focus of effort	Development of people to carry out the improvements	Heavy reliance on technological breakthroughs
Advantage	Very useful in slow-growth economies	Very useful in fast-growth economies
Evaluation of progress	How well small changes are leading to better quality	Profits

Recent research reveals that some of the highest quality firms in the United States report a number of important benefits from their emphasis on incremental, small improvements. These include:

1. **Increased quality of output.**
2. **Greater competitiveness.**
3. **Higher profitability.**
4. **A lower operating break-even point.**
5. **The opportunity to use a participative management approach that allows employees to play a role in decision making.**
6. **A way of learning from past experiences and using this information to set realistic, attainable goals.**[27]

Most important, a continuous-improvement strategy ensures that employees maintain their focus on increasing the quality of goods and services, and they do not stop once a particular productivity goal has been achieved. One way some companies ensure that this happens is by having the quality improvement teams develop lists of problems and improvements that they want to investigate. At AT&T Universal Card Services, these teams have "hit lists" of 10 target areas; when a group resolves one of the problems, it is taken off the hit list and another replaces it. In this way, the team never runs out of projects or problems to resolve. At Honda, managers work closely with suppliers to identify small, simple changes that will increase performance. As a result, the company has been able to raise the productivity of its suppliers by 50 percent.[28]

In a continuing effort to provide world-class service to shippers, FedEx Freight has improved transit times in six U.S. markets involving sixty cities. Reducing transit time supports FedEx's customers who use just-in-time and regional distribution models. FedEx continues to strive for further enhancements to give its customers a competitive edge, while also increasing its own efficiency.[29]

The Human Relations in Action box provides additional insights into some of the strategies that companies use in ensuring that the TQM effort continues.[30]

HUMAN RELATIONS IN ACTION

Keeping the Focus Team Alive

Every organization would like to increase the quality of its goods and services. Getting the effort started is often the easy part. Keeping the focus on quality is much more difficult. Here are five steps that are particularly useful in ensuring that quality teams maintain their focus.

1. *Do not expect too much immediately.* Many total quality management teams begin by attacking a major problem and find that after a couple of months, they have not solved the problem and the commitment of the team members is beginning to wane. A better approach is to start with an easy target that will not take too much time and effort. Then, motivated by this early success, the quality team can set its goals a little higher and try again.

2. *Conduct weekly meetings and keep minutes.* To ensure that quality teams remain active, it is important to have weekly meetings during which the members discuss what they have done since the last meeting, what still needs to be done, and what each person should do by the next meeting. Minutes should be kept of these meetings so that everyone is aware of the group's progress and future objectives.

3. *Choose the team leader and facilitator carefully.* Each quality team should have a leader and a facilitator. The leader's job is to direct the meeting; the facilitator's job is to ensure the discussion remains focused on the relevant issues. The leader and facilitator are critical to the effective performance of a quality team. To the extent that these

people are carefully chosen, the team's potential for increasing quality will increase.

4. *Collect quantifiable data.* Quality teams should collect information that can be quantified. For example, if a team is studying the reasons for low productivity and believes one reason is high rates of absenteeism and tardiness, the group should collect information on how many people have been absent or late during the period under study. If possible, this information should be broken down by day of the week (perhaps more people are absent on Mondays and Fridays than on any other days) or hour of the day (perhaps people are late coming to work on Mondays and Fridays and many are also late in coming back from lunch on Tuesdays, Wednesdays, and Thursdays).

5. *Motivate the participants.* To ensure that everyone on the team remains an active participant, they must be motivated. One simple motivational approach is to acknowledge those who do a good job by calling it to the attention of the other members. For example, the team leader might note, "Betty did an excellent job in gathering the absenteeism data from the shipping department, and Tim's thorough analysis allowed us to see clearly that Wednesdays are the biggest problem day for this department. I'd like to thank both of you for a job well done." If the group has been allocated funds for use in carrying out these tasks, it is always a good idea to set aside some of these moneys for a small party (for example, coffee and cake) after the group has completed its project and to use this time to thank all the participants for a job well done.

Careful Measurement of Performance Results

The purpose of measuring performance results is to evaluate how well things are going and to make any necessary changes. This activity can be accomplished in a number of ways. The Ethics and Social Responsibility in Action box provides insights into the human relations challenges presented by this activity.

At AT&T Consumer Communications Services, for example, customer-related feedback data are analyzed and correlated with other types of information, such as operational performance. In this way, the company can determine how well customer needs are being met. Then, based on the results, appropriate action can be taken. The firm also carries out extensive marketing research to determine customer satisfaction and to track its own performance against that of the competition.

in action

ETHICS AND SOCIAL RESPONSIBILITY IN ACTION

Managing the Productivity Effort with a People Focus

Controlling productivity and quality improvements requires far more than the collection and analysis of operating data. Consideration must also be given to the personnel and the "tools" required to keep them motivated and committed to their work projects. Organizations are finding the following five steps to be particularly helpful in keeping the personnel in focus.

1. Keep everyone openly informed regarding the company's objectives and plans for the future. When an enterprise decides to revise operating procedures and improve efficiency, a great deal of commitment will be required from personnel. Therefore, they should be told up front what management wants to do and why. This helps to instill in workers support for the effort. In addition, these individuals are often the ones best equipped to figure out shortcuts and ways to cut waste and inefficiency. Therefore, their support must be obtained from the outset, and this is where open communication enters the picture.

2. Find out which skills everyone possesses and which skills they will need to increase productivity. Then create the necessary training programs for providing to workers the expertise to move to this next higher level of skill performance. This step is particularly important when organizations decide to purchase new technology. If personnel are unfamiliar with how to use the newly obtained machinery and equipment, performance will be less than ideal.

3. Teach the employees how to focus on the root causes of problems so that they can more quickly isolate the reasons for these problems and the steps that need to be taken to resolve them. In doing this, be sure to empower the workers so that they do not have to check back continually with a higher level manager for approval to proceed. If the personnel are competent and well trained, they will know what to do, and it is a waste of organizational resources to monitor them too closely.

4. Create autonomous work groups and encourage them to look continually for ways of improving performance. This continuous-improvement effort is critically important in ensuring that productivity and quality gains are not lost. In this process, place a great deal of emphasis on the generation of suggestions for improvement. In the best Japanese companies, workers, on average, contribute one idea per month that can be profitably used. In some American firms, management has been able to generate one practical idea per week, which has helped to turn these companies into world-class competitors.

5. Create a reward system that can be used to share productivity gains with the employees. For example, if productivity increases by 10 percent and this generates $100,000 for the company, have a predetermined system for giving part of this money to the workers. Additionally, share these gains on a frequent basis, such as quarterly. Research shows that if these gains are distributed only once or twice annually, their motivational impact tends to diminish. However, if personnel are given productivity bonuses on a monthly basis, they tend to be motivated to continue their efforts toward increasing output and maintaining high quality levels.

The key to productivity success is a well-trained, well-motivated workforce. Of course, having state-of-the-art technology is also important but, in the final analysis, it is the employees who make the system work. Thus, the role of human relations in the productivity equation cannot be overstated.

Sources: Richard M. Hodgetts, Measures of Quality & High Performance *(New York: American Management Association, 1998), chapters 6 and 7; Kate Ludeman, "Motorola's HR Learns the Value of Teams Firsthand," Personnel Journal, June 1995, pp. 117–123; David Chaudron, "The Authority Matrix: Empowerment and Role Clarification," HR Focus, May 1995, pp. 22–23; and Jennifer A. Laabs, "Prudential Measures HR with a Total-Quality Yardstick," Personnel Journal, April 1995, pp. 139–143.*

Another good example is provided by FedEx, which has developed service quality indicators (SQIs) that are used to measure customer satisfaction and service quality. In all, a dozen SQIs are continually tracked:

- *Abandoned calls*—any phone calls in which the caller hangs up when his or her call cannot be answered within ten seconds of arrival.
- *Complaints reopened*—any customer complaint reopened after an unsatisfactory resolution of the initial complaint.
- *Damaged packages*—all packages that contain visible or concealed damage, including weather or water damage.
- *Invoice adjustments requested*—the number of packages for which customers request invoice adjustments, whether or not they are granted, because the company feels that such requests indicate that the customer perceives a problem.
- *Lost packages*—both missing packages and packages that arrive with missing contents.
- *Late pickups*—package pickups made after the customer's requested time.
- *Missing proofs of delivery*—invoices that are not accompanied by proof-of-delivery paperwork, which is something that the company promises to its customers with each bill.
- *Overages*—packages that arrive at a U.S. clearance port without being listed on Customs' clearance documents.
- *Right day late deliveries*—all packages that are delivered after the commitment time (no matter how small the time error) but on the day on which delivery was promised, according to exceptions noted in the terms and conditions of service (such as an incorrect address on the package or an extreme weather-caused delay).

TABLE 7.4	FedEx's 12 Service Quality Indicators	
Indicators		**Weight**
Abandoned calls		1
Complaints reopened		5
Damaged packages		10
Invoice adjustments requested		1
Lost packages		10
Missed pickups		10
Missing proofs of delivery		1
Overgoods (lost and found)		5
Right day late deliveries		1
Wrong day late deliveries		5
Traces		1
International		1

Source: Richard M. Hodgetts, Quality Measures in America's Most Successful Firms *(New York: American Management Association, 1998), p. 121.*

- *Wrong day late deliveries*—all packages delivered after the day on which delivery was promised, according to exceptions noted in the terms and conditions of service (such as an incorrect address on the package or an extreme weather-caused delay).
- *Traces*—proof-of-performance requests from customers that cannot be answered through data in the company's computer tracking system because an employee failed to scan the package's identifying bar code electronically into the computer at each point in the delivery process.
- *International*—a composite score of service quality indicators that includes many of the other eleven indicators just listed as well as other indicators, which are international in focus, such as customs clearance delays.

Each of these SQIs is assigned a relative weight, so FedEx not only tracks its performance for each of these quality indicators but uses the weighting system in arriving at an overall evaluation of how well it is serving the customer. The weights are identified in Table 7.4.[31]

Participative Management Approaches

⑤ LEARNING OBJECTIVE
Relate the value of alternative work arrangements and empowerment to increased productivity and quality

Some approaches to improving productivity and quality are based on getting employees more involved in the effort by giving them greater authority in the workplace. Three of the most popular approaches are alternative work schedules, the use of empowerment, and the development of intrapreneurship attitudes.

Alternative Work Schedules

An *alternative work schedule* is a variation in the times at which employees begin and end work each day. This can be done a number of ways. The three most common are the compressed workweek, flextime, and shift work.

COMPRESSED WORKWEEK

The **compressed workweek** allows an individual to work a shorter workweek than the typical five-day week. The arrangement might involve four 10-hour days or three twelve-hour days. The most common arrangement is the 5-4/9 schedule. Employees work nine hours for eight workdays and eight hours for one workday during a biweekly pay period, and receive one day off biweekly; all basic work requirements apply. Another common arrangement is the so-called 3–4 workweek in which people work three 12-hour days one week and four 12-hour days the next week. When work is compressed into four days, it is typical to find people working Monday through Thursday or Tuesday through Friday. Firemen have long used this arrangement. So have some manufacturing firms, which have found that a four-day workweek reduces cleanup and start-up time and cuts back on three to five paid holidays per year. In industries such as petroleum and chemicals, many people work a three-day, 36-hour schedule.

Some of the major reasons cited for adopting a compressed workweek include:

- Increase in employee leisure time.
- Increase in work quality, production, and employee satisfaction.
- A decrease in employee tardiness, turnover, and accidents.
- Lower setup and cleanup cost.

A compressed workweek has longer individual workdays.

In recent years, European companies have tried to overcome high national unemployment by compressing the workweek and reducing work hours. For example, Volkswagen cut employees from a five-day, 36-hour week to a four-day, 29-hour week in an effort to hire more people.

Is the compressed workweek a good idea? Research reveals that most employees favor it and that it takes only about a month to adjust to the fatigue factor. However, this arrangement does not work well for employees who are carrying out heavy physical or taxing mental work. In these cases, many employees have opted for flextime.

FLEXTIME

Flextime
allows workers to decide when they want to stop and start their workday.

A number of different versions of **flextime** exist, but all require employees to be on hand during certain times known as *core hours*.

- One of the most common arrangements calls for everyone to be at work by 10 A.M. and not to leave before 3 P.M.: 10–3 are the core hours. Those who choose to come in later in the morning can arrive at 10 A.M. and go home at 6 P.M. Those who prefer to arrive at 7 A.M. can leave at 3 P.M.
- Under another common arrangement, employees can take their lunch period any time during the core hours.
- A third arrangement is to allow the personnel to work as many hours in a day as they like just as long as they are present for all core hours and work their total number of hours per week.
- A fourth arrangement is to use the same approach as the third plan except that each employee's hours are checked for completeness on a monthly instead of a weekly basis.

In firms that employ a large number of people, work scheduling often is handled by a computerized system. This system matches employee work preferences with the demand for workers so that the necessary number of employees is on hand at all times.

Many enterprises have had success with flextime. Workers, as well as employers, like the flexible schedules. Some of the reasons why workers like working the flexible schedules include:[32]

- Gives personal control over schedules.
- Experience less traffic congestion and fewer delays.
- Opportunity to work at personal peak times.
- Flexibility to take care of personal business.
- Opportunity to adjust work schedules to meet personal needs.
- Decreased stress.
- Increased job satisfaction.

Employers like offering flexible schedules for the following reasons:[33]

- Expands business hours for local customers.
- Enhances ability to work with other time zones.
- Offers flexibility to workers who need different schedules.
- Increases ability to attract new employees.
- Provides additional cost-free benefit.
- Reduces tardiness and absences.
- Decrease personnel turnover.
- Improves productivity and morale.

As far back as 1985 a study of nine hundred firms, three hundred each in the banking, insurance, and utilities industries, researchers focused on the benefits of flextime among clerical workers. They found some of the major advantages included increased worker satisfaction, higher work quality, greater efficiency, reduced tardiness, lower absenteeism, and less overtime.[34] Overall, the researchers reported that 83 percent of the utilities, 85 percent of the banks, and 97 percent of the insurance firms believed that flextime, in comparison with fixed hours, increased effectiveness.

Recently 28.8 percent of full-time wage and salary workers had flexible work schedules. Men (30.0 percent) were more likely to work flexible schedules than women (27.4 percent). Flexible schedule were most common among managerial and professional specialty occupations, with 45.5 percent of executives, administrators, and managers able to vary their work hours. Although over one in four workers can vary their schedules, only about one in ten are enrolled in a formal, employer-sponsored flextime program.[35]

Many organizations have found that in deciding whether to implement a flextime approach, it is advisable to begin by putting a small number of employees on flextime, work out any problems with the program, and then extend it to include more people. The approach often used in implementing a flextime program is as follows:

1. Get top management's support.
2. Solicit involvement from employees at all levels.
3. Appoint someone who will have the respect of management and workers to oversee the entire program.
4. Set up a committee or task force to coordinate work assignments, hold meetings to explain the procedures necessary to implement the program, and keep two-way communication channels open.
5. Train the management staff by acquainting them with how flextime works, its advantages and drawbacks, and what they need to know about managing their people under this work arrangement.
6. Conduct a pilot test of the program to pinpoint any problems that will have to be overcome before the arrangement is carried to the organization at large.
7. Formulate guidelines for handling problems that may arise.
8. Set up procedures for monitoring work schedules.
9. Evaluate the results.

SHIFT WORK

Most enterprises use **shift work,** with 8–5 or 9–5 being the most common shifts. Some industries have 'round-the-clock shifts because of the demand for output. Manufacturing firms with a large backlog of orders are likely to go to a second, and perhaps a third, shift until the backlog is eliminated. Police and fire departments and hospitals maintain 'round-the-clock shifts every day of the year.

Shift work offers a number of advantages.

- First, the pay usually is better for those on the second and third shifts.
- Second, commuting time usually is shorter owing to less traffic for people on these shifts.
- Third, these shifts are often less hectic and allow the worker more job autonomy.

Reasons given by working an alternative shift include:[36]

- Nature of the job.
- Personal preference.
- Better arrangements for family or child care.
- Better pay.
- It allows time for school.

Is shift work a good idea? Many organizations feel it is. In some cases, no alternative exists. Police and fire departments, for example, have no other way of providing twenty-four-hour protection. In other enterprises, management has found that people soon adjust to their new work shifts and, as their seniority increases, they are able to switch to other shifts that better meet their social and personal preferences. For these reasons, shift work will continue to be an important alternative work schedule.

Use of Empowerment

Empowerment is the process of giving workers autonomy over the way that their jobs are performed and holding them accountable for the results. Throughout history, empowerment

Shift work is assigned on the basis of time shifts such as 8 A.M. to 5 P.M.

Empowerment is the process of giving workers autonomy over the way that their jobs are performed and holding them accountable for the results.

leadership was implemented when "getting the job done" had priority over control. For example, the Chinese brought empowerment leadership styles to California during the 1850s gold rush and in 1864 during the construction of the railroad from Sacramento, California, into the Sierra Mountains. Empowerment gave full control and responsibility of the project to frontline workers. The empowerment concept was so successful most railroad construction companies adapted it. This, however, was not true of the operations of the railroad, where power and control were paramount.[37]

The Panama Canal project in the early 1900s is another example where empowerment leadership made a difference in completing the project. The first chief engineer, John Wallace's leadership style was command-and-control. His workers were treated as machines and the project was failing. The second chief engineer John F. Stevens knew how to organize work environments that energized and motivated workers, which allowed the project to be completed as scheduled.[38]

The empowerment trend gained significant ground in the 1990s and today is one of the primary causes of quality improvement in the workplace. Not only are workers becoming more empowered in the workplace, they are also more empowered as consumers. As online customers, they are shaping online business models by demanding that web sites respond to the privacy preferences of the e-commerce consumer. Consumers are willing to share information with sites in exchange for services, but there is still the issue of trust.[39]

Although a growing body of evidence is showing linkages between empowerment and good governance and growth and improved performance, issues remain about how to measure empowerment. Recently a two-day workshop was held involving eighty World Bank staff, academics, and researchers to discuss how measuring empowerment can better inform policy choices, project design, and assessment of impact on project beneficiaries.[40]

Some of the most recent case examples of empowerment at work are outlined here.

PAINEWEBBER

PaineWebber, a giant stock brokerage firm, uses empowerment. The company concluded that to remain competitive, it would have to install a multimillion-dollar trading and information system for its brokers. This system would enable the brokers to keep track of the latest stock prices and business-related information and perform financial analyses needed by their clients. As a result, PaineWebber upgraded the technology of all 5,200 brokers in 264 offices across the country.

Now brokers are able not only to get the latest stock market price quotations but also to pick any financial software they would like and use it to analyze data for customers and do their own record keeping. This means the broker can provide faster and more accurate information than ever, and everything needed to do the job is at the broker's fingertips.

When introducing the new system, PaineWebber did not stress the technology but the way in which the system could help the broker do a better job. This ensured that the brokers would focus on learning only those things they needed to perform their particular job—and this is precisely what the company wanted. The response of the employees was very positive. Simply put, empowered brokers are helping PaineWebber provide faster, more accurate service than before to an ever more demanding client group.

XEROX CORPORATION

Xerox Corporation is well known for its document equipment, services, and solutions. Xerox is able to stay competitive and lead the market with innovative products and services by using quality principles in all areas of its business. It operates under the guidance of six core values, one of which is valuing and empowering employees.

In one case, a team of virtual sales executives from an eBusiness Teleweb division formed a graphic arts team on that segment of the marketplace. This North American Teleweb Graphic Arts team found there were varying degrees of sales skills and product knowledge, and very little industry-specific knowledge among the team members. Because of specialized market segments, information and training were not available from the immediate Teleweb support team. The newly formed graphic arts team effectively used quality tools,

in action

EMPOWERMENT RULES IN ACTION

Nine Rules for Effective Empowerment Teams

These nine rules are based on the belief that level of elementary problems controls efficiency, quality, and cost. If there are many elementary problems, productivity will be negative; likewise, a low level of problems puts productivity in the positive column. In the typical workforce, there is no recognition for people who spend time on elementary problems, big problems receive all the attention; yet, big problems start as minor and there are people around who are aware of them. Because of leadership attitudes, employees develop the habit of ignoring problems until they explode, at which time they become big problems, and the leaders want to go on record for being problem solvers. Empowered teams correct this attitude. They focus on getting the job done while solving or preventing problems.

1. *Priority 1—Get the job done!!!* In many work environments, the top priority is cost control, which limits the ability to get the job done. While it takes money to control project costs the focus should be on "getting the job done" and what it takes to finish the job, not on what it costs.

2. *Consider employees as an investment, not as a cost.* In any work environment, employees' skills and abilities will reflect the attitude of their leaders. If leadership considers employees a cost, the quality of employees will suffer; likewise, if leadership considers employees an investment, then both sides will be motivated to increase skill quality. Greater efficiency is the result.

3. *Employee attitudes are byproducts of leadership style.* If subordinates' attitudes are negative toward the company, it is because of leadership style. If they are positive, it is because of leadership style. If attitudes need changing, it must start with the leaders.

4. *Sharing knowledge inspires motivation.* People who have an opportunity to share knowledge feel they are a part of the team. Team members want to impress by their ability to contribute valuable information and this motivates the desire to seek information. It maintains a desire to excel, accept challenges, and reject the status quo.

5. *Coach, not control.* People who only follow orders do not assume responsibility, are not motivated, and do not have a desire to excel. Coaching is inspiring people to find solutions to problems. Finding solutions is a motivating force; it also becomes a habit. Coaching is sharing knowledge.

6. *Team responsibility.* Being responsible for results is a highly motivating force. Also, a group of three or more, focused on a common goal, become a highly intelligent force. They are aware of minor problems and have the authority to manage them. The team is recognized for their ability to prevent problems while getting the job done.

7. *Supply quality resources.* Efficiency is as effective as available resources (tools, supplies, work environment) to complete tasks. Teams will work hard to get jobs done, but they need quality resources to be efficient. Resources influence pride, which affects output quality.

8. *Opportunity to learn.* Repetitive tasks kill the desire to learn, an attitude that rejects change and accepts the status quo. There is always a better way of doing a task, including a repetitive task, and better ways are found in empowered teams. Challenges motivate people to learn, and the desire to learn is based on opportunity for challenges.

9. *Wages.* Effective empowered teams require above-average wages. Empowerment is no substitute for low wages. High wages forces leaders to manage in an efficient way. Low wages promotes sloppiness. Wage level influences attitudes and output quality.

*(Robert L. Webb, "Motivation Tool Chest," 2000, **http://www.motivation-tools.com**).*

including employee empowerment, to identify and set improvement goals, determine and prioritize solutions, and to guide the implementation of the team's solutions. It successfully developed the skills and processes for sales, solutions management, and issue management, thereby enhancing the relationships with graphic arts customers. The team put its own training and support mechanisms in place to enable the members to meet increased

Teleweb coverage, excel in their jobs, grow revenue and maximize customer satisfaction. Most importantly, the customer and solutions developed for the customer were the focal point of all team activities.

The team's achievements have been measured in the form of increased sales revenue. It has consistently achieved more than 100 percent of its total revenue goal and expects a 400 percent increase in fulfilled revenue year over year.[41]

LEARNING OBJECTIVE (6)

Define the term intrapreneurship and relate its value to improved organization productivity and quality

An **intrapreneur** *is an entrepreneur who works within the confines of an organization.*

Development of Intrapreneurship Attitudes

An **intrapreneur** is an entrepreneur who works within the confines of an enterprise. Sometimes the individual is known as an *in-house entrepreneur*. In any event, many organizations are beginning to realize that intrapreneurs are critical in an organization's efforts to increase productivity and quality. Brandt has put it this way:

The challenge is relatively straightforward. The United States must upgrade its innovative prowess. To do so, U.S. companies must tap into the creative power of their members. Ideas come from people. Innovation is a capability of the many. That capability is utilized when

time out

ARE YOU AN INTRAPRENEUR?

Many people have intrapreneurial desires and would enjoy working in a job that allows them to fulfill these ambitions. Are you an intrapreneur? To find out, answer the following questions. An interpretation of the responses is provided at the end of the chapter.

Y/N 1. Are you a high risk taker?

Y/N 2. Do you enjoy taking the ideas of others and working to improve them?

Y/N 3. Do you prefer to work alone rather than with others?

Y/N 4. Are you effective at networking with others?

Y/N 5. Do you like to work around rules and regulations by figuring out how to get things done despite all the red tape?

Y/N 6. Would you be willing to risk losing your job to develop or improve a product that could make a great deal of money for the company?

Y/N 7. Are you loyal and true to those who work with you?

Y/N 8. In terms of what motivates you, is money near the top of the list?

Y/N 9. Do you believe luck is a critical factor in the success of most individuals?

Y/N 10. Are your ethics and morals higher than those of the average person?

Y/N 11. Do you like to roll up your sleeves, dive in, and get involved in accomplishing things?

Y/N 12. Do you like to have your boss set goals for you rather than do it yourself?

Y/N 13. Do you believe that to get ahead you often have to do things that are illegal or unethical?

Y/N 14. Are you extremely self-confident?

Y/N 15. Do you like to gather information and examine the facts before you jump into something, as opposed to getting in quickly and going to work on a project?

Y/N 16. Do status symbols such as a big office, a company car, and a key to the executive washroom strongly motivate you?

Y/N 17. Are you good at persuading people to do things?

Y/N 18. Do you often dislike the organizational system but overcome this dislike by working out ways of manipulating the rules and regulations to your own advantage?

Y/N 19. Do you enjoy following orders from above?

Y/N 20. Are you good at generating fresh ideas?

people give commitment to the mission and life of the enterprise and have the power to do something with their capabilities. Noncommitment is the price of obsolete managing practices, not the lack of talent or desire.

Commitment is most freely given when the members of an enterprise play a part in defining the purposes and plans of the entity. Commitment carries with it a de facto approval of and support for the management. Managing by consent is a useful managing philosophy if more entrepreneurial behavior is desired.[42]

Do you have intrapreneurial desires? Take the Time Out quiz and find out. Additional insights into intrapreneurship are provided in Table 7.5. A close reading of these characteristics, along with the information provided in the Time Out quiz, reveals that intrapreneurs provide an interesting blend of behaviors that complement and extend the thinking of traditional managers and entrepreneurs. This helps explain why many firms are interested in promoting an intrapreneurial way of thinking to increase productivity and improve work quality.

TABLE 7.5	*Intrapreneurs: A Comparative Look*		
Characteristic	**Traditional Manager**	**Entrepreneur**	**Intrapreneur**
Primary motives	Wants promotion and other traditional corporate rewards; power-motivated.	Wants freedom. Goal-oriented, self-reliant, and self-motivated.	Wants freedom and access to corporate resources. Goal-oriented and self-motivated but also responds to corporate rewards and recognition.
Time orientation	Responds to quotas and budgets; weekly, monthly, quarterly, and annual planning horizons; the next promotion or transfer.	Uses end goals of 5- to 10-year growth of the business as guides. Takes action now to move to next step along way.	End goals of 3 to 15 years, depending on type of venture. Urgency to meet self-imposed and corporate timetables.
Tendency to action	Delegates action. Supervising and reporting take most energy.	Gets hands dirty. May upset employees by suddenly doing their work.	Gets hands dirty. May know how to delegate but, when necessary, does what needs to be done.
Skills	Professional management. Often business school–trained. Uses abstract analytical tools, people management, and political skills.	Knows business intimately. More business acumen than managerial or political skill. Often technically trained if in technical business. May have had formal profit-and-loss responsibility in the company.	Very much like the entrepreneur, but the situation demands greater ability to prosper within the organization. Needs help with this.
Attitude toward courage and destiny	Sees others being in charge of his or her destiny. Can be forceful and ambitious, but may be fearful of others' ability to sabotage him or her.	Self-confident, optimistic, courageous.	Self-confident and courageous. Many intrapreneurs are cynical about the system but optimistic about their ability to outwit it.

(continued)

TABLE 7.5   *(continued)*

Characteristic	Traditional Manager	Entrepreneur	Intrapreneur
Focus of attention	Primarily on events inside corporation.	Primarily on technology and marketplace.	Both inside and outside. Sells insiders on needs of venture and marketplace, but also focuses on customers.
Attitude toward risk	Cautious.	Likes moderate risk. Invests heavily, but expects to succeed.	Likes moderate risk. Generally not afraid of being fired, so sees little personal risk.
Use of market research	Has market studies done to discover needs and guide product conceptualization.	Creates needs. Creates products that often cannot be tested with market research. Potential customers do not yet understand these products. Talks to customers and forms own opinions.	Does own market research and intuitive market evaluation, like the entrepreneur.
Attitude toward status	Cares about status symbols (such as a corner office).	Happy sitting on an orange crate if job is getting done.	Considers traditional status symbols a joke. Treasures symbols of freedom.
Attitude toward failure and mistakes	Strives to avoid mistakes and surprises. Postpones recognizing failure.	Deals with mistakes and failures as learning experiences.	Sensitive to need to appear orderly. Attempts to hide risky projects from view to learn from mistakes without political cost of public failure.
Decision-making style	Agrees with those in power. Delays making decisions until a feel for what bosses want is obtained.	Follows private vision. Decisive, action-oriented.	Adept at getting others to agree with private vision. Somewhat more patient and willing to compromise than the entrepreneur but still a doer.
Who serves	Pleases others.	Pleases self and customer.	Pleases self, customers, and sponsors.
Attitude toward the system	Sees system as nurturing and protective; seeks position within it.	May rapidly advance in a system; then, when frustrated, may reject the system and form his or her own company.	Dislikes the system but learns to manipulate it.
Problem-solving style	Works out problems within the system.	Escapes problems in large and formal structures by leaving and starting over alone.	Works out problems within the system or bypasses them without leaving.

TABLE 7.5	*(continued)*		

Characteristic	Traditional Manager	Entrepreneur	Intrapreneur
Family history	Family members worked for large organizations.	Entrepreneurial small-business, professional, or farm background.	Entrepreneurial small-business, professional, or farm background.
Relationship with parents	Independent of mother; good relations with father but slightly dependent.	Absent father or poor relations with father.	Better relations with father, but still stormy.
Socioeconomic background	Middle class.	Lower class in some early studies, middle class in more recent ones.	Middle class.
Educational level	Highly educated.	Less well educated, per earlier studies; some graduate work but not doctorate, per later ones.	Often highly educated, particularly in technical fields, though sometimes not.
Relationships with others	Perceives hierarchy as basic relationship.	Perceives transactions and deal making as basic relationship.	Perceives transactions within hierarchy as basic relationship.

Source: Adapted from Gifford Pinchot, Intrapreneuring *(New York: Harper & Row, 1985), pp. 54–56.*

Creating the Right Climate

Many approaches can be used to create and nurture an intrapreneurial climate. Four steps that many enterprises have taken are:

1. **Setting explicit, mutually agreed-on goals so employees know what is expected of them.**
2. **Providing feedback and positive reinforcement so people know how well they are doing and are encouraged to continue their efforts.**
3. **Placing emphasis on individual responsibility that builds confidence, trust, and accountability.**
4. **Giving results-based rewards that encourage risk taking and high achievement.**

Other steps are designed to create an innovative environment. Some of the most useful are:

1. **Encourage action.**
2. **Use informal meetings whenever possible.**
3. **Tolerate failure and use it as a learning experience.**
4. **Be persistent in getting an idea to market.**
5. **Reward innovation for innovation's sake.**
6. **Plan the physical layout of the enterprise to encourage informal communication.**
7. **Expect clever adaptations of other employees' ideas.**
8. **Put people on small teams for future-oriented projects.**
9. **Encourage personnel to circumvent rigid procedures and bureaucratic red tape.**
10. **Reward or promote innovative personnel.**[43]

LEARNING OBJECTIVE

*Explain the impor-
tance for developing
intrapreneurship
strategies*

⑦ Developing Intrapreneurial Strategies

Intrapreneurial strategies are designed to create an environment in which creative, innovative employees flourish. In this environment, the manager often assumes a number of roles, including those of coach, teacher, and mentor. The employees, meanwhile, are encouraged to develop ideas that will result in higher productivity and quality, without concern about making mistakes and losing their jobs. "Very simply put, intrapreneurship is entrepreneurship practiced by people within established organizations." Intrapreneurs "tend to be motivated by the dream of things that conventional wisdom says can't, won't, or shouldn't be done."[44] Intrapreneurship is about making business better. It is not a system , but a process that evolves by using creativity to bring about change. It is not a solo activity, it is a team effort where credit is shared widely. Jobs are done regardless of the job description. An intrapreneurial organization seeks change and responds to it.[45] Intrapreneurial organizations often supplement their strategies with rewards that encourage effort and commitment. Examples include bonus plans, stock incentive plans, stock option plans, and profit sharing.

Even though intrapreneurship has many different interpretations, two intents seem to persist: growth and innovation. As a corporate growth strategy, intrapreneurship might include continuous improvement to bring new or improved products to market to generate new revenue, whereas innovation strategies require breakthrough thinking and action, like being different and creating evolutionary change. The results of a survey of corporate executives conducted by Daniel F. Twomey and Drew L. Harris of Silberman School of Business, Fairleigh Dickinson University, indicates a high correlation between corporate entrepreneurial strategies and intrapreneurial outcomes of employees.[46] Companies willing to promote internal entrepreneurism and foster innovation have their own ideas of intrapreneurism and how it works within the company. For example Thermo Electron, Hewlett-Packard, 3M, and Deere & Co. each have their own ways of fostering intrapreneurism. For the 3M company, the Post-it notes is a legenday billion-dollar idea that the company tried to kill. It survived under a "skunk works" innovation experiment. "Skunk works" allows a committed individual to continue working a bit on a project even after the company has decided not to pursue it.[47]

Intrapreneurial strategies often have two phases. The first phase creates the necessary environment, whereas the second gains participant support. During the first phase, top management will determine the types of entrepreneurial ideas in which it is interested and the rules that will be used in managing intrapreneurs. This includes developing the necessary vision and communicating it to employees. Management will also use this time to identify potential intrapreneurs and target them for attention. The second phase is dedicated to convincing these people to formulate and implement intrapreneurial projects and to helping them to do so. GE is a good example.

> *The company carefully selects young, high-technology people with only a few years' work experience, and often no formal management education, and literally sets them up in businesses. Basically, General Electric gives these new entrepreneurs a product line and a time period and then asks them to make the company grow. They must compete against each other for allocation of funds and resources, and they must learn to assess markets and prioritize and deploy resources. This process is enhanced through the active support of the supervisors, who regularly meet with their intrapreneurs. Finally, at the end of the time period, these venture managers are assessed by how well they have attained their objectives and how much money they have made. Compensation is related to this contribution.*[48]

There are three foundations of intrapreneurialship:[49]

- **Innovation—the ability to see things in novel ways.**
- **Calculated risk taking—the ability to take calculated changes and to embrace failure as a learning experience.**
- **Creativity—the ability to conceive of multiple possible futures and to proactively create the one you most desire.**

The intrapreneur is typically the person who challenges the status quo and fights to change the system and who is inclined to act first and ask for forgiveness rather than to ask for permission before acting.

Regardless of the specific steps taken by an organization, all have similar patterns. They seek a proactive change in the status quo and a new, flexible approach to the management of operations. They also tend to undertake the following steps:

1. **Encourage individuals to assume the challenges of intrapreneurship.**
2. **Give intrapreneurs the authority and freedom to do the job their own way.**
3. **Let the individuals see their ideas through to completion.**
4. **Fund intrapreneurial efforts.**
5. **Have many intrapreneurial projects going on at the same time.**
6. **Encourage risk taking and tolerate mistakes.**
7. **Stick with entrepreneurial ideas long enough to determine whether they will work.**
8. **Encourage people from different departments and areas of interest to pool their interdisciplinary skills.**
9. **Allow the formation of autonomous teams that have full responsibility for developing their ideas.**
10. **Let intrapreneurial teams have authority to use the resources of other divisions and outside vendors if they choose.**

summary

(1) LEARNING OBJECTIVE
Describe the current status and future directions of management efforts to improve productivity and quality

Two of the major challenges facing organizations today are those of increasing productivity and improving the quality of goods and services. Productivity is measured as the relationship between output and input. During the last decade, American productivity has been declining vis-à-vis such foreign competitors as the Japanese and Germans. The same is true for quality. To improve productivity, workers say that conditions for collaboration, commitment, and creativity must be improved. The work needs to be important and management needs to appreciate the workers' efforts. Workers want the opportunity to do interesting, challenging work in a friendly environment.

(2) LEARNING OBJECTIVE
Discuss how total quality management programs are increasing productivity and quality

One step being taken to attack the problem directly is the introduction of TQM programs. TQM is a people-focused management system with the objective of meeting and exceeding customer demands while trying to keep costs as low as possible. The underlying assumptions of TQM are: (1) the quality output of goods and services is everyone's job; (2) the thinking that quality is "good enough" must be replaced by the belief that quality must be continually improved; (3) work can often be done faster without any loss in quality, and (4) everybody associated with the organization needs to be part of the quality effort, including top managers, lower level workers, outside suppliers, and customers.

(3) LEARNING OBJECTIVE
Identify the steps of TQM programs and briefly describe each step

Today, thousands of U.S. firms are implementing TQM programs through the use of five steps: (1) formulation of strategic intent; (2) careful design of organization structure and training efforts; (3) common tools and techniques; (4) emphasis on use of customer value added; (5) use of benchmarking and continuous improvement; and (6) careful measurement of performance results.

Strategic intent focuses on the company's vision and forms the basis for the organization's mission, reason for being in business. A quality council is a group of individuals who oversee the quality initiative. The structural design should allow quality efforts to identify problems, analyze problems, and resolve problems. These teams cannot function effectively unless they are trained properly in quantitative and behavior techniques. Establishing budgets for training is necessary.

A wide variety of tools and techniques are used, such as surveys, charts, bar graphs, and cause-and-effect diagrams. Another way of improving quality is to find out what the customer wants and give it to the individual. This is called customer value added (CVA). To ensure that quality is maintained, companies use benchmarking, an ongoing process of measuring products, services, and practices against leading competitors in the industry. Continuous improvement relies on consistent, incremental gains and occasional innovation. The emphasis is on small improvements achieved on a continual basis. The results are carefully measured to evaluate how well things are going and to make necessary changes.

---

④ LEARNING OBJECTIVE
Explain how Pareto chart analysis, cause-and-effect diagrams, customer-value-added programs, and benchmarking reduce errors and increase quality

A Pareto chart is a special vertical bar graph that helps to identify problems and the order in which they are to be addressed. Cause-and-effect diagrams, often used as a follow-up to Pareto charts, are designed to help identify reasons for the problem. Four basis steps should be used. Customer-value-added programs determine what customers want and follow-up by giving them the products and services they are seeking. Benchmarking measures quality performance against the quality performance of leading competitors in the industry. Each of these tools is a strategy for improving quality and maintaining a competitive position in the marketplace.

---

⑤ LEARNING OBJECTIVE
Relate the value of alternative work arrangements and empowerment to increased productivity and quality

Other approaches encourage participative management. Alternative work arrangements allow people some control in determining when they will come to work and when they will go home. These include such work schedules as the compressed workweek, flextime, and shift work. Empowerment is the process of giving workers authority over the way their jobs are done and holding them accountable for the results. This process is used by a large number of successful firms that are finding it results in cost cutting, increased productivity, and higher-quality output.

---

⑥ LEARNING OBJECTIVE
Define the term intrapreneurship and relate its value to improved organizational productivity and quality

A third major approach in improving productivity and work quality is the introduction of new philosophical approaches. One is the development of intrapreneurship by encouraging entrepreneurial activity within the enterprise. Creating and nurturing an intrapreneurial climate involves setting explicit, mutually agreed-on goals so employees know what is expected of them; providing feedback and positive reinforcement so people know how well they are doing and are encouraged to continue their efforts; placing emphasis on individual responsibility that builds confidence, trust, and accountability; and giving results-based rewards that encourage risk taking and high achievement.

This usually takes two steps. First, the right climate is created. Second, employees are designated as having intrapreneurial potential, are encouraged to engage in intrepreneurial activity, and are rewarded for their efforts. These steps seek a proactive change in the status quo and a new, flexible approach to the management of operations.

KEY TERMS IN THE CHAPTER

Productivity

Total quality management (TQM)

First principle of TQM

Strategic intent

Quality council

Pareto chart

Cause-and-effect diagram

Customer value added

Benchmarking

Compressed workweek

Flextime

Shift work

Empowerment

Intrapreneur

REVIEW AND STUDY QUESTIONS

1. What is meant by *productivity?* Of what importance is productivity to American enterprise?

2. Are American productivity and quality improving or declining? Defend your answer.

3. What is TQM and how does it work?

4. What are some ideas on how the first principle of TQM: "Do it right the first Time," should be implemented?

5. How does a formulation of strategic intent help an organization to increase its productivity and quality?

6. How should training be used to improve quality? Give some examples.

7. What is the purpose of a Pareto chart? Give an example of how to use it.

8. How can a cause-and-effect diagram be used to promote quality?

9. How are firms using the customer value added approach to improve their services to customers? Give examples.

10. What are the basic steps in benchmarking? Of what value is this process in increasing productivity and quality?

11. Why is continuous improvement critical to the success of total quality management efforts?

12. Explain how each of the following work: compressed workweek, flextime, shift work. Give an example of each.

13. In what way do alternative work schedules help to increase work productivity and quality? Defend your answer.

14. How does empowerment of employees work?

15. Why are more and more firms using empowerment in their organizations? Identify and discuss two reasons.

16. What is an intrapreneur? How can organizations encourage intrapreneurship? Cite five examples.

17. How can an intrapreneurial climate be created and nurtured? Discuss at least four ideas.

18. Why would organizations seeking to increase their productivity and work quality be interested in encouraging intrapreneurship?

19. What are two phases in developing intrapreneurial strategies?

20. What are the steps in undertaking the intrapreneurial strategies?

VISIT THE WEB

TECHNOLOGY BUILDING BLOCKS

In this chapter, you discovered a great deal about productivity and the ways in which organizations are attempting to improve the quality of their goods and services. Continually getting better is a major challenge, but some firms are accomplishing this on an almost monthly basis. A good example is the Intel Corporation, which manufactures computer chips. Every 12 months, the power of these chips has been almost doubling, while the price has been continually dropping! How can Intel maintain this momentum? One way is by focusing on productivity and quality improvement. Visit the company's Web site at **http://www.intel.com** and then answer these questions:

1. What new products can we expect from Intel over the next 12 months?

2. How expensive are these products likely to be in contrast to those being offered currently?

MALCOLM BALDRIGE NATIONAL QUALITY AWARD

The Malcolm Baldrige National Quality Award is the nation's highest quality award given to U.S. organizations that have exemplary achievements in seven areas. In 1987, Congress established the award to enhance the competitiveness of U.S. organizations. The award promotes excellence in organizational performance, recognizes the quality and performance achievements of U.S. organizations, and publicizes successful performance strategies. Visit **http://www.nist.gov** and answer the following questions.

1. What are the seven areas where exemplary achievement must be attained?

2. Who are the recent winners of the award? Go to the home page of a winner and learn about the company and why it won.

COMMITMENT TO QUALITY

Eastman Chemical Company was founded in 1920 and today ranks as the fifth largest publicly held chemical company in the United States. Eastman's commitment to quality and values helped the company earn the 1993 Malcolm Baldrige National Quality Award. Along with concern for customers and community, Eastman also has made the environment a top priority. Visit the Web site of the Eastman Chemical Company and answer the following questions. **http://www.eastman.com**

1. What are the steps in the company's Quality Management process?

2. How are teams used to carry out the process?

3. How well is Eastman exceeding customer's expectations?

4. What is the American Chemistry Councils' Responsible Care?

Are You an Intrapreneur?

Give yourself 1 point for each of the following answers.

1. No	8. Yes	15. No
2. Yes	9. No	16. No
3. No	10. Yes	17. Yes
4. Yes	11. Yes	18. Yes
5. Yes	12. No	19. No
6. Yes	13. No	20. Yes
7. Yes	14. Yes	

A score of 15 or more indicates that you have values and beliefs that are similar to those of successful intrapreneurs.

case: A PRODUCTIVE APPROACH

Karl Landis recently bought a collection agency. The agency handles bills that are turned over to it by organizations that believe these debts are uncollectible. Karl's firm receives 40 percent of all moneys collected. The agency also does bill collecting for the county. A large number of parking tickets go unpaid each year, even though residents are denied renewal of their licenses if they have any outstanding violations. Many of these people will not pay until they are forced to do so. However, the county does not want to wait for its money, so it has agreed to give Karl's agency 40 percent of all fines collected.

Collection work can be very time-consuming and costly. For this reason, Karl's firm relies exclusively on telephone collection. This method is fairly effective given the fact that most people would like to pay their bills but are financially strapped. What Karl finds is that most people will pay their overdue bills if they are put on a time payment plan. They just need someone first to coax them into agreeing to it and then to follow up to ensure that they are sticking to the agreement. In the case of overdue parking tickets, most people are surprised to get a call at home and often pay the bill within 10 days. The secret of success in the business is to find the person's telephone number and get through to that person. Sometimes the person has no phone; other times it

is unlisted; still other times the person answering the phone will say the person who is needed is not at home. In the collection business, experienced bill collectors are vital to success.

To maximize his agency's income, Karl has taken five steps. First, he has purchased a computer software program that keeps track of the names, addresses, and phone numbers of every person from whom his agency is trying to collect. This program also is used to keep track of those who have agreed to pay their bills and how much they have paid. The system provides the collection personnel with accurate information when they call back to follow up on slow-paying customers. Second, after a one-week training program in which employees are taught how to collect, Karl turns them loose on their own. He gives each of them full authority to handle the collection process. He does not interfere with his people. Third, he allows his people to set their own hours collectively. Among the group of fifteen full-time people who work for him, some employees prefer to come in around 1 or 2 P.M. Karl does not care when his personnel come and go, just as long as they get the work done. Fourth, Karl requires each person to be on the phone talking to a customer or placing a call at least fifty minutes of every hour. Research shows that one successful collection should occur every fifty minutes, so Karl knows that each employee should succeed in obtaining collections from eight people per day. Fifth, anyone who is responsible for collecting more than $1,000 in any day is given a 5 percent bonus for all sums in excess of this amount.

Since he introduced these five steps, Karl's collections have increased by 55 percent per week. Additionally, he has not lost one employee, although the turnover is extremely high at most collection agencies. In fact, there is a waiting line of job applicants.

QUESTIONS

1. How is Karl using technology to improve productivity?

2. What type of an alternative work arrangement is Karl using? Explain. Do you believe it is the best, or would you recommend another arrangement? Defend your position.

3. What impact does the training program have on employee retention? Explain

4. In what way is Karl encouraging productivity among his people? Give an example.

YOU BE THE CONSULTANT

Now What?

Lowry International is a manufacturing firm that produces electronic handheld games for sale in North America. Lowry manufactures these games under a subcontract from an international conglomerate. In most cases, the conglomerate makes its own games and exports them to the market. However, Lowry's reputation for high-quality production and on-time delivery has made it more profitable for the conglomerate to have its North American merchandise manufactured by Lowry.

One of the terms of the contract allows the conglomerate to return all defective merchandise. In its own plants, the conglomerate has a defect rate of 1 unit per 100. Lowry's rate for the first two years of the contract was 1 unit per 300. However, over the past twelve months, the defect rate has shot up to 5 units per 100. The conglomerate has been returning these defective units and charging them against Lowry's account.

This increasing defect trend is creating two major problems for the company. One is that its profitability goal is based on no more than 1.5 defects per 100. The other is that the conglomerate will soon be choosing a subcontractor to manufacture industrial electronic engine controls, and Lowry would also like to get this contract. However, the company is concerned that its rising defect rate could jeopardize its image and result in the conglomerate rejecting the Lowry bid.

An analysis of the work environment by the quality control people has resulted in the following preliminary recommendations:

1. The personnel have become sloppy in their approach to doing things. A radical commitment to high-quality production is needed.

2. New creative ideas for eliminating time and reducing defects are needed. This can be accomplished in part through the use of participative management techniques, such as quality teams and the empowerment of work teams.

3. Attention should also be given to the use of alternative work schedules and the ways in which this can help to increase productivity and quality.

The quality control people now are waiting for management to give them feedback on their suggestions. Once this is done, they will develop a detailed plan of action.

Your Advice

1. What do you recommend that the company do first?

   ___ a. Form quality teams and use them to attack the productivity and quality improvement problems.

   ___ b. Give everyone total quality management training.

   ___ c. Offer employees alternative work schedules.

2. What did the quality control department personnel mean by their comment about the need to make a radical commitment to high-quality production? Explain.

3. How can a quality-council approach help in dealing with the current problem?

4. How could the company use empowerment in dealing with this situation? Give an example.

EXPERIENCING QUALITY TEAMS AT WORK

Purpose

- To understand better how a quality team works.
- To provide individuals with an opportunity to study and improve a situation that directly affects them.

Procedure

1. In groups of five to eight, choose an activity at your college or university that directly affects you. It may be the long lines at the cafeteria or the bursar's office. It may be the service at the library.

2. Each group member is responsible for researching the cause(s) for the problem. Make assignments in the group to interview personnel who are directly involved, conduct surveys of students using the facility, make observations and record the results, or brainstorm with other groups of students on campus.

3. Meet as a group and review your findings with an eye toward what can realistically be done about the situation. Be as practical as possible, keeping in mind the need to improve quality and reduce costs.

4. Write up your recommendations for action and submit them to the appropriate university or college official.

8

Job Redesign and Job Enrichment

How can modern organizations deal with the challenge of technology and the dysfunctional effects it creates? One of the primary ways is to redesign jobs and enrich them with psychological motivators, such as increased autonomy, feedback, and task variety. In this chapter, we study how this can be done, as well as examine some of the current challenges in job design.

AFTER READING THIS CHAPTER, YOU SHOULD BE ABLE TO:

1. Explain what job design is all about.
2. Describe how job rotation, job enlargement, and job enrichment work.
3. Describe the five core job dimensions and illustrate selected enrichment principles that help to create these dimensions.
4. Explain the significance of MPS and job profile charts.
5. Discuss five job enrichment principles.
6. Cite some illustrations of job enrichment in action.
7. Discuss four current challenges in job design.

Out of Sight, but Not Out of Mind

The technology revolution has changed not just the way employees do their jobs but also the location where some of them work. Thanks to the emergence of high-powered personal computers, cellular phones, fax-modems, and pagers, a growing number of employees now are working at home or other locales outside the office. These individuals, known as teleworkers or telecommuters, are electronically linked to the office and go on-site only periodically, such as to attend meetings or to have a face-to-face conference with a boss. The number of firms that are employing teleworkers is continuing to increase annually.

A good example is Georgia Power, which recently received the annual Innovation Award from the National Telecommuting Advisory Council. The company first implemented its telecommuting effort in 1992 by having fourteen people work from home. The program was part of a citywide effort to help cut air pollution by reducing the number of vehicles on the road. In the process, the firm found that it saved more than $100,000 in annual leased space expenses, as it no longer needed to provide offices for these telecommuters. Today, Georgia Power has approximately 250 employees who telecommute on a casual or full time basis. Each situation is different and is dependent on the type of work done, management discretion, and the equipment provided. Employees can now access the company's network with an Internet connection, and it is as if they were sitting at their own desk at the company office. This gives employees and managers more flexibility in dealing with a more diverse workforce.

Northern Telecom is another example of a firm that has embraced communications technology and revised the way people work. In this case, the concept has been expanded to the upper levels of the structure. For example, when the firm wanted to hire a vice president for global services, it found that the individual did not want to move from Philadelphia, Pennsylvania, to Nashville, Tennessee. Therefore, Northern Telecom reached an agreement with the manager that allows the individual to work from his home in Philadelphia while managing a staff of approximately two thousand people in Nashville and other geographical locations.

Another benefit of teleworking is that it helps organizations to maintain their personnel by allowing them more handily to balance family and work responsibilities. Consider Janna Tess, a buyer for Smith & Hawken, a multimillion-dollar garden store. When her child was born, Janna would have taken maternity leave so she could stay at home with him. However, thanks to teleworking, she was able to log on to her computer and go to work every day without ever leaving home. Now Janna's husband is being transferred to Europe for two years. No problem. Janna will be able to continue working, and the company will not have the added expense of having to find a replacement.

A related benefit of teleworking is that it allows companies to recruit nationwide—and sometimes worldwide. For example, Mazda's North American operations recently began using the Internet to fill a wide range of jobs from materials handlers to accountants. In the past, the company had used newspaper ads and Internet job boards. However, after reviewing the applicants from these sources, the firm decided to create a new Internet recruiting service linked with a corporate Web page. Commenting on the success of this new approach, the company's manager of workforce strategies noted: "What we found most appealing was its almost paperless process. We can put an ad on the Internet and communicate electronically with prospective candidates. It not only saves us time and money, but we're learning that a lot more people are spending more time on the Internet than any other medium, and that means our turnaround time is much quicker compared to the traditional methods of recruiting."

Of course, this strategy can result in a flood of applicants, and someone must wade through all this paperwork and separate from the pile those applicants who are worth pursuing. However, an increasing number of companies are finding that the Internet is a good place to attract applicants and, because everything is done electronically, the opportunity to follow up quickly and bring people in for on-site visits can be expedited. The result, if everything works well, is that such a firm can get a jump on competitive firms that still are using the old approaches (newspaper ads and college recruiters). In the current job market, which is characterized by more jobs than applicants, this edge can spell the difference between hiring outstanding performers or having to choose from the rest of the group. Simply put, a lot more Internet recruiting is likely to be seen in the future.

Source: "Online Recruiting Best Practices," HR Focus, March 2000, p. 14; Scott Hays, "Hiring on the Web," Workforce, August 1999, pp, 77–84; Brad Grimes, Fern Schumer Chapman, and Michael Goodwin, "The Best Places to Work from Home," Money, April 1997, pp. 160–168; Lin Grensing-Pophal, "Employing the Best People—from Afar," Workforce, March 1997, pp. 30–39; and Melissa Lawrence Corbett, "Telecommuting: The New Workplace Trend," Black Enterprise, June 1996, pp. 256–260. Jane Franklin, Georgia Power, correspondence with author, August 4, 2003. **jffrankl@southernco.com.**

Work in America

Many workers today admit that they are bored with their jobs. They feel no challenge or desire to do a particularly good job. There is no excitement in their work lives. What can management do about this? There are four alternatives:

1. **The organization can do nothing.**
2. **Management can offer workers more money for accepting these dull, repetitive, uninteresting jobs.**
3. **The organization can try to replace workers with machines.**
4. **The company can redesign the work so that it has meaning for the employees.**

The most important of these alternatives in the study of human relations is the last. There is a growing need to give workers more challenge, an entire task, an opportunity to use advanced skills, an opportunity for growth, and a chance to contribute their ideas. This philosophy represents a dramatic new way of doing business for many American organizations. In Europe, for example, job enrichment concepts have been employed for decades. Now these ideas are also becoming popular in the United States.

LEARNING OBJECTIVE

Explain what job design is all about

①

Job redesign
refers to any work changes that increase work quality or productivity.

The Nature of Job Redesign

Any activities involving work changes with the purpose of increasing the quality of a worker's job experience or improving a worker's productivity are known as **job redesign.** Under this term can be included such commonly used job redesign techniques as job rotation, job enlargement, and job enrichment. Job redesign is a unique way of improving organizational efficiency. This is true for four reasons.

First, job redesign alters the basic relationship between the worker and the job, which has long been a human relations problem. The scientific managers tried to deal with the problem by blending the physical requirements of the work with the physical characteristics of the workers and by screening out those who did not measure up. When behavioral scientists entered industry, they attempted to refine this process by improving the selection and training of the workers. As with the scientific managers, however, the concentration of effort was still on the people doing the job. The work was treated as a fixed commodity that could not be altered. Job redesign breaks with this tradition and is based on the assumption that the work itself can be a powerful influence on employee motivation, satisfaction, and productivity.

Second, job redesign does not attempt to change attitudes first (such as inducing workers to care about work results in a zero-defects program that is designed to reduce, and then to eliminate, all product errors) but assumes that positive attitudes will follow if the job is redesigned properly. Initial attention is given to determining how the job ought to be performed. Once this is worked out, the individual doing the work will be forced to change his or her old behavior and, it is hoped, will like the new arrangement so much that attitude toward the job then will be positive.

Third, job redesign helps individuals regain the opportunity to experience the "kick" that comes from doing a job well. There is more here than just satisfaction; there is a sense of competence and self-worth in which people feel themselves stretching and growing as human beings.

Fourth, sometimes when an organization redesigns jobs and solves people–work problems, other opportunities for initiating organizational change are presented. For example, technical problems are likely to develop when jobs are changed, offering management the opportunity to smooth and refine the entire work system. Interpersonal issues also are likely to arise, often between supervisors and subordinates, providing the organization a chance to undertake developmental work aimed at improving the social and supervisory aspects of the work system.

Job redesign is a very important tool, for it provides a basis for developing and using the organization's resources. Some experts like to say that it is a way for the enterprise to work smarter rather than harder. In the next section, we examine three job redesign techniques commonly used in this process.

Job Redesign Techniques

LEARNING OBJECTIVE
② *Describe how job rotation, job enlargement, and job enrichment work*

Job redesign techniques are methods used to change work procedures and, depending on the situation, to increase or decrease work demands. These techniques are very useful in dealing with morale problems caused by boring or meaningless work. When employees do not feel challenged by their jobs or believe that their work is of little importance, morale tends to decline. Conversely, if these individuals feel challenged by the work and are convinced that their jobs are important, morale tends to rise and remain high. Job redesign techniques often, although not always, are used to improve morale. The three popular job redesign techniques are job rotation, job enlargement, and job enrichment.

Job Rotation

Moving a worker from one job to another for the purpose of reducing boredom is termed **job rotation.** For example, six workers are charged with assembling, soldering, testing, painting, and packaging a piece of sophisticated machinery. As seen in Figure 8.1, the first person assembles components A, B, and C; the second assembles D, E, and F; and each of the other workers

*In **job rotation,** the worker moves from one job to another.*

FIGURE 8.1   *Job Rotation*

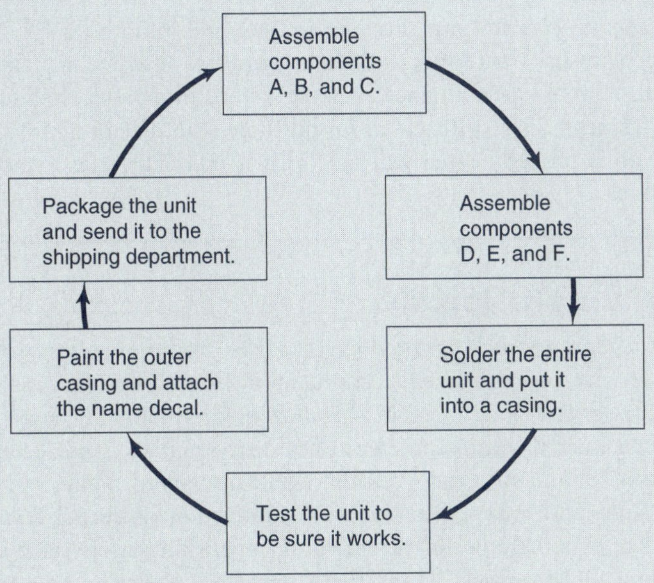

performs a specific function on the unit. The arrows in the figure illustrate how job rotation works. Each person moves to the task immediately following the one he or she has been doing. The person assembling components A, B, and C now assembles components D, E, and F; the worker soldering the unit and putting it into a casing now tests the unit to be sure it works; the individual packaging the unit now moves to assembling components A, B, and C. Continually moving all the workers in this manner can often keep them more interested in their work than if they each did the same thing day after day. Another benefit of job rotation is the perspective it provides the individual as to how his or her activity fits into the overall work flow. A third benefit is that the individual's identification with the final output increases. A fourth benefit is that job rotation turns workers from narrow specialists who can do only one task into broad generalists who can do many. All these benefits can help to increase work motivation.

Job Enlargement

Job enlargement
gives the worker more to do.

Giving the worker more to do is **job enlargement.** Usually this new work is similar to what the person has done before. For example, if Joe is wiring, Ralph is soldering, and Mary is testing the product, the three of them may have their jobs enlarged by allowing each to perform all three functions. One way in which this job redesign can result in efficiency is through the time saved by not having to pass the product from one person to the next. Additionally, a psychological reward is associated with completing a unit as opposed to performing just one small task on a large product. Some researchers have reported that the main advantages of job enlargement appear to be increased job satisfaction and improved quality of work.

Job Enrichment

Job enrichment
gives the worker more authority in planning and controlling the work.

A technique that is more behaviorally sophisticated than job enlargement is **job enrichment,** which attempts to build into the job psychological motivators, as described by Herzberg's two-factor theory. In particular, job enrichment programs attempt to give the worker more authority in planning the work and controlling the pace and procedures used in doing the job.

Industrial research reveals that a number of firms have had success with job enrichment, including American Telephone & Telegraph (AT&T), Campbell Soup, and Travelers Insurance. At AT&T, for example, employees who were handling insurance correspondence with stockholders were chosen for a job enrichment program. Using a test group and a control group, the researchers enriched the jobs of the test group by permitting them to sign their own names to the letters they prepared, encouraging them to become experts in the kinds of problems that appealed to them, holding them accountable for the quality of their work, and providing them with expert assistance in carrying out these duties. After six months, the group's quality, attitudes, and productivity had increased, and their tardiness, absenteeism, and work costs had declined. The control group's performance on these factors, meanwhile, had remained the same. However, job enrichment is not without costs and those who do not approach it with enough determination to do it properly often will fail. This is especially true if they fail to consider core job dimensions.

LEARNING OBJECTIVE

(3)

Describe the five core job dimensions and illustrate selected enrichment principles that help to create these dimensions

Core Job Dimensions

Why do redesign techniques such as the three discussed in the previous section often lead to increases in productivity and higher satisfaction among employees? The answer rests not only in the physical changes that take place in the work environment but also in the psychological changes that take place within the employees. In particular, it has been found that certain dimensions can be built into the work that will bring about higher output, lower absenteeism, higher quality, and greater internal work motivation. Research reveals five **core job dimensions** that are extremely useful in enriching jobs: skill variety, task identity, task significance, autonomy, and feedback. These core dimensions typically are a result of redesigning jobs so that they are more psychologically rewarding and result in higher morale and job

Core job dimensions
are characteristics that make work more motivational.

satisfaction. Research shows that when these core job dimensions are present, morale and job satisfaction tend to increase and, when they are not present, morale and job satisfaction often will decrease.

Skill Variety

The degree to which a job requires the completion of different activities, all of which involve varying talents and capabilities, is **skill variety.** The two most common types of skills are motor skills and intellectual skills. Motor skills help one with performance tasks, whereas intellectual skills are used with "thinking" tasks. If a job can draw on both, it will provide greater variety than if only one type of skill is needed.

Bob Williams is a salesman for a large machine manufacturer. The machine he sells is very complex and requires a technical sales pitch. Advertising is also very important in gaining customer attention and arousing initial interest. The typical sales strategy is to mail an advertising brochure to potential customers and then to follow up by sending a salesperson to meet with those who express interest.

Bob had been the company's number one salesman for three years and had been thinking about quitting because the challenge of selling was losing its excitement. He had begun to feel that the requisite technical sales presentation did not allow him to exercise his creativity. He decided to stay on, however, after the vice president of sales asked him to help write the advertising brochure.

"We need some input from you regarding how to make the initial pitch to the customer," the vice-president told him. "You know how these people think; we'd like to put your ideas into the brochure." Delighted with the chance to do some "think" work, Bob dropped his plans to leave the company.

Task Identity

The degree to which the job requires completion of a whole or identifiable piece of work is **task identity.** The more an individual does on the job, the more likely he or she will identify with the task. Assembly-line employees who put a bolt on a car or weld part of the structure have little task identity. Those who complete a major part of the car (working as a member of a group) have much greater task identity.

Jane Copeland is an assembler-packer for a consumer goods manufacturer. A year ago, Jane used to assemble two parts of a seven-part consumer product. Then, thanks to a job redesign program, she was given all seven parts to assemble as well as the responsibility of packaging the product. As a result, in Jane's group there was a 90 percent decline in absenteeism and turnover and a 7 percent increase in output.

Task Significance

The degree to which a job has a substantial impact on the lives or work of other people is its **task significance.** When employees are able to see how the work they do influences others, they tend to be more motivated to do a good job.

Alice Bodelyn is a manuscript editor for a college textbook publishing firm. Generally, Alice is assigned two manuscripts at the same time and for the next two to three months she reads the material, edits it for grammar, recommends style and substantive changes, and then sends it back to the respective author in batches of three to four chapters for the author's comments. As the edited manuscript reaches completion, Alice discusses the content of the book with a member of the design department, who will work up a cover for the text. Finally, the author visits the publishing house, meets Alice and the cover designer, and spends a few days with them and the marketing people who are putting together the advertising campaign.

Alice has been a manuscript editor for four years, and she has received a personally auto-graphed copy of each book from its author. When asked what she likes best about her work, she says, "I feel an integral part of an important team. When I look at the finished book, I see part of myself in it."

Autonomy

Autonomy
is the degree to which a job provides the worker with freedom in carrying it out.

The degree to which the job provides the worker freedom, independence, and discretion in scheduling the work and determining how to carry it out is **autonomy.** As people begin to plan and execute their assignments without having to rely on others for direction and instructions, they develop feelings of strong personal responsibilities for job success and job failure and are motivated to do the best job possible.[1]

Dick Jackson is a life insurance agent for a large company based in New York. Dick usually begins his workday at 10 A.M., calling on one or two prospective customers and taking a third to lunch. Then he returns to the office to answer correspondence and prepare material for people whom he will be meeting later in the day. From 4 P.M. to 6 P.M., Dick talks to customers in the office, and three days weekly he works evenings. Last year, Dick was again a member of the million-dollar club, having sold $1.92 million of life insurance.

This past week, the district manager asked Dick whether he would like to leave his current job and become an office manager. "What for?" asked Dick. "I've got freedom in my current job. Who wants to be tied down to a 9–5 office schedule?"

Feedback

Feedback
is the degree to which the work provides the worker with performance information.

The degree to which the work required by the job results in the individual's receiving direct, clear information about the effectiveness of his or her performance is **feedback.** Feedback allows people to monitor their own work rather than depend on someone else to do it for them.

Group A is charged with wiring the panels for a complex telecommunications satellite. The incorrect wiring of these panels could result in a malfunction of the entire system during or after launching into earth orbit. To prevent such an occurrence, a few simple tests can be conducted on the panels. Owing to the complexity of the wiring, however, it is not uncommon for each panel to have three or four incorrectly placed wires. When this occurs, errors are caught by the test group and are noted on an error chart. The panel then is returned to Group A for partial rewiring.

Group A has recently protested this procedure, claiming that it is virtually impossible to wire a panel correctly on the first try. They argued that there are bound to be a few errors, and the group is embarrassed when a panel is sent back by the test group. The members of Group A have asked management to redesign their work and incorporate testing as one of their functions while, of course, maintaining a small test group to make a final check of the panel. The company agreed, and over the last four weeks none of the 40 panels sent to the test group has been returned. "Once we know there's an error," said a member of Group A, "we can correct it before sending it on. This type of feedback, from our own group, reduces tension and helps us to do a better job."

LEARNING OBJECTIVE

④

Explain the significance of MPS and job profiling charts

The **motivating potential score** *measures the presence of core job dimensions.*

Motivating Potential Score

Researchers have used the five core job dimensions described in this section to develop a **motivating potential score** (MPS) formula:

$$\text{MPS} = \left(\frac{\text{Skill Variety} + \text{Task Identity} + \text{Task Significance}}{3} \right) \times \text{Autonomy} \times \text{Feedback}$$

Although we do not need to get into the mathematics of the formula, one overriding conclusion can be drawn from it. If the organization wants to redesign jobs so the employees are motivated, it must build in autonomy, feedback, and at least one of the three remaining dimensions. This last statement becomes clear when we observe that if autonomy or feedback is lacking, the MPS will be zero, because these two dimensions are multiplicative. Likewise, if all three other dimensions are zero, the MPS will be zero. Testing of these core job characteristics has provided some breakthroughs in job design. In particular, researchers have found that if these dimensions are present, individuals with high growth needs will be more motivated, productive, and satisfied than if they work on tasks without these dimensions.

Job Profile Charts

In addition, it is possible to construct **job profile charts** so that enrichment programs can more effectively be designed. For example, in Figure 8.2, Job 1 is low on skill variety, task identity, and task significance. Job 2 is low on task significance, autonomy, and feedback. Job 3 is low on skill variety, task significance, and feedback. The first question the organization must answer is: Can the particular job be enriched? That is, can Job 1 be redesigned so that it has greater skill variety, task identity, and task significance? If the answer is yes, then the people charged with the redesign program know where to begin. If the answer is no, the employees must be made to realize that there is nothing that can be done to restructure the job.

Before closing our discussion of this point, we must be very clear on an important point: Some jobs cannot be enriched. There may be no way of increasing the task significance of a dishwasher's job, nor can American automakers' assembly lines, under present conditions, provide a person with skill variety. In some cases, the individual must conform to the work pattern because the work pattern cannot be altered.

How many of these core dimensions can you find in your own job? One way of answering this question is to analyze your work views systematically with the help of the Time Out quiz on how you view your work.

*A **job profile chart** helps to identify core job dimensions.*

FIGURE 8.2

Profile Chart of Core Job Dimensions for Three Jobs

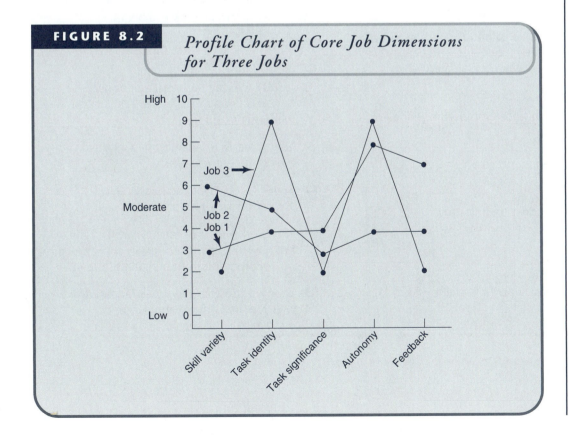

HOW YOU VIEW YOUR WORK

The quiz is designed to provide insights into how you view your work. If you do not currently work full time, refer to your last full-time job in answering the questions. If you have not had a full-time job, think of one you would like to have (be reasonable in your choice), and use it throughout the quiz. Interpretations are provided at the end of the chapter.

A. Read the following job-related questions carefully and decide how accurate each is in describing your job. Then answer each using the following scale:

1 = None
2 = Very little
3 = A little
4 = A moderate amount
5 = Some
6 = Quite a bit
7 = A lot

_____ 1. To what degree does your job allow you to do an entire series of different things, employing a variety of skills and talents in the process?

_____ 2. To what degree does your job allow you to complete an entire piece of work, in contrast to just a small part of an overall piece of work?

_____ 3. How much significance or importance does your job have?

_____ 4. How much freedom do you have to do your job your way?

_____ 5. To what degree does the job itself provide feedback on how well you are doing?

_____ 6. To what degree does your boss or coworkers let you know how well you are doing?

B. Determine how accurately each of the following statements describes your job. Use the following scale to record your answers:

1 = Highly inaccurate
2 = Mostly inaccurate
3 = Slightly inaccurate
4 = Uncertain
5 = Slightly accurate
6 = Mostly accurate
7 = Highly accurate

_____ 1. Your job is simple and repetitive.

_____ 2. Your boss and coworkers never give you feedback on your work progress.

_____ 3. Your job provides you no chance to use personal initiative or judgment in carrying out tasks.

_____ 4. Your job is not really very important.

_____ 5. Your job provides independence and freedom in doing the work your way.

_____ 6. Your job provides the chance to finish completely pieces of work you begin.

_____ 7. How well you do your work really affects numerous other people.

_____ 8. Just by the way the work is designed, you have many opportunities to evaluate how well you are doing.

_____ 9. Your job calls for you to use a lot of complex or high-level skills.

_____ 10. Superiors often let you know how well you are performing your job.

_____ 11. Your work is set up in such a way that you do not have the chance to see an entire piece of work through from beginning to end.

_____ 12. Your job provides few clues regarding how well you are performing your tasks.

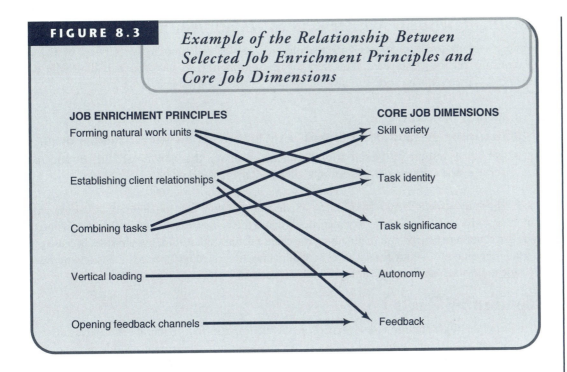

FIGURE 8.3

Example of the Relationship Between Selected Job Enrichment Principles and Core Job Dimensions

JOB ENRICHMENT PRINCIPLES
Forming natural work units

Establishing client relationships

Combining tasks

Vertical loading

Opening feedback channels

CORE JOB DIMENSIONS
Skill variety

Task identity

Task significance

Autonomy

Feedback

Job Enrichment Principles

LEARNING OBJECTIVE
⑤ *Discuss five job enrichment principles*

Many ways exist of enriching jobs so as to provide more meaningful work. In this section, we examine five job enrichment principles:

1. **Formation of natural work units.**
2. **Establishment of worker–client relationships.**
3. **Combining of tasks.**
4. **Vertical loading.**
5. **Opening of feedback channels.**

We study how each principle can be used in redesigning work. Figure 8.3 illustrates how each principle is tied to one or more of the core job dimensions.

Formation of Natural Work Units

In many organizations, the workers all contribute to providing a product or service but do not have any basis for identifying with the work. A secretary in the typing pool types all the correspondence and reports assigned by the supervisor of the pool. On a given day, there may be letters from five or six departmental managers as well as part of a speech for the vice president of human resources. After a while, all the work blurs together, and the secretary identifies with none of it. He or she is simply a producer of typed material. This analogy holds for a person on an automobile assembly line who is installing upholstery. One car looks like another. The job has no real meaning.

One way of enriching jobs such as these is through the formation of natural work units, in which the employee obtains some ownership of the work. For example, responsibility for all the work requested by a single department or person could be assigned to one typist. Instead of typing one part of a large report, the typist now types it all. Over time, the person begins to identify with the task and sees how the material is of value to those who receive the finished product. The formation of natural work units contributes to two core job dimensions: task identity and task significance (see Figure 8.3).

Establishment of Worker–Client Relationships

Workers seldom come in contact with the ultimate user of their product or service. If such a relationship can be established, however, job commitment and motivation will usually be enhanced. Three steps go into establishing worker–client relationships:

1. Identify the client.
2. Determine the most direct contact possible between the worker and the client.
3. Set up a system by which the client can evaluate the quality of the product or service and convey the judgments directly to the worker.

Establishing worker–client relationships can contribute to three core job dimensions: skill variety, autonomy, and feedback. Skill variety increases because the worker has the chance to exercise interpersonal skills in managing and maintaining the client relationship. Autonomy increases because the person is given responsibility for deciding how to manage the client relationship. Feedback increases because the worker has the opportunity to receive praise and criticism for his or her output.

Combining Tasks

The principle of combining tasks is based on the assumption that higher work motivation can result when a series of simple tasks is combined to form a new and larger work module. For example, a few years ago, a Corning Glass Works plant redesigned the job of assembling laboratory hot plates by combining a number of tasks that had been separate. The redesigned job called for each operator to assemble an entire hot plate. Costs declined and motivation increased as a result of the redesign effort. The combining of tasks contributes to two core job dimensions: skill variety and task identity. The enlarged job requires a greater variety of skill and, as the individual begins turning out finished products, task identity increases. The assembler can see the unit taking shape as the various pieces are affixed and soldered.

Vertical Loading

Vertical loading
closes the gap between the doing and controlling aspects of the job.

When the gap between the "doing" and "controlling" aspects of the job is reduced, **vertical loading** occurs. In particular, responsibilities that formerly were reserved for management now are delegated to the employee as part of the job. Some ways of vertically loading a job include the following:

- Give the worker responsibility for deciding work methods and for advising or helping to train less experienced workers.
- Provide increased freedom to the worker, including decisions about when to start and stop work, when to take breaks, and how to assign work priorities.
- Encourage the workers to do their own troubleshooting and manage work crises rather than immediately call for a supervisor.
- Provide workers with increased knowledge of the financial aspects of the job and the organization, and increase control over budgetary matters that affect their work.

When a job is vertically loaded, autonomy increases and workers begin feeling personal responsibility and accountability for the outcome of their efforts.[2]

Opening Feedback Channels

In most jobs, there are ways of opening feedback channels so each worker can monitor his or her own performance. One way, discussed already, is to establish direct worker–client relationships by which the individual can learn what the client likes and dislikes about the product or service being provided. Another is to place as much control as possible in the hands of the worker. For example, rather than having quality checks performed by people in the quality assurance department, let the worker do the checking. Such a move ensures immediate feedback and allows the individual to exercise self-control. Placing quality control functions in the hands of workers can result in higher quantity and quality of output. This principle helps to overcome one of the main human relations problems—failure to tell people how well they are doing.[3]

Job Enrichment in Action

LEARNING OBJECTIVE

6 *Cite some illustrations of job enrichment in action*

Numerous firms have successfully applied the job enrichment concepts discussed in this chapter. Perhaps the best known company is Volvo, the Swedish car manufacturer. Job enrichment has been equally effective in many other organizations, ranging from manufacturing firms to insurance companies. Let us examine some cases of job enrichment in action.

General Electric Company

One of the foremost companies in job enrichment is General Electric (GE), which continues to rely heavily on change and innovation. The focus of many of these efforts is to rewrite the book on management, tap employee brainpower, reduce the role of the boss, and give more authority to the worker.[4] This is accomplished in a number of ways. One is through the use of "workout," an approach in which the personnel are given the opportunity to identify problems and then organize themselves into teams and attack the issues. There is no concern over the fact that these matters are in management's domain. At GE, they are everyone's business and, if there is an easier way to get the job done or if reorganizing can save money, workout sessions allow the personnel to get involved.

A typical workout session lasts two to three days and involves forty to one hundred people from all ranks and functions in the company. The session usually begins with a talk from the boss, who roughs out an agenda, such as thinking up ways of reducing meeting time or eliminating inefficient procedures. A facilitator breaks the employees into groups, then into five or six teams, each of which tackles part of the agenda. When the group is finished (usually a day or two later), the boss returns and the team spokespeople tell him or her what they would like to do. In one case, for example, a group insisted that the company give it the opportunity to bid against an outside vendor to build new protective shields for grinding machines, based on a design an hourly worker had sketched on a brown paper bag. The group was given the authority to do so and ended up bringing in the job for $16,000 versus the $96,000 bid by the vendor.

Work-outs also are used with customers and suppliers in an effort to get their ideas for improving overall productivity and quality. Here is an example.

> A team in the locomotive paint shop in Erie, Pennsylvania, found that a major cause of delays and rework was inconsistency in the paint because GE was buying it from two suppliers. Team members persuaded their boss . . . to use just one [supplier] and asked its chemist to join up. Together they wrote standards for color and consistency, eliminating the need for dual inspections, and hooked up a direct phone line between the two shops. A paint job now takes 10 shifts, down from 11 or 12.[5]

In another case, the company has been able to reduce the time needed to change production and switch from one product line to another as well as reduce inventory for the products. In the appliance division, for example, GE has cut changeover time from four hours to fifteen minutes and has reduced inventory by more than 20 percent. The cost of making these changes was less than $3 million, and the changes already have saved the company more than $300 million. Clearly, by allowing the workers to redesign their jobs, the firm is finding it can achieve dramatic bottom-line results.

A large part of this success is a result of GE's moving into what it calls a "rearchitecting stage," which is characterized by

- **A flat structure with fewer hierarchical levels and more incentives that are broadly shared by employees throughout the organization.**
- **Close cooperation between departments and product groups who share ideas and information and help one another.**

TABLE 8.1		*General Electric's Vision for the Millennium*	
	Strategy	**Organizational Structure**	**Human Resources Management**
Technical	GE's businesses must be no. 1 or no. 2 in their markets. Otherwise, close, fix, or sell. Aim for high-growth businesses.	13 businesses reporting into a central CEO leadership team. Share best practices. Boundaryless organization.	Design pay systems tailored to particular businesses. Make training and development a continuous process.
Political	Achieve synergy across many businesses—or what Welch calls "integrated diversity."	No wedding-cake hierarchy. Demand cross-functional teamwork. Empowerment: decision making pushed to lower levels.	Make rewards very flexible. Have employee appraisals from below as well as from above.
Cultural	Speed, simplicity, and self-confidence. Employees should act like entrepreneurs. Institute "work-out," a process for continuous revolution.	Encourage cultural diversity but common values. Common vision.	Human resource systems designed to produce boundary-lessness. Screen employees for values.

Source: Noel M. Tichy, "Revolutionize Your Company," *Fortune*, December 13, 1993, p. 115.

- **Close cooperation between the company and its suppliers, customers, stakeholders, and competitors, as reflected through supplier and customer teams and alliances with other firms.**

As a result, GE is well on the way to realizing its vision for the twenty-first century. This vision is described in Table 8.1. Table 8.1 shows that the technical, political, and cultural environments of the firm are being changed. As a result, GE's strategy, structure, and human resources management systems are being adapted to meet the challenges of the competitive new century. In the strategy area, for example, the company is aiming only for high-growth businesses, is seeking synergy across the hierarchy, and is encouraging employees to act like entrepreneurs. In meeting these goals, the organization structure is being flattened, employees are being empowered, and everyone is being encouraged to share a common vision. The motivation for all this is being provided through the human resources management changes, including new incentive systems, ongoing training, and the creation of a boundaryless organization. Commenting on this vision by former GE president Jack Welch, one writer noted:

Welch's vision began to emerge from his understanding of the 21st-century organization, which he characterized with the word "boundarylessness." "Old Way" organizations were all about boundaries and compartmentalization and chains of command. The new organization would be free of these increasingly nonproductive strictures. Information would flow freely

HUMAN RELATIONS IN ACTION

Implementing Job Enrichment

Many firms have successfully implemented job enrichment programs, but some company efforts have failed. The reasons some programs have been unsuccessful can often be linked directly to one of the five critical steps in implementing a job enrichment program. Those five steps are as follows:

1. *Be willing to make changes in jobs.* The first step in any job enrichment program is willingness to change work procedures or job requirements to increase the motivational potential of the tasks. Unless an organization is willing to make such changes, there is no chance for a job enrichment program to succeed.

2. *Get the workers involved.* No one knows more about a job than those who are doing it. If the work is boring, excessively demanding, or poorly organized, the workers are aware of this. By getting them involved in redesigning the job, an organization increases the chances that the new work will be more motivational or will result in increased productivity.

3. *Stay the course.* Will a newly designed job result in increased output or improved service? It may, but the results often take time; the company must be willing to wait and see how things turn out. If a job is totally reorganized, for example, the workers may like the new arrangement but need a couple of months to master the new procedures and techniques. Only then can management draw valid conclusions regarding the overall effect of the program.

4. *Be prepared for more changes.* Sometimes changes in one job result in the need for changes in other jobs. For example, if assembly-line workers are given greater authority over their tasks, supervisors' jobs may become less challenging and need to be redesigned as well. This ripple effect may be felt throughout the entire department or plant and result in the need for job redesign in many areas.

5. *Know how to measure the results.* The organization should know how it will measure the results of any redesign effort. Typical examples include productivity, service, and personnel-related results, such as absenteeism, tardiness, and turnover. Is efficiency increasing? This commonly is measured by comparing the amount of output with the cost of producing the goods. Is service improving? This usually is measured in terms of customer feedback. Are absenteeism, tardiness, and turnover decreasing? These typically are measured through time cards, supervisory feedback, and personnel records.

across functional and business boundaries, from where it was developed to where it was needed. The boundaryless corporation would resolve the conflict between organizational size and speed: It would have the might of a large organization and the speed, flexibility, and self-confidence of a small one. Most important, it was the only way GE could get the productivity improvements required to win in all businesses.[6]

This transformation helps to explain why GE continues to outperform the competition.[7] The approach used in implementing job enrichment is often similar from firm to firm (see the Human Relations in Action box).

Southwest Airlines

Southwest Airlines has consistently been rated as one of the best airlines in the country. Its on-time departures and arrivals, baggage handling, and customer satisfaction reports are the envy of the industry. In addition, the company is consistently profitable. One of the reasons for its success is that the airline has created a high team spirit by putting the employees, not the customers, first. Additionally, although the airline is unionized, it has been able to negotiate flexible work rules that enable it to meet its rapid flight turnaround schedule. As a result, pilots helping flight attendants clean the airplanes or assisting the ground crew in loading baggage is not an uncommon sight. In fact, many personnel are trained to fill in on other jobs so that there is never a shortage of personnel to get things done. One way the company has been able to do this is by "hiring for attitude and training for skill." Southwest deliberately looks for applicants with a positive attitude who will promote fun in the workplace and have a desire to "color outside the lines." The firm also has a culture committee that regularly visits all stations across the country, infusing the corporate culture, reiterating the company's history, and motivating the employees to maintain the spirit that has made the airline so successful.[8]

Herb Kelleher, Chairman of the Board, believes that giving people flexibility empowers them to do what is right. Managers can't anticipate all the situations across the system; therefore employees must handle them the best way possible. When employees have the freedom to do their job the way they think it should be done, they will work hard. "Southwest has made living legends of employees who went above and beyond the call of duty to offer exceptional customer service." For exceptional service Southwest Airlines consecutively has won the Triple Crown Award more times than any other airline.

To stay ahead in the industry, Southwest Airlines implements technology and restructures jobs to fit current needs. For example, it was the first airline to establish a home page on the Internet, which has saved the company many dollars over the years and has helped keep Southwest profitable.[9]

LEARNING OBJECTIVE
Discuss four current challenges in job design

(7) # Current Challenges in Job Design

Job design is a very important issue in human relations. After all, designing work so employees achieve a sense of task identity and task significance and are provided with skill variety, autonomy, and feedback stimulates motivation. However, some additional challenges now are becoming prominent in the twenty-first century. These relate to both job design and job enrichment and include new workplace designs, the increasing use of teleworkers, and the challenge in dealing with contract workers (see also the Ethics and Social Responsibility in Action box).

in action

ETHICS AND SOCIAL RESPONSIBILITY IN ACTION

It Provides a Competitive Edge

Job enrichment involves more than just giving people greater autonomy and feedback in their jobs. Many firms now are finding that they need to address the personal concerns of their employees or risk losing them to competitors who will address these concerns. One primary way that organizations are accomplishing job enrichment is by creating an environment that allows employees to meet both their work and family responsibilities. When this happens, research shows, workers tend to be more productive and businesses increase their profit.

Of course, this basic idea is nothing new. Companies have long been interested in helping their people address personal needs. However, today this challenge is far broader and more demanding. Notes *Business Week:*

Disbelievers, skeptics, working stiffs, take note: Work-family strategies haven't just hit the corporate mainstream— they've become a competitive advantage. The exclusive

province of working mothers a decade ago, such benefits now extend to elder-care assistance, flexible scheduling, job sharing, adoption benefits, on-site summer camps, employee help lines, even, no joke—pet-care and law-service referrals.

To help employees focus on their jobs, companies are picking up some of the family and social burdens. For example, at Du Pont, employees who are responsible for caring for children or elder family members are given flexible work hours. At Aetna Casualty, new mothers can take up to six months' parental leave. At Motorola, expectant parents are given a 24-hour nurse hotline and a pager for dad in the last trimester. At Eddie Bauer Inc., the headquarters café stays open late to prepare take-out meals for harried employees to carry home, and each worker is given a paid "balance day" off each year to repay them for all their extra effort. At Hewlett-Packard, every business unit is charged with identifying work-related issues and proposing an action plan as part of its annual business review.

A recent study by the Ford Foundation found something interesting about those family-focused programs that are proving successful. All concentrate on rethinking the work processes rather than finding ways to make people's lives fit the work. The responsibility for how the program would be used by the employees rests squarely with them. They are still responsible for meeting their work obligations. Hence, when Hewlett-Packard's printer group recently faced strong consumer demand and had to increase the number of shifts worked by manufacturing employees, it also investigated alternatives for 'round-the-clock child care. Then, by rescheduling activities that cause peak-period bottlenecks and by providing technology that allowed people to work from home and other sites, employees were able to resolve the problem.

These types of work–family strategies are proving extremely useful in maintaining employee morale and job commitment. They are also proving useful to the company. As one observer put it, "Certainly, employees bear some responsibility for determining their own family balance. But they need help. Companies that recognize the need and adapt work to people's lives will win workers' loyalty—and, with that, a competitive edge."

Source: Keith Hammonds, "Balancing Work and Family," Business Week, September 16, 1996, pp. 74–80.

New Workplace Designs

In an effort to motivate their personnel and create a more conducive work environment, a growing number of organizations now are introducing new workplace designs. Procter & Gamble's 13 million–square-foot building just north of Cincinnati is a good example. The building's design facilitates teamwork by project groups. For example, team members are able to work in open cubicles that are grouped together, so everyone can see everyone else. In addition, file cases are mounted on wheels so they can be easily moved, and office walls can be reconfigured to increase or decrease the enclosed space. Likewise, instead of elevators, escalators move people from floor to floor, because this form of transit encourages the easy flow of communication among individuals, in contrast to elevators, which tend to discourage communication during transit. The building also has "huddle rooms" strategically placed where teams can come together to brainstorm; and electronic whiteboards in the lunchrooms and lounges can be used to convert scribblings and notes into e-mail messages.

> P&G is also among those companies using design to help dual-career families while still boosting productivity. When planning its new building, the company specifically designed in a dry cleaner, a shoe-repair shop, and a cafeteria that prepares food that employees can take home at night. It hits home for Linda Dudek, the mother of two. "The freedom I've felt being here is incredible, and yet I'm leaving the building a lot less. I take my breaks in the fitness center. I have weekly meetings on the stair-steppers. It's cool."[10]

Small firms are also discovering that careful workplace design can increase productivity. For example, at Inhale Therapeutic Systems, a Palo Alto, California, firm that works on novel drug-delivery technology, the president found that everyone was obsessed with having an office close to his. No one wanted to feel left out of anything, so the company redesigned its office layout and now everyone, including the president, sits in large cubicles with four other people of various ranks and functions. There are no walls or barriers of any kind between them. This forces everyone to talk to one another all the time. Moreover, the lack of private space limits gossip, reduces the need for memo writing, and gets top managers scattered among the rest of the employees. Periodically, the president shuffles the workplaces and assigns people to different cubicles. This approach helps maintain morale and productivity.

Another recent development in workplace design is to give people more control over their physical environment. For example, at the West Bend Mutual Insurance Company of Wisconsin, the company had a system installed that allows employees to adjust the temperature, fresh air, and noise in their cubicles. Researchers have found that these workers are 3 percent more productive because of their ability to control their environment, and the novel workstations have become an asset in both recruiting and retaining workers.

Not all workplace design benefits employees. Recently, Kmart, Kroger, A&P, and Home Depot replaced their human cashiers with machines. The "scan-it-yourself checkout lines" are designed to give customers faster checkout service, and they generally pay for themselves in nine to twelve months. A&P labels theirs as "Express Yourself" lanes. IHL Consulting, a retail consultant, predicts that about 90 percent of grocers will have them by 2005.[11]

Yet another recent development in workplace design is provided by Herman Miller Inc., a firm famous for its creation of cubicles in the work area. The firm has now created a system called Resolve that is designed to meet the needs of twenty-first-century workers. The system offers employees a wide number of workplace options. For example, workers can raise or lower a table so that they can work seated or standing. Additionally, if workers use a flat-screen monitor, they can raise or lower the apparatus that holds it, and the table on which the computer sits is wheeled so that it can be rolled to other locations, thus allowing the workers to come together in teams. One designer for the company explained some of the new configurations this way:

> Some workstations have a curved screen that extends from the floor over the desk and connects to the center pole, sort of like a giant leaf. The screen's wheels let workers reposition it to reduce glare on their terminal, to block an air-conditioning vent, or simply to cover their backs for privacy—all solutions to routine complaints. These adjustments may seem minor . . . but for someone who works all day at a terminal, they represent major control over the environment.[12]

Dell Computer Corporation, a successful direct-sales computer company during the 1990s that sold PCs only on the phone and over the Internet, recently expanded its marketing model to include retail store sales. Dell has installed kiosks in shopping malls and launched a trial store-within-a-store with Sears, Roebuck & Co. in Austin, Texas, to allow customers to try out the computers before placing an order. This new workplace design is drawing the attention of Apple Computer, Inc. and Gateway, Inc. These latest moves reflect a drive to increase sales amid a weak economy, which is another example of what motivates companies to make workplace changes.[13]

Increasing Use of Telework

Closely linked to new workplace designs is the use of telework. Telework, or telecommuting, or virtual teams, or global teams, falls under the umbrella of flexible work arrangements and is recognized as a fundamental component in organizational restructuring. According to a survey conducted in May 2001 by the Bureau of Labor Statistics, 3.4 million wage and salary workers had a formal arrangement with their employer to be paid for the time they put in away from the office.[14] These individuals often come to the office only for special meetings or to check in and discuss important matters with their boss or subordinates. Otherwise, they operate out of their homes or work on the road while remaining in electronic contact with their office.

A virtual team is boundaryless with participants linked by telecommunications and technology across organizations, functions, and geography. The advancements in satellite technology have given global access via the Internet and the cell phone. Virtual global teams represent the extreme example of working as a telecommuter. Successful management of these teams requires mutually defining the culture and values applicable to the particular situation, which often are exaggerated by ethnic differences. Virtual teams tend to be geographically dispersed, time dependent and project based. Research has found they work best if members have learned virtual collaborative skills, virtual socialization skills, and virtual communication skills. Typically, teleworkers are better educated and earn higher incomes than most employees. According to *Business Week,* supplies of talent needed to support the New Economy are expected to remain scarce for the next twenty-nine years.[15]

Two of the major human relations challenges that telecommuting presents to firms are those of carefully choosing who will be telecommuters and determining who will supervise these individuals. Recent research reveals that managers typically look for the following traits in individuals whom they are considering for telecommunications jobs:

1. **Self-motivation.**
2. **A high level of job knowledge.**
3. **Flexibility.**
4. **Strong organizational skills.**
5. **A low need for social interaction.**
6. **The ability to be a team player.**
7. **A willingness to take responsibility.**
8. **Trustworthiness and reliability.**[16]

Researchers also have found that managers need to have a series of skills and abilities that allow them to manage their telecommunication work group effectively. The five most important traits are the ability to

1. **Set goals and communicate plans to employees.**
2. **Identify resources and structure the organization.**
3. **Motivate and develop people.**
4. **Foster cooperation and resolve conflicts.**
5. **Monitor performance and evaluate work.**

Researchers have discovered that, although many employees would like to volunteer to be telecommuters, certain behaviors are critical to success. In particular, when people work from home they must be able to put the work first and limit the number of distractions or interruptions caused by family members or personal matters. Organizations are looking for individuals who can work effectively from home, and they want to feel that these employees are indeed committed to their jobs. In the case of people who have been working at the office and would like to become telecommuters, some of the best suggestions for getting this kind of assignment and carrying it out well include the following:

1. **If the organization is looking for a telecommuter, express an interest by explaining how you can do a better job by working from home than by coming into the office. For example, by not having to commute to the office, it will be possible to start calling clients at 8 A.M. rather than at 9 A.M., thus allowing you to get an early start on the business day. However, be careful not to couch your answer in personal terms, such as "this assignment will give me more time to look after my young children." The manager is interested in improving organizational efficiency, so try to see things from this person's point of view.**

2. **If there are children at home who need to be supervised, get them under control by setting firm guidelines regarding when they can interrupt the work routine. For example, before 3 P.M., no one is to come into the work area unless it is an emergency.**

3. Especially during the first month or two as a telecommuter, maintain constant communications with the office. Let people know you are working continuously and try to talk to the boss at least once daily.

4. Leave a strong paper trail showing how hard you are working. Fax the boss about a client who is about to sign a contract; send other team members e-mail messages; and let everyone know you are working hard—but are also available if they need to reach you.

5. If you can find a reason to do so, turn up at the office at least once monthly. This indicates that you are not isolating yourself from the personnel and are committed to the workplace.

6. Because you have been working at the office prior to being assigned a telecommuter job, keep up your contacts with fellow employees. Additionally, make it a point to schedule lunch with them every couple of weeks, so that they mention your name around the office and let the boss know that you are staying in touch with them.

7. Be flexible in your work scheduling so that if they need you in the office for an important meeting, you can break away. This is particularly true if it will look bad if you miss this meeting.

8. Do not be too flexible. Otherwise people will think you are not working very hard at home. Therefore, be selective in your communications with the office and, if you start getting calls beyond office hours, speak up for yourself and let everyone know that you are working from home and keeping the same hours that you did at the office.[17]

Dealing with Contract Workers

A related challenge is dealing with contract workers who are hired on an hourly basis and, as such, typically have neither medical nor retirement benefits. Over the last decade, a growing percentage of the workforce has consisted of contract or hourly employees. One advantage of this arrangement is that it helps many workers to meet specific objectives. For example, an increasing number of retired people are interested in supplementing their social security or organizational retirement benefits and are happy to work twenty hours per week for minimum wage. The same is true for some college students who are going to school part time and financing their education by working four to five hours per week or all day Saturday and Sunday. For example, Angela Gehr works part time for United Parcel Service (UPS). She started at $8 per hour and, within a year, was making $9.25 as a package sorter. When recently asked about her job and her pay, she responded, "Going in I knew that I might only be working 15 hours a week, but that was good for me. I figured that any sacrifice that I would have to make while working there would be worth it because I would get a college degree out of it."[18]

In contrast, though, individuals who depend solely on part-time work find that making a living can be very difficult. Edward Stoess, who also works at UPS, was able to earn $30,000 in one recent year by working 40 hours weekly. However, the next year his shifts were trimmed and he worked only 25 hours per week, cutting his annual income by $11,000. This is not enough to support his wife and two children. Stories like these indicate the challenge that organizations face when they hire part-time employees and rely on them to help keep down costs. Eventually, something must be done to address their problems.

In the case of UPS, the outcome was a major strike that resulted in the company agreeing to a new contract that will give better opportunities to current part-time workers. Specifically, the company has agreed to raise the average hourly wages of full-time and part-time employees. In addition, the new contract calls for a conversion to full-time of two thousand part-time positions per year over five years, for a total of ten thousand jobs. Moreover, five-sixths of new full-time openings from attrition or expansion will be filled by current part-timers, and both pension and benefit increases will be given to full-timers. To ensure that greater opportunities exist for part-timers to work longer hours every week, the company has agreed to phase out the use of subcontractors to help transport packages.[19]

Contracts such as the one between UPS and its union help highlight some of the problems that are facing management as it seeks to deal with the human relations challenges associated with part-time employees. Not only does the work often carry low pay, but also the jobs are not designed to be motivational. They are simply opportunities for individuals to make moderate incomes. However, in the next decade and perhaps years to come, management is going to find that part-time employees need many of the same types of motivation that are provided to full-time workers: interesting and challenging work, an opportunity for advancement in the organization, and medical and retirement benefits that ensure the future well-being of the worker. For the moment at least, these challenges have remained unmet.

Managing Hard-to-Keep Employees

In addition to telecommuters and contract workers are a number of other groups that present challenges to today's organizations. These include single mothers, nonconformists, and others who can make significant contributions to the firm if they are managed properly.

The 2002 statistics from the U.S. Labor Department and the Census Bureau report that 71.4 percent of single mothers are gainfully employed compared to 66.7 percent of married mothers.[20] Many of these women, especially those who have never been married, are not highly educated and, as a result, tend to hold fairly low-paying jobs. This, in turn, can create a problem for management because companies offering better compensation packages are likely to lure such workers away. As a result, many firms now are creating job enrichment programs that are designed to complement their pay packages. Examples, some of which were discussed in chapter 7, include flextime, shift work, and other job-related arrangements that allow personnel to coordinate their work with the needs of their children. For example, many companies now allow single mothers to come to work in midmorning so that they can drop their children off at school. These employees then make up the time later in the day by working until 6 P.M. and then pick up the children from the day care center on the way home. In addition, managers are being trained to interact more effectively with these workers both to encourage productivity and to maintain high levels of job satisfaction, so that they do not leave the organization.[21]

Another group of hard-to-keep employees are nonconformists. These individuals tend to exhibit a number of different needs and attitudes. For example, nonconformists like to set their own work hours. Coming in at 6 A.M. and leaving at 2 P.M. is a common work arrangement and one that many nonconformists like because they feel they are most productive early in the day. Other nonconformists like to work long hours and enjoy being at work six or seven days a week, putting in eighty or more hours. The challenge for management is to balance these personal needs with organizational requirements. Commenting on this, the worldwide managing director of Bain & Company recently noted:

> *Recognizing that no single career model can fit everyone in your organization is an important way to make room for a nonconformist. He or she may value a leave of absence in which to work for a nonprofit organization or take a sailing trip around the world more highly than a promotion or a raise. It's also worth noting that career needs will change over an employee's work life. What works for a 25-year-old MBA may not work for a 55-year-old who's been around your company for decades.*
>
> *An understanding of work habits, life balance, modes of learning, affiliation and career development can help managers meet the needs of nonconformists and incorporate them into the culture.*[22]

A third group of hard-to-keep employees consists of those who are highly educated and experienced and make major contributions to both productivity and profit. These individuals are continually being sought by the competition. In an effort to avoid what is commonly called a *brain drain,* companies now are taking a number of steps to lock in this talent with carefully formulated job redesign and job enrichment programs. Research shows that in addition to compensation packages, companies are offering flexible work schedules, increased job training so that these individuals can qualify for promotion or more challenging work, and job assignments that allow employees to work at home. These strategies help to deal with the most common reasons that high-performing employees leave their jobs including feeling undervalued by the organization, having insufficient opportunity for advancement, and having a job that provides insufficient challenge.[23]

American firms also are looking at how companies in the international arena deal with this problem and are copying some of the ideas they find. For example, in Europe the labor market is becoming tighter, and one of the best ways of attracting new talent is to lure it away from the competition. In an effort to prevent this from happening to them, companies now are designing new retention strategies. At the Laboratoires Boiron, a maker of homeopathic medicines in Lyon, France, the company now sets aside 400,000 francs annually to help employees realize some of their personal desires. As a result, one warehouse worker received nine months off and 25,000 francs to help finance a voyage around the world with her husband and two children. In another instance, the company gave 30,000 francs to a telephone order taker to finance a sculpture and painting studio.

European firms also are altering work schedules to fit the personal needs of their employees. For example, the MFI Furniture Group PLC, a British manufacturer and retailer of full kitchens and other big-ticket household furnishings, recently instituted a program to reduce turnover among its sales staff. To make the job more attractive, MFI stripped out the work responsibilities that were not sales related and beefed up technology training, so that the salespeople could focus on their primary responsibilities and not be bothered with peripheral chores.[24]

In addition to these types of changes, a growing number of companies are putting strong emphasis on providing personal recognition to employees who do exceptional work. Stew Leonard's, the world's largest dairy store, located in Norwalk and Danbury, Connecticut, is known for its outstanding customer service. A fourth store is scheduled to open in 2004 in Farmingdale, New York. With its amusement park atmosphere, combined with its farm fresh foods and outstanding customer service, Stew Leonard's has been recognized as one of the "100 Best Companies to Work For in America" by *Fortune* magazine for the past two years. Not only are its managers accountable for personally recognizing employees' efforts, but also the company supports:

- **A philosophy of promoting from within—90 percent of the managers have been promoted to their current position.**
- **An employee profit sharing program.**
- **A "Mom's Program" that provides working mothers with flexible hours.**

Recently, Stew Leonard's took the feedback from the employees and developed a recognition program to celebrate seniority and added training classes to continue to grow team members.[25]

> *Jill Tavelo, vice president . . . . says employee recognition is tied into the managers' performance review. "We can't have happy customers without happy employees, so we go out of our way to recognize their efforts on a daily basis. We believe that a handwritten note from the manager is very meaningful to our employees, so we actually track how often they send these out." Tavelo says that turnover among their full-time regular staff is among the lowest in the area and well below the industry average.*[26]

Leonards is not alone. A growing number of businesses are developing programs aimed at retaining personnel. At Macy's West, a division of Federated Department Stores in San Francisco, the company has a program for assigning mentors to new managers and telling all managers that

35 percent of their compensation will be linked to how well they retain the people who report to them. At the International Paper plant in Moss Point, Mississippi, morning training sessions are devoted to teaching managers how to give positive reinforcement to their people.[27] The reasoning behind these programs is that satisfied employees are more likely to stay with the firm, and managers play a key role in this process. As one person put it, "People come on board because they want to join a company, but when they quit they do so in order to leave a manager." Thus, to the extent that managers are able to treat their employees well, the likelihood of these personnel leaving is sharply reduced.[28] For obvious reasons, job redesign and job enrichment programs will continue to be important in meeting the human relations challenges of the new century.[29]

summary

① LEARNING OBJECTIVE
Explain what job design is all about

Many workers are bored with their work, feeling no challenge or desire to do a particularly good job. What can management do about this? Various alternatives are available, but the most practical is that of redesigning the work so it has meaning for the employees. Job redesign alters the basic relationship between the worker and the job. It assumes that positive attitudes follow properly redesigned jobs, creating a sense of competence and self-worth in which people feel a sense of stretching and growing as human beings. Job redesign is an important tool for initiating organizational change and a way to work smarter rather than harder.

② LEARNING OBJECTIVE
Describe how job rotation, job enlargement, and job enrichment work

There are a number of ways to accomplish this goal, including job rotation, job enlargement, and job enrichment. Job rotation is a technique for moving workers from one job to another, basically to reduce boredom, whereas, job enlargement involves giving workers more to do, allowing them to complete more tasks on a particular job. The quality of work improves and the workers receive greater satisfaction. Job enrichment is a technique, which attempts to build into the job psychological motivators such as giving workers more authority in planning the work and controlling the pace and procedures for doing the job. Job enrichment is the most commonly used approach.

③ LEARNING OBJECTIVE
Describe the five core job dimensions and illustrate selected enrichment principles that help to create these dimensions

How does one go about enriching jobs? Some of the latest research reveals that five core job dimensions are extremely useful in this process: skill variety, task identity, task significance, autonomy, and feedback. Skill variety is the degree to which the job requires a worker to perform a variety of tasks requiring different skills and abilities. Motor skills help perform tasks, and intellectual skills are used in "thinking" tasks. Task identify is the degree to which the job requires a worker to perform a whole or completely identifiable piece of work. Task significance is the degree to which a job affects the lives of other people within or outside the organization. Autonomy is the degree to which a job provides the worker with freedom in carrying it out. Feedback is the degree to which the work provides the worker with performance information. Researchers have used these five core job dimensions to develop a motivating potential score by which to evaluate a job.

4 LEARNING OBJECTIVE
Explain the significance of MPS and job profiling charts

The Motivating Potential Score formula shows that to redesign jobs so employees are motivated, the work must offer autonomy, feedback, and at least one of the other three core job dimensions. A profile chart illustrates which core job dimensions are the weakest and which ones are the strongest. Redesigning the job to increase the weak areas can increase worker motivation. Some jobs cannot be enriched and workers must conform to the work pattern.

5 LEARNING OBJECTIVE
Discuss five job enrichment principles

The common job enrichment principles that can be used to obtain these dimensions include forming natural work units, establishing worker–client relationships, combining tasks, vertical loading, and opening feedback channels. One way of enriching jobs is through the formation of natural work units, in which the worker obtains some ownership of the work. The worker then begins to identify with the job and begins to see how clients value the job.

Job commitment and motivation are usually enhanced when workers establish a relationship with the clients. The steps are to identify the client, determine the most direct contact possible between the client and the worker, and set up a system for feedback from clients. Combining a series of simple tasks to form a new work unit can provide worker motivation. Assembling a whole unit provides greater satisfaction than repetitive work on one part of the unit.

Vertical loading closes the gap between "doing" and "controlling" aspects of the job. Autonomy increases and workers begin feeling personal responsibility and accountability for the outcome of their efforts. Opening feedback channels allows workers to get direct feedback for clients. People have a need to know how well they are doing and workers need to know as quickly as possible.

6 LEARNING OBJECTIVE
Cite some illustrations of job enrichment in action

A number of successful applications of job enrichment are discussed in this chapter, including those at GE and Southwest Airlines. General Electric uses "work-out" as a way for employees to identify problems and then organize themselves into teams and attack the issues. Work-outs also are used with customers and suppliers to get their ideas for improving overall productivity and quality. A part of GE's success comes through implementing a flatter organization, closer cooperation between departments and product groups, and a closer cooperation between the company and its suppliers, customers, stakeholders, and competitors. The motivation is provided through human resources management changes, including new incentive systems, ongoing training, and the creation of a boundaryless organization.

Southwest Airlines has created a high team spirit by putting the employees, not the customers, first. Its flexible work rules and training allows all jobs to get done quickly, which gives the airline a fast turnaround time record. Employees are encouraged to "color outside the lines." A culture committee infuses the corporate culture throughout the company. Employees are empowered to make decisions at the point of operations. Recognition is an ongoing process for the employees, as well as for the company.

7 LEARNING OBJECTIVE
Discuss four current challenges in job design

In the last part of the chapter, current challenges in job design were examined. One of these is creating new workplace designs that facilitate teamwork, the flow of communication, and employee interaction. A second is the use of telework or telecommuting; a type of flexible work arrangement that creates new challenges for both the organization and the employee. Special skills and attitudes are needed to be a teleworker or telecommuter and to be a manager of these employees. A third challenge involves ways of dealing with contract or part-time workers, many of whom receive neither medical nor retirement benefits. An advantage to this arrangement is that it helps many workers to meet specific objectives, such as spending more time with the family, conducting personal business, or attending college classes. A fourth is strategies for managing hard-to-keep employees. Married and single mothers often need special arrangements to take care of family matters. The nonconformists have a different set of needs and attitudes. They often like to work nontraditional hours, such as 6:00 A.M. to 2:00 P.M. The hard-to-keep employees are the highly educated and experienced who make major contributions to productivity and profit. They need challenging work and job assignments that allow them to work at home. The international arena brings another set of problems and the need to redesign jobs to retain these employees. Personal recognition is important in motivating and retaining employees. People join a company because they want to, but they quit because of their manager.

KEY TERMS IN THE CHAPTER

Job redesign

Job rotation

Job enlargement

Job enrichment

Core job dimensions

Skill variety

Task identity

Task significance

Autonomy

Feedback

Motivating potential score

Job profile chart

Vertical loading

REVIEW AND STUDY QUESTIONS

1. Define job redesign.

2. Identify four benefits for job redesign.

3. Explain how each of the following job redesign techniques works: job rotation, job enlargement, and job enrichment.

4. In your own words, what is meant by each of the following core job dimensions: skill variety, task identity, task significance, autonomy, and feedback?

5. How are the five core job dimensions used to develop a motivating potential score formula? What does the score mean?

6. What is a job profile chart and how can it be used in job redesign?

7. Define each of the following job enrichment principles: formation of natural work units, establishment of worker–client relationships, combining of tasks, vertical loading, opening feedback channels. How does each work?

8. Identify the core job dimensions that fulfill each of the job enrichment principles. Explain, using a figure or drawing to relate each principle to its respective core job dimension(s).

9. How have GE and Southwest Airlines used job enrichment to redesign jobs and increase productivity?

10. How has Southwest Airlines used job enrichment to keep it a profitable company in the shadow of the other major airlines losing money and filing for Chapter 11?

11. What are the current challenges in job redesign? Describe them.

12. How are new workplace designs helping organizations to increase job enrichment? Give an example.

13. In what ways is the increase in teleworkers or telecommuters creating job redesign and job enrichment challenges for managers? Give two examples.

14. Explain some of the issues in dealing with contract and part-time workers.

15. What are some techniques that managers can use to retain hard-to-keep employees?

16. How do the needs and attitudes of working mothers differ form those of highly educated workers?

17. Discuss how companies in the international arena are dealing with managing hard-to-keep employees.

18. Discuss the role of "employee recognition" in retaining employees and keeping them motivated and productive.

VISIT THE WEB

I. Challenging and Rewarding

In this chapter, you studied how enterprises are redesigning jobs and trying to enrich the work. Many companies are interested in doing this, including Lucent Technologies, which is one of the fastest-growing firms in the world. Lucent is on the cutting edge of communications technology, and its people are highly skilled and motivated. As a result, over the next decade you are going to see Lucent becoming an increasingly dominant firm in the worldwide telecommunications market. Visit the company's Web site at **www.lucent.com** and review some of the most recent things it is doing. Then answer these two questions:

1. What are some of the new products that we can expect from Lucent over the next two years?

2. In what way do you think job redesign and job enrichment can help the company bring these products to market at highly competitive prices?

II. Creating a Meaningful Workplace

Job redesign and job enrichment are all about creating a meaningful workplace that encourages employees be productive, resulting in a profitable company. Explore how workplaces are changing. Visit the web site **www.meaningfulworkplace.com** and answer the questions.

1. Identify 22 keys to creating a meaningful workplace.

2. Assume you have the authority to improve morale by creating a meaningful workplace. Using ideas from the web site, discuss what you would do?

III. Flexibility—New Ways of Working

Flexibility, teleworking, and a work-life balance are all workplace issues relative to the 21th century employee. Visit **www.flexibility.co.uk** and learn how the hot workplace issues are being handled. This site contains resources on new ways about working. Look at some of the cases and top stories, then answer the questions.

1. Identify some ways companies are redesigning the workplace to enrich jobs.

2. What are the results from some of the latest research? Discuss.

TIME OUT ANSWERS

How You View Your Work

This quiz is designed to measure the five core job dimensions discussed in the chapter. (Feedback has more questions associated with it because information on feedback from both the job itself and the personnel in the organization was obtained.) Here is how to obtain your score for each dimension: (1) Enter all six of your answers to part A in the appropriate place on the answer sheet; (2) subtract from 8 each of your answers in part B for numbers 1–4, 11, and 12, before entering the result in the appropriate place in the chart; and (3) enter answers in part B for numbers 5–10 in the appropriate place. As you can see, the answers from part B that have an asterisk were handled with reverse scoring; a low answer received a high score, and vice versa.

Skill Variety	Task Identity	Task Significance
A.1. _____	A.2. _____	A.3. _____
B.1.* _____	B.6. _____	B.4.* _____
9. _____	11.* _____	7. _____

Autonomy	Feedback (from the job)	Feedback (from others)
A.4. _____	A.5. _____	A.6. _____
B.3.* _____	B.8. _____	B.2.* _____
5. _____	12.* _____	10. _____

The largest total you can have for any of the foregoing job dimensions is 21 and the smallest is 3. Divide all your answers by 3 to determine your average score per job dimension. Average scores tend to be in the range of 4.3–6.0. If you score lower than 4.3, your job is low on this particular job dimension; if you score higher than 6, your job is high on this particular job dimension. If you do not like your current job, you can probably determine why this is so by examining work from the standpoint of these job dimensions. The reverse is also true; if you like your current job, you should be able to determine why from your totals.

case: THE BEST JOB HE EVER HAD

When Emile Veras was in college, he worked part time for a small accounting firm. His duties were highly routine. Emile would clock in at 4 P.M. and clock out at 8 P.M. every weekday. During these four hours, he was responsible for addressing and mailing all packages and letters left in the to-be-mailed box. He was also responsible for taking phone messages and filing reports, letters, memos, and tax returns.

Emile found the work to be boring, but at $7.25 an hour, he knew it would be impossible to find a higher paying job that required so little mental effort. Additionally, he knew that once he graduated, he would find a job that would be more psychologically rewarding and would start him on a meaningful career.

Eight months ago, Emile finished his undergraduate degree in English and landed a job as a copy editor at a publishing house. The publisher specializes in trade books. Emile's job is to read and copyedit books for the business market. Typical titles include *30 Steps to More Effective Negotiating, Building Confidence in 5 Minutes a Day,* and *Creating Excellence in Your Own Company.* These titles appeal to those interested in how-to-do-it books. They are very popular with businesspeople, especially with young managers and entrepreneurs. Sometimes the books are chosen by business book clubs as the monthly selection. In any event, it is common to find the author being interviewed on radio talk shows and television programs, while the publisher works hard to support the sales effort through newspaper advertising and mail brochures.

Although most authors believe their book can stand on its own merits, Emile's company understands the importance of everyone on the sales team knowing the message the author is trying to convey. For this reason, the publisher will invite the author to its headquarters to meet those who will be working on the project, from the copy editor and the designer to the chief of advertising and the head of the sales force. These individuals will listen to the author explain what he or she is trying to convey in the book, and then they will have the opportunity to ask questions. Once everyone understands the basic message of the book, it is much easier to produce and market it. Advertising has a firmer idea of the book's unique features, and the salespeople know the right

"hooks" that they can highlight in reinforcing why a bookstore should carry the title. Even Emile has found that by listening and talking to an author, he can gain valuable insights for copyediting purposes. "Anyone can copyedit a book," he told his mother. "But to copyedit it with a slant toward the author's message, that is the difference between an average book and a bestseller."

In addition to meeting the author, Emile is assigned to a work team that consists of all in-house personnel who will be responsible for turning out the book. This group is responsible for making all the decisions associated with its publication. Typically, Emile is asked to copyedit a book within twenty working days. The rest of his time on the project is spent discussing the cover with the design artist and the promotion program with the advertising people. When recently asked what he likes about his job, Emile said, "This work really gives me an opportunity to be creative and show what I can do. I love helping turn out a completed project and then watching its release and sale to the public. I feel like I'm helping create something rather than just reworking words on a page. This is the best job I've ever had."

QUESTIONS

1. Which of the core job dimensions are present in Emile's current job? Identify and briefly describe each.

2. How does his current job differ from his previous job? Compare the core job dimensions of the two jobs.

3. Using Figure 8.2 as your point of reference, how do you think Emile would describe his current job? What conclusions can you draw as a result of this profile?

YOU BE THE CONSULTANT

Now It's Meaningful

When Joan Mitchell was hired at the Ogleby Plant, she was brought in as a small-products assembler. Specifically, Joan was given the job of putting together some of the inner assembly of a handheld power drill. This drill, which sells for $39.95 at retail stores nationwide, is a very popular model. Ogleby makes a number of different versions of the machine, and all of them are sold to other, better known firms that, in turn, market the units under their own labels. One of Ogleby's biggest customers is a national retail chain that advertises the power drill as its own. Other customers do the same on a regional basis. Because the machines are different in terms of physical characteristics, customers do not realize that these competitive products are basically the same unit and all are made by Ogleby.

Ogleby has to turn out one thousand of these units every day. Joan is responsible for performing partial assembly on thirty of them per hour. The job is basically boring, but she generally daydreams her way through the workday, and the money is good so Joan does not complain. However, last month the company decided to reorganize the assembly jobs, and the assemblers each put together an entire unit. Now Joan sits in the middle of a U-shaped table with the parts of the machine placed around the table. She assembles the unit moving from left to right and, when she is done, she tests the product to ensure that it works properly. If it does, Joan then places the unit on a tray at the end of the table. If it does not, she disassembles the unit, finds the error, corrects the mistake, and then retests the machine. Joan never has any trouble finding the error; usually it is a loose wire or an improper connection.

Joan was recently asked how she likes the new arrangement. She said she enjoys the work much more now. "I like assembling the entire unit and feeling that I'm personally responsible for the whole machine. I also like the fact that as long as I assemble eighty complete units per day, I can work at my own pace. The fact that I am averaging eighty-four units per day and the company pays a $4 bonus for every unit over eighty is an additional incentive to work fast."

Your Advice

1. What do you recommend that the company do in regard to expanding this idea and using it for nonassembly jobs as well?

   ___ a. It should reorganize all the jobs in the plant the way it has with Joan's job.
   ___ b. It should look into the benefits that might accrue from using job enrichment techniques with nonassembly jobs.
   ___ c. It should leave everything alone, because job enrichment is confined to assembly-type work.

2. Is Joan's story a case of job enlargement or job enrichment? Give an example.

3. In what way has the company vertically loaded Joan's job?

4. In terms of Figure 8.2, how is the new job different from the old one? Prepare a diagram of the old job and one of the new job.

EXPERIENCING JOB ENRICHMENT

Purpose

- To understand the concept of job enrichment and job enlargement.
- To apply these concepts to redesigning specific jobs.

Procedure

1. In small groups, students should choose one specific job to study. It may be the actual job of a group member or of someone whom one of the group members knows well. It should also be a job that the group feels would be well served by job redesign. The person whose job or whose friend's job is being analyzed

should brief the group on the job, giving group members as much detail as possible.

2. The group should develop a job redesign program for the job that would be motivational to the employee yet realistic within the organizational context. (Remember, job enlargement means adding other duties at a similar level of responsibility, whereas job enrichment means adding other duties at increased levels of responsibility.)

3. Each group should describe to the rest of the class its chosen job and the recommended redesign of that job.

4. Discuss the following: Is job redesign as easy as you originally thought it would be? Why or why not?

Source: Adapted from "Redesigning Jobs," in Jane W. Gibson and Richard M. Hodgetts, Readings and Exercises in Organization Behavior *(Orlando, FL: Academic Press, 1985), p. 184.*

The Administrative System

The *administrative* system of organizations is about providing effective leadership and developing, appraising, and rewarding the organization's personnel for doing their job.

THE GOALS OF THIS SECTION ARE TO:

- *Examine the nature of leadership, review some of the leadership and personal characteristics that effective leaders often possess, and examine the assumptions many leaders hold regarding the nature of organizational personnel; investigate four contingency leadership approaches, study four leadership behavior models, and review emerging challenges in developing internal leaders who can deal effectively with difficult employees.*

- *Study what personnel development is all about and how a leader appraises and rewards performance, examine the performance appraisal cycle, review appraisal tools commonly used in employee evaluations, look at some of the problems associated with performance appraisal, examine ways of linking performance and rewards, and examine discipline and methods of employing it.*

When you have finished reading this part of the book, you should have a solid understanding of the administrative system in modern organizations. In particular, you should know the role the leader must play in the organization and the ways in which performance can be measured, rewards can be given, and discipline can be carried out.

9

Fundamentals of Leadership

Leaders direct activities in organizations, but its their leadership skills that determine an organization's level of success. Leadership is a process of influencing people toward achieving results. In this chapter the nature of leadership is examined, leadership behaviors are studied, and contingency leadership models are investigated. Also, the characteristics and personal qualities of effective leaders are examined along with basic managerial assumptions of leaders.

AFTER READING THIS CHAPTER, YOU SHOULD BE ABLE TO:

1. Describe the leadership and personal characteristics related to managerial effectiveness—trait theory, superior intelligence, emotional maturity, motivation drive, problem-solving skills, managerial skills, and leadership skills.
2. Compare and contrast Theory X and Theory Y.
3. Distinguish among four styles of leadership behavior—authoritarian, paternalistic, participative, and laissez-faire.
4. Explain the concept of "self-leaders" and the basic rules of behavior.
5. Describe the two major dimensions of leadership—concern for people and concern for work.
6. Distinguish among the contingency leadership approaches—Fiedler's Contingency Model, the Managerial Grid, Charismatic Leadership, and Transformational Leadership.
7. Describe the leader in the twenty-first century.
8. Discuss emerging leadership challenges.
9. Identify ways of developing internal leaders and dealing with high-potential employees who have bad work habits.

New Leaders Are Emerging

When businesspeople are asked to name the best business leader in the last half of the twentieth century, the overwhelming choice is Jack Welch of General Electric (GE). However, at the beginning of the millennium, GE was faced with a leadership challenge. Jack Welch retired in 2001 and was replaced by Jeffrey Immelt, who had a very different leadership style than Welch. When Jack Welch took the reins in 1981, he spent a good deal of his time getting rid of managers who could not meet their goals. In fact, he soon was dubbed "neutron Jack" because, like a neutron bomb, he got rid of people but left the buildings and machinery intact. As Welch began replacing these managers, however, performance began to increase. In 1981, the company had sales of $25 billion and, by the time Welch retired in 2001, sales had risen to more than $180 billion. Stockholders were delighted with his performance, and Welch loved to note that a person who invested $10,000 in GE in 1981 would have had stock valued at more than $800,000 in 2001.

Immelt's leadership is different from Jack Welch's style. A security analyst who tracks GE stock and operating performance very closely has described Immelt as a person who has "tenacity, intellectual sharpness and results orientation" but, unlike Welch, "is easier to get along with." Additionally, many people, including Welch, believed that GE had effective operating systems in place and the change would go smoothly. Immelt has proven to be an effective leader for GE.

Certainly Immelt had a proven track record as a leader. His previous assignment was head of GE Medical Systems (Gems), a job he held for four years. In his first year at the helm, Gems took in $4 billion and, by the end of the fourth year, it was grossing $7.5 billion. Much of this success was a result of Immelt's working closely with his people to set goals and help them develop their abilities. In particular, Immelt earned a reputation as one of the company's champions of diversity. When he took over at Gems, fewer than twenty women, Hispanics, or African Americans were found in the top ranks. Four years later, there were seventy-five, and Immelt had set up a system by which fast-track minorities and women were to be formally mentored.

Increasing the number of women, in particular, may well be one of Immelt's best strategies, given that recent research reveals that female executives tend to outshine their male counterparts in almost every measure. In one study, 425 high-level executives were each evaluated by 25 people, and female executives had higher ratings on 42 of the 52 skills that were measured. In a second study, women ranked higher than men on 28 of 31 measures. In a third and massive study of 58,000 managers, women outranked men in 20 of 23 areas. In a fourth, evaluations of 2,482 executives from a variety of companies were examined, and it was found that women outperformed men on 17 of 20 measures. In particular, these studies found that female leaders tended to be superior to their male counterparts in motivating others, fostering communication, producing high-quality work, and listening to others. And on another note the debate continues on who is better at multitasking—men or women. "Our society and culture expect women to do it all, so we do, writes Margaret Gottlieb, managing director, Foster Partners Executive Search, Washington." Some employers prefer to hire women on the belief they can get "two-fers or even three-fers" who can multitask. One individual explained the situation this way:

> *Twenty-five years after women first started pouring into the labor force—and trying to be more like men in every way, from wearing power suits to picking up golf clubs—new research is showing that men ought to be the ones doing more of the imitating. In fact, after years of analyzing what makes leaders most effective and figuring out who's got the "right stuff," management gurus now know how to boost the odds of getting a great executive: Hire a female.*

Sources: Claudia H. Deutsch, "G.E.'s New Corporate Face," New York Times, December 1, 2000, pp. C1, C6; Rochelle Sharpe, "As Leaders, Women Rule," Business Week, November 20, 2000, pp. 75–84; Carole K. Barnett and Noel M. Tichy, "Rapid-Cycle CEO Development: How New Leaders Learn to Take Charge," Organizational Dynamics, summer 2000, pp. 16–32; and Matt Murray, "Can House That Jack Built Stand When He Goes? Sure, Welch Says," Wall Street Journal, April 13, 2000, pp. A1, A8." (Sue Shellenbarger, "Female Rats Are Better Multitaskers; With Humans, The Debate Rages On," Wall Street Journal, March 20, 2003, p. D1)

① The Nature of Leadership

Leadership is the process of influencing people to direct their efforts toward the achievement of some particular goal(s).[1] Good leaders have visions of where they want the organization to go, and they have the ability to create enthusiasm among their followers to pursue their goals. Some managers are highly effective leaders, but most are, at best, only moderately successful. What accounts for this difference? Some people believe the answer rests in **leadership characteristics,** such as drive, originality, and tolerance of stress, which, they say, are universal among successful leaders. If you have these qualities, you will do well in leading others; if you lack them, you will be ineffective in the leadership role.

Others argue in favor of **personal characteristics,** such as superior mental ability, emotional maturity, and problem-solving skills. They claim that no universal list of leadership characteristics exists, and so we must turn to personal characteristics that interact with one another to produce the desired outcomes. Only through an awareness of how these characteristics influence managerial effectiveness can we truly understand the nature of leadership. To begin our study of this subject, we examine both approaches—leadership characteristics and personal characteristics—and then address the importance of managerial assumptions regarding the nature of organizational personnel.

Leadership Characteristics

Recent leadership studies have pointed out the importance of environmental influences on leadership effectiveness. However, published research indicates that, regardless of the situation, certain characteristics favor success in the leadership role.

From 1920 to 1950, the study of leadership characteristics, known as **trait theory,** sought to isolate those factors that contribute to leader effectiveness. This approach assumed that such attributes as initiative, social dominance, and persistence were the primary factors in leadership success and failure. Unfortunately, the research studies conducted during this period failed to produce a universal list of traits. Additionally, in most cases, no consideration was given to the possibility that different situations might require different characteristics or that a specific situation might demand so little of the leader or might be so unfavorable that leadership characteristics would be of little, if any, value. Despite the arguments for situational leadership, however, Ralph Stogdill, one of the leading authorities in the field, concluded that a select group of characteristics does, in fact, differentiate leaders from followers, effective from ineffective leaders, and high-echelon from low-echelon leaders.

> *The leader is characterized by a strong drive for responsibility and task completion, vigor and persistence in pursuit of goals, venturesomeness and originality in problem solving, drive to exercise initiative in social situations, self-confidence and a sense of personal identity, willingness to accept consequences of decision and action, readiness to absorb interpersonal stress, willingness to tolerate frustration and delay, ability to influence other persons' behavior, and capacity to structure social interaction systems to the purpose at hand.*[2]

The greatest problem with trait theory, however, is that no common list has been forthcoming. Some traits appear important, but their value is situationally determined. As a result, many researchers have turned their attention to the personal characteristics of effective leaders.

Personal Characteristics

Many personal characteristics appear to be related to managerial effectiveness, but an exhaustive list is beyond our current needs. We will, however, examine some major personal characteristics that significantly contribute to leadership effectiveness. They are superior intelligence, emotional maturity, motivation drive, problem-solving skills, managerial skills, and leadership skills.

SUPERIOR INTELLIGENCE

Research reveals that effective managers tend to have superior intelligence: There is a minimum level of mental ability below which we are unlikely to find successful leaders. Conversely, there may well be a ceiling above which we are, again, unlikely to find effective leaders. Some researchers, for example, report that the intelligence quotient (IQ) of successful leaders typically falls in the range of 115–130.[3]

Keep in mind, however, that intelligence is a relative matter. Some geniuses are excellent leaders, whereas some people with IQs in the 115–130 range lack the personality to manage effectively. Additionally, one can have a superior intellect and be in the wrong job. For example, a person with high verbal skills and abstract reasoning ability and low quantitative ability might do poorly in an accounting firm or a bank, and an individual with low verbal skills and high quantitative abilities might be a total failure as a personnel manager. Yet both have high IQs, and their mental abilities are comparable.

EMOTIONAL MATURITY

Successful leaders are emotionally mature. They are self-confident and capable of directing their subordinates in a calm, conscientious manner. If a subordinate makes a mistake, the effective leader tries to use the experience as an opportunity to teach and counsel the person so as to prevent recurrence of the problem. The leader realizes that little is to be gained from bawling out the subordinate (except maybe to embarrass him or her in front of peers), especially if the person really wanted to do the job right. Effective leaders also have a sense of purpose and meaning in life. They know who they are, where they are going, and how they are going to get there. They are practical and decisive and have confidence in their own abilities. Additionally, the goals they set for themselves are often challenging but realistic.

Finally, because they are emotionally mature, successful leaders are neither ulcer prone nor workaholics. They know how to deal with stress, to delegate work that is either minor in importance or is best handled by someone more technically skilled, and to handle the challenges of the job without resorting to alcohol or drugs. Because they know and understand themselves, they are able to cope with the demands of both their business and personal lives. For example, the divorce rate among successful leaders is no greater than that in the general population.

MOTIVATION DRIVE

Effective leaders have a high motivation drive. In particular, they seem most motivated by the opportunity to achieve the chance for power or control over a situation and by the need to self-actualize. Additionally, as we noted in our discussion of money in Chapter 2, they are motivated by increased personal income, because it is a sign of how well they are doing. Effective leaders often measure their progress in quantitative terms: how much money they are making, how many promotions they have had, how many subordinates they control.

Additionally, we know from research that successful leaders tend to have subordinates who are also interested in fulfillment of self-actualization and esteem needs. Average leaders have followers who are most concerned with esteem and social needs. The least successful leaders have subordinates who are most interested in safety and physiological needs. In short, successful leaders tend to attract a particular type of subordinate, as do the average and least successful leaders, and these subordinates have need drives similar to those of their superiors. In large measure, highly motivated leaders attract or develop highly motivated subordinates.

PROBLEM-SOLVING SKILLS

Effective leaders also possess problem-solving skills. They see a problem as both a challenge and an opportunity to prove their managerial abilities. As such, these skills are closely related to high motivation drives, for without such motivation, leaders might be unwilling to assume the risk that comes with problem solving. These individuals also have a great deal of self-confidence. Conversely, average leaders and, especially, ineffective leaders tend to shun problem solving because they either are unprepared to deal with the issues or have learned through experience that they are not up to the task.

MANAGERIAL SKILLS

Effective leaders, especially at the upper levels of the hierarchy, have managerial skills: **technical, human,** and **conceptual.**

- *Technical skills*—the knowledge of how things work. These skills are very important for lower level managers such as foremen.
- *Human skills*—the knowledge of how to deal with people. These skills are very important for middle-level managers who must lead other managers. Without a solid understanding of such behavioral areas as interpersonal communication, motivation, counseling, and directing, middle-level managers would be ineffective in leading their subordinates.
- *Conceptual skills*—the knowledge of how all parts of the organization or department fit together. These skills cover many activities, from formulating organizational objectives, policies, and procedures, to developing techniques for handling office work flow, to coordinating a host of seemingly unrelated functions that enable the enterprise to operate as an integrated unit.

As shown in Figure 9.1, the leader's place in the hierarchy determines the degree of managerial skill that he or she must possess. As managers prove their effectiveness and begin moving up the ranks, they need to learn more about conceptual skills. In the final analysis, conceptual skills make the difference between leaders who will head the organization and leaders who must be content to manage at the intermediate and lower levels.

LEADERSHIP SKILLS

Although effective leadership style depends on the situation, some personal characteristics seem to contribute to the leadership skills of managers. Some such characteristics are task related, whereas others are more social in nature. The task-related characteristics of effective leaders, as isolated by Stogdill, include initiative, need to excel or achieve, task orientation, drive for responsibility, and responsibility in pursuit of objectives. Some of the social characteristics of

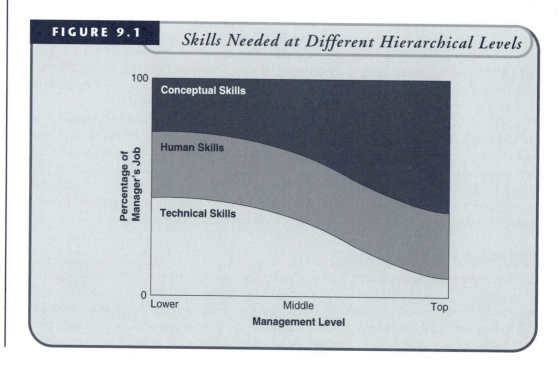

FIGURE 9.1 *Skills Needed at Different Hierarchical Levels*

TABLE 9.1 — Summary of Leadership Skills

Stogdill's Task-Related Characteristics	Stogdill's Social Characteristics	Gallup Organization's Leadership Talents
Initiative	Administrative ability	Goal orientation
Need to excel or achieve	Interpersonal skills	Energy
Task orientation	Tact and diplomacy	Ability to help people grow
Drive for responsibility	Ability to enlist cooperation	A desire to win
Responsibility in pursuit of objectives	Social participation	Willingness to accept challenge
	Cooperativeness	
	Attractiveness	

effective leaders are administrative ability, interpersonal skills, tact and diplomacy, ability to enlist cooperation, popularity, social participation, cooperativeness, and attractiveness.[4] More recently, the Gallup Organization has identified a host of key leadership talents or themes possessed by effective leaders. These include goal orientation, energy, the ability to help people grow, a desire to win, and the willingness to accept challenge.[5] Table 9.1 summarizes the leadership skills of Stogdill and the Gallup Organization.

The profile of today's twenty-first-century CEO leader is fifty-six years old, is male, has been with the company for eighteen years, and is well educated, with 37 percent of them having MBAs. These leaders understand numbers and inner workings of their companies. Some 22 percent have come through finance and another 14 percent have worked in operations. They operate in a complex, imperfect world often balancing the chore of knowing one thing and having to say another, which creates a public debate about whether they know right from wrong. At the top of the organization, they operate alone. A lot can't be shared, which puts them on a razor's edge in how they choose to act and to manage the organization; but a new type of leader is emerging. The corporate scandals of 2002 changed the old CEO epic hero image.[6]

The Nature of Organizational Personnel

LEARNING OBJECTIVE
② Compare and contrast Theory X and Theory Y

Leadership characteristics and personal characteristics provide insights regarding who leaders are. However, it also is important to understand why leaders act as they do.[7] Part of this explanation can be found in the opinions leaders have about their people. Are the subordinates content with satisfying lower-level needs, or do they strive also for esteem and self-actualization fulfillment? How important is money to them? As managers begin to answer these questions, they express their assumptions about the nature of the organization's personnel. The research conducted by Douglas McGregor has provided management with a set of basic assumptions. He called these assumptions *Theory X* and *Theory Y*.[8]

Theory X

Theory X assumptions hold that people are basically lazy and that often it is necessary to use coercion and threats of punishment to get them to work. McGregor summarized the assumptions this way:

1. **People, by their very nature, dislike work and will avoid it when possible.**
2. **They have little ambition, tend to shun responsibility, and like to be directed.**

Theory X
holds that people are basically lazy.

3. Above all else, they want security.

4. To get them to attain organizational objectives, it is necessary to use coercion, control, and threats of punishment.[9]

From this summary of their attitudes, we can arrive at two conclusions regarding Theory X managers. First, they like to control their subordinates because they feel such control is in the best interests of both the organization and its personnel. Second, they believe that people work to satisfy their lower-level needs (security above all else) and that upper-level need satisfaction is not very important. Additionally, because lower-level needs are satisfied with physical rewards, such as money, job security, and good working conditions, Theory X managers will withhold these rewards if the workers do not comply with organizational directives.

Theory Y

Theory Y
holds that, under the right conditions, people will work.

Modern behavioral research has provided the basis for formulating assumptions for a new theory of management, which McGregor called **Theory Y,** which assumes that:

1. The expenditure of physical and mental effort in work is as natural to people as is resting or playing.

2. External control and the threat of punishment are not the only ways of getting people to work toward organizational objectives. If people are committed to objectives, they will exercise self-direction and self-control.

3. Commitment to objectives is determined by the rewards associated with their achievement.

4. Under proper conditions, the average person learns not only to accept but to seek responsibility.

5. The capacity to exercise a relatively high degree of imagination, ingenuity, and creatively in the solution of organizational problems is widely distributed throughout the population.

6. Under conditions of modern industrial life, the intellectual potentialities of the average human being are only partially used.[10]

As you can see, Theory Y presents a much more dynamic view of the organizational personnel. They now are seen as interested in both lower-level and upper-level need satisfaction and as having untapped potential. This theory urges management to reevaluate its thinking and to begin focusing attention on ways of enabling employees to attain their upper-level needs. Motivation is viewed as a problem that must be solved by management. No longer can the leader hide behind Theory X assumptions, claiming that workers are by nature lazy and unmotivated.

Before continuing, however, we should answer one very important question: Is a Theory Y manager always superior to a Theory X manager? Although we have presented Theory Y as a modern, superior view of the workers, it is not without its critics. Some point out that Theory Y can be dangerous because it allows too much freedom to the workers, many of whom not only need but also want close direction and control. Additionally, Theory Y assumes people want to satisfy their needs while on the job. However, many satisfy their needs off the job, as in the case of workers who want a shorter workweek so they will have more leisure time.

Therefore, to put these two theories in perspective, we must acknowledge that some people respond better to Theory X management than to Theory Y management. However, many managers tend to underrate the workers, subscribing much more heavily to Theory X than to Theory Y.

What are your basic beliefs regarding these two theories? You can answer this question by taking the Time Out quiz.

YOUR ASSUMPTIONS ABOUT PEOPLE

Read the following ten pairs of statements. In each case, show the relative strength of your beliefs by assigning to each statement a weight from 0 to 10. The points assigned to each pair must total 10 points. If you totally agree with one statement and totally disagree with the other, give the first one a 10 and the second a 0. If you like both statements equally, give each 5 points. The interpretation of your answers is provided at the end of the chapter.

1. Most employees are fairly creative but often do not have the chance to employ this ingenuity on the job. _____ (a)

    Most workers are not creative at all, but the job does not lend itself to creativity so nothing is lost. _____ (b)

2. If you give people enough money, this will greatly offset their desire for interesting, challenging, or meaningful work. _____ (c)

    If you give people interesting, challenging, or meaningful work, they are less likely to complain about money and fringe benefits. _____ (d)

3. Workers who are allowed to set their own goals and standards of performance tend to set them higher than management would. _____ (e)

    Workers who are allowed to set their own goals and standards of performance tend to set them lower than management would. _____ (f)

4. People want freedom to do work the way that they believe is correct. _____ (g)

    People want to be told what to do; freedom actually makes them nervous. _____ (h)

5. The better an individual knows his or her job, the more likely it is that the person will work just hard enough to produce the minimum amount acceptable to management. _____ (i)

    The better an individual knows his or her job, the more likely it is that the person will find satisfaction in the work and try to produce at least as much as the average worker in the organization. _____ (j)

6. Most workers in a modern organization are not up to the intellectual challenge presented by their jobs. _____ (k)

    Most workers in a modern organization have more than sufficient intellectual potential to do their jobs. _____ (l)

7. Most people dislike work and, if given the chance, they will goof off. _____ (m)

    Most people like work, especially if it is interesting and challenging. _____ (n)

8. Most employees work best under loose control. _____ (o)

    Most employees work best under close control. _____ (p)

9. Above all else, workers want job security. _____ (q)

    Although workers want job security, it is only one of many things they want, and it does not rank first on all lists. _____ (r)

10. It increases a supervisor's prestige when he or she admits that a subordinate was right and he or she was wrong. _____ (s)

    A manager is entitled to more respect than a subordinate, and it weakens the former's prestige to admit that a subordinate was right and he or she was wrong. _____ (t)

Leadership Behavior

Leadership behavior is the way leaders actually carry out their jobs. The four styles of leadership behavior are authoritarian, paternalistic, participative, and laissez-faire (Figure 9.2). On a continuum, they range from high concern for work and people to a general lack of concern for the work and the people. As subordinates have greater input, leadership behavior generally changes to that of helping subordinates rather than supervising them. Depending on the situation, any one of these styles can be ideal.

LEARNING OBJECTIVE

③ *Distinguish among four styles of leadership behavior—authoritarian, paternalistic, participative, and laissez-faire*

FIGURE 9.2   *Continuum of Leadership Behavior*

Task Oriented			People-Oriented
Authoritarian	Paternalistic	Participative	Laissez-Faire
On this end, subordinate's input is small or not wanted			On this end, subordinate's input is large and is expected

Authoritarian Leadership

Authoritarian leadership tends to be heavily work centered, with little attention to the human element.

Leaders who engage in **authoritarian leadership** tend to be heavily work centered, with much emphasis given to task accomplishment and little to the human element. Such leaders fit the classic model of management in which the workers are viewed as factors of production.

These individuals can be very useful in certain situations. For example, when a crisis occurs and the organization needs a "get-tough" leader, the authoritarian manager is often ideal. Attention is focused on objectives, efficiency, profit, and other task-related activities, and this is just to the manager's liking. A good example is Jurgen E. Schrempp, chief executive of Daimler-Chrysler. After the two companies merged, he began instituting a strategy to make Chrysler operate more like Daimler. Chrysler's top management opposed this approach, and most of them ended up either leaving the company or being fired. As a result, Chrysler began experiencing major losses. However, this did not stop Schrempp from continuing to try and force his operating system on Chrysler.[11]

In few instances is an authoritarian manager superior to all others, although a fairly large number of such managers are at work in industry today. These people have authoritarian personalities, often developed because their parents were also authoritarian. They were taught early in life to be submissive toward superior authority and, in turn, have used this parental model to dominate those who hold positions subordinate to theirs. As a result, they tend to be "yes-men" when talking to their bosses and to demand the same type of behavior from their own personnel.

Paternalitic Leadership

Paternalistic leadership tends to be heavily work-centered but has some consideration for the personnel as well.

Leaders who practice **paternalistic leadership** are heavily work centered but, unlike authoritarian leaders, have some consideration for employees. They tend to look after their people the way a father does his family. Their basic philosophy, far out of step with the needs of most employees, is "work hard and I'll take care of you." This style of management was prevalent in the late nineteenth century, when some businesses went so far as to provide the workers with lodging, medical services, a company store, and even churches for religious worship. The Pullman Corporation, famous for the Pullman railroad sleeping car, was such a company and, like other firms that built company towns, it eventually found the workers fighting its paternalism. We know from human relations studies that people do not want to be treated like children or feel that the company owns them.

Many managers in this country are paternalistic leaders; they believe their subordinates want someone to look after them and provide job security, cost-of-living raises, insurance programs, retirement plans, and other extrinsic rewards. Actually, these leaders are confusing management with manipulation. In terms of Theories X and Y, they are soft Theory X managers. Although they do not believe that people are totally lazy or security oriented, they do feel that workers tend to act this way. By playing the role of the parent, these leaders believe they can get the most productivity out of their people. However, most workers resent this type of leadership, although some like it. Employees who have been smothered with affection and security by their parents often welcome a boss who acts the same way. They now have a surrogate parent who takes care of them when they are on the job. However, these people are exceptions to the rule; most workers dislike paternalism.

Participative Leadership

Leaders who have a high concern for both people and work are engaged in **participative leadership.** They encourage their subordinates to play an active role in operating the enterprise, but they reserve the right to make the final decision on important matters. In short, they delegate authority but do not abdicate in favor of subordinate rule. Some management experts have contended that no manager can perform effectively over an extended period without some degree of employee participation. This is certainly true of U.S. managers, for it is an accepted norm in this country that workers have a voice in what goes on.

One way that participative leadership commonly is exercised is through delegating authority to the lowest possible organizational level. A second way is through encouraging feedback from the subordinates. While an authoritarian manager is busy telling the personnel what to do, the participative leader is getting information on what is going well and what is going poorly. From this feedback, the manager is able to decide what should be done next. No leader can be truly effective without the support of the subordinates, and feedback is a key indication of such support. Finally, participative leaders discuss objectives with their people and then give them the opportunity to attain these objectives. This is in contrast to authoritarian leaders, who keep objectives to themselves, distrust their subordinates, delegate very little, and try to do too many things themselves. The participative manager builds esprit de corps by sharing objectives and providing the chance for subordinates to fulfill their esteem and self-actualization needs. The personnel, in turn, like this approach and work harder for the leader.

Laissez-Faire Leadership

Laissez-faire is a French term meaning "noninterference." As we move across the continuum from authoritarian to participative leadership, the subordinates begin playing an increasingly larger role. If a leader continues this transition, however, he or she will come very close to abdicating the leadership position. In Figure 9.3 are diagrammed the comparisons between leadership behaviors that we have discussed. Note that the subordinates in the **laissez-faire leadership** diagram are interacting with one another to get the work done. The leader is merely checking in on occasion to see how things are going.

Although this style is effective for some subordinates, they are not very common. University professors are an example. Very seldom does the department chairperson check up on a professor to see whether the individual is having any problems, meeting classes on time, or conducting appropriate research activities. The chairperson usually meets with the professor prior to the beginning of the academic year to discuss objectives and assignments and relies on him or her to fulfill these obligations by the end of the school year. This approach works for highly skilled professionals in any area. The office manager of a research and development laboratory leaves the scientists alone to get their work done. Only occasionally does the manager check in to see that everything is running smoothly. In a business setting, some managers employ a laissez-faire style with their outstanding copywriters and design people, and a board of directors uses it with a president who has led the company into a new period of prosperity. In each case, the subordinates play a tremendous role in running the show. Keep in mind, however, that although the laissez-faire leadership style can work effectively with some people, it does not work well with most. On average, the participative style tends to be most effective.

Common Leadership Behaviors

To understand effective leadership, it is important to realize that effective leaders try to do a number of things to influence and direct their people. First, they strive to get their subordinates to become "self-leaders"—that is, to learn to motivate and direct themselves. This reduces the amount of time that the leader must spend on direct supervision.[12]

Leaders also support their personnel and provide them with assistance and guidance as needed. In this way, a mutual exchange takes place between the two that is rewarding to both parties. In fact, some researchers have concluded that organizations that promote extraordinary employee

Participative-leaders *have high concern for people and work.*

Laissez-faire leadership *is characterized by a lack of concern for either the people or the work.*

LEARNING OBJECTIVE
④ *Explain the concept of "self-leaders" and the basic rules of behavior*

FIGURE 9.3

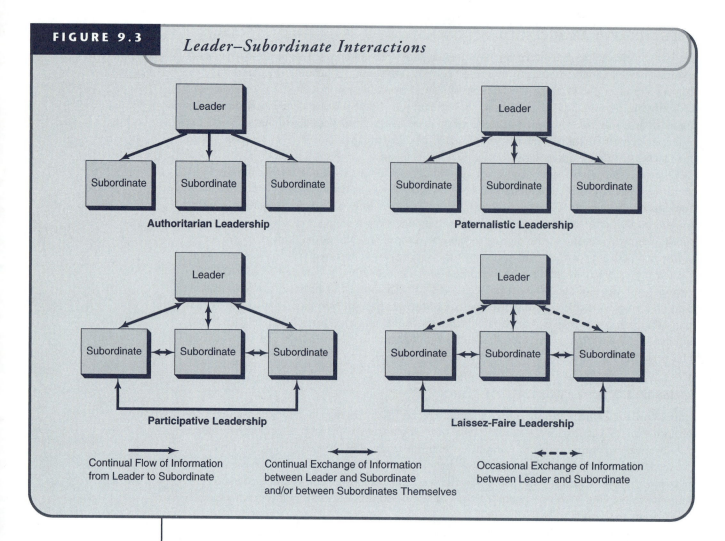

Leader–Subordinate Interactions

Authoritarian Leadership

Paternalistic Leadership

Participative Leadership

Laissez-Faire Leadership

Continual Flow of Information from Leader to Subordinate

Continual Exchange of Information between Leader and Subordinate and/or between Subordinates Themselves

Occasional Exchange of Information between Leader and Subordinate

relations actually function like an extended family. For example, members of strong families gather periodically to communicate, share, celebrate, resolve problems, and enjoy one another's company. The same is true for effective organizations that routinely have meetings and social get-togethers. Additionally, as in families, everyone is accessible to everyone else; there is an open-door policy throughout the company. Another similarity is trust. As in families, effective enterprises trust their people to do the right things and to be honest and fair in their dealings with others.[13]

Leaders also tend to follow basic rules that have proven effective in the past. The following are some examples:

1. **Be decisive.**
2. **Do not promise what you cannot deliver.**
3. **Praise people in front of others for a job well done and reprimand them in private when they have made a mistake.**
4. **When possible, promote from within.**

As seen in the Cultural Diversity in Action box, these leadership behaviors are reflective of successful managers, regardless of gender.

LEARNING OBJECTIVE

(5)

Describe the two major dimensions of leadership—concern for people and concern for work

Leadership dimensions

entail a concern for people and a concern for work.

Leadership Dimensions

Each of the four leadership styles we have just examined contains some degree of concern for work and for people. These two **leadership dimensions**—concern for work and concern for people—have been found to be *independent* dimensions. This means, for example, that someone

CULTURAL DIVERSITY IN ACTION

Women Leading the Way

Over the last decade, the U.S. economy has become stronger than ever. Not only is America the most competitive nation in the world, but also it is the most productive, and a large portion of this economic resurgence and growth can be directly attributed to the fact that an increasing number of women are moving into leadership positions. As a result, companies are finding that they have been overlooking a large pool of highly talented individuals who are capable of both growing the firm and increasing the bottom line. Additionally, recent research reports that, on average, women outscore men in leadership skills. Lawrence A. Pfaff and Associates, a Michigan-based human resource consulting firm, reports that female managers—as rated by their bosses, themselves, and the people who work for them—scored significantly better than their male counterparts. In addition to having better communication, feedback, and empowerment skills, the women also were rated higher in such areas as decisiveness, planning, and setting standards. This study was the second one conducted by Pfaff and Associates and, although the overall results were the same, the differences were significantly better for women this time around. In short, the management and leadership skills of women are even better than those reported in the first study. These latest data led the head of the consulting firm to note that "the statistical significance of these data is dramatic. In two successive studies, men were not rated significantly higher by any of the raters in any of the areas measured."

These findings are not a surprise to most women, especially those who are successful leaders. For example, Stacey Lawson is the senior vice president of product marketing strategy at the Parametric Technology Corporation in Waltham, Massachusetts. After graduating from the University of Washington with a chemical engineering degree, she went to work for IBM in semiconductor processing. However, she did not like her technical job, so she applied to Harvard's MBA program and was accepted. While there, she followed up on an idea she had had at IBM: building content libraries for digitized three-dimensional industrial components, which are needed by companies such as Boeing, John Deere, and Ford to create digital models of their machinery. When she graduated from Harvard in 1996 she founded her own company, InPart,

with an IBM colleague. Soon thereafter, she agreed to sell the company to Parametric Technology, which was working on similar technology. The purchase included jobs for all her employees and made her a senior vice president of product marketing strategy. Today she oversees twenty-five product lines.

Another example of women leading the way is Amanda Klein, director of acquisitions and production for USA Films. Soon after graduating from college, she landed a job that gave her a great deal of real-world experience, including drafting contracts and helping to negotiate multimillion-dollar movie deals. She then moved on to the acquisitions department, where she was responsible for identifying and purchasing hit movie scripts. After eighteen months on this job, USA Films lured her away to be its director of acquisitions and production. In this role, she has been instrumental in bringing to the screen such award-winning films as Hilary and Jackie *and* The Celebration. *Today she is a leading force at USA Films, and many of the scripts that she targets are given the green light by the senior brass.*

Kathryn Cornish is a vice-president at the Wit Capital Corporation, an investment bank that specializes in on-line companies. Kathryn's first job was selling four-color coupon inserts for newspapers. When the company was sold, she stayed on with the chief financial officer to help shut it down and, in her words, "learn[ed] an immeasurable amount about what makes a good company." From here, she enrolled in college and earned a business degree from New York University. On graduating, she became an investment banker at Smith Barney. When this company merged with Salomon Brothers, Kathryn was tapped to work on the integration team. In 1999, Wit Capital made her an offer and she accepted because it had what she was looking for: creative challenge, fast pace, the opportunity to make an impact on smaller companies, and a chance to get in on the emerging world of e-commerce. Today she advises companies such as Barnes and Noble and, with her work group, finds the challenge to be both exciting and energizing.

Ernestina Laura Herrera de Noble is the president and editorial director of Grupo Clarin, the largest media group in Latin America. In addition to owning the country's biggest daily newspaper, the company owns a sports newspaper, a Spanish edition of Elle *magazine, two printing companies, two radio stations, a television station, the*

in action box cont.

Galaxy Entertainment satellite channels, a majority stake in the Multicanal cable company, and part of a cellular phone network. The firm employs 11,500 people. Since Ernestina took over the company after the death of her husband, she has managed to stay ahead of rapid changes in communications technology while maintaining the newspaper's award-winning quality and encouraging new talent through its journalism foundation, which provides both training and scholarships. Under her leadership, the group has grafted its brand reputation into other diverse media ventures. In addition, she has teamed up with some powerful partners, including the United States-based Hughes Electronics company.

Nancy Lublin was a first-year law student at New York University when she received a $5,000 check from the estate of a relative. She used the money to realize her vision of finding a way to get professional clothing to low-income women seeking employment. When her nonprofit company, Dress for Success, opened its doors, it generated such a positive response from companies such as Avon, Coach, and Garfield & Marks that she dropped out of law school to tend the organization full-time. As executive director, her job is to bring in big sponsors. For example, Avon gives the company imitation pearl earrings and necklaces for the clients as well as thousands of pairs of stockings; Coach donates twelve thousand pairs of shoes annually; and Garfield & Marks contributes one thousand suits. Today Dress for Success has fifty employees and locations across the United States as well as in Vancouver and London. In each city, local social services networks—homeless shelters, domestic violence groups, job training and substance abuse programs, and unemployment agencies—refer job applicants eager for a new look and a new life. In its latest year, the company suited more than fifteen thousand women.

Sources: Michele Wucker, "Clout: The 20 Most Powerful International Business Women," Working Woman, November 1999, p. 61; Lynne Sanford, "20 Under 30," Working Woman, September 1999, pp. 46–56; and Elaine McShulskis, "Women Outscore Men in Management and Leadership Skills," HR Magazine, December 1996, p. 14.

can be high in one of the dimensions without having to be low in the other. As a result, there are four basic leadership behaviors:

- **High concern for work, high concern for people.**
- **High concern for work, low concern for people.**
- **Low concern for work, high concern for people.**
- **Low concern for work, low concern for people.**

Figure 9.4 is a leadership grid incorporating these behaviors. Although effective leaders have a preferred style of leadership, at times each of these four basic styles will be used. For example, a high concern for work and people typically is employed when the leader wants to develop high teamwork, wants to set challenging goals, or must act decisively. A high concern for work and low concern for people often is used when the leader strongly needs to control the personnel, must have strict compliance, or is faced with an emergency that must be quickly resolved. A low concern for work and high concern for people often is used when the leader is eager to help, is sympathetic because of a personal problem facing a worker, or wants to praise someone for doing a good job. A low concern for work and people often is used when the leader feels that a situation will work itself out without any personal intervention, as when a new worker has been told how to do a job and must now be left alone to accomplish the task. Although the leader may want to help, he or she may feel that the best approach is to allow the new worker to carry out the task without any interference or assistance. Later the leader and the worker can evaluate the situation and decide what needs to be done. For the moment, however, a low concern for the work and the people is the preferred leadership style.

Keeping in mind that any one of these can be an effective leadership style, let us examine some specific examples of each style and place them in the grid in Figure 9.5. First, let us take

FIGURE 9.4

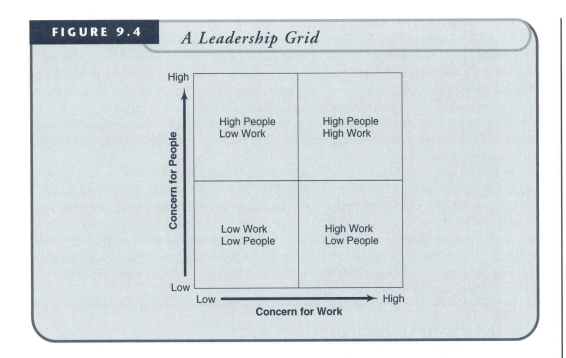

A Leadership Grid

the supervisor on an assembly line. The supervisor is charged with seeing that the workers keep up with the line. The most effective style for such a person is usually one that stresses high concern for work (for this is where the emphasis is needed) but low concern for people. (After all, what can a supervisor do for the workers, as the entire operation is automated?)

Conversely, the manager of a successful sales group has little need to be concerned with a work emphasis. The people are doing the job; sales are very high. The leader can therefore concentrate attention on praising the salespeople and encouraging them to keep up the good work. The individual needs a style with high concern for people and low concern for work.

The president of a large corporation, meanwhile, has to have high concerns for work and for people. This individual must be concerned with long-range planning, budgets, and programs and must be friendly, approachable, and willing to look out for the personal welfare of all the employees.

FIGURE 9.5

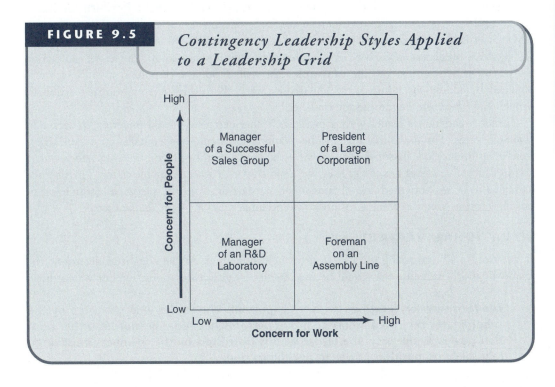

Contingency Leadership Styles Applied to a Leadership Grid

Finally, in the lower left corner of Figure 9.5 is the manager of a research and development laboratory. This individual has highly competent personnel, so there is no need to be concerned with production. These workers are self-motivated. Likewise, there is no need for the manager to praise them for a job well done, because they are skilled scientists who receive intrinsic satisfaction when their peers praise them. Such praise from their boss means very little to them, because the manager of such a laboratory usually is not a scientist and so would be less able to value their work. As a result, the most effective style for the leader is low concerns for both people and work. The manager should be prepared to help them if called on but, for the most part, he or she should stay out of the way.

We should keep one thing in mind about this discussion. The examples we have used in Figure 9.5 are all presented to conform to one of the four leadership dimension combinations. However, we are not saying that every supervisor on an assembly line should have high concern for work and low concern for people or that every president of a large company ought to have high concerns for both work and people. It all depends on the situation. To understand leadership more fully, many researchers have turned to an investigation of contingency leadership models. This represents the latest development of leadership theory, and every student of human relations should be familiar with it.

LEARNING OBJECTIVE

(6)

Distinguish among the contingency leadership approaches— Fiedler's Contingency Model, the Managerial Grid, Charismatic Leadership, and Transformational Leadership

Contingency Leadership Models

Today we are in a *contingency* phase of leadership study. The human relations manager must adapt his or her style to meet the situation. Drawing on our discussion of leadership and personal characteristics, we now address the question: "What specific style of leadership is best in which type of situation?" To answer this question, we need to match styles with environmental demands. In this section, we examine three contingency approaches: (1) Fiedler's Contingency Model, (2) the Managerial Grid, and (3) Charismatic and Transformational Leadership.

Fiedler's Contingency Model

The best known contingency model of leadership effectiveness was developed by Fred Fiedler and his associates.[14] **Fiedler's contingency model** represents a significant departure from earlier trait and behavior leadership models, because Fiedler contends that group performance is contingent on both the motivational system of the leader and the degree to which the leader can control and influence the situation. To classify leadership styles, Fiedler and his colleagues developed the least preferred coworker scale.

The **least preferred coworker** (LPC) **scale** uses a questionnaire asking the leader to describe the person with whom he or she can work least well. From the responses, an LPC score is obtained by adding the item scores. This score reveals the individual's emotional reaction to people with whom he or she cannot work well.

Fiedler found that a leader with a high LPC score describes a least preferred coworker in favorable terms. The individual tends to be relationship-oriented and obtains great satisfaction from establishing close personal relations with the group members. Conversely, a leader with a low LPC score describes his or her least preferred coworker in unfavorable terms. The individual tends to be task-oriented and obtains much satisfaction from the successful completion of tasks, even if it comes at the risk of poor interpersonal relations with the workers.

SITUATIONAL VARIABLES

In addition to administering the LPC test to each individual, Fiedler sought to determine the major situational variables that could be used to classify group situations. He discovered three:

- **Leader–member relations** are very important. The leader who is trusted by the subordinates can often influence group performance regardless of his or her position power. Conversely, the leader who is distrusted by the members must often rely solely on position power to get things done.

Fiedler's Contingency Model
holds that leader effectiveness is determined by leadership style and situational variables.
The **least preferred coworker scale** *describes the individual with whom the respondent can work least well.*

Leader–member relations
are determined by how well the two parties get along.

- **Task structure** is the degree to which the leader's job is programmed or specified in step-by-step fashion. If the job is highly structured, the leader knows exactly what is to be done and, if there are any problems, the organization can back the leader. If the job is highly unstructured, no one correct solution to the problem is identifiable, and the leader will have to rely on personal relationships in getting the group to do things his or her way.
- **Leader position power** is the authority vested in a leader's position. For example, the president has more power than the vice president, and the division head has more power than the unit manager.

FIEDLER'S FINDINGS

Fiedler then brought together the LPC scores (which identified leadership style) with the situational variables to find what leadership style works best in each situation. Figure 9.6 illustrates all the variables in the model. At the bottom of the graph are the eight possible combinations of situational variables (leader-member relations, task structure, and leader position power). Note that in situation 1, on the left, things are very favorable for the leader; leader–member

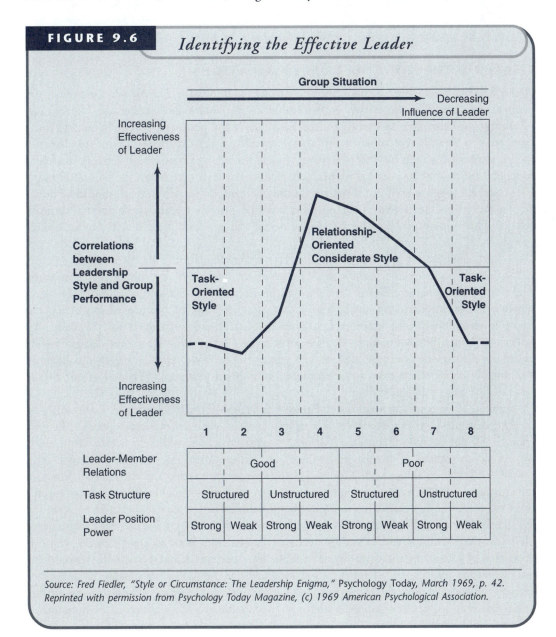

FIGURE 9.6 *Identifying the Effective Leader*

Source: Fred Fiedler, "Style or Circumstance: The Leadership Enigma," Psychology Today, March 1969, p. 42. Reprinted with permission from Psychology Today Magazine, (c) 1969 American Psychological Association.

relations are good, the task is highly structured, and leader position power is strong. Meanwhile in situation 8, on the right, things are very unfavorable for the leader. Leader–member relations are poor, the task is unstructured, and the leader's position power is weak. As we move across the continuum from the first to the eighth situation, things get progressively worse for the leader.

What type of individual does best in each of these eight situations? As can be seen from the model, a task-oriented leader does best in very favorable situations (1, 2, and 3) or very unfavorable situations (7 and 8), and a relationship-oriented leader does best in the moderately favorable and moderately unfavorable situations (4, 5, and 6). Fiedler explained it this way:

> The results show that a task-oriented leader performs best in situations at both extremes—those in which he [or she] has a great deal of influence and power, and also in situations where he [or she] has no influence and power over the group members.
>
> Relationship-oriented leaders tend to perform best in mixed situations where they have only moderate influence over the group. A number of subsequent studies by us and others have confirmed these findings.
>
> The results show that we cannot talk about simply good leaders or poor leaders. A leader who is effective in one situation may or may not be effective in another. Therefore, we must specify the situations in which a leader performs well or badly.[15]

FIEDLER'S THEORY AND HUMAN RELATIONS

Fiedler's theory offers several important alternatives for improving human relations. First, the organization, as well as the leader, is responsible for the latter's success, because a leader can be effective or ineffective depending on the situation. Many personnel psychologists and managers tend to view the executive's position as fixed and must turn their attention to changing the person's basic leadership style. However, this is the wrong approach. To change a leader's style, one must want to alter his or her personality. This can take from one to several years; a few lectures or some brief but intensive training will not do it. What, then, should be done? The answer is first to develop training programs that provide a leader with the opportunity to learn which situations he or she can perform well and in which situations he or she is likely to fail.

Second, engineer the job to fit the leader. This recommendation is based on the fact that it is a lot easier to change the leader's work environment than to change his or her personality. Any one of the three situational variables can be altered. For example, the leader's position power could be improved by giving him or her a higher rank, or be reduced by forcing the leader to consult with the subordinates rather than make unilateral decisions. Similarly, the leader's task can be made more explicit or can be changed to be more vague. Finally, leader–member relations can be altered: The group can be made more homogeneous or more interdisciplinary, or the leader can be reassigned to a group that gets along well or one that is continually engaged in squabbling.

Applying these recommendations to Figure 9.6, we can move the leader back and forth on the grid depending on our objectives. For example, a task-centered manager operating in situation 5 will not be very effective; a relationship-centered leader would do better. However, if we can do something to change leader–member relations from poor to good, we will have moved the leader to situation 1. (You can verify this by comparing the three major variables for situations 1 and 5 and noting what happens when the leader–member relations are changed.) Likewise, a relationship-oriented manager operating under the conditions in situation 8 will be ineffective. However, the same person would do well in situation 4. This can be arranged simply by working to improve the leader–member relations from poor to good. (Again, you can prove this by comparing the three major variables for situations 8 and 4 and noting what happens when the leader-member relations are modified.) If the leader were aware of his or her strengths and weaknesses, the individual could try to change the group situation to match his or her leadership style. In addition, leaders can profit from the ideas presented in the Human Relations in Action box.

HUMAN RELATIONS IN ACTION

Leading Effectively

A great deal of research has been conducted on leadership. Drawing together much of this information from a human relations standpoint, we find there are four things managers should know in their quest to lead effectively.

1. *Know your biases.* Are you a Theory X person? A Theory Y person? A combination of the two? If the latter, do you lean more to the X side or the Y side? If you can answer these questions accurately, you know something about your leadership biases. This is important because, like it or not, you eventually resort to that leadership style with which you feel most comfortable.

2. *Know the situations in which you function best.* Do you do well when there is a crisis? Are you good at handling situations that are out of control? Or are you best when things are on an even keel? In answering these questions, think of a time when you have done extremely well as a leader. Then think of a situation when you performed poorly. What was the difference in the two situations?

Your answer helps you to understand your "best" environments.

3. *Understand the leadership preferences of your people.* What leadership style do your subordinates like best? Your answer will undoubtedly include a range of behaviors, but group them all under one of the four basic styles: authoritarian, paternalistic, participative, and laissez-faire.

4. *Match your style with the situation and the people.* Pull everything together: your style, the demands of the situation, and the needs of the subordinates. Do the best you can to lead from your strengths by employing that style with which you have had the most success. You may have to alter this style a bit, but stay within the leadership parameters you know best. Use Fiedler's ideas to change the environment to suit your style rather than vice versa. Also, remember that in the short run, you may have to use a style you do not prefer. Be flexible and adapt to this brief inconvenience while working to get things back to where you can enjoy your most effective style.

The Managerial Grid

The grid approach is most closely associated with Robert Blake and Jane Mouton.[16] The **managerial grid** consists of two dimensions: concern for production and concern for people. As can be seen in Figure 9.7, nine gradients or degrees are associated with each dimension, resulting in eighty-one possible combinations of concern for production and concern for people. A *1* represents low concern for the dimension, and a *9* represents high concern.

Rather than trying to direct attention to all eighty-one combinations, grid development practitioners tend to focus on five crucial combinations. The combinations are usually referred to by number and, when people become familiar with the grid, they know what the numbers mean. Although they are briefly described in Figure 9.7, let us examine each combination in more detail.

THE FIVE CRUCIAL COMBINATIONS

The **1,1 managerial style** is used to describe the *do-nothing manager*. This individual tends to put people in jobs and then leave them alone. He or she does not check up on their work (concern for production) or try to interact with them by offering praise and encouraging them to keep up the good work (concern for people).

The **9,1 managerial style** describes the *production pusher*. This manager has a high concern for production and a low concern for people. He or she plans the work and pushes to get it out. Little interest is shown in the workers; if they cannot keep up, they are replaced by others who can.

The **1,9 managerial style** has been called *country-club management* because of a high emphasis on concern for people's feelings, comfort, and needs. The manager is interested in obtaining

The **managerial grid** *addresses concern for production and concern for people.*

The **1,1 managerial style** *shows a low concern for both people and work.*
The **9,1 managerial style** *shows a high concern for work and a low concern for people.*
The **1,9 managerial style** *shows a high concern for people and a low concern for work.*

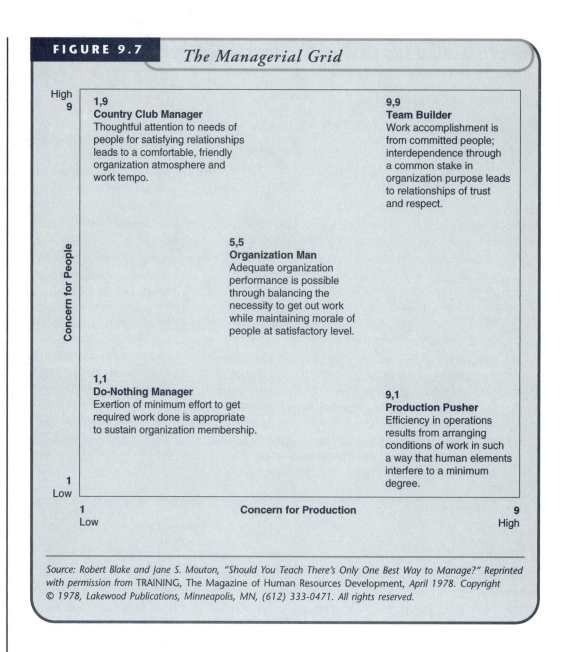

FIGURE 9.7 *The Managerial Grid*

High
9

1,9
Country Club Manager
Thoughtful attention to needs of people for satisfying relationships leads to a comfortable, friendly organization atmosphere and work tempo.

9,9
Team Builder
Work accomplishment is from committed people; interdependence through a common stake in organization purpose leads to relationships of trust and respect.

Concern for People

5,5
Organization Man
Adequate organization performance is possible through balancing the necessity to get out work while maintaining morale of people at satisfactory level.

1,1
Do-Nothing Manager
Exertion of minimum effort to get required work done is appropriate to sustain organization membership.

9,1
Production Pusher
Efficiency in operations results from arranging conditions of work in such a way that human elements interfere to a minimum degree.

1
Low

1   Concern for Production   9
Low   High

loyalty from the subordinates and tries to motivate them to do their work without putting pressure on them.

The **5,5 managerial style** typifies the *organization manager*. This person assumes that an inherent conflict exists between the concerns for production and people. Therefore, he or she tries to compromise and balance the two dimensions.

The **9,9 managerial style** is used by the *team builder*. By many **9,9** is regarded as the ideal style, as the one that both managers in particular and the organization in general should employ. This style focuses on people's higher-level needs, involves subordinates in decision making, and assumes that the goals of the people and the goals of the organization are in harmony. As a result, the **9,9** manager believes that maximum concern for both dimensions will result in the greatest overall efficiency.

Which of these basic styles is best? The answer will depend on the needs of the subordinates, the manager, and the organization. *There is no such thing as one ideal style for all situations.* This can be made clear by giving you the opportunity to choose a leadership style on your own.

IDENTIFYING YOUR STYLE

A modern manager must perform many functions. Four of the most important are planning, decision making, leading, and controlling. In carrying out these functions, various degrees of

The 5,5 managerial style shows a moderate concern for both people and work. The 9,9 managerial style shows a high concern for both people and work.

concern for both people and work can be employed. In Figure 9.7, we have listed for each of these functions five leadership behaviors that can be used to implement them. Read the five behavior descriptions that accompany each function and place a 1 next to the behavior that you feel is *most* descriptive of you. Put a 2 next to the second most descriptive behavior, and so on, to a 5 for the *least* descriptive. If you are not currently a manager, imagine that you are in a managerial position while you take the test.

When you have finished assigning numbers to all the behaviors, write your answers in the columns at the bottom of Figure 9.8. Be sure to enter the numbers properly. If you assigned a 3 to alternative b in the planning part of the figure, put a 3 in column I in the table. If you gave a 5 to alternative d in the planning part, put a 5 in column II. Then add each column and put the total on the bottom line of each. The short survey quiz is designed to determine the type of leadership style you use in carrying out each of the four functions we discussed. Which overall leadership style is your favorite? That will depend on the total scores of the columns. Remember, the *lower* the total, the *higher* your support for that leadership style. (You assigned a 1 to your favorite choice and a 5 to the least preferred one.)

Column I reveals your preference for the 5,5 style; column II measures your preference for the 1,1 style; columns III, IV, and V measure preference for the 9,1 style, the 9,9 style, and the 1,9 style, respectively. Which is your most preferred style? Which is your least preferred style? Could you have predicted this, or are the findings a surprise to you?

The grid is important in the study of human relations because it offers the opportunity to close the gap between one's current and ideal leadership styles. The current style is the one identified in the management style test. The gap is the difference between the current and ideal styles. For example, if a person feels that the 9,9 leadership style would be most effective but currently is relying most heavily on the 5,5 style, that person must become more people- and work-oriented. On the other hand, if the person's current style is 1,9, he or she must become more work-oriented.

Charismatic and Transformational Leadership

In recent years, many human relations experts have concluded that the contingency theory of leadership does not fully explain the nature of leadership. As a result, attention is now being directed toward charismatic and transformational leadership.

CHARISMATIC LEADERSHIP

Charismatic leaders are those who lead by the strength of their personal abilities. Researchers characterize these leaders as self-confident, ideological, confident of their subordinates, having high expectations of subordinates, and leading by example. Followers of charismatic leaders identify with the leader and his or her mission, are loyal and have strong confidence in the leader, emulate the leader's values and behaviors, and derive personal esteem from their relationship with the leader. Here are five examples of commonly cited charismatic leaders:

- *Herb Kelleher,* Southwest Airlines, a chain-smoking, bourbon-loving maverick, he inspires employees to break the rules and have fun. His enthusiasm has helped to make the airline profitable every year since 1979.
- *Oprah Winfrey,* Harpo Entertainment, whose telegenic charm and empathetic personality have helped make her America's hottest businesswoman. She manages employees the same way she does her audience—with emotion and intimacy.
- *Carly Fiorina,* Hewlett-Packard, broke the stereotypes when she became CEO. She is one of the most scrutinized chief executives in America today. Being absorbed with a mission, staying focused on why she was hired, being confident, and sometimes assertive, she pulled off the acquisition of Compaq while dealing with difficult board members.
- *Charlotte Beers,* Ogilvy & Mather Worldwide, is regarded as unpredictable and difficult to work for. At the same time, her humor, charm, and ingenuity have helped her turn around this giant advertising agency.[17]

Charismatic leaders
lead by the strength of their personal abilities.

FIGURE 9.8

Management Style Identification Test

Planning

a. ＿＿ I sit down with my people, review the whole picture, and get reactions, ideas, and commitments from them. Schedules, goals, responsibilities, and control points are developed during this interaction period.

b. ＿＿ I plan the work for each of my people after discussing such things as targets and schedules with the person involved. I then make individual assignments but also ensure that each person knows to check back with me whenever further assistance is needed.

c. ＿＿ I suggest steps and offer assistance to my people in arranging their activities.

d. ＿＿ I let my people have planning responsibilities for their own parts of the job.

e. ＿＿ I plan for my people, set quotas where they are needed, and assign steps to be followed. I also establish checkpoints that can be used for measuring performance.

Decision Making

a. ＿＿ I make decisions, and after they are made, I stick with them.

b. ＿＿ My decisions follow the thinking of my boss; I think as he or she does.

c. ＿＿ I discuss decisions with those who will be affected by them, give them the facts from my point of view and, in turn, get facts from them. After evaluation of alternatives, decisions are reached based on mutual understanding.

d. ＿＿ I sit down with each person who is affected by the decision and listen to the person's point of view. Then I make the decision and communicate it to those who will be affected, along with my reasons for making that particular decision.

e. ＿＿ I try to get a picture of what the subordinates want and use it as a basis for my decision.

Leading

a. ＿＿ Once assignments and plans have been clearly explained, I keep up with each person's performance and review their progress with them. If someone is having difficulty getting the job done, I lend assistance.

b. ＿＿ After assignments have been given to the people, I prefer to take little on-the-spot action. I think it is best for people to solve their own problems.

c. ＿＿ Once upcoming assignments are discussed, I keep in touch with my people to show I am interested in how each is getting along.

d. ＿＿ Once plans have been determined, I keep up with the progress of the subordinates. I contribute time and effort as required by defining problems and removing roadblocks.

e. ＿＿ After I have set out plans and instructions, I keep a close eye on the subordinates' work performance and make changes as necessity dictates.

Controlling

a. ＿＿ As work progresses, if any problems or changes need to be made, I make them on the spot. When the job is completed, I evaluate everyone's performance, correct those who have done a poor job, and recognize those who have performed well.

b. ＿＿ I sit down with my subordinates and review progress in detail and, when the job is totally finished, I study how the entire operation was handled. Correct decisions, good work, errors, and misjudgments all are noted and examined in detail so that the former can be reinforced and the latter can be prevented in the future. When deserved, recognition for contribution is given on both a joint and an individual basis.

c. ＿＿ When I receive a reaction to their work, whether it is praise or a complaint, I pass this information on to the respective subordinates.

d. ＿＿ I compliment my subordinates when they do a good job and invite their suggestions for improvements. I believe that criticism tends to arouse tension and make people defensive.

e. ＿＿ I point out weaknesses as well as strengths to each subordinate. Each person then gets a chance to introduce his or her own suggestions for improvements.

	I	II	III	IV	V
Planning	b. ＿＿	d. ＿＿	e. ＿＿	a. ＿＿	c. ＿＿
Decision making	d. ＿＿	b. ＿＿	a. ＿＿	c. ＿＿	e. ＿＿
Leading	a. ＿＿	b. ＿＿	e. ＿＿	d. ＿＿	c. ＿＿
Controlling	e. ＿＿	c. ＿＿	a. ＿＿	b. ＿＿	d. ＿＿
Total	＿＿	＿＿		＿＿	＿＿

- *Michael Dell,* Dell Computer, a highly innovative individual who has surrounded himself with skilled personnel who have a strong grasp of the industry. He is also highly optimistic and able to capture the imagination of both employees and customers.[18]

There is a link between charismatic leadership theory and Fiedler's contingency theory in that charismatic leaders often perform best in crisis situations or when followers are dissatisfied with the status quo. However, more research on the theory is needed before we can understand fully the nature, scope, and value of charismatic leadership. Additionally, some researchers have suggested that this type of leadership is actually just one of other, broader-based emerging theories of transformational leadership.[19]

TRANSFORMATIONAL LEADERSHIP

Transformational leaders are visionary agents with a sense of mission who are capable of motivating their followers to accept new goals and new ways of doing things. In contrast to the charismatic leader, the transformational leader gets followers to change rather than follow. In recent years, Lou Gerstner, head of IBM, has used his transformational leadership skills to bring the company back to its previous prominence, and David Glass, CEO of Wal-Mart, is using his style to maintain the company's dominance.

Transformational leaders are distinct from most other leaders, who are best defined as transactional leaders. A **transactional leader** exchanges rewards for effort and performance and works on a something-for-something basis. Table 9.2 compares the characteristics and approaches of

Transformational leaders
are visionary agents who motivate people to do things differently.

Transactional leaders
exchange rewards for effort and performance.

TABLE 9.2	*Transformational and Transactional Leaders: A Comparison*
Transformational Leader	**Transactional Leader**
Provides a vision and a sense of mission to followers	Sets goals and encourages employees to pursue them
Attempts to instill pride, respect, and trust in employees	Uses reward and punishment systems to generate compliance
Communicates high expectations and expresses important purposes in simple ways	Lets everyone know the objectives
Promotes rationality and careful problem-solving	Is interested in results rather than problem-solving process
Gives employees individual attention, coaching, and advising	Carefully spells out rewards for accomplishing objectives
Is a courageous change agent	Tends to support the status quo
Is able to deal with complexity, ambiguity, and uncertainty	Avoids complexity and uncertainty by delegating responsibility to subordinates
Leads by example	Watches for mistakes or deviations from rules and regulations and then takes corrective action
Is a lifelong learner	Relies on past knowledge to deal with future problems

Source: Adapted from Bernard M. Bass, "From Transactional to Transformational Leadership: Learning to Share the Vision," Organizational Dynamics, Winter 1990, p. 22.

transformational and transactional leaders. This comparison illustrates why transformational leaders often head organizations that are superior, whereas transactional leaders often head mediocre organizations. In the future, it is expected that researchers will continue their efforts to understand fully why transformational leaders are effective and how this knowledge can be incorporated into organizational training programs, thus helping to create a larger pool of transformational leaders.

Another current area of leadership inquiry is the role of transformational leaders as sponsors, facilitators, and individuals who encourage teamwork by breaking down organizational barriers. In this role, leaders share information, focus on results, and view themselves more as internal consultants and coordinators than as directive managers. Transformational leaders are also able to take time off, reflect, and think about where their organization is going and the role they need to play. In this process, researchers find these leaders to be objective, continually learning new things, self-confident, prepared to assume personal responsibility, able to deal with uncertainty and ambiguity, and prepared to take action. In the future, greater attention will be focused on understanding how and why leaders do these things.

UNIVERSAL LEADERSHIP BEHAVIORS

In drawing together all the current information on leadership, it would seem reasonable to ask: Are there some leadership behaviors that are more effective than others? Recent research by Bernard Bass reveals that there are. After gathering leadership data from around the world, Bass has grouped leadership behaviors into five categories. The first category, which Bass calls the "4 I's," is a series of interrelated factors that help to define a leader's charisma:

- *Idealized influence* results in followers admiring the leader and having pride, loyalty, and confidence in the individual's vision.
- *Inspired motivation* is the ability of the leader to articulate the vision and provide a sense of meaning regarding what needs to be done.
- *Intellectual stimulation* is the ability to get followers to view the world from new perspectives and paradigms.
- *Individualized consideration* is the ability to address personally the needs of the followers.

These 4 I's are presented in Figure 9.9, top right box. As can be seen, they represent the most effective leadership behaviors. Next in importance (again see Figure 9.9) are contingent reward (CR) behaviors, which are widely used by transactional leaders. The CR leader clarifies what needs to be done and exchanges both psychic and material rewards with followers who comply accordingly. Third in importance is what Bass calls the active management-by-exception (MBE-A) leader, who monitors follower performance and takes corrective action when deviations from standards occur. The next leader, ineffective in performance, is the passive management-by-exception (MBE-P) person, who intervenes only when standards are not met. Finally, the least effective leader is the laissez-faire (LF) individual, who avoids intervening or accepting responsibility for follower action. Commenting on his findings, Bass reports:

> *According to a higher-order factor analysis, the eight factors can be ordered from lowest to highest in activity: 4 I's, CR, MBE-A, MBE-P, LF. Correspondingly, the eight factors can be ordered on a second dimension—effectiveness. The 4 I's are most effective; CR, second most effective; MBE-A, next most effective; MBE-P, even less effective; and LF leadership, least effective (or most ineffective).*[20]

Bass has found that transformational leaders also use transactional leadership to supplement their approach. Hence, both the 4 I's and the CR leadership style are important to them as shown in Figure 9.9. Less effective leaders tend to use styles that do not include the

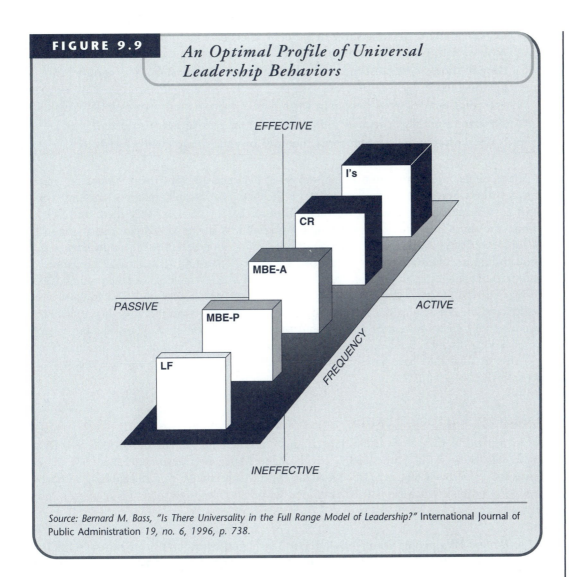

FIGURE 9.9 *An Optimal Profile of Universal Leadership Behaviors*

Source: Bernard M. Bass, "Is There Universality in the Full Range Model of Leadership?" International Journal of Public Administration *19, no. 6, 1996, p. 738.*

4 I's and may use contingent-reward leadership only cursorily. Additionally, Bass reports that various modifications of these findings are extant, depending on the culture of the country. For example, in some nations, leaders employ the 4 I's in an autocratic manner, whereas in others the leaders use a more participative approach. For example, he reports that transformational leaders in India and Japan tend to be more participative than those in Pakistan and Taiwan.

These latest findings help to bring together much of what is currently known about leadership. In particular, they point out the importance of charismatic behaviors in the leadership process.

Leaders in the Twenty-First Century

LEARNING OBJECTIVE
⑦ *Describe the leader in the twenty-first century*

Patrick McKenna, a partner at consultancy Edge International, Edmonton, Canada, and David Maister, an expert on management professional services, believe that "today's leaders have to be kinder, gentler, more empathetic—and able to show genuine interest in whatever their charges are trying to achieve." The authors argue that executives must move past outdated notions of what makes a good leader and move toward genuine affection and empathy as essential management tools. Another argument is that professionals develop confidence and achieve peak performance at the office through a leader's inspirational techniques. McKenna and Maister present five questions to reflect on, which can inspire employees:

1. **Do you show a genuine interest in what each of your group members wants to achieve with his or her career? (This is a critical part of any group leader's role.)**
2. **Do you show an interest in the things that mean the most to your people in their personal lives?**
3. **Are you there for your people in their times of personal or professional crisis?**
4. **Do you informally "check in" with each of your people every so often?**
5. **Do you offer to help when some member of your group clearly needs it?**[21]

Inspiration comes from within and it's the job of the leader to create the environment, which inspires others. Study after study shows that it is the intangible variables that motivate employees such as "full appreciation for a job well done, being a part of decisions that affect them, open communications, interesting and meaningful work, and having good relationships at work."[22] What is interesting is that these items require "little if any money, but rather simply some time, thoughtfulness and creativity" on the part of the leader. Successful leaders today take time to show genuine interest in their employees. For example, Robert Whitehead, recently retired CEO of SunTrust Bank, states that the leader's role is to treat people well and to help employees understand the end results of a project and why it will be better than it is now. If people know you champion their cause, they will buy into your cause and line up on your side, but it can't be done long distance. It takes a lot of time to meet with people, to look them in the eye and to listen to what they have to say. People also will watch what you do and say and will act accordingly.[23]

Leading Virtual Teams

As we learned in Chapter 8, teleworking is growing. These individuals and groups need leadership, like those working in an office environment. Managing teleworkers has its own set of issues and problems. Caroline Davis, President, Worth Collection, a women's clothing company has surrounded herself with a stellar team of teleworkers. Her suggestions for managing long distance are:

- *Hiring*—Hire people who work independently and who don't need supervision. She uses a written "personal profile" test to gain insight into a prospective employee's work habits.
- *Communication*—Connect everyone by e-mail, voicemail, and fax so communication flows much as it would in a single location. Davis has weekly conference calls with all levels of management and requires managers to meet in New York every ten to twelve weeks for additional long-term strategic planning.
- *Culture*—"We pay more attention to our corporate culture than if everyone were in one place and we took it for granted," says Davis. Sometimes books or newspaper articles are discussed and to help keep people connected, a company newsletter goes to everyone on a regular basis.[24]

Multitasking Skills

Leaders are constantly being asked to do more with less, make more decisions, and get more stuff done with fewer people and fewer resources. As an economy slows down, leaders are asked to do more with less, often creating impossible expectations. A feeling of being overworked and being overwhelmed sets in. How do leaders remain sane? They must become very good at multitasking. Effectively using technology and communications is key to successfully multitasking. For example, voicemail, conference calls, e-mail, Web cast, advanced voicemail functions, face-to-face meetings, and instant messaging all provide a means for accomplishing several tasks at the same time and in several locations around the world at the same time. The fast pace world of the twenty-first century requires leaders to be connected and to be fast paced as well.[25]

Au: Refer
no. added
ok since
treating it
Notes?

Emerging Leadership Challenges

LEARNING OBJECTIVE

8 *Discuss emerging leadership challenges*

Over the last decade, the U.S. economy has seen unparalleled growth. This, in turn, has created a demand for leaders. Today large and small firms alike are finding themselves facing the challenge of both attracting and developing leadership talent. Moreover, given that the pool of such talent is smaller than the demand, more and more organizations now are working to hire and develop leaders through careful training and mentoring. What abilities and skills will these individuals need? According to a recent survey conducted by Andersen Consulting, over the next decade the best leaders will have to do the following:

1. **Create a shared vision for everyone in the firm.**
2. **Ensure customer satisfaction.**
3. **Live the values that are critical to the company.**
4. **Build internal teamwork and external partnerships.**
5. **Think globally.**
6. **Appreciate cultural diversity.**
7. **Develop and empower people.**
8. **Be able to anticipate opportunity.**
9. **Learn how to achieve competitive advantage.**
10. **Embrace change.**
11. **Share leadership.**
12. **Demonstrate personal mastery of the job.**
13. **Show technological savvy.**
14. **Encourage constructive challenge.**[26]

A number of approaches are proving particularly helpful in dealing with these challenges. One is to develop an internal cadre of leaders who can meet the varied challenges being confronted by their organizations. A second is to learn how to lead high-potential employees who need careful direction.

Developing Internal Leaders

LEARNING OBJECTIVE

9 *Identify ways of developing internal leaders and dealing with high-potential employees who have bad work habits*

Every successful company identifies the results it needs to achieve. The challenge, then, is to get the leaders to reach these goals. At Cisco Systems Inc., for example, senior-level executives carefully spell out the results that are expected from the managers. In this way, the managers know what they have to do as leaders. Additionally, they know how they are going to be evaluated, as their performance is tied directly to their compensation.[27] At the same time, leaders at Cisco work to develop leaders in their group so that, as the company grows, it has leaders to help handle the new business. This sometimes is labeled *managing the law of explosive growth.* John Maxwell, a world-renowned expert on leadership, explains the logic this way:

> *Leaders who develop followers grow their organization only one person at a time. But leaders who develop leaders multiply their growth, because for every leader they develop, they also receive all of that leader's followers. Add ten followers to your organization, and you have a power of ten people. Add ten leaders to your organization, and you have the power of ten leaders times all the followers and leaders they influence.*[28]

Firms such as GE, Motorola, Wal-Mart, IBM, and Hewlett-Packard, among others, use this approach to meet the impending shortage of leaders. This was not true years ago when companies would be able to hire leaders from other firms by offering more attractive compensation packages. Today, however, the best leaders often are unwilling to leave because their current employers are giving them generous compensation as well as challenging jobs that are personally fulfilling. As a result, a growing number of firms now are training their managers to develop

Developing In-House Talent:
Followers Versus Leaders

Leaders Who Develop Followers	Leaders Who Develop Leaders
Develop the bottom 20 percent of their people.	Develop the top 20 percent of their people.
Focus on the weaknesses of their people.	Focus on the strengths of their people.
Have a need to be needed.	Have a need to be succeeded.
Hoard power.	Give away power.
Spend time with others.	Invest time in others.
Grow by addition.	Grow by multiplication.
Affect only people they touch personally.	Affect people far beyond their own reach.
Treat all their people the same in order to be fair.	Treat their leaders differently to allow them to make an impact on the organization.

Source: Adapted from John C. Maxwell, The 21 Irrefutable Laws of Leadership *(Nashville: Thomas Nelson, 1998), p. 210.*

leaders from their work groups so that the firm can handle its needs on an internal basis. The old approach of developing followers now is being replaced by a strategy of developing leaders. Table 9.3 illustrates the differences between these two approaches.

Leading High-Potential Employees

Many organizations have employees who are innovative, highly skilled, or strongly motivated but who, at the same time, are creating problems for other personnel because their approaches to doing things are disruptive. The challenge for the leader is to help these people overcome their bad habits while still remaining high performers. Waldroop and Butler, two psychologists, have identified six patterns of behavior—hero, meritocrat, bulldozer, pessimist, rebel, and home-run hitter.[29]

1. The *hero* is an individual who works long and hard every day. This person continually pushes himself or herself as well as those in the work team. The problem is that many of these team members do not like the continual stress that is created by the hero, and they feel that this individual does not consider their needs. The hero is interested in maximum effort and wants everyone to contribute to this goal regardless of his or her personal situation. In dealing with this person, leaders must do three things.

   a. First, express appreciation for all the hero's accomplishments and then note the negative effect that this maximum effort is having on the workers.

   b. Second, discuss the importance of the hero paying closer attention to the workers and noting when they are being worked too hard.

   c. Third, encourage the individual to focus more attention on long-range projects and stop emphasizing short-run goals, because this is what often causes problems for the other team members.

2. The *meritocrat* believes that recommendations, ideas, and suggestions will be accepted based on their merit. What the person fails to realize is that sometimes

even the best ideas need to be sold, negotiated, or shaped to meet political and organizational realities. In leading this individual, the manager needs to support the person's ideas while also helping the meritocrat to understand that often new ideas must be sold to others, which means that networking and politicking are necessary. Often the manager will ask the meritocrat, "Do you want to be right or do you want to be effective?" Once the individual realizes that good ideas do not always sell themselves, he or she is often more willing to add realism to the situation and begin seeking support from others for these ideas.

3. The *bulldozer* is a person who runs roughshod over others in a quest for power. This individual typically intimidates and alienates others in an effort to get his or her ideas accepted. In dealing with this person, the leader must be equally blunt in making the individual aware that he or she is not liked by many of the people in the organization and that the person's confrontational style must change—or the leader will have to replace him or her. Once the person realizes this, the leader must then work with the individual to mend fences.

4. The *pessimist* focuses on the downside of things and worries aloud about what could go wrong if changes are introduced. The leader's objective must be that of getting the pessimist to look at the positive side of things by pointing out where this individual's fears were unjustified in the past. The leader must then help the pessimist to evaluate better the risk associated with change, so that the individual realizes that some changes are going to work just fine and others have a small degree of risk and should be accepted. In this way, the pessimist begins to take a more realistic view of things and abandons the continual negative attack on all proposed changes.

5. The *rebel* automatically fights against authority and convention. The leader's role here must be that of co-opting the individual and getting him or her to stop making negative comments and become a team player. One of the most popular initial approaches is to have the individual spend a week or two noting the way people in the department go about interacting with one another, how they align in groups, and how decisions are made. The rebel then is assigned to write up this information in a report for the manager.

> Once the rebel has gathered that information, ask him this: "If you were a real revolutionary fighting somewhere against a dictatorship, would it be better to stand out or to blend in?" The answer is clear, so push the rebel to the logical conclusion. "You have a choice. You can work to change things here or you can follow your old pattern and just be an irritant. If you choose the latter, your career will stall and your influence on the organization will never amount to much. I hope you make the other choice, because you're right—this place isn't perfect, and we need people like you to help improve it."[30]

This approach typically gets the rebel to see how he or she can be more effective. As a result, the individual often drops the negative attitude and begins turning his or her energies toward constructive criticism. This does not happen immediately, but the ultimate result is often beneficial for both the organization and the pessimist.

6. The *home-run hitter* tries to do too much too soon and, as a result, often ends up failing. This type of individual is like a baseball player who always swings for the fences. He or she hits a fair number of home runs but also strikes out often. In getting this person to slow down and focus on doing less, the leader needs to work with the home-run hitter in setting smaller goals that can reasonably be accomplished. The leader also needs to encourage the individual to work more closely with others and to remind this employee that a successful career track in the company often begins with slow progress (hitting a lot of singles) that adds to the bottom line. Then, as the individual begins to make headway in achieving these small goals, the leader must continually praise the employee and show him or her how this progress will contribute to career success.

These approaches to dealing with individuals with bad habits can be very helpful to leaders in getting everyone to contribute as a team member. They are also useful in developing productive team members.[31]

summary

① **LEARNING OBJECTIVE**
Describe the leadership and personal characteristics related to managerial effectiveness—trait theory, superior intelligence, emotional maturity, motivation drive, problem-solving skills, managerial skills, and leadership skills

Leadership is the process of influencing people to direct their efforts toward the achievement of particular goals. What makes a leader effective? Some people believe the answer rests in leadership characteristics, such as drive, originality, and the tolerance of stress. The greatest problem with this trait theory approach, however, is that it does not take the situation into account. A leadership style that is effective in one situation may not be effective in another.

In an effort to address the situational nature of leadership, many people have turned to personal characteristics. Some of the most commonly cited personal characteristics of leaders include superior intelligence, emotional maturity, motivation drive, problem-solving skills, managerial skills, and leadership skills. The degree and importance of each are determined by the situation. For example, some situations require the leader to rely heavily on human skills, but others demand conceptual skills.

Intelligence is a relative matter, but there is a minimum level of mental ability below which successful managers are unlikely to be found, as well as a ceiling above which effective leaders are generally not found. Successfull leaders are emotionally mature, self-confident, and capable of directing their subordinates in a calm, conscientious manner. They have a sense of purpose and meaning in life, know how to deal with stress, delegate work, and handle challenges of the job. Effective leaders have a high motivation drive. They like money, power, and control and measure success in quantitative terms. Effective leaders possess problem-solving skills and see problems as both challenges and opportunities to prove their managerial skills. They have technical skills, human skills, and conceptual skills. Their leadership style depends on the situation. Some leader characteristics include initiative, need to achieve, task orientation, drive for responsibility and the pursuit of objectives, interpersonal skills, tack and diplomacy, ability to enlist cooperation and help people grow, desire to win, and willingness to accept challenge.

② **LEARNING OBJECTIVE**
Compare and contrast Theory X and Theory Y

To lead personnel effectively, one must also form some opinions about the personnel. Some managers are adherents of the Theory X philosophy, which holds that people are basically lazy and that, to get them to work, it often is necessary to use coercion and threats of punishment. Other managers support Theory Y, which holds that people are interested in both lower-level and upper-level need satisfaction, have untapped potential and, if given the right rewards, exercise self-direction and self-control in attaining organizational objectives.

③ **LEARNING OBJECTIVE**
Distinguish among four styles of leadership behavior—authoritarian, paternalistic, participative, and laissez-faire

Leadership styles also vary. Some situations require authoritarian leadership behavior, but others call for a paternalistic leader; some are best handled with a participative leadership style, and others require a laissez-faire manager. Authoritarian leaders are work centered and task directed, with little emphasis on the human element. They are good in crisis situations and when tough leaders are needed. Paternalistic leaders also are work centered, but they have some consideration for employees. Participative leaders have a high concern for both work and people and encourage subordinates to play an active role in operations. They delegate to and seek feedback from subordinates. Under laissez-faire leaders, subordinates play an increasingly larger role. The subordinates are highly skilled professionals requiring their leaders to provide resources and to check on the progress of the job.

---

④ LEARNING OBJECTIVE
Explain the concept of "self-leaders" and the basic rules of behavior

Self-leaders motivate and direct themselves, reducing the amount of time required for supervision. These leaders support their employees and provide them with assistance and guidance as needed. Examples of basic rules leaders follow are: be decisive; do not promise what you cannot deliver; praise people in front of others for a job well done and reprimand them in private when they have made a mistake; and when possible, promote from within.

---

⑤ LEARNING OBJECTIVE
Describe the two major dimensions of leadership—concern for people and concern for work

Each of the four leadership behavior styles can be described in terms of two dimensions: concern for work and concern for people. Every leader exercises some degree of each and, because these dimensions are independent, the individual can exercise a high degree of one style without having to sacrifice another style. A person can exercise a high degree of two styles or, for that matter, a low degree of both.

---

⑥ LEARNING OBJECTIVE
Distinguish among the contingency leadership approaches—Fiedler's Contingency Model, the Managerial Grid, Charismatic Leadership, and Transformational Leadership

Today, we are in a contingency phase of leadership study. The best known contingency model is that of Fred Fiedler, who has found that task-centered leaders do best in very favorable or very unfavorable situations and relationship-oriented leaders are most effective in situations that are moderately favorable or moderately unfavorable. He recommends matching the leader to the situation rather than trying to change the individual's personality to fit the job. The situation will determine the degree of the leader's success.

The managerial grid approach is well liked by practicing managers. It consists of two dimensions: concern for production and concern for people. It is useful in helping participants to understand the five basic styles of leadership and to close the gap between current and desired leadership styles. The 1,1 managerial style is described as the do-nothing manager. The leader lets people do their job. The 9,1 managerial style is described as the production pusher, who is more concerned with production than with people. The 1,9 is called country-club management because of a high emphasis on concern for people's feelings, comfort, and needs. The 5,5 managerial style typifies the organization manager who compromises and balances the concern for production and concern for people. The 9,9 managerial style is used by the team builder and is regarded as the ideal style. It focuses on employee's higher level needs, involves subordinates in decision making, and assumes the goals of employees and the goals of the organization are in harmony.

Current attention also is being directed toward better understanding of charismatic and transformational leadership. Charismatic leaders use the strength of their personal abilities to get things done. Transformational leaders are visionary agents who have strong confidence in their employees and who encourage them to accept challenges and do things in new, more effective ways. This is in sharp contrast to transactional leaders, who give rewards in return for effort and performance. Researchers today are studying the roles of leaders as internal consultants, coordinators, and advisors who reflect on their roles and deal effectively with uncertainty and ambiguity. Bass found that the 4 I's—idealized influence, inspired motivation, intellectual stimulation and individualized consideration—are important to transformational leaders. Effective leaders tend to use them.

⑦ LEARNING OBJECTIVE
Describe the leader in the twenty-first century

Leaders must be kinder, gentler, more empathetic, and show genuine interest in what each team member wants to achieve and in their personal lives. Leaders support team members in times of personal crisis, check in on their progress, and offer to help them. Employees expect leaders to appreciate a job well done, allow them to be a part in decisions that affect them, use open communications, assign interesting and meaningful work, and have a good working relationship. Many leaders must manage virtual teams or teleworkers, which requires dealing with issues and problems different from those with in-office workers. To accomplish many tasks simultaneously in a fast-paced global world, leaders use multitasking skills. Technology and communications help leaders successfully complete several tasks in several locations at the same time. Voicemail, e-mail, and instant messaging are examples of ways to stay connected. Leaders live in a 24/7 world.

⑧ LEARNING OBJECTIVE
Discuss emerging leadership challenges

As the economy changes, so do the needs for leadership skills. Hiring qualified people and developing them through training are constant challenges. Abilities and skills needed in the future include: being able to create a shared vision for everyone in the firm, endure customer satisfaction, live the values that are critical to the company, build internal teamwork and external partnerships, think globally, appreciate cultural diversity, develop and empower people, be able to anticipate opportunity, learn how to achieve competitive advantage, embrace change, share leadership, demonstrate personal mastery of the job, show technological savvy, and encourage constructive challenge. To meet the shortage of leaders, many firms are training their managers to develop leaders from their work groups. The new approach to leadership is to develop leaders instead of followers.

⑨ LEARNING OBJECTIVE
Identify ways of developing internal leaders and dealing with high-potential employees who have bad work habits

Some of the latest trends in leadership include strategies for dealing with high-potential employees who have bad habits that must be changed. The hero works long and hard every day causing stress among team members. The meritocrat believes that recommendations, ideas, and suggestions will be accepted based on their merit, but fails to realize that ideas have to be sold, negotiated or shaped to meet political and organizational realities. The bulldozer seeks power and typically intimidates and alienates others in an effort to get his or her ideas accepted. The pessimist focuses on the downside of things and worries about what can go wrong if changes are introduced, instead of looks at the positive side of things. The rebel automatically fights against authority and convention and must be trained to be a team player. The home-run hitter tries to do too much too soon, often ending up failing. With the proper training and development, these individuals with bad habits can be productive team members.

KEY TERMS IN THE CHAPTER

Leadership	Theory X
Leadership characteristics	Theory Y
Personal characteristics	Authoritarian leadership
Trait theory	Paternalistic leadership
Technical skills	Participative leadership
Human skills	Laissez-faire leadership
Conceptual skills	Leadership dimensions

Fiedler's contingency model

Least preferred coworker scale

Leader–member relations

Task structure

Leader position power

Managerial grid

1,1 Managerial style

9,1 Managerial style

1,9 Managerial style

5,5 Managerial style

9,9 Managerial style

Charismatic leader

Transformational leader

Transactional leader

REVIEW AND STUDY QUESTIONS

1. How do leadership characteristics differ from personal characteristics?

2. What are the leadership characteristics that appear to account for success in the leadership role?

3. Identify six personal characteristics of successful managers. Tell why each is important to the success of the manager.

4. In terms of motivation drive, how do successful leaders differ from least successful leaders?

5. What are the three types of managerial skills that every leader must have? Define each. Which skill is more important to top managers? Why?

6. What are the basic assumptions of Theory X? How accurate are they? What are the basic assumptions of Theory Y? How accurate are they?

7. Is a Theory Y manager always superior to a Theory X manager? Explain.

8. Compare authoritarian leadership with paternalistic leadership. Compare participative leadership with laissez-faire leadership. Compare authoritarian leadership with laissez-faire leadership.

9. Who are "self-leaders"? Why is the concept important to successful leadership?

10. Identify four basic rules that have proven effective in leadership. Why do they make a difference in leadership?

11. The two leadership dimensions—concern for work and concern for people—have been found to be independent dimensions. What does this statement mean?

12. What type of leader would do best in a situation requiring high concern for work and low concern for people? High concern for both? Low concern for both? Explain your answers.

13. According to Fiedler, in which types of situations are task-oriented leaders most effective and in which types of situations are relationship-oriented leaders most effective? Be complete in your answer.

14. In what way is Fiedler's theory useful in the study of human relations?

15. What is meant by each of the following: 1,1 management, 9,1 management, 1,9 management, 5,5 management, 9,9 management?

16. Of what value is the managerial grid in the study of human relations?

17. How do charismatic leaders go about leading their people? Give two examples.

18. How do transformational leaders differ from transactional leaders? Identify and discuss three differences.

19. Describe the leader in the twenty-first century. Identify the skills that are required and tell how they differ from skills used by leaders of the twentieth century.

20. Identify some emerging leadership challenges. How can developing internal leaders meet these challenges?

21. How do effective leaders go about dealing with meritocrats? Pessimists? Bulldozers? Home-run hitters?

VISIT THE WEB

I. When You Want to Send the Very Best

In this chapter, you learned about effective leadership and that every manager needs to be a leader. When the organization is industry-dominant, the leadership challenge is greater than ever. This is certainly the case for Hallmark Cards, which continues to succeed in the face of ever-growing competition. Visit the company's Web site at **http://www.hallmark.com** and find out some of the latest developments that are taking place at Hallmark. Then answer these two questions:

a. What are some of the major leadership challenges of Hallmark's senior-level management?

b. What type of leadership style do you think is the most effective in accomplishing these challenges?

II. Tom Peters, The Guru of Management

Tom Peters, a well-known expert and spokesman in management, has revolutionized and shaped management for the past several decades. Within the next decade, Tom Peters believes a "White-Collar Revolution" will transform 90 percent of the white-collar jobs. The jobs will disappear or will be refigured. The revolution will bring a different kind of work and different careers. To learn more, visit **http://www. tompeters.com** Answer the following questions.

1. Click on "new world of work." What are some new ideas about work, leadership, and/or management? Summarize the key points.

2. Who is Tom Peters? Summarize the important points you discovered from the web site or contacts you made from the web site

3. Why might a company want to hire Tom Peters to conduct a workshop or give a speech to employees?

TIME OUT ANSWERS

Your Assumptions About People

This test measures your tendency to support Theory X and Theory Y beliefs. To determine your scores for each, fill in the answer sheet and then plot a graph by placing a dot at the point where your Theory X and Theory Y scores intersect.

Theory X Score   **Theory Y Score**

_____ (b)   _____ (a)

_____ (c)   _____ (d)

_____ (f)   _____ (e)

_____ (h)	_____ (g)
_____ (i)	_____ (j)
_____ (k)	_____ (l)
_____ (m)	_____ (n)
_____ (p)	_____ (o)
_____ (q)	_____ (r)
_____ (t)	_____ (s)

Look at the dot you have placed on the graph. Now draw a line from the origin through the dot and on outward to the end of the graph. At the end of this line place an arrowhead. This line points the direction in which your beliefs about people move. Based on the direction of the arrow, you can determine whether you are basically a Theory X person, a Theory Y person, or a blend of the two.

case: MAKING SOME NECESSARY CHANGES

Helen Knighter and Sam Schwede are assistant store managers for a large retail chain located throughout the mid-western and southern parts of the country. Helen began her career with the firm three years ago. The company was hiring people for its human resources department, and Helen's degree in psychology helped land her the job. Although most of the new hires were put into training and development, Helen was assigned to counseling. In this job, she talked to store people who were having a variety of personal problems, from drinking to failure to interact effectively with customers. Helen's job was to provide them assistance and guidance in straightening out their lives. After a six-week training program, she was assigned a number of cases and performed well. Her performance ratings were always in the top 10 percent of the department.

Although Helen liked her job, she realized that there was a limited career track for people in counseling. If she wanted to succeed with the firm, she needed to get a job in one of the firm's retail stores. At the end of her second year, she applied for a position as assistant store manager and was assigned to a unit four months ago. Since then, Helen has worked very hard to learn her job. Last week she attended a managerial training program. During one of the sessions, the participants measured their leadership style. Before interpreting this style, the trainer asked each of the participants to identify the style that he or she thought would be most effective for getting their particular jobs done. Helen chose the 9,9 style. When her test results were interpreted, however, it turned out that Helen was using the 1,9 style.

Sam Schwede was sitting next to her during the training program. Sam has been with the company for only four months. He was hired directly out of college, where he majored in management and minored in marketing. Because Sam has had little experience in retail management, his store manager sent him to the training program. Like Helen, Sam identified the 9,9 style as the one that would be ideal for him in managing the store personnel. However, his leadership style test indicated that he was using a 5,5 style.

When the trainer discussed the results of the test with both Helen and Sam, he pointed out that both will have to make changes to bring their current styles more into line with their desired style. "This won't be as hard as it seems," he told them, "but it will take some work on your part."

QUESTIONS

1. Describe the five basic styles on the managerial grid.

2. What changes will Helen have to make? Be complete in your answer and tell why.

3. What changes will Sam have to make? Explain.

Back to Square One

Ted Abbott was brought into Kendrick Works to straighten things out. Ted had worked for one of Kendrick's competitors for eight years and had earned an enviable reputation during this time. Starting out at the foreman level, Ted worked his way up to senior vice-president. Along the way, he streamlined the company's operations, brought in new machinery and equipment that increased productivity, cut waste and inefficiency, and reduced the overall payroll from 55 percent of total expenses to less than 42 percent. Ted was in line for promotion to president when Kendrick contacted him and asked if he would consider taking over its reins. Since it would be at least five years before his firm's president stepped down, Ted accepted Kendrick's offer.

For more than three years, Kendrick had been losing money. Top management hoped that under Ted's direction this could be changed. Over the next two years, they were not disappointed with their decision. Ted started cutting waste and inefficiency and getting the firm on a more competitive basis. Within six months, the company began to show a profit. A year later, the board announced that it was paying back its outstanding long-term debt and was issuing a special dividend on all stock. The firm was making more money than it ever had before.

Then things started to turn around. Costs began to rise and employee turnover increased. At the lower and middle ranks of management, more and more people began leaving. The union entered into prolonged negotiations with management, arguing that with the increase in profit, the firm should raise wages by 10 percent more than was standard in the industry. When Ted held the line, there was a 45-day strike, which worsened the company's position. Kendrick soon found itself heading back into the red.

Over the last 18 months, Kendrick has continued losing money and at a faster rate than when Ted took over. Some members of the board of directors have suggested that they get rid of Ted and bring in someone else. One of them put it this way: "What good is Ted to us? Thanks to him we're back to square one." On the other hand, Ted has a strong following on the board, and they are unwilling to let him go. As one of them argued, "Look, the guy turned things around before. We all know that. Well, here's a chance for him to work his magic again. I don't know anyone else who can straighten out a mess better than he can, and a mess is certainly what we have. I recommend we keep Ted and see what we can do to help him turn things around."

Your Advice

1. What should the board do?

   ____ a. Keep Ted as president.
   ____ b. Replace Ted as president.
   ____ c. Wait six months and then make a decision on the matter.

2. What type of a leader is Ted? (Refer to Figure 9.7 in your answer.)

3. Why was Ted effective in turning the company around?

4. Why is Ted having problems now?

EXPERIENCING FOUR SYSTEMS OF LEADERSHIP

Purpose

- To better understand leader-subordinate interactions under authoritarian, paternalistic, participative, and laissez-faire leadership.
- To analyze leadership behavior under these four systems.

Procedure

1. The class is divided into four groups, and each group organizes itself around one of the four systems, as assigned by the teacher. A leader is identified in each group. A nonparticipating observer also is assigned and, before continuing, each group should discuss how leaders and members behave under the assigned system. For example, those in the paternalistic group need to consider how the leader will behave with respect to his or her employees. How do members typically respond?

2. After 10 minutes of such discussion, the group solves the problem presented in the "Situation," keeping strictly in the assigned character. Each group has 10 minutes to come to a decision.

3. Each group relates to the class its decision, how it was reached, and how they as individuals are satisfied. Each observer comments on how the group acted. Did they stay in character?

4. Discuss the following:

    ____ a. Which group came to the fastest decision? Why?
    ____ b. Which group was most committed to the decision reached? Why?

Situation

The group consists of a plant manager and first-line supervisors. Budgetary problems require that they lay off two production employees immediately. Chances are they will not be rehired. Who is laid off?

- Robert Sanderson, age twenty-five, good producer, six months with the company, unmarried, attending night school for a bachelor's degree in business administration.
- Mark Riley, age thirty-two, average producer, B.S. degree, seven years with the company, married with two kids, one on the way.
- Marilyn Smith, age thirty, excellent producer, five years with the company, no degrees, married and pregnant.
- Cheryl Whitman, age fifty, average producer, technical school graduate, fifteen years with the company, married with three grown kids.
- Mary Sampson, age twenty-five, average producer, four years with the company, enrolled in high school equivalency program, unmarried.
- Raul Sanchez, age twenty-one, excellent producer, one year with the company, high school dropout, no family in the United States.

10

Developing, Appraising, and Rewarding Personnel

An effective leader develops productive subordinates. From a human relations viewpoint, every employee is affected by the way the organization recruits, develops, appraises, and rewards its personnel. In this chapter techniques, practices, and tools for completing these processes are explored, along with ways for linking performance and rewards, while dealing with discipline issues and methods.

AFTER READING THIS CHAPTER, YOU SHOULD BE ABLE TO:

1. Identify and describe the stages in the process for developing personnel.
2. Discuss the performance appraisal cycle.
3. Explain how graphic rating scales, paired comparison, management by objectives, and 360-degree evaluations can be used in appraising performance.
4. Describe four major problems associated with performance appraisal.
5. Explain ways of dealing with appraisal problems.
6. Examine the link between performance and rewards.
7. Identify ways for rewarding performance.
8. List the types of discipline used when performance is inadequate.

A Diversified Workforce: The 55 and Over Group—Productive and Still Going!

According to recent research, the organizations that are most successful in besting the competition are those that have adopted innovative human resource strategies that help them to deal with myriad new human relations challenges. Among other things, these companies hire people regardless of age, religion, or sexual preference, and they provide mentoring programs and senior management commitment to meeting diversity challenges. As a result of their leading edge recruiting, developing, appraising, and rewarding programs, they are able to outperform the competition.

A good example is the Clearwater, Florida–based Home Shopping Network (HSN), an electronic retailer that broadcasts twenty-four hours per day to more than seventy-nine million U.S. households. HSN recognizes the continued need to bring in diverse talent into all areas of the business, and has implemented benefit programs and internal training and recognition programs to support such diversity. For example, HSN offers same-sex domestic partner medical and dental insurance, a discounted pet "insurance" plan, flexible work schedules, and many on-site conveniences to support its various cultures and employees. HSN respects that employees have diverse backgrounds, interests, and lifestyles, and supports those individuals as employees and as members of the community. To that end, HSN offers every employee the opportunity to participate in one paid community service day per year to help out in the local community, whether it be a company-sponsored event or one of their own choosing. In 2002, over thirteen hundred HSN employees donated over ten thousand hours of community service to their favorite charity. Over seventy-five various agencies, schools, and nonprofit organizations have benefited from HSN volunteerism in just the past year.

HSN also offers internal diversity training to illustrate the benefits of respecting diversity and recognizing its value in the workplace. Diversity is also a recruitment component for talent acquisition at all levels. HSN ensures that its recruitment advertising reaches many diverse groups and, through the Internet, has played a significant role in allowing HSN to reach out to minority groups, which they otherwise might not be able to target. For example, the company has posted available positions on Web sites such as **http://www.blackvoices.com, http://www.gaywork.com, http://www.ivillage.com,** just to name a few. Diversity in all areas of HSN's business is essential to their growth. Diversity is more than merely a value practiced at HSN, it is truly embedded in the company's culture.

Another good example is McDonald's, which has developed special strategies for recruiting a diversified group of employees, especially the older employee. Many retired people who have an interest in working for McDonald's end up in units run by college graduates who are still in their twenties. When these managers interview older applicants, they are taught not to ask such standard questions as "What are your career goals?" Instead, interviewers focus on talking about how older candidates can share their skills and experiences with others, and they sell McDonald's as a career opportunity based on scheduling flexibility and the fact that older employees will not jeopardize their own social security earnings. Additionally, to minimize older workers' fears of moving into the workforce, McDonald's has set up a buddy system so that each older worker has someone to help him or her acclimate to the way things operate in the firm. Workers can choose one restaurant position in which they're particularly interested, or they can choose to learn a variety of positions.

Do older employees make better employees? Statistics show that often they do. For example, only 3 percent of workers older than fifty change jobs in any given year, in contrast to 10 percent of the workforce at large and 12 percent of those between the ages of twenty-five and thirty-four. Additionally, older workers are more careful: Studies show that although workers fifty years of age or older now make up 24.8 percent of the workforce, they suffer only 10 percent of all workplace injuries. They also are healthier. Research from the University of Southern California has found that people older than fifty tend to use fewer health care benefits than do workers with school-age children. This helps to explain why such employers as McDonald's actively seek the well-seasoned employee.

By 2010, as seventy-six million baby boomers begin to hit retirement age, the United States will have ten million more jobs than it will have workers to fill them, according to the Bureau of Labor Statistics. There won't be enough Generation X or Y workers to fill the gap. Companies are so caught up in today's issues, they are not thinking about the future, but now is the time that "companies should start thinking about how workplaces are going to recruit, retain, and accommodate people of 70 to 80 years."

Companies like to retain their older employees because these people are extremely productive. For example, consider the case of Fort Worth–based Texas Refinery Corporation. The firm's number two salesperson is seventy-four years old—and he isn't alone. Among its sales force of more than three thousand, the company employs more than five hundred people who are sixty years of age or older. The company works hard to retain these people for purely selfish reasons: They are productive. As the president said, "Age is immaterial to us. We put a great deal of value on life experience, and we think that in relationships, often an older, more experienced person probably has a distinct advantage." Many of the company's salespeople are hired as independent contractors who receive commission and benefits based on their sales. This is fine with the fifty-plus crowd, as seen in the case of Elvin Briggs, a seventy-one-year-old sales representative who has been with the company for nineteen years. He averages fifty hours per week, drives one hundred miles per day, and still climbs ladders to inspect roofs of industrial buildings.

Why are companies that hire older workers so productive? One reason is that these workers have excellent attendance. Another is that they are committed to quality. Other key reasons include solid performance records, practical knowledge, the ability to get along with others, solid experience, and emotional stability. All these assets add up to profit for the firm.

Sources: Dayton Fandray, "Gray Matters," Workforce, July 2000, pp. 27–32; Stephen Baker and Paul Judge, "Where IBM Goes, Others May Follow," Business Week, October 7, 1996, p. 39; Anne Fisher, "Wanted: Aging Baby-Boomers," Fortune, September 30, 1996, p. 204; and Charlene Marmer Solomon, "Unlock the Potential of Older Workers," Personnel Journal, October 1995, pp. 56–66. E-mail from Kathy Aitken, HSN, April 4-4-03; telephone discussion with Texas Refinery Corporation, 4-07-03. Carroll Lachnit, "Brave New World," Workforce, March, 2003, p. 8. **http://www.workforce.com**

LEARNING OBJECTIVE

Identify and describe the stages in the process for developing personnel

(1) # Developing Personnel

The development of personnel begins when individuals enter the organization and does not end until they leave. From a human relations standpoint, this subject is important because every person in an organization will be affected by the ways in which the enterprise recruits and develops its people. This overall process typically involves recruiting, screening, selecting, orientation, training, appraising, and rewarding.

Recruiting

Recruiting is the process of attracting qualified applicants to apply for available positions. Applicants can come from *internal sources*—employees who want to change positions, or be promoted within the organization and from *external sources,* those outside the organization. Examples include resume databases, ads in newspapers and industry journals, job fairs, employee referrals, the firm's Web site, cold calls, and recruiting firms. By developing a job profile that accurately defines the duties, responsibilities, and skills required for the job, the recruiter can begin the search for the person who has the appropriate technical and personal skills to do the job and more importantly can fit into the culture of the firm. "Recruiters need more than just a list of job skills to find candidates. They need to understand the culture and environment," says Tom Lucas, senior vice president of HR and employee relations at Adecco North America, an international employment firm headquartered in Melville, New York. "What you want is for the recruiter to find people who fit into your environment," says Cathy Fyock, President of Innovative Management Concepts, Crestwood, Kentucky.[1]

Tom Peters, a management expert and consultant, believes that women are an underutilized talent source in this new economy. His conviction is that "women's increasing power—leadership and purchasing power—is the strongest and most dynamic force at work in America. This is bigger than the Internet." In our complex world, leaders must see the world in bigger terms. "It's not just enough to inspire a shared vision about the corporate mission, strategy and vision, leaders must inspire a greater vision of the world we all live in, reports Melinda Davis, a management consultant.[2] With the composition of the workforce changing, recruiters in the next decade will be challenged to look beyond the traditional sources of applicants. Getting a diversified and qualified pool of applicants is the job of the recruiter.

"Choosing a recruiter is all about personality," says Bill Jones, vice president of operations of Point2Point Global Logistics, a video-game distribution house in Houston, Texas. "The relationship you build with your recruiter is an important thing."[3] Recruiters must understand a firm's value system and understand its intangible needs in order to fill positions with people who will fit into a firm's culture and who can work effectively with other employees, creating good human relations within the firm. Each year companies spend a vast amount of money on recruiting and staffing. For example, in 2002 they spent $58.9 billion worldwide, and that is expected to increase to $85.5 billion by 2007.[4]

Screening and Selecting

Screening is the process of eliminating applicants who are unlikely to be successful on the job. **Selecting** is the process of determining which applicants will be offered jobs. The challenge is to screen and select accurately the best individuals from the pool of applicants.

Organizations do this in a number of ways. One example is checking an applicant's education, previous employment, credit history, driving record, and criminal record. Although this process can cost anywhere from $50 to $200 per applicant, a growing number of firms are finding that this is money well spent, because it reduces the likelihood that they will hire the wrong person.[5]

Another useful screening and selecting tool is the job interview. Recruiters often use a number of human relations techniques in this process. One is the *structured interview,* in which all applicants are asked the same questions. This approach then allows interviewers to make comparisons among job candidates based on responses to identical questions. A second is the *unstructured interview,* which focuses on specific objectives but allows the interviewer to determine the direction that the interview will take, thereby permitting interviewers to judge a wide range of candidate abilities.

In the interview process not only should applicants be interviewed, but also applicants should ask their own questions to learn more about the job and firm. In Figure 10.1 are listed some common questions often asked of hiring managers. How many of these questions have you used in the past job interviews?[6]

Regardless of the type of interview used, in recent years interviewers have begun relying more and more heavily on situational questions. A situational question describes a scenario— typically a problem likely to occur on the job—and asks applicants what they would do in that situation. These questions are designed to help evaluate how well applicants can express themselves, examine problem situations and offer recommendations, and think on their feet. Situational questions often are very effective in distinguishing those who have true self-confidence from those who merely express bravado in the interview situation.[7]

Attitude, and not a fixed set of skills or experiences, is what Southwest Airlines is looking for in applicants. The company needs employees with a "perfect blend of energy, humor, team spirit, and self-confidence to match Southwest's famously offbeat and customer-obsessed culture." Often applicants participate in group testing where applicants are scored on a scale ranging from "passive" to "active" to "leader."[8] Last year only 5,042 applicants were hired out of 243,657 people who applied for work at Southwest Airlines.[9]

Another common approach is the use of *screening tests.* Various types of screening tests are available. One general category is the demonstration test, which is used to identify proficiency in a specific job-related skill, such as the ability to use a word-processing program to produce monthly reports. Another general category is the professional test, used to select individuals for such areas as managerial positions by identifying the individual's knowledge and familiarity with the technical and managerial aspects of a position. Regardless of the type of screening test used, however, the company must be careful that it does not discriminate against an applicant.

Screening
is the process of eliminating applicants who are unlikely to be successful on the job.
Selecting
is the process of determining which applicants will be offered jobs.

Inquiries that invade privacy provide a good example of discriminatory practices in hiring. Job applications and job interviews cannot delve into areas that are not job related. For example, the Supreme Court has ruled in *Shelton v. Tucker* that requiring public school teachers to disclose all organizations in which they have held membership in the previous five years is a violation of their right to association. In *Shuman v. Philadelphia,* a federal court found that inquiry into people's sexual conduct was a violation of their right to privacy. At the same time, however, there are forms of inquiry that do not violate privacy. For example, in *McKenna v. Fargo,* a federal court held that personality testing of firefighter applicants was designed to determine whether they could stand the pressures of the job and that, therefore, the city's interest in ensuring public safety outweighed the privacy rights of the applicant.[10]

Orientation

Orientation
is the process of introducing new employees to their jobs.

Orientation is the process of introducing new employees to their work group, their superior, and their tasks. Some of the most common items on an orientation agenda are a brief discussion of the company's history and general policies, a description of its services and products, an explanation of the organizational structure, a rundown of personnel policies, an explanation of general regulations, and a formal introduction to the group in which the individual will be working. In small organizations, much of this is handled orally; in large organizations, new employees typically are given booklets or brochures that explain and elaborate on the oral presentation.

Many important advantages are associated with an effective orientation. Among them are:

1. A reduction in the costs of instruction.
2. A lessening of anxiety regarding job failure.
3. A reduction in employee turnover.
4. A saving in time spent on assistance.
5. An increase in the employee's job satisfaction.

Numerous studies have been conducted on the benefits of orientation programs. For example, one group of new employees in a manufacturing firm was given a standard orientation; and another group, a more detailed, comprehensive orientation. It was found that the latter group exhibited 50 percent less tardiness and absenteeism, required 50 percent less training time, and had 80 percent less scrap work. Well-designed orientation programs do indeed pay off.

Training

Training of employees can take many forms. The first step, however, is to identify the objectives of the training: What does the individual need to know? The answer to this question will determine the appropriate training method. The basic principal types of employee training are apprentice, vestibule, on-the-job, off-the-job and virtual training.

- *Apprentice training* is given to people who are new to a job. The training is designed to teach them the rules for getting the work done and to provide an opportunity for applying these procedures. Apprentice training is done both on and off the job.
- *Vestibule training* takes place in an environment that simulates the actual workplace. For example, a trainee who is being taught to run a lathe will be sent to a special area of the plant where a trainer will provide close supervision. Once the trainee learns the job, he or she will then be sent to the shop floor and assigned to a lathe.
- *On-the-job training* is provided by the immediate superior and by fellow workers. It can be formal or informal in nature and usually consists of coaching the individual in the most effective ways of getting the job done. The major benefit of on-the-job training is that it teaches the individual the right way to do the job, bypassing the inefficiencies of trial and error.
- *Off-the-job training* is done away from the workplace. Often it is used when people need to be trained in activities or ideas that are nontechnical in nature, such as effective communication, motivation, and leadership. Trainers who teach both theory and practice can best handle these instructional areas.
- *Virtual training* uses a computer and a well-designed learning program, more commonly known as e-learning. Self-paced components are often combined with computer-driven components.

These training methods help an individual to learn a job quickly and correctly. They assist in matching an individual to a job and improve a person's chance of receiving a good performance appraisal.

A number of interesting developments have occurred in the training arena in recent years. One is the increased scope and depth of training that companies now offer to their employees. According to the American Society for Training and Development (ASTD) in Alexandria, Virginia, the average company spends $770 a year on training per eligible employee. Small companies spend even more. They shell out $966 per worker each year.[11]

After the events of 9/11, the economy slowed down and budgets became tight. Money budgeted for training was cut and companies had to find new ways to train employees. The virtual classroom, commonly known as e-learning, gained momentum and is predicted to be the vehicle for training in the future. Advantages of e-learning are flexibility learning and cost effectiveness, provided the program is designed correctly. "The content must be measurable and performance-based. People have to know going in what they are expected to learn, how they are expected to apply that on the job, and how the experience will benefit them and the company."[12] Bob Dean, CLO for Grant Thornton, global accounting, tax, and business advisory firm in Chicago believes that training is a strategic tool for achieving business results. Dean states that, "daily learning is a key to competitiveness and profit." Its management is focused on building a continuous learning culture. Through the Grant Thornton University, a Web-based corporate learning portal, employees have "access to more than 1,000 hours of self-paced training, live Webcasts, and virtual-classroom courses." The learning paths are broken down by competencies and skill requirements, and then tied to job performance. Dean believes the blended model of combining self-paced modules with live virtual-classroom components is critical for learner success.[13]

Cisco Systems, a producer of hardware and software for routing traffic on the Internet, "is changing, experimenting and rethinking the way it recruits, hires, and trains its employees and how it will maintain its winning culture." Cisco is using a computer software program called Pathfinder to fill positions within the firm. "The software allows Cisco employees to search for jobs that interest them and contact the supervisors directly to set up interviews." This program allows Cisco to shift its talent to the most promising places within the firm and to develop skills that facilitate Cisco's goal of relying on internally nurtured talent.[14]

In late 2000, Circuit City, a consumer electronics retailer, used Digital Think to roll out a company-wide custom e-learning program. Within a year, Circuit City employees had completed more than one million courses. Its success is attributed to two significant factors: tracking and certification. To tie training to performance, Circuit City initiated its e-learning certification program in 2002. "Product lines are now tied to specific certificate tracks, and in order to sell those products, associates must first complete the learning for that track and pass the certification exam." "The combination of tracking and certification is enough to induce most Circuit City associates to seek out training opportunities," says Bill Cimino, director of public relations. That "is why the learning program is such a success." Cimino states that, "e-learning returned its investment within months after implementation and continues to add value every day."[15]

Honeywell, one of the largest companies in America, is challenged to find talented employees. The company recently rolled out what may be the world's learning management system, which will serve about 111,000 employees on five continents. Mark Sullivan, corporate director of learning technology and operations stated the system will help Honeywell "make sure we have the right people with the right skills doing the right jobs at the right times." The Saba system will help measure, track, and deliver the training. For example, the system helps transfer the knowledge needed for the "20-30-something crowd" to fill positions of retired employees.[16]

Another development is the use of diversity training, which is designed to teach managers how to deal with America's changing workforce. Many managers are accustomed to supervising only white men and have had very limited experience in managing women, older workers, or people of color. Demographic data show that the U.S. workforce composition is changing and, by the year 2010, an increasing number of women will be in the workforce. Although this trend has been evident for more than three decades, many managers are experiencing great difficulty in meeting this challenge. Many also are accustomed to older workers retiring. Now that mandatory retirement is a thing of the past in most organizations, managers must learn how to supervise older workers. The same is true for people of color. Between now and the year 2010, African American, Hispanic, and Asian American employees will enter the workforce in unprecedented numbers. Managers must be better trained to understand, motivate, and lead these employees.

A third development in the training arena is the creation of in-house programs. In many cases, enterprises rely on colleges and universities for assistance, although some of the larger firms now are becoming self-reliant. For example, Wal-Mart ended its training relationship with a major university and took its Wal-Mart Institute in-house. Company personnel now train all new store managers. Recently Wal-Mart implemented a twenty-week training program for all managers, assistant managers, and new management trainees. A designated store in each district conducts the training. Likewise, Mervyn's, a retail chain store and McDonald's, a fast-food restaurant, both have their own universities for training personnel.

More common, however, are firms that combine in-house and university-linked training for their people. As Motorola's corporate change agent and a world-renowned corporate university, Motorola University brings time-tested and highly refined business improvement practices to leading organizations around the world. Motorola University (MU) has full-time professionals who are providing annual training to almost ninety-seven thousand employees. At the lower levels of the company, these programs extend from one day to fifteen days and include a wide range of topics from technical (manufacturing, operations, engineering) to behavioral (time management, effective communication, leadership). At the upper levels, Motorola has a senior executive program that is conducted annually for two hundred top managers worldwide. Topics range widely and, in the past, have dealt with the challenge of Asian competition, rethinking offshore manufacturing strategies, and developing more effective customer-driven programs. At the same time, Motorola has a formal agreement with Northwestern University's Kellogg School of Business to deliver a two-week development program for senior executives, and it has licensed community colleges to teach Motorola courses. Still another example of university training linkages is provided by Nynex, the New York telecommunications utility, which has designed a degree in telecommunication technology in association with its union and the State University of New York.

The learning philosophy at Motorola University reveals the commitment Motorola has made to training and to its personnel.

> *Motorola has a time honored and valued tradition of commitment to the growth and development of its people. Continuous learning is a strategic investment that represents one of the only remaining sustainable sources of competitive advantage. To maximize our investment, employee development and learning must be aligned with our business strategies and needs. All Motorola managers have a clear obligation to budget strategic development funds in areas that yield the greatest return for our business and in employees they wish to attract, develop, and retain.*
>
> *Motorola managers and employees are in a crucial developmental partnership to select the developmental opportunities that best meet the unique needs of the business and the associate. Employees have an essential responsibility to ensure that their personal competence and capability is growing to meet the increasing performance challenges of our changing business environment. To achieve this end they must create and enact development plans that align with business needs, meet their personal development goals, and are financially supported by the business. Managers have a duty to evaluate, approve, plan, and budget for the development and learning needs in their respective business units.*[17]

Appraising Subordinates

Every effective organization wants to reward its best performers and ensure that they remain with the enterprise. How does one separate the best from the average or poor performers? The answer is through a well-designed performance appraisal process. If this process is carried out properly, and the employees realize that management intends to be equitable in its reward system, personnel morale will be high and teamwork can be both developed and nurtured by the enterprise.

To understand fully the performance appraisal process, we must:

1. **Examine the performance appraisal cycle, which describes how the entire evaluation process should be conducted.**
2. **Examine the appraisal tools that can be used in carrying out the evaluation.**
3. **Compare the attributes of appraisal techniques.**
4. **Learn to recognize the problems that can accompany a performance appraisal and the ways to reduce or avoid them.**

The **performance appraisal cycle** *helps managers to set goals and evaluate subordinate performance.*

Performance Appraisal Cycle

Performance appraisal is a four-step process known as the **performance appraisal cycle.**

First, there must be some *established performance standards* that specify what the worker is supposed to be doing. These standards are often quantified; that is, the machinist is supposed to process twenty-five pieces an hour or the typist is expected to type an average of sixty words per minute. Such performance standards establish a basis against which to evaluate the individual.

Second, there must be a *method of determining individual performance.* To say "Barry does a good job" or "Kathleen is an asset to the department" is not a sufficient measure of individual results. The organization needs appraisal instruments that measure desired performance. In the case of the machinist, we would want to consult daily output records to determine whether his or her average is twenty-five pieces per hour or the Word Processor is expected to key an average of sixty words per minute; in the case of the typist, we would want to check the number of pages of material turned out in a typical day. Of course, appraisals will not be conducted on a daily basis but, if proper evaluation instruments are designed, output can be recorded periodically and evaluated later.

Third, there must be some *comparison of performance against standards.* At some point, usually once annually, the individual's work record should be compared with the standards set for the job.

Fourth, an *evaluation of performance* should be made on the basis of the comparison. This process can take several forms. Sometimes the boss meets with the subordinate, reviews progress in general terms, and then announces the basic direction for the upcoming year. At other times, the manager has a detailed work report on the subordinate and is able to pinpoint strengths and weaknesses in great detail. In either case, this step is not finished before the manager has told the subordinate how well he or she is doing. The more definitive the manager is, the more useful the feedback will be in directing and motivating the subordinate. Once this fourth step is completed, the manager and the subordinate are ready to establish performance standards for the next evaluation period. Building on current successes (and sidestepping failures), the two can determine the department's needs and the subordinate's abilities and then work to mesh them. This overall performance appraisal cycle, presented in Figure 10.2, provides the primary basis for any evaluation program.

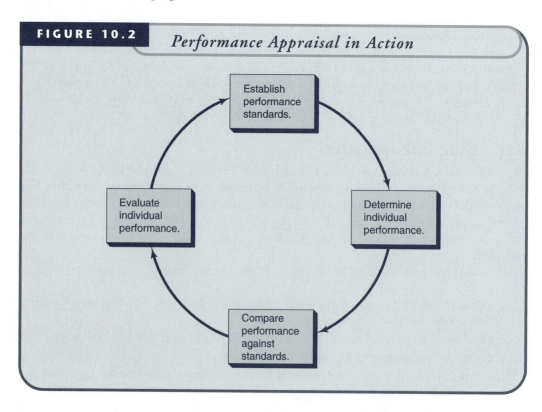

FIGURE 10.2 *Performance Appraisal in Action*

Establish performance standards.

Determine individual performance.

Compare performance against standards.

Evaluate individual performance.

FIGURE 10.3 *Illustration of a Graphic Rating Scale (Partial Form)*

Employee ______________________ Date ______________

Department ______________________ Rater ______________

Rating / Factor	1 **Unsatisfactory** Totally inadequate	2 **Fair** Meets minimal requirements	3 **Good** Exceeds minimal requirements	4 **Superior** Always does above the basic job requirements	5 **Exceptional** Is consistently outstanding
Quantity The volume of output produced					
Quality The accuracy and thoroughness of the output					
Supervision The need for direction, correction, and/or advice					
Attendance Dependability, regularity, and promptness					

Performance Appraisal Tools

Many kinds of appraisal tools can be used to evaluate employee performance. Four of the most common are graphic rating scales, the paired comparison method, management by objectives, and 360-degree evaluations.[18]

3 LEARNING OBJECTIVE

Explain how graphic rating scales, paired comparison, management by objectives, and 360-degree evaluations can be used in appraising performance

GRAPHIC RATING SCALES

The most widely used of all performance appraisal tools are **graphic rating scales.** One major reason is undoubtedly the ease with which they can be developed and applied. Figure 10.3 illustrates such a scale. In the chart, the factors on which the employee is to be evaluated are identified and the degrees of evaluation are spelled out. The rater, usually the subordinate's boss, has merely to read each of the factors and then check the appropriate box. By totaling the value associated with every factor degree (i.e., from 1 for unsatisfactory up to 5 for exceptional), the rater can obtain a total score for the subordinate.

Graphic rating scales *evaluate personnel on the basis of predetermined factors.*

Each rating level communicates a different message and has a different outcome, so what is the best number of rating levels. Some advantages and disadvantages for five levels, four levels, and three levels are:

Five Levels

Advantages

- Provides for the finest distinctions in performance
- More consistent with bell-curve distribution
- Most managers believe they can discriminate among five levels of performance
- Consistent with familiar "A-F" school-grading model
- Most familiar rating scheme—less training required

Disadvantages

- May be harder for supervisors to communicate how to attain higher performance levels
- Typically only four levels are used
- Middle rating usually perceived negatively—as average, or mediocre, or a "C" student
- May encourage central tendency

Four Levels

Advantages

- Does not include a middle rating which may be perceived as "average"
- Eliminates "central tendency" rating error
- May skew raters in a positive or negative direction
- Provides for finer distinctions than a three-level scale

Disadvantages

- May not provide a way to distinguish between those who can improve and those who should be terminated
- May skew raters in a positive or negative direction
- Typically, only three levels are used

Three Levels

Advantages

- Supervisors find it easy to categorize performance into three categories
- Supervisors tend to be more consistent if given fewer choices—higher reliability
- Some jobs may be better appraised on a "pass/fail" basis
- Only three levels of performance can be proved empirically
- Middle rating implies expected performance, not average performance
- More consistent with TQM principles

Disadvantages

- May not provide fine enough distinctions in performance
- Managers frequently alter system by adding plusses and minuses
- Does not distinguish between those who can improve and those who should be terminated
- Typically only two levels are used
- Does not allow for identifying the truly exceptional 2–5 percent

---

Reference: "Pros and Cons of Performance-Appraisal Rating Systems, Now Solutions, Workforce, *Source: Grote Consulting Corporation Adapted from* The Performance Appraisal Question and Answer Book, *Copyright 2002, by Dick Grote, Published by AMACOM Books, a division of American Management Association, New York, NY. Used with Permission. All rights reserved.* **http://www.amacombooks.org**

PAIRED COMPARISON METHOD

*The **paired comparison method** compares each person against all others being evaluated.*

Many managers regard the **paired comparison method** as superior to the graphic rating scale because it is more discriminating in its approach. Rather than just providing an overall evaluation of a person, in which each worker might end up receiving an exceptional score, this method compares each employee to every other one in the group with respect to a number of factors (see Figure 10.4). In this way, although everyone may be doing good work, it still is possible to determine who is best and who is poorest. It is no longer simply a matter of how well a person is performing the job but of how the individual compares with all the other

FIGURE 10.4 — Paired Comparison Method for Rating Employees

On the Basis of Work Quantity

	Personnel Being Rated				
As compared to:	Anderson	Brown	Carpenter	Davis	Evans
Anderson		−	+	−	+
Brown	+		+	+	+
Carpenter	−	−		−	+
Davis	+	−	+		+
Evans	−	−	−	−	

Evans has the highest ranking for work quantity.

On the Basis of Work Quality

	Personnel Being Rated				
As compared to:	Anderson	Brown	Carpenter	Davis	Evans
Anderson		−	+	+	+
Brown	+		+	+	+
Carpenter	−	−		+	+
Davis	−	−	−		−
Evans	−	−	+	+	

Davis has the highest ranking for work quality.

Note: A plus (+) indicates higher than and a minus (−) indicates lower than (the coworker against whom an individual is being compared). The individual with the greatest number of pluses is the one with the highest ranking.

workers. In Figure 10.4, work quality and quantity are measured. A rater may end up with five to ten paired comparison forms before compiling the scores and getting an overall evaluation for each employee. Regardless of the number of factors rated, however, only one person ranks at the top of the list when all the ratings are completed.

MANAGEMENT BY OBJECTIVES

Management by objectives (MBO) is an overall appraisal system used at all levels of the employment hierarchy. Many organizations prefer MBO because it is systematic, all encompassing, and easy to understand. Because of its great popularity, we shall study it in much greater depth than we have the other appraisal tools. Before doing so, however, let us define the term. **Management by objectives** is a process in which the superior and the subordinate jointly identify common goals, define the subordinate's major areas of responsibility in terms of expected results—objectives, and use these measures as guides for operating the unit and assessing the contribution of each member. It is a goal-setting process initiated by Peter Drucker, a management guru.

Management by objectives
is a process by which superior and subordinate jointly set goals that then are used for evaluating the individual.

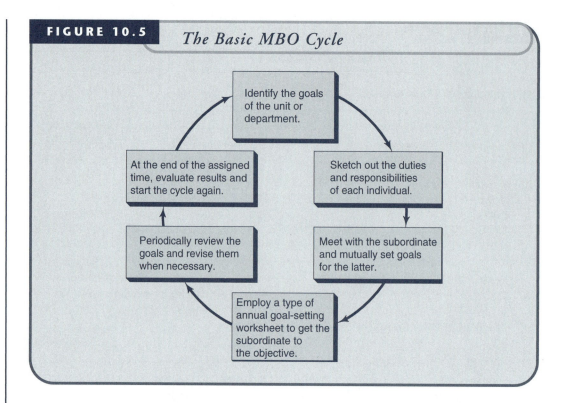

FIGURE 10.5   *The Basic MBO Cycle*

Identify the goals of the unit or department.

Sketch out the duties and responsibilities of each individual.

Meet with the subordinate and mutually set goals for the latter.

Employ a type of annual goal-setting worksheet to get the subordinate to the objective.

Periodically review the goals and revise them when necessary.

At the end of the assigned time, evaluate results and start the cycle again.

How MBO Works   The MBO process consists of six basic steps. Figure 10.5 illustrates the typical cycle employed in implementing it.

First, the manager identifies the goals that his or her unit should pursue over the next evaluation period. These goals can often be expressed in terms of profit, revenues, margins, competitive position, or employee relations.

Second, the organization must be clearly described. Who is in the department? What does each person do? Having answered these questions, the manager then reviews each individual's work, noting what can be expected of that person.

Third, the manager sets objectives for the next evaluation period for the workers individually. This is achieved by:

1. **Asking each subordinate to list those objectives that he or she has in mind for the next year and setting a date for discussing them.**
2. **Making a personal list of objectives that the manager would like to see the subordinate attain.**
3. **Reviewing both lists and then jointly agreeing on a final set of objectives for the subordinate.**
4. **Typing two copies of the final draft of objectives, one each for the superior and the subordinate.**
5. **Making oneself available to help the subordinate accomplish the assigned goals.**

Fourth, an annual goal-setting worksheet is designed to help the subordinate reach these objectives. Figure 10.6 is an example. As can be seen in the figure, the worksheet is divided into three parts: objectives, major steps for achieving the planned objectives, and the way in which progress is to be evaluated—in short, what is to be done, how it will be accomplished, and the methods that will be used to show how well it is being accomplished.

Fifth, during the year, each subordinate's goals are checked to determine whether the objectives are being reached. In particular, the manager needs to know how close the person is coming to attaining these targets, whether any of the goals need to be amended, and what kinds of assistance the person requires to reach the goals.

FIGURE 10.6

An Annual Goal-Setting Worksheet (Partial Form)

NAME Hal Lymer   DATE January 2, 2001

POSITION Superintendent of Engine Manufacturing   SUPERVISOR Les Rodgers

Objectives	Major Steps for Achieving Planned Objectives	The Way in Which Progress Will Be Evaluated
Increase the number of production hours in the engine departments from 30,000 to 40,000.	Conduct methods study of the bottleneck operations in engine assembly and make necessary changes. Reduce machining time on the planer type mill by employing an assistant operator during peak periods. Add three floating supervisors to give 'round-the-clock supervision to the bottle-neck operations.	Progress will be measured in terms of shipments reported on the monthly cost control report.
Reduce supervisory overtime by cross-training supervisors.	Cross-train supervisors in the large-machine, small-machine, and engine assembly departments. Determine how general supervisors can be used as substitutes for forepersons and assistant forepersons. Use these general forepersons on at least four Sundays per calendar quarter.	In the first 6 months of last year, fore-persons and assistant forepersons in engine manufacturing worked an average of 20 of 26 Sundays. The target for the first 6 months of this year is to reduce this to no more than 15 of 26 Sundays.
Reduce scrap cost from 4 percent to 3 percent of production.	In conjunction with quality assurance, have manager conduct a study to identify the specific causes of scrap losses. Determine ways to measure scrap and rework costs by shift. Put together a task force for determining alternative ways to reduce this scrap. Develop an incentive plan for rewarding the shift with the best scrap record. Determine the feasibility of disciplining employees who cause major scrap losses.	Measure progress in terms of scrap and rework costs reported on the monthly cost control report.

Sixth, results are measured against goals. Near the end of the MBO cycle, which commonly coincides with the budget year, the superior asks each subordinate to prepare a brief statement of performance. Then the two meet to review how well the subordinate has done and to establish objectives for the next budget year.

Advantages of MBO   MBO has proved to be a very popular approach because it is both comprehensive and easy to understand. One of its primary advantages is the attention given to the subordinate in the goal-setting process. Rather than the individual being told what goals he or she should pursue, the manager and subordinate now engage jointly in a give-and-take process.

Another advantage of this approach is that MBO places a strong emphasis on quantifiable objectives that are tied to a time dimension. For example, performance standards are stated in specific, measurable terms, such as percentages, dollars, ratios, costs, and quality. If a manager is going to reduce tardiness, this goal will be stated in a percentage: "We will cut tardiness by 18 percent." In addition, a period will be set for the attainment of the objective. Expanding the foregoing statement, then, we can bring together the quantifiable goal and the time dimension in this way: "We will cut tardiness by 18 percent within the first six months of the upcoming fiscal year." Some of the following might be objectives for other major areas of organizational performance:

- **Raise return on investment to 15 percent within the next four operating quarters.**
- **By December 31, complete the management control reporting system for all operating decisions.**
- **Install the new computerized information system by April 30.**

Note that each objective is written in such a way that what is to be attained (the goal) and when it is to be attained (the time dimension) are clearly stated.

A third advantage of MBO is that there is a concentration on the organization's key goals. Each manager ties his or her unit's objectives to the goals of the organization at large. As a result, all units are working in the same direction.

In the MBO approach, emphasis is given to working with a small, manageable number of objectives. The number of objectives assigned to each person usually is limited to five or six. The accomplishment of these objectives will satisfy the key goals assigned to the manager in a specific work area. When these objectives are accomplished, the manager is effective. Limiting subordinates' objectives makes it easier for employees to channel their energy toward accomplishing the objectives that fit into the goals assigned to their specific work area and for the superior to monitor progress and to review performance.

MBO helps to coordinate the activities of the units by linking each with those above, below, and on the same level. For example, Mary is in charge of department B. When, to determine her objectives, she meets with her boss, Ted, who is in charge of a group of departments, Ted integrates her objectives with his own. He will do the same for the other departments, A and C, that report to him, as will Mary with the subordinates in her department who report to her.

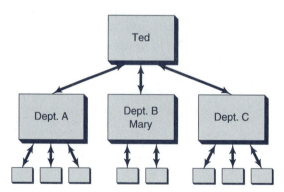

Another advantage of MBO is that it encourages the manager to delegate time-consuming activities and to devote his or her energies to overall planning and control. Using MBO, the manager knows what everyone is supposed to be doing. The initial delegation of authority is very systematic. Additionally, MBO helps the manager to evaluate subordinates and to learn what each can do well and what each does poorly. With this information, the manager can then determine what work to delegate to each subordinate in the future. Who does job A well? Who is best assigned to job B? Who is the best performer on job C? In delegating these tasks, the manager is able to pass off much of the busywork that he or she has performed in the past, because now the manager knows better the strengths of the subordinates. Additionally, the manager's boss will encourage such delegation. One of the primary benefits of MBO is its philosophy of delegating busywork and concentrating one's time on "think-work." An effective top manager will not let the subordinate manager delegate work that should be handled personally while hanging on to time-consuming activities.

Overall, MBO has been well accepted in many organizations. In particular, managers like its systematic approach and the emphasis it gives to the key managerial functions of planning, organizing, and controlling. In both public and private sectors, it holds a great deal of promise for the future.

360-Degree Evaluation Reviews In recent years, a growing number of companies have begun using 360-degree evaluation reviews.[19] These companies include Alcoa, Bank of America, Hewlett-Packard, Johnson & Johnson, Procter & Gamble, and Shell Oil.[20] These reviews are carried out not just by the individual's superior but also by the person's subordinates, peers, work group, and others with whom he or she comes in frequent contact.[21] A good example of the 360-degree evaluation process is provided by General Electric Plastics. In all, the organization uses six steps:

1. The employee and manager agree on the list of individuals who will be used to evaluate the employee, and each of these individuals receives an evaluation form.
2. The evaluators complete the forms and return them to the managers.
3. The manager collects and summarizes the data.
4. The manager and the subordinate meet and discuss the results and agree on a developmental plan of action that will help the employee address any problems as well as expand his or her knowledge, experience, and other job-related skills and abilities.
5. The 360-degree summary and action plan are used to evaluate the individual, and these become part of the employee's personnel file.
6. The action plan is used as a guide in providing the individual with overall leadership direction and serves as a basis for the next 360-degree evaluation.

A key part of the evaluation process is the determination of how well the individual has performed during the measurement period. At GE Plastics, the focus is on what the person accomplished, and this result is expressed in terms of a *1, 2,* or *3* rating:

1 = excellent performance
2 = fully satisfactory performance
3 = significant improvement needed

Coupled with this is an evaluation of the means that were used in accomplishing these goals. This part of the evaluation is based on how others view the person's company business values, including vision, accountability, receptivity to change, teamwork, empowerment, involvement, energy, and speed. In this case there are three evaluations—*A, B,* and *C:*

A = significant strength
B = some development needs exist
C = significant development is required

The two sets of ratings (*1, 2,* or *3;* and *A, B,* or *C*) then are brought together in a nine-block matrix. Figure 10.7 provides an illustration. This matrix is used to summarize an individual's strengths and identify development needs.

As noted earlier, the final step in the 360-degree evaluation review is the creation of a development action plan. This consists of a dialogue between the manager and the employee regarding long- and short-term development needs and the options available for meeting these needs. This overall development process is linked very closely to the firm's business strategy, so that all new skills, knowledge, and training will help the individual do a better job of meeting both personal and team goals. In turn, these goals will assist the operating unit in attaining its goals.

On the basis of the development meeting, an action plan is formulated. This plan is a result of agreement between the employee and the manager regarding the performance areas (outputs, competencies) that need improvement or that hold high payoff potential for the employee's long-term career goals. The two individuals also discuss ways in which the employee can obtain any assistance that is needed. Examples include coaching, one-to-one instruction, assignment

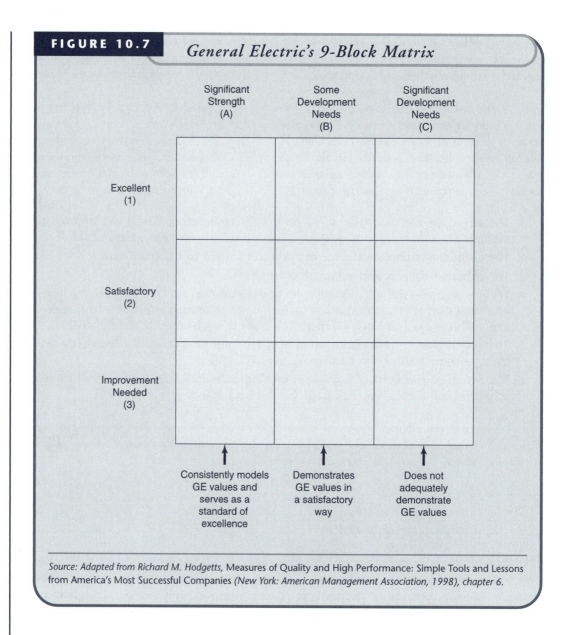

FIGURE 10.7 *General Electric's 9-Block Matrix*

	Significant Strength (A)	Some Development Needs (B)	Significant Development Needs (C)
Excellent (1)			
Satisfactory (2)			
Improvement Needed (3)			

↑ Consistently models GE values and serves as a standard of excellence

↑ Demonstrates GE values in a satisfactory way

↑ Does not adequately demonstrate GE values

Source: Adapted from Richard M. Hodgetts, Measures of Quality and High Performance: Simple Tools and Lessons from America's Most Successful Companies *(New York: American Management Association, 1998), chapter 6.*

changes, task-force work, project leadership, classes, courses, workshops, and personal reading assignments of books and articles.

Once the action plan has been formulated, it is the employee's responsibility to take charge and begin implementing the agreed-on steps. The manager, of course, remains available to assist, but it is the employee who ultimately is responsible for his or her development. Then, at the end of the agreed-on time, the 360-degree evaluation process begins again.[22]

One reason that 360-degree reviews have proven to be so popular is that they help organizations more effectively deal with performance evaluations. For example, a recent Korn/Ferry—Columbia Business School study found that minority executives report that they often are treated harshly or unfairly by whites,[23] which can negatively affect their career opportunities. The objectivity of 360-reviews can help to eliminate this problem.

LEARNING OBJECTIVE

④

Describe four major problems associated with performance appraisal

Performance Appraisal Problems

Performance appraisal helps the manager to identify those who should be rewarded for adequate or superior performance and those who should not. However, such an approach can yield erroneous results if the appraisal form is designed improperly or if the rater is biased.

Clarity of the Appraisal Form

One of the most common appraisal problems relates to clarity of the form. If every appraiser does not have an identical interpretation of what the factors and their ratings mean, uniformity is impossible. In Figure 10.3, for example, quantity, quality, supervision, and attendance are defined briefly, as are the ratings for each. But how does the appraiser determine when a person should get a rating of fair and when he or she should be rated as good? Unless the factors are defined precisely and this information is made available to the evaluator, an employee might be rated fair by one manager and good by another. The situation is even worse if the factors or their ratings are not described at all. If each manager is using only his or her own judgment, performance evaluations will not be uniform throughout the organization.

To overcome this problem, it is necessary to describe on the evaluation form the factors and degrees on which the employee will be evaluated and to ensure that the appraisers apply a uniform interpretation. When is an individual's performance to be considered good? When is it to be rated superior? Many organizations find it very helpful to schedule a meeting of all the people who are rating a particular group of employees, such as salespeople, to discuss the evaluation form and determine the ground rules for the appraisal. In this way, all employees doing similar work can be rated in uniform terms.

The Halo Effect

A **halo effect** occurs when the appraiser gives a worker the same rating on all factors, regardless of actual performance. For example, the manager has noticed that Paul is occasionally late for work. The manager believes that Paul does not care much for his job, and this impression carries over to the manager's rating of Paul. Regardless of how much work Paul does or how high the quality of the work output is, he continually receives a fair rating. Conversely, Mandy is always on time for work and has a very pleasant personality. This biases the manager's rating of her, and she is always rated excellent in all categories. Many firms find that a training program can alleviate this problem by helping the manager to identify these built-in biases and work to correct them.

*A **halo effect** occurs when the appraiser gives a worker the same rating on all factors, regardless of actual performance.*

Central Tendency

A second common rater-generated problem is that of **central tendency,** in which everyone receives an average rating, regardless of how effective he or she has been. For example, Andy is one of the department's poorest workers and Karl is one of the best, yet their performance ratings are always identical. The manager continually rates both as good. Such an approach helps Andy, who should be given a rating of fair, but it punishes Karl, who should be given a rating of superior.

One of the greatest problems faced by managers who rate their people this way is that the best workers begin looking for new jobs. After all, their chances for increased salary or promotion are being severely limited. Another problem is that the evaluations are now useless. The organization cannot rely on them to identify those who should be advanced and those who should be terminated. One way of overcoming this problem is to use a paired comparison evaluation or an MBO approach, in which results are quantified or described in such terms that the manager is required to give each person a more precise rating.

*With **central tendency,** everyone receives an average rating.*

Leniency

A third common rater-generated problem is that of **leniency,** in which managers give all their people the highest possible rating. Here again, failure to distinguish between those doing an outstanding job and those doing a poor job results in inaccurate ratings. Many organizations in recent years have worked around this problem through use of a paired comparison evaluation.

*With **leniency,** the highest possible ratings are given out to all.*

Dealing With Appraisal Problems

⑤

The rating form or the rater is generally the cause for appraisal problems. By investigating the various advantages and disadvantages of each rating approach, an organization can determine which one best meets its needs. Additionally, training the raters in how to use the selected form can eliminate many bias problems.

Validity
means that the instrument measures what it is designed to measure.
Reliability
means that the instrument measures the same factor repeatedly.

Remember, two major issues must be dealt with in performance appraisal: validity and reliability. By **validity,** we mean that the instrument measures what we want it to measure. If work quantity is important, then this factor should be on the rating form. If cooperation with others is of no value because the individual works alone, it should not appear on the form. By **reliability,** we mean that the instrument measures the same factor repeatedly. If we are interested in work quality but not work quantity, we want to be sure the raters understand this. Otherwise, the way a person is rated by two managers might differ.

In recent years, a wealth of research has shown that validity and reliability continue to be problems when appraising individuals. For example, one study of interview panels of police officers found that race was an influencing factor when screening officers for promotion. People on interview panels tended to give a higher evaluation to candidates who were the same race as themselves.[24] In another study, which examined the impact of both physical attractiveness and gender, researchers found that individuals who were above average in attractiveness tended to receive higher evaluations than those who were below average. Additionally, women tended to be ranked lower than men, and those women who were of below-average attractiveness did poorest of all. However, the researchers also found that the extent of bias was less among experienced managers than among those who were less experienced.[25] Still another study found that the accuracy of performance evaluations often is influenced by how well the manager remembers subordinate performance and, when memory is inaccurate, so too is the evaluation.[26]

Fortunately, there are ways of dealing with appraisal problems. Some are presented in the Human Relations in Action box. Another is to require managers to justify their evaluations. Researchers have found that when people are required to explain why they gave the evaluation they did, they are more careful about how they carry out the process, and their evaluations tend to be more accurate.[27] Still other useful ways include the following:

1. **Involve employees more in the design, development, and administration of the appraisal process. Participation creates ego involvement and a sense of commitment.**

2. **Invest time and effort in training managers to use the system for evaluation purposes, and teach them how to communicate this information effectively to those being rated.**

3. **Create an environment in which performance information is viewed as a resource that managers can use in developing their subordinates rather than as a method for punishing them.**

4. **Make performance appraisals the responsibility of the ratee—not the rater—by teaching employees how to use feedback on their job performance to help them manage their own careers and to rely less on their superior in determining their progress.**

5. **Reduce reliance on just one reviewer by building a system that allows multiple raters to provide input. This reduces bias and helps to provide a clearer, more complete picture of the ratee's strengths and weaknesses.[28]**

⑥

Rewarding Performance

The manager is in a position to reward (or not reward) a subordinate on the basis of the performance appraisal. In determining the type and degree of reward to give, it is necessary to examine three important areas: extrinsic and intrinsic rewards; performance and rewards; and discipline. The first two areas were discussed in Chapter 2, but here we want to apply them directly to performance rewards. Discipline is important because sometimes the manager must give out negative rewards.

HUMAN RELATIONS IN ACTION

Conducting an Effective Performance Appraisal

Managers need to know many things about carrying out an effective performance appraisal. The following five guidelines present much of this information in abbreviated form.

1. *Be familiar with the jobs being evaluated.* The best way to make an effective appraisal is to know what the person has been doing. Some people can look productive while performing simple or meaningless tasks. They could be overrated. Conversely, an effective worker might be underrated by someone unfamiliar with the job. There is no substitute for work familiarity.

2. *Know the factors to be evaluated.* The following criteria can be used in deciding how well the individual is performing the job: work quantity, work quality, speed, accuracy, ability to get along with others, and communication effectiveness. These factors should be job-related so that individuals who do well on the job also receive high ratings.

3. *Let employees know the factors being evaluated.* This has a number of advantages. One is that the

workers are aware of what they need to do to receive a good evaluation. A second is that the amount of tension and anxiety often associated with being evaluated tends to decline. A third is that it lets the workers know that the evaluation is job-related and not tied to such personal factors as an ability to get along with the boss.

4. *Measure the evaluation criteria appropriately.* Some jobs can be measured on a daily or weekly basis. For example, secretaries or office workers often handle short-term assignments. Progress can be evaluated from week to week. In contrast, salespeople often experience certain seasons of the year that are better than others, and so their overall performance cannot be evaluated until you see how well they have done during the best sales months.

5. *Use the evaluation to help people do better.* Evaluations should not be punitive instruments. Using them to show people where they have made mistakes creates anger and resentment. Instead, evaluations should be used as learning tools for showing people where their performance needs to be improved. An effective evaluation can serve as a basis for personnel training and development.

Extrinsic and Intrinsic Rewards

Extrinsic rewards are external and physical, taking such forms as money, increased fringe benefits, and use of a company car. **Intrinsic rewards** are internal and psychological, taking such forms as a feeling of accomplishment, increased responsibility, and the opportunity to achieve.

Money is both an extrinsic and an intrinsic reward. In and of itself, money is extrinsic, but with it often come psychological rewards, such as esteem ("I'm important; look how much the organization is paying me"), a feeling of accomplishment ("Well, I did it: I finally made $75,000 in one year"), and a sense of achievement ("I'm good at what I do, a real achiever; that's why I'm being paid so much").

Intangible rewards and recognition are much more powerful motivators than money. A recent nationwide survey sponsored by Katzenbach Partners LLC found "that employees—by a more than three to one margin—would rather feel proud of their work than receive a higher salary." The study found that slightly more than half of the employees strongly agreed or mostly agreed with the following statement: "feeling proud of your work is more important to you than getting a raise."[29]

The effective leader realizes that a mixture of extrinsic and intrinsic rewards is needed. Which mix will be best depends on the subordinate and, to be more definitive in our answer, we must apply expectancy theory to the specific situation.

Remember that expectancy theory can be expressed as: motivational force = valence × expectancy. *Valence* is the individual's preference for an outcome; for example, John may prefer a $100-per-week raise to a company car. *Expectancy* is the perceived probability that a particular

Extrinsic rewards
are external and physical.
Intrinsic rewards
are internal and psychological.

act will be followed by a particular outcome: If John has the highest sales in the region he will be given a one-week, all-expenses-paid trip to San Francisco. Knowing a person's valence and expectancy is no easy task. However, effective leaders understand their people and soon learn to know which rewards will motivate them.

> *Maureen Wilson is the head of advertising for a large cosmetics firm. Maureen is making more than $100,000 annually in salary and 50 percent more in bonuses tied directly to sales. The more effective the advertising program, the more likely that sales, and her bonus, will rise.*
>
> *Realizing that money will not motivate Maureen very much, her boss has scheduled her to go to sales meetings in London, Paris, and Rome during the next month. The boss knows Maureen likes to travel and that her husband, who owns a successful retail store, can get away any time he wants. The two often can spend three weeks in Europe, and the cosmetics firm will pay most of their expenses. Next year Maureen will be going to the Far East.*

It is obvious that Maureen's boss knows how to motivate her. The reward schedule is designed to meet Maureen's specific needs. The boss gave her a combination of extrinsic and intrinsic rewards. The free travel saved her the cost of going to Europe on her own. (Her income tax bracket is very high, so if the cost of her trip were $8,000, she would have to make around $12,000 to have this amount after taxes.) It also shows her how much the firm appreciates her talents.

On the other hand, some people want extrinsic rewards and are little influenced by psychological payoffs. This is especially true for people just starting their careers and raising a family at the same time.

> *Tony Farino is a middle manager in a manufacturing plant. He is married and has three children. He bought a house for $140,000, and his car is two years old. Tony's salary is $55,500 but, with overtime, including Saturday and occasional Sunday work, he can gross $67,500. Last month, there was an opening for a manager in the purchasing department. This department has had more than its share of problems. The company's sales are growing so quickly that the department is in a constant state of turmoil trying to check on orders, verify deliveries, and see that suppliers are paid promptly.*
>
> *When the department manager resigned, Tony was offered the job. The salary was $65,000, with the opportunity of making another 25 percent through overtime. Tony accepted and so far has been very happy. Although he is working harder than ever before, he feels the higher pay more than compensates. Also, with the increased salary, he and his wife are planning to take the family on a week's vacation, something that would have been impossible with his former salary. Tony realizes he is working long hours and not seeing very much of his family, but he feels that within 12 to 18 months, things will turn around. The car will be paid for, and the cost-of-living increase that management gives the employees will raise his salary enough to ease the burden of the house payments. Then he will be able to relax and spend more time with the children. For the time being, however, he is willing to sacrifice his leisure time for increased extrinsic rewards.*

In both our illustrations, the manager knows how to motivate the subordinate, offering each what he or she wants. Involved in the two cases was the issue of equity, something that merits closer attention.

LEARNING OBJECTIVE

Identify ways for rewarding performance

⑦ # Linking Performance and Rewards

One of the most important questions in modern compensation theory is: How closely should performance and rewards be linked? This question is particularly critical because dozens of studies show how people who expect to receive a reward for completing a task successfully often perform no better than those who expect no reward at all. Therefore, management must carefully design its reward system.[30] The compensation system can offer three types of rewards: wages, incentive programs, and benefit programs.

Wages, Incentive Programs, and Benefit Programs

Wages are agreed-on or fixed rates of pay. For an hourly employee making $12 per hour, we need merely multiply the number of hours worked by $12 to determine the person's pay for the period under consideration. Most people, however, do not work for an hourly wage; they are salaried. Managerial personnel, in particular, are paid an annual amount, such as $52,000 per year. This salary then is broken down by pay period—that is, $1,000 per week before taxes and other deductions.

Some organizations also have **incentive payment plans.** When offered on an individual basis, they typically take the form of production or sales incentive plans. In a production incentive plan, a worker is paid a higher rate for producing output over and above an established level. For example, a firm might pay $2.00 per manufactured piece per week up to two hundred pieces and $2.25 for any output in excess of two hundred pieces. In a sales incentive plan, the salesperson's pay is tied to sales dollars generated. Often the individual receives a guaranteed draw, such as $100 per week, and a percentage of sales, such as 5 percent of all receipts generated. In the last couple of years, these incentive plans have begun to gain popularity. Hiring bonuses and retention bonuses, which are used to attract and to keep talented people, also are becoming more popular. A recent survey by Bucks Consultants found that a growing number of firms are using these types of bonuses.[31]

One of the best examples of the use of individual incentive plans is Lincoln Electric, the Cleveland-based manufacturer of arc-welding equipment. In recent years, more than seventy-five people on the shop's floor have been able to earn in excess of $100,000 annually thanks to the firm's incentive program.

Group incentive programs can also be found in many organizations. In these cases, the program is similar to the individual incentive plan. For example, the production output of the group, or the sales of the unit, are combined in determining how much of an incentive has been earned by these employees.[32] In the case of Lincoln Electric, every year there is a bonus pool that is shared by the employees at large. In recent years, this pool has been in excess of $60 million and, in many years, has been equal to 50 percent of each person's base salary.

Some organizations have found they can save money by instituting an organization-wide incentive program. In this case, everyone in the enterprise participates. The logic is simple. Management believes that with a joint worker-management effort increased efficiency and cost savings can be affected. Table 10.1 provides a comparison of these three different types of incentive plans.

Benefit programs also come in many different versions. Some of the most common include life, health, and accident insurance; sick leave; workers' compensation; pension plans; and unemployment insurance. An increasing number of organizations also are making use of "cafeteria benefits," in which each worker can pick and choose the benefits he or she wants within a dollar limit established by the firm.[33] This allows people to tailor the benefit package to meet their particular needs.

Causal Link?

Is there a link between people's performance and their rewards?[34] Research by Towers Perrin, the consulting firm, reveals that high-performance companies more closely link pay to performance than do their less effective counterparts. For example, the firm has found that 79 percent of the high-performing companies they studied use merit increases for hourly nonunion workers, as compared to 58 percent for other firms.[35] Thus, the first step is to institute the proper rewards system. In recent years, many companies have shown a willingness to set up a compensation plan that promotes this link between pay and performance, and the latest research reveals that more and more firms are doing so. In fact, currently a revolution is taking place in employee rewards: pay-for-performance plans. At Chicago-based Ameritech, for example, all employees are compensated with a variable pay approach. Some part of their pay is tied to performance and, if the employees do not meet the established level of performance, they will not receive their variable pay percentage. In some cases, variable pay accounts for 35 percent of an individual's

Incentive payment plans *tie rewards directly to output.*

TABLE 10.1

A Comparison of Individual and Group and Organization-wide Incentives

Individual Incentive Plans	Group and Organization-wide Incentives
Typical Characteristics of the Plan	
Rewards are based directly on what the individual produces.	Rewards are based on group performance.
Performance is determined by the individual worker.	A committee typically determines performance standards.
Rewards are provided every payday.	Performance is only indirectly controlled by employees.
Individuality and competitive spirit are encouraged.	Rewards are paid on a monthly, quarterly, semiannual, or annual basis.
The incentive relies heavily on monetary rewards.	Teamwork and unity are encouraged.
Commonly Cited Advantages	
There is a strong sense of individualism.	The incentive motivates a large number of employees.
Rewards are in direct proportion to output.	The approach can be used for a wide variety of tasks.
	All employees in the organization can be included.
	Group cooperation is encouraged.
Commonly Cited Disadvantages	
Seldom are all the employees included in the plan.	Employees are not all rewarded according to their own productivity.
This incentive tends to be restricted to mass-produced and relatively simple operations.	Individual initiative and effort often are discouraged.
The incentive cannot be easily adapted to high-quality jobs.	
Employee grievances are a continual headache.	

total compensation, so there is strong motivation to perform.[36] At Taco Bell, managers are given moderate salaries and the rest of their income is based on the unit's performance; effective store managers can earn as much as 10 percent to 20 percent of their base pay in performance-related bonuses.[37]

Many of these pay-for-performance plans make use of what are called *nontraditional rewards,* such as profit sharing, bonuses, individual incentives, gain-sharing programs that divide cost reductions among all members of the organization, small-group incentives, payment for knowledge, the granting of earned time off in lieu of a monetary reward, stock options and employee stock purchase plans (ESPP).

Business Week reported that stock options and employee stock purchase plans (ESPP) are often misunderstood and underutilized as employee benefits. They "are available at more than 4,000 companies, including Cisco Systems, Southwest Airlines, and Starbucks." These benefits allow employees to buy shares of company stock at a discount of 10 to 15 percent. The National Center for Employee Ownership surveyed 80 companies and found that "only 55% of the companies' employees participate in their plan." Often employers fail to educate employees about them.[38]

Another interesting trend is taking place among service companies. Organization structures are being flattened, positions are being removed, and everyone is being given a greater opportunity to share in the reward system. For example, at the Hard Rock Cafe, as many as three times annually the company president will walk into a unit and ask the managers to nominate and the staff to vote for the best employee of the quarter. The winner is given an all-expense-paid, one-week trip to Hawaii. In most service-driven organizations, however, incentives are not spontaneous. They are a result of a plan that has been communicated to the personnel. For example, at the Peasant Restaurants, headquartered in Atlanta, the General Manager of the Year award winner receives a trip for two to Europe. To win the incentive, the individual must meet the demands of the company's five-part formula:

1. **Have the five highest scores overall on regional inspections.**
2. **Have the highest scores on dining experience as rated by the corporate staff.**
3. **Have a superior training program.**
4. **Have an accurate and timely administrative record.**
5. **Postpositive sales growth.**

Meanwhile, at Chi Chi's of Louisville, Kentucky, the company annually awards twenty-two trips to field managers who increase liquor sales during Cinco de Mayo festivities. In addition, there are five $1,000 employee of the year awards, $100 employee of the quarter awards, and $25 employee of the month awards. At Wendy's, the company gives quarterly cash bonuses to managers who meet a variety of performance goals related to sales, profits, and cost control. In addition, there are six levels at which agents can redeem points for prizes ranging from a Disney vacation to a gift.[39]

Offering the right rewards and benefits is crucial to hiring, motivating, and retaining employees. However, over time employees' needs change and they want different types of rewards and benefits. For example, Lee Hecht Harrison conducted a survey in 2003 of 1,680 managers and employees. He compared the results to a similar study completed in 1999. The results show:[40]

Reward/Benefit	2003	1999
Ongoing training opportunities	76% want it	41% wanted it
Flex time	73%	57%
Cell phones/laptops	71%	52%
Outplacement	69%	53%
Tuition reimbursement	53%	40%
Use of company car	28%	53%
Health club membership	45%	58%
Child care	19%	32%
Concierge services	16%	31%

In closing our discussion, it is important to remember that an organization can link rewards and performance only when four conditions are present:

1. **Individual performance can be measured objectively.**
2. **There is a low degree of interdependence among the individuals in the system.**
3. **It is possible to develop measures for all the important aspects of the jobs.**
4. **Effort and performance are closely related over a relatively short period.**

In establishing this link, many managers find it helpful to focus on actions that reward people for work well done. Some of the specific steps in this process are as follows:

1. *Reward solid solutions instead of quick fixes.* Specifically identify what people are to do and then evaluating their performance over the long term rather than every three to six months.
2. *Reward risk taking.* Encourage people to take well thought out, calculated risks and be willing to encourage those who fail and those who succeed.
3. *Reward applied creativity.* Give people bonuses and other forms of monetary payment when their creative ideas result in profits for the organization.
4. *Reward decisive action.* Encourage people to set deadlines and make decisions within this period rather than continually procrastinating and doing more thinking and research, thus falling victim to "paralysis by analysis."
5. *Reward people for working smarter rather than merely harder.* Give people the information and tools they need to get the job done right, correct poor work habits, and let them go home when they have attained their goals rather than making them sit around and wait until closing time.
6. *Reward simplification.* Encouraging people to use direct communications, such as calling on the phone rather than writing a memo, to avoid creating bureaucratic red tape and to simplify procedures, do this.

in action

ETHICS AND SOCIAL RESPONSIBILITY IN ACTION

Maintaining a Diverse Workforce

Recent research reports that more and more women are now in the management ranks. Additionally, a growing number of women are breaking through the glass ceiling and making it into the executive suite. Examples include Cristina Morgan, codirector of investment banking at Hambrecht & Quist; Carol Bartz, chief executive officer of Autodesk; and Linda Sanford, general manager of the S/390 Division of IBM. However, there is still a long way to go, given that women constitute less than 1 percent of the highest-paid officers and directors of large industrial and service companies. This is true for a number of reasons, including the fact that many women feel that if they are going to get ahead, they must switch jobs. What can organizations do to stem this exodus? In addition to financial rewards, companies are finding the following are proving to be extremely effective tools:

1. Fast-track promotions.
2. Mentoring programs that link senior professional women with new female managers entering the company.
3. Maternity leave with pay and provision for leaves to attend sick children.
4. Organizational training designed to deter bias against women.
5. Reduced pressure to accept relocation as a prerequisite for career advancement.
6. Encouragement of women's support networks within the organization.
7. Career counseling for women who are targeted as up-and-coming managers.
8. Assistance for employee spouses in conducting a job search in the event of relocation.
9. Leave policy for care of older dependents.
10. Provision of referral services for child care.

Sources: Valerie L. Williams and Stephen E. Grimaldi, "A Quick Breakdown of Strategic Pay," Workforce, December 1999, pp. 72–79; Rana Dogar, "The 10 Most Important Women in Tech," Working Woman, September 1997, pp. 54–55; Benson Rosen, Mabel Miguel, and Ellen Peirce, "Stemming the Exodus of Women Managers," Human Resource Management, Winter 1991, pp. 475–491; and Diane Harris, "Does Your Pay Measure Up?" Working Woman, January 1994, pp. 26–32.

7. *Reward quietly effective people.* Do not let the squeaky wheel get all the attention and rewards but rather seek out and reward the quiet heroes who are responsible for getting things done.

8. *Reward quality.* See that people are well trained, encourage them to improve their techniques and methods, and give recognition and monetary rewards to those who produce the highest-quality output.

9. *Reward loyalty.* Providing job security, promoting from within, keeping communication lines open, offering fair pay and benefits, and providing people continuous education, training, and development are ways to reward loyalty.

In recent years, organizations have been finding it particularly challenging to develop reward systems that help them to attract and retain women. The Ethics and Social Responsibility in Action box spells out some of these problems and the solutions firms are using to solve them. At the same time, firms are instituting penalties for executives who leave the company to go elsewhere. At General Motors, for example, a special committee now determines how and when bonuses are awarded to top managers, and the committee can hold back a large percentage of this bonus until the person retires. If the individual leaves the firm, of course, the retirement portion of the bonus is forfeited.

Discipline

LEARNING OBJECTIVE

8 *List the types of discipline used when performance is inadequate*

Sometimes, instead of giving rewards to employees, the leader must discipline some of them. Often this is known as a *negative reward.* The use of this approach will depend on the employee and the situation. For example, as seen in Table 10.2, problem employees can be divided into four categories. In dealing with people in each category, the manager must consider the primary and secondary goals to pursue. For purposes of human relations, the manager must integrate this information with an understanding of both the types of discipline and the manner in which discipline should be administered.

TABLE 10.2	*Types of Problem Employees*	
Type	**Primary Goal**	**Secondary Goal**
Type I does not intentionally violate the rules but does so unintentionally and infrequently.	To correct the behavior, to inform and train.	To maintain the individual's motivation.
Type II will violate the rules when he or she considers some treatment unfair and does so only occasionally.	To correct the behavior and to avoid discipline problems with others.	To identify and deal with why the person feels unfairly treated, so that future problems can be avoided.
Type III will violate the rules whenever he or she can get away with it, generally creates problems, and often is disciplined.	To avoid discipline problems with others.	To document the use of discipline (toward eventual termination).
Type IV is not so much a problem employee as an employee with a problem.	To get help for the individual and to provide a reason to use that help.	To document whether the individual is unwilling to seek help or the problem recurs.

Source: John Seltzer, "Discipline with a Clear Sense of Purpose," Management Solutions, February 1987, p. 34.

Types of Discipline

Most formal disciplinary processes employ what is called *progressive discipline,* beginning with an oral warning and, if things do not straighten out, terminating with firing (see figure 10.8). If an employee breaks a rule, especially a minor one, the first step usually is a clear **oral warning,** pointing out that repetition of the act will result in discipline. At this point, the manager hopes that the worker will refrain from breaking the rule in the future. If the employee breaks the rule again or if the first offense was a major one, some firms require **written warnings.** These become part of the employee's records and can be cited as evidence if it is decided to terminate the individual's employment in the future.

A **disciplinary layoff** is the next most severe form of discipline. In this case, the employee is required not to come to work for a specified period and to forfeit pay for that period. A lay-off varies in length from one day to two weeks. Some organizations, however, do not use disciplinary layoffs because of their inability to find a replacement for a few days or weeks. Instead, they simply fire the employee.

Discharge is the ultimate penalty. In recent years, this approach has been used less and less, principally because the penalty often is regarded as too harsh. The effective leader strives to avoid this situation by preventing rule violations. When such violations do occur, the leader must be consistent and impersonal in employing discipline. In discharging someone, Suters recommends the following six guidelines:

1. **Be firm and unemotional and present the decision as irrevocable.**
2. **Give straight, honest reasons for the dismissal.**
3. **Do not be drawn into an argument or counterproductive discussion over the reasons for the termination.**
4. **Ease the blow by pointing out that the action is a mutual disappointment.**
5. **Do not terminate anyone's employment when you are upset.**
6. **Do not blame the decision on anyone else.**[41]

The "Red-Hot-Stove Rule"

One of the most effective methods of employing discipline is the **red-hot-stove rule.** This rule draws an analogy between touching a red-hot stove and receiving discipline. When someone

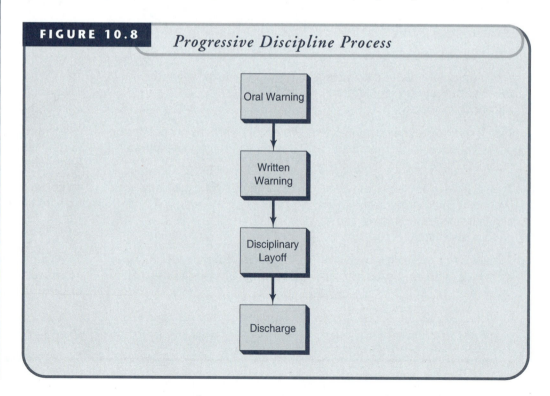

FIGURE 10.8 *Progressive Discipline Process*

Oral Warning

↓

Written Warning

↓

Disciplinary Layoff

↓

Discharge

An **oral warning** *involves orally pointing out an infraction of a rule.*

A **written warning** *is a warning that is placed in an employee's personnel file.*

A **disciplinary layoff** *involves sending a person home without pay for a predetermined time.*

Discharge *is the separation of the individual from the organization.*

The **red-hot-stove rule** *applies discipline immediately, consistently, and impersonally.*

touches a red-hot stove, the burn is *immediate*. There was *advance warning* in the form of heat emanating from the stove, which should have alerted the person to the danger. Anyone who touches the stove is burned, and this *consistency* holds for everyone else who touches it. The burn is *impersonal* in that everyone touching the stove is burned, regardless of who they are. These four characteristics can be applied to discipline.

DISCIPLINE SHOULD BE IMMEDIATE

As soon as the manager knows that a worker has broken a rule, discipline should follow. If the manager waits, the worker may not associate the disciplinary action with the violation of the rule, and bitter feelings are likely to result.

By immediate discipline we do not mean hurried action. The facts of the case should be clear, and only if there is an obvious infraction of the rules should discipline be given. In many organizations, a worker is suspended until the investigation is complete. If the worker is found innocent, he or she is reinstated and given back pay for the suspension period. Conversely, if the worker is found guilty of the offense, the prescribed discipline is carried out.

THERE SHOULD BE ADVANCE WARNING

The organization should make its rules clear, and the employees should know what the penalties are for breaking them. One of the most common ways of doing this is to familiarize workers with the rules during the induction period. Any future rule changes should then be communicated by the immediate superior or, if workers are unionized, should be included in the union contract.

Management must follow two important guidelines in giving advance warning. *Never have too many rules.* If people are given 5 rules to follow, they will generally adhere to them. However, if they are asked to abide by 105 rules, they will generally ignore them. The degree of importance tends to decline as the number of rules increases. *Clearly state and uniformly apply the penalties for infractions.* If management does otherwise, the workers will protest disciplinary procedures. For example, if Paul, a new worker, sees people walking around the construction site without hard hats, he will feel discriminated against if the supervisor disciplines him for not wearing his hat. In addition, when such cases go to arbitration, it is likely that the company will lose because disciplinary action has not been taken for previous offenses. "Why," the arbitrator will reason, "should the firm suddenly decide to start enforcing the rule now?"

DISCIPLINE SHOULD BE CONSISTENT

If two people commit the same offense, each should be given the same discipline. The biggest problem for the manager is that of identifying everyone who breaks the rules. If the manager can catch only 20 percent of the workers who violate a particular rule, those who are caught often are angry because discipline seems to be more a matter of chance than anything else.

DISCIPLINE SHOULD BE IMPERSONAL

The manager should make it clear to the workers that they are all on the same team but that this does not mean the workers can violate the rules with impunity. Some workers are more productive than others. Some are informal group leaders and others are followers. Obviously, the manager would want to cultivate the friendship of the more productive or leading workers. However, this cannot be done at the expense of either the other workers or the organization.

On the other hand, the manager should not be excessively harsh when disciplining a worker. After ensuring that the worker has indeed broken the rule, the effective manager tries to learn why and then to work with the individual to prevent another violation.

If the manager handles the situation properly, it often is possible to prevent feelings from being hurt. To a large degree, the manager's success in handling the disciplinary matter will be determined by his or her negotiating ability. In fact, appraising, rewarding, and disciplining employees requires effective skills. Before proceeding, take the accompanying Time Out quiz to rate your effectiveness in reward-discipline situations, as measured by your negotiating ability.

HOW GREAT IS YOUR NEGOTIATING ABILITY?

Performance appraisal, the allocation of rewards, and the effective use of discipline require a manager to be, among other things, a skilled negotiator. The individual must be able to evaluate performance diplomatically and effectively *and withstand the pressures that come about when subordinates complain that they are being treated unfairly. How great is your negotiating ability? Decide whether each of the following 16 statements is basically true or basically false in describing you.*

	Basically True	Basically False
1. I really like to be liked.	_____	_____
2. I am not a very good listener, but I am an excellent talker.	_____	_____
3. I try not to do formal preparation for any performance appraisal because it detracts from my spontaneity and creativity; I prefer to play things by ear.	_____	_____
4. I am not really much of a compromiser; I know what I want and I fight to get it all.	_____	_____
5. Under pressure, I can really handle myself well.	_____	_____
6. People who know me well find me to be both tactful and diplomatic.	_____	_____
7. I find that most things in life are negotiable.	_____	_____
8. No matter what salary increase is offered to me, I try to get more.	_____	_____
9. I take what people say at face value.	_____	_____
10. Whenever possible, I try to avoid conflict and confrontation.	_____	_____
11. I do not care how the other side feels about the results of my negotiation efforts; that is their problem, not mine.	_____	_____
12. I do not like to haggle with people over salaries; I pay what is asked or walk away from the negotiation.	_____	_____
13. A person's facial expressions often tell me more about what is being said than do the words.	_____	_____
14. I am not particularly adept at expressing my point of view.	_____	_____
15. In most cases, I am not willing to compromise on issues.	_____	_____
16. I find it easy to smile even when engaged in a serious discipline situation.	_____	_____

The interpretation of your self-assessment can be found at the end of the chapter.

Dismissal and the Law

Over the last few years, a new dismissal-related problem has arisen. Employees who have been discharged by their firms now are suing their former employers, and many have been winning large settlements. One reason is because the employees can prove discrimination. In the most recently reported year, 29,910 lawsuits were filed with the Equal Employment Opportunity Commission on the basis of race. In addition, 25,536 individual filings charged gender discrimination, and another 19,921 lawsuits claimed discrimination based on age.[42]

At the heart of the matter are the issues of employment at will, which means that the organization has a right to dismiss an employee at any time, regardless of cause, and the right of employees to expect fair and equitable treatment from the employer. Sometimes these two issues are in conflict. A good example is when a loyal long-time employee is fired for a minor rule infraction or is summarily dismissed even though he or she has been receiving very good performance evaluations. Do employees have the right to continued employment, or is this provided at the discretion of the employer?[43]

Most states currently give employees the right to sue for "wrongful discharge." This means that if an employee believes that he or she has been fired without just cause, he or she can bring a lawsuit. At the present time, twenty-five thousand wrongful discharge lawsuits are pending in the United States, as compared with only two hundred lawsuits ten years ago. In an effort to deal with this emerging social phenomenon, Montana has passed a law that requires employers to submit these cases to arbitration and limits to four years' back wages the damages that can be awarded. The law also prohibits firing anyone who has completed a probationary period, unless there is just cause for such action.

Many firms now are developing procedures for handling these situations. One is to institute a lawsuit of their own, asking the court to throw out the case.[44] However, the most popular is an arbitration procedure that relies on neutral outside arbitrators to listen to the facts and then make a ruling. The Northrop Corporation has used this procedure for decades. BankAmerica, NBC, Aetna Life Insurance and, most recently, Chrysler Corporation have followed suit. Coors has taken this idea a step further and developed a peer-review appeals process for handling appeals of grievance decisions. All appeals are referred to a small group of workers and managers who are chosen by an employee-relations manager. The group reviews a grievance appeal and decides what to do. Coors's appeal groups have reversed 12 percent of the original disciplinary decisions, modified 33 percent of them, and upheld the remaining 55 percent.[45] The company and the employees are both pleased with the program because they believe that it provides a balanced, equitable approach to resolving grievances.

Some employers are beginning to fight back by having their employees sign statements that indicate they can be dismissed at the discretion of the company. However, except in the case of new employees who sign these forms at the beginning of their employment, the courts are setting them aside and allowing wrongful-discharge suits, which, in many cases, are proving to be costly to employers. Consequently, a continued trend toward impartial arbitration is likely in handling these matters.

summary

(1) **LEARNING OBJECTIVE**
Identify and describe the stages in the process for developing personnel

In this chapter, we addressed the issues of personnel development, performance appraisal, and performance rewards. Personnel development should begin with an effective recruiting, screening and selecting, and orientation program. Another important phase of personnel development is training. The basic types of training are apprentice, vestibule, on-the-job, off-the-job, and virtual.

Qualified candidates must be made aware of available positions. This process is called *recruiting*. Recruiters can use internal sources—postings on bulletin boards, e-mail, newsletters, and meetings—or external sources, such as advertisements in the classified section of newspapers, cold calls, or recruiters. *Screening* is the process of eliminating applicants who are unlikely to be successful on the job, whereas *selecting* is the process of determining which applicants will be offered jobs. Several strategies are used in this process. (1) By checking the applicant's education, previous employment, credit history, driving record, and criminal record the possibility of hiring the wrong person can be reduced. (2) The interview gives the interviewers a chance to judge a wide range of the candidate's abilities. Two types of *interviews* are used. One is the *structured interview* where all applicants are asked the same questions and another is the *unstructured interview* where candidates are placed in decision-making scenarios. This allows the interviewer to determine how the applicant might behave in a similar situation. (3) Screening tests are another common approach to selecting the right applicant. One type of test is the demonstration test, which identifies proficiency in certain skills. Another test is the professional test used to screen candidates of managerial positions. Regardless of the type of screening and selection device used it must not invade privacy issues.

Orientation is the process of introducing new employees to the company, their work group and their tasks. Some items covered are the company history, policies, procedures, structure, and benefits.

Training focuses on teaching new knowledge, skills, or improving skills. Apprentice training focuses on teaching employees a new job with an opportunity to apply the procedures. The training is done both on and off the job. Vestibule training is conducted in a similar setting away from the employee will actually work. The immediate supervisor and fellow workers provide on-the-job training, whereas off-the-job training is done away from the workplace, usually in workshops, seminars, or class courses. Virtual training, more commonly called e-learning, uses a computer and a well-designed learning program.

Several trends in the training include an increase in training budgets; an increase in diversity training; an increase in the creation of in-house programs, namely, e-learning programs, and a combination of in-house and university-linked training.

Appraising performance is the process of monitoring, comparing, and correcting weaknesses. Employees with positive results are rewarded, whereas employees who fail to improve, even with training, are generally fired.

---

② LEARNING OBJECTIVE
Discuss the performance appraisal cycle

We next considered the four-step process of performance appraisal: (1) Performance standards are established, (2) individual performance is determined, (3) a comparison of individual performance and performance standards is made, and (4) overall performance is evaluated. When this fourth step is completed, the cycle begins again.

---

③ LEARNING OBJECTIVE
Explain how graphic rating scales, paired comparison, management by objectives, and 360-degree evaluations can be used in appraising performance

Many kinds of appraisal tools can be used to evaluate employee performance. The simplest is the *graphic rating scale*, in which all the factors (and degrees of each factor) on which the employee is to be evaluated are listed. The manager's job then is to check the appropriate degree of every factor and to total the value associated with each to arrive at an overall score for the individual.

The *paired comparison method* of evaluation requires the manager to compare each employee in the group with every other. Often there are five to ten factors on which all are compared. On the basis of the comparisons on all factors, the manager is able to rank the workers from the best to the poorest.

Management by objectives (MBO) can be used at all levels of the employment hierarchy. The MBO process consists of six steps: (1) identifying the goals of the unit or department, (2) describing the duties and responsibilities of the personnel, (3) meeting with the subordinate and mutually setting goals for this individual, (4) employing a goal-setting worksheet to help the subordinate work toward the objective, (5) periodically reviewing the goals and revising them as necessary, and (6) evaluating the results and starting the cycle anew.

The *360-degree evaluation review* gathers input from an individual's superior, subordinates, peers, work group, and others with whom the individual comes into frequent contact. The purposes of the evaluation are to determine the person's performance and to serve as a basis for creating a developmental action plan for improvement. This evaluation and the results of the action plan then serve as the basis for the next 360-degree review.

---

④ LEARNING OBJECTIVE
Describe four major problems associated with performance appraisal

In every performance appraisal, the manager must be aware of problems. The most common problems are attributable to (1) lack of clarity of the form itself, (2) the halo effect, (3) central tendency, and (4) leniency. On the rating form, the levels on which employees are rated should be clearly defined. When employees are given the same rating on all factors regardless of performance, the halo effect occurs. Central tendency occurs when all ratings are marked average, and when all ratings are marked high, a leniency problem occurs.

⑤ LEARNING OBJECTIVE
Explain ways of dealing with appraisal problems

In noting the ways of dealing with appraisal problems, we stressed the need for validity and reliability in performance appraisal instruments. A testing instrument that measures what we want it to has *validity* and when the instrument repeatedly measures the same factor, it has *reliability*. Other ways of dealing with appraisal problems include: involving employees in the design, development, and administration of the appraisal process; investing time and effort in training managers to use the system, creating an environment in which performance information is viewed as a resource in developing employees; making performance appraisals the responsibility of the ratee; and reducing reliance on just one reviewer by building a system.

⑥ LEARNING OBJECTIVE
Examine the link between performance and rewards

The last part of the chapter was devoted to the subject of performance rewards. After reviewing common types of extrinsic and intrinsic rewards, we discussed the link that the organization establishes between performance and rewards. Some organizations attempt to do this through the use of incentive payment plans; others make strong use of performance appraisal. In most cases, the reward-performance link is not very great, and the manager must rely most heavily on providing an environment in which workers can attain psychological rewards. Most people, however, want extrinsic rewards.

⑦ LEARNING OBJECTIVE
Identify ways for rewarding performance

The most common ways of rewarding performance are: wages or salary, incentive programs, and benefit programs. *Wages* are fixed rates of pay and *salary* is an annual amount of pay. Incentive payment plans include receiving a higher rate for production beyond a stated amount, hiring bonuses, retention bonuses, and group bonuses. *Benefit programs* come in many versions. They usually include life, health, and accident insurance; sick leave; workers' compensation; pension plans; and unemployment insurance. Research shows that high-performance companies more closely link pay to performance than do their less effective counterparts. It is important to implement the proper rewards system. *Pay-for-performance plans* make use of nontraditional rewards such as profit sharing, bonuses, individual incentives, and gain-sharing program. The needs and wants of employees change over time. Therefore, it is important to keep abreast of current changes in employees needs and be ready to change the system or it will no longer provide the needed motivation to keep up performance and retain employees.

⑧ LEARNING OBJECTIVE
List the types of discipline used when performance is inadequate

The manager must also exercise discipline, sometimes labeled a *negative reward*. Most formal disciplinary processes employ *progressive discipline*, beginning with an *oral warning* and moving to a *written warning*, a *disciplinary layoff* and, ultimately, *discharge*. In carrying out discipline, many managers use the *red-hot-stove rule*. Effective discipline has four characteristics: (1) It should be immediate, and (2) there should be advanced warning of discipline penalties. If the individual still violates the rule, the discipline should be (3) consistent and (4) impersonal. If dismissal is required, just cause should be provable, in case the dismissed person files a discrimination suit.

KEY TERMS IN THE CHAPTER

Screening

Selecting

Orientation

Performance appraisal cycle

Graphic rating scales

Paired comparison method

Management by objectives

Halo effect

Central tendency

Leniency

Validity

Reliability

Extrinsic rewards

Intrinsic rewards

Incentive payment plans

Oral warning

Written warning

Disciplinary layoff

Discharge

Red-hot-stove rule

REVIEW AND STUDY QUESTIONS

1. What are the stages of the overall development process? Identify and define them.

2. Why is recruiting an important part of the development process?

3. What are the differences between internal recruiting and external recruiting?

4. Why is a well-designed screening and selection program critical to organizational effectiveness?

5. How is a structured interview different from an unstructured interview?

6. What are some examples of the most common screening tests?

7. Of what value is an orientation program? What are some of the benefits it offers?

8. There are five basic types of training. Identify and describe each type.

9. What are three developments/trends in training in the past several years?

10. How does the performance appraisal cycle work? Be sure to discuss all four steps.

11. How does the graphic rating scale help the manager to appraise subordinates?

12. How does the paired comparison method work?

13. Why is management by objectives so popular? How does MBO work?

14. How does a 360-degree evaluation work?

15. What are four major performance appraisal problems?

16. What is meant by *validity? Reliability?* Which is more difficult to attain? Why?

17. When it comes to rewarding performance, which is more important: extrinsic rewards or intrinsic rewards? Why?

18. How can performance and rewards be linked? Identify five human relations steps.

19. What are the steps in the progressive discipline process? Identify and define each.

20. If an individual must be discharged, what guidelines should the manager follow? Discuss four.

21. According to the red-hot-stove rule of discipline, what are the four characteristics of appropriate discipline? Explain each.

22. Can an employer dismiss an employee regardless of cause? Why or why not?

Can Proper Training Prevent Lawsuits?

Every year thousands of employees file discrimination lawsuits against companies. In 2002, for example, 84,442 individual charges were filed. The number of individual charges was up from 80,840 in 2001 and up from 72,302 ten years ago. Why is this so? In this chapter you learned about training and its importance in developing employees. And one would think that employers would provide the type of training needed and would take corrective action to prevent such discrimination. Research several recent cases posted on the Web site: **http://www.eeoc.gov**

1. Click on "News/Press Releases" and read several different types of cases.

2. Analyze each case and determine what you believe is the cause for the problem(s).

3. Ask yourself: With proper training, could this case have been avoided?

4. Assume you are responsible for redesigning the training program at the firm where you work. How would you train employees about discrimination issues? What would you include in the training program? Identify the key components that focus on discrimination training that you would include in the newly designed training program. Tell why you believe each component is important.

How Well Do You Measure Up?

Your level of technical and personal skills will determine your success in getting hired for a job and retaining the job. In fact, skills drive the whole development process starting with the recruitment stage through the development, appraising, and rewarding stages. Do you know your strengths and weaknesses? How well do your skills measure up? Take time to check your skills using some of the free tests posted on the Internet. Visit Web site: **http://www.brainbench.com** and complete the following exercise.

1. Review the free skills tests in the area of management.

2. Select a free test and take it.

3. Check your score and learn how well you measure up against your peers.

4. See where you need to improve.

5. Write an assessment of what you learned about your management skills and what you need to do to improve.

How Great Is Your Negotiating Ability?

Compare your answers to the self-assessment quiz to the answers that follow. For each answer that is identical to the scoring key presented here, give yourself one point.

1. Basically false	7. Basically true	13. Basically true
2. Basically false	8. Basically true	14. Basically false
3. Basically false	9. Basically false	15. Basically false
4. Basically false	10. Basically false	16. Basically true
5. Basically true	11. Basically false	
6. Basically true	12. Basically false	

Your total score, assuming your self-evaluation is correct, provides some insights regarding your ability to negotiate well. The following is a general breakdown regarding your negotiation effectiveness:

14–16 Excellent. You are a true negotiator.

11–13 Good. You have real negotiating potential.

 8–10 Average. You do not see yourself as much of a negotiator.

 0–7 Below average. You do not see yourself as a negotiator.

How can you improve your negotiating ability? The best way is by examining your incorrect responses and trying to change your behavior appropriately.

case: ACADEMIC EVALUATION

A large urban university in the Midwest offers three classes of business law at 7:30 A.M. on Mondays, Wednesdays, and Fridays. All three are taught by practicing attorneys who meet the class and then go downtown to their law offices. The three lawyers all teach the same basic class, but they have totally different grading policies. One of them is a very difficult grader. Most of his students receive C's. Over the last four semesters, the breakdown of his grades has been A's, 10 percent; B's, 15 percent; C's, 50 percent; D's, 15 percent; and F's, 10 percent. Regardless of how well the students perform in this class, the professor grades them on a bell-shaped curve. The highest 10 percent of the class will receive an A, whereas the lowest 10 percent will get an F. Of course, the top 10 percent seldom have a 90 average, and the lowest 10 percent always have an average well below 50. Therefore, the professor merely decides how much of a curve to put on the grades in fitting them into his predetermined bell-shaped grading format.

The second lawyer is the most lenient of the three. Most of the students in her class receive either A's or B's. The breakdown on grades over the last four semesters in this class has been A's, 33 percent; B's, 50 percent; and C's, 17 percent. The student body is well aware of this professor's grading practices, and her classes are always filled to capacity during the first day of registration. This woman always divides her final grades into three groups. Those in the top third are given A's regardless of their final score, the lowest one-sixth all get C's, and everyone else is given a B.

The third lawyer has grading policies similar to the first. Over the last four semesters, his grade breakdown has been A's, 10 percent; B's, 20 percent; C's, 50 percent; D's, 15 percent; and F's, 5 percent. However, he has a soft spot for people who are working their way through college. The students are aware of this and, as a result, many of them show up in work clothes so the professor will realize that they hold jobs in the city. Some of them make it a point to walk out to the parking lot with the professor, while discussing their jobs with him. Realizing that some of them will attempt to pull the wool over his eyes, the professor always asks the dean's office to give him a list of those students who are working full-time (this information must be turned into the dean's office) and thus sidesteps such maneuvers.

Some students objected to the grading policies of the first and third professors (none had anything but praise for the second one) and asked the dean to insist that the professors change their rigid approach to performance evaluation. However, the dean declined to get involved and suggested that the matter be turned over to a university committee. After visiting with the committee and learning that committee members feel that any attempt to interfere with the professors would be viewed as an infringement of academic freedom, the students decided to drop their action and learn to live with the situation.

QUESTIONS

1. In terms of performance appraisal errors, what error(s) is (are) the first lawyer making? What about the second lawyer? The third lawyer? Explain.

2. Is the grade evaluation of each lawyer valid? Is it reliable? Support your reasoning.

3. Are the lawyers properly rewarding the students for their performance? What suggestions would you make to each lawyer? Explain.

4. How closely is performance linked to rewards (grades)? Discuss.

YOU BE THE CONSULTANT

Clock-in Time

Fred Winslow is a shop steward in a New York City manufacturing firm. He is well liked by the management and the workers. The management feels that Fred is particularly helpful in working out union-management grievances before they reach arbitration. Several times, Fred has served as an intermediary and has always been able to establish harmony between the disagreeing factions.

Last month, for example, one of the unionized employees was charged with stealing some supplies. The supervisor laid the man off immediately and recommended that he be fired. Fred, as the shop steward, came to the man's defense and said that the punishment was too great for "accidentally" walking off the job with $10 worth of supplies. After talking to the man and getting his side of the story, Fred approached the supervisor and suggested a compromise. The worker would admit that he accidentally took some supplies from the premises and would submit to punishment of five days off without pay. The supervisor agreed that the compromise was fair, and everyone was pleased.

In the last two weeks, however, the supervisor, who also happens to be Fred's boss, has encountered a problem. A company rule states that anyone who comes in late must be docked an hour's pay for any tardiness of less than sixty minutes, two hours' pay if the lateness extends into the second hour, and so on. In addition, a worker who is late twice in one week is laid off for one week. If a worker is late three times in a four-week period, the penalty is a layoff of two weeks. Finally, if the worker is late four times in any four-week period, he is dismissed.

Two weeks ago, Fred was late thirty minutes one day and was docked an hour's pay. He said that the train had been delayed. Earlier this week, Fred was again late by thirty minutes and was docked an hour's pay. The supervisor is worried, however, because Fred was late again today. He came in at 8:15 A.M. and immediately went to his workstation. The supervisor noticed this, because he had been waiting since 7:30 A.M. to talk to Fred. At 7:55 A.M., when he had gone to check for Fred's time card, it had not yet been punched.

When the supervisor finally saw Fred enter the work area, he immediately went over to talk to him. The supervisor said nothing about Fred's tardiness, although Fred said he was sorry he was late getting to his workstation but that he had been talking to one of the men in another part of the plant about a union matter.

What has the supervisor concerned is this: Fred must clock in by 8:00 A.M., regardless of union activities, although he then is allowed to go to other parts of the plant on union business. If he is late, the supervisor feels, Fred should be penalized, regardless of his position in the union and his value to management in helping solve union-company problems. The actual proof, of course, is the time card, which should have

Fred's actual arrival time on it. After talking to Fred, the supervisor went over to check the card, which showed a clock-in time of 7:58 A.M. Now the supervisor is unsure of what to do, for he is certain that Fred was not in the building before 8:15.

Your Advice

1. If you were the supervisor, what would you do first?

     ____ a. Call in Fred, let him know you are aware of what is going on, and enforce the rule.

     ____ b. Call in Fred, let him know you are aware of what is going on, and tell him not to do it again.

     ____ c. Call in Fred, tell him the facts as you understand them, and ask him if he has anything to say before you make your decision.

2. If you found Fred to be guilty of tardiness, what specifically would you do?

3. If you were the supervisor's boss and he came and told you he had proof that Fred was late but wanted your advice before doing anything, what would you recommend? Explain.

4. Is there anything the supervisor can do to prevent this type of practice from recurring? Explain.

EXPERIENCING MANAGEMENT BY OBJECTIVES

Purpose

- **To understand how the MBO process works.**
- **To construct an annual goal-setting MBO worksheet.**

Procedure

1. In groups of three to five students, consider the course you currently are taking. Identify a goal you should be pursuing. List three or four objectives for accomplishing the goal, identifying them as quantitatively as possible. Relate what you specifically want to accomplish. Your particular objectives may be somewhat different from those of others on the team, but the desired results should be similar.

2. Write down your goal and objectives on a goal-setting worksheet similar to the one provided in Figure 10.6.

3. Write down the major steps that should be taken in pursuing each objective that you have identified.

4. Write down the way in which you will evaluate progress toward each objective.

5. Discuss your individual worksheet with the other members of the team and, where you see the need for change or improvement, make it. Discuss the value of a goal-setting worksheet in preparing course assignments and studying for exams.

Behavioral Effectiveness

part V

In this part of the book, we examine the two most important areas for ensuring behavioral effectiveness: communication and the management of change.

THE GOALS OF THIS SECTION ARE TO:

- *Explore how modern organizations go about communicating for effectiveness, describe the communication process, discuss the selection of a medium appropriate to the intended communication, and examine some common barriers to effective communication and investigate ways to achieve effective communications.*

- *Study the management of conflict and change, discuss the nature of conflict and ways to manage it, describe the nature of change and how to manage change, examine how both processes work, and discuss the role of participation and communication in the change process.*

When you have finished reading this part of the book, you should have a solid understanding of the communication process and of how modern organizations attempt to manage change. You should also understand the importance of behavioral effectiveness and know how communication and the management of change help to ensure this result.

11

Communicating for Effectiveness

One of the most common causes of organizational inefficiency is poor communication. In this chapter, we study ways that managers can communicate effectively.

AFTER READING THIS CHAPTER, YOU SHOULD BE ABLE TO:

1. Describe the communication process.
2. Discuss how to choose the appropriate communication medium.
3. Explain how perception, inference, language, and status can lead to communication breakdown.
4. Identify eight ways to overcome barriers to communication and achieve effective communication.
5. Outline the four steps in the communication process and describe how they can help improve a manager's communication skills.
6. Describe the importance of using simple, repetitive language and empathy and understanding body language in achieving effective communication.
7. Discuss ten guidelines for developing effective listening habits.
8. Identify four ways for improving writing skills.
9. Explain the four parts of PLAN (purpose, logistics, audience, nonverbal communication) for improving speaking skills.
10. Discuss gender differences in communication style.
11. Describe technology's impact on communication.

Making Communication Pay Off

Many organizations are finding that effective communication is the key to their overall ability to compete. One reason is that the frequency with which changes occur makes it necessary continually to inform personnel about what is going on—and why. Consider the case of Wright Builders, a custom builder based in Temple, Texas. Steve Wright, president and owner of Wright Builders, began his business as a framing contractor in 1976, soon becoming a premier framing source in the Central Texas area.

Innovative ideas, supported by a solid reputation for dependability, directed the company to expand into a diversified profile of custom and commercial building along with versatile remodeling services. Eager to continue offering Central Texans the finest opportunities for new homes, Temple Southwest Development Company was formed in 1994. This project involved the development of an exclusive subdivision of Timber Ridge and the construction of custom executive homes. The success of the project exemplifies the professional standards of Steve and his associates.

The goal of Wright Builders is total customer satisfaction. Steve Wright recently states:

> We believe that the pursuit of excellence in every aspect of our business enables us to meet this goal. This pursuit, which has been a twenty-seven year endeavor, begins with craftsmanship, the exceptional ability to produce a quality product with distinction. Attention to detail is the hallmark of this level of workmanship. The process continues by providing superior service to our customers, attained by striving to meet the individual needs of each client.

Over the years Steve Wright has been the recipient of many awards and recognitions for his excellent work in the building industry. His latest award, Temple Area Builders Association's President's Award of Excellence, was presented in 2002. So why is Wright Builders so successful? You only need to ask his staff. They will readily tell you, "It is organization and communication." Every associate and staff member, his team, feels a part of the building process—from the time a potential client enters the front door of the office until the project is completed. To make this work, Steve and his team meet regularly to gather input from all phases of operations and to keep everyone posted on the progress of the project; in fact, he calls them "brainstorming" sessions. No one in particular handles each meeting; everyone shares in a roundtable fashion. By keeping his team informed, questions from clients, suppliers, vendors, bankers, carpenters, plumbers, electricians, and roofers can be answered quickly and accurately by whomever answers the phone, which builds rapport and results in excellent working relations. Because his team is knowledgeable about each phase of the project, no task in the office is left undone; anyone can jump in and finish uncompleted tasks on any project. Even though each staff member has specific duties, it is the participation of all staff members that enable this process to work effectively and efficiently. Each member has the authority to make decisions when needed. This professionalism along with a positive attitude are true keys to success.

Since the team concept is working at Wright Builders, how is it affecting the firm's organization structure? The structure looks like a bubble of concentric circles interconnecting with communication lines flowing between the circles. Refer to Figure 11.5, on page 356. For example, Steve Wright is in the A circle. His associates and office staff fill the B circles. The clients, vendors, subcontractors, suppliers, lending institutions fill the C circles; whereas city inspectors, state regulators, or other government agents fill the D circles. This structure allows open communication to flow in all directions throughout the entire firm.

"Communication is the most essential key to providing the best customer service available," states Steve, who works hard at establishing a relationship with each client and with all subcontractors. This enables the decision-making process to be as easy as possible. When he interviews clients, he listens to what they want and the effect they want to achieve. Steve follows a printed outline listing an array of questions that guides him through the process. Pictures, illustrations, and samples of products may also be used to clarify points. By spending quality time in the first phase of the project, both the client and Steve's team have an understanding of the project. Estimating and monitoring the cost of the project are critical communication issues. Here is where Wright Builders depends on technology to give an accurate projection of the cost of the project. Jobs are entered into an estimator software program, Builders Software Enterprises. It tracks the project for job costing and variance. Immediately changes can be spotted and communicated to the appropriate party for adjustments. This eliminates overrun cost surprises at the end of the project and happier clients.

Steve can be described as a walking communication machine—constantly meeting face to face with clients, subcontractors, and suppliers on site or keeping in touch by cell phone. Close monitoring, follow up, and communication build a high level of trust between his company and all partners in the project. All partners continually are informed about what is going on, which makes them feel important to the project; therefore, they build a quality product. Communication is what makes Wright Builders successful.

Financial Information Trust (FIT), a small company of approximately 275 people in Des Moines, Iowa, is another good example of how firms are making communication pay off. The company was founded about twenty years ago by a group of savings and loan institutions to provide data-processing services to the group. As downsizing hit the savings and loan industry, FIT was forced to cut back its staff. In the beginning, these layoffs came without warning, and the survivors soon were looking over their shoulders to see who would be next. At this point, management changed its communications approach. Now all functional heads were required to review their expected staff needs for three months into the future and, if someone's employment was going to be terminated, the individual was given ample advance notice so that he or she could begin looking for work elsewhere. However, the identity of the people was not revealed to the rest of the group. Instead, when the next downsizing took place, management announced it and told everyone that those who would be affected by the decision had already been informed. This strategy reduced anxiety. Involuntary terminations dropped, production and morale increased, and customer satisfaction reached new heights. Through a carefully formulated communication strategy, FIT was able to build trust, even though it was going through hard times.

Sources: Jac Fitz-Enz, The 8 Practices of Exceptional Companies *(New York: Amacom, 1997), pp. 98–105; and Peter Lowry and Byron Reimus, "Ready, Aim, Communicate!"* Management Review, *July 1996, pp. 40–43. Personal interview with Steve Wright and his staff on March 3, 2003, Temple, Texas.*

<table>
<tr><td>

LEARNING OBJECTIVE

Describe the communication process

</td></tr>
</table>

LEARNING OBJECTIVE

Describe the communication process

(1) # The Communication Process

Communication is the process of transmitting meanings from sender to receiver. These meanings are conveyed through a medium such as e-mail, a telephone call, a fax, a memorandum, or a conversation. This **communication** process entails five essential elements: (1) the sender, (2) the message being transmitted, (3) the medium used to carry the message, (4) the receiver of the message, and (5) the interpretation given to the message. In conveying meanings from sender to receiver, three functions must be performed.

Communication
is the process of transmitting meanings from sender to receiver.

- First, the message must be encoded, or put into a form that will be understood by the receiver.
- Second, it must be conveyed through the proper medium or channel.
- Third, it must be decoded, or interpreted properly, by the person to whom it was directed. These functions are described in Figure 11.1.

Encoding

Encoding
is translating a message into an intelligible code.

Before a message can be sent from one person to another, it must undergo **encoding,** or be expressed in a code (words, facial expressions, gestures) that is intelligible to the receiver. For

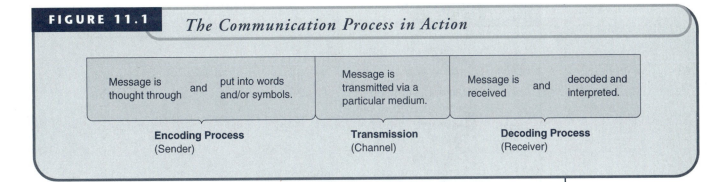

FIGURE 11.1   *The Communication Process in Action*

| Message is thought through | and | put into words and/or symbols. | Message is transmitted via a particular medium. | Message is received | and | decoded and interpreted. |

Encoding Process (Sender)   **Transmission** (Channel)   **Decoding Process** (Receiver)

example, when Americans agree with something that is being said and they want to encode this response, they often will smile and nod their heads. This tells the speaker that the listener understands and is supportive of the idea that is being communicated. In contrast, Japanese often will smile and nod their heads to indicate politeness, but this does not mean that they either understand or agree with the speaker. Unfortunately, because many Americans are unaware of the differences in the encoding process between the two cultures, they erroneously believe that their Japanese listeners are supportive of their ideas. Another example is when Steve Wright, a custom home builder, interviews clients, he must translate technical building terms into words the client understands. Effective encoding requires an understanding of the receiver's level of knowledge.

The encoding process involves two important steps.

1. **The sender thinks through the ideas to be communicated.**
2. **The sender translates these ideas into some code or symbol, which in this case was a combination of facial expression and gesture.**

Medium

In describing the encoding process, we have already noted two common forms of communication: facial expressions and gestures. Other forms include conversation, pictures, diagrams, and charts. For example, when one is advertising a product, one frequently uses pictures to convey the idea, as in newspaper ads and billboards. Diagrams and charts often are used when managers communicate with one another. Large amounts of business data are conveyed in these forms.

In addition, we need to consider nonverbal forms of communication. Body language is one example. People transmit meanings by their facial expressions, eye movements, and how close (or far away) they sit or stand in relation to other people. Even the way they walk tells us something about them.

The physical environment in which people live has an influence on their communication. Dentists' offices have comfortable chairs and pleasant decor in the waiting rooms so that patients will be less nervous. Restaurants offer dim lighting and soft music, which encourage people to talk softly and stay longer. Even the colors of the room can have an effect on people's mood, resulting in a particular communication pattern. Table 11.1 lists the moods commonly associated with certain colors. If the boss is going to communicate important news to a subordinate and has him or her wait in an orange room, the subordinate may surmise that the news is bad (orange tends to create a distressed, disturbed mood), but if the subordinate is waiting in a yellow room, he or she might begin to expect good news (yellow tends to create a cheerful, jovial mood).

Finally, we must consider that the medium also is used in directing the message toward certain people and away from others. It must be decided how the communication be delivered. For example, will it be delivered face-to-face, over a phone call, by a fax message, in an e-mail message, printed in a letter or memo, posted on a bulletin board, sent by instant messaging, or some other medium? This selective process was examined in Chapter 5 in the discussion of informal communication networks and the high degree of selectivity that exists among organizational personnel. Some people are passed information, whereas others are deliberately bypassed.

TABLE 11.1	*The Association of Moods With Colors*	

Mood	Color
Exciting, stimulating	Red
Secure, comfortable	Blue
Distressed, disturbed, upset	Orange
Tender, soothing	Blue
Protective, defending	Red
Despondent, dejected, unhappy, melancholy	Black
Calm, peaceful, serene	Blue
Dignified, stately	Purple
Cheerful, jovial, joyful	Yellow
Defiant, contrary, hostile	Red
Powerful, strong, masterful	Black

Source: Lois B. Wexner, "The Degree to Which Colors (Hues) Are Associated with Mood-Tones," Journal of Applied Psychology, December 1954, pp. 433–434.

Decoding

Decoding *is interpretation of the message by the receiver.*

The last phase of the communication process involves **decoding,** or interpreting of the message by the receiver. In understanding how this decoding process works, we must consider three areas: the sender's meaning, the receiver's interpretation, and the degree of overlap between them. Let us consider an exaggerated example of very little overlap.

Eddie Jones spent two weeks in South America consulting for the local branch office. The branch manager assigned him an office assistant and an office. A few days before his assignment was over, Eddie told the branch manager that he wanted to show his gratitude to his office assistant for a job well done. He planned on getting her a small present on his last day there. The branch manager told Eddie the office assistant would appreciate such a gesture. Following up on his promise, Eddie brought the office assistant a dozen roses.

Imagine his surprise when the office manager came by to tease him later. "When you said you were going to get her a gift, I thought you were going to buy her something for her home. I should have asked you beforehand what you wanted to get. You see, giving flowers in this country is a sign of romantic interest!"

In this example we can see that the office manager sent too little information for Eddie to decode the message accurately. The office manager assumed Eddie knew the customs of gift giving in the country. When senders make assumptions about receivers, problems in communication can occur. Receivers decode from their base of knowledge and experience and may not know enough to ask the proper questions. Even though Eddie decoded the message accurately, the message failed to contain sufficient information for Eddie to act appropriately, which resulted in an embarrassing situation for Eddie and his office assistant.

The hospital administrator told Roy Jones, his associate administrator, that the board of directors would be visiting the hospital the next day and would be looking at the new wing that had just been built. The wing had seven stories, and the top five stories contained patients' rooms. "The beds and other furniture arrived yesterday and we should get them put into the rooms as soon as possible," the administrator told Roy, "so the board members can see what the rooms look like when they're finished." Roy rounded up all the help he could get on short notice and began moving the furniture and arranging the rooms. It took until 1:00 A.M just to get all the furniture up in the rooms but, by the time the board members arrived at 9:00 A.M., everything was ready. The members examined the first two floors of the building, took the elevator to the third floor to look at some of the patients' rooms, and then returned to the main part of the hospital for lunch.

Later, the hospital administrator told Roy, "I didn't realize that you were going to furnish all the rooms. I should have told you that they would only be looking at one of the patients' floors! All of them are the same, so there was really no need for them to go on up any further. Nevertheless, it's better to have done too much work than too little. We would have had to put all the furniture in those rooms later in the month anyway."

In this case, we can see that more-than-adequate information was conveyed. However, the hospital administrator failed to explain to Roy Jones that the board of directors would only inspect one floor of patients' rooms. Roy Jones, the receiver, failed to get clarification of his understanding—decoding—of the message and made an assumption that all the furniture was to be arranged in all the rooms.

Choosing a Medium

LEARNING OBJECTIVE
② *Discuss how to choose the appropriate communication medium*

In communicating effectively, it is important to choose the proper medium, and there is a wide range of choices. The *Wall Street Journal* recently reported that the average U.S. employee sends and receives more than two hundred messages daily.[1] The breakdown was as follows:

Telephone	51
E-mail	36
Voice mail	22
Postal mail	19
Interoffice mail	19
Fax	14
Post-it notes	12
Telephone message slips	9
Pager messages	8
Cell phone	4
Overnight couriers or messengers	4
Express mail	3

Two important considerations are associated with determining which medium to use. One is information richness, and the other is complexity.

The Matter of Information Richness

The best choice of medium is the one that provides the appropriate degree of richness and that helps the parties to the communication deal with the complexity of the situation or problem. **Information richness** has been defined as "the potential information-carrying capacity of data."[2] If the medium carries a great deal of information, it is high in richness; if it conveys very little information, it is low in richness. Hence, alternative media can have varying degrees of information richness.

This richness can be measured by four factors.

1. **Feedback, which can range from immediate to very slow.**
2. **The channel that is used to convey the information and can range from a combination of audio and visual to limited visual.**
3. **The type of communication, such as personal versus impersonal.**
4. **The language source that is used, including body language, natural, or numeric.**

Information richness
is the potential information-carrying capacity of data.

TABLE 11.2

Information Richness for Different Media

Information Richness	Medium	Feedback	Channel	Type of Communication	Language Source
High	Face-to-face	Immediate	Visual, audio	Personal	Body, natural
High–Moderate	Telephone	Rapid	Audio	Personal	Natural
Moderate	Personal written	Slow	Limited visual	Personal	Natural
Moderate–Low	Formal written	Very slow	Limited visual	Impersonal	Natural
Low	Formal numeric	Very slow	Limited visual	Impersonal	Natural

Source: Adapted from R. L. Daft and R. H. Lengel, "Information Richness: A New Approach to Managerial Behavior and Organization Design," in B. M. Staw and L. L. Cummings, eds., Research in Organizational Behavior *(Greenwich, CT: JAI Press, 1984), p. 197.*

Table 11.2 categorizes the information richness of five types of media in terms of these four factors.

The richest form of communication is face-to-face. It provides immediate feedback and is a check on how well the information has been comprehended. In addition, this form permits the communicating parties to observe language cues such as body language and voice tone. Another form that is high in richness is the telephone, both landlines and cell phones, although they are not as rich as face-to-face communication. On the other hand, formal numeric media such as quantitative computer printouts or video displays have low richness. These forms provide slow feedback, limited visual information, and impersonal data.

The Issue of Complexity

In communicating information for the purpose of passing on data or discussing problem situations, managers must match their choice of media with the complexity of the issue. For example, the communication of a decision to downsize some of the company's divisions is a complex situation. Those who are going to be affected by the message will have questions, concerns, and fears that must be addressed. Therefore, the company will have to communicate this situation in a deliberate, detailed way. In contrast, low-complexity situations are routine and predictable and can be handled through the use of rules or standard operating procedures. An example is a communiqué to all salespeople reminding them that their expense reports are due by the fifteenth of the month. The challenge for the manager is to choose the appropriate medium. Daft and Lengel have suggested that there are three zones of communication effectiveness.[3]

1. The *most effective zone* is the one in which the complexity of the problem or situation is matched appropriately with the richness of the medium. For example, when faced with a simple situation, a manager should choose a medium that is low in richness. Conversely, if a problem is very complex, the manager should opt for a medium that is high in richness. If the individual does not correctly match the situation and the medium, the individual will be in one of the other two zones, the overload zone or the oversimplification zone.

2. The *overload zone* is one in which the medium provides more information than is necessary. An example is the use of face-to-face communication to convey a simple, routine matter such as reminding someone to attend a weekly meeting; an e-mail or voicemail could easily accomplish this.

3. The *oversimplification zone* is one in which the medium does not provide the necessary information. For example, posting on the bulletin board a memo that relates

that management has decided to downsize and terminate 10 percent of the work-force is going to cause a great deal of concern and anxiety. The personnel will want to know more about the decision, who will be affected, and how management intends to handle the matter. A more detailed, medium-rich approach is needed.

Research studies have revealed that media usage is significantly different across organizational levels.[4] Senior-level managers tend to spend much more time in face-to-face meetings than do lower-level managers. Given that these executives are far more likely to be dealing with ambiguous and complicated situations, these results are consistent with those noted here regarding the importance of matching the situation and the media richness.

Barriers to Communication

③ LEARNING OBJECTIVE

Explain how perception, inference, language, and status can lead to communication breakdown

All communication flows are subject to barriers that prevent the receiver from getting the sender's meaning. Some of the most common barriers are (1) perception, (2) inference, (3) language, and (4) status.

Perception

As noted in Chapter 3, **perception** is a person's view of reality, and this reality can be influenced by many factors, including age, gender, noise, and lifestyle. For example, recent research reveals that some younger managers feel older employees lack the skills and abilities to keep up with competitive demands and that this influences the way the older employees are managed.[5] Research also shows that many men perceive women as unsuitable for top management positions,[6] although this perception now is beginning to change[7] as evidenced by Carly Fiorina, CEO of Hewlett-Packard; Celia Swanson, executive vice president of membership, marketing, and administration for SAM'S CLUB; Meg Whitman, CEO of eBay; Andrea Jung, CEO of Avon; and Indra Nooyi, CEO of PepsiCo, just to name a few. Another factor that can influence perception is secret salaries. When the amount of money that personnel is being paid remains a secret, many people have the perception that they are being paid less than others who are doing the same work.[8] Conversely, when salary information is made available to everyone, it often results in higher employee satisfaction because the workers realize that they are not being shortchanged and that their perception was incorrect.[9] Another perception-related problem is the common belief that the listener has the same knowledge as the communicator. However, often this is not true, and so the listener is unable to follow the conversation because he or she lacks the necessary information: The result is communication breakdown.[10] Noise can even affect perception. Consumers expect a vacuum cleaner to be loud because they believe that there is a relationship between noise and how well the unit is working. In contrast, people expect a copy machine to purr quietly—a sign of efficiency.[11] Lifestyle is another example. For example, Americans perceive those who work long hours as being hard-working and responsible, whereas many Germans place greater value on leisure, work about twenty percent fewer hours than Americans, and find it difficult to perceive why people in the United States are so committed to work.[12] Clearly, when communicating with others, one's perception can influence the outcome.

Nonetheless, to communicate effectively, people do not need to have *identical* perceptions. It is necessary only that one party transmit sufficient information for the other party to take appropriate action. The major question for the manager is, "What constitutes 'sufficient' information?" Some messages may be well thought out and still may be misunderstood by the receiver. Other messages may be vague, but the receiver may have no trouble understanding them.

These two ideas—clear and vague—can be placed on a communication continuum as in Figure 11.2. The messages on the left deal with ideas that are easily understood and do not involve matters of opinion or issues that are open to interpretation. "George, beginning tomorrow you are to occupy Ralph's office. He is being transferred to the Denver office, and you are

Perception
is a person's view of reality.

FIGURE 11.2 *A Communication Continuum*

Clear Communications → Vague Communications

next in line in seniority, so the office is yours." This is a clear message. We can expect George to clean out his desk and move the contents into Ralph's office tomorrow. We would be surprised if we found that George moved into his boss's office, because that would indicate quite a deviation from the originally transmitted message.

"George, if you do well in your current position, you can expect a promotion to the Denver office as well." This message is much more vague than the previous one. Note that the sender of the message does not make clear what is meant by "if you do well." It is implied that George knows, but does he?

As one moves across the communication continuum in Figure 11.4, there is a point at which the messages become extremely difficult to comprehend. However, it is erroneous to believe that all clear communiqués are error-free. Often people see and hear what they want or expect to see and hear. When this happens, communication breakdown can occur. Let us take an example. After this paragraph, there is a sentence containing all capital letters. Read the sentence slowly and carefully so you understand its entire meaning. When you are finished, go on to the paragraph that follows.

FINISHED FILES ARE THE RESULT OF YEARS OF SCIENTIFIC STUDY COUPLED WITH THE EXPERIENCE OF MANY YEARS.

Before reading further, you may read the foregoing sentence one more time. When you have finished, and *only* when you have finished, continue reading down this page.

The capitalized sentence that you have read consists of seventeen words. It is a somewhat long, although not particularly difficult, sentence containing a handful of ideas. Within this sentence are a number of different letters: fourteen E's, four A's, and so on. Count the number of times another letter appears in the displayed sentence, adhering to the following ground rules:

First, you may not use your finger, pen, or pencil in rereading the capitalized sentence; you may use only your eyes.

Second, you are to read the sentence as quickly as possible, taking no more than ten seconds to do so. (If possible, time yourself.) When you have finished reading the sentence, you may continue to the next paragraph. Ready? Okay. Begin reading the capitalized sentence and count the number of times the letter F appears. Go!

How many times did you find the letter F in the sentence? The most common answers are two, three, four, five, six, and seven. Was your answer one of these? One of these numbers is correct. Regardless of the number you arrived at the first time, go back to the sentence and read it *slowly* and *deliberately*, counting the number of F's very carefully.

If you have counted three—no more, no less—you are typical of most people. Actually, there are six F's in the sentence (*finished, files, scientific,* and the three *of*s). Most people miss these last three because they are accustomed to reading past short words, skimming over them too quickly to notice the spelling. This exercise demonstrates that even when it comes to "clear" messages, people make errors because they do not perceive what actually is there.

Let us take another illustration, this time using a vague message. Following this paragraph are nine dots. After studying them for a minute, connect all nine dots with four straight lines. Here are the rules:

1. **You may not take your pen or pencil off the paper.**
2. **If you retrace a line by, for example, going from left to right and then back again to the point of departure, you have used two lines.**

3. The lines must indeed be straight; do not curve them in any way.

After you have finished this exercise (take no more than five minutes with it), you can check your answer with the solution given at the end of the chapter. As you will see, going outside the perimeter formed by the nine dots is the only way to solve the puzzle. If you try to stay within this square area, you cannot solve the problem without using at least five straight lines.

When managers communicate, they often believe their messages are clear. Often, however, they are vague, and the receiver ends up asking, "What did the boss mean by that?"

Inference

Another common communication problem, closely associated with perception, is inference. An **inference** is an assumption made by the receiver of a message. Inferences are most often present in messages that are very long or that involve a large number of facts. In interpreting their meaning, the receiver often is forced to make assumptions, because the facts are not all clearly transmitted. The Time Out quiz is an illustration. How well did you do? Check your answers with those at the end of the chapter. Most people get no more than eight correct answers.

Inference occurs whenever the sender of the message fails to communicate clearly and completely. In face-to-face communication, many of these problems can be overcome, as the listener can quickly stop the conversation and ask a question. However, with written messages, this is more difficult because the receiver is forced to use his or her own best judgment in deciding what the message actually means.

Language

Language is used to convey meaning in the communication process. This is as true in written as in spoken communication. However, sometimes language proves to be a communication barrier. One of the most common reasons is that people are unfamiliar with some of the words that are being used or associate different meanings with them. For example, in recent years, a number of new words have become part of many people's lexicon. Examples include *home page, browser, chat room, netiquette, URL, search engine,*[13] and *householding.* Even the terms *telecommuting* and *teleworking* are used and defined in many different ways and include both flexible scheduling and the use of advanced information technology. Another example is words that have technical meanings. For example, in engineering firms, the word *burn* often means "to photocopy." Imagine the surprise of a manager when he or she tells a new office assistant to burn a copy of the original blueprints and then finds that they must be redrawn!

Every profession has its own meanings for words. In the medical profession, *OD* stands for overdose. However, in the field of management, *OD* signifies organizational development, a strategy used to introduce planned change. Or consider *OB,* which in the medical profession stands for obstetrics but in the management profession signifies organizational behavior, an academic discipline taught in accredited schools of business. Communications theorists like to point out that meanings are not resident in words but in the people who use them. When we employ language for communication purposes, we sometimes do not associate the

An **inference** *is an assumption made by the receiver of a message.*

time out

A MATTER OF INFERENCE

Instructions

Read the following story very carefully. You may assume that everything it says is true, but be aware that parts of the story are deliberately vague. You can read the story twice if you desire, but once you start reading the statements that follow, do not go back to either the story itself or any previous statements. Simply read each statement and decide whether it is true (the story said so), false (the story said just the opposite), or inferential (you cannot say whether it is true or false; you need more facts). Write your answer (T for true, F for false, I for inferential) on the line after the statement. When you are finished, check your results with the answers given at the end of the chapter.

The Story

Bart Falding is head of the research and development (R&D) department of a large plastics firm located in New England. Bart has ordered a crash R&D program in hopes of developing a new process that will revolutionize plastics manufacturing. He has given five of his top R&D people authority to spend up to $250,000 each without consulting him or the R&D committee.

He has sent one of his best people, Mary Lou Rasso, to a major midwestern university to talk to a Nobel Prize winner there who has just applied for and received a patent that Bart believes may provide the basis for a breakthrough in the plastics field. Three days after Mary Lou left for the university, Bart received a call from her. Mary Lou was very excited and said she and the scientist were flying in to see Bart the next day, although she declined to discuss the matter over the phone.

Bart believes he will have very good news for the company president when they meet for their biweekly lunch early next week.

The Statements

1. Bart is head of the research and development department of a large plastics firm. _____

2. The company is located in Los Angeles, California. _____

3. Bart received orders from the president to engage in a crash R&D program. _____

4. Bart's R&D budget is in excess of $1 million. _____

5. Bart assigned five of his best people to work on developing a new process for revolutionizing plastics manufacturing. _____

6. Mary Lou was sent to talk to a Nobel-Prize–winning professor. _____

7. Mary Lou works for the plastics manufacturing department. _____

8. Mary Lou was authorized to spend up to $250,000 without approval from the R&D committee. _____

9. Bart's company wants to buy the patent from the university professor. _____

10. Bart believes that Mary Lou has already offered the professor a deal and the latter is prepared to accept it, but Mary Lou first wants to discuss the matter with top management. _____

11. Mary Lou has agreed to pick up all the scientist's expenses if the latter will consent to come and talk to Bart in person. _____

12. The scientist must be interested in some type of financial or business arrangement with Bart's firm, or the scientist would not have agreed to fly in and meet with Bart. _____

13. The scientist received the Nobel Prize for work he did in the area of plastic processes. _____

14. Bart and the company president have lunch on a biweekly basis. _____

15. Bart believes he will have good news for the president, for he is sure the scientist will agree to sell the patent to the company if the firm makes a sufficiently high offer. _____

same meaning with a word as does the receiver, and so communication breakdown is all but inevitable.

Another common language-related problem is reading. Many schools no longer teach students to read and write properly. Grammar, sentence construction, and reading skills are not stressed. Students now enter the workforce unprepared to communicate effectively.

Status

Status, as defined in Chapter 4, refers to the relative ranking of an individual in a group. In the formal organization, those at the top tend to have much higher status than those at the bottom. When people communicate, status affects the process, because they often monitor what they say or write on the basis of who is going to receive the message, and they distort what they hear by judging its accuracy according to who said it. For example, many people do not share good news or useful ideas with their boss because they believe their information will be ignored or, if it has any practical value, the boss will use the information for his or her personal gain. Peter Lilienthal, president of InTouch Management Communication Systems, has reported that surveys conducted by his firm reveal that 90 percent of employees believe they have good ideas for improving the effectiveness of their firms but only 50 percent of them ever share these ideas with the company.[14]

Another example involves status between management and union members. Management may regard a complaint it receives from the union as nothing more than union rhetoric. However, if a member of management tells the president that the complaint is accurate, the union's message takes on a higher degree of credibility. Conversely, if a union employee is late for work and is laid off for three days, the shop steward may fight to have the punishment reduced. However, if people in the employee's area tell the steward that the employee is always late for work, is unproductive in assignments, and altogether is more of a hindrance than a help, the shop steward may not argue the employee's case very hard.

One way to motivate people is to give them status symbols. The personnel may want equality, but most people want to be just a little more equal than others. In short, status is important. We all want to feel special. As a result, the organization cannot remove status symbols, so it must learn to adjust to the problems that accompany them, including communication breakdown.

Status
is a person's relative rank.

Achieving Effective Communication

The barriers we have just examined can prevent the sender from conveying his or her meaning to the receiver, but this need not happen. There are ways to overcome the barriers and achieve effective communication. Some of the most useful are:

1. **Knowing the steps in the communication process.**
2. **Using simple, repetitive language.**
3. **Using empathy.**
4. **Understanding body language.**
5. **Learning how to receive and give feedback.**
6. **Developing effective listening habits.**
7. **Improving writing and speaking skills.**
8. **Understanding gender differences.**[15]

LEARNING OBJECTIVE
④ *Identify eight ways to overcome barriers to communication and achieve effective communication*

Knowing the Steps in the Communication Process

If a manager knows the steps in the communication process, many of the breakdowns we have just discussed can be avoided. The four steps in communication are (1) attention, (2) understanding, (3) acceptance, and (4) action.

Attention

Only when the listener has screened out all the disturbances or other distractions that can interrupt his or her concentration is **attention** possible. The sender can help in this process by remembering that many listeners are confronted with message competition. Listeners have

LEARNING OBJECTIVE
⑤ *Outline the four steps in the communication process and describe how they can help improve a manager's communication skills*

Attention
is the overcoming of message competition.

other things on their minds—telephone calls that must be returned, memos and reports that need to be read, people who have asked them for assistance and are awaiting replies. If the sender does not keep the message interesting and informative, there is a good chance that the receiver will begin to daydream or ponder some of the other messages competing for his or her attention.

Understanding

Understanding
involves comprehension of the message.

Comprehension of the message results in **understanding.**[16] The receiver must grasp the meaning. In trying to accomplish this step, many managers ask their people, "Do you understand what I'm saying?" However, this is the wrong approach. One should never ask people *whether* they understand, because the pressure is on them to answer yes. Rather, the manager should ask them *what* they understand. In this way, the listener is forced to restate the message in his or her own words, and the manager can judge the accuracy of understanding. Following is an illustration.

> **Manager:** Dave, we need this report typed up and sent to the division manager. I want you to get to it as soon as possible.
>
> **Dave:** Uh, okay. I'll get to it as soon as possible.
>
> **Manager:** Are you sure you understand?
>
> **Dave:** Sure.
>
> **Manager:** What are you going to do?
>
> **Dave:** Well, I'm going to drop that rush job I'm working on and get going on this report for the division manager.
>
> **Manager:** No, Dave, that's not what I meant to say. I want you to finish that rush job and *then* do the report for the division manager.
>
> **Dave:** Oh, okay. I misunderstood. I'm sorry.
>
> **Manager:** That's all right, Dave. The important thing is that we now understand each other. In the future, if you have any questions about what I mean, don't hesitate to ask.

Note that the manager initially asked *whether* the subordinate understood but avoided a problem by then asking Dave *what* he understood. The manager also encouraged him to ask questions in the future to ensure continued understanding. The Cultural Diversity in Action box offers additional insights to the area of understanding. "The Black Hole in Corporation Communication in Action" is another example of what happens in the absence of real information.

Acceptance

Acceptance
means compliance.

When the receiver is willing to go along with the message, **acceptance** occurs. Only in rare cases do subordinates refuse to comply with directives from the boss. They usually obey without giving the matter much thought. However, people balk if they think that the order is detrimental to their best interests.

> **Manager:** Jane, I've just gotten a phone call from Morris, and they're shipping over the supplies we ordered last week. They'll be here in about forty minutes. I'd like you to wait, sign for the supplies, and put them in the storeroom.
>
> **Jane:** I've got a night class at the university that starts at 6 P.M. If I don't leave right now, I'll miss it.

Obviously, the manager can try to force Jane to stay. However, if the boss reads the feedback signs, he should be able to see that Jane's acceptance will at best be slow in coming. The manager must be aware of these negative vibrations and either press for acceptance or ask someone else to wait for the supplies. In this case, asking someone else appears preferable.

CULTURAL DIVERSITY IN ACTION

A Black Hole in Corporate Communication in Action

I was in New York last week with my friend Ray, who works for a multinational financial services firm. He and his coworkers from around the country had gathered in the city for a week to review marketing plans and revenue goals, which they did. But during the meetings, the Pooh-Bahs in his division also cryptically mentioned the possibility of a division-wide restructuring: something they called a "re-org."

After the second day of meetings, I returned to the Embassy Suites to find Ray sitting on the couch, staring into space, his shirt rumpled and untucked.

This worried me. Ray is never rumpled. I asked if he was okay.

"What do they mean by re-org?" he asked, still staring straight ahead. "I'll tell you what they mean. They mean job cuts. I think I'm okay—but maybe not. Maybe I'm not okay. Do you think I'm okay?" He didn't wait for an answer. "I should've talked more during the meeting today," he said. "I should've gone to the dinner last night. I should've worn black shoes. I looked too casual."

I told him I thought layoffs were rarely decided on the basis of shoe color.

"YOU don't know these people," he shouted, as red blotches bloomed across his neck. "I just don't understand why they're doing this."

Ray crossed his arms over his chest and began rocking back and forth, clearly on the edge of a gale-force panic attack. I tiptoed from the room and shut the door. From down the hallway, I could hear him repeating the phrase "re-org, re-org, re-org" like a stuck 45 on a diner jukebox.

At the time, I felt that Ray's behavior was a tad extreme. After all, his company's restructuring was far from certain—and besides, no one knew what it would entail. But the next day I went to an exhibit on Albert Einstein at the American Museum of Natural History and experienced, firsthand, the panic and conjecture that come from not knowing how to interpret information. Physics will do that to you.

The exhibit started off well enough. I entered the hushed museum and learned about Einstein as a young boy. I reviewed a copy of his report card, which refutes the myth that he was not a motivated child. I saw a replica of the compass that launched Einstein's fascination with the forces of nature. And, in something that belongs in the "who knew?" category, I read one of the many love letters he wrote to one of his many mistresses. Apparently, Einstein was a hottie in his day, a babe-magnet with a large romantic appetite.

But then, as I began to read about Einstein's theories, my sunny enjoyment of the day disappeared behind a dark cloud of ignorance.

I read about his general theory of relativity, which overturned the classic Newtonian view of gravity, which said that apples never fall far from the tree, or some such thing.

I read about the imaginary gravity of projected black holes, which helps to explain why SUVs plow into sinkholes on rainy days.

I learned about Einstein's search for a grand unified theory that would explain everything about everything, including, I presume, why Michael Jackson thinks he's Peter Pan.

See, the more I read about Einstein's work, the less I understood it. And the less I understood it, the more I felt compelled to fill in the gaps with my own interpretation. Even though I listened to the curator's talk, and watched a film narrated by Alan Alda, and reviewed the seventy-two handwritten pages that make up Einstein's theory of relativity, I couldn't grasp what his theories really meant.

I started to get agitated and sped through the exhibit. Gravitational warps? The space–time continuum? Yeah, yeah, whatever.

By the time I hit the gift shop at the end of the exhibit, I had a massive headache caused, no doubt, by an unprecedented cerebral failure. I sped past the wall of books on Einstein and picked up a souvenir writing pen. Ahhhh. This was something I could understand. So simple. So elegant. I held it to my chest until my breathing returned to normal.

And when it did, I thought about my friend Ray and his company's re-org. I began to understand his panic over the proposed restructuring. He didn't understand why it was necessary. He didn't understand how it could affect him. He didn't understand why he'd been told that information. And in the absence of all that understanding, he filled in the black holes with his own warped view of the outcome.

As Einstein might explain it, Ray was suffering from an extreme case of $E = MC^2$, which I believe means that expectations are driven by management communication—or the lack thereof.

Reference: Shari Caudron, "A Black Hole in Corporate Communication," *Workforce*, April 2003, p. 24.

Action

Action
requires that the receiver do what was expected.

The final step in the communication process, **action**, requires the receiver to follow up and do what was requested. A purchase order may have to be placed, a report filed, or a meeting held. It would appear that, if the sender gets to this action stage, the communication process would attain completion with no further problems. However, this is not always so. Sometimes the receiver will encounter unforeseen difficulties. The purchase order may not be filled because the supplier is temporarily out of raw materials; an executive assistant may be on vacation so a particular report may have to wait to be filed until she returns; a vice president may be on an extended business trip so a meeting may have to be delayed until he or she returns. In all these cases, the message will not get through the action stage.

Another cause for inaction can be found in the receiver, who may be incapable of carrying out the order. For example, if Mary tells Bob to fill out Report A and send it to the comptroller but Bob has never been told how to perform this task, the report may be completed incorrectly or it may not be filled out at all. The message may not reach the stage of completed action. Alternatively, if Bob asks Mary for help and she is too busy to see him, he will fill out Report A as best he can, with the same result.

If the action stage is to be completed, the sender must be available to answer questions and provide assistance to the receiver. If a problem develops, the receiver then has someone to whom he or she can turn. The action stage ensures that there is feedback in case of trouble. Remember, the sender's communication responsibility does not end until the desired action is completed.

LEARNING OBJECTIVE
Describe the importance of using simple, repetitive language and empathy and understanding body language in achieving effective communication

⑥ Using Simple, Repetitive Language

The simpler a message is, the more likely it is that it will be understood and acted on properly. Consider the advertisements you see in the daily newspaper. Research shows that the shorter the ad, the higher the reader rate, and the greater the likelihood that the material will be remembered.

Unfortunately, many managers do not carry this simple rule to the workplace with them. They tend to communicate long messages in a hurried fashion. The receivers are unable to follow everything said but, because the sender is in such a rush, they are afraid to interrupt either to ask questions or to get the sender to repeat the more difficult portions of the message. If the message is in writing, the sender tends to use vague terms and incorporate too many ideas into one sentence. When the receiver has read the memo, only part of the message has been properly decoded.

Effective managers know that every message should be understandable. If the subject matter is complex, the communication should be done in "small bites," giving the listener the opportunity to ask questions or seek clarification. In addition, the sender should, from time to time, review part of the message so that the listener finds it easier to follow the flow of information. We illustrate how this can be done further on in this chapter.

Using Empathy

Empathy
means putting oneself in another person's place.

Putting oneself, figuratively, in another person's place is termed **empathy**. In so doing, one begins to see things as the other person does. Barker has put it this way:

Empathy means deep understanding of other people, identifying with their thoughts, feeling their pain, sharing their joy. Such empathy is typical of strong, healthy relationships. Indeed, empathetic communicators know each other so well that they can predict the responses to their messages. For example, Mario says to himself, "I know if I tell May that I'm not crazy about her new dress, she'll be hurt. So instead I'll say 'May, that dress looks great on you, but I think the green one is even more becoming.'"[17]

We know that successful managers empathize with their subordinates. They know when to be task oriented and when to be people oriented, because they are capable of putting themselves in a subordinate's place and answering the question, "What kind of direction does this person need?"

Empathy is particularly important at two stages of the communication process: acceptance and action. When the manager gives an order that the subordinate is reluctant to accept, the manager should be tuned in to pick up the hesitancy. Apparently the subordinate does not understand how important the matter is and how significant his or her role will be. The manager needs to clarify the situation further and explain why the subordinate is being asked to handle the task. If a manager lacks empathy, it is likely that he or she will ignore the hesitancy. The astute manager knows that the problem or issue should be dealt with immediately and laid to rest.

Empathy also helps in the action stage. When the subordinate has trouble carrying out a directive, the empathetic manager is quick to give assistance. He or she realizes immediately that help is needed and does not let the subordinate down. Conversely, the manager who lacks empathy does not check on worker progress and, on learning that the subordinate is having trouble, lets the subordinate work it out alone. Research shows that empathetic managers are more effective than are managers who lack empathy.

Empathy is also important in knowing *how* to talk to people. A training and consulting executive has noted that when speaking to the boss, for example, it is important to understand the individual's preferred communication style. Here are some examples of bosses and the style that works best with them:

- *The director:* **This person has a short attention span, processes information very quickly, and is interested in only the bottom line. Therefore, it is best to present this individual with a bulleted list of conclusions and forget all the background information.**
- *The free spirit:* **This manager is a creative, big-picture type of person who likes to consider alternative approaches to doing things but is not very good on follow-through. In dealing with this individual, it is important to be patient and to be prepared for changes in direction. This manager often likes to assimilate what he or she is being told and to consider several alternatives before making a decision.**
- *The humanist:* **This person likes everyone to be happy and is very concerned with the feelings of others, so any suggestions or recommendations that are given to him or her will be passed around the entire department for full consensus before any action is taken. In dealing with this person, patience and tact are very important.**
- *The historian:* **This manager likes to know the complete picture and thrives on details. He or she wants to be given a thorough analysis and background information, especially if it is presented in linear fashion. The individual does not jump from subject to subject but instead remains focused on the topic under consideration until it has been exhaustively reviewed and a decision has been made.**[18]

Uunderstanding Body Language

Body language is one of the most important forms of nonverbal communication. People use this communication form to pass messages to one another, although in many cases they are unaware that they are doing so. Common examples of body language include the way a person moves his or her eyes, where an individual stands in a room in relation to others, the way a person shakes hands or touches another on the shoulder, and the way a person dresses.

In regard to eye movement, many managers believe that if people are lying, they will not look the listener in the eye. This is untrue. Effective liars often do look their listeners right in the eye; they know such eye contact increases their credibility. However, there are things managers can learn by looking at the other person's eye movements. In particular, it is possible to tell when the other party is under stress or emotional strain. For example, right-handed people tend to look to the left when they are trying to deal with an issue on an emotional level, and they tend to look to the right when they are unemotional or rational. The reverse is true for left-handed people.

Posture is a second important body language sign. Slouching, looking down, or hanging back in the crowd are typical examples of individuals who are unsure of themselves. Mehrabian, a communications expert, has discovered a relationship between how near a person stands to another and how relaxed the individual is.[19] Some of Mehrabian's findings include the following:

1. A high degree of relaxation generally indicates a lack of respect or a dislike of the other person, whereas a lesser degree of relaxation indicates a liking for the other person.
2. An absence of relaxation indicates the person feels threatened or is being threatening to someone else.
3. Relaxation is related to status, with higher-status people being generally more relaxed than their lower-status counterparts.
4. Women consistently demonstrate greater immediacy and consequently deliver more positive feelings.

Touch is another important body language sign. When American businesspeople shake hands, a vigorous or firm handshake often is regarded as a sign of self-assurance. This type of touching is used to define power relationships. Causal touching or unwanted touching in the office can lead to lawsuits for sexual harassment. Some countries are regarded as "touch-oriented" countries where touching between men, such as holding hands while walking down a street, is a sign of great friendship and respect, not being homosexual as Americans might think. The Middle East, Italy, and the Latin countries are examples of touch-oriented countries, whereas, Japan is not regarded as a touching society. As business operations become more global, cultures are colliding over this dilemma of "to touch or not to touch." This is an issue managers confront while working with diversified groups of employees. For example, a manager who wants to emphasize an order must know how an employee feels about touch before grasping the employee's arm while issuing the order, or if the manager wants to congratulate the employee, can he or she pat the person on the back.[20]

time out

PHYSICAL LOCATION AND BODY LANGUAGE: A QUIZ

Assume you are Person A. You would like very much to be cooperative and open to Person F. Are you seated in *a correct chair or should you switch chairs with someone else? Think about this for a minute and then compare your answer to that at the end of the chapter.*

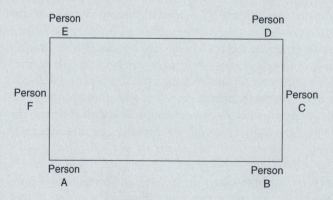

Physical location is a fourth important form of body language. This subject is known as **proxemics** and deals with the way people use physical space to communicate. The quiz on physical location and body language in the Time Out box illustrates this idea. Take a moment to complete the exercise in the Time Out box. Where people sit or stand in relation to one another also communicates a message. For example, when communicating personal information, individuals often stand within two feet of each other. When conveying general or social information, the parties generally stand two to six feet apart. When the message is less personal, the distance will be greater between the people. Of course, these cultural guidelines only hold in the United States and other Western countries. When dealing with Arabs or other people from the Middle East, for example, it is customary to conduct general business discussions within a few feet of one another. This nearness often makes Americans feel uncomfortable but, if they back away and try to establish a greater distance, they will usually find their Arab counterparts coming closer. The use of proxemics is culturally determined. Figure 11.3 draws together many of these comments about empathy and body language. As you examine the figure, notice the differences between the two groups: aggressivians (Americans being a good example) and passivians (most other countries of the world).

Proxemics
deals with the way people use physical space to communicate.

Learning to Receive and Give Feedback

A manager can improve his or her communication ability primarily by learning when his or her messages are being transmitted poorly and by working to overcome the breakdown. One way to do this is to solicit feedback. Let's look at some effective openers:

"Could you give some more information about . . . ?"
"You've given me some things to think over. I'd welcome any other ideas you might have about . . . "
"I think the proposed reorganization plan is a good one. What do you think?"

Notice that in each of these opening remarks the sender is encouraging the receiver to give feedback. The channel is being opened.

In discouraging feedback, the sender closes the channel by either threatening or belittling the receiver. In those cases the receiver is likely to say nothing. The following are illustrations:

"Let me say straight off that there is no way that I'll go along with any recommendation other than the one that J. R. proposed yesterday."
"While you may not be aware of all the constraints I'm working under . . . "
"Of course, that may be the way you see it, but let's look at the facts."

In each of these statements, the sender is closing down the feedback channel. In the first example, the sender is apparently backing up a top manager and daring the receiver to argue the point. In the second, the sender seems to be saying that he or she is overworked and does not want any disagreement or argument from the receiver. In the last example, the sender appears to be labeling the receiver as stupid. Unless the receiver is looking for an argument with the manager, there is little chance that he or she will say anything in response.

Once the manager starts getting feedback, it is important to sustain the flow of information. Numerous stock phrases or statements can be used for this. Here are some of the most effective:

"Could you tell me more about . . . ?"
"I see."
"Right, right. Go on."
"I appreciate your saying that."
"Am I going into sufficient detail?"
"What else?"

FIGURE 11.3

Culture Behavior Characteristics: Aggressivians Versus Passivians

Aggressivians	Passivians
Body Language	
Frequently uses gestures and facial expressions when speaking	Never uses gestures or facial expressions when speaking
Enjoys prolonged eye contact; stares intently at others when engaged in conversation	Avoids eye contact as much as possible
Smiles constantly	Never smiles
Stands and sits erectly	Slouches when standing and sitting
Personal Space	
Likes closeness; requires little personal space	Likes distance; requires much personal space
Stands and sits as close as possible to others	Stands and sits at a distance from others whenever possible
Touches others frequently	Never touches others
Concept of Time	
Believes time is money	Believes time is relatively unimportant
Believes decisions should be made within strict deadlines	Believes making a sound decision is more important than meeting deadlines
Is always in a hurry	Never rushes
Wants to discuss only the facts	Wants to discuss all aspects of a problem and how various decisions affect others involved
Wants to reach a decision as soon as possible	Wants to reach a decision only after all evidence has been thoroughly discussed and carefully evaluated
Vocal Qualities	
Speaks loudly	Speaks softly
Speaks rapidly	Speaks slowly
Speaks with exaggerated vocal inflections	Speaks in a monotone
Personality	
Is extremely self-centered	Is extremely group-oriented
Frequently uses *I, me, my,* and *mine*	Frequently uses *we, us,* and *ours*
Is rarely willing to help others unless a personal benefit results	Is always willing to cooperate and help others
Constantly fosters his or her personal rights at the expense of others	Frequently relinquishes personal rights in deference to those of others
Never tries to understand the views of others	Always tries to understand the views of others
Always feels better than or more important than others	Never feels better than or more important than others
Negotiating Style	
Is brutally frank	Frequently uses euphemisms to avoid hurting others
Demonstrates no concern for the feelings of others	Is extremely concerned about the feelings of others
Likes to argue for the sake of arguing	Always avoids arguments and conflict
Talks *at* rather than *with* people	Talks *with* rather than *at* people
Always assumes he or she is right and others are wrong	Listens carefully and never interrupts others
	Accepts the fact that others may think differently and that there may be more than one correct viewpoint

Source: Jack E. Hulbert, "Overcoming Intercultural Communication Barriers," The Bulletin, March 1994, p. 42.

Finally, we must consider the subject of giving feedback. Sometimes the subordinate will not ask questions about matters that merit further discussion or explanation. At these times, the effective manager needs to know how to introduce feedback into the process. Some of the best opening lines are these:

"Would you be interested in my reactions to . . . ?"
"You may be at a good point right now for me to give you some feedback on . . ."
"I like what you did. What sets it apart is . . ."

In each of these instances, the sender (manager) has approached the feedback issue from the standpoint of the receiver (subordinate). Each comment conveys something of help or value to the receiver. For example, in the first opening, the manager is going to give reactions to some matter that apparently involved the subordinate. Note, however, that the manager did not attempt to give these reactions unsolicited. The manager asked if the subordinate would be interested in them. If the subordinate feels feedback will be of little value, he or she can say so, but the opportunity for feedback is there if the subordinate wants it. In the second and third openings, it is obvious that the subordinate is going to be given feedback that is important and, in the last case, laudatory.

These effective openers contrast significantly with ineffective openers that commonly lead the subordinate to tune out the message. Some common examples follow:

"You really ought to know better than to . . ."
"How many times do I have to tell you not to . . . ?"
"Now, Bob, you're just too critical of . . ."

In each case, the listener is not really being given feedback as much as being criticized for particular behavior. The most common response is to ignore it. How does a manager overcome these common pitfalls and learn how to both receive and give feedback? The answer rests in analyzing one's messages and putting oneself in the receiver's shoes (empathizing).

Developing Effective Listening Habits

⑦ LEARNING OBJECTIVE
Discuss ten guidelines for developing effective listening habits

Listening is difficult business. Research reveals that most people speak at a rate of approximately 125 words per minute but are capable of listening to more than 600 words per minute. This leaves a listener's brain a great deal of slack, which can be used for such things as daydreaming or thinking up responses to issues the speaker raises. Instead of really listening to what the person is saying, the listener is trying to formulate a response. This is unfortunate, because effective human relations are based heavily on good listening skills. For example, individuals who are poor listeners are typically also poor negotiators. As a result, they are unable to learn what the other party wants or is willing to settle for, and so they end up with a less-than-ideal settlement. Poor listeners are also ineffective in crisis situations. During this period, these individuals need to gather as much information as possible in determining how to handle the situation. However, they often shut out incoming signals and make decisions that are based on incomplete information. Research by Maritz Poll recently revealed that almost a fourth of the American workers—23 percent—don't think that their company listens to or cares about them, and 28 percent disapprove of the ways that their organizations communicate with them.[21]

Fortunately, a number of techniques can be used to improve one's listening skills. One is to ask questions that will help provide feedback and increase understanding. Another is to remain objective and not get upset by what the other person is saying. A third is to empathize, put yourself in the other person's shoes, and try to see things from that individual's point of view. These suggestions are designed to encourage the listener to hear what the other person has to say and to put the information into proper perspective before saying anything. Further suggestions are discussed in the in the Action Box. Other useful guidelines include the following:

1. Do not label the speaker as either boring or uninteresting merely because you dislike his or her delivery. Listen to *what* is being said rather than *how* it is being said.
2. Tell yourself that the speaker has something to say that will be of value or benefit to you. Give him or her a chance to communicate.
3. If the speaker starts talking about something you find boring, ask a pertinent question to influence him or her toward more interesting subject matter.
4. If the presentation becomes too technical or difficult to understand, fight the tendency to tune out the speaker by increasing your determination to listen, learn, and remember.
5. Note the techniques used by the speaker to determine whether you should adopt any of them yourself. Did he or she use a lot of facts? Was an emotional appeal ever employed? When? Were either of these approaches effective in presenting the message? Could you use these techniques to improve your own communication skills?
6. Evaluate the relevance of what is being said. Are any new or useful data being communicated that can be of value to you?
7. Listen for intended meanings as well as for expressed ideas. Are there any hidden messages that the speaker is trying to convey?

in action

HOW TO BECOME A MORE ACTIVE LISTENER

Effective listening involves more than just paying attention. It includes active, empathetic, and supportive behaviors that tell the speaker, "I understand. Please go on." This is the way an active listener behaves. However, watch out for four other types of listener: directing, judgmental, probing, and smoothing. Here is a brief description of each.

The directing listener leads the speaker by guiding the limits and direction of the conversation. This individual likes to use such phrases as "If I were you I'd . . ." and "Don't worry about it, everybody agrees that . . ." The directing listener really does not listen; he or she takes control of the situation.

The judgmental listener introduces personal value judgments into the conversation. This individual offers advice or makes statements regarding right or wrong conduct. Some of the most common statements he or she might use include: "Well, you're just going to have to understand that . . ." or "You're right to say that Bill is tough to get along with because . . ." Rather than hearing the speaker out, the judgmental listener tends to impose his or her own personal values.

The probing listener asks a lot of questions in an effort to get to the heart of the matter. In the process, this person attempts to satisfy his or her personal needs rather

than those of the speaker. A probing listener will ask such questions as, "What has this person done to you that prevents your getting along with him?" or "When did all of this start?" The probing listener tends to be inquisitive to the point of frustrating the speaker.

The smoothing listener adopts a strategy designed to reassure the speaker. The individual often says such things as, "Don't let that worry you because . . ." and "I understand exactly how you feel about . . ." This individual believes that conflict is bad and should be avoided at all costs.

The active listener tries to encourage the speaker to express himself or herself. This listener creates an environment in which the speaker feels free to develop his or her thoughts. The active listener commonly says such things as, "You sound upset about . . ." or "It seems that you are willing to go ahead and implement your ideas regarding . . ." The active listener gives the speaker neutral summaries of what is being said. These summaries encourage the other party to continue speaking.

The most effective listener is the active listener because this person maintains the role of listener. The other four types of listener are characterized by their attempts to influence or dominate the speaker. Work on avoiding the habits of these ineffective listeners and strive to become a more active listener.

8. **Integrate in your mind what the speaker is saying so that it all fits into a logical composite. If any information does not fit into this overall scheme, place it on the sidelines but seek to integrate it later.**

9. **Be a responsive listener by maintaining eye contact with the speaker and giving him or her positive feedback, such as nods and facial expressions.**

10. **Be willing to accept the challenge of effective listening by telling yourself that it is a skill that you need to develop.**[22]

Another way to improve one's listening skills is to become an active listener. How do you rate in terms of being a good listener? One way of finding out is by taking the accompanying Time Out quiz. It is not always easy to follow these ten guidelines for effective listening. In fact, many effective managers report that when they first decided to become better listeners they had to force themselves to follow these guidelines. Effective listening is not simply doing what comes naturally. *Listening is a developed skill.* This is why, in many organizations today, managers are being given effective listening courses in which they are taught how to become active listeners. In large degree, listening is starting to be regarded as partly a science (rather than totally an art) that can be improved by training and practice.

---

time out

ARE YOU A GOOD LISTENER?

Read the statements in this section and rate yourself on each by using the following scale:

A = Always
B = Almost always
C = Usually
D = Sometimes
E = Rarely
F = Almost never
G = Never

1. Do you let the speaker completely express his or her ideas without interrupting her or him? _____

2. Do you become upset or excited when the speaker's views differ from your own? _____

3. Are you able to prevent distractions from disrupting your ability to listen? _____

4. Do you make continuous notes on everything the other person says? _____

5. Are you able to read between the lines and hear what a person is saying even when hidden messages are being conveyed? _____

6. When you feel that the speaker or topic is boring, do you find yourself tuning out and daydreaming about other matters? _____

7. Are you able to tolerate silence by sitting quietly and allowing the speaker time to gather his or her thoughts and go on with the message? _____

8. As you listen, do you find yourself trying to pull together what the speaker is saying by thinking of what has been said and what seems to be coming? _____

9. As you listen to the speaker, do you note that person's body language and try to incorporate this into your interpretation of the message? _____

10. If you disagree with what the speaker is saying, do you provide immediate feedback by shaking your head no? _____

11. Do you move around a great deal when listening, changing your posture, crossing and recrossing your arms or legs, and sliding back and forth in your chair? _____

12. When you listen, do you stare intently into the speaker's eyes and try to maintain this direct contact throughout the time the person is speaking? _____

13. When the other party is finished speaking, do you ask pointed and direct questions designed to clarify and amplify what was said? _____

14. If the speaker has been critical of you, do you try to put down that person before addressing the substantive part of the message? _____

The interpretation of your answers appears at the end of the chapter.

⑧ Improving Your Writing Skills

Whenever communication is discussed, talk usually centers on reading, speaking, and listening; writing typically is given a low priority. Why is this so? Perhaps the main reason is that most managers do not write well, and they hate to be reminded of it. Yet written communication is an important part of their job, as evidenced by the fact that managers are always writing memos, reports, evaluations, and so on. In fact, thanks to electronic mail and facsimiles, written communication is becoming increasingly more important. E-mail is so popular that every day millions of these messages are sent,[23] and some executives report that they spend more than an hour daily reading and responding to them. Research shows that the use of these new electronic tools can result in better memos and reports.[24]

How can you improve your writing skills? There are a number of steps you can take.

- **First, force yourself to write and rewrite material. If you do this frequently enough, your writing will become much more effective. Professional writers admit that writing is difficult work, but you can get better at it if you make yourself do it.**

- **Second, make it a point to write at least three drafts of everything you do. The first draft is for gathering ideas. The second draft is for assuring that the material is accurate. The third draft is for polishing and making the material read smoothly and interestingly.**

- **Third, see if you can get someone in your organization to review your written work and comment on it. There may be four or five problems that account for 90 percent of your inability to write effectively. Once you identify the problems, you can correct them in your writing.**

- **Finally, if possible, sign up for a college course and force yourself to learn more effective writing skills. If this is either too time consuming or threatening, put together your own checklist of the most important things to look for in written communiqués and compare your written work with this checklist.**

⑨ Improving Your Speaking Skills

Speaking skills can also be improved.[25] In fact, research among managers reveals that speaking skills are one of the basic shortcomings of many college graduates. How can verbal skills be improved? One way is through what is called a PLAN approach.[26] The acronym stands for *p*urpose, *l*ogistics, *a*udience, and *n*onverbal communication:

- ***Purpose:* What is the reason for the presentation or speech?**
- ***Logistics:* When and where will the meeting be held?**
- ***Audience:* Who will be present?**
- ***Nonverbal communication:* How can the room layout and the use of presentation tools—PowerPoint, charts, and other audiovisual equipment—be used effectively?**

These human relations considerations can greatly improve message delivery, as can a careful evaluation of the audience. Figure 11.4 provides a method for doing this. This audience analysis grid considers the friendliness of the audience and the group's knowledge and receptivity to learning. By combining consideration of the two, an effective strategy can be formulated for delivering the message.

⑩ Understanding Gender Differences

In recent years, growing attention has been focused on the difference in the communications styles and approaches of men and women.[27] A number of reasons exist for these gender-based differences. One is **linguistic style,** which refers to a person's speaking pattern and includes

FIGURE 11.4 *An Audience Analysis Grid*

	Friendliness Continuum →			
	Friendly	Neutral	Disinterested	Hostile
Resistant to Learning	(A) Show them personal profit from presentation	(B) Need a dramatic start to grab interest	(C) Stress benefits of this presentation given the fact they're there anyway	(D) Find and emphasize important benefit for them
Neutral to Learning	(E) Get them involved in the presentation	(F) Use icebreakers or humor to get their attention	(G) Get their interest fast!	(H) Concentrate on benefits of learning
Little Knowledge: Eager to Learn	(I) Pedagogy important for best results	(J) Quickly give them the facts they want	(K) Give them the facts; don't waste time trying to be friends	(L) Emphasis on education
Knowledgeable	(M) Straightforward presentation	(N) Warm them up by referring to their expertise	(O) Find a point to grab their interest	(P) Identify source of hostility and try to diffuse it

Knowledge Continuum (vertical axis)

such things as pacing, pausing, word choice, directness, and the use of jokes, figures of speech, stories, and questions.[28] This style is culturally generated and is used both to convey information and to interpret the meaning of messages from others.

The reason for these differences currently is being debated as a nature-versus-nurture issue. Some researchers believe that the differences can be explained in terms of the inherited biological differences between the sexes. For example, supporters of the "nature" argument contend that men communicate more aggressively and hide their emotions because they have an inherent desire to be attractive to women. These innate desires carry over into the organization setting and manifest themselves in male behavior at work.[29] Supporters of the "nurture" argument contend that men and women learn communications skills and habits in their social environment. Boys are taught skills that focus on status and hierarchies and learn to use communications to negotiate skillfully and to achieve and maintain the upper hand. This increases their need to maintain independence and avoid failure. Girls are taught to view communication as a network of connections in which conversations are negotiations for closeness and to use this orientation to seek and give confirmation and support.[30]

Regardless of the reasons, research reveals that men and women communicate differently in a number of ways.[31] Men like to boast about themselves, give blunt feedback, withhold compliments, and not admit weaknesses or faults. Women are more likely to give carefully worded feedback, share credit for success, ask questions for clarification, and tactfully tell others what to do. Table 11.3 provides some examples of these and other contrasts. However, it is important to remember that these generalizations do not extend to all men and women. At the same time, they do point out the need for both groups to understand better how to communicate

TABLE 11.3 — Some Communication Differences Between Men and Women

Linguistic Characteristic	Men	Women
Asking questions	Not very likely to do so	More likely to do so than men
Giving feedback	Tend to be blunt and direct	Tend to be tactful and to temper criticism with praise
Offering compliments	Restrictive with their praise	Fairly generous with their praise
Showing confidence	Not very likely to indicate when they are unsure about something	More likely to indicate uncertainty about an issue
Making apologies	Tend to avoid saying they are sorry because it makes them "look bad"	More likely to say "I'm sorry" when they make a mistake
Taking credit	More likely to take credit for achievements ("I did that")	More likely to share credit ("We did that")
Use of indirectness	More likely to be indirect when admitting they do not know something or admitting that they made a mistake ("The report was late" rather than "I was late submitting the report")	More likely to be indirect when telling others something that needs to be done ("This is what needs to be done" rather than "This is what I want you to do")

Reprinted by permission of Harvard Business Review. Deborah Tannen, "The Power of Talk: Who Gets Heard and Why," September-October 1995. Copyright Harvard Business School Publishing Corporation; all rights reserved.

with the other. Many men need to be more patient and less dominant; many women need to speak up and be more forceful in presenting their ideas and opinions. One way in which a growing number of organizational training departments are addressing this issue is by having trainees adopt the linguistic characteristics of the other gender, examine this group's perceptions and behaviors, and discuss the strengths and limitations of this linguistic style. Simply put, communication between the sexes can be improved by realizing that both groups have different ways of communicating the same ideas.

LEARNING OBJECTIVE

Describe technology's impact on communication

(11)

Technology's Impact on Communication

Technology is changing the way communication works in firms and affecting the way people interact. Technology speeds up communication and gives immediate access to information that was not available before. For example, on January 13, 2003, Shannon Syfrett, a fifteen-year-old ninth-grader at Central Academy in Macon, Mississippi, launched a chain letter over the Internet for her science fair project. The objective was to learn where and how fast information travels. She sent out twenty-three e-mails and expected to get 2,000 to 3,000 replies in six weeks, but got 160,478 e-mails from 189 countries and 50 states in 25 days, when she had to pull the plug due to the volume of replies. "Shannon's first e-mail reply arrived 2 hours after lunch, and her first overseas reply arrived 11 hours after that from Schleswig-Holstein, Germany."[32]

Regardless of the technology used to exchange information, the basics of the communication process remain constant and are important to the effectiveness of the communication. It is the communication networks and electronic machines and gadgets that are changing. They impact how we communicate and how we interact in the workplace and in our job. For example, managers today are linked to a computer in the office, a laptop they take on the road, and a computer at home. They carry cell phones and pagers that use satellites to transmit messages. Information can be sent to anyone, anyplace, and be received from almost anywhere in the world nonstop, twenty-four hours a day, seven days a week. The number of people owning cell phones is growing. "Telephia, a number-crunching firm for the wireless industry, reports that more than half—about 51%—of the overall U.S. population living in major metropolitan areas now own a mobile phone and subscribes to a wireless-phone service." And according to a Harris Interactive survey, approximately 66 percent, or two-thirds, of all Americans were online in 2002.[33]

Communication technology is changing the workplace. Managers today must be computer and "Internet literate in order to take advantage of real time information and data on their operations," states Jim Moore, Director of Workplace Development for Sun Microsystems, Inc. CEOs are expected to retrieve their own information and not depend on an office assistant.[34] Although the phone, fax, and cell phone are standard business communication devices, the Internet, Intranet, and Extranet networks; e-mail; and instant messaging are fast becoming standard for businesses, even small ones of 250 employees. According to the Small Business Administration, 57 percent or 21.3 million small U.S. companies use the Internet. "About 32% of those not online today said they expect to be within the next year." (Perman) To enhance communication, firms are installing voice recognition systems and video-conferencing systems. Teleworking (telecommuting) is on the rise. It was discussed in Chapter 8.

As the workplace becomes more mobile, new patterns of communication will emerge. The traditional systems of downward, upward, and horizontal communication will no longer be the dominant patterns of communication. We will see new patterns emerge allowing all group members to have greater access to receiving and sending information across the organization. The way information flows will change to meet the needs of the technology used. For example, the flow of information among workers in remote locations is different from that used by employees working in an office. Each group will form its own unique system of communication.

Changes in organizational structure also affect patterns of communication. For the past one hundred years, rank has equaled authority. The old hierarchy business structure placed people and functions in boxes, and some even developed a pyramid with the CEO sitting on the top, keeping watch over his workforce. In the past decade massive changes in global competition, technology, philosophy, and leadership have forced organizations to transform their organizations. The old way of doing business did not work any more, as Frances Hesselbein, editor-in-chief of Leader to Leader, president and CEO of the Drucker Foundation, and former chief executive of the Girl Scouts of the USA, learned when she worked for the Girl Scouts organization. She developed "a new organizational structure where people and functions move across three concentric circles, with the CEO in the middle looking across, not at the top looking down." It is known as "the bubble chart" or "the wheel of fortune." In this organization people communicate across the circles of the organization. See an illustration in Figure 11.5.[35] As discussed in the opening vignette, Steve Wright uses this type of structure with his staff at Wright Builders. He admits that organization structure and communication are keys to the success of his business.

Researchers at Hewlett-Packard have "developed a way to use e-mail exchanges to build a map of the structure of an organization. The map shows the teams in which people actually work, as opposed to those they are assigned to. People working for big institutions tend to divide organically into informal collaborative networks, called communities of practice." This information is used to "construct a communications graph in which lines—each denoting a

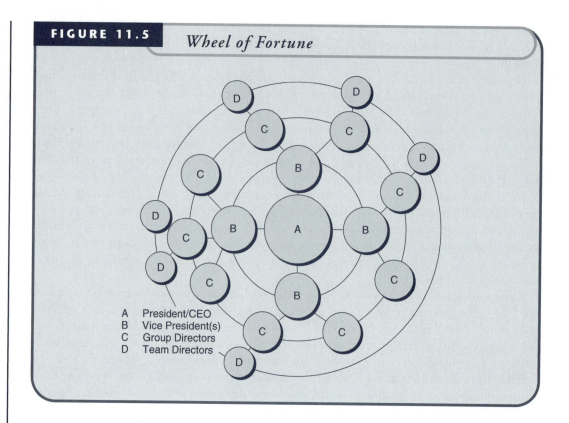

FIGURE 11.5   *Wheel of Fortune*

A   President/CEO
B   Vice President(s)
C   Group Directors
D   Team Directors

direct e-mail exchange—link nodes that correspond to individuals." At Hewlett-Packard the researchers found sixty-six communities.[36]

When technology is used to communicate information, there are some drawbacks that managers must address. For example:

- *Information-Security is a problem.* The wrong party can intercept the communication and use the information in the message to their advantage, such as during the Iraqi Freedom War when the U.S. military intercepted messages among members of Saddam Hussein's regime. Security has long been an issue and firms are working hard to remedy the problem. For example, in post-September 11, firms have increased their Information-Security budgets (IS budgets) at the expense of their Information Technology budgets (IT budgets). "According to Vista Research, a financial research and reporting firm, 48% of primary decision makers have increased information-security budgets since September 2001. Half of those indicated the increase was 10% or more." Over half indicated they would increase that amount in the next twelve months. (Perman)

- *Privacy issues are a concern.* Firms are doing a better job of protecting private information and convincing consumers that their personal information is protected on the firm's Web site. As a result, consumers are gaining confidence and are using the Internet to shop. According to the Commerce Department, online retail sales were up 34 percent. "E-shops are growing at a faster pace than their bricks-and-mortar counterparts." (Perman)

- *The workday is extended.* Communication can occur anytime, anyplace, not just during office hours.

- *Nonverbal clues are missing.* Facial expressions and gesturing provide clues to the receiver's level of understanding of the message. Voice defection can sometimes give the sender a clue.

- *Multitasking is increased.* People can make a phone call and send an e-mail at the same time or work on another message.

- *The volume of information is overwhelming.* Processing e-mails can take a block of time from a manager's day.
- *The interaction among team members changes.* Everyone has an equal chance of participating and not be overlooked or dominated by stronger team members.
- *Small talk and social interaction is reduced.* People tend to get to the point and not engage in small talk, as they might in a face-to-face meeting.[37]

summary

① LEARNING OBJECTIVE
Describe the communication process

One of the best ways to achieve behavioral effectiveness in the workplace is to communicate properly. In this chapter, we reviewed the ways in which effective communication can be attained. First, we examined communication, which is the process of transmitting meanings from sender to receiver. In this process are five essential elements: (1) the sender, (2) the message, (3) the medium, (4) the receiver, and (5) the interpretation given to the message. In conveying the message, three functions must be performed: encoding of the message, choice of a communication medium, and decoding of the message.

② LEARNING OBJECTIVE
Discuss how to choose the appropriate communication medium

To communicate effectively, the proper medium must be chosen. Two important considerations are associated with determining which medium to use. The first is the matter of information richness—the potential amount of information-carrying capacity of data. Four factors measure richness (1) feedback, (2) the channel used to convey the information, (3) the type of communication—personal or impersonal, and (4) language source used including body language, natural or numeric. The richest forms of communication are face-to-face and the telephone. Computer printouts and video displays provide low richness and are impersonal.

The second consideration is the issue of complexity. There are three zones of communication effectiveness. If the message is simple, a medium in low richness can be selected; whereas, when a problem is complex, a medium that is high in richness should be used. Media usage is significantly different across organizational levels.

③ LEARNING OBJECTIVE
Explain how perception, inference, language, and status can lead to communication breakdown

We learned that many barriers can prevent effective communication, including perception, inference, language, and status. Perception is a person's view of reality. Because no two people have the same experiences and training, no two people see things in exactly the same way. For this reason, there are degrees of perception, and what is crystal clear to the sender may be very vague to the receiver. Inference is an assumption made by the receiver of a message. Whenever messages are long, involved, or nonspecific, there is a good chance that an inference will be made. Language is a barrier whenever two people associate different meanings with the same word. Status is a problem whenever people modify messages according to who is receiving or sending them.

④ LEARNING OBJECTIVE
Identify eight ways to overcome barriers to communication and achieve effective communication

These barriers can lead to communication breakdown, but there are ways of overcoming them. Some of the most helpful are (1) knowing the steps in the communication process; (2) using simple, repetitive language; (3) using empathy; (4) understanding body language; (5) learning how to receive and give feedback; (6) developing effective listening habits; (7) improving writing and speaking skills; and (8) understanding the impact of gender differences on communication style. Of these ways, the two that warrant most consideration are the first and the sixth. By knowing the steps in the communication process, it is possible for the manager to be aware of breakdowns and to work to overcome them. By being an effective listener, the manager ensures a closed loop in the communication process. The subordinate sends back a message to the manager, and the manager can use it to correct any problems that have occurred in the communication process.

(5) **LEARNING OBJECTIVE**
Outline the four steps in the communication process and describe how they can help improve a manager's communication skills

Many breakdowns in communication can be avoided when the following four steps in the communication process are followed: (1) attention, (2) understanding, (3) acceptance, and (4) action. A sender must get the full attention of the receiver, who must block out any competition for attention. Understanding involves comprehension of the message. Asking appropriate questions help to reveal levels of understanding. Acceptance means compliance—going along with the message. The final step, action, requires the receiver to follow up and do what was requested.

(6) **LEARNING OBJECTIVE**
Describe the importance of using simple, repetitive language and empathy and understanding body language in achieving effective communication

The simpler a message, the more likely it will be understood and acted upon. Shorter messages have higher reader rates and are more likely to be remembered. Complex messages should be broken down into small bites giving listeners more opportunities to ask questions or seek clarification. In addition parts of the message should be repeated and reviewed.

Empathy means putting oneself in another person's place. You can identify with their thoughts, feelings, and joys because you have been there yourself. Empathy is especially important in the acceptance and action stages of the communication process. Empathy determines how quickly the receiver will respond and to what degree of importance the receiver attaches to the message. Empathy is important in knowing how to talk to people. The style of communication should fit the type of person to whom you are communicating. Four types are: (1) director, (2) free spirit, (3) humanist, and (4) historian.

People use body language to pass messages to others, but in some cases they are not aware they are doing it. Common examples of body language are eye movements, where a person stands or sits in relation to others, handshakes or touches, and the way a person dresses. Posture gives off language signals, such as, a high level of relaxation indicates a lack of respect. The type of grip in the handshake sends signals as does a pat on the back. Proxemics deals with the way people use physical space to communicate.

Communications can improve by learning how to analyze poorly transmitted messages and learn why they did not work effectively. Learn to ask sufficient questions for classification. Another way is to put oneself in the receiver's shoes (empathizing).

(7) **LEARNING OBJECTIVE**
Discuss ten guidelines for developing effective listening habits

Listen to what the speaker is saying, not how it is being said. Tell yourself that the speaker has something to say that will be of value or benefit to you. If the speaker gets boring, ask a pertinent question. Increase your determination to listen in times when the presentation gets technical or difficult to understand. Note the techniques of the speaker to determine whether you should adopt any of them. Evaluate the relevance of what is being said—any new or useful data. Listen for intended meanings as well as for expressed ideas. Integrate in your mind what the speaker is saying. Be a responsive listener by maintaining eye contact and giving positive feedback—nods or facial expressions. Be willing to accept the challenge of effective listening by telling yourself that it is a skill that you need to develop.

---

(8) LEARNING OBJECTIVE
Identify four ways for improving writing skills

Four steps for improving writing skills include: (1) Force yourself to write and rewrite material. (2) Make it a point to write at least three drafts of everything you do. (3) See if you can get someone in your organization to review your written work and comment on it. (4) If possible, sign up for a college course in writing and force yourself to learn more effective writing skills.

---

(9) LEARNING OBJECTIVE
Explain the four parts of PLAN for improving speaking skills

The parts of the PLAN are: P = the purpose for the presentation or speech; L = logistics is when and where the meeting will be held; A = audience is who will be present; and N = nonverbal communication involves the layout of the room and the effective use of presentation tools—PowerPoint, charts, samples, and so forth.

---

(10) LEARNING OBJECTIVE
Discuss gender differences in communication style

Research finds differences in the communication styles and approaches of men and women. One reason is linguistic style, which refers to a person's speaking pattern and includes things such as pacing, pausing, word choice, directness, and use of jokes, figures of speech, stories, and questions. Some researchers believe that some of the differences can be explained in the inherited biological differences between the sexes. Boys are taught skills that focus on status and hierarchies and they learn to use communication to negotiate skillfully to achieve and maintain the upper hand. Whereas, girls are taught to view communication as a network of connections in which conversations are negotiations for closeness and to use this orientation to seek and give confirmation and support.

---

(11) LEARNING OBJECTIVE
Describe technology's impact on communication

Communication technology is changing the way people communicate in firms and affecting the way people interact. The increase in communication networks and electronic machines have people connected twenty-four hours a day seven days a week—at work, on the road, and at home—extending the day to anytime, anyplace. Over half the population in major metropolitan areas now own a mobile phone and subscribe to a wireless-phone service, and two-thirds of the population are online.

Communication technology is changing the workplace. New patterns of communication are emerging, forcing some traditional downward, upward, and horizontal organizational structures to become bubble charts or wheels. Communication flows across the lines creating systems of webs. Firms can use technology software to detect functioning teams versus assigned teams by studying e-mail transmissions and analyzing patterns of communication within the firm.

There are drawbacks in using technology to communicate information. They include: (1) information-security is a problem, (2) privacy issues are a concern, (3) the workday is extended, (4) nonverbal clues are missing, (5) multitasking is increased, (6) the volume of information is overwhelming, (7) the interaction among team members changes, and (8) small talk and social interaction is reduced.

KEY TERMS IN THE CHAPTER

Communication   Understanding
Encoding   Acceptance
Decoding   Action
Perception   Empathy
Inference   Proxemics
Status   Information richness
Attention   Linguistic style

REVIEW AND STUDY QUESTIONS

1. What are the five essential elements in the communication process? Explain each.

2. Describe what happens in the encoding process. Include two basic steps.

3. Give several examples of nonverbal forms of communication. What message do they send?

4. Explain how the decoding process works.

5. In choosing a communication medium, when is face-to-face the most effective choice? When is it a poor choice? Explain.

6. What does the issue of complexity in communication have to do with selecting a medium?

7. In what way can perception be a communication barrier?

8. What is an *inference?* In what way is it a communication barrier?

9. Is status a communication barrier? How? Explain.

10. What are the four steps in the communication process? Describe each.

11. In what way can simple, repetitive language lead to more effective communication? Explain.

12. How can empathy on the part of the manager help to achieve effective communication?

13. What does a manager need to know about body language? Cite some specific examples.

14. What are some of the most effective ways of getting feedback? Giving feedback? Give some examples.

15. What are some of the important ways to develop effective listening habits? List at least six.

16. How can managers improve their writing skills? Offer at least three useful suggestions.

17. How can speaking skills be improved? Explain PLAN.

18. How do men and women differ in the way that they communicate?

19. How is technology impacting communication in the workplace? Discuss several changes.

20. What are some drawbacks that firms must address when using technology communication? Identify eight issues.

VISIT THE WEB

Anybody, Anywhere

In this chapter, you studied about the communication process and the ways in which managers go about transferring meanings. This process is important in all companies, especially such large enterprises as Motorola, which has worldwide operations that extend from North America to South America, Europe, Asia, and Africa. The company's pagers and cellular telephones rely on wireless communication that allows the user to communicate with anybody, anywhere in the world. Visit the company's Web site at **http://www.motorola.com** and then answer these two questions:

(1) How do the products that the firm produces help managers to communicate?

(2) In addition to helping these managers do a better job, what communication challenges or problems do these products present for the managers?

Test Your Communication Skills

In this chapter, you learned the basics of communicating effectively, but how effective are you at communicating? Being a good communicator is crucial to effective human relations and to building interpersonal relationships required in all types of jobs. Take a few minutes and access your communication skills by answering the thirty-four questions in the "Communication Skills" test in this Web site at **http://www.queendom.com**

1. Visit the Web site and click on "Interpersonal Tests." Scroll down until you see the list of free tests. Click on the "Communication Skills" test.

2. Take the test and learn how effective you are at communicating. You will receive an overall score from the test results. If you want an analysis of the six parts of the test, you must pay a fee, which is not required for this course.

3. Write a summary on how you feel about the results. What is your overall score? Were you surprised? If so, why? What do you need to do to make changes?

Are You Convinced?

In this chapter you studied the basics of effective communication. Now let's see if you can apply those principles to a Web site. Visit the Web site at **http://www. ralcorp.com** and assess the effectiveness of its communication.

1. Did you easily understand what the company does? If so, what is it?

2. How educational is the communication? What new things did you learn?

3. How persuasive is the message? How will it impact your buying habits? Give an example.

4. What are the communication strengths and weaknesses of the Web site?

5. What did you learn about communication from this Web site?

SOLUTION TO THE NINE-DOT PROBLEM

Note that you can solve the problem only by going outside the square formed by the dots.

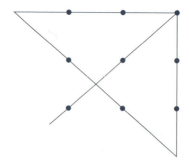

TIME OUT ANSWERS

A Matter of Inference

1. True. The first sentence of the story says so.

2. False. Although we are never told exactly where the firm is located, we do know that it is in New England.

3. Inference. We are never told who gave Bart the order to engage in the crash R&D program.

4. Inference. We are never told the size of Bart's budget. The $250,000 he has allowed his top R&D people to spend might be coming from a special fund created for this purpose by the president of the firm and so may not be included in his regular budget.

5. Inference. We do not know what the five people are supposed to be doing with the money. They may be working to develop a new process or they may be trying to buy the process from someone else. The story is unclear on this point.

6. Inference. We do not know that the individual to whom Mary Lou is talking is a professor. The story refers to the person as a scientist, who may not hold a professorial rank.

7. False. The story says Mary Lou is one of Bart's best people, so she is in the R&D department, not the plastics manufacturing department.

8. Inference. We do not know whether Mary Lou is one of the five people authorized to spend up to $250,000 or is a sixth member of Bart's department.

9. Inference. We do not know that the company wants to buy the patent. Even if the company does want it, it might be interested in giving the scientist stock in the firm and a position that pays about what the scientist currently is receiving but offering better fringe benefits. In short, it may want to trade for the patent, not to buy it.

10. Inference. Bart may believe this. However, he may believe the scientist is wavering and needs to be convinced by someone in higher authority who can spell out the terms of an agreement. Even this conclusion, however, is inferential.

11. Inference. We do not know why the scientist is coming with Mary Lou. Additionally, he or she may have decided not to accept any reimbursement of expenses so that there is no implied obligation to go along with the company's offer.

12. Inference. Again, we do not know for sure why the scientist is coming to see Bart. Could it be that Mary Lou has told him or her that the firm will build a special research facility far better than that at the university and that this is motivating the scientist to fly in and talk to Bart?

13. Inference. We do not know in what area the scientist received the Nobel Prize. We also do not know that the scientist is a man.

14. True. The story says Bart and the president have lunch on a biweekly basis.

15. Inference. We do not know the basis for Bart's belief that he will have good news for the president. Might it be that the president assigned Bart to another project, which is coming along so well that Bart knows that the president will be pleased?

ANSWER TO PHYSICAL LOCATION AND BODY LANGUAGE

You are seated in a correct chair. Individuals seated at an angle to each other are more likely to engage in cooperative interaction than are those seated either side by side or completely opposite each other. You and Person F can move closer to each other or further away, making the corner position the ideal one for the two of you.

TIME OUT ANSWERS

Are You a Good Listener?

Using the scoring key given, determine the total number of points you earned for the answers that you gave.

Question	Points Earned for Answer							Score
	A	B	C	D	E	F	G	
1.	7	6	5	4	3	2	1	_____
2.	1	2	3	4	5	6	7	_____
3.	7	6	5	4	3	2	1	_____
4.	1	3	5	7	5	3	1	_____
5.	7	6	5	4	3	2	1	_____
6.	1	2	3	4	5	6	7	_____
7.	7	6	5	4	3	2	1	_____
8.	7	7	6	4	3	2	1	_____
9.	7	6	5	4	3	2	1	_____
10.	1	2	3	4	5	6	7	_____
11.	1	2	3	4	5	6	7	_____
12.	1	3	5	7	5	3	1	_____
13.	7	6	5	4	3	2	1	_____
14.	1	2	3	4	5	6	7	_____
						Bonus point	+2	
						Grand total		_____

Scoring Interpretation

90–100	Excellent. You are an ideal listener.
80–89	Very good. You know a great deal about effective listening.
70–79	Good. You are an above-average listener.
60–69	Average. You are typical of most listeners.
Less than 60	Below average. You need to work on developing more effective listening habits.

Sandra Shelby is a training officer for a large metropolitan community. The community spends approximately $400 million per year on a variety of services, including transportation, garbage collection, and police and fire protection. The training and development department has a budget of $7 million and is responsible for providing orientation to new community employees as well as ongoing training to all public personnel.

Each year, the board of commissioners of the community enacts a budget. Because funds are limited, each department within the community must present and defend its budget requests. An effective presentation can result in a department getting all the funds it requests, whereas a poor presentation can result in a department getting as little as 60 percent of its request.

Sandra has been chosen to make this year's presentation. The talk is to run twenty minutes, followed by approximately ten minutes of questioning by the commissioners. In an effort to make the best possible presentation, Sandra plans on interviewing the manager and assistant manager of her department to find out which programs they feel are critical. She then intends to compare this year's proposed budget with last year's proposed budget in order to ensure that she has not left out any requests.

Sandra also knows that the six commissioners have very fixed views regarding the area of training and development. Two of the commissioners believe that the community is not spending enough money on training, two feel that too much is spent, and the remaining two tend to listen to the arguments that are made at the meeting and vote accordingly. Sandra believes that it would be wise to talk to the two commissioners who support training and development and get some information from them regarding what might be included in the report. She would also like to talk to the two who do not make up their minds until the meeting itself to determine whether she can learn from them some of the key facts that would influence their decision. The commissioners are easily approachable, and Sandra knows that she will have no trouble getting in to see the four of them.

Sandra intends to take all this information and condense it into a twenty-minute talk. She believes that the easiest way to present the information will be on a point-by-point basis. She intends to use PowerPoint presentation projected onto a large screen that easily can be seen by all the commissioners. "It will help the commissioners clearly focus on the points I want to make," she told her assistant. "In addition, I need to be prepared to answer their questions. So I am going to run through my talk with you as my only audience. When I am finished, we will critique the presentation and see how it can be strengthened. Then, after we finalize the talk, I want you to make up 20 questions that you believe they will ask me, and we will discuss the proper responses."

Sandra believes this approach will be effective in ensuring that her department gets its budget request. However, she is remaining flexible in her approach and, if anyone in the department has constructive ideas, she intends to incorporate them into her presentation.

QUESTIONS

1. In handling this assignment, how can the PLAN approach help Sandra? Explain how Sandra will incorporate each phase of PLAN.

2. How can the use of Figure 11.3 be of value to Sandra? Prepare a list of suggestions for Sandra to follow in giving her presentation. Give at least one suggestion for each of the six factors.

3. How can Sandra benefit from the information in the Audience Analysis Grid, Figure 11.4? Give examples of how Sandra can use the information to improve her presentation.

4. What other things would you recommend that Sandra do in preparing for her presentation?

Looking to Move Up

George Rather is a store manager for an eastern discount chain. When he took over the New Jersey unit a little over a year ago, the store's sales were down and employee turnover was high. However, George was not particularly concerned because he had faced situations similar to this before. He had taken a unit in Ohio and turned it into a winner and, before that, he had turned around a company store in the Los Angeles area.

When George's boss asked him to take over the management of the New Jersey store, George was not pleased. "I've done more than my share of turning around unsuccessful stores," he said. "I want to move up from store manager to district manager. I've proven I can handle things at this level and I think I should be promoted." His boss agreed that George had done an excellent job at the store level. "I'm going to recommend you for the next opening that occurs at the district level. However, for the moment I need you in New Jersey."

A month ago, there was an opening at the district level. Three people applied for the job. In addition to George, the manager of the largest store in the system and the manager of the store that had the greatest sales increase last year both applied. Two weeks ago, top management announced its decision. The manager of the largest store was given the promotion. George was crushed. He had been certain he was going to get the job. On hearing the news, he called his boss. "I thought you said that I was going to get the next job opening at the district level. I had your word on it," he complained. His boss was embarrassed over the decision and did not hesitate to say so. However, he also pointed out that he had not guaranteed George the next promotion. "I don't have the authority to do that," he noted. "However, I did vote for you and did everything I could to help you secure the position. For what it's worth, you are a shoo-in for the next opening." George thanked him for his encouraging words and hung up.

Yesterday, George announced he would be leaving to join a competitive firm. He is to be their district manager. His boss called him up and wished him the best. "I know things didn't work out the way you and I wanted them to. I hope you find what you're looking for with your new firm."

Your Advice

1. What might George have done differently to ensure that his boss would go to bat for him and fight harder to get him the promotion?

   ____ a. He could have told the boss that he would leave the organization if he did not get the job.
   ____ b. He could have asked the boss to explain what "I'm going to recommend you for the next opening" meant and how likely it was that this support would land him the job.
   ____ c. He could have checked with the boss a few days prior to the time the final decision was made and ensured that this person would fight hard for him during the meeting.

2. What communication barrier caused George to believe he was going to get the next promotion to district manager? Identify and describe this barrier.

3. How could this problem have been overcome or minimized? What should George have done? What could the boss have done? Explain.

4. What does this case illustrate about communication breakdown? What lessons that can be drawn from this case? Identify and describe three.

Purpose

- To identify commonly understood gestures.
- To understand the importance of gestures in nonverbal communications.

Procedure

1. Students should form groups of three to five. Individuals should jot down five examples of commonly understood gestures—for example, waving goodbye or signing "okay."

2. Group members then should take turns displaying one of their gestures for their group. Is it, in fact, commonly understood? For those gestures that are not, what is the problem?

3. When each group member has displayed his or her five gestures, make a list of all those that were considered commonly recognizable. List them from most easily recognized to least easily recognized. Make a second list of those that were confusing or unrecognizable. Share these lists with other groups.

4. As a class, discuss these questions:

   ____ a. How rich a source of meaning are gestures?

   ____ b. How may gestures be used to complement verbal content? To contradict?

   ____ c. Are gestures culturally bound—that is, would they be identically interpreted in other countries or cultures?

12

Managing Conflict and Change

As discussed in Chapter 11, one of the most important duties of the manager for achieving behavioral effectiveness is to communicate well; however, this alone will not ensure overall effectiveness. Two of the most common reasons are conflict and change, topics that are the focus of this chapter.

AFTER READING THIS CHAPTER, YOU SHOULD BE ABLE TO:

1. Define *conflict* and explain some of the major types of conflict.
2. Relate some of the most effective ways of managing conflict.
3. Discuss how change occurs.
4. Explain four common responses to change—rejection, resistance, tolerance, and acceptance.
5. Identify three dimensions of change.
6. Describe the five basic steps in the change process.
7. Describe the characteristics of a change leader.
8. Explain how participation and communication can help the manager implement change, and how structural changes can be used as change interventions.
9. Discuss how organizational development interventions can be effectively employed in dealing with change.

Using Change to Lead a Revolution

As the U.S. auto industry entered the twenty-first century, foreign competition was continuing to gain market share. Chrysler, which had been acquired by Daimler-Benz a few years earlier, was reeling from major financial losses, and General Motors, which once held more than 55 percent of the American market, now controlled only 28 percent of the market and announced that it was dropping its Oldsmobile line. Ford Motor was in a better position than its two major rivals, thanks to its ability to deal effectively with the United Auto Workers union and to maintain its market share in the range of 25 percent. One of the reasons for this success has been the company's ability to deal with change. The company accomplishes this in part through its Leadership Development Center, where managers are taught how to assess risk, make decisions, and follow through by ensuring that the implementation is carried out correctly.

One graduate of these training programs is Nancy Gioia, a chief program engineer leading a team of engineers, designers, marketers, and purchasing managers who work on the Ford Thunderbird. In addition to the leadership training she has received, Gioia mentors participants in the training programs. The advice she gives them is a result of her work experience and the way in which she has used the training in her own job. Commenting on how to deal with change and keep Ford on the cutting edge in the industry, she dispenses a wide variety of advice. Some of her ideas include the following: (1) Pick one or two challenging things that you want to learn in the training programs and concentrate on them. (2) Have a bias for action. Anyone can set a series of objectives for themselves, but the best leaders implement a plan for attaining these goals. (3) Learn to work in groups and use this team to create a network for getting things done. (4) Be prepared to both listen to and accept change.

Ford's training programs are designed to help people take risks, make decisions, and cope with change. In particular, the company wants its managers to create discomfort among the personnel because this is how both learning and improvement come about. By getting the personnel to cope with problem areas and take the necessary action, the company is building a cadre of employees who can deal with change. One manager, after having been to the company's New Business Leader program, noted that, "It was a great week. It renewed for me the idea that I'm not supposed to look around for leadership. I'm working on a project that could change the nature of Ford's relationship with its customers. People often ask me how this project applies to my job. Well, it doesn't. But in order to drive change, I have to step out of my functional competency. This idea *will* get implemented—if not by my team then by someone else. Either way, Ford wins."

At the present time, Ford is putting approximately two thousand people annually through its New Business Leader program. The company is convinced that changes in the auto industry over the next decade are going to change radically the way that things are done. Those who are not prepared for these changes will find themselves falling further and further behind. The old way of doing things will not be enough. New approaches are going to be needed to meet this impending revolution—and Ford intends to be ready to lead the way by making the changes that are needed to ensure its position in the automobile market. In the first decade of the twentieth century, Ford was the premier automobile firm in America. The company believes that if it can meet the challenges of the new century, it will be able to reclaim its position in the first decade of the current century.

Sources: Keith H. Hammonds, "Grass Roots Leadership: Ford Motor Co.," Fast Company, April 2000, pp. 137–152; Edmund L. Andrews, "Daimler Says Chrysler's Problems Are Worsening," New York Times, December 19, 2000, p. W1; and Jeffrey Ball, "DaimlerChrysler Official Expects Restructuring, Change Next Year," Wall Street Journal, December 20, 2000, p. A4.

LEARNING OBJECTIVE 1
Define conflict and explain some of the major types of conflict

The Nature of Conflict

Conflict
is opposition or antagonism toward other individuals or things.

Conflict is opposition or antagonism toward other individuals or things. For example, Martha has beaten out Robert for a promotion, and now there is conflict between the two because Robert feels he was better qualified and should have gotten that job. Similarly, Tim and Tina

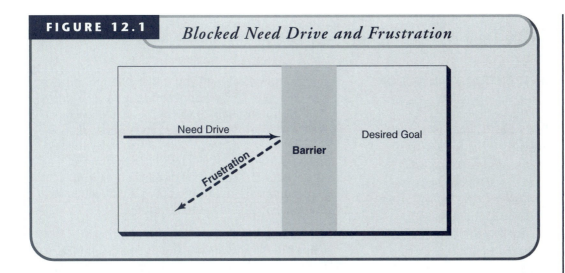

FIGURE 12.1 | *Blocked Need Drive and Frustration*

Need Drive

Frustration

Barrier

Desired Goal

believe the new monthly cost control report is a waste of time and have decided to file their reports late and incomplete. Both have a conflict with this new report.

In overall terms, two types of conflict are important in the study of human relations. One is conflict at the *individual* level. The other is conflict at the *organizational* level. Each type of conflict has its own characteristics.

Individual Conflict

Whenever the needs of individuals in the organization are at odds, conflict can develop. Two of the most common reasons are frustration and interpersonal conflict.

FRUSTRATION

Frustration is the result of a blocked need. In the example just given, Robert was frustrated because his need to reach a desired goal (the promotion) was blocked by a barrier (only one person could receive the promotion). Figure 12.1 provides an illustration of Robert's frustration. Another good example is provided by the worker who is unable to accomplish a task because of interference by other employees or because of a failure of the equipment that is provided for doing the job.

What the manager needs to realize is that the stronger the worker's motivation to reach a desired goal, the greater the person's frustration with failure. Because the manager wants to encourage high motivation, it is imperative that some form of assistance be provided in helping the individual deal with this frustration. For example, in many cases the manager can intervene and remove the roadblocks that are preventing goal attainment. An example is to give an employee access to the information needed to complete the task in a timely manner or to find the resources needed to get the job done. Another common cause of frustration is unfair or discriminatory treatment in the workplace. In some organizations, minorities are not accorded the same treatment as others. For example, research shows that blacks and women, on average, have lower salaries than do their white male counterparts.[1] Additionally, women sometimes are subject to sexual harassment. The Ethics and Social Responsibility in Action box describes some of the steps that organizations now are taking to ensure that this practice is terminated.

INTERPERSONAL CONFLICT

Closely related to the idea of frustration is that of **interpersonal conflict,** which arises when disagreements occur among personnel. For example, when Daimler-Benz acquired Chrysler, its objective was to establish a strong foothold in the American auto market and to give Chrysler greater entry into the European market. Within a short period, however, the senior-level

Frustration
is the result of a blocked need.

Interpersonal conflict
is a result of disagreement between personnel.

in action

ETHICS AND SOCIAL RESPONSIBILITY IN ACTION

Dealing with Sexual Harassment

Many women in the workplace feel that they are sexually harassed. In the past, involvement in this problem was confined to the woman and the person who was doing the harassing. This no longer is true. Additionally, the number of sexual harassment complaints that have been filed since 1990 has surged from 6,000 annually to more than 14,000 today, and the nature of sexual harassment is beginning to be expanded by the courts. In a recent ruling, the Supreme Court held that it is sexually harassing to create a "hostile environment" in which individuals are subjected to such behaviors as sexually suggestive comments, mental abuse, and obscenities. In response, many organizations have now created formal policies that specifically forbid sexual harassment in all forms. In addition, experts in the area recommend that managers know how to deal with this problem when it arises. In particular, they suggest that managers adhere to five guidelines:

1. *Know the organization's policy on sexual harassment.* If you do not have a copy of the rules, get one and read it. If there is no written policy, assume any complaint by a female worker that she is being "bothered" by a male employee will be construed by the courts to be sexual harassment.

2. *If there is a formal policy, ensure that everyone in your work unit knows about it and understands it.* If there is no formal policy, tell your personnel that sexual harassment will not be tolerated and urge those who feel they have been victims to report the matter to you.

3. *Take all complaints seriously.* Do not assume that someone has hidden motives and is trying to get another worker in trouble. Meet with the complaining employee, taking notes and asking any

questions that will help you to get a better understanding of what has happened. Also make it clear that the organization does not tolerate sexual harassment in any form and that you will not allow it in your work unit. It is important to convey the seriousness with which you approach this matter. If it ever gets into court, one of the first things the prosecution will attempt to prove is that you knew of the situation and treated it lightly.

4. *Act immediately.* Call in whomever has been named in the sexual harassment charge and talk to the person. Try to resolve the situation at this point. Perhaps this person regards the entire matter as nothing more than a joke. Make it clear to the person that these matters are not funny. Perhaps the individual says that the other person misunderstood some innocent remark. Make it clear that any remarks that can be misconstrued as sexual harassment can get an individual into serious trouble. If, in your view, the matter is sufficiently serious, have the person who brought the charge present at your meeting with the worker who has been accused and make it clear to both of them that you expect no further problems along this line. It may be embarrassing to the person bringing the charge to be present at the meeting but, if it will help you to convey the seriousness of the matter to the other employee, you should have the person there.

5. *Follow up on your actions.* After a week has gone by, check with the woman to be sure she is not being subjected to further harassment. Let her know that you have not forgotten the matter and that, if it arises again, you want to know about it at once.

It is unlikely that you can stamp out sexual harassment in the workplace. However, you can reduce its occurrence and its negative impact by following these five guidelines.

Sources: Stephanie N. Mehta, "What Minority Employees Really Want," Fortune, July 10, 2000, pp. 181–186; Jennifer Steinhauer, "If the Boss Is Out of Line, What's the Legal Boundary?" New York Times, March 27, 1997, pp. C1, C4; Paul S. Greenlaw and John P. Kohl, "Creative Thinking and Sexual Harassment," SAM Advanced Management Journal, winter 1996, pp. 4–10; and Jennifer J. Laabs, "What to Do When Sexual Harassment Comes Calling," Personnel Journal, July 1995, pp. 42–53.

German management was engaged in an interpersonal conflict with their American counterparts regarding how Chrysler should be run. The Germans felt that the American executives were paid too much money and the Americans felt that the Germans did not understand how the U.S. auto market operated. As a result, when Chrysler began losing money, the German executives began replacing the senior American staff with their own executives.

This, in turn, created interpersonal conflict and resulted in even further deterioration of relations between the two groups.[2]

Organizational Conflict

When viewed from an organizational level, conflict can be categorized into two groups: institutionalized and emergent.

INSTITUTIONALIZED CONFLICT

Institutionalized conflict results from organizational attempts to structure work assignments. For example, three major departments are fighting for increased budgets, but insufficient moneys are available for all to receive their requests. Each department fights to gain increases at the expense of the others. In the end, at least one department will not get its request and, possibly, none of them will end up with what they want. Ultimately, conflict often ensues, with each department harboring a grudge against the others.

Another example of institutionalized conflict occurs when employees refuse to share information because it results in their losing informal power. For example, when Buckman Labs, a specialty chemical company, implemented an electronic network to enable knowledge sharing by all employees so that complex customer problems could be quickly resolved, the new system faced institutional conflict. In particular, it threatened many employees who had developed a great deal of informal power by hoarding their valuable expertise. Therefore, when employees tried to make use of the electronic network to obtain necessary information, those who could provide the data refused to do so while offering a variety of reasons, including "You don't need to know this information."[3]

EMERGENT CONFLICT

Emergent conflict arises from personal and social causes. For example, there may be disagreement between the formal and informal organizations regarding how much work personnel should perform. Another example is conflict that emerges when subordinates feel they know a great deal more than their boss regarding how to improve efficiency. Although the boss has the formal authority to run the department and make decisions related to work assignments, the personnel are in conflict with these decisions because they feel the boss lacks the necessary knowledge and experience to do the job as well as they can.

Managing Conflict

Conflict can be managed in a number of ways. One of the most common is general counseling. However, in some cases, such as that of troubled employees or individuals who are drug abusers, the approach must be more carefully planned. Other approaches to managing conflict include mutual problem solving, expansion of resources, smoothing, and compromise. The following sections examine these ways of managing conflict.

General Counseling

Counseling is the discussion of an emotional problem with an employee for the purpose of eliminating or reducing the problem. Many people in the workplace need counseling because the demands of their jobs create emotional problems for them. The overall purpose of counseling is to provide emotional support for employees. In this function, the manager's job is to increase the employee's understanding, self-confidence, and ability to work effectively as a member of the team. Managers typically use four approaches in carrying out this function.

ADVICE

When the manager advises a subordinate, he or she lays out a course of action to be followed. The manager takes the lead, and the subordinate follows. Some professional counselors have

Institutionalized conflict
results from organizational attempts to structure work assignments.

Emergent conflict
arises from personal and social causes.

LEARNING OBJECTIVE
(2) *Relate some of the most effective ways of managing conflict*

Counseling
is the discussion of an emotional problem with an employee for the purpose of eliminating or reducing the problem.

pointed out the dangers in trying to understand another person's complicated emotions and to recommend a path of action. Despite the possible dangers, however, this approach to counseling is widely used, because managers believe they should provide such guidance and workers expect them to do so. Many employees admit that they would rather have the manager suggest a course of action (even if it might be wrong) than to plan one themselves.

REASSURANCE

Closely related to advice is reassurance. Some people, for example, encounter stress because they are unsure of how well they are performing their jobs. The manager may tell a subordinate that he or she is doing fine and may encourage him or her to keep it up. To a worker who is experiencing job stress, the manager may point out, "This is all temporary. Our busy season ends next week, and everything will return to normal." Sometimes reassurance is just what the person needs to reduce frustration or stress. In other cases, the individual needs to be assured that organizational rules will be enforced. A good example is sexual harassment on the job. Managers not only need to be aware of this form of behavior, they must be prepared to take action as soon as they learn about it.

RELEASE OF EMOTIONAL TENSION

Many times, all a worker needs is a sympathetic ear. The tension declines, once he or she pours out what has been bottled up inside. Of course, this may not solve the problem, but it often removes mental blocks and permits the worker to face the problem squarely. Few people can resolve their problems when seething with anger and tension. This counseling function can help to alleviate such emotions.

REORIENTATION

Sometimes employees need to be reoriented. They require additional training for a new job, a revision of their aspirations so that these are more in line with their abilities, or a rethinking of their current goals and values vis-à-vis those of the organization. The manager can sometimes handle these problems but, if they are severe, professional help must be engaged. If, for example, an executive is an alcoholic, helping him or her become reoriented may be beyond the ability of most managers. When one's subordinate has this problem, it is best to let professional counselors take over.

Dealing With More Serious Problems

Sometimes employees will need more than general counseling. Their problems are serious and troubling, may be resulting in mental depression, and could be a result of alcohol or drug abuse.

TROUBLED EMPLOYEES

Sometimes employees will be troubled over job-related or home-related problems. If the manager feels the problem is best handled by letting it go, of course, no action is required. However, if the manager believes that some action is needed, three courses are available:

1. **Tell the employee to shape up or ship out.**
2. **Discipline the person.**
3. **Discuss the problem with the employee in an effort to work out a solution.**

This last approach requires effective counseling or coaching by the leader. Some of the most useful guidelines that can be employed include the following:

- **Talk to the employee early in the workweek rather than just before the weekend. In this way, you can follow up the next day if additional coaching or counseling is needed.**

- Talk to the employee early in the day rather than just before quitting time. This will allow you ample time to at least cover your main points and give the worker a chance to respond.
- Talk to the individual privately, away from other workers and managers. Let the person know that just the two of you are involved—at least at this stage.
- Get to the point immediately. Describe the problem situation or behaviors you have been noticing and present them from *your* point of view rather than someone else's. The following are some examples:

Do say:

I am becoming concerned about the number of accidents you are having.

As opposed to:

Your nervousness is causing you to have too many accidents.

Do say:

I am upset over your failure to follow my instructions.

As opposed to:

You make me mad by failing to follow my instructions.

Do say:

I have some concerns about your work.

As opposed to:

Some concerns have been voiced about your work.

- If the worker finds it difficult to talk, provide reassurances and let the individual proceed at his or her own pace. Acknowledge what the person says without passing judgment or giving advice.
- When the employee is done talking, discuss how he or she can improve work performance. Let the person know you are available if assistance is needed.
- If the individual's problem requires professional counseling, do not offer it yourself. The problem is beyond your training. Help to identify the problem and then have the organization's counseling service handle the matter. If no such service is available, prepare a list of community referral services to which the worker can turn. Typical examples of problems for which referrals should be made include:
  - recurring bouts of anger, sadness, or fear.
  - feelings of loneliness, isolation, moodiness, or depression.
  - suicidal thoughts.
  - inability to concentrate or sleep.
  - lack of self-confidence.
  - family problems.
  - high stress levels.
  - constant anxiety.
- Respect the employee's confidentiality. Do not discuss his or her situation with coworkers or others who have no need to know about the matter.

ALCOHOLISM

Frustration and stress are very common in modern organizations. In dealing with these problems, some people turn to alcohol because they believe that it helps them to unwind. The unfortunate fact is that alcoholism in industry has now become a major problem resulting in accidents, absenteeism, wasted time, ruined materials, and premature job termination. Moreover, the Office of Applied Studies of the Substance Abuse and Mental Health Services Administration reports that more than 8 percent of employees were heavy drinkers in 2000 and in 2002 over 7 percent of these workers were dependent on abusing alcohol. In the construction industry the number of heavy drinkers increases to over 14 percent.[4]

Observable Behavior Patterns of Alcohol Abuse

	Stage	Absenteeism	General Behavior	Job Performance
Alcohol Addiction Line	I Early	Tardiness Quits early Absence from work situations ("I drink to relieve tension")	Complaints from fellow employees for not doing his or her share Overreaction Complaints of not "feeling well" Makes untrue statements	Misses deadlines Commits errors (frequently) Lower job efficiency Criticism from the boss
	II Middle	Frequent days off for vague or implausible reasons ("I feel guilty about sneaking drinks"; "I have tremors")	Marked changes Undependable statements Avoids fellow employees Borrows money from fellow employees Exaggerates work accomplishments Frequent hospitalization Minor injuries on the job (repeatedly)	General deterioration Cannot concentrate Occasional lapse of memory Warning from boss
	III Late middle	Frequent days off; several days at a time Does not return from lunch ("I don't feel like eating"; "I don't want to talk about it"; "I like to drink alone")	Aggressive and belligerent behavior Domestic problems interfere with work Financial difficulties (garnishments, etc.) More frequent hospitalization Resignation; does not want to discuss problems Problems with the laws in the community	Far below expectation Punitive disciplinary action
	IV Approaching terminal stage	Prolonged unpredictable absences ("My job interferes with my drinking")	Drinking on the job (probably) Completely undependable Repeated hospitalization Serious financial problems Serious family problems; divorce	Uneven Generally incompetent Faces termination or hospitalization

Source: Gopal C. Pati and John I. Adkins Jr., "The Employer's Role in Alcoholism Assistance," Personnel Journal, 1983. Copyright © July 1983. Reprinted with permission of Personnel Journal, Costa Mesa, CA. All rights reserved.

How does a manager know when one of the workers is drinking too much? Answering this question is difficult, but there are some signs for which a manager can remain alert (see Figure 12.2). Among white-collar workers, these include such things as elaborate (and often bizarre) excuses for work deficiencies, pronounced and frequent swings in work pace, avoidance of the boss and associates, and increased nervousness. Among blue-collar workers, the clues include a sloppy personal appearance, signs of a hangover, frequent lapses of efficiency leading to occasional damage to equipment or material, increased nervousness, and increased off-the-job accidents. Perhaps the biggest problem managers must face in dealing with alcoholics is that they are skillful in denying the problem, especially when confronted by the boss.

Alcoholic employees have an uncanny knack for manipulating the feelings of supervisors. In many cases, they sense the onset of angry outbursts and know how to play for the counter feelings that will block supervisory urges to act decisively. A favorite ploy is the "whipped child" syndrome, characterized by the hang-dog look and the "I can't do anything right" verbalizations. Almost invariably, these behaviors tug at parental heart-strings, and suddenly a supervisor finds himself or herself comforting and supporting the alcoholic employee rather than confronting the individual. At other times, outbursts of righteous indignation by an employee will frighten the supervisor and cause him or her to back off.

Alcoholics have a great deal of experience at playing these games. Unless they know what is going on, supervisors do not have a chance.[5]

Regardless of how effective they are in initially hiding their problem, however, it eventually becomes obvious to the boss. This is particularly true if the organization has trained its managers in how to identify the excessive drinker. At this point, the problem worker should be sent either to the firm's medical department or human resources department for counseling or further referral. Because the manager is not likely to be an expert on alcohol rehabilitation, the individual must be careful about what he or she says. For example, it is a mistake for the manager to moralize to the employee about the dangers of drinking or to try to diagnose why the person has become a problem drinker. Instead, the manager should stress that the problem will be handled confidentially and that alcoholism can be successfully treated. From here, it is a matter of providing assistance to the person in getting the necessary treatment. Many organizations have their own program designed to deal with alcoholism; this is the ideal situation.

Some firms have found that managers do not like to be the ones to confront a subordinate about a drinking problem. The confrontation can be awkward, and the manager is often defensive about having to take the action. As a result, some firms now are using a team approach, in which a subordinate's associates and peers are involved in the evaluation process. As Edwards and Sproull have noted, "An alcoholic may be able to hide behaviors from a boss, but it is unlikely that . . . associates will be fooled."[6]

DRUG ABUSE

Employee drug use is widespread in industry, and its impact on the bottom line can be significant. Some of the latest statistics, for example, reveal that:

1. **Absenteeism is 66 percent higher among drug users than nondrug users.**
2. **Almost half of workplace accidents are drug related.**
3. **Disciplinary actions are 90 percent higher among drug users.**
4. **Employee turnover is significantly higher among drug users.**[7]

In addition, the U.S. Department of Health reports that 77 percent of drug users are employed full-time.[8]

Various reasons account for this rise in drug use. Generally, people take drugs at work to reduce the boredom, tension, or anxiety that accompanies the work. The symptoms of drug abuse are similar to those of alcoholism: slurred speech, dilated eyes, an unsteady walk, lack of dexterity, and uncontrollable laughter or crying. Also like alcoholism, programs have been developed for dealing with drug abusers. A typical program, in a large organization, will be designed and implemented in four stages:

1. **A committee is formed. If the firm is unionized, the union will be adequately represented. One representative in the group will be from the firm's medical department, if such a department exists.**
2. **A policy statement expressing the philosophy of the organization toward the effect of drug abuse on job performance will be developed.**
3. **If the firm is unionized, a joint labor-management policy statement recognizing the effect of drug abuse on health and behavior will be developed.**

4. Supervisors and management personnel will be trained in identifying drug-related problems and the proper ways to deal with them most effectively, including monitoring rehabilitation progress as measured by job performance.

Those found to be using drugs are removed from the workplace and often provided with assistance. If they accept this help and overcome their drug dependency, no disciplinary action is taken. Otherwise, they are dismissed.[9]

In recent years, disagreement has arisen regarding the use of drug testing and what to do when people test positively. Testing often is conducted before employment, randomly, and for cause (as in the case of someone involved in a job-related accident).[10] Research indicates that drug testing has increased over the past decade. Part of this increase is a result of state and local drug testing ordinances that permit pre-employment and random testing and, if there is reason to suspect the use of drugs, testing "for cause" as well. At the same time, it is important to remember that testing can result in false positive results; some experts contend that the error rate in drug testing can be as high as 30 percent. For example, evidence shows that the ingestion of codeine can produce positive results for heroin, some brands of aspirin have resulted in people testing positive for marijuana, and some cough medicines have resulted in individuals receiving positive test results for the use of amphetamines.[11] Clearly, drug testing has its limitations. This undoubtedly helps to explain the current move toward relying less on drug testing and more on educating personnel about the dangers of drugs and encouraging them to be intolerant about substance abuse by other employees.

How else should drug testing be handled? Many experts recommend that an employee assistance program (EAP) be created that offers confidential and professional help to those employees who are drug abusers. Many firms have an alcohol-related EAP, so it is merely a matter of expanding the program's focus. Rather than putting the emphasis on catching drug users and firing them, however, attention is devoted to prevention and rehabilitation. This is a frontline defense for many organizations in their fight to deal with drug abusers in the workplace.[12] Firms, however, need to do a better job of informing employees about these programs. Recently, the Office of Applied Studies in the Substance Abuse and Mental Health Services Administration reported about 53 percent of workers were aware of substance use employee assistance program (EAP) at their workplaces. Those workers in administrative support occupations were more likely than workers in other occupations to be aware of written workplace policies about employee substance use. Although workers in the transportation, communication, and other public utilities industries were more likely than workers in other industries to be aware of substance use testing at their workplaces.[13]

Drug use among workers is related to a series of workplace outcomes dealing with health, productivity, and performance. For example, a survey conducted by the National Household Survey of Drug Use revealed that employees using drugs compared to those not using drugs were more likely to have worked for three or more employers in the past year, skipped one or more days of work in the past month, or have voluntarily left an employer in the past year.[14]

Other Common Approaches

Counseling is an important method of resolving conflict. However, other approaches also are commonly used. The following sections examine four of these, in addition to offering some useful guidelines.

MUTUAL PROBLEM SOLVING

Mutual problem solving involves bringing together all the parties to a conflict and discussing the issues face-to-face. For example, if two groups in the department are having a problem working together, the manager will sit down with both groups and discuss the matter jointly. Each group will be given the opportunity to explain why it is having trouble with the other. Then the manager will work to create ground for common understanding, will discuss how the current conflict can be resolved, and often will require the two groups to determine mutually how they will resolve their own conflict. Through this process

Mutual problem solving
involves bringing together all the parties to a conflict and discussing the issues face-to-face.

of sharing concerns and communicating with each other, mutual problem solving often brings about intergroup harmony.

EXPANSION OF RESOURCES

Sometimes conflict can be resolved through an expansion of resources. For example, the department may need five computers but has a budget for only three. However, by talking the finance people into delaying the purchase of other equipment, there will be more money left for departmental computers. Alternatively, the company may be reorganized and some people given early retirement, thus freeing up funds for computer equipment. An expansion of resources involves a reworking of the budget for the purpose of determining how additional funds can be found.

SMOOTHING

Smoothing is the playing down of differences between individuals and groups while emphasizing their common interests. This approach often is useful only in the short run, as it involves ignoring or overlooking the major reasons behind the conflict. However, smoothing can be important in that it provides a temporary respite from the bickering and backbiting that often accompany conflict. Then, after all parties have had a chance to cool off, the problem can be reviewed and readdressed.

COMPROMISE

Compromise involves each side giving up something, such that neither side emerges as the big winner. Compromise is an important conflict resolution approach because it often allows each side to gain at least some of what it is seeking. In union-management negotiations, compromise commonly is used. If each side is able to feel that it did better with a compromise than it would have done with a prolonged conflict, the problem may be resolved permanently. However, if one side to the conflict feels that it gave up far too much, then the conflict is likely to reemerge.

ADDITIONAL USEFUL GUIDELINES

Recent research in the area of conflict has also generated a series of practical suggestions for managers.[15]

- One is not to promote conflict as "healthy competition." No empirical data support this assumption, and firms that do so often invite trouble for themselves.
- A second suggestion is to remember that it is better to avoid conflict from the beginning than to determine how to manage it when it appears.
- A third guideline is to realize that when conflict cannot be averted, it is extremely important to address some of its effects (distrust, anxiety, escalation of feelings) and to accept the fact that sometimes the elimination of conflict is not feasible.
- A fourth suggestion is to identify, if possible, the major reasons for the conflict. The manager should then try to set up trades in which each side acquiesces on issues that have low costs for it and relatively high payoffs for the other side(s).
- A fifth suggestion is that managers adopt a pragmatic approach to managing conflict by using techniques that are reasonable and, when possible, also inexpensive.[16]

The Nature of Change

Any modification or alteration of the status quo is **change** and, in recent years, virtually every organization has had to deal with rapid and often unpredictable changes, and often people are clueless about what's causing the change and how it affects them. Companies are not fine tuned machines that can be copied easily; they are "living, breathing, changing organisms that interact with millions of other living, breathing, changing organisms."[17] Commenting on the nature and severity of change in today's world of work, one expert recently wrote:

Smoothing
is the downplaying of differences between individuals and groups while emphasizing their common interests.

Compromise
involves each side giving up something such that neither side emerges as the big winner.

Change
is any modification of the status quo.

HOW MUCH DO YOU KNOW ABOUT THE CHANGE PROCESS?

Before studying the management of change, take a minute to examine how well you understand the change process.

Presented here are a dozen statements that relate to change. Read each carefully and then check whether it is basically true or basically false. Answers are given at the end of the chapter.

	Basically True	Basically False
1. Because change is so much a part of everyday life, most modern workers like new work procedures and policies.	_____	_____
2. Most work changes lead to an immediate increase in productivity.	_____	_____
3. Many employees like the status quo; change scares them.	_____	_____
4. If a computer designed to help them do their work were available, most employees would try to learn how to use the machine as quickly as possible.	_____	_____
5. Most organizational changes that are introduced are truly designed to increase efficiency.	_____	_____
6. If their friends at work are opposed to a change, most workers will also oppose the change.	_____	_____
7. Most people who resist change do so because they enjoy giving the organization a hard time.	_____	_____
8. People prefer to be told about new changes just before they are to be implemented.	_____	_____
9. People tend to be more supportive of changes they helped to fashion than of those forced on them.	_____	_____
10. Most managers tend to overrate the time needed to implement changes effectively.	_____	_____
11. Change always results, if only in the short run, in an increase in work output.	_____	_____
12. Unions tend to reject new work changes.	_____	_____

Change is sudden, nonlinear, and constant. Its amplitude and direction can't be forecast. Killer apps can come from anywhere; new competitors are lurking everywhere. Markets emerge, flourish, inspire imitators, breed competitors, and disappear seemingly overnight. Brands, which once took years to establish and which, once established, seemed unassailable, now burst on the scene like a new strain of virus, finding competitive spaces and market niches that were previously invisible. Internet buzz can make a product overnight—or break it. There is more choice than ever, more challenge than ever—and more change than ever. As a result, products and markets are continuously morphing, so organizations that want to prosper over the long term need to practice the art of continuous change.[18]

Moreover, sometimes change results in resistance from those who are encountering it.[19] Before examining the importance of change in the field of human relations, let us look at the nature of change by studying how it occurs and by answering the question, "Is resistance to change always a bad thing?" (Before continuing, take the Time Out quiz.)

LEARNING OBJECTIVE

Discuss how change occurs

③ How Change Occurs

When change takes place, three things happen: (1) There is a movement from one set of conditions to another; (2) some force(s) causes the change to come about; and (3) a consequence results from the change. The consequence is an alteration in the way things now are done. For example, to keep better track of inmates in prisons and to ensure that the wrong person is not accidentally released or transferred to another cell block, some prisons have introduced "eyedentity" technology. A high-technology machine takes a photo of an inmate's eye and, because no two people have the same eye configuration, the machine can identify each prisoner individually. Before someone is moved to another cell block or transferred out of the facility, the individual is required to look into the machine and have his or her "eyedentity" determined. The introduction of this new technology has dramatically improved the ability of prisons to keep track of their inmates. This is an excellent example of change that is quickly accepted by the organizational personnel because it helps them to do their jobs more efficiently. However, not all change is quickly accepted. Sometimes there is resistance.

Many forms of work-related technology provide a good example. The introduction of microcomputers often frightens personnel, because they believe the machines will require them to do more work or will be used to replace them. The same is true for other types of machinery from production equipment to facsimile machines. Another major reason for resistance is that personnel do not know how to use the technology or do not understand its value to them. Many people have found it difficult to learn computer operations, and each time they make a mistake they feel more defeated. (Many students who now use a personal computer for writing term papers can remember their own early problems in using the computer. One of the most common horror stories typically involves a time when they accidentally erased material or failed to save their work and had to rewrite part of a paper.) As long as people do not know how to use the new technology, resistance is likely.

Is Resistance Bad?

Some people believe that resistance to change is inevitable. In many cases, this is true, for when an organization's employees weigh the benefits associated with the status quo against those that they believe will result from the change, they opt for maintaining things the way they are. "Change, as it is usually orchestrated, creates initiative, overload and organizational chaos, both of which provoke strong resistance from the people most affected."[20] As a result, they resist alteration of the status quo.

Such resistance is not necessarily bad. Several important functions are served by it. First, resistance forces those supporting the change to build a case against the status quo, thereby providing management a chance to weigh the pros and cons. Here is an example.

> *The Almuth Public Library is one of the largest in the city, housing more than 700,000 volumes. Six months ago, the city council voted to appropriate the necessary funds to computerize the library. Many of the staff were delighted with the news, but some opposed computerization, claiming it would be very difficult to implement and would make exorbitant demands on their time. However, after a general meeting in which both sides had the opportunity to air their concerns, it was agreed that everyone would work together to implement the computerization. After the meeting, one of the employees, who initially had opposed the move, said, "After hearing the pros and cons, I realize computerization would not increase our workload or threaten our jobs. So now I'm all for it."*

A second benefit of resistance to change is that it encourages the organization to look before it leaps. This is particularly important when implementation of the change will be expensive and, if wrong, could mean major problems for the enterprise. In dealing with resistance and ensuring that change is properly implemented, the first place to begin is with careful planning. This involves consideration of three issues: (1) whether there should be a change; (2) if so, what type of change is needed; and (3) how the change should be implemented.

In many cases, change is good for the entire organization. For example, many technological innovations, from personal computers to cellular telephones to fax machines, are making it easier and cheaper to communicate information. Nonetheless, employees will not necessarily go along with a change. Change calls up many different responses. Some are a result of rational reasoning; others can be a result of unjustified concerns or biases brought about by fear, prejudice, or lack of trust.[21] What ever the reason, it is important to realize that the response to change can take numerous forms.

LEARNING OBJECTIVE

Explain four common responses to change—rejection, resistance, tolerance, and acceptance

④ # Responses to Change

People's reactions to change will depend on the benefits that they think will result from it. If they believe they will profit from the change, they will support it; if they feel they will lose status, prestige, earning power, or the job itself because of change, they will fight it. If we think of change as a stimulus, personnel can make numerous responses with varied outcomes and effects on the organization. For example, in Figure 12.3, eight workers are being subjected to the same change. As you can see, there are many responses: increase in absenteeism, resignation,

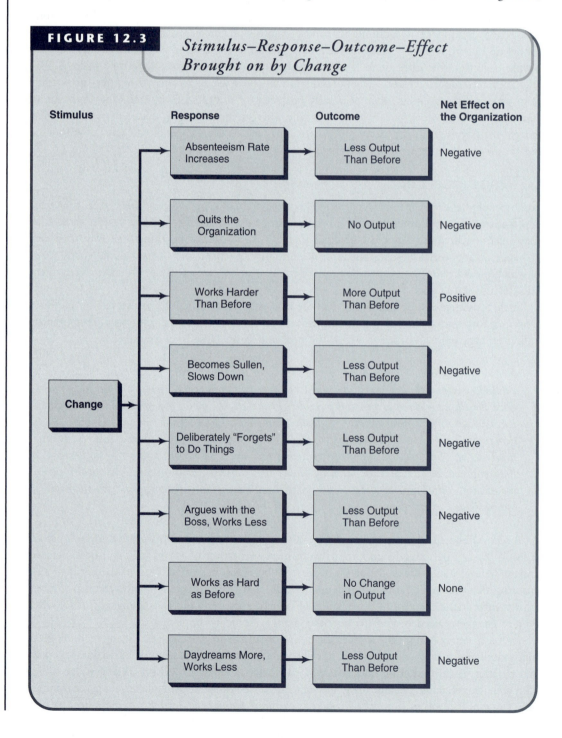

FIGURE 12.3 *Stimulus–Response–Outcome–Effect Brought on by Change*

Stimulus	Response	Outcome	Net Effect on the Organization
	Absenteeism Rate Increases	Less Output Than Before	Negative
	Quits the Organization	No Output	Negative
	Works Harder Than Before	More Output Than Before	Positive
Change	Becomes Sullen, Slows Down	Less Output Than Before	Negative
	Deliberately "Forgets" to Do Things	Less Output Than Before	Negative
	Argues with the Boss, Works Less	Less Output Than Before	Negative
	Works as Hard as Before	No Change in Output	None
	Daydreams More, Works Less	Less Output Than Before	Negative

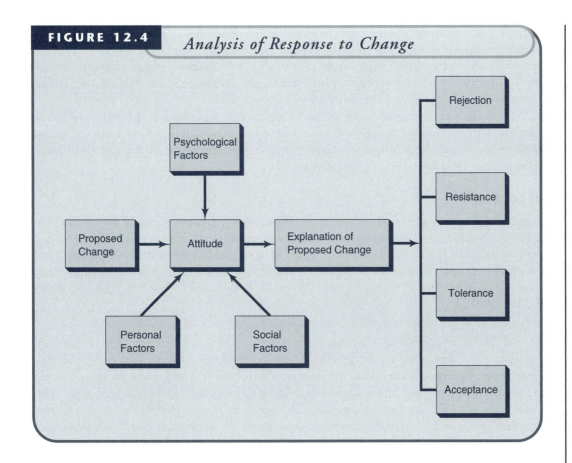

FIGURE 12.4 *Analysis of Response to Change*

working harder than ever, slowing down, arguing with the boss, and so on. Overall, however, there is a negative effect on the organization. In this case, we may conclude that most of the workers do not like the change or that it was not properly introduced.

In examining the situation further, we need to take a closer look at the stimulus (change) and response (outcome) relationship. We can view the change or stimulus as a causal variable and the response or outcome as an end-result variable. For human relations purposes, however, we need to investigate why different people respond in different ways to the same stimulus.

Some psychologists believe the answer can be found in an individual's attitude toward the stimulus. A person's attitude is a reflection of psychological factors, personal factors, and social factors. These factors will result in a particular evaluation of the change. In turn, the evaluation will lead to one of the four reactions: rejection, resistance, tolerance, or acceptance (Figure 12.4).

One of the most important psychological factors affecting attitudes is the individual's reaction to stress, a topic discussed earlier in the text. Some workers are rather comfortable under stressful or high-anxiety-producing conditions, but other employees shun stress and seek a calm environment.

One of the most important personal factors is experience: People who have encountered similar changes in the past draw on the results of those changes to evaluate the current or pending change. For example, if the last time it changed work procedures a company tried to increase output requirements by 15 percent, the workers probably will fight the management's new attempt to change work procedures again. They are likely to believe that if they give in, management will once more increase output requirements.

Conversely, we can take the example of the organization that introduced a new hospitalization plan to save the employees money: The next time the company announces a change in the hospitalization plan, there is likely to be warm support for the move because the employees had a good experience with a similar change.

The social factors refer to the group in which the individual works. If there is a great deal of cohesion in the group, all members will tend to stick together. If the proposed change conflicts with the norms and values of the informal group, members will not go along with management's attempt to introduce change. Conversely, if the change is supportive of its norms and values, the group will accept the change. Keep in mind that when we talk about group acceptance, one of the primary norms is always group unity. If management makes any reorganizational changes that will break up the group, the members will oppose plans.

As a result of psychological, personal, and social factors, an employee will form an attitude regarding the change. This attitude will assist him or her in evaluating the impact of the change to determine whether it is acceptable. On the basis of this evaluation, the employee will reject, resist, tolerate, or accept the proposed change.

REJECTION

When the change is perceived as potentially destructive, **rejection** occurs. Those being subjected to the change view it as totally unacceptable. In this case, it is not uncommon to find workers resigning their jobs or going on strike. At best, management can expect to encounter increased turnover, alienation, and dramatic reductions in productivity and job satisfaction.

RESISTANCE

Whenever workers feel threatened by or extremely anxious about a particular change, they are likely to resist. The resistance can be either overt or covert. **Overt resistance** is observable; management can see it. Work slowdown, the setting of lower informal production norms, and outright sabotage are examples. **Covert resistance** is not readily observable because it is done under the guise of working as usual. For example, the management has brought in a group of consultants to study operations and make efficiency recommendations. The workforce is concerned that some of them will lose their jobs or will be transferred to other departments. In an effort to thwart the consultants' efforts, the workers use veiled resistance. When the consultants ask for some data on a particular topic, a worker hands them a massive report containing the information. However, it will take the consultants two or three hours to find the material. In short, the workers are not refusing to go along; they are simply making it more difficult for the consultants to do their job.

TOLERANCE

If the workers are neutral about the change or have equal positive and negative feelings, they will have **tolerance** for the change. For example, management decides that, in the future, all people who work in Section D must wear safety equipment when they are in the work area. Because of the particularly high noise factor created by the machinery there, management wants every worker to wear plastic earmuffs that will screen out the noise and prevent damage to hearing. Many of the workers admit they are not particularly eager to wear the earmuffs, but they can understand management's point of view, so they will go along with management's request. They have no particularly strong feelings either way.

ACCEPTANCE

Sometimes the positive factors favoring the change are weighed much more heavily than the negative ones. In these cases, the workers' acceptance of the change is likely. For example, instead of asking workers to wear regular plastic earmuffs, the management has a set of earmuffs specially wired for each person. Music can be piped through the set so that workers can listen to music and do their jobs at the same time. Changes such as this have been widely accepted in many industrial settings. Printing companies, especially large newspaper firms, often give this kind of earmuff to their press operators, who, according to research, like the changed environment.

Why Is There Resistance to Change?

In most cases, workers do not reject change outright nor do they accept it. Rather they tend either to resist it or tolerate it. In our study of human relations, resistance is the reaction of greatest interest to us. After all, if the workers tolerate a particular change, there is really nothing for the manager to be concerned about. However, if they resist, the manager should find

Rejection
is the refusal to accommodate a particular condition or change.

Overt resistance
is observable.
Covert resistance
is not readily observable.

Tolerance
involves putting up with a change.

out why and then should determine how this resistance can be reduced or eliminated. Let us discuss in detail the most common causes of resistance to change.[22]

OBSOLESCENCE OF JOB SKILLS

A bookkeeper, who has worked for the same company for twenty years, learns that the bookkeeping functions are going to be transferred to a computer will fight the change. An assembly-line welder who learns that the company has just bought automatic welding machinery that will weld things faster and more efficiently than can be done by hand will oppose the change. Additionally, whereas organizations will attempt to find these people other positions in the firm, the meaningful alternative jobs require special training that the displaced workers lack.[23] These people have been on the job for so long doing the same thing day after day that their knowledge about other work is obsolete. Also, they do not qualify for the jobs being given to college-educated engineers and business specialists. In short, they have no real marketable skills, so they fight for the status quo.

FEAR OF THE UNKNOWN

Fear of the unknown can create a great impasse for change. The unknown brings uncertainty; and for some individuals, a natural resistance. For example, conservative individuals tend to resist change. "This factor has been measured and demonstrated in numerous studies and stands to reason on its own."[24] Introducing technology into a firm brings fear and uncertainty, especially for older workers. As a result, they may develop a negative attitude toward their work.

FEAR OF ECONOMIC LOSS

Another reason for resistance to change is fear of economic loss. Sometimes workers are replaced or fired or find themselves in dead-end jobs. Technology often plays a key role here, turning rather demanding jobs into simple ones that can be done by anyone. When this occurs, the lower demands of the job often are reflected by a new pay rate, and the workers now find that salary raises are much lower than before. After all, who needs highly paid people if the job is automated so that anyone can do it?

EGO DEFENSIVENESS

Sometimes a change will make a person look bad, so he or she will fight it. For example, Roberta has an idea for expanding the market effort out of the eastern part of the country and into the western states. If things go well there, the effort will then be expanded to the national market. However, her boss, Chuck, is reluctant to go along with her suggestion because it will make him look bad with his colleagues, who will all realize that Roberta was the one who thought up the new sales effort. Rather than allow this to happen, Chuck continually claims that he needs to develop the market in the east more fully before considering expansion.

THE COMFORT OF THE STATUS QUO

Change is disturbing to many people. They feel more comfortable working in established routines and procedures than taking risks by entering into new ventures or undertakings. Any attempt to alter this status quo meets with resistance.

SHORTSIGHTEDNESS

Many people know what is going to happen in the short run but not the long run. Therefore, they look only at the short-run effects of any change. We can illustrate this through an analysis of the impacts of autocratic and democratic, or participative, leadership. In the short run, if a manager changes from autocratic to participative leadership, his or her department often will suffer short-term decreases in productivity (Figure 12.5). This will not last indefinitely, however; long-term increases eventually will follow. Research reveals that it takes time for such a change to bring about increased productivity. Unfortunately, many managers are not interested in riding out the short-run declines to reap long-run benefits and so are not interested in changing their leadership style.

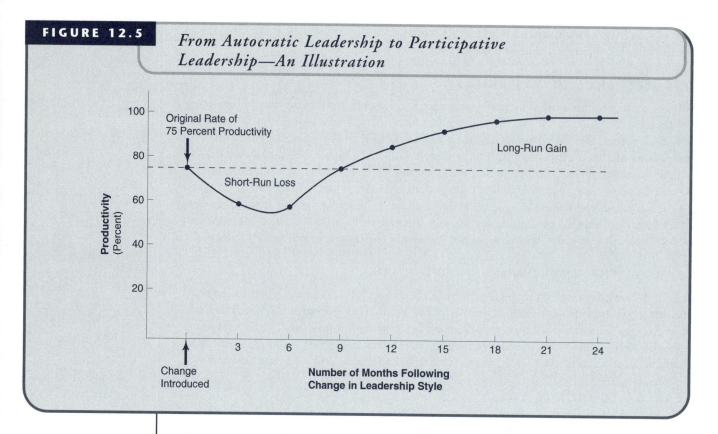

FIGURE 12.5 *From Autocratic Leadership to Participative Leadership—An Illustration*

Original Rate of
75 Percent Productivity

Short-Run Loss

Long-Run Gain

Productivity
(Percent)

Change
Introduced

Number of Months Following
Change in Leadership Style

PEER PRESSURE

Many times, people refuse to accept change because their peers are unwilling to go along with it. Remember, as noted in the discussion of group cohesiveness, if there is high cohesion, the group will stay together. If change is introduced, therefore, the group may collectively agree to resist it.

LACK OF INFORMATION

Whenever people do not know what is going to happen, they are likely to resist the change. The unknown scares them. Consider how you would feel if a doctor told you that you were very sick and had to have an immediate operation. Not knowing what is wrong with you, what kind of operation you need, or what the effect of the operation will be, you would probably be very nervous, and unless you were convinced that the operation was indeed warranted, you would resist the doctor's advice.

SOCIAL DISPLACEMENT

Whenever changes are introduced, it is possible that work groups will be broken up and social relationships will be disturbed. People usually enjoy working with their fellow employees and, when these friendships are interrupted, a psychological letdown occurs. Research shows that in combat situations, soldiers often fight the tendency to make friends among the other members of their platoon because, if one member is killed or injured, the effect on the others can be disastrous. They would not be totally prepared to do their jobs and could be injured or killed themselves. When social relationships have been developed, people tend to want to maintain them and to fight social displacement.

Managing Change

Until now, we have been discussing how people respond to change and why they often resist it. Now we consider how the manager should introduce and manage change properly.[25] Admittedly, change causes problems, but if the manager analyzes the situation properly, follows some basic steps, and remains aware of the important areas of implementation, he or she can effect

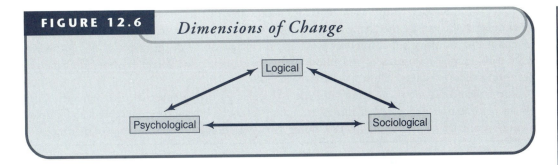

FIGURE 12.6 *Dimensions of Change*

Logical

Psychological ←→ Sociological

many changes to the benefit of both the personnel and the organization.[26] In particular, the manager needs to

1. Understand the three dimensions of change.
2. Know the basic steps in the change process.
3. Understand the characteristics of change leaders.
4. Be aware of the importance of participation and communication.

The Dimensions of Change

The first things a manager must know are the three dimensions of change (see Figure 12.6).

1. First is the **logical dimension,** which is based on technological and scientific reasons. Why is the change needed, from an organizational standpoint? The logical answer is found in such responses as increases in profit, productivity, or efficiency and decreases in cost, worker fatigue, monotony, or machine downtime.
2. Then there is the **psychological dimension,** the logic of the change in terms of the workers who would be affected. Do these people feel the change will be good for them? Is it in line with their values? If the answer is affirmative, the psychological dimension has been satisfied.
3. Finally, there is the **sociological dimension,** which refers to the logic of the change in terms of the work group. Will the change be consistent with the norms of the group? Will it help to maintain teamwork? Will the group members be able to live with it?

Unless the manager considers all three of these dimensions, implementation of the change will be less than ideal.

The Basic Steps in Change

If the three dimensions of change have all been adequately considered, attention can then be focused on the basic steps in change. There are five basic steps in securing effective change, and each is vital to maximum effectiveness.

First, the manager must answer the question, "Is this change *truly* necessary?" The benefits and costs must be weighed. If the manager has examined the dimensions of change that we have discussed, the answer to this question must be affirmative before further consideration of the change process is undertaken.

Second, the manager must consider whether the proposed change is the right one. In many cases, alternative changes exist, any one of which might accomplish the desired result. The manager must choose one that will provide the best results for both the organization and the personnel.

Third, and often most important, the impact of the change must be evaluated. What will be the effect of the change in the short run and in the long run? These may be difficult questions to answer, but the manager should attempt some investigation to compare the impact of various proposed changes.

Fourth, the manager must work to secure acceptance of the change. In this case, workers most directly affected by the change hold the key to success. Their anxieties and fears must be calmed if the company hopes to effect a successful change. Some of the steps for doing this are dealt with in the discussion of the importance of increasing the forces pushing for change, decreasing those pushing against the change, or both.

Fifth, there must be some follow-up. After the change is implemented, the manager must obtain information on how well things are going. Has the change been accepted and implemented properly? More important, is it doing what was desired or was it a waste of time?

LEARNING OBJECTIVE

Describe the characteristics of a change leader

⑦ Leading the Change

Many organizations lead change from the top. For example, senior-level management may decide to expand operations into Canada and Mexico and set a goal of achieving 20 percent of all revenue from these two locales by the year 2006. Then all members of the management team cooperate in helping to gain support for the new program throughout the enterprise.

In recent years, researchers have found that change can also be effectively initiated and led from lower levels of the hierarchy. Moreover, there appear to be seven characteristics that are common to these lower-level change leaders.

One is that such leaders are easily identified by their actions. These people are not afraid to stand up, challenge the status quo, and suggest ways that change can be constructively implemented.

A second characteristic is that these individuals often are not on the company's "high potential" list. They have not been identified as people who are likely to be the senior leaders and managers of the future. In fact, many of them come from the firm's rank-and-file.

A third characteristic is that these change agents are loyal to the enterprise but are willing to go beyond their current job and take the initiative to perform additional tasks that will help to carry the changes forward.

A fourth characteristic is that these personnel are willing to learn new ideas and skills in order to make the change successful.

A fifth is that they are internally driven to make a difference and are unwilling to be chained to their desk and simply carry out their day-to-day routines.

A sixth is that they are action-oriented and have a sense of urgency for accomplishing changes. As a result, they do not wait for approval; they simply move forward and implement the changes they feel are needed.

Finally, researchers have found that people with this personal initiative tend to focus far more on results than on teamwork. They do not wait for others to agree to join them in getting things done; they are willing to move forward on their own, if this will ensure that the necessary results are achieved.[27]

Leading change is an important managerial responsibility. Several important recommendations for managing change initiatives include:

1. **Accept the fact that change is nonlinear.**
2. **Involve more people in the process.**
3. **Pay closer attention to the pockets of resistance.**

LEARNING OBJECTIVE

Explain how participation and communication help the manager implement change, and how structural changes can be used as change interventions

⑧ For these initiatives to be successful, they need an organized framework that clarifies the reasons for a change, or they will fail.[28]

Participation and Change

In most cases, personal initiative is not the primary way that change is implemented. Typically, management announces the changes that are to be made, often including them as part of the annual strategic plan or performance evaluation criteria. In this case, participation and communication by the leaders of the change are critical. Participation is important in the change process because, as we know from research, people will be more supportive of changes that they helped bring about than of changes that were either assigned to them or forced on them. Additionally, if some problem occurs with implementation of a change with which they have assisted, the workers will help to eliminate or work around the problem. However, if they have had no input regarding the change, they will sit on the sidelines and let management figure out how to solve the problem.[29]

A good example of successful change with employee participation is Seiko, the Japanese multinational corporation. When the company decided to make major organizational changes (by expanding its product lines and looking for more lucrative markets), employees resisted these changes because the company was doing so well. To bring about change, the company president and board of directors decided to diversify the company into electronic equipment. At this point, the president got the senior-level managers involved in the change effort. Each manager was asked to propose a three-year plan for the division and departmental levels, which would incorporate diversification into electronic equipment. Once the board accepts these plans, the junior-level managers were integrated into the change process and asked to develop implementation plans at their respective levels of operation. The result: Seiko reached its diversification objective four years early and developed a new line of sophisticated graphic devices that accounted for 50 percent of sales.[30] By communicating with employees and getting them to participate in the change process, Seiko overcame the negative effects that typically accompany change.[31]

Another good example is provided in the Human Relations in Action box, which shows that one primary reason for the success of Japanese firms in the United States is their ability to promote participation and communication in the change process.

in action

HUMAN RELATIONS IN ACTION

The Japanese Way

Manufacturing plants opened by the Japanese in the United States have proven to be some of the most productive in the industry. Why? One of the primary answers is that the Japanese know how to use participative management and communication in introducing and managing change. Some of the basic principles that Japanese firms use are the following:

1. Japanese managers identify closely with the workers and spend a great deal of time interacting with them. This allows the managers to understand the workers' concerns and needs better and, when change is introduced, the managers have excellent insights regarding how the change will be perceived and what types of barriers will have to be overcome.

2. Japanese firms get the workers actively involved in the change process. By gathering employees' ideas and opinions, management learns the concerns and fears of the personnel and can then develop an effective strategy for dealing with them.

3. In dealing with change, Japanese managers carefully examine what needs to be done and what problems are likely to result. They spend much more time analyzing the situation than do their American counterparts. This has led some observers to note that Japanese managers follow the cliché, "Don't do something . . . stand there!" which is the direct opposite of the way American managers do things. As a result of the Japanese approach, although formulation of a change may take a great deal of time, implementation often proceeds smoothly.

4. If something does go wrong, management does not blame the workers; it blames the system. There must have been an error in the way the change was handled. Management did not do its job properly.

5. Japanese firms use much flatter organizational structures than do American firms. This reduces bureaucratic red tape and encourages open communication on the part of the personnel.

Sources: Richard M. Hodgetts and Fred Luthans, International Management, *4th ed. (Burr Ridge, IL: Irwin/McGraw, 2000), chapters 5–7; Noboru Yoshumura and Philip Anderson,* Inside the Kaisha *(Boston: Harvard Business School Press, 1997); and Philip R. Harris and Robert T. Moran,* Managing Cultural Differences, *4th ed. (Houston: Gulf, 1996), pp. 267–273.*

Using Organizational Structural Interventions

Reorganizing, implementing new reward systems, and making cultural changes are all examples of how organizations make changes.[32] Many factors dictate when and why firms reorganize. The most common factor is the state of the economy. When the economy is weak, firms cut costs by eliminating unnecessary functions, resulting in reorganizing the operations to be more cost effective.

The purpose of a reward system is to attract talented people and motivate them in their job. The best designed reward system may not work in a firm because it was designed for another company. For example, too much emphasis may be placed on the wrong rewards, the wrong behavior is being rewarded or there is too much time between the performance and receiving the reward, or one reward is expected to fit everyone. Changing the reward system to fit employees' needs can result in improved individual performance, resulting in greater productivity for the firm. So everyone wins: the employees as well as the firm.

An organization's culture reflects the value systems and the norms preferred by the organization. It is important to reevaluate periodically the culture to determine if it in essence reflects what the firm values. Is the culture focusing on the main goals of the organization? By more directly aligning the culture with the goals and values of the firm, employees have a greater identification with the organization and will generally make a greater commitment to the firm. Changing an organization's culture is another way to intervene change in an organization.

Organizational development *is an effort to improve an enterprise's effectiveness by dealing with individual, group, and organizational problems.*
An **OD intervention** *is a method used in carrying out the OD process.*
An **OD change agent** *is a person who carries out or leads on OD intervention.*
Role playing *is the spontaneous acting out of a real-life situation.*

⑨ Using Organizational Development Interventions

Sometimes change is created through the use of organizational development interventions, which are typically conducted by an outside behavioral expert. Outside consultants are used to avoid political agendas and biases from within the organization. **Organizational development** (OD) is an effort to improve an enterprise's effectiveness by dealing with individual, group, and overall organizational problems from both a technical and a human standpoint. "For OD to work, its users must believe that people are important, not mere 'human resources' to be used and discarded. By bringing out the best in their people, organizations can reach optimal effectiveness and increase profits."[33] The methods used in this process are called **OD interventions,** and they take such forms as role-playing, team building, and survey feedback. The individual who carries out or leads the intervention is called an **OD change agent.** This person's job is to introduce the intervention, get the personnel involved, and show them how the particular intervention can help them deal with the problems they face. People can affect systems as much as systems affect people.

ROLE PLAYING

One of the most common forms of training used in OD is **role-playing.** It consists of the acting out of a realistic situation that involves two or more people. The purpose of the training is to acquaint one or more of the participants with the proper way of handling a given situation. For example, one person may be told that he or she is a plant supervisor and that absenteeism and tardiness at the plant have been increasing dramatically. The supervisor's job is to reduce these irregularities by sending everyone home who arrives late, thereby penalizing the latecomer a day's pay. Another person is to play the role of a late worker who is trying to talk the supervisor out of sending him or her home. As the two people begin acting out their roles, the rest of the participants watch. When the scene is over, the trainer and the participants all have the opportunity to give their analysis of what each said and did. Then the trainer gives the participants and the other members of the group some *do*s and *don't*s for handling similar situations.

The benefit of role-playing is that it puts the participants in a situation that they are likely to face in the future, gives them a chance to react to the situation, and then provides feedback on performance. When these people return to the real work environment and face a similar situation, they experience less tension and anxiety regarding how to handle the matters because, for all practical purposes, they have been in that situation before.

TEAM BUILDING

Currently, the most popular form of OD consists of approaches directed toward improving the effectiveness of regular work groups. The overall term given to these approaches is **team building.** A number of different team-building interventions exist. Some focus on intact, permanent work teams, and others are directed toward special teams or newly constituted work groups. The following are some common objectives pursued by team-building interventions:

1. Increasing task accomplishment by improving the group's problem-solving ability, decision-making skills, and goal-setting approaches, or defining the roles and duties of the individual managers.
2. Building and maintaining effective interpersonal relationships, including boss-subordinate relationships and peer relationships.
3. Understanding and managing group processes and intergroup relations.
4. Improving intergroup relations and resolving interpersonal or intergroup conflict.
5. Developing more effective communication, decision-making, and task-allocation skills, both within and between groups.

One of the most popular methods of team building consists of asking two work groups who are having trouble working with each other to adjourn to separate rooms and draw up a list of those things that each group dislikes about the other group and a list of those things that each believes the other group will say it dislikes about them. Then the two groups are brought together, and each reads its first list. The only questions permitted are those that allow the person reading the list to clarify what the group means by a listed item. When both groups are finished, each then reads its second list (what it believed the other group would say about it).

Having now identified their real and imaginary problems, the two groups begin discussing the issues. Some issues are disposed of very quickly because they had been caused by lack of communication or simple misunderstandings. From this point, a list of the major problems that still exist between the two groups is constructed, and ways of solving the problems are identified. Then the groups put together a timetable for solving the problems and list the specific steps that will be taken in problem solving. Having developed an action plan, the two groups then work together and follow the timetable to overcome their mutual problems. In most cases, the OD change agent checks back with the two groups to determine whether they are making progress in resolving the problems or whether further meetings are needed to revitalize their efforts.

Most OD practitioners have great faith in team building, which undoubtedly helps to account for the approach's current popularity. However, some problems are common to this intervention. The major difficulty is that one work group may fail to be honest with the other group, holding back feelings because it is afraid of being too forthright with people it has learned to distrust. However, this problem can be overcome early in the intervention if the change agent keeps everyone honest.

> *The early stages of these interventions—making lists and sharing them and using the fishbowl technique—lead the participants to experience feelings of success in dealing with the other group. Feelings of anxiety, apprehension, and hostility start to give way to feelings of competence and success as the early stages of the interventions produce better communication and understanding than the participants had expected. Nothing succeeds like success, and both groups usually perceived the early stages as a success experience. This leads to the optimistic realization that "We can work together with those people."*
>
> *Participants are watching for subtle cues of defensiveness, resistance to the data, stubbornness, and the like, and the controlled nature of the process makes most of these unnecessary. This starts building momentum for feelings of competence and success.*[34]

If carried out competently, team building can be very beneficial to both the personnel and the organization.

Team building
is an OD intervention for resolving group problems.

FIGURE 12.7

Sample Survey Feedback Questions

	Strongly Agree	Agree	Undecided	Disagree	Strongly Disagree
There is a lot of teamwork in my work group.	____	____	____	____	____
Very few people in this organization listen to one another.	____	____	____	____	____
Management is as interested in the people as it is in the work.	____	____	____	____	____
Most important decisions are made by management and then announced to the workers without any input from the latter.	____	____	____	____	____
This organization is a good place to work.	____	____	____	____	____

In your opinion, what are the three biggest problems currently facing the firm? Write your answers in the space below, and use the back of the page if necessary.

SURVEY FEEDBACK

Survey feedback *is an OD intervention based on the collection of data and the feeding back of this information to the organizational personnel.*

Another important and widely used intervention is that of **survey feedback**, a comprehensive OD intervention. The technique entails three distinct steps:

1. **A systematic collection of data on the current state of the organization, usually obtained through questionnaires, interviews, or both.**
2. **A feedback of the findings to the organizational personnel.**
3. **The development of an action plan for dealing with the problems that have been identified.**

Gathering the Data   Data in the survey feedback intervention is often gathered by means of an objective-subjective questionnaire such as the one illustrated in Figure 12.7. The survey usually is designed by a specialist in attitude measurement and is administered to the total organization, to a department, or to a representative sample of either.

Feeding Back the Information   After the information is collected and analyzed, the results are revealed to the survey participants. In a nutshell, the OD change agent is saying, "Here's an overall view of what you told me about the organization. These are the things that everyone seems to like. These are the things that most people feel need to be corrected. Let us look at this information and decide what should be done about the situation."

Developing an Action Plan   The last phase of the survey feedback intervention involves the development of an action plan. This plan is formulated by individuals at all levels of the group(s) that participated in the original survey. Often included in the action plan is a time limit for following up to see that the proposed plan is implemented. The follow-up prevents the OD effort from becoming only a short-lived, interesting experience.

When the results are communicated back to employees, survey feedback has proven to be an effective change technique. Otherwise, employees become frustrated and feel their input was never really wanted. Telling people the results of the survey builds respect and cooperation. But more than knowing the results, employees want to know what real changes have been made to improve the organization.[35] Bowers, for example, has reported that a study evaluating the effects of different change techniques in twenty-three organizations revealed that survey feedback was more effective than many other types of change strategies.[36] However, to keep these results in perspective, we should note that these survey feedback programs may have been better rated because they were more comprehensive than other programs. The positive results may reflect the superiority of more comprehensive programs to less comprehensive ones. On the other hand, some researchers have also noted that survey feedback is a cost-effective means of implementing a comprehensive program, making it a highly desirable change technique.[37]

① **LEARNING OBJECTIVE**
Define conflict and explain some of the major types of conflict

Conflict is opposition or antagonism toward other individuals or things. Conflict can exist at the *individual level* in such forms as frustration and interpersonal conflict. It can also exist at the *organizational level* in such forms as institutionalized and emergent conflict.

Frustration is the result of a blocked need and managers must understand that the stronger the worker's motivation to reach a desired goal, the greater will be the individual's frustration with failure. Unfair and discriminatory treatment in the workplace creates frustration. *Interpersonal conflict* arises when disagreements occur among personnel. If not handled properly, it can deteriorate relations between the parties involved.

Institutionalized conflict occurs when assignments, resources, and information are not fairly distributed and shared among personnel and departments. Personal and social issues can cause *emergent conflict*. For example, differences between formal and informal groups, the boss and workers, and authority of the boss and the boss's lack of knowledge.

② **LEARNING OBJECTIVE**
Relate some of the most effective ways of managing conflict

Managers often try to manage conflict through general counseling, such as providing advice, reassurance, release of emotional tension, and reorientation. If the problem is more serious, as in the case of troubled employees or individuals suffering from alcoholism or drug abuse, more carefully structured counseling may be necessary, including the use of outside professional assistance.

With troubled employees three courses of action are needed: (1) Tell the employee to shape up or ship out, (2) discipline the person, or (3) discuss the problem with the employee in an effort to work out a solution.

Some employees turn to alcoholism to help them deal with frustration and stress on the job. They are skillful at denying the problem, making it difficult for managers to confront these people. Drug abuse causes absenteeism, accidents on the job, and an increase in employee turnover, resulting in costs to the firm.

Methods for resolving conflict are numerous. Four of the most common are mutual problem solving, expansion of resources, smoothing, and compromise. *Mutual problem solving* brings the parties in a conflict together face-to-face to jointly resolve the issues. Reorganization and budget increases can make available *additional resources*. *Smoothing* is the process of playing down the differences between the parties in conflict, while emphasizing their common interests; whereas, *compromise* involves each side giving up something. If one side feels it gives more than the other side, the conflict may rise up again.

③ **LEARNING OBJECTIVE**
Discuss how change occurs

Change is any modification or alteration of the status quo. When change takes place, three things occur: (1) There is movement from one set of conditions to another, (2) some force(s) causes the change to come about, and (3) a consequence results from the change.

Some people believe that resistance to change is inevitable. Although this may be true, there are some very good reasons for resistance. One is that it compels the prochange forces to build a case against the status quo. Another is that it encourages the organization to look before it leaps. Change is generally good for the entire organization.

In dealing with resistance and ensuring that change is properly implemented, begin with planning (1) whether there should be a change, (2) what type of changed is needed, and (3) how the change should be implemented.

④ LEARNING OBJECTIVE
Explain four common responses to change—rejection, resistance, tolerance, and acceptance

How do most people react to change? Their reactions to change will depend on the benefits they think will result from it. Some psychologists believe the answer can be found in an individual's attitude toward the stimulus. A person's attitude is a reflection of psychological factors—reaction to stress, personal factors—experience, and social factors—group makeup.

There are many responses to why people resist change, but most can be categorized as rejection, resistance, tolerance, or acceptance. Of these, the most common is resistance to change. Rejection is simply refusing to accommodate a change. Resistance can be observed and not so readily observed depending on the individual worker. Tolerance is a condition of putting up with the change when the worker is neutral about the change. Acceptance is the response of going with the change.

More reasons for resistance to change include: obsolescence of job skills, fear of the unknown, fear of economic loss, ego defensiveness, the comfort of status quo, shortsightedness, peer pressure, lack of information, and social displacement.

⑤ LEARNING OBJECTIVE
Identify three dimensions of change

Despite the various pressures and tendencies to resist change, it is possible to alter the status quo if the change is introduced and managed properly. One of the first things the manager must do is be aware of the three dimensions of change: logical, psychological, and sociological. The *logical dimension* of change is based on scientific reasons—productivity, decreases in cost, worker fatigue or machine downtime. The *psychological dimension* of change is based on how the individual will be affected. Will the worker feel the change is good? The *sociological dimension* of change is based on how the change will affect the group—work group members, teamwork, and group norm.

⑥ LEARNING OBJECTIVE
Describe the five basic steps in the change process

The manager should know the five basic steps in the change process. (1) Is this change necessary? (2) Is the change the right one? (3) What will be the impact of the change? (4) How will the manager get acceptance of the change? (5) Has the change been accepted and implemented properly?

⑦ LEARNING OBJECTIVE
Describe the characteristics of a change leader

The leaders are (1) identified by their actions, (2) not on the company's "high-potential" list, (3) loyal to the company and willing to go beyond their current job, (4) willing to learn new ideas and skills in order to make the change successful, (5) internally driven to make a difference, (6) action oriented and have a sense of urgency for accomplishing changes, and (7) focused far more on results than on teamwork.

⑧ LEARNING OBJECTIVE
Explain how participation and communication can help the manager implement change, and how structural changes can be used as change interventions.

Participation is important in the change process because people will be more supportive of changes if they have helped bring about the change. If problems occur, workers will be more eager to assist and help eliminate the problems. Effective communication is critical in the change process. Workers have a need to be informed of what is going that will affect them and why.

Organizations can use reorganization, new reward systems, and culture change as change interventions. Reorganizing is necessary when the company is no longer cost effective. Reward systems should reward performance, meet the expected needs of the employees, and motivate employees to continue to perform excellent work. The culture of an organization reflects the values and purpose of the business. When employees feel an identity with the organization, they are more committed.

⑨ LEARNING OBJECTIVE
Discuss how organizational development interventions can be effectively employed in dealing with change

Organizational development is an effort to improve an enterprise's effectiveness by dealing with individual, group, and overall organizational problems from both a technical standpoint and a human standpoint. At the heart of OD is a concern for improving the relationships among the organization's personnel. This often is accomplished through *OD interventions*. The person who carries out or leads the intervention is called the *OD change agent*.

Many kinds of OD interventions exist. Some relate exclusively to the individual and seek to improve behavioral skills. One such intervention is role playing. Other OD interventions, such as team building, are designed to improve intragroup and intergroup performance. Finally, there are overall or comprehensive interventions. One of the most popular is survey feedback.

KEY TERMS IN THE CHAPTER

Conflict	Covert resistance
Frustration	Tolerance
Interpersonal conflict	Logical dimension
Institutionalized conflict	Psychological dimension
Emergent conflict	Sociological dimension
Counseling	Organizational development
Mutual problem solving	OD intervention
Smoothing	OD change agent
Compromise	Role-playing
Change	Team building
Rejection	Survey feedback
Overt resistance	

REVIEW AND STUDY QUESTIONS

1. What are two common forms of conflict at the individual level? Describe each.

2. What are two common forms of conflict at the organizational (group) level? Describe each.

3. What is the overall purpose of counseling? Describe four basic approaches managers can use in carrying out counseling.

4. How should a manager counsel a troubled employee? Describe at least five useful guidelines.

5. What do managers need to know about alcohol- and drug-related employee problems?

6. What are the four stages in designing a program for dealing with drug abusers? Identify and describe each stage.

7. How can each of the following approaches help to resolve conflict: mutual problem solving, the expansion of resources, smoothing, and compromise? Give an example for each approach.

8. Describe three things that happen when change occurs.

9. Is resistance to change bad for the organization? In your answer, be sure to make a case both for and against resistance.

10. What is the behavior of the worker who engages in each of the four responses to change: rejection, resistance, tolerance, and acceptance? Describe the behavior in each situation.

11. One of the primary reasons for resistance to change is the fear of economic loss. What does the statement mean?

12. Why does the lack of information impact a resistance to change?

13. What are the three dimensions of change? Why are they important to the manager in the change process?

14. What are the five basic steps in the change process? Describe each.

15. How do participation and communication play important roles in the introduction of change?

16. How can reorganization, reward systems, and culture changes be used as change interventions?

17. Role-playing is one of the most common forms of training used in OD. How does role-playing work?

18. How does the team-building intervention work? Why is this intervention so well liked by OD practitioners?

19. What are five common objectives pursued by team-building interventions?

20. What are the three distinct steps in survey feedback?

21. How effective is the survey feedback approach as a change technique? Why?

VISIT THE WEB

The Dominant Firm

In this chapter, you studied how organizations go about dealing with conflict and change. Change is certainly the name of the game for Microsoft, which dominates its industry and has provided myriad computer-related products. In fact, the company's president, Bill Gates, is one of the richest people in the world, thanks to his firm's industry dominance. To maintain this leadership, however, Microsoft must continue to change. Visit the firm's Web site at **http://www.microsoft.com** and then answer these two questions:

1. What are some of the new products we are likely to see from Microsoft over the next two years?

2. In bringing these products to market, in what ways will the company's personnel have to deal with change?

Alcoholism and Drug-Related Issues

As discussed in this chapter, managers must know how to deal effectively with employees who have alcohol- and drug-related problems. The first step in educating oneself about handling alcohol and drug-related problems is to learn as much as possible about the issues involved and the programs available for assistance. Visit the

Web site: **http://www.samhsa.gov/oas/work.htm** and explore the wealth of information available. Answer the questions:

1. What are some "dos" and "don'ts" you need to know about dealing with alcohol and drug issues? Make a list of each.

2. Investigate the "Model Plan for Comprehensive Drug-Free Workplace Program." Outline key points that should be covered in the

   a. Supervisory Training Program.
   b. Employee Education Program.

3. Summarize several important points you learned from exploring this site that will help you manage alcohol- and/or drug-related problems in your workplace. If you are an employee and not in management, how will the information help you deal with coworkers who have alcohol- and/or drug-related problems.

TIME OUT ANSWERS

How Much Do You Know About the Change Process?

1. Basically false. Most changes scare people and they, at least initially, tend to dislike them.

2. Basically false. Most changes take time to be accepted so, if anything, there is an immediate decrease in productivity.

3. Basically true. Most changes scare people, as explained in number one.

4. Basically false. They would regard it with fear or concern, wondering if the machine would have them do more work or even replace them.

5. Basically true. This is usually the objective of all organizational changes.

6. Basically true. Workers tend to stick together, especially when change is involved.

7. Basically false. People resist because they are afraid of losing their jobs.

8. Basically false. Advance notice is crucial, and the greater the change, the more advance notice that should be given.

9. Basically true. Participation in the change process is one of the most effective ways of ensuring successful implementation of the change.

10. Basically false. They tend to underrate the time needed to implement change effectively and end up pushing the change too quickly. The result is resistance from the workers.

11. Either answer can be right here so take one point regardless of your response— if the change is a positive one, it often results in a short decline in work output before things turn around and vice versa.

12. Basically true. Unions usually fight change because they are afraid of the effect of the change on worker employment.

   Total the number of your correct responses. How well did you do? Use the following to measure your current knowledge of the change process:

11–12 correct	Excellent
9–10 correct	Above average
7–8 correct	Average
6 or fewer correct	Below average

Regardless of how well you did, you will find the answers to these questions in the chapter, so take heart and read on.

Nine months ago, Private Hospital was taken over by the county. The population in the local area had grown by approximately 125 percent in the last decade, and the hospital was unable to keep up with local needs. The people who owned the hospital felt that too great an investment was needed for additional emergency and patient rooms and their requisite equipment and inventory. They proposed that the county buy and run the hospital, and the county agreed.

Since the takeover, hospital personnel has increased by almost 50 percent, while the budget has risen by 44 percent. As a consequence, a number of new cost controls have been implemented. County management is particularly concerned about controlling expenses. A number of prominent citizens as well as the local newspaper have questioned the purchase of the hospital and are saying that it will cost millions of dollars more each year to run a county hospital than it would to have the hospital run by a private group. In response to these charges, the county wants to ensure that the hospital is run as efficiently as possible.

One of the changes introduced was a monthly cost control report. This report is specially designed to provide information to central accounting as well as feedback to the various departments.

Now that the reports have been in use for three months, it has become evident that some departments understand them, fill them out completely, and use them as a source of feedback in controlling their costs and expenditures. Other departments seem confused about the report, do not know what to put into it or leave out, and do not appear to be using the data to control their costs and expenditures.

Phil Albright, head of central accounting, decided to check out the situation for himself by visiting one of the departments that was filling out the form properly and one that was not. The first department is run by Pat Rogers and, after talking to both Pat and her personnel, Phil confirmed that Pat's people are familiar with the form, know the kinds of information that are supposed to go into it, and are aware of how to use the data for control purposes. Much of their understanding stems from a meeting that Pat had with her personnel at which they discussed the report at length. By the end of the meeting, everyone in the department was familiar with the format of the report and was prepared to provide the necessary data.

Conversely, Paul Heckman's department is having all sorts of problems with the report. All three times it was submitted, it was both incomplete and late. In addition, Paul's department is currently 21 percent over budget. In talking to the personnel, Phil learned that Paul had not discussed the report with his department. Rather, he had sent a photocopy of the form to each person, announcing that the report was to be submitted monthly to accounting. He told his people that he wanted them to decide what they thought should go into the report and to send this information to his secretary. He then would incorporate the data in the monthly cost control report. Phil realizes that this way of introducing the report undoubtedly accounts for most of the problems that Paul's department is having with it, but he is unsure of how to begin discussing the matter with Paul.

QUESTIONS

1. How important is participation and communication in effecting change? Give examples from this case.

2. How has Pat's approach helped to reduce the anxiety that often accompanies change?

3. What did Paul do wrong? Explain.

4. What would you recommend that Phil say to Paul? Why?

Saturday Meetings

Marcy Schuller works for a medium-sized airline. For the last three years, Marcy has been a manager and, given her performance, she is likely to be promoted to a director within the next three years. A director coordinates the activities of a group of managers. Within five years a director can expect to be promoted to vice president.

A large degree of Marcy's success is a result of her ability to keep morale up, maintain high customer satisfaction, and reduce the infighting that sometimes occurs among the departments and two major cliques. The previous manager was unable to control these two cliques and, as a result, had affected customer service. That individual lasted only six months on the job.

Last week, the company's central office sent out a new policy statement. All employees who are not working on weekends are expected to attend regional planning meetings every other week. These meetings take place on Saturday mornings and typically entail a question-and-answer period involving local employees and a representative from headquarters. This is management's way of keeping track of what is going on in airline operations in all the regions and getting feedback on the problems and concerns of the employees. The meetings have already been introduced outside of Marcy's region.

On hearing the news, most of the employees expressed their displeasure to Marcy. "We work five days a week," one of them explained. "Why do we have to come in for a half-day on Saturday as well? We all like you and know that you would not have supported this policy if they had asked your opinion. However, the management at headquarters really doesn't care about us, and most of us don't care about them."

A majority of the employees agree with these sentiments. However, in an effort to accentuate their differences, members of one clique have announced that they fully support management's new policy, so now it is only members of the other clique who are in opposition.

Marcy has informed the director that there may be a problem getting the employees to go along with the Saturday morning meetings. However, the director responded that it is Marcy's job to ensure that everyone is present at the meetings. As a result, Marcy has decided that the best way to handle the situation is to sit down with the second clique and try to help them resolve their differences with the company so that they will agree to attend the meetings. The director is also trying to be helpful. He called back to say that Headquarters maintains an organizational development team that is part of the training and development department. "If you would like them to come out and help you in any way, perhaps by conducting an organizational development intervention such as survey feedback, they'd be happy to do so. We've used them at other stores around the region, and they have worked out very well." Marcy thanked him for his assistance, and said she would get back to him after she had given the idea more thought.

Your Advice

1. What should Marcy do first?

    _____ a. Make a list of reasons why the workers should go along with management's decision.

    _____ b. Encourage members of the clique that is willing to go along with management to put pressure on the other clique.

    _____ c. Continue with her present plan of sitting down with the second clique and discussing the problem.

2. Why are the employees resisting the change? Give several reasons.

3. How can Marcy use participation and communication to help to persuade the members of the second clique to attend the Saturday morning meetings? Give several specific examples.

4. If the organization were to use survey feedback with the employees, how would this be done? Explain the process and the potential payoffs for the department and the airline.

EXPERIENCING TEAM BUILDING

Purpose

- To introduce the reader to the concepts of team building.
- To participate in an authentic team-building activity.

Procedure

1. As a class, generate as many responses as possible to the question: How can this group (class) function more effectively to meet our goals—that is, successfully completing the course objectives? List as many ideas as possible. None should be evaluated or judged at this time, although clarification may be sought.

2. Next, separate into four subgroups. Discuss each of the suggestions, group similar ones, and discard those believed by the entire group to be inappropriate. List in order of importance the ones that are left.

3. As a class, discuss each group's first priority. Why was it given top priority? Do other groups agree or disagree? Continue until all items are again listed and discussed.

4. As a class, choose the top five items. How can they be implemented to better meet class objectives?

5. Discuss what was learned about team building and mutual problem solving in this exercise. What would you do differently next time?

Looking to the Future

part **VI**

Thus far in this book, we have studied the entire field of human relations, which, as you will remember from Chapter 1, we defined as a process by which management brings workers into contact with the organization in such a way that the objectives of both groups are achieved. Now we consider two important questions:

- *What are the future challenges of human relations?*

- *How can you use your human relations knowledge to help you obtain employment and move ahead in your chosen career?*

We answer these questions by first examining some of the developing trends that will have a major impact on human relations. These include the growth of international business, the need for a greater focus on innovation, commitment to quality, and changing social values, the need to examine human relations practices in the best-managed firms, and how the knowledge of human relations can be of value to you.

THE GOALS OF THIS SECTION ARE TO:

- *Define a multinational enterprise; discuss why firms become multinational companies; study international culture, with a particular emphasis given to the four dimensions of culture; examine the impact of international culture in the workplace, paying specific attention to work attitudes, motivation and the way people deal with time; and study the types of cross-cultural training used by multinational enterprises.*

- *Examine the area of innovation and the ways in which organizations are trying to nurture and sustain creativity, look at how the nature of work is changing and the implications that this will have for human relations during the next decade, study the ways in which businesses are meeting the diversity challenge, and examine world-class organizations that are leading the way in the twenty-first century.*

- *Discuss the ways of choosing a career, including how to evaluate yourself; study the ways of actually finding a job by writing an effective resume and carrying out a successful job hunt; identify some of the most important steps in managing your career effectively; and examine the responsibilities and challenges for the modern manager.*

13 International Human Relations

Each year, more and more organizations begin conducting business overseas. In fact, an increasing number of firms now earn more revenues from international operations than ever before. As a result, international human relations is emerging as a major area of study for managers.

AFTER READING THIS CHAPTER, YOU SHOULD BE ABLE TO:

1. Define the term *multinational enterprise* and discuss four major reasons why companies become multinational enterprises.
2. Identify the term *culture* and relate four basic dimensions of international culture.
3. Discuss the value of country clusters in understanding the impact of culture in the international arena.
4. Relate the ways in which culture affects work attitudes, motivation, and how people deal with time.
5. Describe the ways in which cross-cultural training is used to prepare personnel to deal with international cultures.

Mickey Has a Human Relations Problem

The Walt Disney Company is one of the world's premier entertainment firms. Disneyland in Anaheim, California, and Walt Disney World in Orlando, Florida, have been immensely successful. Hence, when the company decided to create EuroDisney, everyone was sure it would be another success. The park opened in April 1992 near Paris, France, and drew record opening-day crowds. However, by 1993, EuroDisney had lost $1 billion and, by 1994, the operation had to be totally overhauled. What went wrong? There are several answers, and many of them relate to poor human relations. Here are some examples:

- Management had been very successful with its American theme parks and went into the EuroDisney deal believing that its approach would transfer directly to Europe. This attempt to run a European venture with American values and attitudes led to a series of operating mistakes.

- Disney got carried away with its desire to build a high-quality park. As a result, the firm spent exorbitant amounts of money to ensure that the facility was not a carbon copy of Disneyland or Walt Disney World, by constructing larger and more detailed buildings. The outcome was a venture that cost millions of dollars more than expected, resulting in the need to charge increased admission prices—something at which many European customers balked.

- The company discovered that it had built far more hotel rooms than were needed. In the United States, most visitors stay at Disney theme park hotels for three or more days. However, at EuroDisney, the park is smaller and can be seen in one or two days. Many guests arrive at their hotel early in the morning, rush to the park, come back late at night, then check out the next morning before heading back to the park.

- Disney failed to realize that many Europeans are economical. A room at the EuroDisney Hotel costs about $340 per night—the same as a premiere hotel in Paris. As a result, most visitors find accommodations elsewhere or stay only one night at the Disney hotel.

- The firm failed to realize that many Europeans enjoy walking. Therefore, the trams that were built to take guests from their hotels to the park went unused, resulting in a needless investment of approximately $250,000.

- Disney misunderstood the eating habits of Europeans. The policy of serving no alcohol in the park (which has since been changed) caused astonishment in a country where a glass of wine with lunch is common. Management also thought that Europeans did not eat breakfast, so restaurants were downsized. However, the demand for breakfast was often ten times the restaurants' seating capacity, and waiting lines were extremely long.

- Disney management underestimated the number of people who would be arriving by bus. In the United States, most people come to the parks by car. As a result, the parking space for buses was far too small to accommodate the two thousand buses that arrived on peak days.

- The company failed to realize that peak days in Europe are different from those in the United States. Disney was used to having a light Monday crowd but a very heavy Friday crowd. However, just the opposite occurred at EuroDisney.

Since opening EuroDisney, the Walt Disney Company has made a number of important changes designed to address better the needs of its European customers. However, this has not corrected all the problems—at least in the minds of the stockholders. For example, although revenue increased moderately every year between 1995 and 1999 and is now approaching $1 billion, net income has not been very high. In 1998, EuroDisney netted only $45 million on sales of nearly $825 million and, in 1999, this fell to $24 million on sales of $850 million. Worse yet, the stock was one of the poorest performers in the European hospitality and leisure industry. The price peaked at nine euros (approximately $9 at that time) when the park opened its doors but, by the end of 2000, it was trading at less than one euro (around 60 European cents). In addition, by this time the French chairman and chief executive officer of the company had left and been replaced by an American which, critics charged, hampered the managerial autonomy and motivation of EuroDisney's senior executives; most of whom are European. The goal of the company was to forge ahead with plans for a mammoth retail center and Disney Studios, in order to lure more visitors to the still-developing site.

This goal has proved to be successful for EuroDisney. "Despite the generally weak tourism environment caused by the ongoing geopolitical uncertainties, revenues during the first half of 2003 increased 8% reflecting strong improvements in all key operating drivers for the Resort, including theme park attendance, hotel occupancy and average guest spending." This growth was driven by the significant investments made in the Walt Disney Studios Park, which opened in 2002. The Walt Disney Studios Park is expected to benefit from the opening of additional on-site hotel capacity with the first phase of 1,450 rooms having been completed by the summer of 2003.

The President and Chief Operating Officer of EuroDisney S.A., Yann Caillére, recently stated that "Disneyland Resort Paris continues to be the most visited tourist destination in Europe and our momentum is growing. This momentum was driven by the investment in Walt Disney Studios." The Resort continues to focus on improving revenues through marketing and sales initiatives and to respond more quickly to changes in guest demand. Recently Andre' Lacroix, the former President of Burger King International, was nominated to the position of Chairman and Chief Executive Officer of EuroDisney S.A. "His experience and management skills uniquely qualify him to take on the challenge of propelling Disneyland Resort Paris into a new era becoming a resort destination where families can come together to create magical memories that they will cherish for a lifetime."

Although it was not easy, EuroDisney, Paris, survived and celebrated its tenth birthday in 2002. Critics, however, wondered whether the park ever would prove to be a sound business investment or whether the Disney management was trying to superimpose on a European market, which presents a variety of significantly different human relations challenges, a strategy that works well in the United States.

Sources: "First Half 2003 Results," EuroDisney S.C.A., Financial Statements, **http://www.eurodisney.com** *May 12, 2003; Paulo Prada, "EuroDisney Does Nicely. So Why Are Investors Grumpy?"* Wall Street Journal, *September 6, 2000, p. A20; Victoria Griffith, "Mortgaging the Mouse,"* Magazine for Senior Financial Executives, *August 1997, pp. 71–73; Peter Gumbel and Richard Turner, "Fans Like EuroDisney but Its Parents' Goofs Weigh the Park Down,"* Wall Street Journal, *March 19, 1994, pp. A1, A12; and Stewart Toy and Paula Dwyer, "Is Disney Headed for the Euro-Trash Heap?"* Business Week, *January 24, 1994, p. 52*

LEARNING OBJECTIVE

Define the term multinational enterprise and discuss four major reasons why companies become multinational enterprises

① Why Firms Become Multinational Enterprises

A **multinational enterprise (MNE)** is a company that is headquartered in one country but has operations in two or more countries.[1] Table 13.1 lists the twenty MNEs that recently were ranked by *Fortune* as the world's most admired firms.[2] Thousands of others are much smaller and not as well known, but they too play a significant role in the international arena. Table 13.2 lists *Fortune's* top twenty world's largest MNEs for 2002. Only five companies are listed in both tables. This illustrates that the largest companies are not always the most admired companies. During the first decade of this millennium, international business will touch almost every enterprise—hence, the importance of international human relations.

A company will become an MNE for a number of reasons.

One reason is to protect itself from the risks and uncertainties of the domestic business cycle. By setting up operations in another country, a firm often can secure a hedge against economic volatility in its home country. For example, General Motors (GM) has begun producing a small car in China for the local market.[3] Although the firm's share of the American auto market has declined in recent years, GM hopes to profit from this new emerging market.

A second, and complementary, reason is to tap the growing world market for goods and services. For example, many foreign MNEs have targeted the Untied States because of its large

*A **multinational enterprise** is a company headquartered in one country but having operations in two or more countries.*

TABLE 13.1	*The World's Most Admired Companies*	
Rank	**Company**	**Industry**
1	General Electric	Electronics, electrical equipment
2	Cisco Systems	Network communications, Internet technology
3	Microsoft	Computer hardware, software
4	Intel	Computer hardware, software
5	Wal-Mart Stores	Retail: general and specialty
6	Sony	Electronics, electrical equipment
7	Dell Computer	Computer hardware, software
8	Nokia	Network communications, Internet technology
9	Home Depot	Retail: general, specialty
10	Toyota Motor	Motor vehicles
11	Southwest Airlines	Airlines
12	Lucent Technologies	Network communications, Internet technology
13	Goldman Sachs	Securities, diversified financials
14	Berkshire Hathaway	Insurance: property, casualty
15	Coca-Cola	Beverages
16	Charles Schwab	Securities, diversified financials
17	Johnson & Johnson	Pharmaceuticals
18	Citigroup	Securities, diversified financials
19	Ford Motor	Motor vehicles
20	Pfizer	Pharmaceuticals

population and per capita income. Americans have both a desire for new goods and services and the money to buy them. The same is true for many other industrialized nations, which helps to explain why American MNEs have been targeting Europe and Asia as primary expansion areas. For example, in recent years, Wal-Mart has been slowly opening stores in China and now grosses more than $100 million annually in that market.[4] The firm also is expanding in Germany and is becoming a major competitor there.[5]

A third reason is to respond to increased foreign competition. Using a follow-the-competitor strategy, the MNE will set up operations in the home countries of competitors. This strategy serves a dual purpose: It takes business away from competitors, and it lets other firms know that, if they attack the MNE in its home market, those firms will face a similar situation. This strategy is particularly important when MNEs want to communicate the conditions under which they will retaliate.

A fourth reason is the desire to reduce costs. By setting up operations close to the customer, MNEs can eliminate transportation costs, avoid the expenses associated with having intermediaries handle the product, develop a more accurate and rapid response to customer needs, and

TABLE 13.2 World's Largest MNEs for 2002

Global 500 Rank	Company	Industry	Revenue ($ in millions)
1	Wal-Mart	Retail: General and specialty	219,812.0
2	Exxon Mobil	Oil and gas	191,581.0
3	General Motors	Motor vehicles	177,260.0
4	BP	Oil and gas	174,218.0
5	Ford Motor	Motor vehicles	162,412.0
6	Enron	Energy	138,718.0
7	DaimlerChrysler	Motor vehicles	136,897.3
8	Royal Dutch/Shell Group	Oil and gas	135,211.0
9	General Electric	Electronics, electrical equipment	125,913.0
10	Toyota Motor	Motor vehicles	120,814.4
11	Citigroup	Banking and finance	112.022.0
12	Mitsubishi	Motor vehicles	105,813.9
13	Mitsui	General trading company	101,205.6
14	Chevron Texaco	Oil and gas	99,699.0
15	Total Fina Elf	Oil and gas	94,311.9
16	Nippon Telegraph & Telephone	Communications	93,424.8
17	Itochu	Trading company, telecommunications	91,176.6
18	Allianz	Insurance	85,929.2
19	Intl. Business Machines	Computers	85,866.0
20	ING Group	Integrated financial services	82,999.1

Source: Adapted from "The 2002 Global 500: The World's Largest Corporations," Fortune, July 22, 2002
(http://www.fortune.com/fortune/global5)

take advantage of local resources. A good example is Ford Motor, which is now building a small, economic car, the Ikon, in India. In fact, it is the only car Ford makes in India. After conducting a great deal of research, the company was able to determine the features that were most appealing to buyers in India. As a result, sales have more than met projected forecasts.[6]

A fifth reason is to overcome tariff walls by serving a foreign market from inside. The European Union (EU) provides an excellent example.[7] Firms exporting their goods to France are subject to tariffs, but those that are producing the goods in France can transport them to any other country in the EU without paying tariffs. The same is true in North America, where the North American Free Trade Agreement (NAFTA) binds Canada, the United States, and Mexico into an economic bloc that has almost as much purchasing power as that of greater Europe. As a result of the EU and NAFTA, more and more businesses are now finding it profitable to do business in other nations as well as to enter into partnerships or joint venture agreements with foreign firms that conduct business locally.

The Nature of International Culture

Culture is the acquired knowledge that people use to interpret experience and to generate social behavior.[8] This knowledge forms values, creates attitudes, and influences both individual and group behavior. Culture is learned through education and experience and is shared so that members of a group, an organization, or a society have a common culture. Moreover, culture is passed from one generation to another, so it is enduring. At the same time, cultures undergo change as people adapt to new environments. As a result, in most countries, the culture of the first decade of this millennium is different from that of the 1980s, although, as seen in the Ethics and Social Responsibility in Action box, a wide variety of biases still exist.

LEARNING OBJECTIVE

(2) Identify the term culture and relate four basic dimensions of international culture

Culture
is the acquired knowledge that people use to interpret experience and to generate social behavior.

in action

ETHICS AND SOCIAL RESPONSIBILITY IN ACTION

Women in International Management

Many American businesses are surprised to find that human resource practices that are commonplace in the United States are frowned on or ignored in overseas markets. A good example is the hiring of women for management positions. In the United States, companies that hire and promote women are viewed as role models and are held up for emulation. Perhaps this helps to explain why women in 2002 made up 41.4 percent of the management, business, and financial occupations workforce in this country. In the management occupations alone, 36.4 percent in the workforce were women. However, in other industrialized nations such as the Netherlands, Denmark, and Sweden, women account for less than 30 percent of the workforce. Similarly, in the Middle East, for example, men hold most management positions, and women are confined to secretarial or support roles. The situation is not much better in India or China and, even in such advanced countries as Germany, women generally are not regarded as management timber. This is highly surprising given that current international labor statistics show that women are entering the workforce in record numbers. For example, in the last decade in Singapore, the number of married women in the labor force has grown from 33 percent of the total to more than 45 percent and, in Malaysia, women now make up half the workforce.

However, research reveals that many of these stereotypes are beginning to disappear. One reason for this change is that MNEs realize that to be successful they must judge people based on their worth to the organization and not on social custom alone. Firms such as IBM Europe have long espoused equality for women in the workplace and, if only to prevent this company from getting a big jump on them, other computer MNEs have followed suit. In addition, governments in Europe and Asia now are enacting and enforcing legislation to promote equality in the workplace.

Although this is a step in the right direction, the challenge for many American MNEs is to realize that social values in the United States often differ from those in other countries, and some cultures have difficulty dealing with female managers or company representatives. The firm must be careful not to present itself as aggressive and unconcerned about local custom. To ease the way, many American MNEs first promote a woman into the upper ranks of the overseas subsidiary and then, after the local business community is accustomed to dealing with this person, into the top job. In some cases, MNEs are finding that women are able to open doors that are closed to men, because foreign managers are impressed by the fact that a multinational company would send a woman rather than follow the usual procedure of appointing a man. In many cases, women report that top managers are willing to give them appointments, whereas their male counterparts have never been able to get in to see these managers. Women also report that many of these foreign managers believe that women are better listeners and more receptive to the needs of their enterprise. They view the women as putting the client's needs ahead of their own MNE's profit. These recent findings help to explain why more and more American women are willing to accept overseas assignments. They realize that international cultures are different, but they also know that excellent opportunities exist in the international arena.

Sources: Richard M. Hodgetts and Fred Luthans, International Management, *4th ed. (Burr Ridge, IL: Irwin/McGraw, 2000), chapter 4; Alan M. Rugman and Richard M. Hodgetts,* International Business, *2d ed. (London: Pearson Education, 2000), pp. 595–600; "Nordic Career Track,"* Across the Board, *May 2000, p. 78; and Bonnie Michaels, "A Global Glance at Work and Family,"* Personnel Journal, *April 1995, p. 90.*

Two major human relations problems associated with culture arise for those doing business internationally: first, understanding the cultures of other countries and, second, learning how to adapt to these cultures.[9] It is a known fact that "few managers are trained in how to motivate workers and provide the kind of environment that supports optimal performance."[10] These failures often are a result of ethnocentrism and misconceptions.

Ethnocentrism is the belief that one's way of doing things is superior to that of others. Ethnocentric behavior can be found among both people and organizations. In the case of individuals, it often takes the form of "we're better than anyone else." In the case of organizations, it is typified by an MNE that uses the same strategies abroad that it employs at home because it is convinced that the way business is done in the home country is superior to that used by the competition overseas.

A second major reason for people's lack of understanding of international culture is the misconceptions that they hold regarding these other people. A good example is provided in the case of the United States and Russia. Before the recent thaw in international relations, many Russians believed a large percentage of Americans not only lived in poverty but, were street people who roamed the cities and slept on park benches and in subways. As a result, most Soviets concluded that life in America was much worse than that in Russia. Americans also have misconceptions about other countries.

Some misconceptions occur because of differences in gestures of the eyes, the face, and the hands. For example, in the United States when listening to a speaker, it is customary to look at the speaker's mouth, and when speaking, to make intermittent eye contact with the listener; however, in China, a speaker maintains unbroken eye contact. In North American and northern European cultures, eye contact displays openness, trustworthiness, and integrity; whereas in Arab cultures, intense eye contact and concentration on the eye movement is used to read intentions, and in the Japanese culture, people do not make direct, intense eye contact. Hand shaking is a way to greet and to depart from people. How it is done varies among cultures. For example, in Austria, the hand shake is firm with direct eye contact and with women first; in Germany, the hand shake is firm with one or two pumps custom among men with women offering their hand first; in Spain, the hand shake is accompanied with a pat on the back with a slight embrace; in Saudi Arabia, the hand shake is light with the left hand touching the forearm, elbow, or the shoulder; and in Mexico, the hand shake is gentle, whereas women friends embrace and kiss the cheek. General gestures of the hand can vary by geographic locations, as well. Gestures made by people living in the southern part of the United States can mean something very different from the same gesture made by people living in the north.[11]

Table 13.3 illustrates a comparison of cultural values by priority among Americans, the Japanese, and the Arabs.

The most effective way of dealing with misconceptions is by learning about international culture. Before doing so, however, take the Time Out quiz to determine how much you currently know about Japanese business.

Cultural Dimensions

In recent years, researchers have attempted to develop a composite picture of culture by clustering or grouping these differences. This has been accomplished in two ways.

First, attention has been focused on finding cultural dimensions that help to identify similarities and differences between cultures.

Second, researchers have attempted to integrate these findings and to group countries into clusters that contain nations with similar cultures.

Geert Hofstede, a Dutch researcher, has found four cultural dimensions that help to explain how and why people from various cultures behave as they do:

1. **Power distance.**
2. **Uncertainty avoidance.**
3. **Individualism.**
4. **Masculinity.**[12]

Ethnocentrism *is the belief that one's way of doing things is superior to that of others.*

TABLE 13.3 — *Comparison of Cultural Values by Priority*

Americans	Japanese	Arabs
Freedom	Belonging	Family security
Independence	Group harmony	Family harmony
Self-reliance	Collectivity	Parental guidance
Equality	Age/seniority	Age
Individualism	Group consensus	Authority
Competition	Cooperation	Compromise
Efficiency	Quality	Devotion
Time	Patience	Patience
Directness	Indirectness	Indirectness
Openness	Go-between	Hospitality

Source: Carolena Lyons Lawrence, "Teaching Students How Gestures Communicate Across Cultures," Business Education Forum, February 2003, p. 39. Reprinted with permission from Business Education Forum C2003 by the National Business Education Association, 1914 Association Drive, Reston, VA 20191.

POWER DISTANCE

Power distance is the degree to which less powerful members of organizations and institutions accept the fact that power is not distributed equally. People in societies in which orders are obeyed without question live in a high-power distance culture. Many Asian and Latin countries, such as Malaysia, the Philippines, Panama, Guatemala, Venezuela, and Mexico, are typified by

Power distance
is the degree to which less powerful members of the society accept the fact that power is not distributed equally.

time out

DOING BUSINESS IN JAPAN

Here are nine statements about Japanese business. Read each carefully and decide whether it is true or false. Answers are provided at the end of the chapter.

T/F 1. The Japanese produce better-quality products than do the Americans.

T/F 2. Japanese productivity per worker is higher than that of the American worker.

T/F 3. Under Japanese management approaches, workers have higher work satisfaction than do their American counterparts.

T/F 4. Japanese employees work harder than do American employees.

T/F 5. The Japanese management approach is more humanistic than the American approach.

T/F 6. The Japanese have a technological advantage over the Americans.

T/F 7. The Japanese are better educated than Americans and thus are able to be trained more quickly in sophisticated operations.

T/F 8. The Japanese provide their personnel with better orientation and training than do Americans.

T/F 9. Japanese companies make better use than do American companies of modern human resources management techniques, such as quality circles and cooperative union relationships.

high power distance. In contrast, the United States, Canada, and many European countries (such as Denmark, Great Britain, and Austria) have moderate to low power distance.

In countries demonstrating high power distance, managers make autocratic and paternalistic decisions and the subordinates do as they are told. Close control of operations and a fairly weak work ethic usually are extant. Organization structures tend to be tall, and managers have a fairly small number of subordinates reporting directly to them. In countries with moderate to low power distance, people put a high value on independence, managers consult with subordinates before making decisions, and the work ethic is fairly strong. Organizational structures tend to be flat, and managers directly supervise more subordinates than their counterparts in high–power-distance enterprises.

UNCERTAINTY AVOIDANCE

Uncertainty avoidance
is the extent to which people feel threatened by ambiguous situations and have created institutions for minimizing or avoiding these uncertainties.

Uncertainty avoidance is, for Hofstede, the extent to which people feel threatened by ambiguous situations and have created institutions and beliefs for minimizing or avoiding these uncertainties. Countries with high uncertainty avoidance try to reduce risk and to develop systems and methods for dealing with ambiguity. There is strong uncertainty avoidance in Greece, Uruguay, Guatemala, Portugal, Japan, and Korea but weak uncertainty avoidance in such countries as Singapore, Sweden, Great Britain, the United States, and Canada.

Countries with high uncertainty avoidance tend to structure organizational activities and depend heavily on rules to ensure that everyone knows what he or she is to do. There often is high anxiety and stress among these people, they are very concerned with security, and decisions are often a result of group consensus. Low-uncertainty avoidance societies offer less structuring of activities and encourage more risk taking by managers. People tend to take things as they come, have more acceptance of dissent and disagreement, and rely heavily on their own initiative and ingenuity in getting things done.

INDIVIDUALISM

Individualism
is the tendency of people to look after themselves and their immediate family only.
Collectivism
is the tendency of people to belong to groups that look after each other in exchange for loyalty.

For Hofstede, **individualism** is the tendency of people to look after themselves and their immediate family only. This dimension is in direct contrast to **collectivism,** the tendency of people to belong to groups that look after each other in exchange for loyalty. Economically advanced countries tend to place greater emphasis on individualism than do poorer countries. For example, the United States, Great Britain, the Netherlands, and Canada have high individualism. In contrast, Ecuador, Guatemala, Pakistan, and Indonesia have low individualism.

Countries with high individualism expect all workers to take care of themselves. The strong emphasis is on individual initiative and achievement. Autonomy and individual financial security are given high value, and people are encouraged to make individual decisions and not rely heavily on group support. In contrast, countries with low individualism place a great deal of importance on group decision making and affiliation. No one wants to be singled out for special attention, even if it is praise for an outstanding job. The workers believe they collectively account for all success and that to praise one person more than the others is embarrassing to that individual because it implies that he or she is better than the others. Countries with low individualism emphasize belonging and draw strength from group affiliation.

MASCULINITY

Masculinity
is the degree to which the dominant values of a society are success, money, and material things.
Femininity
is the degree to which the dominant values of a society focus on caring for others and on the quality of life.

Masculinity, for Hofstede, is the degree to which the dominant values of a society are success, money, and material things. This is in contrast to **femininity,** which Hofstede perceives as the degree to which the dominant values of a society focus on caring for others and on the quality of life. Countries with high masculinity are Japan, Austria, Venezuela, and Mexico. Countries that have low masculinity (or high femininity) are Norway, Sweden, Denmark, and the Netherlands. The United States has a moderate to high masculinity score, as do other Anglo countries.

Countries with high masculinity scores place a great deal of importance on earnings, recognition, advancement, and challenge. Achievement is defined in terms of wealth and recognition. These cultures often favor large-scale enterprises, and economic growth is viewed as very important. In school, children are encouraged to be high performers, and boys are expected to think about work careers where they can succeed. Less emphasis is given to this for girls because the opportunities for women in upper-level jobs are limited. Countries with low masculinity scores place great emphasis on a friendly work environment, cooperation, and employment security. Achievement is defined in terms of human contacts and the living environment. There is low stress in the workplace, and workers are given a great deal of freedom.

Integrating the Dimensions

LEARNING OBJECTIVE

③ *Discuss the value of country clusters in understanding the impact of culture in the international arena*

For Hofstede, the four dimensions just described influence the overall culture of a society and result in a unique environment. No culture is identical to another; however, some similarities exist among most cultures. This can be illustrated by examining the effect of pairs of dimensions on culture. (Figure 13.1 provides an example.) In this case, the effects of power distance and individualism-collectivism are presented. (See Table 13.4 for the names of the countries and regions used in Figure 13.1.)

The United States is located in the lower left quadrant. It has high individualism and moderate power distance. American culture is characterized by a desire to do things personally, and individuals in authority do not overly impress people. Notice that other Anglo cultures are located nearby, including Australia, Great Britain, and Canada. In the same quadrant, directly above this group, are a host of Western European countries, including Sweden, Switzerland, Denmark, and Ireland. In the lower right quadrant are some of the other Western European countries, including Italy, Belgium, France, and Spain. They have cultures similar to those of their European neighbors. Most of the remaining countries and regions examined by Hofstede are in the upper right quadrant, including Latin countries, Asian nations, East and West African countries, and Arab nations. Moderate to low individualism and moderate to high power distance characterize these nations. It is particularly interesting to note that of all the Asian nations, Japan is most similar to the United States, indicating that technology and affluence may well have an impact on a culture and make it more like other nations with these same characteristics.

A second example of pairs of cultural dimensions is provided in Figure 13.2, in which masculinity–femininity and uncertainty avoidance are plotted. In this case, the United States is in the upper right quadrant. American culture encourages uncertainty avoidance, and moderate emphasis is placed on masculinity. Once again, some of the countries surrounding the United States are Anglo nations characterized by similar religious leanings, history, and economic development and speaking the same language.

In the upper-left quadrant are most of the Scandinavian countries, whereas Latin and Asian nations are located in the lower half of the figure, characterized by high uncertainty avoidance and varying degrees of masculinity. Notice that Japan is by itself in the lower right quadrant. That country is characterized by high uncertainty avoidance and high masculinity.

Figures 13.1 and 13.2 are only two of the six figures that can be constructed using the four cultural dimensions. However, they are sufficient to illustrate the effect of culture on behavior. As we examined the two figures, we noted that some countries tend to cluster near one another, thus indicating the effect of similar cultural values. In recent years, other researchers have taken Hofstede's work and used it to study attitudinal dimensions and country clusters.

Attitudinal Dimensions

An overall assessment of the similarities and differences among the fifty countries and three geographical regions would be difficult to make on the basis of the data provided in Figures 13.1 and 13.2. The location of each area in relation to the others changes from one figure to the next. Using Hofstede's findings, however, researchers have been investigating the similarities and differences in work values and attitudes between countries. Early work by Simcha Ronen and Allen Kraut led these researchers to conclude that "countries could be clustered into more or less

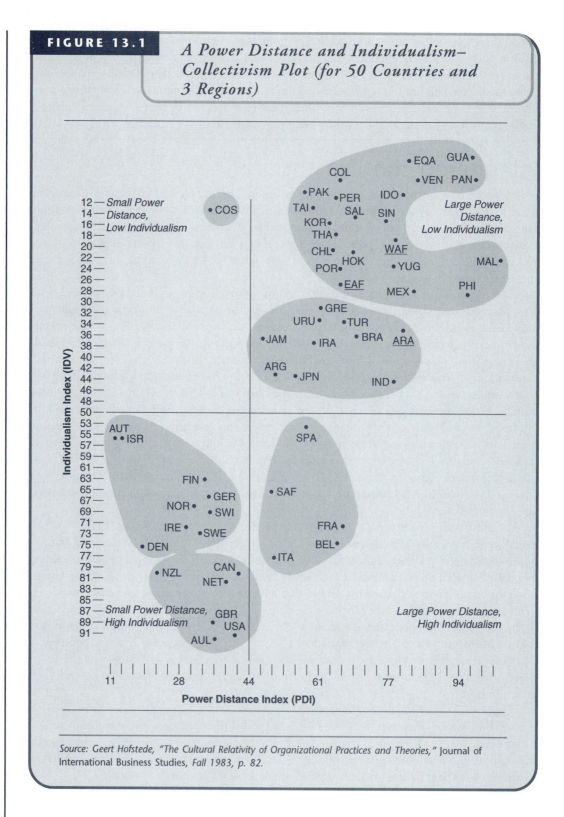

homogeneous groups."[13] The two researchers sought to cluster countries by using a mathematical technique that allowed them to identify how close countries were to one another in terms of overall culture. They identified five different country clusters: Anglo, Nordic, South American, Latin European, and Central European. Since the time of their research, additional multicultural studies have been conducted, and the number of countries and clusters has been expanded.

The most integrative analysis to date has been offered by Ronen and Oded Shenkar, whose review of the literature revealed that eight major cluster studies had looked at four major cultural areas:

TABLE 13.4 — Countries and Regions Used in Hofstede's Research

ARA	Arab countries (Egypt, Lebanon, Libya, Kuwait, Iraq, Saudi Arabia, United Arab Emirates)	ITA	Italy
		JAM	Jamaica
		JPN	Japan
ARG	Argentina	KOR	South Korea
AUL	Australia	MAL	Malaysia
AUT	Austria	MEX	Mexico
BEL	Belgium	NET	Netherlands
BRA	Brazil	NOR	Norway
CAN	Canada	NZL	New Zealand
CHL	Chile	PAK	Pakistan
COL	Colombia	PAN	Panama
COS	Costa Rica	PER	Peru
DEN	Denmark	PHI	Philippines
EAF	East Africa (Kenya, Ethiopia, Zambia)	POR	Portugal
		SAF	South Africa
EQA	Ecuador	SAL	El Salvador
FIN	Finland	SIN	Singapore
FRA	France	SPA	Spain
GBR	Great Britain	SWE	Sweden
GER	Germany	SWI	Switzerland
GRE	Greece	TAI	Taiwan
GUA	Guatemala	THA	Thailand
HOK	Hong Kong	TUR	Turkey
IDO	Indonesia	URU	Uruguay
IND	India	USA	United States
IRA	Iran	VEN	Venezuela
IRE	Ireland	WAF	West Africa (Nigeria, Ghana, Sierra Leone)
ISR	Israel		
		YUG	Yugoslavia

Source: Geert Hofstede, "The Cultural Relativity of Organizational Practices and Theories," Journal of International Business Studies, Fall 1983, p. 79.

1. The importance of work goals.
2. Need deficiency, fulfillment, and job satisfaction.
3. Managerial and organizational variables.
4. Work role and interpersonal orientations.[14]

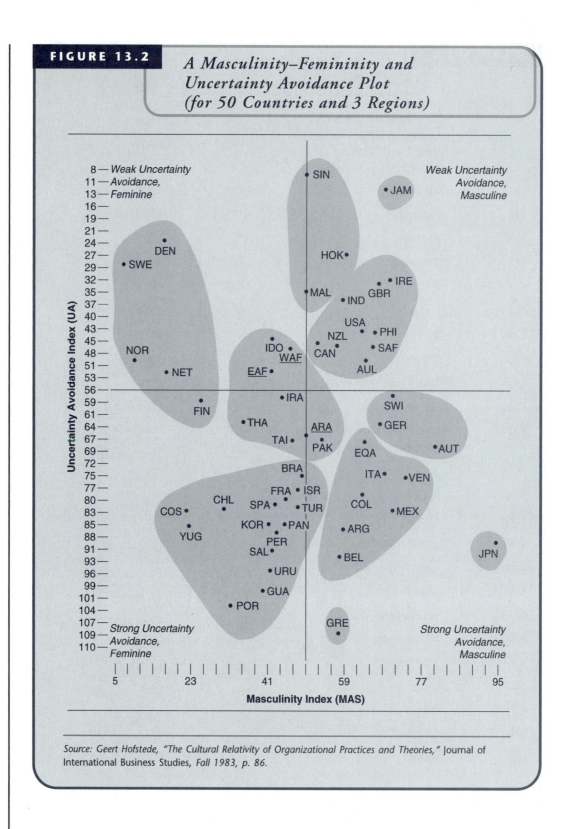

FIGURE 13.2 *A Masculinity–Femininity and Uncertainty Avoidance Plot (for 50 Countries and 3 Regions)*

Source: Geert Hofstede, "The Cultural Relativity of Organizational Practices and Theories," Journal of International Business Studies, Fall 1983, p. 86.

The problem with the studies was that each examined different countries and regions. However, after carefully reviewing the studies, Ronen and Shenkar were able to identify eight country clusters and four countries that were independent and did not fit into any of the clusters. Their findings are presented in Figure 13.3.

Each country in Figure 13.3 that has been placed in a cluster shares values, attitudes, and beliefs with the other countries in that cluster. Additionally, the closer to the center of the overall circle that a country is located, the higher is its gross national product (GNP). Those nations

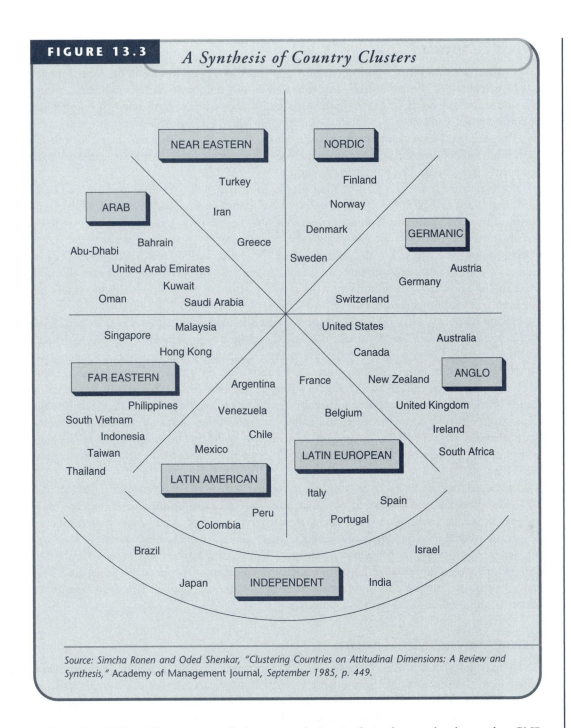

FIGURE 13.3 *A Synthesis of Country Clusters*

NEAR EASTERN

Turkey

Iran

Greece

ARAB

Abu-Dhabi
Bahrain

United Arab Emirates

Kuwait

Oman
Saudi Arabia

NORDIC

Finland

Norway

Denmark

Sweden

GERMANIC

Austria

Germany

Switzerland

United States

Canada

Australia

FAR EASTERN

Singapore
Malaysia

Hong Kong

Philippines
South Vietnam
Indonesia
Taiwan
Thailand

Argentina

Venezuela

Chile

Mexico

France

Belgium

New Zealand

ANGLO

United Kingdom

Ireland

South Africa

LATIN AMERICAN

Peru
Colombia

LATIN EUROPEAN

Italy

Portugal

Spain

Brazil

Israel

Japan
INDEPENDENT
India

Source: Simcha Ronen and Oded Shenkar, "Clustering Countries on Attitudinal Dimensions: A Review and Synthesis," *Academy of Management Journal, September 1985, p. 449.*

with similar GNPs will not necessarily have intercluster similarity but to the degree that GNP influences values and culture, they will have converging cultural values.

Not everyone agrees with the data in Figure 13.3; some researchers have formulated different international clusters. However, the figure does provide a basis for investigating the international cultural environment, and it is particularly useful to the study of international human relations. In particular, multinational enterprises can benefit from knowledge of the impact of local culture on business attitudes and practices.

International Culture's Impact at Work

Culture directly affects the way that people work. It influences their attitudes, motivation, and even the way that they deal with time. The following sections examine the impact of culture in each of these areas.

LEARNING OBJECTIVE

4 *Relate the ways in which culture affects work attitudes, motivation, and how people deal with time*

Work Attitudes

Work attitudes can influence both the quality and quantity of employee output. Americans are taught to believe in the work ethic, but this ethic is not unique to the United States. Many people around the world believe in hard work, and it shows in their attitudes. In many Asian countries, job attendance is viewed as a major responsibility, and everyone comes to work every day. Another common cultural work attitude among Asians is that they remain on the job for the entire workday, in contrast to many Americans who believe that if people can get their work done early they should be allowed to go home.

However, there must be a limit to what people do or they will collapse from stress and over-work, and many managers report that they face these conditions on a daily basis. In fact, a recent survey of managers in twenty-four countries found that British managers, in particular, are more heavily stressed than those from any of the other countries where managers were surveyed. Long working hours and the lack of job security were the major reasons for this condition.[15] The study also reported that stress among American managers was not very high. However, this may be changing given that, in recent years, the number of hours worked annually by Americans has been continually increasing.[16]

On the matter of overwork, it is Japanese workers who seem to suffer most. In particular, the incidence of *karoshi,* or overwork, is rising especially among forty- to fifty-year-old men, and this trend is likely to continue because many employees in this age category report that they have no intention of changing their work habits. In a poll taken by an insurance company in Japan, 40 percent of the employees surveyed said they feared they might fall victim to *karoshi,* but almost none of them said they were going to change their work habits. Fortunately, signs indicate that younger managers and employees are willing to change and adopt healthier work attitudes. However, MNEs doing business in Japan will have to remain aware of the dangers presented by *karoshi* and be prepared to encourage the employees to slow down and take more days off.

The population of Japan is growing older, causing changes in the workplace. "By around 2007, the proportion of the population over sixty-five will have jumped to 20 percent from 10 percent in just twenty-one years, which is nearly twice as fast as any other major nation." To get the work done, the elderly are working longer and harder. The work available is changing, for example, major auto Japanese companies, like Nissan, Toyota, and Honda are shifting their assembly operations out of Japan and are not opening any new operations in Japan. These actions affect pension benefits, consumption levels, and the standard of living. In time other countries also, will be faced with this problem.[17]

Achievement Motivation

A second cultural factor, closely linked to work attitudes, is achievement motivation. How achievement-driven are people from other countries? Research reveals that achievement drive in Eastern Europe is not very high. Industry managers in Czechoslovakia, for example, have much lower achievement drive than American managers. On the other hand, as Eastern Europe makes the transition from a command economy to a market economy, this is likely to change. After all, the need for achievement is a learned need and is determined largely by the prevailing culture. Another good example is provided by China, where researchers have found little evidence of high achievement drive. Workers in China have low scores on challenge, promotion, and earnings, all work goals that would be particularly important to high achievers. Conversely, whereas high achievers would not give high scores to affiliation- or safety-related goals, such as security, benefits, physical working conditions, or time for nonwork activities, Chinese workers rate these variables as very important.

These results help to illustrate why culture is so important to MNEs as they formulate their strategic plans. MNEs are looking for countries and geographical regions that encourage economic activity and achievement drive. In places such as Eastern Europe and China, the company would have to plan on sending its own managers to head the enterprise, if only in the short run, and would have to look for ways of creating and nurturing high achievement drive among the employees it hires.

Time and the Future

A third element of culture that will affect an MNE is the society's view of time and how it should be spent. In some areas of the Far East, people believe they will be reincarnated, so they do not worry about whether they will get something done in this lifetime. In some African cultures, time is not a constraint. In fact, lateness is acceptable behavior. As noted earlier in the text, the same is true in many Latin cultures of both South America and Europe, although in countries such as Spain, the traditional *siesta* now is being radically modified and, in some cases, eliminated by companies.[18]

In follow-up research on culture, Hofstede has added a fifth dimension: long-term orientation.[19] This dimension was a result of work by both Hofstede and a colleague in Hong Kong, who measured basic values through the use of an instrument known as the *Chinese values survey*. This survey clearly indicated that Asians have a much longer-term orientation than do Occidentals. Hofstede believes that this cultural dimension may help account for such developments as the willingness of Asians to save greater amounts of their income and invest it in economic growth, thus helping spur the rise of such economies as Japan, Hong Kong, Korea, Taiwan, Singapore and, most recently, China. However, the long-term orientation does not end here. It can also be extremely useful in helping companies to make decisions.

For example, Asians are known to take a long time making up their minds to do something. However, once they have decided on a plan of action, implementation usually follows in short order. This is in direct contrast to many Western cultures, where decisions to proceed are made quickly but implementation is extremely slow. Thus, among firms that value rapid implementation, Asian cultures can be ideal.

American MNEs have also found that firms in the Far East, especially Japanese companies, are more long-range in their planning efforts and do not expect to generate a fast return on their investment. These firms are willing to invest today and wait five to ten years to make an adequate profit. This makes them particularly attractive to U.S. firms looking for investors. A good example is the Walt Disney Company, which raised almost $1 billion from Japanese investors in the last decade. In return, the investors are limited partners in movies made by Disney and will share in the future profit of these films. The arrangement is ideal for both sides. Disney gets interest-free capital that it can use to make films, and the investors have future earnings that, if the movies are successful (as are most Disney films), will provide a handsome return on investment.

Sending upscale jobs offshore, such as basic research, chip design, engineering, and even financial analysis, is a trend in globalization that is saving U.S. companies 50 to 60 percent in costs. This is "one of the biggest trends reshaping the global economy. The driving forces are digitization, the Internet, and high-speed data networks that girdle the globe."[20] Now that knowledge work of all kinds can be done anywhere in the world, Forrester Research Inc, analyst John C. McCarthy states "You will see an explosion of work going overseas." Intel, Inc., and Texas Instruments, Inc., for example, are using engineers from India and China, and the Hewlett-Packard Company has employed over three thousand engineers in India. Whereas the rise in a globally integrated knowledge economy is helping developing nations, it is unclear what it means for the United States. "Our comparative advantage may shift to other fields," says City University of New York economist Robert E. Lipsey, a trade specialist.

By tapping the world's best talent, "companies like American Express, Dell Computer, and Eastman Kodak can offer round-the-clock customer care while keeping costs in check."[21] On the flip side, some nine hundred big companies have complained of problems in communicating and meeting deadlines. Another concern is what will happen to the displaced white-collar workers. Until now the concern has only been with blue-collar workers. From a human relations position, foreign workers are definitely making a cultural change.

Global outsourcing is causing the financial industry to undergo a major change. For example, processing insurance claims, selling stocks, and analyzing companies can all be done by workers in Asia. Outsourcing experts say the big job migration won't happen until 2010. Companies are just beginning to work out the bugs in the systems and to develop standards, and issues concerning human relations must be resolved. This trend is currently in its initial stages and will directly impact human relations issues in the next decade.

LEARNING OBJECTIVE

Describe the ways in which cross-cultural training is used to prepare personnel to deal with international cultures

⑤ International Human Resource Management Challenges

A host of international human resource management challenges will face companies during the first decade of this millennium. Two major challenges are the appropriate selection and training of personnel for international assignments and the need to develop a global perspective that allows firms to manage their far-flung operations in a cohesive and integrated way. We examine these challenges in the next sections.

Selection and Training of Personnel

One of the current international human relations challenges facing organizations is that of choosing the appropriate personnel for international assignments. Should the company send people from the home office or select local managers? In recent years, a growing number of enterprises have been opting for local managers, although the top positions often are reserved, if only in the beginning, for home office personnel. Sometimes this is done because there is a shortage of talented senior-level managers in the other country.[22] In other cases, management simply wants to have someone in charge who understands what headquarters wants done and is able to communicate effectively with those at the home office. For example, Ford Motor owns a significant share of Mazda Motors of Japan and has assigned one of its own managers to run Mazda and integrate the company's operations into that of Ford.[23]

In choosing the best personnel to fill overseas positions, a growing number of companies have been focusing on identifying selection criteria that can be used to select the people most likely to do the best job.[24] Typically, both technical and human skills are evaluated. Some of the most common criteria are:

1. **The ability to adapt personally to an overseas assignment.**
2. **Technical competence.**
3. **The ability of one's family to adapt.**
4. **Human relations skills.**
5. **Previous overseas experience.**[25]

In addition, many firms use interviews as part of the screening process. In the case of managers, these interviews typically are held with both the candidate and the candidate's spouse. The objective of this screening is to ensure that there is a strong fit between the person's abilities and talents and the demands of the position.

In many cases, those who are selected for overseas assignments are given special types of training prior to their departure. The two most common are cultural training and language training. Cultural training is designed to familiarize the individual with the ways life is lived in the country and typically includes a wide array of considerations from social customs to business practices.[26] Some of this training is generic and is designed to provide general information about how things are done in the country. For example, the overall cultural highlights and specific guidelines that often are provided regarding how to do business in China include such information as the following:

- **The Chinese place a great deal of emphasis on trust and mutual connections, so it is important to spend time building good relationships with those with whom you will be doing business.**
- **Business meetings typically start with pleasantries such as tea and general conversation about your trip to the country, local accommodations, and family. In most cases, the host will have already been briefed on your background.**

- When a meeting is ready to begin, the Chinese host will give the appropriate indication. Similarly, when the meeting is over, the host will indicate that it is time for you to leave. Be alert for these signs.
- Chinese businesspeople tend to be slow in formulating a plan of action but, once they decide what they want to do, they generally proceed at a fairly good rate. When the plan begins to be implemented, it is important to be fully prepared to do your part.
- In negotiations, reciprocity is important. If the Chinese make concessions, they expect something in return. Additionally, it is common for them to slow down negotiations in order to take advantage of Westerners (Americans, in particular) who are eager to conclude a deal. The objective of this tactic is to extract further concessions. Therefore, be patient in your negotiations.
- Because negotiating can involve a loss of face, it is common to find Chinese carrying out the process through intermediaries. This allows them to convey their ideas without fear of embarrassment.[27] As a result, you typically will find that no one in the negotiation has the authority to sign off on the deal.

Information such as this often is provided in two ways. One is through the use of cultural assimilators and the other is by individuals who have been stationed in the country and can speak from firsthand experience.

CULTURAL ASSIMILATORS

A **cultural assimilator** is a programmed learning technique that is designed to expose members of one culture to some of the basic concepts, attitudes, role perceptions, customs, and values of another culture. Cultural assimilators are developed for pairs of cultures, such as to familiarize managers from the United States with the culture in Germany. The approach almost always takes the same format: The person being trained is asked to read a short episode of a cultural encounter and then to choose an interpretation of what has happened and why. If the person's response is correct, the individual goes on to the next episode. If not, the person is asked to reread the episode and make another choice. Table 13.5 provides an illustration.

Cultural assimilators use critical incidents as the basis for training, and these incidents typically are provided both by managers who have served in the particular country and by members of the host nation. Once the incidents are written, they are tested on people who have had experience in this country in order to ensure that the responses are realistic and that one choice is indeed preferable to the others. Typically 150–200 incidents are developed, and then the list is pruned to 75–100 incidents that eventually are included in the assimilator booklet.

Assimilators can be expensive to create. However, for MNEs that are continually sending people to a particular overseas location, the cost can be spread over many trainees, and the assimilator package can remain intact for a number of years. For example, a $100,000 assimilator package that is used by five hundred people over a five-year period will cost the company only $200 per person, and the cost of revising the program often is very small. Thus, over the long run, cultural assimilators can be cost-effective as well as being extremely helpful in developing effective international human relations-oriented personnel.

LANGUAGE TRAINING

Language training is another area that often is regarded as important for those who are going to work in the international arena. During the 1980s, when Japan was the most competitive nation in the world and its economy was booming, a number of major MNEs with operations in that country began encouraging their people to learn Japanese. Certainly, to the extent that it can help multinational managers interact more effectively with the local personnel, the ability to speak the local language is a benefit. It also is useful in learning about the culture of the country, because it allows the individual to read the newspapers and listen to local radio and television and thus get a very good grasp of what is going on in the country. Other benefits of knowing the language are that it helps one interact socially with both the personnel and clients,

*A **cultural assimilator** is a programmed learning technique that is designed to expose members of one culture to the values of another culture.*

TABLE 13.5

A Cultural Assimilator Situation

Sharon Hatfield, a schoolteacher in Athens, Greece, was amazed at the questions that were asked of her by Greeks whom she considered to be only casual acquaintances. When she entered or left her apartment, people would ask her where she was going or where she had been. If she stopped to talk, she was asked questions such as, "How much do you make a month?" or "Where did you get that dress you are wearing?" She thought that the Greeks were very rude.

Page X-2

Why did the Greeks ask Sharon such "personal" questions?
1. The casual acquaintances were acting like friends do in Greece, although Sharon did not realize it.

Go to page X-3

2. The Greeks asked Sharon the questions to determine whether she belonged to the Greek Orthodox Church.

Go to page X-4

3. The Greeks were unhappy about the way in which she lived, and they were trying to get Sharon to change her habits.

Go to page X-5

4. In Greece, such questions are perfectly proper when asked of women but improper when asked of men.

Go to page X-6

Page X-3

You selected 1: The casual acquaintances were acting like friends do in Greece, although Sharon did not realize it.

Correct. It is not improper for in-group members to ask these questions of one another. Furthermore, these questions reflect the fact that friendships (even casual ones) tend to be more intimate in Greece than in America. As a result, friends generally are free to ask questions that would seem too personal in America.

Go to page X-1

Page X-4

You selected 2: The Greeks asked Sharon the questions to determine whether she belonged to the Greek Orthodox Church.

No. This is not why the Greeks asked Sharon such questions. Remember, whether or not some information is personal depends on the culture. In this case, the Greeks did not consider these questions to be too personal. Why? Try again.

Go to page X-1

Page X-5

You selected 3: The Greeks were unhappy about the way in which she lived, and they were trying to get Sharon to change her habits.

No. There was no information given to lead you to believe that the Greeks were unhappy with Sharon's way of living. The episode states that the Greeks were acquaintances of Sharon.

Go to page X-1

Page X-6

You selected 4: In Greece, such questions are perfectly proper when asked of women but improper when asked of men.

No. Such questions are indeed proper under certain situations. However, gender has nothing to do with it. When are these questions proper? Try to apply what you have learned about proper behavior between friends in Greece. Was Sharon regarded as a friend by these Greeks?

Go to page X-1

Source: Reprinted from Fred E. Fiedler, Terence Mitchell, and Harry C. Triandis, "The Cultural Assimilator: An Approach to Cross-Cultural Training," Journal of Applied Psychology, April 1971, pp. 97–98. Copyright © 1971 by The American Psychological Association. Reprinted by permission.

and it can be particularly useful in recruiting local talent. On the other hand, the recent trend has been toward minimizing language training for American managers, because English is so dominant and, for all intents and purposes, has become the primary language of the business world. One expert in the area explained the new trend this way:

> By happy coincidence, English has become the lingua franca of international business. It would be quite impossible, after all, for all the people in the world to learn all the languages of the people they do business with. When Germans and Japanese meet to strike a deal, the chances are the negotiations will take place in English.
>
> An increasing number of people in the business world speak English. Many European companies require their employees to speak English as a condition of employment. In most parts of the world, children learn English in elementary school. Generally speaking, as you go higher in the corporate hierarchy of a foreign company, more people speak English and speak it better. But even at lower levels, speaking English is an important skill in many foreign firms.[28]

Development of a Global Perspective

In recent years, a growing number of businesses have begun expanding internationally. In most cases, this has been accomplished by setting up overseas operations in conjunction with a local partner. These joint ventures have proven very popular. Another way that MNEs have been expanding their operations is through the use of mergers and acquisitions. For example, Daimler-Benz bought Chrysler, and Unilever, the Anglo-Dutch consumer products company, purchased Bestfoods, the maker of Skippy Peanut Butter and Hellmann's Mayonnaise.[29] In each of these instances, the companies have found themselves having to adjust to a new culture. After all, the way Daimler does business in Europe is going to be somewhat different from the way Chrysler carries out business in the United States. In an effort to ensure that all of their operations, domestic and foreign, are working together, MNEs now are developing and refining a global perspective. In particular, they are blending the overall corporate culture with the local culture of their international operations. The following are some representative examples:

- **At Costco's warehouse in Korea, employees dine at the corporate cafeteria. As this is traditional in other companies in Korea, Costco is following local customs.**
- **Siemens of Germany has a feedback tool called *management dialogue* that is used to judge the effectiveness of managers. Once annually, employees provide feedback about their supervisor. However, this tool is not used in China because that culture has a strong respect for hierarchies, and employees do not feel comfortable making comments about their boss.**
- **Wal-Mart offers stock options to its American employees in order to build morale. However, the company uses different forms of motivation in Germany, because stock options violate local laws.[30]**

Simply put, MNEs are working to strike a balance between creating a unifying corporate culture and addressing local differences.[31] A goal of Omron, a Japanese electronics manufacturer headquartered in Kyoto, Japan, is to make itself a multilocal company by promoting business operations that meet the particular characteristics of the local market in which it operates and that contribute to the local community, and at the same time, it must be unified on a global scale. In some cases, a company will insist that its overseas subsidiaries do things the way they are done in the home country because there must be a uniform culture in these areas. A good example is language: More and more firms now are insisting that everyone communicate in English. Omron, has designated English as the company's official language, and all international meetings are conducted in English. The company believes that the use of one language among all executives enhances communications and helps to reinforce the global nature of its business.[32] Omron also has standardized its software to eliminate compatibility issues and ensure a smooth exchange of information among its offices worldwide. To set the course for the future and at the same time maintain a balance, the company has formulated three key management concepts for its "Grand Design 2010" plan:

1. *Self-reliance.* To encourage each internal business company to operate more autonomously.
2. *Coexistence.* To maintain harmony with individuals, countries, the environment, and society.
3. *Creativity.* To offer higher added value and enhance Omron's corporate value by strategically combining hardware production.[33]

In addition, MNEs are beginning to develop systems for sharing information worldwide. For example, Ernst & Young, an international consulting firm, has its people share knowledge and discuss different approaches to doing business in other countries. One reason for this knowledge sharing is that a solution that worked well in India may be of value to a consulting team in the United Kingdom. A second reason is that this information can help other company consultants understand the culture of other countries and note the ways in which the local Ernst & Young consulting team modified its approach to address the local culture. In particular, understanding cultural nuances and how they shape customers' behaviors can help MNEs plan business operations to suit customer requirements better. For example, customers worldwide tend to use the same computer hardware, but the way in which they use their software often varies. Wolfgange Bothe, chairman of BETA Systems Software Inc., offers this example:

> . . . people in some cultures read an operational manual from cover to cover. Others expect instruction directly for BETA staff, while others sit quietly in a group to study and discuss the manual before they begin to install the software. "We have to understand first how different cultures learn, and then give them the information the way in which they need it," says Bothe. Thus, knowing how our client companies work affects the level of information in BETA's written software documentation for customers, as well as the number and caliber of people needed to staff its technical support centers.[34]

This approach is very important in helping BETA develop a global perspective, and the company is not alone. At Skoda Automobilova, a Czech Republic carmaker, the company has trained its managers in Western management techniques so that they are better able to work with the firm's MNE partner. At the same time, Skoda has taught its partner, Volkswagen, how business is conducted in Czechoslovakia. The result is that both groups now work together more productively.

Another example is provided by Wal-Mart, which has found that some facets of its corporate culture can be easily exported to foreign operations, whereas others require modification or do not work at all and must be abandoned. For example, when the company entered the German market in 1997, it brought along the culture that it had successfully used in the United States. One of these cultural activities was the company "cheer," in which a person stands in front of the associates and yells, "Give me a W!" and everyone shouts "W." The individual then continues with the Wal-Mart cheer by saying, "Give me an A!" and so on until the company's name is spelled out. The German personnel had no problem participating in this activity. However, other Wal-Mart activities were not well received. One is the Ten-Foot Rule, which states that an employee must greet any customer who is within a ten-foot radius. Neither the employees nor the customers felt comfortable with this custom, so it is not used in Germany.

MNEs are working very hard to ensure that their corporate culture and the culture of both their business partners and their customers fit together. This is particularly important given that, in one investigation of the reasons that business alliances fail, 75 percent of the companies said it was a result of an incompatibility of their corporate culture and the other firm's culture.[35] In dealing with this challenge, many MNEs now are developing their own in-house programs. At Nokia, for example, all new employees must attend the firm's "cultural awareness" class.

Companies also are reinforcing the development of a global perspective at salary review time. At Gillette, managers consider an employee's commitment to corporate culture as part of the individual's overall performance. At Siemens, when evaluating people for salary raises and promotions, managers look carefully at how well employees are working in accordance with the firm's core beliefs. The company's executive vice president put it this way:

> The goal is not to develop one "mind" in every part of the world but rather to achieve a meeting of the minds. That's what distinguishes companies with a truly global culture from those without. Employees and divisions across borders can work together because they all operate from the same basic beliefs. While a transplanted culture doesn't guarantee success, the lack of unifying corporate beliefs can only lessen a company's chances of being a major global player.[36]

The value of this is going to be even more important in the future, because of the growing number of alliances that are taking place between MNEs. For example, Airbus, the aircraft manufacturer, is allied with more than one hundred partners with whom it works in designing and building planes; and Sprint, Deutsche Telekom, and France Telecom, members of the Global One joint venture, serve seventy-five countries and work to function as one firm in addressing the global telecommunications needs of corporations. Unless the group can develop a uniform global perspective, the venture is likely to flounder.[37] As a result, international human relations will continue to be an important consideration in the new millennium.

summary

① LEARNING OBJECTIVE
Define the term multinational enterprise and discuss four major reasons why companies become multinational enterprises

A multinational enterprise is a company that is headquartered in one country but has operations in two or more countries. More and more firms are expanding into the international arena for a number of reasons, including protecting themselves from the domestic business cycle, tapping the growing world market for goods and services, and responding to foreign competition.

② LEARNING OBJECTIVE
Identify the term culture *and relate four basic dimensions of international culture*

Culture is the acquired knowledge that people use to interpret experience and to generate social behavior. Culture creates two major problems for those doing business internationally: understanding the cultures of these other countries and learning how to adapt to these cultures.

③ LEARNING OBJECTIVE
Discuss the value of country clusters in understanding the impact of culture in the international arena

In recent years, researchers have attempted to develop a composite picture of culture by clustering or grouping people based on these differences. One way, which this clustering has been accomplished, is through the use of cultural dimensions: power distance, uncertainty avoidance, individualism, and masculinity. Another way in which clustering has been performed is through an analysis of work values and attitudes between countries.

④ LEARNING OBJECTIVE
Relate the ways in which culture affects work attitudes, motivation, and how people deal with time

MNEs are particularly interested in the effect of country and geographical cultures on their international operations. In particular, they are concerned with the ways in which work attitudes, achievement motivation, and the society's view of time will affect the productivity and performance of the unit. They also are interested in taking steps to ensure that their enterprise is able to deal effectively with other cultures.

⑤ **LEARNING OBJECTIVE**
Describe the ways in which cross-cultural training is used to prepare personnel to deal with international cultures

Cross-cultural training has proven to be very effective in accomplishing this goal, especially language training and the use of cultural assimilators. In addition, MNEs now are working to develop a global perspective that helps them to integrate worldwide operations.

KEY TERMS IN THE CHAPTER

Multinational enterprise
Culture
Ethnocentrism
Power distance
Uncertainty avoidance

Individualism
Collectivism
Masculinity
Femininity
Cultural assimilator

REVIEW AND STUDY QUESTIONS

1. Why are so many firms now expanding internationally? Identify and discuss three reasons.

2. In your own words, explain what is meant by *culture?*

3. In what way are ethnocentrism and misconceptions about other cultures major problems for those doing business internationally?

4. In what way do power distance and uncertainty avoidance influence the way people in different cultures behave? What implications does this have for the study of human relations? In your answer, be sure to define each term.

5. In what way do *individualism* and *masculinity* influence the way that people in different cultures behave? What implications does this have for the study of human relations? In your answer, be sure to define each term.

6. Of what value is Figure 13.3 in understanding international human relations? In your answer, compare and contrast two different clusters.

7. In what way does culture influence work attitudes? Are work attitudes in the United States the same as those found in Asia? Why or why not? What does your answer relate about the importance of understanding international human relations?

8. In what way does culture influence achievement motivation? Give two examples.

9. In what way is time a cultural element that is of interest to MNEs? Explain.

10. Why is language training so useful in preparing people for overseas assignments?

11. How does a cultural assimilator work? Of what value is it in helping people to understand international human relations? Explain.

12. What are some steps that MNEs now are taking to develop a global perspective? Identify and describe two.

Addressing Global Communication Needs?

Deutsche Telekom, one of the world's leading communications companies in Germany, is addressing global communications needs of corporations. The company is represented in sixty-five countries on all six continents. Visit the Web site **http://www.deutschetelekom.com** and learn what the company is doing, then answer the questions.

1. Identify the four strategic divisions of the company. Prepare a profile for each division.

2. Review the latest press releases to learn what the company is currently doing. Describe the latest innovations and tell how they are making a difference in global communications.

3. Comment on your thoughts about what the company is doing and how the innovations will impact your life.

Working Abroad?

As businesses become more global in operations, so will the jobs and employment. Have you thought about working in another country? Do you know what it would be like to work in Germany, France, or Brazil? Visit the Web site: **http://www. careerjournal.com** and find out. Under "Manage Your Career" click on "Working Abroad." Under "Country Profiles," select a country. Complete the exercise.

1. Select a country. Use the following list to learn about the people and customs in that country.

   a. The people.

   b. Meeting and greeting.

   c. Body language.

   d. Corporate culture.

   e. Dining and entertainment.

   f. Dress.

   g. Gifts.

   h. Helpful hints.

   i. Especially for women.

2. Select another country and learn about its people and customs.

3. Compare the two countries and select one country in which you would like to work. Discuss why you would rather work in that country versus the other one.

4. What would you need to do to make working in a foreign country a reality?

Doing Business in Japan

1. Basically true, although for some products American quality still is regarded as superior (such as computers, telephone equipment, and commercial aircraft), and the Americans have greatly closed the quality gap in many consumer products.

2. False. The American worker has had the highest productivity for well over a half century.

3. False. Researchers have found that American workers tend to have higher work satisfaction than do their Japanese counterparts.

4. False. Both groups work about equally hard.

5. False. Many Japanese admit that they work in an environment in which they are told what to do and in which failure to comply carries strong penalties. Democratic leadership is far less prevalent in the Japanese workplace than many people realize.

6. Partially true. The Japanese tend to lead in areas in which applied concepts are important, but they are behind in areas in which theoretical knowledge is critical.

7. Partially true. The Japanese provide a better basic education to their people but, at the university level, they are inferior to the United States, which is the acknowledged world leader in upper-division education. This is particularly evident given the number of Japanese students who come to the United States for university and graduate study.

8. True. The Japanese do an excellent job in providing their people with orientation and training.

9. True. Japanese companies work hard at developing quality circles and cooperative company-employee teamwork, and they are very successful in their efforts.

Source: Richard M. Hodgetts and Fred Luthans, "Japanese HR Management Practices: Separating Fact from Fiction," Personnel, *April 1989, pp. 42–45.*

case: MORE OF THE SAME

Barbingry, Inc., is an electronic retail chain located in southeastern United States. The company is headquartered in Miami, and 25 percent of its business comes from international sales. These sales are from two major sources: visitors to Miami who buy merchandise to take back home and buyers from large retail stores throughout South America and Europe.

Barbingry has decided to expand operations by opening two large overseas stores. One is to be located in Madrid, Spain, and the other in Bogotá, Colombia. The company plans to stock the stores by shipping goods from the United States, as well as by using local suppliers in both overseas locations. Barbingry estimates that it will double current sales within three years because of the large forecasted increase in these international markets.

The company plans to use some of its bilingual managers in Miami to head the overseas operations, while hiring 90 percent of the personnel locally. Barbingry feels that Miami is such an international Latino market currently that operations in Madrid and Bógota will not pose a cultural problem for the firm. Barbingry estimates that last year, Latinos in Miami accounted for approximately 54 percent of all sales in south Florida.

"We believe that the markets in South America and Spain are going to be very similar to what we have encountered here in Miami," the chairman of the board told a reporter for the *Miami Herald.* "Additionally, since both of these international markets will have similar cultures, we can train our managers here in Miami for positions in either location, and we can transfer personnel from one overseas location to another without having to retrain them. I think it's an excellent idea to pick locations on different continents that have similar cultures because of this interchangeability factor. Once our people know how to interact with the Latino culture, we can send them on their way. And, in many cases, they are getting this training right here in Miami, where over half the local population is Latino. In fact, 45 percent of the management people we have hired over the last five years speak fluent English and Spanish. So I'd say we're ideally suited for the international Latino market, and I can't wait for us to implement this overseas expansion."

QUESTIONS

1. When it comes to cultural dimensions as power distance and individualism, how similar are Spain and Colombia? Give an example.

2. When comparing the degree of uncertainty avoidance and masculinity in these two markets, how similar are they?

3. Since the personnel being sent overseas will speak Spanish, what types of cultural adaptation would you recommend for these managers? Explain your answer.

YOU BE THE CONSULTANT

Look Out World, Here We Come

Roxling, Inc., a consumer appliance firm, plans on expanding internationally. The company designs and manufactures small, lightweight appliances. The organization has many patents on its products and is widely considered to be one of the foremost firms in this growing industry.

In the past, a number of companies from other countries have approached Roxling and asked for the right to manufacture or distribute its products overseas. Roxling has refused because it wants to maintain total control of both the production and the distribution of its products. Six months ago, the firm concluded that it is now in a position to begin expanding internationally. The company would like to move into three countries—England, China, and Saudi Arabia—within the next six months.

Roxling's initial plan is to train salespeople for the overseas market. These people will operate out of small offices in these countries and will send their sales reports back to headquarters. These orders then will be shipped from the United States to the overseas customers. Over the next two years, this approach will be modified, with the company opening up manufacturing plants in both Europe and the Far East. This strategy will reduce both delivery time and transportation costs.

Some members of Roxling's board of directors have suggested that the company spend more time preparing for this overseas expansion. "You really don't know much about these overseas countries," one of them explained. "You are going to have to find out a lot more about the culture and methods of doing business there than we know currently. Doing business in Saudi Arabia, for example, is a lot different from doing business in Chicago. We can't assume that our methods are going to fit in overseas and that we can simply send people over and have them go out and get orders."

The company president agrees with these comments but is unsure of the specific types of training to give his salespeople. "We are going to be selling products that have worldwide appeal," he explained. "This is going to help overcome a lot of the cultural barriers that most firms have to deal with. Also, there is no better way to learn the culture of a country than to go and live there, and this is exactly what we are going to have our salespeople doing. They are going to be within a day's drive of their customers and, if there are any problems, they can quickly resolve them."

The firm intends to start its sales training program within the next three weeks. After completing the training program, the salespeople will be scheduled for their overseas locations. Roxling intends to have a sales force in the field within six months.

Your Advice

1. What is your evaluation regarding the decision to go into England, China, and Saudi Arabia?

   _____ a. It is an excellent idea and the company should proceed to implement this plan.

   _____ b. England and China are acceptable, but the cultural change is so great in Saudi Arabia that the firm should hold off until it is more familiar with how to do business internationally.

   _____ c. The firm knows relatively little about expanding internationally and should focus on England for the moment while it builds up international experience.

2. What are the cultural differences among the three countries in which Roxling is considering doing business? Prepare a table listing your results.

3. What type of language training should the company implement for its personnel going overseas?

4. How can a cultural assimilator be useful? Explain.

EXPERIENCING THE IMPACT OF INTERNATIONAL CULTURE

Purpose

- **To understand the impact of culture on human relations.**
- **To learn the types of cultural barriers that must be overcome when expanding internationally.**
- **To apply these concepts to on-the-job situations.**

Procedure

1. The class should divide into groups of three or four students each. With the exception of the Anglo cluster, each group is to choose one of the country clusters in Figure 13.3. If there are more than seven teams, the independent clusters (Brazil, Japan, India, Israel) may be used.

2. Each group should then choose one of the countries within this cluster and gather information on the cultural problems that would be faced by the company described in the situation. Interviews with foreign students and professors with specific knowledge of this country, as well as library research, should be employed.

3. After identifying the major cultural problems that the company would face and the ways in which the firm should deal with these problems, present your findings to the rest of the class.

4. Note the similarities and differences faced by firms operating in the various cultures.

Situation

You are working for a firm that plans to open an overseas branch to sell its industrial machinery directly to customers in this foreign country. Your firm has never before directly sold its products outside the United States. You are to present your boss with a list of the major cultural barriers that must be surmounted if this sales effort is to be successful.

14

Human Relations Challenges of the Future

Myriad human relations challenges will confront managers in the twenty-first century. The overriding objective of this chapter is to identify and examine some of the major challenges.

AFTER READING THIS CHAPTER, YOU SHOULD BE ABLE TO:

1. Describe the characteristics of creative people.
2. Explain how creativity in an organization setting can be both encouraged and nurtured.
3. Discuss some of the reasons why the nature of work is changing and the role that reengineering, flowcharting, and training are playing in this process.
4. Review the current state of diversity in the workplace.
5. Explain how awareness-based, skill-based, and integrated-based training programs are being used to deal with the challenge of diversity.
6. Identify the major pillars of world-class organizations and explain how organizations are using the pillars.
7. Describe several human relation challenges facing managers in the next decade.

Developing the Boundaryless Organization

Many human relations changes currently are under way that will revolutionize the way organizations manage their people in the next decade. One of the most interesting is that of the "boundaryless" organization, an idea that is being developed by General Electric (GE), among others. The concept is simple: GE wants to create an environment in which no internal boundaries exist among the people in the company. Ideas and suggestions are allowed to flow up and down the enterprise as well as across departments. The objective is to create an internal team that is able to work as a cohesive unit and focus all its energies on addressing external problems, such as customer needs and competitive strategies.

One way in which GE began developing its boundaryless organization was by establishing "work-out" sessions, for which forty to fifty people would meet for three days at a local hotel. There they would divide into three or four groups, each of which would be asked to identify low-value work that could be eliminated or streamlined. Each group, led by an outside facilitator, then would focus on ways in which reports, approvals, meetings, policies, and practices could be streamlined. After each group had identified its list of improvements, action plans were developed and a champion was assigned for each plan. Then, on the last day of the session, the manager of the business would come in with four to six assistant managers, and they would listen to these ideas. The managers then would either approve or disapprove each proposed change on the spot. As a result of these work-out sessions, GE was able simultaneously to downsize and increase productivity.

Today GE continues to use work-out sessions. However, instead of two- to three-day meetings at a local hotel, the sessions now are carried out at the job site. In contrast to years past, when senior-level management would insist that all managers attend these work-out sessions, today the sessions are held on a regular basis in-house, because everyone realizes they are useful. The sessions cut down on bureaucratic red tape, and they provide motivation for personnel. As they say at GE these days, "In the past, work-out sessions used to be orchestrated; today they are spontaneous."

Another approach used by GE is that of empowering individuals so that decision-making takes place at the lowest level "where a competent decision can be made." This last qualifying phrase is emphasized by GE, because the company wants to point out that empowerment is not a process of turning a company into a democracy; rather, it's a way of ensuring that the best decisions be made at the lowest possible levels and that individuals who have no need to be involved in the process are systematically excluded. This process requires GE managers to ask themselves three questions: What value am I adding by making a decision? What information keeps me from letting my subordinate make this decision? What factors keep me from giving that information to subordinates and letting them make the decision?

A third human relations strategy is the introduction of wide banding, a process of decreasing the pay grades so that it is easier to give people salary raises. With narrow banding, the pay grade for a particular job might range from $9 to $14 per hour. A boss who wanted to give someone a salary raise in excess of $14 per hour would first have to get the person assigned to a new pay grade, which took time. Today, thanks to wide banding, there are fewer pay grades at GE, and the grades cover greater ranges. Hence, a particular pay grade might encompass a number of jobs and range from $9 to $30 per hour. If a boss wants to raise a $14-an-hour employee's wage to $15 per hour, the boss now has authority to do so. In this way, GE has empowered its bosses and given them more opportunities for motivating the workers.

Are these human relations ideas paying off? According to recent reports, GE is one of the most competitive companies in the world and, in most markets, it is growing faster than its major competitors. A large degree of this success can be tied directly to the firm's ability to build a boundaryless organization in which everyone works together as a team. It is a model that many other organizations are seeking to develop in order to compete effectively in the next couple of decades.

Sources: Geoffrey Colvin, "Changing the Guard," Fortune, January 8, 2000, pp. 83–99; Thomas A. Stewart, "See Jack. See Jack Run," Fortune, September 27, 1999, pp. 124–127; John. Curran, "Jack Welch's Secret Weapon," Fortune, November 10, 1997, pp. 116–126; Richard M. Hodgetts, "A Conversation with Steve Kerr," Organizational Dynamics, spring 1996, pp. 68–79; and Ron Ashkenas, David Ulrich, Steve Kerr, and Todd Jick, The Boundaryless Organization: Breaking the Chains of Organizational Structure (San Francisco: Jossey-Bass, 1995).

Greater Focus on Innovation

During the next decade, organizations are going to do more than merely try to understand how innovation works; they are going to focus their attention on using human relations ideas to help their people be more innovative.

Creativity and Personnel

LEARNING OBJECTIVE
(1) *Describe the characteristics of creative people*

Most people are a great deal more creative than they believe. Additionally, most organizational jobs do not tap the full potential of the employee, so the latter does not use all of this creative potential. Figure 14.1 illustrates this idea. Notice that the job requires only a fraction of the employee's ability. The organization must learn to tap this asset. One way of doing so is to make employees aware of how creative they truly are. Most people believe that only geniuses are creative. However, this ability is much more widespread than is believed, and individuals in the general population possess varying degrees of creativity. The following are some characteristics of creative people:

- **Creative people tend to be bright rather than brilliant.**
- **Creative people have a youthful curiosity throughout their lives.**
- **Creative people are open and responsive to feelings and emotions and the world around them.**
- **Creative people tend to have a positive self-image.**
- **Creative people have the ability to tolerate isolation.**
- **Creative people frequently are nonconformists.**
- **Creative people enjoy finding imaginative solutions to problems.**
- **Creative people are persistent.**

FIGURE 14.1 *Job Requirements Distribution Superimposed on Ability Distribution*

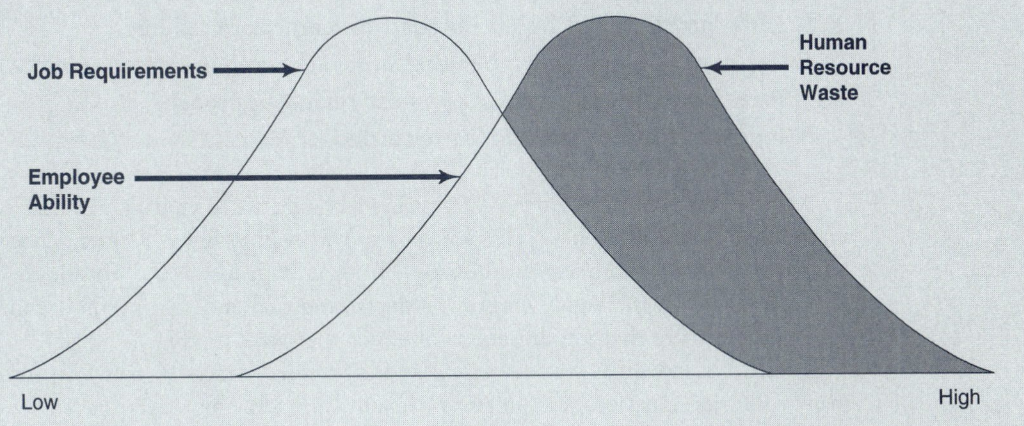

② Encouraging Creativity

One reason why people are not creative is that they approach creativity in the wrong way. For example, many have erroneous, preconceived ideas about innovation that actually stifle their creativity. Here are some illustrations of these myths:

Myth 1: *Innovation is planned and predictable.* In truth, innovation is highly unpredictable and can be introduced by anyone from a scientist in the research and development laboratory to a clerical worker who has discovered a better way to file invoices.

Myth 2: *Innovation is the result of exaggerated daydreaming.* Actually, most accomplished innovators are practical people who base their ideas on realistic, down-to-earth developments, such as piggybacking on someone else's invention and generating a smaller, cheaper, higher-quality, or faster-working model.

Myth 3: *Innovation is the result of carefully drawn technical specifications.* In most cases, this approach takes too long. Successful innovators often rely on a try–test–review approach. Sometimes this is jokingly addressed as "ready, fire, aim." Only after innovators have seen the quality of their completed work do they make the necessary modifications.

Myth 4: *Large projects produce more innovative results than do small ones.* This is untrue; research reveals that small project teams working with limited budgets typically produce better results because the participants have an opportunity to share their ideas, brainstorm, and quickly implement modifications and changes. There is no bureaucratic red tape such as exists in larger projects.

Myth 5: *Technology is the driving force behind innovation and success.* Although technology is one source for innovation, the most important ingredient is people who are able to modify new discoveries so the market accepts them. In production work, for example, American firms have spent billions of dollars annually to improve the quality of their output, yet they have been unable to close the gap between this country and Japan. Why? Part of the answer is that American businesspeople have not focused enough attention on the human element.[1]

If individuals were aware of these myths, it would help to improve their creativity. Organizations can also help by implementing time-proven principles, such as:

1. **Personnel must be encouraged to search actively for new ideas, opportunities, and sources of innovation.**
2. **Ideas that are pursued should have practical application.**
3. **Projects should be small and well focused.**
4. **An initial schedule of events or milestones should be drawn up even if the project falls behind and does not meet all these deadlines.**
5. **Participants should be encouraged to learn from failures.**
6. **Personnel should remember that innovation requires hard work and persistence.**
7. **Participants should follow a try–test–review approach.**
8. **Innovative activity should be rewarded.**

Another way of improving creativity is to engage in mental games that require clever or imaginative solutions. (The Time Out quiz provides an example.) Often, creativity and innovation are a result of improving on the ideas of others both inside and outside the organization. In past years many of the highly creative products produced and sold by the Japanese, for example, were nothing more than modifications of goods that were produced initially by American firms. This practice is known as *creative swiping* and is practiced widely by many organizations located in many countries. One Japanese professor explained the idea this way:

When we want to do something, we just try to learn and absorb all the possible answers, alternatives, and developments not only in Japan but in Europe, in developing countries, and

IMPROVING YOUR CREATIVENESS

There are many ways to improve personal creativeness. One is by engaging in mental exercises that stir the

imagination. This creativity test requires you to think of two rhyming words that describe a specific definition. Write your answer to the right of each definition.

Examples

Definition	Answers	
1. Highest-ranking officer in the police department	Top	cop
2. A fat porker	Big	pig
3. The amount of difference between two very similar points of view	Fine	line
1. An angry father	_____	_____
2. A happy young boy	_____	_____
3. A person who steals from a library	_____	_____
4. A cloak worn by a gorilla	_____	_____
5. An obese feline	_____	_____
6. A beverage with very little alcohol	_____	_____
7. A heavy crying spell	_____	_____
8. A quick meal	_____	_____
9. Food with very few calories	_____	_____
10. A sickly escargot	_____	_____

in the U.S. Then, by combining and by evaluating the best of all this, we try to come up with the optimum combinations which are available. . . . we are very sophisticated copycats.[2]

Innovativeness and Human Relations

In addition to helping their personnel become more creative, a growing number of organizations now are working to ensure that their own human relations programs are innovative. In fact, the most successful enterprises, according to the latest research, are leaders in human relations programs, and this is as true at the top of the organization as at lower levels. One group of researchers, for example, has found that high firm performance is associated with placing strong emphasis on innovation and creativity when selecting top managers.[3] Those at the executive level must be prepared to think "out of the box" in meeting the organization's emerging challenges. These findings are echoed by Philip Mirvis, based on his analysis of the data provided in the well-known Laborforce 2000 study. Mirvis has found that companies that are human relations leaders tend to develop innovative ways of managing people. In particular, he reports:

In the Laborforce 2000 study, leaders and fast followers invested somewhat more on high tech than companies that were slow-to-innovate or laggards. But they were two and three times more apt to invest substantially in "high touch" workplace improvements—work redesign, TQM [total quality management], and employee involvement programs. HR [human relations] leaders downsized as much as other firms in the sample, yet they retrained over 84 percent of their workforce in the aftermath as compared with laggards, who retrained only 39 percent. And . . . leaders also regularly train workers in new technologies, take innovative steps to attract and prepare newcomers, and have specialized programs to respond to changes in workforce demographics.[4]

TABLE 14.1

Characteristics of Human Relations Innovators: Investments in Human Capital

Characteristic	Leaders (n = 44)	Fast Followers (n = 157)	Slow Followers (n = 151)	Laggards (n = 43)
Workplace Improvement				
Redesign jobs for teamwork	61%	51%	37%	28%
Employee involvement programs	61	45	30	26
Percentage of workforce retrained after downsizing	84	69	51	39
Education and Training				
Involved in public schools	70	58	52	39
Annually retrain workers	52	33	34	28
Workplace Flexibility				
Job-sharing option	66	53	39	33
Work-at-home option	45	31	24	16
On-site child care	27	10	7	5
Managing Diversity				
Senior management commitment	75	57	40	37
Management training in diversity	80	69	56	49
Mentoring programs	50	33	19	12
Programs for Older Workers				
Phased retirement	32	25	16	12

Source: Philip M. Mirvis, "Human Resource Management: Leaders, Laggards, and Followers," Academy of Management Executive, May 1997, p. 53.

Firms that are leaders in human relations programs and efforts also are more likely than other organizations to invest in training and development. This is particularly true for entry-level personnel, many of whom begin work straight out of high school and have poor math, science, and communication skills that are critical for effective job performance. Human relations leaders take on the responsibility of providing remedial education and basic skills training. Additionally, these firms focus a great deal of attention on redesigning the workplace, launching employee involvement programs, introducing total quality management tools and techniques, and retraining those personnel whose skills need updating. Table 14.1 provides additional data related to Mirvis's findings.

The three primary factors that have been found to influence human relations innovativeness are customers, new technologies, and changes in the demographics of the workforce. Leading firms are acutely aware of what customers want and the types of programs that are needed to address these desires. They also tend to be on the cutting edge in terms of acquiring, mastering, and using state-of-the-art equipment. Perhaps most important, however, is that they show evidence of a stick-to-it philosophy. This cultural mindset is reflected in their belief that people make the difference in an organization's success. Attention to these three factors—customers, new technologies, and demographic changes in the workforce—are proving critical in helping leading firms to sustain their competitive advantage. At the same time, these changes are creating a challenge, and a possible problem, for organizations that are not on the human relations cutting edge. Mirvis has put it this way:

> . . . certain hothouses of innovative thinking—and companies with the money and imagination to invest in the human resource frontier—may continue to enhance their leading edge status and gain a competitive edge from these new human resource innovations. But fast followers, who would next be expected to try out these ideas and practices, may not adopt them so easily or capitalize as readily on their potential. And firms that are slow-to-innovate or that wait for these practices to prove themselves may be left behind at a crucial competitive disadvantage and have neither the resources nor the residual talent needed to undertake a corporate transformation. The risk is that the innovators will get richer and more responsive to change while the rest will at best muddle through or simply wither away.[5]

The Changing Nature of Work

LEARNING OBJECTIVE
③ *Discuss some of the reasons why the nature of work is changing and the role that reengineering, flowcharting, and training are playing in this process*

As noted in the opening vignette, work assignments are changing and the way work used to be done is being radically altered. A work revolution is under way in America, and it is going to affect employees, who will perform their jobs differently, and their managers, who must learn how to lead in this new environment. Ways in which organizations are meeting this new challenge are:

1. Through the use of reengineering and flowcharting.
2. By complementing the organizations' product selling with a strong emphasis on services.
3. The way in which companies now are hiring and retaining the best talent.

We examine these approaches in the next sections.

Reengineering and Flowcharting

In describing these new changes, perhaps the most widely used term is *reengineeing.* As defined by Hammer and Champy, **reengineering** is the fundamental rethinking and radical redesign of business processes to achieve dramatic improvements in performance.[6] This approach does not simply modify a process; it redoes the process from the ground up. Many organizations are finding that reengineering is critical to their success. Union Carbide, for example, has used reengineering to reduce fixed costs and GTE has used the process to deliver large benefits to its telephone operations—in some cases, doubling revenues or halving costs. Sun Life Assurance Society has eliminated most of its middle managers and reorganized its customer service representatives into groups that handle customer claims from beginning to end, thus reducing by almost 50 percent the time required to settle claims. In the process, of course, these changes lead to downsizing, which can create human relations problems. This is why it is so important for managers to learn to deal effectively with the negative effects of these actions. The Human Relations in Action box provides some insights regarding how this can be done.

Reengineering *involves the fundamental redesign of business processes to achieve dramatic results.*

Other organizations are opting for a less dramatic approach to reengineering their jobs, preferring to use *job modification,* in which work is changed but not radically reengineered. A good example is provided by organizations that use flowcharts to identify and map out the steps used in performing a job. A **flowchart** is a pictorial representation of the steps in a work process. Figure 14.2 provides an example of how a flowchart can be used to reduce work time. Some of the steps commonly used in flowcharting include

A flowchart *is a pictorial representation of the steps in a process.*

1. Eliminating all steps that are unnecessary or redundant.
2. Reducing the amount of time needed to carry out the remaining steps by computerizing or streamlining them.
3. Carrying out some of the work in tandem, so that two or more steps are being done simultaneously.

in action

HUMAN RELATIONS IN ACTION

Managing Effectively with Less

Downsizing can be traumatic on the remaining personnel. For example, one recent survey found that middle managers who remained with the firm reported that they were working longer hours, were under more stress, were in less control of what was going on around them, and seemed to be close to psychological exhaustion. What can organizations do to help overcome these negative effects of downsizing? Experts recommend the following steps.

Make it difficult for anyone else to be let go. *As long as the reductions in force continue, people will be nervous and concerned that they are on the "hit list." One way of removing these fears is by eliminating work that does not contribute to overall productivity and moving these people to other jobs where they can make a substantive contribution. In many cases, this means retraining, but most people will go along with this approach as long as they can remain with the firm. At the same time, the organization is less likely to cut someone who has just been retrained for more productive work.*

Overcommunicate. *During a reduction in force (RIF), the rumor mills grind out new messages at a rapid rate. To combat these rumors and put everyone at ease, it is necessary to let personnel know why the company is cutting back and where these cuts are likely. If personnel realize that the firm is losing money every month, they also will understand why RIFs are necessary. They are even likely to support the effort and to determine how they might help.*

Give increased attention to those remaining on board. *Survivors of a cutback need much reassurance and support. This means telling each person why he or she is valued, letting each employee know his or her unique contributions, and discussing each employee's future with the organization. It also means keeping in touch with personnel on a regular basis, giving them time to talk about their feelings and concerns, and encouraging them to be open and frank about anything that is troubling them. This concern for their well-being often results in growing trust and increased productivity.*

Attend to your personal well-being. *Managers are not above feeling the same concerns and fears as do their subordinates. Employees look to their manager for guidance, but they also look to the individual for cues regarding how they should react to situations that arise. If the manager's morale is low, their morale will suffer. If the manager appears not to trust higher-level management, they will not trust this group either. The manager must serve as a positive role model whose behavior says, "I'm not concerned about the future of this organization, and you shouldn't be either."*

Sources: Diann R. Newman and Richard M. Hodgetts, Human Resource Management: A Customer-Oriented Approach (Upper Saddle River, NJ: Prentice Hall, 1998), pp. 375–376; Gene Hall, Jim Rosenthal, and Judy Wade, "How to Make Reengineering Really Work," Harvard Business Review, November–December 1993, pp. 119–131; Dan Rice and Craig Dreilinger, "After the Downsizing," Training and Development Journal, May 1991, pp. 41–43; and Ron Zemke, "The Ups and Downs of Downsizing," Training, November 1990, pp. 27–33.

A close look at Figure 14.2 shows that the old approach for handling customer complaints was reduced from 34 minutes to 3.5 minutes.

The major human relations challenge is introducing these changes without negatively affecting worker morale and output. As organizations reduce their workforces and streamline the work of the remaining personnel, they must address the concerns of these employees. One way is to train workers and give them authority to do their jobs. Another way is to teach managers to work within this new environment by serving as a team leader rather than a boss.

Tom Peters believes work as we know it today will be reinvented in the next ten years. An example is the rise in the outsourced economy, which is creating a whole new set of management challenges. Companies are finding that it is easier to pay someone else to do tasks such as the accounting, human resources, and claims processing. "Recently, greater savings have been realized by moving these tasks overseas, often to low-wage locales such as India, the Philippines, and the Caribbean. The competitive differentiation for companies will come from how they manage outsourced relationships, says John K. Halvey, a partner who heads the outsourcing practice at New York law firm Milbank, Tweed, Hadley & McCloy LLP."[7] This may mean companies will need to revamp their management structures.

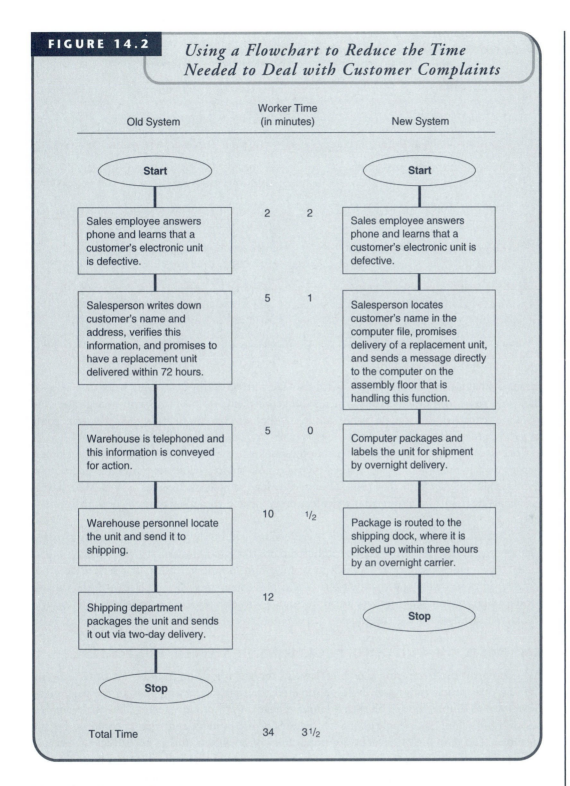

FIGURE 14.2

Using a Flowchart to Reduce the Time Needed to Deal with Customer Complaints

Old System	Worker Time (in minutes)		New System
Start			**Start**
Sales employee answers phone and learns that a customer's electronic unit is defective.	2	2	Sales employee answers phone and learns that a customer's electronic unit is defective.
Salesperson writes down customer's name and address, verifies this information, and promises to have a replacement unit delivered within 72 hours.	5	1	Salesperson locates customer's name in the computer file, promises delivery of a replacement unit, and sends a message directly to the computer on the assembly floor that is handling this function.
Warehouse is telephoned and this information is conveyed for action.	5	0	Computer packages and labels the unit for shipment by overnight delivery.
Warehouse personnel locate the unit and send it to shipping.	10	1/2	Package is routed to the shipping dock, where it is picked up within three hours by an overnight carrier.
Shipping department packages the unit and sends it out via two-day delivery.	12		**Stop**
Stop			
Total Time	34	3 1/2	

Emphasis on Service

Another major change that now is taking place is an emphasis on teaching employees how to provide world-class service. This is being accomplished by teaching workers to follow the three laws of service and to build strong customer relationships.

THE THREE LAWS OF SERVICE

The three laws of service provide an umbrella under which effective human relations principles are brought together. The **first law of service** is: Satisfaction equals perception minus expectation. This

*The **first law of service** is: Satisfaction equals perception minus expectation.*

TABLE 14.2	Product Versus Relationship Selling

Product Selling	**Relationship Selling**
• The focus is on the product.	• The focus is on the customer.
• The seller serves as the expert.	• The seller serves as a resource.
• The seller gives the customer information.	• The seller listens to the customer and gets information.
• The seller works to educate the customer.	• The seller works to create a partnership with the customer.
• The primary objective is to sell the product.	• The primary objective is to sell a solution.
• If the seller does his or her job well, the buyer will purchase this time.	• If the seller does his or her job well, the buyer will purchase this time and be inclined to buy in the future as well.

means that customers evaluate how satisfied they are with service by comparing what they believed they were going to get to what they actually did get. If their perception of service was greater than what they expected, they will be highly satisfied. If they received less than they felt they were going to get (regardless of how much service they actually got), they will be less satisfied.

The **second law of service** is: First impressions are the most important. Most customers make up their mind about a company's products and services within five minutes of the time they initially interact with that firm. This is why, for example, such stores as Wal-Mart have a greeter at the front of the store who welcomes everyone and tries to establish a good first impression.

The **third law of service** is: Service attitude alone will not assure good service. This means that an organization also must have an infrastructure that promotes and delivers service. In particular, as an enterprise grows, the firm must hire more people to ensure that service does not suffer. Additionally, the appropriate policies and procedures must be in place; and the organization must have the requisite amount of technology to ensure that personnel are able to meet the service demands of the customers.

EMPHASIS ON BUILDING RELATIONSHIPS WITH CUSTOMERS

As a complement to applying the three laws of service, a growing number of firms now are training their people in ways to build personal relationships with customers. In the past, many organizations simply directed all their training efforts toward product selling. The main emphasis was on teaching salespeople about the features of the product and what it could do for the customer. Today, though it remains an important consideration, this is not sufficient, because it fails to give the enterprise an enduring competitive edge. As a result, there has been a movement toward complementing product selling with what is called *consultative selling,* which is characterized by a strong emphasis on developing personal relationships with customers.

Consultative selling is the process of finding out what the customer wants before trying to sell anything to the individual. This approach differs from the typical product selling because it focuses on providing service to the customer. Table 14.2 lists some of the contrasts between product and relationship selling. In particular, emphasis by leading human relations firms now is given to developing a relationship with the customer regardless of the medium used—direct face to face, telephone, or online.

Training in relationship selling is becoming increasingly popular for a number of reasons. One reason is that this approach keeps customers coming back. Initially, of course, many people will buy because a company offers a product that has special features or because it can perform better than any other on the market. The product sells itself and, once the customer sees what is being offered, the individual is pleased and buys. Over time, however, competitors will emulate the company's product and try to erode its market share. To retain business, companies now are finding that their people must offer superior customer service. When this happens, customers continue to buy because they like the seller and have developed a warm, personal relationship with the individual. Although many organizations can provide look-alike products, they do not have a sales force that is skilled in consultative selling. They have not trained their people in the latest human relations approaches for capturing and holding market share as an economy changes, for example, the market changes resulting after the disaster of September 11, 2001. In contrast, leading-edge firms have done so, and they are continuing to develop the human relations skills and talents of their personnel. As a result, consultative selling helps such leading firms to retain customers' business.

HIRING AND RETAINING THE BEST TALENT

When a professional baseball player signs a multimillion dollar contract to play baseball with the Texas Rangers, baseball enthusiasts note that exceptional talent now commands huge salaries. The same is true in industry, as more and more companies realize that skilled employees are in great demand and that, to attract and retain these people, new motivation packages must be developed. Unlike baseball, however, the motivational part of these packages is heavily geared to the non-financial side. The logic of this approach is that when people like working for an organization, they are unlikely to leave merely because they are offered more money. They like their coworkers; the job is challenging; the prerequisites (perks, for short) are extremely good; and they are happy with their work. Russell Campanello, chief people officer at Nervewire Inc., recently acquired by Wipro Limited of Bangalore, India, put it this way, "The number-one reason why people leave their jobs is to pursue personal development—the chance to learn something new. If you want to hold on to your best people, you've got to make sure that they're learning, growing, and changing."[8] The challenge, of course, is to develop the appropriate environment for making this happen, and a growing number of firms are doing just that.

For example, CheckFree, headquartered in Atlanta, serves nine million consumers initiate online payments through services managed by CheckFree that tap into the market with real-time, customized information. CheckFree personnel work very hard in a campus work environment. CheckFree strives to set the standard for quality in online billing and payment.[9] Among other perks, a company fitness center remains open 'round-the-clock, and a basketball court, racquetball courts, a swimming pool, a bowling alley, a sauna, a hot tub, a big-screen TV, and a pool room are available to personnel. When the company recruits people, one of the first things it does is take them on a tour of the firm's facilities. No one goes away unimpressed. Explaining its strategy, the company's president says, "We work very hard. We try to compensate with a more peaceful, relaxed environment. That's what it's about—trying to create the right atmosphere."[10]

BeFree Inc., a subsidiary of ValueClick, located in Marlborough, Massachusetts, offers a variety of cost-effective and measurable ways to attract customers and increase online sales using partner marketing and an automated merchandising assistant. It maximizes return and eliminates waste, turning limited online marketing dollars into quality customers and sales.[11] Some of the perks the company has provided include a popcorn machine, fresh fruit delivered twice weekly, a well-stocked ice cream freezer, a pool, and onsite auto oil changes. In addition, when someone did something that merited attention, the person received a check and an e-mail that was copied to all of his or her coworkers. The company also has sponsored monthly lunches with the chief executive, giving personnel an opportunity to share ideas and discuss matters of concern.[12]

Cognex, a New England computer manufacturer, tries to create a community such that people want to come to work. The company's motto is "work hard, play hard." Like other firms trying to create a motivational environment, Cognex offers a wide variety of perks including a fitness center, an on-site cafeteria, and a game room that remains open at all times. Yet what the employees enjoy most are the surprises that the company offers, such as calling a halt to work so that everyone can attend an impromptu barbecue or taking everyone to a show in Boston or renting an amusement park for the day. One of the most recent surprises was to put a lunch bag on everyone's desk inside of which were a "Get Out of Work Free" ticket and $50. A few hours later, a bus took the employees to a shopping mall, where they could spend the money.

Although the impact of the economy after September 11, 2001, resulted in some companies eliminating perks offered to employees, other companies have retained employee perks in order to recruit and retain top-notch workers in a competitive industry, according to Frank Scanlan, a spokesman for the Society for Human Resource Management. Perks also are used to reward commitment of the company. For example, Altru Health System recently started a "worklife center" to help employees with personal errands during the work day, such as tending to oil changes for personal vehicles, taking care of dry cleaning, and even procuring concert tickets. Phillips International, Inc., a Washington, D.C.-area publishing house, took its full- and part-time employees and their families on a three-day cruise in September 2003.[13]

"J. M. Family Enterprises, A Deerfield Beach, Florida, Toyota distributor recently added more perks on its already lavish list of benefits—which include on-site hair salons, a medical clinic staffed with two physicians, a lap pool, and recognition cruises on a company yacht. In the past year, it opened an on-site child-care center and began offering retirees with 10 years' service a health-insurance plan in which the premium is split 50-50."[14]

Applied Creative, Inc., a graphic design, advertising and marketing communications agency in Scottsdale, Arizona, has created a stimulating work environment by using creative art, bright color throughout, and open office space. The kitchen is stocked with snacks and drinks so employees can fuel their energy at any time. A satellite television provides a temporary escape and a quiet room with a futon is provided for a quick nap.[15]

In addition to the examples just cited, others include leasing BMWs for all full-time employees, offering free flying lessons, providing dry cleaning pickup and delivery, and setting up hammocks in the lounge so that employees can take midday naps. These perks all are designed to make the company a place where people like to work. As a senior director of human resources put it, "You have to pay people competitively, but people don't leave a company because of salary. They leave because they don't like working for you; they don't enjoy the environment."[16] Table 14.3 provides additional examples of perks that the best companies are providing for their employees.[17]

TABLE 14.3	*Ten of the Best Companies for Which to Work*

Company	Some of the Perks That Create an Appealing Environment
SAS Institute (Cary, NC)	
Cisco Systems (San Jose, CA)	
Fenwick & West (Palo Alto, CA)	
Born Information Services (Wayzata, MN)	
Goldman Sachs (New York, NY)	
American Century Investment (Kansas City, MO)	
MBNA America Bank	
American Skandia	
First Tennessee (Memphis, TN)	
American Management Systems (Fairfax, VA)	

Source: Robert Levering and Milton Moskowitz, "The 100 Best Companies to Work For," Fortune, January 8, 2001, pp. 148–149. © Time Inc. All rights reserved.

Meeting the Cultural Diversity Challenge

4 **LEARNING OBJECTIVE**
Review the current state of diversity in the workplace

The workforce is more diverse than ever before. More young people (age twenty-five and under) are entering the workforce, and more older people (age sixty-five and over) are staying on the job.[18] In addition, women, African Americans, Hispanics, and Asian Americans are entering the workforce in record numbers. The result is a major diversity challenge for companies everywhere. Among the reasons for this are the following:

- Many of today's managers are accustomed to supervising Anglo men and have had limited experience leading a diverse workforce.
- Women and other nontraditional managers often are not given the necessary organizational support for developing their skills.
- Many businesses have failed to develop the talents of their nontraditional employees, thus denying both them and the enterprise an opportunity to succeed.
- Many firms have failed to examine the career and family needs of their employees and to work out plans for helping the personnel balance both these demands. Such concerns are particularly evident given the current status of women and minorities in today's workforce.

Women and Minorities

Women and minorities in the workforce continue to remain largely untapped resources. In an effort to change this condition and to achieve equality in the workplace, companies will need to take a number of steps. Let's examine some of these challenges. Although some progress has been made in recent years, women still are being paid less than men. According to recent government statistics, women's weekly earnings are less than 80 percent of those of men.[19] Women also have a more difficult time securing management positions, and many of them report that they are subjected to sexual harassment. In response, a number of lawsuits have been filed in recent years and, in some cases, significant settlements have resulted. For example, Merrill Lynch & Company and the Salomon Smith Barney unit of Citigroup were accused of gender-based discrimination. To date, in total, Citigroup has paid out almost $100 million to implement and settle with all but about 70 of 1,920 women in the suit. Two cases have gone to arbitration with $3.2 million being paid to one female stockbroker, and the other case was dismissed. Currently, Deborah McCrann's case is scheduled to appear before a private arbitration panel hearing. Her case is unique in that whereas "she had an impressive title and annual compensation hitting $920,000, she alleges that she was paid less than her male counterparts and wasn't given as much responsibility" and "was passed over for several jobs in favor of men with less experience."[20]

In another case, Mitsubishi agreed to pay $34 million to hundreds of women who worked in its auto factory in central Illinois and to submit to outside monitoring of complaints of harassment and discrimination.[21] In still another recent instance, Landis Plastics was charged with placing women in the lowest paying, most strenuous, most dangerous jobs and failing to promote them, whereas new male workers were given easier, better-paying work. The company agreed to pay $782,000 to settle these discrimination charges.[22]

Dena Zechella, a former employee of Outback Steakhouse, was recently awarded $2.2 million. Outback paid her considerably less than a similarly situated male employee who performed the same job duties. The jury also found that Outback had subjected Zechella to different terms and conditions of employment because of her sex and terminated her in retaliation for having complained about the discriminatory treatment.[23]

In June 2002, two cases were settled for $47 million between a class of over five thousand women and Rent-A-Center, based in Plano Texas, the nation's largest rent-to-own company with over twenty-two hundred stores. Payments went to women who claimed they were fired or forced out of the company, were denied promotions or were demoted, and made claims of sexual harassment on the job.[24]

In 2003, the U.S. Department of Labor settled two cases involving discrimination against women. Jimmy Dean Foods, a division of Sara Lee Corporation, discriminated against forty-eight female applicants for laborer jobs at its Newbern, Tennessee, meat-processing plant. The settlement was valued at $900,000 and Jimmy Dean Foods agreed to hire forty-eight female applicants and pay more than $240,000 in back pay.[25] In the second case, Swissport USA, Inc., of Anchorage agreed to pay $94,065 in back pay and interest to seventeen female and minority job applicants for refusing to hire them into ramp worker positions at the Anchorage, Alaska, Airport.[26]

People of color have also filed complaints with the Equal Employment Opportunity Commission (EEOC) and have brought lawsuits for racial discrimination. One of the most publicized was a lawsuit brought by African Americans against Coca-Cola. The suit charged the Coca-Cola Company with discriminating against Blacks in promotions, evaluations, terminations, and pay. The case eventually was settled, and Coca-Cola agreed to pay more than $192 million and to relinquish broad monitoring powers to a panel of outsiders.[27]

In another recent development, more than three hundred employees of Nextel Communications Inc., a wireless communications carrier, filed a series of complaints with the EEOC charging the company with both sexual and racial discrimination.[28]

Other Forms of Discrimination

Although women and people of color often face discrimination in the workplace, they are not alone. Researchers have found that personal appearance often influences the way that people are treated at work. This is particularly true for those who are overweight and has led some experts in this area to conclude "weight may now draw more open and widespread discrimination than race or gender or age."[29] People who are overweight agree with this statement, and many of them report that they often are denied jobs or are ridiculed by their coworkers. These individuals are more likely to make less money than their counterparts. In fact, one study by Mark Roehling, a professor in the Department of Management, Western Michigan University, found that obese women earn 24 percent less than their thinner coworkers and moderately obese women earn about 6 percent less. After reviewing twenty-nine studies of obese people in the workplace, Roehling found evidence for discrimination at every stage of the work process: "selection, placement, compensation, promotion, discipline, and discharge. Overall the evidence of consistent, significant discrimination against overweight employees is sobering."[30]

Some of the reasons given for not hiring obese people include concerns about health insurance premiums and worries that customers will respond negatively to them. As a result, in the opinion of the company, operating costs will rise and revenues will decline. Moreover, although some obese people have argued that obesity is a disability, the courts have ruled that the Americans with Disabilities Act provides protection to them in some cases but not in others, depending on the circumstances.

What can be done to address these problems? Firms are taking a number of steps, some of which are tied to well-designed diversity training programs. Others are described in the Ethics and Social Responsibility in Action box.

LEARNING OBJECTIVE

⑤

Explain how awareness-based, skill-based, and integrated-based training programs are being used to deal with the challenge of diversity

Diversity Training

Companies are developing diversity-training programs to meet their human relations challenges in a number of ways. The focus of these programs tends to fall into three categories: making personnel aware of the diversity issues, helping personnel to develop skill-based approaches for dealing with such issues, and combining both awareness- and skill-based methods and objectives into an integrated-based approach.

AWARENESS-BASED DIVERSITY TRAINING

Awareness-based diversity training helps participants to discover the nature and causes of diversity and helps them to understand their own assumptions and tendencies to stereotype. People typically judge the behavior of others by comparing their own cultural values to those of others. When others act differently, people may experience discomfort and anxiety. For example,

ETHICS AND SOCIAL RESPONSIBILITY IN ACTION

Developing Diversity Programs

Many companies are developing diversity programs designed to ensure that women and other minorities are not just given equal employment opportunities but are provided with mentors and training so that their full potential can be tapped. At the same time, diversity training is given to all employees so that everyone is better able to work as a member of the organization's team. Texaco, UNUM, and GTE provide three examples of such organizations.

In recent years, Texaco, the giant energy company, has been focusing more and more attention on developing the capabilities and talents of its personnel. One of these efforts is a new diversity strategy that is being implemented via a four-phase plan. The first phase is the formation of a cross-functional team to look at the organization's promotion process and find ways to improve it. The second phase educates workers on how to achieve promotion. The third phase is the development of a diversity training program for all managers in the organization. The fourth phase brings diversity training to all employees, so that everyone learns how to work with people of widely varying backgrounds and experiences. Texaco believes this program helps maintain its global competitive edge.

UNUM, a Portland, Maine, life insurance company, is not as well-known as some of its competitors, but the firm is large (more than $13 billion of disability and special risk insurance in effect) and has an extremely active diversity program. The company's efforts in this area began when it started experiencing high turnover among minority workers, a group it was trying very hard to recruit and maintain. After investigating the situation, UNUM concluded that it needed to create a diverse workforce. One of the first steps taken by the company was to hold meetings between the senior executives and members of the minority groups. From these dialogues came a three-day diversity workshop designed to build cultural competence. In addition, the firm has begun publishing a newsletter addressing diversity issues and has started surveying employees regarding the company's diversity activities. As a result, UNUM reports that its efforts to hire and retain minority employees are proving to be highly successful.

Finally, GTE, the telecommunications giant, has been actively pursuing a diversity strategy because it believes that this is critical to its global efforts. Some of the firm's diversity programs include minority recruitment, employee career advancement, training in managing and being part of a diverse workforce, and the celebration of multicultural awareness events. One of its specialized educational programs for minorities is its 18-month associate development program that gives "high-potential" individuals exposure to line and management positions and a chance to interview for appropriate positions within GTE. The company also regularly sponsors a two-day seminar, Managing Personnel Diversity, which is open to all managers. Through these types of programs, GTE has increased minority and female representation among its managers. In addition, 45 percent of new management recruits are now women and 35 percent are minorities. And in its last annual employee satisfaction survey, the firm received an 80 percent approval rating.

Sources: Elizabeth Olson, "In a First for Swiss, Women in Geneva Gain Maternity Benefits," New York Times, December 17, 2000, p. 10y; Kenneth Labich, "Making Diversity Pay," Fortune, September 9, 1996, pp. 177–179; Genevieve Capowski, "Managing Diversity," Management Review, June 1996, pp. 13–19; Jenny McCune, "Diversity Training: A Competitive Weapon," Management Review, June 1996, pp. 25–28; and Michel Galen and Ann Therese Palmer, "Diversity: Beyond the Numbers Game," Business Week, August 14, 1995, pp. 60–61.

researchers have found that men and women often think differently when it comes to situations, such as ethical dilemmas, that call for moral reasoning. Here are some contrasts:

Women are likely to:	Men are likely to:
• Respect the other person's feelings	• Respect the other person's rights
• Avoid being judgmental	• Value the importance of being decisive
• Search for a compromise	• Seek a solution that is objectively fair
• Rely on communication	• Rely on rules
• Be guided by emotion	• Be guided by logic
• Challenge authority	• Accept authority[31]

Awareness-based training increases employees' knowledge and sensitivity to diversity issues. Some of the specific objectives of this type of training include:

1. Providing participants with information about diversity.
2. Heightening awareness and sensitivity by uncovering hidden personal assumptions and bias.
3. Assessing participants' attitudes and values.
4. Correcting myths and stereotypes that these individuals may have.
5. Fostering an environment in which individual and group sharing of information can take place.

Awareness-based training also focuses on developing effective intercultural communication. In doing so, it works to achieve long-range goals, such as improving morale, productivity, and creativity, and contributing to the organization's competitive position. The training strives to promote feelings of unity, tolerance, and acceptance with the existing organizational culture and structure. Many different approaches are used in attaining these goals. Some programs focus on heightening diversity awareness by providing information on the cultures of the various ethnic groups in the workplace. Others are process-oriented and uncover unconscious cultural assumptions and biases by using experiential exercises that help people to get in touch with their feelings about diversity.

One problem with awareness-based training programs is that they may make the participants more knowledgeable about their feelings but they do not always lead to a change in attitudes. This is why many organizations combine this approach with skill-based training.

SKILL-BASED DIVERSITY TRAINING

Skill-based diversity training is behavioral in nature and provides participants with tools for effectively interacting in a heterogeneous work setting.[32] "The training goes beyond consciousness-raising; it provides workers with a set of skills to enable them to deal effectively with workplace diversity."[33]

Four common objectives of this type of training are:

1. Gaining a better understanding of how and why culturally different Team members act the way that they do.
2. Eliminating intercultural communication barriers, such as semantic difficulties and perception problems.
3. Creating facilitation skills that allow participants to mediate differences and negotiate misunderstandings.
4. Teaching participants to be more flexible and adaptable when working with others.

Some of the skills that are taught in this type of training typically include:

- *Self-awareness.* The ability to recognize the assumptions one has about those who are perceived as different.
- *Clear-headedness.* The ability to overcome stereotypes and rely on individual character and skills assessments when making job assignments, recommending promotions, or rendering other key decisions.
- *Openness.* A willingness to share knowledge about the "rules of the game" with outsiders and to provide them with access to mentors who can help them to penetrate invisible barriers and move up in the organization.
- *Candor.* The ability to engage in constructive dialogue about differences, whether they are individual, ethnic, cultural, or organizational.
- *Adaptability.* The willingness to change old rules to allow the full benefits of diversity to the organization.
- *Egalitarianism.* A commitment to encourage employees to grow professionally and to participate fully in the success of the organization.

INTEGRATED-BASED DIVERSITY TRAINING

Integrated-based diversity training combines both awareness- and skill-based methods and objectives. Some companies integrate their diversity training into existing training programs, such as management development, team building, and leadership training programs. This requires working with all appropriate groups with the company.

Regardless of the type, most diversity training address the same issues: race, gender, stereotypes, business objectives, work–family issues, age, sexual harassment, national demographics, disabilities, and sexual orientation.

Diversity training is not always successful. It takes more than requiring employees to attend classes. The program must be designed to fit the company, which starts with an assessment of the needs within the company. Some well-intentioned diversity training fails for several reasons, such as:[34]

1. The training is driven by EEO or affirmative action.
2. The training is considered the moral thing to do.
3. Training is the only activity; appropriate interventions are not included.
4. There is management support, but no management commitment.
5. Training is "off the shelf" or "canned" and does not fit the organization.
6. Only external consultants are used.
7. Training is conducted without a needs assessment.
8. Training is awareness-based only.
9. There are no internal resources after training.
10. There is no follow-up plan to training.

Diversity will continue to be a major issue for organizations; research indicates that many are willing to take the necessary steps to meet this challenge. More important, much of this

---

time out

IS YOUR COMPANY IN NEED OF A DIVERSITY OVERHAUL?

To determine how diverse your company might be, ask the following questions:

1. What percentage of women at your company rank on the managerial level or higher?

2. What percentage of minorities at your company rank on the managerial level or higher?

3. Does your company include "sexual orientation" in its anti-discrimination policy?

4. What kind of mentorship programs does your company sponsor?

5. Does your company provide benefits to single-sex domestic partners?

6. What kind of assistance does your company give to employees with small children?

7. Does your company offer part-time opportunities for parents with small children? Do part-time employees receive benefits?

8. Is there a private forum or source that employees can turn to with a diversity-related problem?

9. What percentage of minorities stay at the company long enough to attain senior-level positions?

10. Does your company endorse or sponsor clubs and associations to women, gays and lesbians, and/or minorities?

If the answers to even a few of these questions are restrictive or negative, your company may be in need of some kind of diversity training.

"Industry Overview: Is Your Company in Need of a Diversity Overhaul?" New Jersey Technology Council Online Career Center, **http://www.njtc.com**

desire is not a result of response to government mandates or social pressure: Rather, it is generated by senior management's belief that it is critical to the survival and growth of the enterprise. Such strategies certainly are going to help businesses meet this important human relations challenge.[35] They also will play a major role in helping an enterprise toward becoming a world-class organization.

LEARNING OBJECTIVE

Identify the major pillars of world-class organizations and explain how organizations are using the pillars

*A **world-class organization** can compete effectively on a global basis.*

⑥ Becoming a World-Class Organization

Businesses cannot afford to stand still. They must improve their ability to deliver higher-quality goods and services at competitive prices or they will soon fail to exist. This trend has resulted in the emergence of **world-class organizations** (WCOs), enterprises that can compete effectively on a global basis. This does not mean that the organization must do business in an international setting. However, if a multinational enterprise (MNE) sets up operations locally, the WCO must be able to compete effectively or, if it is a supplier, it must make a competitive bid to supply the MNE with the desired goods. Simply stated, businesses now use their competitive advantage to invade international markets, and local companies must meet that challenge. As illustrated in Figure 14.3, this means being more than just a total quality or adaptive organization. It means learning how to anticipate and stay ahead of impending changes (characteristics of learning organizations) and continuously improving to maintain a competitive advantage. What do organizations need to do to become WCOs? As shown in Figure 14.4, there are six pillars of WCOs, and each presents a human relations challenge.[36]

CUSTOMER-BASED FOCUS

The most important characteristic of a WCO is its customer focus. All organizations are designed to meet the needs of external and internal customers. As a result, the enterprise can deliver goods and services that the customer wants and can do so when needed. A good example is Pitney Bowes,

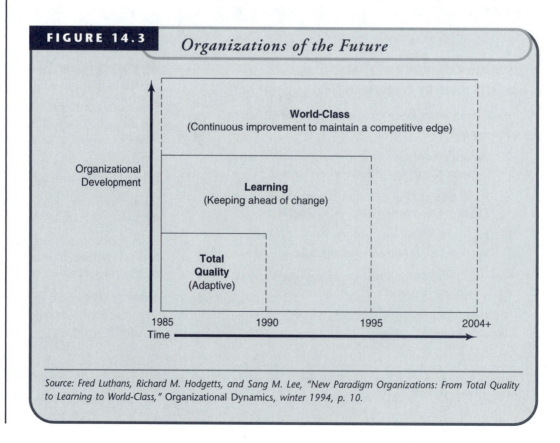

FIGURE 14.3   *Organizations of the Future*

Organizational Development

World-Class
(Continuous improvement to maintain a competitive edge)

Learning
(Keeping ahead of change)

Total Quality
(Adaptive)

1985   1990   1995   2004+
Time ➤

Source: Fred Luthans, Richard M. Hodgetts, and Sang M. Lee, "New Paradigm Organizations: From Total Quality to Learning to World-Class," Organizational Dynamics, winter 1994, p. 10.

The Major Pillars of World-Class Organizations

World-Class Organizations

Customer-Based Focus	Continuous Improvement	Fluid, Flexible, or "Virtual Organizations"	Creative HRM	Egalitarian Climate	Technological Support

Source: Fred Luthans, Richard M. Hodgetts, and Sang M. Lee, "New Paradigm Organizations: From Total Quality to Learning to World-Class," *Organizational Dynamics, Winter 1994, p. 15.*

Inc., long known as an innovator in the postage meter business. Pitney has developed creative products that have made the firm indispensable to the U.S. Postal Service and to many domestic and international customers. Today, Pitney has expanded its focus from the postal business to the entire mailing business and has become a WCO in this niche because of its drive to go beyond serving its customers to creating new products and services for them. In doing so, Pitney has had to address important elements that support the customer-based pillar of the WCO, including:

1. Teaching its personnel to share a single vision for customer service.
2. Redesigning its structure and jobs to better serve the customer.
3. Empowering teams to generate new ideas and approaches that result in improved customer service.
4. Designing compensation systems that reward and motivate its employees.

CONTINUOUS IMPROVEMENT

World-Class Organizations are not content to be the best at what they do: They want to maintain their status. To do this, they create continuous improvement strategies that encourage employees constantly to strive to do better. The use of reengineering and flowcharting, which help the organization identify bottlenecks and streamline operations, is one way that this is accomplished. Another way is by teaching employees to use laptop computers, pagers, and cellular phones to create virtual offices at home or when traveling. For example, AT&T, IBM, and Dun & Bradstreet have given their employees the latest technology, which allows them to spend less time in the office and more time in the field with customers. WCOs maintain continuous improvement efforts in several ways, including:

1. Benchmarking the best-in-class companies, and copying or adapting their approaches.
2. Reengineering work processes and procedures.
3. Empowering employees to take actions that will cut through red tape and get things done faster and more efficiently.
4. Using outsourcing to purchase goods and services from vendors that cannot be provided as efficiently in-house.
5. Developing innovation-based reward systems that encourage employees to keep up their continuous improvement efforts.

CREATION OF FLEXIBLE OR VIRTUAL ORGANIZATIONS

World-Class Organizations know the importance of getting things done efficiently and effectively. They do not build facilities when it is cheaper to rent them. They do not produce products that can be purchased for less from outside vendors. They do not develop a particular expertise when they can enter into a business alliance with a partner that already has such expertise. These strategies help to create what is called a *virtual organization.* This term refers to an enterprise that lacks the facilities or the ability to produce large amounts of goods and services but acts as if this lack does not exist because it is able to compensate for it through its business arrangements with other firms. The company acts just as if it were a giant producer—hence, the term *virtual.*

The Daimler-Chrysler operation in the United States is a good example of a virtual organization. The firm outsources more than 50 percent of all parts needed to build its cars. Another example is Dell Inc., which relies on outside suppliers for just about everything that goes into its computers.

In creating flexible or virtual enterprises, World-Class Organizations:

1. **Train workers to employ multiple skills.**
2. **Rely heavily on cross-training and job rotation of employees.**
3. **Create multifunctional work teams.**
4. **Empower employees.**
5. **Use innovative approaches that reduce the time needed to deliver goods and services.**

CREATIVE HUMAN RESOURCE MANAGEMENT

The human resource management (HRM) programs of World-Class Organizations are tailored to help employees provide state-of-the-art goods and services to customers. One way of accomplishing this goal is by teaching employees to think and act creatively. Another is to help them develop empowered teams that work well together. A third is to create employee suggestion systems that encourage new ideas, which can be used by workers throughout the organization. At the heart of these HRM programs is well-designed training.

Many important steps are involved in bringing about creative resource management. These include:

1. **Constant training.**
2. **Employee suggestions systems.**
3. **Empowered teams.**
4. **Promotion of those who take risks, whether they succeed or fail.**
5. **Creation of an effective reward system that encourages teamwork and effort.**

EGALITARIAN CLIMATE

Another key pillar of World-Class Organizations is an egalitarian climate in which everyone values the contributions of other personnel and respects the people in the organization as well as those that the company services. This climate is critical in ensuring teamwork within the organization and proper response to the needs and expectations of those outside the enterprise walls. WCOs promote an egalitarian climate in many ways; among them are:

1. **Developing open communication channels with all internal and external customers.**
2. **Sharing the organization's vision with everyone and ensuring their commitment to these same values and beliefs.**
3. **Developing an effective mentoring, coaching, and buddy system for creating the most effective employees possible.**
4. **Sponsoring community, wellness, and family programs.**
5. **Developing a code of business ethics and community citizenship and adhering strictly to these guidelines.**

TECHNOLOGICAL SUPPORT

Many of the creative, innovative, and productive approaches of WCOs are a result of the organizations' ability to use modern technology effectively: telecommunications networks, distributed database systems, interorganizational information systems, multimedia systems, and executive information systems. When organizations compete in the global market—where speed, information, and resilience are essential in developing a competitive edge—technological support is critical. The most important factor, of course, is not technology but the way that creative people use it. For example, American Express recently launched a new company—AmeriTax—that has created an electronic link between the Internal Revenue Service and the tax preparation firm. Through the use of this interorganizational information system, AmeriTax not only offers tax return preparation service to its customers, it also develops a basis for offering a larger set of financial products and services, lending or borrowing some $70 billion. For the Internal Revenue Service, this system has reduced costs and improved overall accuracy. WCOs develop technological support in a number of ways by:

1. **Offering continuous technical training to the personnel.**
2. **Modernizing all information and telecommunication systems.**
3. **Pushing decision making down to the lowest possible level in the organization.**
4. **Creating effective technology–human interfaces.**
5. **Encouraging information sharing so that everyone who needs the data has access to them.**

A Final Word

The six pillars of World-Class Organizations are not new. They have been discussed throughout this book. However, by bringing them together here at the end, the objective has been to illustrate their value to organizations in the twenty-first century. Close analysis of these pillars shows how important human relations practices are to each of them. Regardless of the amount of technology needed to produce goods and services, an enterprise succeeds or fails based on its human resources, for it is the personnel who must use the organization's assets in achieving its goals. If employees are treated well and committed to the vision and objectives of the company, the business will succeed. If the employees feel they are being exploited and are not committed to the same vision and objectives as management, the business will fail. In the final analysis, it all comes down to human relations. Before we close our study of this topic, we want to look at some trends predicted for the next decade that will provide human relations managers with a variety of challenges.

Human Relations Challenges in the Future

LEARNING OBJECTIVE
⑦ *Describe several human relation challenges facing managers in the next decade*

The disaster of the twin towers in New York City on September 11, 2001, changed the world forever. For example, on Wall Street, a parade of corporate scandals put executives in handcuffs and led companies to restate billion on their balance sheets. A succession of bankruptcy-court filings made history. The downfall of Enron was just the beginning of uncovering many business scandals involving CEO greed, fraud, and creative accounting practices used to inflate earnings that mislead shareholders.[37] To survive the aftermath of these disasters, companies were forced to change the way they do business. In many companies, technology perpetuated the change, which will continue to impact decision-making and how things get done in business. This means human relations management will continue to be challenged on a daily basis.

In June 2003, *Workforce Magazine* published a list of 25 predictions that will alter the world of workforce management over the next decade. The list was compiled by forward-thinkers and trend-spotters who make it their business to look into the future. These trends may serve to inform and intrigue all of us who manage people.

25 Trends That Will Change the Way You Do Business in the Future[38]

1. *E-mail.* New capabilities will be added and at the same time senders may have to match a predetermined list—either by name, company, etc.—or find themselves blocked. Powerful information-management and collaboration tools are also likely to emerge. Unified messaging will allow workers to check e-mail, voicemail, mobile messaging, and fax machine form a single inbox.

2. *Organized Labor.* Despite declining membership and overwhelming odds, labor unions aren't in danger of dying any time soon. More than five hundred thousand workers formed new unions just last year.

3. *Business Goes to Kindergarten.* All signs indicate that corporate involvement in public schools—already redefining kindergarten-through-high-school education—will continue to increase over the next decade.

4. *Going Euro.* As American companies engage in more multinational activities, they may need to reverse their policies on workplace privacy and increasingly look to Europe as the standard. For example, in Europe, snooping at employees' e-mail isn't only considered bad form, but is often flat-out illegal.

5. *Companies Won't Sleep.* In a quest to reach new customers in foreign time zones and to speed up production and services, more and more companies in the future will be open for business around the clock, seven days a week. The migration to a 24/7 workplace will make human resources managers' jobs far more complex.

6. *Artificial Intelligence.* As the Web and the data warehouses grow, artificial intelligence will solve problems that are beyond the reach of the human brain. AI's strength is that it can uncover patterns and spot problems amid a mountain of data.

7. *The Simmering Malaise.* Employers who ignore workplace discontent run the risk of periodic productivity slumps as skilled staffers depart for higher-paying positions whenever the labor market surges. Smart companies that make employees feel valued will gain a crucial competitive edge.

8. *Office Design.* Human resource managers will be more actively involved in the design process. Most cubicle-dwelling employees probably won't have a room—or a door—of their own. There is an office movement toward more shared workspace coupled with private desk areas. This promotes a more collaborative work environment.

9. *Defined Benefit Plans.* Attracting the best and brightest employees in the future will become nearly impossible without a defined benefit plan. Companies will have to offer retirement plans that provide a floor level of retirement income.

10. *Telework Has a Part-Time Future.* By the year 2010, more than half of American wage earners will spend more than two days a week working outside the office. There will still be a central location where people come to work. Some people need to stay connected.

11. *Consumer-Driven Health Care Reigns.* Ten years from now the notion of health-care dollars employees can spend as they see fit will be routine. The Internet and a push for greater openness about corporate finances will allow employees to see exactly what health care will cost them and they will be able to make comparisons to other plans. The critical pieces for the success of consumer-driven programs are "education, advocacy, and assistance."

12. *Child Care.* Access to quality child care will continue to be a major issue for working moms and their employers. It is expected that a number of companies will offer backup-care arrangements employees can use in the event of emergencies.

Employees often are willing to pay a fee for the care, so all the company may have to provide is the space.

13. *Help Wanted: Ten Million Workers.* The convergence of several trends—declining births, retiring baby boomers, and expected business growth—will create more jobs than there will be workers to fill them by 2010. Pressure will be put on baby boomers to remain in the workplace. Older workers won't show up in sufficient numbers and the problem will be aggravated by the shortage of skilled, educated workers already occurring in manufacturing, health care, and various technical fields.

14. *Outsourcing.* Double-digit growth is expected in the multibillion-dollar outsourcing market, dramatically gobbling up traditional human resources tasks and significantly altering people management. Growing even faster will be the one-stop shopping market, where companies bundle different human resources management services into one large contract rather than serving it up piecemeal.

15. *Recruiting Older Workers.* With the graying of the workforce, American business is going to have to pay attention to what older workers want and how to recruit them. Companies must use terminology that better reflects age diversity such as "experienced workers" and "age-diverse." They work not only for money but also for enjoyment and a sense of purpose. They want time off and flexible schedules, health-care benefits, insurance, and good pension benefits.

16. *Mergers.* In the coming years, people management will play a far more pivotal role in corporate mergers. One of the principal reasons why mergers and acquisitions have failed in the past is that workforce management isn't brought into negotiations until the deal is consummated.

17. *Freelancers and Consultants.* The corporate workplace will evolve into a continually shifting mix of employees and freelancers, to the point where it will become difficult to distinguish one from the other. This may lead to profound changes in health care, retention, and career development and an increased freedom to move in and out of corporate positions.

18. *Pay for Wellness Performance.* Instead of waiting to pay for the treatment of sick employees, some employers will soon turn to the concept of wellness management—with a twist. They'll give employees a concrete financial incentive to participate. The process, which is handled through an outside organization to preserve privacy and HIPAA compliance, begins by having employees and their covered spouses take a voluntary health-risk appraisal each year. Health-care couching and monitoring may be involved. The employee's insurance premiums are reduced as long as the employee participates. The purpose is to head off major health problems. Fifty percent of disease is ultimately preventable.

19. *Spirituality at Work.* Americans eat too much and spend too much money. They are obese and in debt and worried about personal safety and job security—especially since 9/11 and the economic downturn. These are some of the reasons they're increasingly looking for spiritual comfort. The biggest change in the workplace is the interest in spirituality. It's about doing the right thing. It's not about religion. It's about job satisfaction. Jobs in the future will have to be meaningful. Pay won't be as important as a good job.

20. *Women at Work.* With steeply mounting numbers of educated women, glass ceilings are going to shatter in the coming years. More women than men are receiving four-year degrees. More women will be moving in management jobs and more men will move into women's jobs like nursing and teaching. The line between men's and women's work will blur and fade.

21. *Skills Shortage.* A job-skills shortage is already reality in the manufacturing industry and is likely to spread to other industries over the next ten to fifteen years as baby boomers retire. Well-trained workers will be needed in information technology and the global-energy and electrical-utility industries. Shortages are expected in the global competition for managers, engineers, technicians, skilled craftspeople, and frontline workers, mostly jobs requiring a college degree or technical education.

22. *Security Versus Privacy.* As technology becomes more sophisticated, the ability of those who administer company—and government—computer networks to monitor the comings and goings of workers will grow exponentially. In the future, the cat-and-mouse war between businesses and crooks will lead to more sophisticated surveillance, the standard use of data encryption, and sophisticated data mining techniques that spot potential problems and risks by analyzing patterns. The threat of terrorism is raising the stakes. We're living in a new era.

23. *Accounting for People.* More information will be printed in corporate publications about a company's most important assets—its people. More statistics will be printed on turnover, absenteeism, and revenue per employee. The basis for competition in the twenty-first century is a person's ability to think through complex problems, serve the customers better, and be more creative. Wall Street analysts will want to see what corporations know about the people who are winning patents for the company and closing big deals.

24. *Universal Health Care.* As costs soar and the number of uninsured Americans—both employed and unemployed—rapidly expands, there are about as many predictions about where health care is headed as Carter's little pills. Some dramatic change is likely. The country is indeed moving toward some form of universal health care system.

25. *The End of HR as We Know It.* Conventional wisdom says that human resources finally has achieved its sought-after seat at the table. But the ability of human resources to add value at a strategic level "is currently more promising than reality." Today's managers still are most comfortable with traditional human resources activities. Human resources must reinvent itself. The old approaches and models are not good enough.

Workplace Changes Impact Human Relations Management

As the workplace changes, it will bring new issues before human relations managers. For example:

Identity Management (IM). Identity management (IM), "the integrated set of processes, services, and architectures that provide secure and appropriate access to organization system assets"—is growing in importance as security issues and risks get bigger and the challenges more acute. "Collaborative commerce is emerging as another reason to prioritize IM."[39]

Building Design. New warehouses and distribution centers are taking on a luxurious look—from skylights to lush greenery to air-conditioned lounges.[40]

Video Cameras and Privacy. Big brother will be watching over us. "One industry consultant predicts that about 15 million Americans will be carrying camera-phone in three years; world-wide, some 100 million." Video cameras already are found in many places—retail stores, offices, manufacturing plants, and street corners—to name a few.[41]

Cost-Cutting Labor Practices. In tight markets, employers find job seekers willing to accept less. Businesses make common cost-saving moves by swapping expensive labor with lower-paid workers. The position is not eliminated, but rather the high-paid person in the position is eliminated. Deciding which employees to keep and which to discard involve human relations decisions that impact all employees in the company.[42]

Impact of Global Events. Major events in the world can change the way business is done. For example, when Wal-Mart was unable to send buyers to China because of the outbreak of SARS, it had to come up with an emergency alternative to product-development trips. Buyers accustomed to doing business face-to-face on Asian soil had to improvise.[43]

Opportunities for Older Employees. Another human relations issue concerns the lack of opportunities for advancement for managers in their forties and fifties. These managers feel underutilized and are stuck in jobs they have mastered. The challenge will be to find ways to motivate these workers in the next ten years.[44]

Impact of Technology. As technology grows, so do the opportunities to slack off at the office. Davis Wiskus, a Denver technosupport worker, "installed a program on this Handspring Visor hand-held that allowed him to manipulate the screen on his office computer from a booth at a local diner." New options and strategies allow diehard slackers to crack into program settings to make themselves appear perpetually available. Mr. Wiskus was eventually fired for habitual lateness.[45] Technology has allowed business to eliminate human contact. As more self-serve devices are added, what will it mean for human relations management? The travel industry struggling for cost-cutting measures is in the forefront of eliminating human contact. For example, you can book a plane ticket on the Internet, pick up the ticket at a check-in kiosk, take a shuttle to the car lot, pick your vehicle, swipe your membership card and drive off, then use a self-service machine at the hotel to check in and out faster.[46]

Collaboration Between Employees—Young and Old. "Fostering interaction between the younger and older workforces within a company is a necessary step in preparing younger workers for senior leadership roles while preserving valuable institutional memory," said Tom Silveri, President, Drake Beam Morin. In a survey of human resource professionals, forty percent felt their companies were unsuccessful in encouraging the collaboration of younger and older generations in the workplace. Some strategies organizations should consider include:

- **Educating employees of different age groups on what each contributes to the work environment and organizational goals.**
- **Motivating older workers to continue acquiring new skills.**
- **Enabling workers of all ages to recognize their transferable skills and seek opportunities within the organization before taking their experience and knowledge elsewhere.**
- **Implementing a corporate mentoring program.**
- **Equipping employees of all ages to network across generations, forming connections internally and externally.[47]**

As you can see the job of human relations management is an ever-changing process that brings with it a multitude of challenges. Hence, we close our study of this topic as we opened it—by defining *human relations,* the process by which management and workers interact and attain their objectives.

summary

(1) LEARNING OBJECTIVE
Describe the characteristics of creative people

The twenty-first century is bringing to light a number of important human relations challenges. One is a greater focus on innovation. Most people are more creative than they believe themselves to be, and creativity is widespread in the population. Some characteristics of creative people are: they are bright, have a youthful curiosity throughout their lives, are open and responsive to feelings and emotions, have a positive self-image, have the ability to tolerate isolation, are nonconformists, enjoy finding imaginative solutions to problems and are persistent.

(2) LEARNING OBJECTIVE
Explain how creativity in an organization setting can be both encouraged and nurtured

To encourage creativity, organizations must debunk some of the myths about innovations, such as innovation is planned and predictable, innovation is the result of exaggerated daydreaming, innovation is the result of carefully drawn technical specifications, large projects produce more innovative results than do small ones, and technology is the driving force behind innovation and success. They also must implement innovation principles, such as promoting the active search for new ideas, encouraging people to learn from their failures, and rewarding those who are most innovative.

Many organizations are working to ensure that their own human relations programs are innovative. These organizations are more likely to invest in training and development. They provide remedial education and basic skills training. Additionally, these firms redesign the workplace, launch employee involvement programs, and implement total quality management tools and techniques.

Three factors that affect human relations innovativeness are customers, new technologies, and changes in the demographics of the workforce. Attention to these factors can provide a competitive advantage.

---

(3) LEARNING OBJECTIVE
Discuss some of the reasons why the nature of work is changing and the role that reengineering, flowcharting, and training are playing in this process

Another major human relations challenge is the need to redesign work to accommodate changes caused by technology and competition. Reengineering, flowcharting, focus on service, hiring and retaining the best talent, and the creation of the appropriate environment are some of the approaches that now are being widely used. However, these will not be successful unless the organization also implements an effective training program that helps employees adapt to these new conditions. This is particularly true because of the increasing amount of education that workers will need to meet the challenges of this new century.

Reengineering is the fundamental rethinking and radical redesign of business processes to achieve dramatic improvements in performance; whereas, flowcharting involves mapping out the steps used in the process. Providing better service requires understanding three basic principles: Satisfaction equals perception minus expectation, first impressions are the most important, and service attitude alone will not assure good service.

An emphasis on building relationships with customers requires training employees how to find out what customers want before trying to sell anything to them regardless of the medium used. It keeps customers coming back. Hiring the best talent possible and retaining them calls for developing a program and an environment that allows employees to learn and grow on the job. Perks are used to reward commitment to the company. Employees must be paid competitively. People leave a company because they don't like to work for it, not because of the salary.

---

(4) LEARNING OBJECTIVE
Review the current state of diversity in the workplace

As the number of women and other minorities in the workforce increases, businesses will have to learn how to adapt to the needs of these individuals. At present, a great deal of discrimination against women and minorities still exists. To tap the full potential of the workforce, businesses must make major changes in the way that people are managed and led. Cases continue to be filed for gender, unequal pay, and sexual discrimination in the workplace. Larger and larger settlements are occurring. Obesity is another form of discrimination. It occurs in every stage of the work process: selection, placement, compensation, promotion, discipline, and discharge. One reason for not hiring obese people is the concern over health insurance premiums.

---

(5) LEARNING OBJECTIVE
Explain how awareness-based, skill-based, and integrated-based training programs are being used to deal with the challenge of diversity

Awareness-based diversity training programs help participants to discover the nature and causes of diversity and help them to understand their own assumptions and tendencies to stereotype. It increases an employee's knowledge and sensitivity to diversity issues and focuses on developing effective intercultural communication. The training strives to promote feelings of unity, tolerance, and acceptance with the existing organizational culture and structure.

Skill-based diversity training is behavioral in nature and provides participants with tools for effectively interacting in a heterogeneous work setting. It goes beyond consciousness-raising; it provides workers with a set of skills to enable them to deal effectively with workplace diversity. Some of the skills include: self-awareness, clear-headedness, openness, candor, adaptability, and egalitarianism.

Integrated-based diversity training combines both awareness- and skill-based methods and objectives. This training is sometimes integrated into existing programs. Regardless of the type of training, it covers the same issues: race, gender, stereotypes, business objectives, work–family issues, age, sexual harassment, national demographics, disabilities, and sexual orientation.

---

⑥ LEARNING OBJECTIVE
Identify the major pillars of world-class organizations and explain how organizations are using the pillars

A major challenge is that of becoming a world-class organization—or at least a sufficiently competitive organization locally to ensure the survival of the enterprise. The six pillars of a world-class organization help to ensure this: a customer-based focus, continuous improvement, the use of flexible or virtual organizations, creative human resource management strategies, development of an egalitarian climate, and proper technological support. Attention to these areas will ensure that organizations employ effective human relations, the process by which management and workers interact and attain their objectives.

---

⑦ LEARNING OBJECTIVE
Describe several human relation challenges facing managers in the next decade

Trends that will impact how business is done in the next decade include: the use of e-mail, forming new labor unions, businesses becoming involved in public schools, privacy issues facing global transactions, 24/7 operations, use of artificial intelligence, workplace discontentment, office design, defined benefit plans, telework, consumer-driven health care and child care, older employees working longer and having different needs, outsourcing, using people management in mergers and acquisitions, more freelancers and consultants, pay for wellness performance, spirituality at work—doing the right thing, more women in management, skills shortage, security versus privacy in a technology world, more information printed about employees in corporate publications, universal health care, and HR as we know it today will have to reinvent itself.

Additional changes that are impacting human relations are: identity management (IM)—providing appropriate access to organization system assets, warehouse and distribution centers taking on a new luxurious look, video cameras being used everywhere—big brother watching, and high-salaried employees being replaced by lower-paid employees. Major events in the world are increasingly impacting business policies and practices in companies located around the globe. Companies must find ways to motivate older employees, where advancements are not possible. Technology not only helps conduct business faster and more efficiently but also allows employees to manipulate the system for their own pleasure.

KEY TERMS IN THE CHAPTER

Reengineering

Flowchart

First law of service

Second law of service

Third law of service

Consultative selling

World-class organization

REVIEW AND STUDY QUESTIONS

1. What do most people believe about creative people?

2. What are some characteristics of creative people? List five.

3. What are some of the myths about creativity? Identify and discuss three of them.

4. How can an organization improve its innovation? Identify five useful principles.

5. Identify three primary factors that have been found to influence human relations innovativeness. Describe each one.

6. How does reengineering work? Why would an organization want to use reengineering?

7. How does flowcharting work? When would an organization use this approach? Give an example.

8. Describe three principle laws of service and tell why each is important.

9. How can a company build relationships with customers?

10. What are some major challenges in retaining good employees?

11. Companies everywhere are facing a diversity challenge. What are some of the reasons for this challenge?

12. One of the most common forms of diversity training focuses on awareness-based objectives. How does this training work?

13. Another very common form of diversity training focuses on skill-based objectives. How does this training work?

14. What is integrated-based diversity training? How does it work?

15. What is a world-class organization (WCO)? How do customer-based focus, continuous improvement, and creation of flexible or virtual organizations help to create a WCO?

15. How do creative human resource management, an egalitarian climate, and technological support help to create a WCO?

16. What are some things that will impact business in the future? Identify ten trends that will change the way business is done in the next decade.

17. What is Identity Management (IM)?

18. How will video cameras invade employee privacy?

19. Describe how employees are being treated in cost-cutting practices.

20. What are some negatives of using technology in the workplace?

VISIT THE WEB

Unlimited Potential

In this chapter, you studied about human relations challenges facing organizations in the next decade. Organizations need to do a number of things to succeed. No one knows this better than Nokia, the Finnish company that is the world's leading developer of digital handsets and wireless data. Visit their Web site at **http://www.nokia.com** and then answer these three questions:

1. Where does Nokia have offices around the world?

2. What do the most recent press releases reveal about Nokia and its products?

3. What is the next step for Nokia? Prepare a timeline of the history of the company and describe the next step it must take to maintain its world-class organization.

Why Is Pitney Bowes, Inc. a World-Class Organization?

Pitney Bowes, Inc. has become a world class organization because it serves its customers by creating new products and services that go above and beyond the expected. Visit **http://www.bp.com** and learn what Pitney Bowes is doing to provide special services. Answer the following questions.

1. Identify some of the special services provided by Pitney Bowes.

2. Explain several of Pitney Bowes small business solutions. (Click on Small Business Solutions.)

3. Review the company's Global Diversity Leadership statement. How will this statement help the company meet human relations challenges in the future? Give an example.

TIME OUT ANSWERS

Improving Your Creativeness

1. mad dad	6. near beer
2. glad lad	7. deep weep
3. book crook	8. fast repast
4. ape cape	9. lean cuisine
5. fat cat	10. frail snail

Score	Interpretation
8–10	Excellent
6–7	Above average
4–5	Average
1–3	Below average

Regardless of how well you did, remember that creativity can be improved. Individuals who like crossword puzzles or enjoy puns tend to do best on these rhyme-type tests. Your creative interests may lie in other areas, so do not be disheartened. This test is only one of many that can give you insights to your creativeness.

case: AFTER THE STORM

The Garrett Manufacturing Company has been in business for twenty-eight years. Much of its early success was a result of flexible manufacturing techniques that allowed the company to offer a wide array of products. As a result, Garrett became a supplier to a large number of well-known firms in the auto and computer industries.

Recently, however, the company has experienced a downturn. The company's primary customers have started giving their business to other suppliers. The primary reason is that Garrett's quality has not kept up with its competition. Once Garrett realized this, it began making dramatic changes. In particular, three strategies have been initiated in the last four months.

First, the company has completely overhauled its machinery and equipment and purchased twelve new high-tech units that can increase output by 40 percent while driving down costs by almost 50 percent. At the same time, Garrett scheduled 60 percent of its machinists for specialized training so that they can efficiently operate these new units. Now the company is completely reengineering the production area and revising work procedures and job assignments.

Second, the company has begun a diversity program for all its employees. The reason for this move is that more than 75 percent of the workforce consists of Hispanics and African-Americans, although 90 percent of the managers are Anglo men. The president of the company, Ty Garrett, believes that, in order to increase productivity further, the firm must get everyone working as a team. "This means we have to learn to better understand and respect each other," he noted recently. "This is an area we have neglected until now, but I see a lot of world-class manufacturing firms moving in this direction, and I think we have to follow suit." Within the next month, Ty is offering two types of training to his people. The first program will deal with diversity awareness. The second will focus on skill-based diversity training.

The third strategy is to begin downsizing the company and letting go of approximately 25 percent of the workforce. The new technology and the need to be competitive are forcing the firm to cut its labor and overhead costs. Even with this reduction in staff, Garrett will be able to increase output and quality and generate a higher profit than it has in six years.

Ty Garrett's main concern now is implementing the strategy effectively. "I know what I'm doing is right, but I have to be careful about implementing these changes correctly," he explained to one of his senior-level managers. "We've had to dig in and weather a competitive storm, and we've done that. Now we've got to take advantage of the situation and not drop the ball at the last minute."

QUESTIONS

1. How does reengineering work? How would Garrett use it in the production area to improve quality?

2. How can diversity training be of any practical value to the company? Explain.

3. What can Garrett do to reduce the trauma that employees may be feeling as a result of the downsizing? Offer three suggestions.

YOU BE THE CONSULTANT

New Ideas, New Products

The Global Insurance Products Company has increased its annual premiums from $172 million to $886 million over the last five years. The primary reason for the increase in revenue is that the firm has been able to develop and market a wide variety of new insurance offerings. One of its most successful products has been a term insurance policy tied directly to the homeowner's mortgage. This policy has sold very well among young homeowners with small children.

The biggest problem Global faces is competitive products that offer basically the same form of coverage at a lower price. Typically, Global will develop a new offering and, once competitors realize that the product is doing well, they will enter the marketplace. This is upsetting to some of Global's top management, but the president, Neal Sedanno, is philosophical: "If all the competition can do is copy us," he notes, "they'll never get ahead. All they can do is follow behind."

To ensure a continual flow of new products into the marketplace, Neal has formed product teams to study, develop, and bring to market new insurance coverage that currently is unavailable. In recent months, the company has done very well offering ecological damage coverage to homeowners living on the West Coast. Any oil spills in Alaska are likely to drift south and affect the beach property of West Coast home-owners. Although the possibility of such an occurrence is remote, the cost of annual coverage is less than $10 per $1,000 of insurance. This coverage was developed by one of the product teams, which consist of an actuary, a salesperson and, depending on the situation, three additional people. In this case, a geologist and a marine biol-ogist were part of the team. By examining scientific data and then brainstorming, the group was able to develop the new coverage.

Every year, the company comes out with five new product lines, four of which are usually successful. By the time the competition has copied the coverage, Global is established in the market and is moving to add still more lines.

Your Advice

1. How can Neal help the teams to maintain their high creativity?

    ____ a. Upgrade computers so the teams can use these machines to help them generate even more creative ideas.

    ____ b. Encourage the groups to do more formal planning so their thinking is better focused.

    ____ c. Keep the focus on one project at a time rather than allowing the groups to consider five to ten different areas in which they might develop new forms of coverage.

2. Why are Global's product teams so creative?

3. Could other insurance companies be successful if they followed this new product team approach?

4. What are three time-proven principles that could be helpful to those using Global's approach?

EXPERIENCING CREATIVE THINKING

Purpose

- **To provide students with a creative thinking exercise.**
- **To allow participants to share their information with and gain information from others.**
- **To show how interaction with others can result in more creative solutions than can working alone.**

Procedure

1. Examine each of the definitions that follow and try to come up with two rhyming words that describe the definition. If you want to obtain more insights into how this works, review the Time Out box, *Improving Your Creativeness*, which appears in this chapter.

2. After you have finished writing down your descriptive words for each definition, work in groups of three or four and try to complete the items for which you have no answer.

3. After the instructor gives you the remaining answers, discuss how exercises of this nature can help individuals to increase their creativity.

Definitions

1. An SST that has been caught in a torrential downpour

   _____   _____

2. An ocular growth that prevents someone from seeing clearly

   _____   _____

3. A light red colored potable

   _____   _____

4. An illegitimate business that takes cars and cuts them up for their parts

   _____   _____

5. A police officer who stops all drivers who fail to obey a traffic light

   _____   _____

6. An FBI agent who is secretly working for Russia

   _____   _____

7. A location fifty yards outside an oasis on the equator

   _____   _____

8. An auto located a great distance away

   _____   _____

9. A man who badly needs a glass of water

   _____   _____

10. A drop to the ground from the top of the Eiffel Tower

    _____   _____

15

Human Relations and You

Having studied the field of modern human relations, we now turn our attention to how you can use human relations to help you obtain employment and move ahead in your chosen career. Before reading further, test yourself using the Time Out quiz on "Interviewing Effectively" to see how much you know about applying human relations to a job interview.

As college students, many of you are still undecided about a career. The aim of this chapter is to help you begin to focus on your career. Several ideas for choosing a career are discussed, including how to evaluate your skills and abilities. The results can give you insight into your strengths and weaknesses, which can be used in preparing your resume. The interviewer, as well, may ask questions concerning your strengths and weaknesses. A well-prepared resume often can make a difference in who gets the job. To be promoted and move ahead in your career, you must learn how to manage effectively your career. This means you must learn to meet the responsibilities and challenges afforded you in the future; regardless of whether it is developing alliances, showing you are a star, training your replacement, managing your time and stress, finding a mentor, or organizing your office.

AFTER READING THIS CHAPTER, YOU SHOULD BE ABLE TO:

1. Identify key questions that should be asked in carrying out a self-evaluation.
2. Write an effective résumé.
3. Discuss six important points in carrying out a successful job hunt.
4. Describe some of the major guidelines that you should follow in managing your career effectively.
5. Explain the major steps for getting ahead in your job.

It's a Whole New Ball Game

In the recent past, job applicants would send their résumés to companies and hope that the firm would contact them for an interview. Today that approach is passé. A growing number of firms now are actively seeking qualified people and then making rapid hiring decisions, ensuring that they get the candidates they want before the competition has a chance to hire them. The Vignette Corporation of Austin, Texas, provides a good example. The company makes software applications for online businesses and now is locked in a race for market share in the highly competitive business-to-business Web industry. In recent years, the firm's revenues have grown rapidly. To maintain this momentum, Vignette needs both to attract and to keep talented personnel. Therefore, the company hires only people with information technology experience. In this way, the new hires hit the ground running.

Vignette uses a number of approaches in recruiting the best people, but all have one thing in common: They radically cut the time between receiving an applicant's résumé and making the individual an offer. As a result, even though the company's Web site receives more than one hundred résumés daily, each can be quickly processed. In fact, within seconds after a résumé is submitted to Vignette, an alert pops up in a recruiter's e-mail box, and this individual will evaluate the applicant. If the person appears to be qualified for the posted position, he or she will be given a telephone interview that same day in most cases. Those who pass this phone screening then are brought in for a round of interviews within a couple of days' time.

The on-site interview consists of a series of face-to-face meetings with a variety of company personnel, each of whom has a different area of expertise. For example, a master programmer will assess the candidate's technical skills and the manager for whom the individual will be working will evaluate the applicant's ability to fit into Vignette's fast-paced, autonomous culture. Once a person is hired, the company works hard to keep the individual on board. In an industry where annual turnover is more than 20 percent, Vignette's annual attrition goal is less than 10 percent. They accomplish this goal through offering the employees interesting and challenging work, providing many opportunities for two-way communication, conducting an annual employee survey, a strong performance management program, and the opportunity to gain equity in the company through performance-based stock options grants.

By creating a partnership with Adecco, a recruiting firm, Moen, Inc., a producer of residential and commercial plumbing products of North Olmsted, Ohio, reduced its turnover rate by 10 percent at its final-assembly plant in New Bern, North Carolina. It is Adecco's job to keep the New Bern facility manned with between 175 and 200 hourly temps and to keep the full-time hourly positions filled. Together Adecco and Moen have built a unique full-time placement program called Adecco To Moen. Every full-time employee begins as a temp and goes through the program.

The program starts with Adecco's recruiting activities, which are based on a system of evaluation and specific competencies. "For example, employees should be team workers, require limited supervision, and be flexible and deadline oriented." They must be comfortable working in a high-pressure environment. Once the temps are hired, they receive points based on their performance, attendance, safety, and discipline. When they gain sufficient points to be hired for full-time employment, their names are put into a pool of candidates. Then when a full-time employee is needed, the names of the top performers—the ones with the most points—are selected from the candidates' pool. Because this system is based on a point system, it takes the emotion out of the hiring process and reduces the chances of hiring poorly qualified candidates. The temps who score poorly usually take themselves out of the system before their assignment is over. Bart Rovins, HR manager at the New Bern plant feels "it's reasonable to assume that the program has helped us make better hiring decisions." This program demonstrates that in the area of human resources development, for Moen and many other companies, it's a whole new ball game.

Sources: Information on the Vignette Corporation was provided courtesy of the Vignette Corporation, August 12, 2003; Sarah Fister Gale, "Permanent-Hire Program Reduces Turnover," Workforce, July 2002, pp. 74–77.

Choosing a Career

LEARNING OBJECTIVE

1 *Identify key questions that should be asked in carrying out a self-evaluation*

The value of human relations is not confined to managing others. It can also be used in choosing a career and succeeding in that choice. When applied this way, human relations concepts can be employed to evaluate one's self accurately and to succeed in a job hunt.

Conduct a Self-Evaluation

The most important initial step in applying human relations concepts to your career is that of evaluating yourself. What do you do well? What do you do poorly? In conducting this evaluation, some of the most important questions are the following:

1. What do you do best?
2. What do you like to do?
3. What do you dislike doing?
4. Do you work well with others or do you work best by yourself?
5. Do you know your own talents and abilities? What are they?
6. What do you think you would like to do for a living? Has your education prepared you for this career, or is further training necessary?
7. How hard are you willing to work?
8. What are your work habits? Do you work at a steady pace or in short bursts of intensive effort?
9. Have you sought any information or professional advice regarding your career choice(s)? What have you learned?
10. How will you go about beginning your employment search?

These questions require you to apply to your own career development many of the ideas that you have studied in this book. Included in this group are such concepts as motivation, personality, values, group behavior, job design, leadership, communication, and your ability to deal with change. This type of self-analysis is helpful because it provides basic direction in assessing where you are and where you would like to go. This preparation also is important in helping you to identify both the preparation and basic skills that will be needed for a successful career. For example, many companies require applicants for management jobs to have a college degree and, in some cases, the degree must be in a particular area. Supervisors and first-line managers typically do not need to have concentrated in any specific area, although many firms do like to hire business majors for these positions. Salespeople often are hired from all areas, except when the product is highly technical and the firm knows that engineers make the best salespeople. Other jobs require specific training: Accountants must major in accounting; at advertising agencies, advertising majors have the inside track over other applicants; and most human resources departments will give the nod to those who have majored in human resource management.

An understanding of your basic skills is important, because it helps direct both your educational and your career choice. If you are a highly analytical person, you should look for a career in which this trait is a key factor for success. Examples include banking, market research, operations management, and stock brokering. If you have high social and personal or interactive skills, you should consider such career choices as advertising, personal services, sales, and training and development.

In addition, you should think about your future goals and what you seek in a career. Recent research shows that 75 percent of college freshmen believe that hard work counts more than luck in succeeding, 65 percent want to do work that offers opportunities to help others, and 57 percent are willing to work more than 40 hours weekly to reach their career goals. Only 33 percent report that they want to earn a high salary.[1] How do you feel about these areas, and what other things do you desire from an employer?[2] Now is a good time to answer these types of questions.

DO NOT UNDERRATE YOUR ABILITY

In your self-analysis, be sure not to underrate your ability. Otherwise you will be selling yourself short. One way of approaching this subject is to keep in mind that you not only possess ability but that you probably have more than enough ability to undertake most jobs. (This idea was illustrated in Figure 14.1.) People often have more ability than is required by the job.

If you do feel that you are above average in ability, be sure to take this into consideration. What may be an interesting or challenging job for the average person could prove quite boring to you. Try to match your interests and abilities with the requirements of the job. At the same time, remember that you may not have the opportunity to use all your abilities and talents immediately. Sometimes, the first year or two entail a great deal of technical, boring work, and you will not find the job highly rewarding until you receive one or more promotions. You must be willing to persevere if you want the chance to use your ability.

Develop an Overall Plan of Action

Once a self-evaluation has been completed, the next major step is to formulate an overall plan of action. What jobs are available? What career choices have you identified? How should you go about writing your résumé? What steps need to be taken to ensure the most successful job interview? These questions should be put into the form of a checklist, so that you do not forget to do something important. Figure 15.1 provides a sample checklist that can be used for this purpose.

FIGURE 15.1 — *Career Preparation Checklist*

This exercise helps you to understand what you need to do to prepare for a successful career search. Evaluate yourself in the six areas covered in this program. Use the following scale when responding:

YES! = strong agreement with the statement
Yes = agreement with the statement
yes = slight agreement with the statement
no = slight disagreement with the statement
No = disagreement with the statement
NO! = strong disagreement with the statement

Getting Started

	NO!	No	no	yes	Yes	YES!
I know how to manage the emotions I may experience during my career search.	1	2	3	4	5	6
I know what to say and what not to say to people who can help me.	1	2	3	4	5	6
I know the general characteristics that all employers seek when hiring people.	1	2	3	4	5	6
I know what I should be doing *now* to maximize my career potential and satisfaction.	1	2	3	4	5	6

Looking at Options

I can describe just what I need and prefer from a new job.	1	2	3	4	5	6
I am clear about the skills and abilities I bring to a career.	1	2	3	4	5	6
I am prepared to discuss what I have accomplished with potential employers.	1	2	3	4	5	6
I know how to determine whether a career fits my goals and abilities.	1	2	3	4	5	6

Applications and Résumés

I am prepared to fill out employment applications.	1	2	3	4	5	6
I understand the different types of résumé formats.	1	2	3	4	5	6
I know how to write each part of my résumé.	1	2	3	4	5	6
I know how to write cover letters that will catch attention in a positive way.	1	2	3	4	5	6

FIGURE 15.1 (*continued*)

The Game Plan

I know how to increase my chances for success when responding to advertisements.	1	2	3	4	5	6
I know how to select and work with agencies and counselors.	1	2	3	4	5	6
I know how to approach companies that are not advertising jobs openings but that may have them.	1	2	3	4	5	6
I know how to develop a network of personal contacts to find opportunities.	1	2	3	4	5	6

Telephone Skills

I understand the advantages of using the telephone in my job search.	1	2	3	4	5	6
I know how to use the phone to gather information about careers and companies.	1	2	3	4	5	6
I can discuss my strengths on the phone in a way that makes a positive impression.	1	2	3	4	5	6
I know how to use the phone to follow up effectively on correspondence.	1	2	3	4	5	6

Interviewing

I know how to make a positive first impression in interviews.	1	2	3	4	5	6
I am prepared to answer the typical questions interviewers ask.	1	2	3	4	5	6
I know how to ask questions that convey my interest in working for the company.	1	2	3	4	5	6
I know how to follow up after an interview.	1	2	3	4	5	6

Scoring the Preparation Checklist

Add up your scores for each of the six areas of career management and record them below. Then add your six scores to calculate a total score for the checklist.

Score for *Getting Started* _____
Score for *Looking at Options* _____
Score for *Applications and Résumés* _____
Score for *The Game Plan* _____
Score for *Telephone Skills* _____
Score for *Interviewing* _____
Total Score _____

Interpreting Your Scores for Each Area of Job Hunting

≥20   You are quite well prepared in this area. Concentrate on skills that need polish.
15–19   You are somewhat prepared in this area. Spend extra time on skills that are weak.
≤41   You are not prepared in this area. Practice each skill with your coach or a friend.

Interpreting Your Total Score

≥120   You are quite well prepared to manage your career. Work through each unit, concentrating on areas that need polish.
90–119   You are somewhat prepared to manage your career. Work through each unit, spending extra time on areas that are weak.
≤89   You are not prepared to manage your career. Take each unit seriously, practicing all skills with your coach or a friend. Make the effort to prepare fully and not lose out because you are unprepared.

Complete this sentence: "I would describe my level of preparedness as _____."

Source: Florida International University.

Finding a Job

After conducting your self-analysis, the next step is finding a job. This requires you to do two things:

First, you must write a résumé that attracts attention and points you out as someone whom the organization should pursue.

Second, you must conduct yourself properly during the job hunt, especially the interview.

LEARNING OBJECTIVE
Write an effective résumé
②

A résumé is a summary of your experience and training.

The Effective Résumé

Regardless of the job you are seeking, you should put together a **résumé,** or summary of your qualifications, education, work experience, and training. The résumé is typically the first step to the interview. After reviewing résumés of job applicants, an organization will choose those applicants who look most promising and extend to them an interview. Without an effective résumé, you will never get to the interview stage.[3] If you are just starting out in a career, your résumé should be simple, straightforward, and factual. A good rule is to make it only one to two pages long, preferably one page. It is best to gear the résumé specifically to the company where you are applying. Otherwise, it can be more general if you are applying to several related companies in the same industry. The following are some of the most important guidelines you should apply in drafting your résumé:

1. Group your information into four to six categories, such as personal data, employment objective, education, work experience, special interests, and references.
2. Start by listing your name, address, and telephone number; then move on to your education and job experience, listing your most recent degree or job first and working backward.
3. If you have a specific employment objective, state it, but avoid the use of generalities, such as "want a challenging position" or "desire to work with people." These do not tell the reader a great deal.
4. Use a format that is easy to read, has eye appeal, and provides a positive impression about you and your goals. If you feel it is necessary or useful, underline or capitalize some words.
5. Retain duplicate copies of your résumé if you intend to interview with more than a handful of firms; these should be made by a professional printer so that each copy looks identical to the original.
6. If you want to send along a picture of yourself, do so. However, attach it to the résumé; do not have it printed as part of the résumé. In this way, if the organization is prohibited by state law from requiring pictures or simply does not want a photograph as part of the résumé, the picture can be removed.
7. References are optional. If you are just starting out, it is useful to list them. If you have been working for a number of years, you may not want anyone to contact your references without your approval; in this case, simply state that these are available on request.

The seven suggestions all draw on human relations concepts, and they help you to present yourself in a positive light. Figures 15.2 through 15.4 provide examples of résumés that follow these suggestions.

The first is the *chronological résumé,* which presents information in descending order, the most recent events being listed first under each heading. This type of résumé is easiest to prepare, and it is the most popular and brings the best results.

The second is the *functional résumé,* which focuses on skills, aptitudes, and qualities that can be applied in a number of situations. This résumé is particularly appropriate for those who

FIGURE 15.2   *Chronological Resume*

MIKE TOWERS   SALES PROFESSIONAL
                                                        323-555-1212 ~ mt@support.com

QUALIFICATIONS

Bilingual, customer-focused individual with a proven track record of increasing department and store sales through effective merchandising, superior product knowledge, and comprehensive staff training. Recently honored as *Employee of the Month* at Century Hardware for exceeding company goals by 35% in a weak market. Spearheaded drive for in-store home improvement classes to showcase high-end products, including *Andersen Windows, Black & Decker Power Tools, Behr Paint,* and *Burlington Carpets.* Fluent in English and Spanish with excellent communication skills to easily interact with all levels of management, peers, staff, vendors, and customers.

PROFESSIONAL EXPERIENCE   1991–Present

CENTURY HARDWARE, Los Angeles, California
Department Manager/Sales Associate

- Train, schedule, and conduct performance reviews for up to 50 employees.
- Attend manufacturer-sponsored informational classes and review product updates to ensure superior merchandise knowledge for customer satisfaction.
- Maximize customer traffic and increase sales through product displays and promotional events, including the *Deck Days of Summer* that showcased building materials, stains, and sealants.

Accomplishments
- Awarded *Department Supervisor of the Month* in March, April and September of 2002.
- Increased sales 40% by reorganizing the hardware department to market high-end products.
- Boosted garden department sales from $5 million to $10 million+ annually and same store sales by 30% through effective management.

CALIFORNIA HOME CENTERS, Los Angeles, California   1989–1991
Sales Associate

- Educated customers on product brands, rang sales, and maintained merchandise appearance.

Accomplishments
- Doubled department sales by providing personalized customer service.
- Increased store sales, on average, 35% by creating a *shopper-friendly* environment with attractive merchandising and prominent displays.

EDUCATION

STATE UNIVERSITY, San Francisco, California
Bachelor of Arts in Business Administration, Marketing Emphasis, 1988

6689 Ocean Boulevard,#12   **Los Angeles, California 90001**
Source: **http://www.resumeedge.com.** *Printed by permission of ResumeEdge.com, a Peterson's site.*

---

have had a variety of jobs or assignments not directly related to their career targets but include relevant functions or responsibilities or have changed jobs often. This form works well for technical jobs.

The third is the *combination résumé,* which uses parts of the chronological and functional résumés. The combination *résumé* is often the best choice for people who have a great deal of experience and many jobs or for those who are changing careers.

Over the last few years, a number of new developments have occurred in the area of résumé writing. Two of the most important relate to attention-getting résumés and the use of the Internet.

FIGURE 15.3 *Functional Resume*

TONI BURNS, MBA

6684 Baca Grande Drive
Albuquerque, New Mexico 87101
505-555-1212/trburns@net.net

QUALIFICATIONS
Business Analyst with superior analytical skills applied to contract negotiations, business processes, data collection and management for major health providers, including *Health First.* Consistently promoted to positions of increased responsibility, advancing three times within a one-year period. Excellent communicator with fluency in English and Spanish. Proven leadership in training employees and conducting formal presentations to all levels of management. Outstanding academic credentials in business, international management, and analytical finance.

SELECTED ACCOMPLISHMENTS

- Completed contracting for 6,000+ providers within 6 months for CHAMPUS contract.
- Improved production 20% through the establishment of department production standards.
- Launched marketing department for the State of New Mexico.

PROFESSIONAL EXPERIENCE
Financial & Business Analysis

- Performed complex analyses for system-wide negotiations, projections, and line-of-business reviews in addition to analysis of population distribution, claims/utilization, and cost.
- Identified, collected, and organized data from multiple sources for input into monthly, quarterly, annual, and ad hoc reports provided to contracting/finance departments and senior management.
- Designed and implemented database applications used in contract rate and risk management analysis as well as the identification and correction of data errors and discrepancies.

Management & Supervision
- Analyzed, interpreted, and resolved claims with authorization for payments up to $75,000.
- Directed activities of 40 claims analysts at a large project site.
- Increased daily with enrollment, claims, utilization/quality management, and customer service to resolve provider issues.

EMPLOYMENT HISTORY
HEALTH FIRST, Albuquerque, New Mexico
Manager, Contract Analysis/Senior Financial Analyst   1997–2003

FEDERAL HEALTH SERVICES, Albuquerque, New Mexico
Manager, Provider Relations   1994–1997

CROSS HEALTH CARE, Albuquerque, New Mexico
Risk Analyst   1993–1994

GROUP SERVICES, Albuquerque, New Mexico
Senior Claims Analyst/Project Manager   1990–1993

EDUCATION
GRADUATE SCHOOL OF BUSINESS, Albuquerque, New Mexico
Master of Business Administration, 1992

NEW WEST UNIVERSITY, Albuquerque, New Mexico
Bachelor of Arts in Business, 1989

Source: **http://www.resumeedge.com.** *Printed by permission of ResumeEdge.com, a Peterson's site.*

FIGURE 15.4 *Combination Resume*

JENNIFER RIVERS
1543 Central Park Drive ~ New York, New York 10001

212.555.1212   pro@news.net

MARKETING EXECUTIVE
Product Launches ~ Overseas Partnerships ~ Presentations

Accomplished, multilingual Professional consistently recognized for achievement and performance in the fuel industry. Innovative and successful in mining new sales territories and establishing business alliances, including the recent partnership with *MJM Oil* in Korea. Proven leader with special capabilities in building teams, strategizing, and implementing workable marketing plans employing television, radio, Internet, and print media. Fluent in English, Korean, Japanese, and French.

BUSINESS SKILLS

Marketing
- Launch gasoline exports in conjunction with new production plant start-up; target overseas markets.
- Initiate sales of ULS, an environmentally-friendly new product launched in the European market.
- Establish joint venture partnerships in Europe and Far East; implement marketing for aviation fuel and asphalt as a value-added commodity.

Market Planning
- Analyze regional import/export economics and the interregional oil markets.
- Participate in contract negotiations for strategic alliances with major European and Asian concerns.
- Achieved $25 million in revenue by developing offshore storage programs that fulfilled seasonal market trends in the region.

Product Planning
- Optimize production mode by selecting appropriate refinery; research product specification revisions by country.
- Propose and participate in the Plant Operation Committee, a team effort between production and sales.

PROFESSIONAL EXPERIENCE

TTR CORPORATION, New York, New York
Vice President, Overseas Business Division   1993–Present
- Promoted to position in March 1996; selected as one of three employees to attend an MBA course in 2003.
- Named *Employee of the Year* in 1996 based on professional achievements.

FUEL INDUSTRY OF AMERICA, New York, New York   1989–1992
Manager of Marketing
- Provided analysis on fuel industry, drafting report for the White House.
- Awarded the *Honor Prize* in 1992 based on performance evaluations of oil producers.

EDUCATION

UNIVERSITY OF NEW YORK, New York, New York
Bachelor of Arts in Communications, 1988

Source: **http://www.resumeedge.com.** *Printed by permission of ResumeEdge.com, a Peterson's site.*

ATTENTION-GETTING RESUMES

Most résumés appear very similar. In an effort to distinguish one's résumé from that of the others, however, a growing number of applicants now are personalizing their résumé so that it stands out from the rest. For example, a person applying for a marketing manager post recently took along with her a personalized compact disk. On the compact disk were seven songs that described her work ethic and background, and the accompanying résumé appeared in the form of liner notes. The company was impressed with this creative approach. Here is another example:

> When . . . Peter Shankman sought a public-relations job in New York a few years ago, he didn't want to mail out a bunch of résumés. Instead, he printed out his résumé on two 4-foot–by–3 foot poster boards, sandwiched himself between them, stood on a Manhattan corner on a cold January day, and handed out 1,000 résumés from 6 A.M. UNTIL 7:15 P.M.

The stunt was a raving success. After two hundred phone calls, forty-five interviews, and twenty job offers, Mr. Shankman took a job as a director of new media for the New Jersey Devils hockey team. Although he admits his stunt was off the wall, Mr. Shankman says he was successful because he met people face to face. "At least they could see I was a nice nutcase," says Mr. Shankman, who wore a business suit and an overcoat that day.[4] At the same time, it is important to remember that a résumé that is too creative may be viewed as inappropriate. Simply put, applicants must be careful about going too far. For example, in one case, a graphic designer seeking a job with a veterinary company, sent her résumé wrapped in a faux diamond-studded collar with a bone-shaped identification tag that sported her name and title. In another case, a manager in Florida applied for a job up north and, in addition to sending his résumé, included a zipper-lock bag containing sand from the nearby beach and fake gold coins, meant to imply that he was a hidden treasure in need of discovery. In a third instance, an applicant sent out garden spades to employers with a note saying, "hire me and watch your company grow." None of these creative efforts resulted in any interest from the employers. Clearly, creative approaches can end up proving to be worthless.

"College students make job-hunting tougher with weak résumés." To help graduates write resumes and prepare for interviews, Brad Karsh recently launched JobBound in Chicago. He states that some common mistakes on resumes of college graduates include:

- **The lack of a clear objective.**
- **Using generic job descriptions that omit tangible accomplishments.**
- **Selling short your assets and omitting cutting-edge skills.**
- **Failing to list jobs in reverse chronological order.**
- **Cramming résumés with extraneous information.**[5]

According to several top headhunters and outplacement specialists, "90% of the resumes they see are riddled with errors or misrepresentations, including "sales manger" for sales manager, "skilled in massaging" for messaging and "on contract with the state" "(in jail)." They suggest you consider hiring a résumé doctor to help you prepare your résumé. Recently *Business Week* magazine contacted twenty-one firms to remake a résumé. Among those they felt who helped "craft the clearest, most data-filled résumés were: Mike Jeans of New Directions, Jack Downing of WorldBridge Partners, John Lybarger of Career Architects and Tamar Shay of Shay & Tannas. Because the field is unregulated, you must be careful in selecting a firm to help you. It is best to ask for samples of previous work before you make a commitment.[6]

Applicants who have stopped out of work to raise a family or retire early may have gaps in their résumés. In this case, you will need to evaluate your unpaid experiences and decide which ones support the qualifications needed in the position for which you are applying and then list them as skills. If a company you once worked for has merged, then acknowledge both company names. This practice indicates you are keeping abreast of current business changes. Some experts suggest "that re-entry candidates sprinkle a résumé with the latest buzzwords for a targeted occupation." Doing so indicates you know what's hot.[7]

By reading classified ads, you can find out the type of employees businesses are seeking. This information is helpful in preparing your résumé. For example, in today's newspapers the popular words are "go-getter, hard-charger, team player, self-starter, multitasker, goal-oriented, results-oriented, win-oriented, 24/7." Only those with these skills and attributes need apply. These ads are indicators of what is important within the business environment and they also reflect social changes within society.[8]

USE OF THE INTERNET

The Internet is now becoming a popular tool for job hunting. Among other things, an increasing number of job applicants are posting their résumés on Web sites. In turn, employers can easily access these sites and identify those individuals whom they would like to contact. Likewise, many college and university placement services are creating Web sites that can be accessed by employers who are looking for applicants. As a result, e-mailed résumés are becoming increasingly popular, and many recruiters are finding this to be a convenient and efficient way to handle job applications. The important points that must be remembered by applicants who wish to use the e-mail route is that their résumés must be simple and they must refrain from using symbols, pictures, or other embellishments that can be altered in transmission.[9]

A search on the Internet will reveal many sites that provide information, samples, and assistance in preparing résumés. One site for example is **http://www.ResumeEdge.com,** the net's premier résumé writing and editing service. There you will find a discussion of the "12 Step Resume Writing" process.

One drawback of the Internet is that these Web sites often are not very secure. Hence, anything in a résumé can be read by anyone gaining access to the site. To protect the privacy of applicants, university placement service personnel now recommend that applicants use a confidential number in lieu of their name and a post office box rather than a home address. In this way, an employer who wants to contact the individual can do so, but the applicant can screen the communication. Additionally, many university placement services have begun charging employers an access fee for the right to review résumés that have been placed at the Web site, thus ensuring that the only people who review the résumés are individuals seeking job applicants.

Here is a list of six Internet sites that offer résumé-writing services. Some of them also offer job-posting and job-hunting services. These sites should help you get started in writing an effective resume.

- **http://www.ResumeEdge.com.** A premier résumé writing and editing service.
- **http://www.careercity.com. or http://www.truecareers.com.** An online board for finding professional, degreed candidates quickly and easily; includes information on interviewing.
- **http://www.sampleresumes.net.** Shows examples of résumés.
- **http://www.free-resume-tips.com.** Lists ten tips for writing an effective résumé.
- **http://www.provenresumes.com.** Provides access to 60 free résumé and job search workshops.
- **http://www.resumes2000.com.** Will prepare a résumé in a hour for a fee.
- **http://www.shaytannas.com.** Has steps for constructing a dynamite résumé and how to master the art of interviewing.

Another recent development is the use of readily available Web sites that can be accessed by job applicants. These sites allow you to become your own personal headhunter, and, in most cases, no fees are associated with going to these sites and searching for jobs. Here are several sites that offer mostly job search and posting, but some also offer career building, résumé writing, and interviewing tips.

- **http://www.bakosgroup.com.** Has assisted over 1+ million job seekers, search 3+ million jobs from 275+ employment search sites. The site offers a free test to determine your Motivational Appraisal of Personal Potential (MAPP). The results reveal your natural motivations, interests and talents for work.
- **http://www.careerbuilder.com.** Reports on more than 400,000 jobs and includes résumé writing, in addition to providing a host of tips regarding how to interview.
- **http://www.careermart.com.** Helps job seekers search jobs and offers free resume posting.

- **http://www.careersite.com.** Provides a national network supporting over 150 newspapers with over 70,000 employers and 2.5+ million job seekers. The Résumé Tune-up section offers tips on résumé writing. The site includes twenty-eight common mistakes in preparing cover letters and shows examples of cover letters.
- **http://www.FlipDog.com.** Collects job postings directly from employers and puts them in one central location. It is a good source for finding where jobs are available in the United States and the number of jobs available; click on a state, then the city, and the industry.
- **http://www.monster.com.** Reports on more than 800,000 jobs, in addition to allowing applicants to post their résumés for employers to view.
- **http://www.4work.com.** Reports on thousands of jobs and is a low-cost online posting service that offers a fast response and pinpoints candidates who are qualified. It boasts more than 300,000+ job seekers.

It is not always easy to find a job online. "The unpleasant truth, according to job seekers, career counselors and even some companies, is that applying for jobs on corporate Web sites is often a complicated and frustrating process." Job seekers often feel their résumé has gone into a black hole, never to return, while automated systems scan their résumé for certain key words and return an automated response. Some job seekers complain that real-life recruiters don't enter the hiring process often enough.[10]

LEARNING OBJECTIVE
Discuss six important points in carrying out a successful job hunt
③

The Successful Job Hunt

If you have written an effective résumé, the next step is to get it into the right hands. One of the easiest ways to accomplish this, if you are about to graduate, is by signing up at the college placement office with prospective employers who will be recruiting on campus. Another way is to contact directly organizations that have job openings and to send them your résumé. If things go your way, you will be interviewed and hired. From a human relations standpoint, however, you need to know several important points.

Silence Can Be Golden

If you already have a job and are looking for another, do not advertise this fact to everyone. Keep quiet about your search, seeking help only from friends or business associates who can provide leads or introductions. If your boss will hit the ceiling or jeopardize your career should he or she find out you are looking for other employment, ask all potential employers to treat your application confidentially.

On the other hand, if this is your first career job, you should go out of your way to advertise it. Interview with all campus recruiters who have job openings similar to your career objectives. Give all your major professors a copy of your résumé for distribution to any employer whom they may meet who is looking for someone with your qualifications.

Don't Answer Every Employment Ad

Many firms place help-wanted ads in newspapers and trade journals. Most identify themselves and describe their job openings; some merely provide a brief explanation of the individual they are seeking and a coded box number to which one can send a résumé. The former ads, which seem to offer those opportunities you are seeking, are worth pursuing; the latter are not. In most cases, blind ads, as these are known, do not result in responses. The organization usually is trying to gauge the labor supply in the field or determine salary levels for certain types of jobs, so you may be wasting your time by applying.

Know How To Be Interviewed

When you get an interview, you are halfway toward your goal of a job offer. Now you want to be sure that you do not flub your chance. The first thing you should do is learn something

INTERVIEWING EFFECTIVELY

One of the most important steps in obtaining the job you want is to impress the interviewer. Often, this individual will interview a dozen people and then recommend three or four for further consideration. If you cannot pass this initial screening, you will not get the job. Read and answer the following questions related to effective interviewing. Answers are provided at the end of the chapter.

T/F 1. Know something about the firm and make the interviewer aware that you have done this background research.

T/F 2. Don't just answer questions; ask some. Interviewers like this feedback because it shows an interest on your part.

T/F 3. If you are asked whether you would be willing to relocate, say no, because this answer indicates your willingness to take a position and stay with it.

T/F 4. If you are unsure of how to dress for the interview, it is better to be too formal than too informal.

T/F 5. It is important that you be on time for the interview, even if the interviewer is running late.

T/F 6. If you are asked to give a starting salary that you desire, give a figure that is about 20 percent higher than the going rate, because you can always negotiate downward.

T/F 7. If you are asked about interviews that you have had with other firms, make it a point to note that you were not very impressed with these other firms but are impressed with the current one.

T/F 8. Be sure to ask detailed questions about the company's benefit and retirement program. This is one way of communicating a genuine interest in the job.

T/F 9. If you smoke or chew gum, do so during the interview, because this indicates a degree of individualism and most interviewers will be impressed by this.

T/F 10. When the interview is over, make it a point to ask the individual when you can expect to hear from the firm.

about the company: What goods or services does it produce? How much did it gross last year? What is its reputation? What qualities is it looking for in applicants? Some of the most common qualities are perseverance, drive, integrity, and good communication skills.[11] If you know about the company, this is likely to impress the interviewer and improve your chances of a job offer. However, do not stop here. Develop some questions that demonstrate your knowledge of your field. Let the interviewer know that you know what you are talking about. Be prepared to go on the offensive.

Also keep in mind that the interviewer is checking to determine whether personal chemistry might exist between you and the organization. "While degrees, experience and skills count, they are only part of the overall picture. It's a straightforward concept: hire the right people and build a better—and more profitable—organization."[12]

Southwest Airlines, a Dallas-based carrier, which earned $5.5 billion in 2002 and employs nearly 34,000 people, spares no effort to find the perfect blend of energy, humor, team spirit and self-confidence. The first step in its hiring process is to take a group of applicants into a room and observe how they interact. Southwest's vice president of people, Beverly Carmichael, might ask a dozen or so participants to tell about a time when their sense of humor helped them or what their personal motto is. Although most responses aren't memorable, they provide clues as to how a person thinks and copes. "It's not necessarily the answer but the way a person answers," she says.[13]

UPS, which has 360,000 employees worldwide, is another company that focuses its entire recruiting, training, and internal-promotion process on attitude. Applicants "undergo at least two levels of behavioral interviews that focus on issues such as motivation, commitment and building working relationships."[14]

How you dress, act, and talk are all important. Keep things on a positive note. If you are asked about your ability to interact well with others, talk about your personality strengths. If you are asked why you are leaving your current job, discuss your desire for increased responsibility and challenge. Do not talk negatively about either yourself or your current employer. Such discussion casts a pall over the interview and can result in a missed job offer.

Interviewers tend to ask typical questions, such as the following:

- **Aside from the information on your résumé, what else have you done that would prepare you for a job with this company?**
- **What are you looking for in an employer?**
- **Why did you apply with us?**
- **Where do you hope to be after ten years with this firm?**
- **What are your long-range objectives?**

If you are prepared with answers for the most likely questions, your interview is more likely to proceed smoothly. Figure 15.5 offers some additional guidelines for handling interviews, especially difficult ones.[15]

During the course of the interview, you will want to learn more about the company. Prepare a list of no more than a dozen premeditated questions that can be grouped into four categories. Take these questions with you to the interview.

1. **Company questions—market share, projected growth, new products.**
2. **Industry questions—growth, change, technology.**
3. **Position questions—responsibilities and duties, travel, compensation.**
4. **Opportunity questions—potential for growth, advancement, promotion.[16]**

There are times when it is more difficult to find a job. During these times, you should "relax and realize that you may not be doing anything wrong in your job search." Don't let rejections wear you down. Go to every interview with a positive attitude and a yearning to work for the company. Also, individuals often do strange things that don't help them get the job, such as failing to attach a résumé to an e-mail or to a cover letter, failing to use correct spelling, failing to address qualifications in the ad, and failing to arrive on time for the interview.[17]

Downplay Salary

How do you answer the question, "What salary do you want?" If possible, sidestep the question by explaining that salary is only one of your considerations and you would prefer to learn more about the job. If you are pushed into an answer, cite a range, such as $30,000–$35,000, rather than a single figure, such as $33,700. If the employer is willing to pay $33,200 for the job, you are in the ballpark with a salary range but too high with a set number. Additionally, because they truly want the job, some individuals will drop their asking price to a lower level, such as $32,700. In this case, such people have given up $500, as the employer seldom is inclined to pay more than is necessary.

If you are just starting out, you do not have to be concerned with knowing how much to request. Most employers have a specific salary range for positions and, if they do not, you can compare starting salaries and job requirements at interviews before deciding which job to take.[18] You can also go on the Internet at **http://www.salary.com** or **http://www.salaryexpert.com** and get information regarding how much employers currently are paying for the job that you are seeking.[19]

A basic rule to follow is to never, ever bring up the subject of salary or benefits. If the interviewer asks if you have any questions, then you can discuss your concerns. It is best to focus on what you can do for the company.[20]

FIGURE 15.5

Acing a Tough Interview

Any job interview can be tense, but in today's tough job market, more and more executives are using a technique called the stress interview. Their goal is not to verify the claims on your résumé—that can be done easily—but to see how you react when you're pressured and to test your professionalism and confidence. Typically, the interviewer sets up the job seeker with softball questions and a friendly manner, then tries to throw her off balance by switching suddenly to much tougher queries. The biggest mistake you can make is to take the probing personally and respond with anger. Instead, phrase your answers in a way that demonstrates positive rather than negative traits, sell yourself to the interviewer, and try to turn the discussion back to the job itself. And take heart: Only top candidates are put through the wringer this way. (The job seeker's words are in screened boxes.)

PROBE FOR WEAKNESS Your résumé does a fine job of pointing out your professional strengths and skills, but I'd like to find out more about you as a person. For example, what would you say is your greatest weakness?

POSITIVE "WEAKNESS" I always give 110% to whatever project I'm working on, so I get very frustrated when other members of the team don't pull their weight. I've been trying very hard lately to lead by example rather than express my frustration openly.

FORMER WEAKNESS When I started in sales, I tended to overbook my appointments. Then I realized I wasn't devoting enough time to each call, giving short shrift to some clients. Since then, I've learned not to schedule more calls than I can handle effectively.

JOB-HISTORY PROBE Going over your résumé, I notice that you've changed jobs several times in the past few years. Why is that?

LAST-JOB PROBE You've been out of work for a long time. Since you clearly didn't leave your last job for a new one, I assume you were let go. Why?

STAGNATION PROBE You've been with XYZ Company in the same position for five years now. Why haven't you been able to move up?

JOB-HISTORY DEFENSE As you can see, my job moves haven't been lateral; they've all led to positions of greater responsibility. Now that I've gained the experience, I'm looking to settle down with a company that will keep me challenged—like this one.

LAST-JOB DEFENSE Like so many places these days, my company was looking to cut payroll costs and wound up eliminating hundreds of jobs last year. I volunteered for the buyout program because I felt I'd reached the limit of what I could do there anyway.

STAGNATION DEFENSE The new positions that have opened up have gone to employees who have a lot more seniority than I do. That's why I'm looking for a company that offers a real opportunity to move up. What can you tell me about the possibilities for advancement here?

JOB-HISTORY FOLLOW-UP With your history of job-hopping, I'm not sure that you'd be content to stay in one place for long. Would you say you're the kind of person who gets bored easily?

LAST-JOB FOLLOW-UP You've been looking for a new position for several months now, apparently without any luck. What seems to be the problem?

STAGNATION FOLLOW-UP Being in the same job at the same company for such a long time can make you stale. How will you cope with the challenge of a new job in a new organization?

CLOSING JOB-HISTORY DEFENSE Not at all. But I do enjoy being challenged. In fact, what's been most exciting in my previous positions has been finding new ways to keep a product fresh in our customers' eyes. Am I right in thinking that's a crucial part of the job here?

CLOSING LAST-JOB DEFENSE I'm not looking for just another paycheck. My severance was generous enough to allow me to take the time to find a company that's really right for me, where I can make a real contribution. Can you tell me more about precisely what this job entails?

CLOSING STAGNATION DEFENSE It's precisely because I don't want to get stale that I'm looking for new opportunities. From what I understand, your company offers just that. Can you tell me more about the kind of challenges I'd face in this job?

Source: Stephen M. Pollan and Mark Levine, Lifescripts, ©1996. John Wiley & Sons, Inc. This material is used by permission of John Wiley & Sons, Inc.

Strive for Originality

Most organizations will be interviewing more than one person for each job opening. If you are a typical candidate, you will do all the usual things: write an interesting résumé, dress well, and act properly. However, if possible, try to do something different also. Look for a way to distinguish yourself from the others. Although this requires some degree of creativity, it does not have to be unique. Your level of confidence and your attitude will show in the way you shake hands, greet the interviewer, walk, talk, and sit. Your behavior should indicate you are eager and ready to help the company meet its goals and objectives. Never display a negative attitude or talk negatively about a previous employer or boss.

Do Not Lose Hope

As you delve further into your job search, you may discover yourself sending out thirty résumés and receiving fifteen responses, of which only ten or fewer potential employers express any interest. You may also find that you interview with seven of these firms and only two make you an offer, neither of which you feel is truly competitive. As a result, you may decide to restart the process and send out résumés to new organizations. The important thing to remember is not to despair. Keep a positive attitude. You will eventually find something that will satisfy you.

To find a job, you must sell your capabilities, and tired or unenthusiastic salespeople do not make sales. You cannot let the stress of the job hunt lead you to undervalue your potential or

in action

HUMAN RELATIONS IN ACTION

Asking the Appropriate Questions

No matter how much you may want a particular job, some important questions should be asked before you agree to accept the position. In asking these questions, remember that you must be direct while also being friendly. Six of the most important of these questions are:

1. *What happened to the last person to hold this job?* If the person was promoted, ask why. Now you have an idea of what the firm is looking for from the person who holds this job. If the person was fired, find out why. This tells you what *not* to do.

2. *May I talk to someone who is doing the same basic type of job that I'll be doing?* This will help you to find out what is good and bad about the department. No one knows better than the personnel, and they very often are willing to share this information with new people.

3. *How, and by whom, will my performance be measured?* Find out what the organization expects from you and how they will determine whether you are doing a good job. To head off confusion later, keep the criteria as objective and measurable as possible.

4. *What is the salary range for this job, and what other compensation do you offer?* This may appear too direct, but most firms like to talk about their financial package. If you are moving from another job, this question is particularly important

because you should not move for less than a 20 percent salary increase, unless you are very eager to join the company. Additionally, you should find out about any bonuses, perks such as a company car or club membership, vacations, health insurance, pension, and profit-sharing plans. Obtain all the financial data so that you know exactly what you will be getting in terms of remuneration.

5. *If relocation is involved, how much will the company help?* If you are commuting across town, the firm will not give you any assistance. However, if you must relocate, this will take time and money. In many major cities, you will end up paying a fee to secure an apartment. If you have to sell your house and buy another, a broker's commission on the sale and financial points on the new loan will be incurred, as will (in all likelihood) a higher rate of interest. If the firm is unwilling to absorb any of these expenses, you must add them into the cost of taking the job. Often, a move to another location is financially unwise unless the firm agrees to help with costs.

6. *Would you mind putting all of this in writing?* It never hurts to ask for the agreement in writing. This is particularly true if your employment arrangement contains anything other than standard items, such as salary, benefits, and vacation time. In this way, you do not have to worry about some manager later saying, "We never agreed to that. We don't pay those expenses for anyone." You will have the agreement in writing.

restrict your options. There is no logical reason to despair. You know the kind of work you are capable of doing. The big catch is meeting the person who needs someone like you to do a job. Logic says that this will happen sooner or later. When that job does arrive, be sure to ask the right questions before accepting it. The Human Relations in Action box provides some of these questions.

Getting Ahead

After you have secured a job, human relations knowledge can continue to benefit you, by assisting you in managing your career effectively, finding a mentor, and organizing your office properly.[21]

Manage Your Career Effectively

LEARNING OBJECTIVE ④ *Describe some of the major guidelines that you should follow in managing your career effectively*

After you have secured employment, your challenge becomes one of managing your career effectively. The most successful people do not allow their career paths to develop randomly.[22] They take steps to ensure that things go their way and, when they do not, these people know how to adjust their career course. Some useful management guidelines include the following:

1. **Don't wait for things to happen; manage your own career.**
2. **You will make four to six career moves. Make the most of them.**
3. **Mobility and maneuvering produce greater returns than does misguided loyalty. Your first loyalty should be to yourself.**
4. **Outside contacts are important to a career. These people can be of help to you, so build a good outside network of friends and associates.**
5. **Work in-line jobs, not staff jobs. The more important your contribution to the firm, the more highly prized you will be.**
6. **Don't be lured by long-run rewards that will not materialize for twenty years. Consider the shorter run.**
7. **Always be prepared to leave so that, if things go badly in the organization, you will have a plan of action.**
8. **As millions of companies are operating in the economy, do not limit yourself to just the largest industrials.**
9. **After your employment interview, do not forget to send a thank you note.**
10. **Whom you know will always be more important than what you know. Effective career planning is often a matter of knowing the right people.**

Additional major steps toward getting ahead are discussed next.

Know Your Job

LEARNING OBJECTIVE ⑤ *Explain the major steps for getting ahead in your job*

In every job, a basic set of skills must be mastered. For engineers, these skills are technical in nature; for human resources specialists, they are behavioral in content; for managers, they are a combination of technical and behavioral. Discover which skills are most important to your job and learn and master them as quickly as possible. A good example is found in the case of individuals whose careers require them to have some international experience. Research shows that a working knowledge of a second language can be particularly helpful. The Cultural Diversity in Action box explains why.

Know How You Will Be Judged

Most people are judged on two types of criteria: formal and informal. Formal criteria tend to be measurable and often take such forms as volume of work output or productivity, sales

CULTURAL DIVERSITY IN ACTION

A Matter of Bilingualism

Many people today are finding that if their job requires them to work overseas or with international clients, knowledge of a second language can be very helpful. Of course, English will continue to be the primary language of international business. However, training in the host country's language can be particularly useful, and those who are willing to learn another language often find that their career opportunities improve.

One of the most popular languages is Spanish. A large percentage of the world's population speaks this language, including most people in Latin America. A second popular language is French, which is widely spoken in Europe as well as in certain areas of Africa and Asia. Learning both these languages is fairly easy for Americans, as the pronunciation and rules of grammar are not as "foreign" as are those of Russian and Chinese.

Students in other countries often are taught a second language at both the high school and college levels, with English continuing to be the most popular. In China, for example, more people speak English than any other language, because there are so many variations of Chinese that people from one part of China are unable to understand those from another part. Similarly, it may be difficult initially for people from the midwestern United States to understand people from Scotland (who also speak English) because of their pronunciation, but this problem will be overcome once Americans become attuned to the accent.

Americans must become bilingual so that they can communicate with others around the world and will not have to rely on other nationals to speak English. In business operations, for example, many international clients like doing business with individuals who speak their language, even if the person does not demonstrate fluency in this language: Specifically, businesspeople often feel that fewer misunderstandings ensue if the participants in a professional pursuit all speak the same language, and they feel most comfortable using their native tongue. Hence, those Americans who have learned a second language are at a distinct advantage when it comes to career opportunities because, during the next decade, more and more firms will be increasing their international operations. Those who can communicate fluently in the language of the country where the firm does business will have an advantage over other job applicants.

Another reason that companies prefer individuals who can speak the language local to their international enterprises is that it helps the firm to monitor the competition. Multinational firms often locate near their major competitors, because new developments by these firms are most likely to be reported in local newspapers and other sources. For the cost of such a publication, it often is possible to learn more about what a competitor is doing than one could ever find out if the investigation were conducted from headquarters. For this reason, many foreign multinational organizations employ personnel who read and speak English fluently and can peruse the Wall Street Journal, The New York Times, *and American industry publications on a daily basis and compile folders on the strategies of their U.S. competitors.*

Of course, not every job applicant is going to be bilingual. However, those who are not can always learn a second language after they are hired. The important thing to remember is that as multinationalism increases, bilingualism is going to become a more important asset for those who are seeking increased career opportunities.

increases, or profit. Those who do well in these areas receive greater raises or faster promotions than those who do not.[23] Your performance on formal criteria is measured by some document or evaluation instrument. If you are determined to win the career promotion game, you must concentrate on doing well on these formal criteria and let other things go.

On the other hand, if you find that formal criteria include the earlier-stated objectives as well as such qualitative criteria as personality, interpersonal skills, leadership styles, and work attitudes, you must broaden your attention and address these criteria as well. In some firms, you may find that most people do well in pursuing the quantitative objectives and that it is the qualitative objectives that separate the most promotable employees from the others. In this case, concentrate most of your attention on qualitative criteria, as this is where your career progress in that firm will be decided. Informal criteria are more difficult to describe, because your boss often determines them. Typical examples include the way you dress, whether you seem interested in your job, and whether you fit in as a member of the work group. The best way to meet these challenges is to watch successful members of your department or group and emulate how they function.

Keep a Hero File

The formal evaluation system is used by the organization to reward you for your contributions. However, at some point during your career, you may decide to move to another enterprise. How will you be able to show your new prospective employer how good you are?

- **One way, of course, is by pointing to your past promotions and current salary.**
- **A second way is by having your boss write a letter of recommendation for you (assuming he or she would comply).**
- **A third way, and best of all, is to keep a hero file that contains all your accomplishments.**

Typical examples include memos congratulating you on your work, awards given to you by the organization, and samples of your work (a major report you wrote, an advertisement you designed, a financial analysis you conducted) that show the quality of your performance. Remember, modesty has its place, but sometimes it pays to blow your own horn!

Develop Alliances

Very few loners succeed in modern organizations. You must be able to get along with others if you are going to advance. This requires the development of alliances. In developing alliances, begin with your subordinates by creating an effective work relationship with them. This will show others that you are qualified in your job and will begin to open doors at the management level. Next you should begin developing peer group relationships with others who occupy the same level in the hierarchy as do you. Finally, you should seek ways of developing work relationships with higher-level managers.

If you violate this "from the bottom up" approach, you may find it very difficult to develop meaningful alliances. Your peers will regard you as an apple polisher or someone who is trying to succeed at their expense; when possible, they will look for ways to undercut your performance and your reputation. Your subordinates will look on you as someone who is more interested in his or her own career than in helping them to get things done. They will retaliate by giving you minimum performance and helping create a reputation for you as someone who is not very effective in managing work teams. Because both of these groups can be just as harmful to you as they can be helpful, it is best to win their support and create an alliance with them as soon as possible. Learn to be a team player.

"Networked people are smarter people. The reason they get smarter is that they talk to each other, sharing the benefits of past experience." The onset of the Internet provided workers with the tool to increase their knowledge and expertise in every area of operations. This has resulted in companies treating employees with more respect and has impacted the age-old adversarial relationship that has existed between labor and management. The bottom line is that corporate behavior is beginning to change from control to being a partner.[24]

Show That You Are a Star

Strive to prove that you are a star on the rise. You can do this by turning in a top-notch performance. When your work is outstanding, word gets around, and people begin to notice you.

A second way of proving that you're star material is by realizing the truth in the cliché that great performance is 99 percent perspiration and 1 percent inspiration. In modern organizations, most people succeed because of hard work; it is still the key to great performance.

A third way is by making yourself a crucial part of the work team. The more your boss relies on you, the greater are your chances for success. As your supervisor goes up the chain of command, he or she is likely to take you along. Of course, you may find that your boss is at a dead end. A classic example of the Peter Principle, he has risen to his level of incompetence. In this case, get out: Find another position in the organization or look elsewhere. Your mobility is limited. How do you know when your boss is no longer a fast-track manager? Simply compare the average time between promotions for other managers and for your boss. Typically, managers are promoted every three to five years. If your boss has been in the same position for seven years, he or she is probably not going anywhere. If you remain in the department, the same will be true for you.

A fourth way of demonstrating that your star is rising is by getting continuous feedback on how well you are doing. Stay alert to comments from your boss on what you are doing well and the areas in which you need improvement. Treat this feedback as a source for personal action. Sure, it may hurt when the individual tells you, "Your report was incomplete," or "Jones tells me that you were late for the meeting yesterday afternoon," or "I want you to start paying closer attention to the cost data I'm sending you; your work group's efficiency is falling down." However, you can use this feedback to improve your performance. Accept it in a positive light and use it to help correct your shortcomings.

A fifth way is by standing out from the crowd. How do you distinguish yourself from others? What is your brand? This is what marketers try to accomplish in every advertisement—to sell products. You must take the initiative to sell your skills, talents, and accomplishments. Your leaders—bosses—are too busy promoting their own career to focus on your career. How do you make a difference and set yourself apart from the average employee? Do something that sets you apart. Take an assignment that provides you the opportunity to present your findings to the board of directors. Agree to serve on a committee that has representatives from all management levels and go out of your way to impress them. Volunteer for extra assignments that you feel you are qualified to handle and no one else wants. Gain exposure by giving talks to outside groups and writing articles in magazines and journals, thus establishing yourself as an expert in a management-related area.[25] As you try to separate yourself from the crowd, remember that your strategy has its risks. If you fail, your career may be jeopardized, so be somewhat conservative and do not bite off more than you can comfortably chew.

Train Your Replacement

If you are a rising star, your promotion will leave a void unless you have a replacement. In some cases, your promotion may be delayed until there is someone to take your place. You can speed up your career progress by training your replacement early. If you are being promoted to another department or unit, your boss will be reluctant to let you go because he or she will be left without adequate assistance—hence, the need for a replacement.

Periodically Reassess Your Career

As you begin to learn your job and show those around you that you are capable of higher-level tasks, continually reassess your career. Sometimes, opportunities for you to be promoted in your current organization are minimal. If your boss is five years younger than you are and it appears that he or she, in all likelihood, is content with the organization, you are not going to be promoted over him or her. You are going to have either to go around him or her by finding a job elsewhere in the organization or to seek employment in another enterprise.[26]

Career reassessment can help you to decide exactly what you should do. Set some objectives for yourself, and, if you do not attain them, consider moving. The following are examples of typical objectives:

- If I do not receive two promotions in the first five years, I will leave.
- If I do not receive an average raise of 10 percent each year for the first three years, I will leave.
- If I am not in a middle-management position, with a group or unit of at least seven subordinates within five years, I will seek employment elsewhere.
- If I feel that I am not going to be in top management by the time I am age forty-five, I will leave.

None of these examples is meant to serve as a definitive guideline.[27] However, all are representative of the types of goals high-achieving people set for themselves in reassessing their careers.

It also is helpful to examine where you are in your career and what lies ahead. For example, many people start out on a very fast track but after receiving a series of promotions, their careers plateau. Can they get back on a fast track, or is it time to move on? This requires careful analysis of where the company is heading and what role you will play. Often the best initial strategy is to sit down with your boss and discuss what your future looks like. If you like the scenario that is presented, you can stay. Otherwise, start looking around to learn what other opportunities are available either within the organization or in another firm. Perhaps your career field is no longer a growing one. Table 15.1 provides a list of some of the occupations that are anticipated to be most in demand between now and 2008. Over the 2000–2010 period, total employment is projected to increase by 22.2 million jobs. By 2010, women are projected to account for 48 percent of the total labor force.

Of all the major occupational groups, *professional and related occupations* are projected to increase the fastest (26 percent) and add the largest number of jobs (7 million) between 2000 and 2010. Examples of occupations are: computer software engineers; database administrators; desktop publishers; medical records and health information technicians; and special education, preschool, and elementary teachers. Among health care practitioners, registered nurses should account for more than a third of all new jobs in this category.[28]

One final note: If you do decide to leave for new employment, do so at your convenience and on a good note. Furthermore, regardless of why you leave, stay on good terms with

TABLE 15.1	New Jobs for the New Economy: The Ten Fastest-Growing Occupations (In Thousands of Jobs)			
	Employment		Change	
Occupation	1998	2008	Number	Percentage
Computer engineers	299	622	323	108
Computer support specialists	429	869	439	102
Systems analysts	617	1,194	577	94
Database administrators	87	155	67	77
Desktop-publishing specialists	26	44	19	73
Paralegals and legal assistants	136	220	84	62
Personal care and home health aides	746	1,179	433	58
Medical assistants	252	398	146	58
Social and human services assistants	268	410	141	53
Physician's assistants	66	98	32	48

Source: U.S. Bureau of Labor Statistics, 2000.

TABLE 15.2	Ten Rules of Time Management for Effective Leaders

1. Carry a to-do list with you; jot down notes on those things you have to do and cross out those that you have finished.
2. When reading memos, mail, or short reports, do so standing up. You read faster in this position.
3. As you read memos and letters that call for a reply, answer each as you go along. Otherwise you will have to read each again later when you get around to formulating a response.
4. Concentrate your efforts on one thing at a time.
5. Give your primary attention to those tasks that are most important and work at delegating minor jobs to your subordinates.
6. If you have an appointment to visit someone, bring work with you so that if you are forced to wait, you can put the time to good use.
7. When you finish a particularly important or difficult task, give yourself time off as a special reward.
8. Try not to work on weekends.
9. Examine your work habits for ways of streamlining your current procedures and saving time.
10. If you do not get all you wanted accomplished in a given day, tell yourself you will get to it the next day. Do not feel guilty over any failure to meet your daily work plan. As long as you are doing your best, tell yourself that this is good enough.

everyone. Bosses tend to remember your last days on the job more vividly than they do most other days. If you need them to say something about you in the future, you want them to give positive and complimentary responses.

Manage Your Time Well

Successful people know how to manage their time. They are not afraid to delegate work to their subordinates while they focus their attention on matters that require their personal attention. They also prioritize their activities so that the most important jobs get highest priority, and they use time management principles, such as those in Table 15.2, to help them lead effectively.[29]

Manage Your Stress Effectively

Everyone in an organization is under stress, and research shows that stress can help people work more efficiently. However, too much stress can result in poor judgment, low performance, and even burnout.[30] Burnout is a particular problem for individuals with *Type A personalities,* characterized by a desire to get more and more done in less and less time. This is in contrast to *Type B personalities,* who are evenly paced and do not constantly feel overly pressed by time constraints. Are you a Type A person? Take the Time Out quiz to find out.

In dealing with stress, some of the most effective steps include:

1. Staying alert for signs of stress.
2. Maintaining a positive mental attitude at all times.
3. Making time in your daily work schedule to put everything aside and just relax for ten to fifteen minutes.
4. Being prepared to make changes in your work routines or career if stress becomes too great.

ARE YOU A TYPE A OR TYPE B PERSON?

Here are ten combinations of statements related to your work and personal habits. In each case, read the A and B statements and decide which is most descriptive of you. If A is totally descriptive of you and B is not at all descriptive, give 10 points to A and none to B. If both

statements are descriptive of you, divide the 10 points between A and B based on their degree of descriptive accuracy. If B is totally descriptive of you and A is not at all descriptive, give 10 points to B and none to A. An interpretation of your score is provided at the end of the chapter.

Points

1. _____ A Even when it is not necessary I find myself rushing to get things done.
   _____ B I seldom rush to get things done, even if I am running late.

2. _____ A I often get upset or angry with people, even if I do not show it.
   _____ B I seldom get angry with people if there is no real reason for it.

3. _____ A When I play a game or compete in an event, winning is my primary objective.
   _____ B When I play a game or compete in an event, my greatest enjoyment comes from the social interaction with others.

4. _____ A I am a tense, anxious person, but I try to cover this up by smiling a lot and trying to be social.
   _____ B I am basically a relaxed, easygoing individual; I seldom get tense or uptight.

5. _____ A Even when I am sitting down watching TV, I am usually moving about, checking my nails, tapping my foot, or carrying out some similar physical activity.
   _____ B When I sit down to watch TV, I get totally involved in the program and seldom move about or change position.

6. _____ A I set high goals for myself and become angry if I fail to attain them.
   _____ B I set reasonable goals for myself and, if I fail, I try not to let this get me down.

7. _____ A I write down how I intend to spend my day, and I rigidly stick to this schedule.
   _____ B I note objectives that I want to attain during the day but try to remain flexible; if something is not finished today, I will get to it tomorrow morning.

8. _____ A I hate to wait for people; it makes me edgy and nervous.
   _____ B If I have to wait for others, I try to spend the time doing something relaxing such as reading, talking to others, or quietly walking around.

9. _____ A Meals interrupt my schedule, and I often find myself doing work while I am eating.
   _____ B I enjoy meals and eat them slowly and in a relaxed fashion; if there is any work to do, it can wait until I am finished eating.

10. _____ A At the end of the day, I often find myself extremely tired and run down.
    _____ B I like to get things done but not at the cost of physical exhaustion.

Find a Mentor

Another important aspect of getting ahead is to find a mentor. A **mentor** is a person who coaches, counsels, teaches, or sponsors others. Although it is possible to succeed in a large organization without having a mentor, it is easier to succeed if you have one. In fact, such firms as AT&T, Bell Labs, Johnson & Johnson, NCR Corporation, and Merrill Lynch have all created formal mentoring programs.

What, in particular, makes a mentor so useful? The primary answer is that individual's willingness to share knowledge and understanding with younger managers, helping them to develop

A **mentor**
is a coach, counselor, and sponsor of others.

into effective leaders. The mentoring process is particularly important to individuals between the ages of twenty-five and forty. These people are still in the learning and growing period of their career.[31]

Mentors and Female Executives

Hennig and Jardim, writing about the managerial woman, have reported that mentors are particularly important to the success of female executives.[32] Recent research continues to support these findings. Statistically speaking, women are more likely to have mentors than are their male counterparts and tend to have more of them. For example, Reich has found that women place a higher value on the mentoring process than do men. Some of his other findings include the following:

1. More female than male protégés consider political aid, such as career guidance and counseling on company politics to be important.
2. A higher percentage of women feel that they gained greater self-confidence through the mentor relationship and that it enhanced their awareness of their strengths.
3. More women than men report that mentors stimulate their thinking, give them feedback about their weaknesses, and allow them to set their own job goals.
4. Women assign higher values than men to helping young people improve their managerial skills.[33]

Trends

Today, the trend toward mentoring continues with approximately 75 percent of all executives younger than forty having a mentor. As these people continue their climb up the career ladder, they eventually lose their need for a mentor but begin taking on protégés of their own. Hence, mentoring begets mentoring.

To a large degree, this process is inevitable. Given today's complex and rapid-paced environment, increased demands are being put on managers. One of the best ways to meet these demands is by seeking out individuals from whose experience one can learn. Of course, you can succeed in any organization without a mentor, but it will help if you have one (or more) who can provide you with assistance and advice along the way. A mentor cannot guarantee that you will succeed, but he or she can give you that extra push that will help you move out from the pack.

Organize Your Office Properly

Another important success variable is the way that you organize your office. If you have an office, you can employ psychological principles that will help you to arrange it most effectively. The first rule is that, no matter how small it is, make your office look spacious and less crowded by arranging the furniture appropriately. The desk should be given initial priority. If the office is small, keep the desk fairly small or it will crowd the rest of the room. Conversely, if the office is spacious, get a fairly large desk that takes up more room. If at all possible, have a wooden desk or one that looks like wood. In contrast to metal desks, wood connotes power and authority and will help to increase your status. Your own physical dimensions will dictate the size of the desk chair. If you are a tall or large person, a small chair will make you look like an ogre. If you are a short or slender person, a large chair will dwarf your appearance. Choose a chair proportional to your size and, if possible, one that has a back that comes up to the back of your head.

If you have your choice of chairs, get two that match your desk chair. Some of the most acceptable colors for these chairs are natural leather, rich brown, or deep maroon. Black, the most commonly manufactured color is not as effective, because it lacks the richer look of these other colors.

Visitors' chairs should be placed in front of your desk. Do not put any of them on the side of your desk because this reduces your power and authority in relation to other people.

If space allows, you can place a couch, a coffee table, or easy chairs in your office such that the room is divided in two. The area with the desk is for day-to-day business, whereas the part with the couch or easy chairs is for small-group work or conferences. Finally, for maximum psychological results, you must try to set up the office so that it draws attention to you. You must "frame" yourself so that when people enter your office, they are directed toward you, the central person there. This can be accomplished in one of two ways: by placing your desk in front of a window or by placing a picture on the wall directly behind your chair. In either case, the desk should be positioned symmetrically in front of the window or picture. Otherwise, visitors will feel that your desk is off center or the picture is askew.

A final test of your office's effectiveness is to take a picture of it and take pictures of several friends' offices who are in the same line of work. Give these pictures to other managers (outside your organization) and ask them to rate the importance of the office holder based on the office arrangement. This will give you a good idea of how your office compares.

Consider Career Switching

Many people switch careers.[34] In most cases, this occurs because the individual has not been as successful as he or she would like and is looking for better opportunities. Common examples are:

1. **People who have been passed over for a promotion.**
2. **Those who believe that their organization is falling behind the competition and who want to work for an industry leader.**
3. **Individuals who are being moved onto a career track that will not get them to their long-range goals.**

Most people who switch careers do so because there is no alternative. A sales analyst who has been laid off because of cutbacks in the industry—especially during times of economy slowdown—may conclude that the only way to salvage a career is to change jobs and become a salesperson. A stockbroker who is laid off may look for a job in a bank or a real estate firm. Notice in both of these illustrations that the individual is seeking new employment in a related field. This is the easiest, and oftentimes wisest, approach, because the person is entering an arena of which he or she has some knowledge or indirect experience. Businesspeople who decide to change careers often take jobs in business colleges, teaching subjects that they know firsthand.

A second common career switch is to go into business for oneself. Becoming self-employed has occurred with increasing frequency in recent years as middle- and upper-level managers have concluded that it is more profitable to break away from their large firms and set up their own operations. Many of these managers have been carrying out all the important functions needed to run a competitive company, so breaking away to start a new venture is not a high-risk decision. Similarly, many salespeople have found that by leaving their firms, they are able to take some of their customers with them and build successful businesses from this initial base.

A third common career switch is to move to a job in an unrelated field. This can be a risky decision but, for many people, it is the only available choice. A mechanic who dislikes his work may be willing to try a job as a salesperson for an insurance company. A social worker who dislikes the bureaucracy may be willing to start anew as a bank teller. Every year, millions of people begin new careers.

The important point to remember about career switching is that it typically requires additional training and education. This is particularly true when one is changing to an unrelated field. Not only is it necessary to learn new procedures and policies but many jobs require the individual to know how to operate machinery and to learn how to interact effectively with customers and clients. As hiring practices change, just remember that after periods of economy slowdown and layoffs, for example, after 9/11, companies try to upgrade their work-forces by being very selective and bringing on better people. They want the A-players, people who can add value to an organization. "You have to be ready to work 20% longer and 20% harder," says Tom Johnson, founding partner of executive-search firm, WorldBridge Partners in Cleveland.[35]

summary

① LEARNING OBJECTIVE
Identify key questions that should be asked in carrying out a self-evaluation

Our overriding objective in this chapter has been to illustrate how human relations concepts can be of value to you personally. Human relations play a big role in choosing a career and succeeding in it. Human relations concepts are employed in evaluating one's self accurately and in developing a plan for finding a job. A series of questions you should ask yourself include: What do you do best, what do you like and dislike doing, do you like to work with others or alone, do you know your talents and abilities, how hard are you willing to work, what are your work habits, and how will you begin your employment search, just to list a few.

An understanding of your basic skills will help direct your educational and career choices. It is important not to underrate your abilities or you will be selling yourself short. Once the self-evaluation is completed, prepare an overall plan of action that focuses on jobs that are available, your career choices, preparing an effective résumé, and ways to ensure a successful job interview.

② LEARNING OBJECTIVE
Write an effective résumé

After conducting a self-evaluation, the next step is finding a job. This requires writing a résumé that attracts attention and conducting yourself properly during the job hunt. A *résumé* is a summary of your qualifications including skills, education, work experience, and training. It is best to make the résumé one page long, definitely no more than two pages, and gear it to the company to which you are applying.

Guidelines for drafting your résumé include: grouping your information into personal data, employment objective, education, work experience, and special interests. Start the résumé with your name, address, and telephone number. Then move to a summary of qualifications or employment objectives and a list of skills followed by your education and/or work experience—listing the most recent degrees and jobs first. List them in reverse order. Make your résumé easy to read and have it paint a positive impression of you. Pictures, if sent, should be clipped to the résumé and not printed on the résumé. References are optional, usually printed on a separate sheet.

Three types of résumés are used. The first is a chronological résumé, which presents information in descending order. The second is the functional résumé, which focuses on skills, aptitudes, and qualities that can be applied, in a number of situations. The third type is a combination résumé, which uses parts of the first two types.

Your résumé should grab the attention of the interviewer. By personalizing your résumé, you set yourself apart from other applicants. Résumés fail to get attention because of the lack of clear objectives, errors, failing to focus on the job description, failing to use proper résumé form, and cramming too much extraneous information into the résumé.

The Internet is a useful tool for learning how to write an effective résumé and conducting a successful interview, searching for available jobs, and applying for them. Internet sites are not always secure and may be hard to use.

(3) LEARNING OBJECTIVE
Discuss six important points in carrying out a successful job hunt

A series of six steps designed to improve your chances of a successful job hunt are outlined. These steps include: Keep quiet about your search, don't answer every employment ad, know how to be interviewed, downplay salary, strive for originality, and don't lose hope. In pursuing another job, you don't want to lose your present job, so be careful about whom you tell and which ad you answer. Before going on an interview learn something about the company, which should impress the interviewer. You may have the degrees and skills, but you also need to be the right fit for the company. Dress properly and stay positive, and don't ask about salary until the interviewer brings it up. Try to distinguish yourself from others by displaying a level of confidence and a "can-do" attitude. But most of all, don't lose hope. When employment times are tough, you may receive several rejections before the right job comes along. Stay focused, don't give up, and approach each interview with a positive attitude.

(4) LEARNING OBJECTIVE
Describe some of the major guidelines that you should follow in managing your career effectively

Successful people manage their careers; they don't wait for things to happen. They take the risk and make career changes as needed. Mobility and maneuvering produce greater returns than does misguided loyalty, but be loyal to yourself. Build an outside network of contacts through associations and friends. Your contributions are more important in in-line positions than in staff positions. Don't be lured by long-term rewards; consider shorter-run rewards. Always be prepared to leave the company; that way you won't be surprised in tough times when layoffs occur. Don't limit yourself to just the largest industrials. After an interview, always send a thank you note. And remember that whom you know is more important than what you know.

(5) LEARNING OBJECTIVE
Explain the major steps for getting ahead in your job

How well you get ahead in your job will be determined in part by how well you know your job, manage your time, manage your stress, use mentors, organize your office properly, and switch careers. You will be judged not only by your performance but also by the way you dress and how you conduct yourself in the workplace. These are the formal and informal criteria on which you are judged by your boss and co-workers.

You should keep a file of your accomplishments, promotions, and letters of recommendation. These are helpful in seeking promotions or in finding a new job. Remember, modesty has its place, but sometimes it pays to blow your own horn.

You must be able to get along with others if you are going to advance, which requires the development of alliances, teams, and networks. Start with your subordinates; then move to group relationships and on to higher-level managers. Networked people are smarter people.

Show that you are a star by turning in a top-notch performance, work hard, make yourself a crucial part of the work team, seek continuous feedback, and distinguish yourself from the others. If you want to be promoted, train your replacement. Continually reassess your career. After examining where you are in your career and what lies ahead, set objectives for yourself. Manage your time effectively by not being afraid to delegate. Learn to prioritize activities. Stress must be managed. Learn to deal with stress by staying alert to the signs of stress and maintaining a positive mental attitude at all times. Make time in your daily work schedule to put everything aside and just relax for ten to fifteen minutes. Be flexible and ready to make changes as needed.

Mentors can help you get ahead. They coach, counsel, teach, and sponsor others. Mentors can help younger managers develop into effective leaders. Today the majority of managers use mentors to get ahead.

Another important success variable is the way you organize your office. Arrange it to appear spacious and not cluttered. The furniture should fit the size of the room. Place visitor's chairs in front of the desk to improve your power and authority position. The arrangement must draw attention to you. Place the desk in front of a window or of a picture placed on the wall.

Consider switching careers to improve your success. Most people who switch careers do so because there is no alternative—in times of layoffs and industry cutbacks. Others take the risk and enter an unrelated field, which can prove to be rewarding, whereas others find it rewarding to start their own business. In switching jobs, businesses want the A-players who can add value to an organization.

KEY TERMS IN THE CHAPTER

Résumé   Mentor

REVIEW AND STUDY QUESTIONS

1. What types of questions should a person ask when conducting a career-related self-evaluation? List several questions.

2. Why should you understand your basic skills? Explain.

3. What is the purpose of developing an overall plan of action? Identify several important items that should be included in the plan.

4. What are seven important guidelines you should apply in drafting your résumé? Identify and briefly describe each.

5. How do the three types of résumés differ? Describe each.

6. Explain how you can set your résumé apart from other résumés and make it an attention-getting résumé.

7. How can the Internet be used in your job hunt?

8. In conducting a successful job hunt, what are six things the applicant should know? Identify and describe each.

9. A friend is preparing a résumé and she would like to be as effective as possible. What are some suggestions you would offer her? Be complete in your recommendations.

10. What are some important points to remember in conducting a successful job hunt? Discuss each one.

11. What are seven major steps you should follow in managing your career effectively? Be specific in your descriptions.

12. What are six steps in getting ahead in your job? Explain each one and tell why it is important.

13. Periodically reassessing your career requires setting career objectives. What are some examples of typical objectives?

14. What are two important strategies for managing your time more effectively? Describe them.

15. What are several steps for dealing with stress?

16. What is a mentor? Of what value are mentors? Will their use increase or decline during the next decade?

17. Your best friend has just been hired by a large corporation and wants to make a good impression. What would you tell this person regarding how to organize his or her office? Be complete in your answer.

18. Why do people switch careers?

VISIT THE WEB

Get a Job

In this chapter, you learned some useful ideas regarding how to write an effective résumé and successfully do a job hunt, but where are the job opportunities today? Find out by visiting **http://www.FlipDog.com.** It provides a wealth of information regarding available job opportunities. Select several states and cities where you might like to work. Then select the industries in which you are interested and finally learn which companies have available jobs. Follow the instructions in the site. Good Luck!

1. List the states and cities where you might like to work. Which companies have available jobs for you?

2. What did you find to be the most useful in this Web site?

3. Using the information from the Web site and your textbook, prepare a list of things to do before applying for your next job.

What Do I Need to Know to Find a Job?

It takes more than a well-prepared résumé to get a job. You need to know what interviewers are looking for and how to address the factors that will make your interview stand above the rest. These factors often change, as the economy changes; and it is wise to check out these changes before applying for a job. Visit the Web site: **http://www.careerjournal.com** and learn what the experts are saying about finding a job.

1. Explore the Web site, particularly the articles.

2. Make a list of things that are important to finding a job in today's job market.

3. What did you learn that surprised you?

How Do Your Interviewing Skills Measure Up?

How do your interviewing skills measure up? Find out by working through six exercises listed in the Web site: **http://www.thomasmore.edu** Click on "Search Our Site." Under "Advanced Search" type in "job interview quiz" and click on "Search." Complete the six exercises by following the directions given on the site.

1. What did you learn about interviewing?

2. Which skills do you need to improve?

3. What will you do differently the next time you go on an interview?

TIME OUT ANSWERS

Interviewing Effectively

1. True. This often is regarded as a positive sign that you are interested in the job.

2. True. This indicates a genuine interest in the job.

3. False. This may result in your being rejected. Many firms want to relocate their new people, so you should be flexible on this point.

4. True. It is better to overdress than to underdress.

5. True. Especially for a first meeting, promptness is imperative.

6. False. In most cases, the company will pay you a competitive rate regardless of who you are. If you ask for too high a starting salary, this may result in your being dropped from further consideration.

7. False. Never say anything bad about the other firms, because this reflects poorly on you. Simply point out that you have interviewed with these other companies and let it go at that.

8. False. Most interviewers are unimpressed by interest in the benefit and retirement program. After all, you are not going to be retiring for years, so why spend much time discussing these matters now?

9. False. This will indicate that you lack social graces and is likely to count against you.

10. True. You have a right to know and should not hesitate to ask.

Are You a Type A or Type B Person?

Add up your total points for the A statements and for the B statements.
If your total for A is:
80–100   You exhibit strong Type A behavior.
60–79   You exhibit moderate Type A behavior.

If your total for B is:
80–100   You exhibit strong Type B behavior.
60–79   You exhibit moderate Type B behavior.

Any other combination is a mixture of Type A and Type B behavior that does not exhibit a clear pattern.

case: GIVING IT HIS BEST SHOT

Within a day of the time that the placement service at his university listed the firms that would be interviewing on campus later that month, Jim Richardson had signed up to meet with five of the representatives. Jim's first choice was a nationally known consumer goods firm. The company typically hires six to eight graduates from Jim's university every year. He wants very much to be one of them.

Jim's interview took place three weeks ago. Unfortunately, Jim had been so busy preparing for a science exam that he overslept. When he arrived at the placement office, the head of the office was waiting outside. "Where have you been?" he asked. "I've been stalling the inter-

viewer for almost 15 minutes. Go to Room 4 immediately. I'll get the man from my office and bring him down." After being introduced, Jim immediately told the interviewer that he was sorry for his tardiness but that he had studied until after 2 A.M. and had overslept. The recruiter shrugged it off. "Don't be concerned. I've done it myself on occasion." Then, after some general pleasantries, the interview began.

The recruiter started to tell Jim about his company and then stopped. "Are you familiar with us?" he asked. Jim admitted that he did not know much about the consumer goods firm, although he did add, "but you are my first career choice." The recruiter then proceeded to give Jim some brochures that described the firm and its operations and began to describe some of the company's major product lines and activities.

Later in the interview, the recruiter asked, "What starting salary would you be looking for?" Based on his discussions with the head of the placement office, Jim learned that the going rate was approximately $23,500. "I'd like to start around $27,500," he said "with an opportunity to increase my salary by about 10 percent through overtime." The recruiter did not respond to this statement but did write something on the piece of paper in front of him.

When the interview concluded 15 minutes later, Jim shook the man's hand and asked, "When can I expect to hear from you?" The recruiter told him he would have a response within three weeks. Yesterday two of Jim's friends who had interviewed with the consumer goods firm received letters of acceptance. Today Jim received a letter. It said that because the company was able to hire only a limited number of applicants, it would be unable to offer him a position but wished him luck in his job search.

QUESTIONS

1. Was showing up late a big mistake on Jim's part? Why or why not?

2. How should Jim have handled the question about salary? Explain.

3. Why did Jim not get the job? Defend your answer.

4. What should Jim do to prepare for the next interview? Prepare a list of suggestions for preparing for the next job interview. Prepare another list of how Jim should conduct himself in the interview. Be specific in both lists.

YOU BE THE CONSULTANT

Formulating a Career Plan

Pauline Caruthers has just graduated from State University. She currently is interviewing with several large organizations in Chicago. One in particular has impressed her. It is a finance firm, and its growth over the last five years has been phenomenal. The organization has offices in eighty-four locations throughout the United States and intends to double this number within eighteen months. Its biggest location is the home office, and this is where the firm will want Pauline to work, if she gets the job. This is convenient for her, because her family lives nearby and she would like to stay in the vicinity.

During her day-long visit at the firm, Pauline was introduced to a number of different managers. The one for whom she would be working is Charles Cooper, an up-and-coming young executive. Charles has been with the firm for three years and has been promoted every year. He currently is in charge of one of the largest offices in the firm's headquarters, and everyone has tagged him as top management timber. Charles and Pauline chatted for more than 45 minutes during her interview. Additionally, she had the opportunity to talk with some of the personnel in Charles's department. It is obvious from her conversation with them that when Charles moves up, he intends to take some of these people with him. Charles appears to be a mentor for at least three of them. During her conversation with Charles, he made it clear to her that she too could expect to move along with him. "I need effective people on my team and I have a couple of them in the department right now," he told her. "You would be another. This job is too big for one person. However, with the right team of three to four people, it can be a stepping stone up the line. Along the way, my objective is to develop a cadre of management talent. Too many people try to get to the top by going it alone. In today's world, the person who can succeed in that approach is rare. You need to use a team approach, and the best way I know of putting together an effective team is through a well-thought-out mentoring program."

Your Advice

1. If Charles offers Pauline a job today at a salary $5,000 higher than what she is likely to get anywhere else, what should she do?

   ____ a. Accept it and seal the deal as quickly as possible.

   ____ b. Tell him she'll get back to him on the offer within a week.

   ____ c. Take the opportunity to negotiate for even more money with the objective of sealing the deal at a salary $2,500 higher than what Charles has just offered.

2. Why is it a good idea for Pauline to know the criteria Charles will use in evaluating her performance before she agrees to go to work for him?

3. In what way would working for Charles help Pauline to follow the career management rule: develop alliances?

4. How long would you recommend Pauline work before she makes her first periodic assessment of her career? Explain.

EXPERIENCING INTERVIEWS

Purpose

- To understand the dynamics of employment interviews.
- To experience interview questions and answers.

Procedure

1. The instructor will describe a job vacancy for which applicants are being interviewed.

2. One student will be chosen to act as the interviewee; the instructor will be the interviewer. The two people will engage in a role-playing exercise for about ten to fifteen minutes.

3. After the role-playing exercise is completed, class discussion should center on assessing the performance of the interviewee. Were questions answered adequately? Confidently? What could have been done better?

4. Another student is chosen to take the part of the interviewee and step 2 is repeated.

5. In small groups, discuss ways in which you can prepare for job interviewing. Consider the following:

   a. What questions are almost sure to be asked?

   b. What questions should you ask?

   c. How should you dress?

Notes

CHAPTER 1

1. Adapted from Rensis Likert, *The Human Organization* (New York: McGraw-Hill, 1967), pp. 4–10.

2. For a complete account of the program, see Alfred J. Marrow, David G. Bowers, and Stanley E. Seashore, *Management by Participation* (New York: Harper & Row, 1967).

3. William F. Dowling, "At G.M.: 'System 4' Builds Performance and Profits," *Organizational Dynamics,* winter 1975, pp. 23–28.

4. Sam Deep and Lyle Sussman, "Eight Management Principles You Can't Work Without," *Working Woman,* June 1991, pp. 61–63.

5. C. Northcote Parkinson, *Parkinson's Law* (Houghton Mifflin, 1957), p. 24.

6. Fred N. Kerlinger, *Foundations of Behavioral Research,* 2d ed. (New York: Holt, Rinehart and Winston, 1973), p. 6.

7. For more on this, see B. F. Skinner, *Contingencies of Reinforcement* (New York: Appleton-Century-Crofts, 1969) and Fred Luthans, *Organizational Behavior,* 8th ed. (New York: McGraw-Hill, 1998), chapter 8.

8. Michael Schrage, "Will Evolving Corporate Strategy Be Dar-win-win-ian?," *Fortune,* June 21, 1999.

9. Amy Barrett et al., "Jack's Risky Last Act," *Business Week,* November 6, 2000, pp. 40–45.

10. Jack Ewing, "Sharing the Wealth," *Business Week Online,* March 19, 2001.

11. Thomas L. Davenport and Laurence Prusak, *Working Knowledge: How Organizations Manage What They Know* (Boston: Harvard Business School Press, 2000), p. xxiii.

12. Louisa Wan, "Making Knowledge Stick," *Management Review,* May 1999, p. 25.

13. Stephanie N. Mehta, "What Minority Employees Really Want," *Fortune,* July 10, 2000, p. 183.

14. Julie Forster and Ann Therese Palmer, "That's It, I'm Outta Here," *Business Week,* October 9, 2000, p. 96.

15. "More Businesses Look at Diversity as an Obligation, Not a Choice," *HR Focus,* October 1993, p. 14.

16. See David A. Andelman, "Too Tight a Grip on Diversity," *Management Review,* June 1996, pp. 21–23.

17. Ann M. Van Eron, "How to Work with a Diversity Consultant," *Training and Development Journal,* April 1996, pp. 41–44.

18. Geresa Brady, "The Downside of Diversity," *Management Review,* June 1996, pp. 29–31.

19. "Pay Disparity Between Sexes Persists," *Miami Herald,* May 30, 2000, p. 7B.

20. Toddi Gutner, "The Rose-Colored Glass Ceiling," *Business Week Online,* September 2, 2002.

21. For more on the glass ceiling, see Debra E. Meyerson and Joyce K. Fletcher, "A Modest Manifesto for Shattering the Glass Ceiling," *Harvard Business Review,* January–February 2000, pp. 127–136.

22. **http://www.avon.com** press release, "Avon Selected as One of the Top Ten 'Best Corporate Citizens' by *Business Ethics Magazine,*" April 22, 2002.

23. **http://www.jcpenney.com** "Our Commitment".

24. Linda Himelsteen and Stephanic Anderson Forest, "Breaking Through," *Business Week,* February 17, 1997, p. 66.

25. "The Interview," *Time Magazine,* December 30, 2002/January 6, 2003, p. 59.

26. Special Report, "The Whistle Blowers," *Business Week Online,* January 13, 2003.

27. Keith Naughton, "The CEO Party is Over," *Newsweek,* p. 55, January 6, 2003.

28. Heesun Wee, "Corporate Ethics: Right Makes Might," *Business Week Online,* April 11, 2002, **http://www.businessweek.com**

29. Q&A, "To Cure Fraud, Start at the Top," *Business Week Online,* October 18, 2002.

30. Adapted from Carl Pergola's interview, "To Cure Fraud, Start at the Top," *Business Week Online,* October 18, 2002.

31. Hall, William D. *Making the Right Decisions.* New York: John Wiley and Sons, Inc., 1993, p. 44.

32. Heesun Wee, "Corporate Ethics: Right Makes Might," *Business Week Online,* April 11, 2002, **http://www.businessweek.com**

33. Full Text of President Bush's speech at the Regent, *Wall Street Journal,* July 9, 2002.

34. Keith Naughton, "The CEO Party is Over," *Newsweek,* p. 55, January 6, 2003.

35. Code of Business Conduct, The Coca Cola Company, 2003. **http://www.cocacola.com**

36. "MBAs Need More Than Ethics 101," Reader Survey Results, *Business Week Online,* January 21, 2003.

37. Walter B. Wriston, "A Code of Our Own," *Wall Street Journal,* January 16, 2003.

38. News Release, "GM Endorses New Corporate Accountability Initiatives," August 6, 2002. **http://www.generalmotors.com**

39. "Making a Plus on Downsizing," *Business Week Online,* January 22, 2003.

40. From Interview with M. Daris, Agent, State Farm Insurance, 2003.

41. **http://www.eeoc.gov** Age Bias Discrimination Case, December 11, 2002.

42. Linda Greenhouse, "Justices, in a Unanimous Decision, Make It Easier to Sue for Discrimination on the Job," *New York Times,* June 13, 2000, p. A21.

43. See, for example, Constance L. Hays, "Coca-Cola Reaches a Settlement with Some Workers in a Bias Suit," *New York Times,* June 15, 2000, section C, pp. 1, 6; Patrick McGeehan, "Morgan Stanley is Cited for Discrimination Against Women," *New York Times,* June 6, 2000, section C, pp. 1–2; and Charles Gasparino and Randall Smith, "U.S. Agency Calls Morgan Stanley Biased Against Female Executive," *Wall Street Journal,* June 6, 2000, section C, pp. 1–2.

44. Jennifer Steinhauer, "If the Boss is Out of Line, What's the Legal Boundary?" *New York Times,* March 27, 1997, pp. C1, C4.

45. Press Release from EEOC, January 2, 2003. **http://www. eeoc.gov**

46. Press Release from EEOC, January 15, 2003. **http:// www.eeoc.gov**

47. David Hancock, "Judge: Channel 10 Discriminated on the Basis of Age," *Miami Herald,* February 13, 1996, section B, pp. 1B–2B.

48. Carey Goldberg, "Fat People Say an Intolerant World Condemns Them on First Sight," *New York Times,* November 5, 2000, p. 30y; Wade Lambert, "Obese Workers Win On-the-Job Protection Against Bias," *Wall Street Journal,* November 12, 1993, pp. B1, B7; and Tamar Lewin, "Workplace Bias Tied to Obesity Is Ruled Illegal," *New York Times,* November 24, 1993, p. A10.

49. Lucinda Harper, "Good Looks Can Mean a Pretty Penny on the Job, and 'Ugly' Men Are Affected More than Women," *Wall Street Journal,* November 23, 1993, p. B1.

50. Antonio Regalado, Laurie McGinley, and Sarah Lueck, "Cloning Claim Spurs Ethics Debate," *Wall Street Journal,* December 30, 2002, p. A3.

51. **http://www.xerox.com** Stephen Perry, "Knowledge Sharing—The Xerox Approach" and "Knowledge Sharing for the Enterprise," February 2002.

52. "The Great Migration in Numbers," *Fast Company,* July 2000, p. 205.

53. William B. Johnston, "Global Work Force 2000: The New World Labor Market," *Harvard Business Review,* March–April 1991, pp. 115–116.

54. Howard W. French, "Women Win a Battle, but Job Bias Still Rules Japan," *New York Times,* February 26, 2000, p. A3.

55. Also see Richard M. Hodgetts and Fred Luthans, *International Management,* 4th ed. (Burr Ridge, IL: Irwin/McGraw, 2000), p. 76.

56. Cara Buckley, "Worldwide Music Piracy Costs Industry $5 Billion," *Miami Herald,* October 3, 2000, section C, p. 1; and Craig S. Smith, "Piracy a Concern as the China Trade Opens Up," *New York Times,* October 5, 2000, p. W1.

CHAPTER 2

1. "Conseco Files for Chapter 11; Insurance Unit Remains Sound," *Wall Street Journal,* December 19, 2002, and "Wendt Quits as Conseco CEO but Remains Board Chairman," *Wall Street Journal,* October 2, 2002.

2. Gemmy Allen, Professor of Management, Northlake College, DCCCD, Dallas, TX. **http://ollie.dccc.edu/ mgmt1374/book-intro.html**

3. Roy J. Blitzer, Colleen Petersen, and Linda Rogers, "How to Build Self-Esteem," *Training and Development Journal,* February 1993, pp. 58–60.

4. Paul Kirby and Dominic Di Mattia, "A Rational Approach to Emotional Management," *Training and Development Journal,* January 1991, pp. 67–70.

5. See David C. McClelland, J. W. Atkinson, R. A. Clark, and E. L. Lowell, *The Achievement Motive* (New York: Appleton-Century-Crofts, 1953); David C. McClelland, *The Achieving Society* (Princeton, NJ: Van Nostrand, 1961); and Richard Davidson, "Motivating the Underachiever," *Supervisory Management,* January 1983, pp. 39–41.

6. Srikumar S. Rao, "The Superachiever's Secret," *Success,* June 1991, pp. 28–31.

7. Abraham H. Maslow, "A Theory of Human Motivation," *Psychological Review,* July 1943, pp. 388–389.

8. Frederick Herzberg, Bernard Mausner, and Barbara Bloch Snyderman, *The Motivation to Work* (New York: Wiley & Sons, 1959).

9. For other examples of dissatisfiers, see Dean R. Spitzer, "The Seven Deadly Demotivators," *Management Review,* November 1995, pp. 56–60.

10. Dean R. Spitzer, "Power Rewards: Rewards That Really Motivate," *Management Review,* May 1996, p. 47.

11. Wendelien Van Eerde and Henk Thierry, "Vroom's Expectancy Models and Work-Related Criteria: A Meta-Analysis," *Journal of Applied Psychology,* 81, no. 5, 1996, pp. 575–586.

12. Victor H. Vroom, *Work and Motivation* (New York: Wiley & Sons, 1964).

13. Lyman W. Porter and Edward E. Lawler III, *Managerial Attitudes and Performance* (Homewood, IL: Richard D. Irwin, Inc., and Dorsey Press, 1968).

14. In some cases, however, pay for performance has not proven acceptable. See, for example, Dirk Johnson, "Teachers Reject Linking Job Performance to Bonuses," *New York Times,* July 16, 2000, p. A16.

15. Also see "Raises and Praise or Out the Door," *Wall Street Journal,* June 21, 1999, p. B1.

16. See, for example, Greg Winter, "Coke Issuing Widespread Pay Increases," *New York Times,* October 20, 2000, pp. C1–C2; and "Soaring Salaries: It's Payback Time," *Business Week,* October 9, 2000, pp. F24–F30.

17. "The Big Picture," *Business Week,* July 31, 2000, p. 10.

18. See *Business Week,* April 17, 2000, p. 16. Also see Gary McWilliams, "Dell to Cut Back on Stock Options, Pay Cash Bonuses," *Wall Street Journal,* May 6, 2003, p. A3.

19. Working at Lincoln Electric, 2003. **http://www. lincolnelectric.com**

20. Eric Wahlgren, "CEO Pay Tomorrow: Same as Today," *Business Week Online,* August 21, 2002.

21. Janet Wiscombe, "Can Pay for Performance Really Work?" *Workforce,* August 2001, pp. 28–34.

22. Janet Wiscombe, "How MetLife Measures Core Behaviors for Leaders, Managers, and Employees," *Workforce,* August 2001, p. 30.

23. Wiscombe, pp. 28–34.

24. **http://www.incomesdata.co.uk/** extracted from IDS Management Pay Review 259, September 2002.

25. G. Karen Jacobs, "The Broad View," *Wall Street Journal,* April 10, 1997, p. R10.

26. A White Paper by Effective Compensation, Incorporated, "Broad Banding: A Management Overview," 2001.

27. **http://www.incomesdata.co.uk/broad banding;** IDS Management Pay Review 259, September 2002 Simply put, broad banding is proving to be an effective tool in maintaining employee motivation.

28. Steven Kerr, "Practical, Cost-Neutral Alternatives That You May Know, But Don't Practice," *Organizational Dynamics,* summer 1999, p. 68.

29. **http://www.recognition.org/walker.htm** (June 2000).

30. **http://www.recognition.org/brief_summary** (September 20, 2002).

31. "Companies Are Working to Improve Recognition Programs," *The Conference Board,* p. 7

32. "Morale Maintenance," *Across the Board,* January 2000, p. 79.

33. Judy Artunian, "Small Business Building Loyalty," *Chicago Tribune,* North Sports Final, pp. 7, 11–12, 2002.

34. Ibid.

CHAPTER 3

1. Milton Rokeach, *The Nature of Human Values* (New York: Free Press, 1973).

2. Gordon W. Allport, Philip E. Vernon, and Gardner Lindzey, *Study of Values,* test booklet (Boston: Houghton Mifflin, 1960).

3. Aaron Bernstein, "Is America Becoming More of a Class Society?" *Business Week,* February 26, 1996, p. 86.

4. Joanne Cole, "The Art of Wooing Gen Xers," *HR Focus,* November 1999, p. 8.

5. Michelle Neely Martinez, "FMLA: Headache or Opportunity?" *HR Magazine,* February 1994, pp. 42–45.

6. Dale D. Buss, "Planters' M. G. Boron: Producing a Worker-Friendly Plant," *Food Processing,* March 1994, pp. 89–90.

7. Joann S. Lublin, "Memo to Staff: Stop Working," *Wall Street Journal,* July 6, 2000, pp. B1, B4.

8. Charlene Marmer Solomon, "Workers Want A Life! Do Managers Care?" *Workforce,* August 1999, pp. 54–58.

9. Edward I. Powers, "Employee Loyalty in the New Millennium," *SAM Advanced Management Journal,* summer 2000, pp. 4–8.

10. David Cay Johnston, "I.R.S. More Likely to Audit the Poor and Not the Rich," *New York Times,* April 16, 2000, pp. 1, 33.

11. Nicholas Kulish, "Postal Service Is Satisfying Its Customers," *Wall Street Journal,* May 15, 2000, p. A2.

12. Will Ruch, "How to Keep Gen X Employees from Becoming X-Employees," *Training and Development Journal,* April 2000, pp. 40–43.

13. Scott Hays, "Generation X and the Art of the Reward," *Workforce,* November 1999, p. 46.

14. Tom Terez, "What Works: The Power of Nice," *Workforce,* January, 2003, pp. 22–24.

15. "Employee Attitudes," 2002 Workplace, CRN News.

16. Beverly Kaye and Sharon Jordan Evans, "Wake Up, and Smell the Coffee: People Flock to Family-Friendly" excerpts from *"Love'Em or Lose'Em: Getting Good People to Stay,"* Business Week Online, January 28, 2000.

17. Unmesh Kher, "How to Sell XXXL," *Time Magazine,* January 27, 2003, pp. 43–46.

18. SCORE, Service Corps of Retired Executives, "Good Employee Attitudes Help You Make Money," News & Information.

19. Jill Neimark, "The Power of Positive Thinkers," *Success,* September 1987, pp. 38–41.

20. Jack Stack, "Measuring Morale," *Inc.,* January 1997, pp. 29–30.

21. Also see Stephen Fineman, ed., *Emotion in Organizations,* 2d ed. (London: Sage, 2000).

22. Daniel Goleman, *Working with Emotional Intelligence* (New York: Bantam, 1998), p. 317.

23. Ibid., p. 19.

24. "Can you answer the real question about emotional intelligence?" Emotional Intelligence At Work **http://equatwork.com/Unlinked/the_case_for_eq.htm** (June, 2003).

25. For more on EI in the workplace, see Tony Schwartz, "How Do You Feel?" *Fast Company,* June 2000, pp. 297–313; Jennifer Laabs, "Emotional Intelligence at Work," *Workforce,* July 1999, pp. 68–71; and Scott Hays, "American Express Taps into the Power of Emotional Intelligence," *Workforce,* July 1999, pp. 72–73.

26. Goleman, op. cit., p. 318.

27. Cary Cherniss Ph.D., "The Business Case for Emotional Intelligence," Consortium for Research of Emotional Intelligence in Organizations, **http://www.eiconsortium.org/research/business_case_for_ei.htm** (June, 2003).

28. Helen Fisher, *The First Sex: The Natural Talents of Women and How They Are Changing the World* (New York: Random House, 2000).

29. Cynthia E. Griffin, "Vive La Difference!" *Entrepreneur,* November 1999, p. 52.

30. Psych Self Help, "Methods for Developing Skills," Mental Health Net, **http://www.mentalhelp.net**

31. Lynn Z. Bloom, Karen Coburn, and Joan Pearlman, *The New Assertive Woman* (New York: Dell, 1976), pp. 175–176.

32. Barbara Moses, *The Good News About Careers* (San Francisco: Jossey-Bass, 2000).

33. For more on these profiles, see Barbara Moses, "Degrees of Motivation," *Black Enterprise,* November 2000, pp. 155–162.

CHAPTER 4

1. For more on this, see John Beck and Neil Yeager, "Moving Beyond Team Myths," *Training and Development Journal,* March 1996, pp. 51–55.

2. For more on this, see Joyce Ranney and Mark Deck, "Making Teams Work: Lessons from the Leaders in New Product Development," *Planning Review,* August 1995, pp. 6–13.

3. David Chaudron, "How to Improve Cross-Functional Teams," *HR Focus,* August 1995, pp. 4–5.

4. For more on virtual teams, see Leigh Thompson, *Making the Team* (Upper Saddle River, NJ: Prentice Hall, 2000), pp. 247–250; and Regina Fazio Maruca, "How Do You Manage an Off-Site Team," *Harvard Business Review,* July–August 1998, pp. 22–26.

5. Charlene Marmer Solomon, "How Virtual Teams Bring Real Savings," *Workforce,* June, 2001, p. 62.

6. Lewis Brown Griggs and Lente-Louise Louw, "Diverse Teams: Breakdown or Breakthrough," *Training and Development Journal,* October 1995, p. 27.

7. Ellen Van Velsor and Jean Brittain Leslie, "Why Executives Derail: Perspectives Across Time and Cultures," *Academy of Management Executive,* November 1995, p. 65.

8. Griggs and Louw, op. cit.

9. For more on groups in this stage, see Susan A. Wheelan, *Creating Effective Teams* (Thousand Oaks, CA: Sage, 1999), pp. 28–30.

10. Ellen Hart, "Top Teams," *Management Review,* February 1996, pp. 43–47.

11. Wheelan, op. cit., pp. 62–64.

12. Also see Margaret Coles, "Call in a Therapist to Boost Team Morale," *Sunday Times,* July 23, 2000, section 7, p. 24.

13. "Size is the Key," *Fast Company,* November 2000, p. 118.

14. For more on this topic, see Robert F. Bales and Edgar F. Borgatta, "Size of Group as a Factor in the Interaction Profile," in A. P. Hare, Edgar F. Borgatta, and Robert F. Bales, eds., *Small Groups* (New York: Knopf, 1955), pp. 396–413; and Lyman W. Porter and Richard M. Steers, "Organizational, Work, and Personal Factors in Employee Turnover and Absenteeism," *Psychological Bulletin,* August 1973, pp. 151–176.

15. For more on the use of this organizational arrangement, see Douglas A. Saarel, "Triads: Self-Organizing Structures That Create Value," *Planning Review,* August 1995, pp. 20–25.

16. See A. J. Rowe and R. O. Mason, *Managing with Style: A Guide to Understanding, Assessing and Improving Decision Making* (San Francisco: Jossey-Bass, 1987).

17. Bertram Schoner, Gerald L. Rose, and G. C. Hoyt, "Quality of Decisions: Individuals Versus Real and Synthetic Groups," *Journal of Applied Psychology,* August 1974, pp. 424–432.

18. Dorwin Cartwright, "Risk Taking by Individuals and Groups: An Assessment of Research Employing Choice Dilemmas," *Journal of Personality and Social Psychology,* December 1971, pp. 361–378; Russell D. Clark III, "Group Induced Shift Toward Risk: A Critical Appraisal," *Psychological Bulletin,* October 1971, pp. 251–270; and Dean G. Pruitt, "Choice Shifts in Group Discussion: An Introductory Review," *Journal of Personality and Social Psychology,* December 1971, pp. 339–360.

19. Earl A. Cecil, Larry L. Cummings, and Jerome M. Chertkoff, "Group Composition and Choice Shift: Implications for Administration," *Academy of Management Journal,* September 1973, pp. 413–414.

20. *Fast Company,* April 2000, p. 100.

21. Michael A. West and Neil R. Anderson, "Innovation in Top Management Teams," *Journal of Applied Psychology,* December 1996, p. 691.

22. See, for example, Warren Bennis and Patricia Ward Biederman, *Organizing Genius: The Secrets of Creative Collaboration* (Reading, MA: Addison Wesley, 1997).

23. Cheryl Comeau-Kirschner and Louisa Wah, "Who Has Time to Think?" *Management Review,* January 2000, pp. 16–23.

24. Suzy Wetlaufer, "Common Sense and Conflict: An Interview with Disney's Michael Eisner," *Harvard Business Review,* January–February 2000, p. 119.

25. Richard L. Priem, David A. Harrison, and Nan Kanoff Muir, "Structured Conflict and Consensus Outcomes in Group Decision Making," *Journal of Management,* 21, no. 4, 1995, pp. 691–710.

26. Larry Armstrong, "Nurturing an Employee's Brainchild," *Business Week,* Special Issue, December 1993, p. 196.

27. Arthur B. Van Gundy, *Idea Power* (New York: American Management Association, 1992), chapters 10 and 11.

28. Sue Barrett, "How to Brainstorm and Be Creative," *Workforce.* **http://www.workforce.com.**

29. Dorothy Leonard and Jeffrey F. Rayport, "Spark Innovation Through Empathic Design," *Harvard Business Review,* November–December 1997, pp. 102–103.

30. See, for example, Gary Hamel and C. K. Prahalad, *Competing for the Future* (Boston: Harvard Business School Press, 1994).

31. Paco Underhill, *Why We Buy: The Science of Shopping* (New York: Simon & Schuster, 1999).

32. Millard Fuller, "A Hammer as a Way to Help People," *Fast Company,* November 2000, p. 130.

33. H. David Aycock, "Selfish People Spell Doom for a Team Effort," *Fast Company,* November 2000, p. 128.

34. Jeanie Duck, "Don't Shortchange Your Startup," *Fast Company,* November 2000, p. 142.

CHAPTER 5

1. David Krackhardt and Jeffrey R. Hanson, "Informal Networks: The Company Behind the Chart," *Harvard Business Review,* July–August 1993, p. 105.

2. Richard Rapaport, "How to Build a Winning Team: An Interview with Head Coach Bill Walsh," *Harvard Business Review,* January–February 1993, pp. 111–120.

3. K. Michele Kacmar and Gerald R. Ferris, "Politics at Work: Sharpening the Focus of Political Behavior in Organizations," *Business Horizons,* July–August 1993, pp. 70–74.

4. Bruce Fortado, "Informal Supervisory Social Control Strategies," *Journal of Management Studies,* March 1994, pp. 251–274.

5. Some of these ideas can be found in Ken Myers, "Games Companies Play," *Training,* June 1992, pp. 68–76.

6. David De Long and Patricia Seemann, "Confronting Conceptual Confusion and Conflict in Knowledge Management," *Organizational Dynamics,* summer 2000, p. 39.

7. Dennis A. Gioia and Clinton O. Longenecker, "Delving into the Dark Side: The Politics of Executive Appraisal," *Organizational Dynamics,* Winter 1994, p. 50.

8. Herminia Ibarra, "Race, Opportunity, and Diversity of Social Circles in Managerial Networks," *Academy of Management Journal,* June 1995, pp. 673–703.

9. Glenn R. Carroll and Albert C. Teo, "On the Social Networks of Managers," *Academy of Management Journal,* April 1996, p. 433.

10. Also see Patricia A. Wilson, "The Effects of Politics and Power on the Organizational Commitment of Federal Executives," *Journal of Management,* Spring 1995, pp. 101–118.

11. For more on e-mail and the Internet, see "We've All Got Mail," *Newsweek,* May 15, 2000, p. 73K.

12. Leigh Thompson, *Making the Team: A Guide for Managers* (Upper Saddle River, NJ: Prentice Hall, 2000), p. 236.

13. Keith Davis, *Human Behavior at Work: Organizational Behavior,* 6th ed. (New York: McGraw-Hill, 1981), p. 339.

14. Daniel C. Feldman and Carrie R. Leana, "A Study of Reemployment Challenges After Downsizing," *Organizational Dynamics,* summer 2000, pp. 64–74.

15. Jeffrey Ball, "DaimlerChrysler Official Expects Restructuring, Change Next Year," *Wall Street Journal,* December 20, 2000, p. A4; and Edmund L. Andrews, "Daimler Says Chrysler's Problems Are Worsening," *New York Times,* December 19, 2000, p. W1.

16. For more on setting goals, see Lynda McDermott, Bill Waite, and Nolan Brawley, "Putting Together a World-Class Team," *Training and Development Journal,* January 1999, pp. 47–51; and Dale Buss, "The Entitlement Generation Wants it All—And They Want It Easy. How Dare They?" *Wall Street Journal,* May 22, 2000, p. R23.

17. See, for example, Gordon W. Allport and Leo Postman, *The Psychology of Rumor* (New York: Holt, Rinehart and Winston, 1974), p. 33.

18. Also see "What Makes a Good Boss?" *HR Focus,* March 2000, pp. 10–11.

19. Gareth R. Jones and Jennifer M. George, "The Experience and Evolution of Trust: Implications for Cooperation and Teamwork," *Academy of Management Review,* July 1999, pp. 531–546.

20. Julie Forster and Anne Therese Palmer, "That's It, I'm Outta Here," *Business Week,* October 9, 2000, pp. 96, 98.

21. Davis, op. cit., pp. 337–338.

22. Also see Alan M. Webber, "Will Companies Ever Learn?" *Fast Company,* October 2000, pp. 275–282.

23. Amy Zipkin, "The Wisdom of Thoughtfulness," *New York Times,* May 31, 2000, p. C1.

24. Jay Knippen, "Grapevine Communication: Management Employees," *Journal of Business Research,* January 1974, pp. 47–58.

25. Cheryl Comeau-Kirschner, "The Sharing Culture," *Management Review,* January 2000, p. 8.

CHAPTER 6

1. Alvin Toffler, *Future Shock* (New York: Bantam Books, 1971).

2. Allen R. Myerson, "Superhuman Feats from a Subhuman Diver," *New York Times,* July 13, 1994, p. C4.

3. Amy Barrett, John Carey, Michael Arndt, "Feeding the Pipeline," *Business Week Online,* May 12, 2003.

4. Neil Gross, "How Johnny Could Learn Calculus," *Business Week,* May 24, 1999, p. 55.

5. Press Release from Casio, Inc., January 9, 2003. **http://www.casio.com**

6. Catherine Arnst, "This Smart Bomb Targets Cancer Cells," *Business Week,* May 31, 1999, p. 115.

7. Ellen Licking, "Reading What's Written on the Wind," *Business Week,* September 20, 1999, p. 82.

8. Neil Gross, "Stem Cells That Stem Damage," *Business Week,* November 20, 2000, p. 141.

9. *Science Year, 2003, The World Book Annual Science Supplement,* World Book Encyclopedia, pp. 106–109.

10. *Science Year, 2003, The World Book Annual Science Supplement,* World Book Encyclopedia, p. 283.

11. Jeffrey Ball, "U.S. Auto Makers to Rev Up Output of 'Hybrid' Vehicles," *Wall Street Journal,* October 24, 2000, p. B4.

12. Press release from American Honda Motor Co., Inc, 2/06/03, **http://www.honda.com**

13. Anne Marie Squedo, "21st Century Armor," *Wall Street Journal,* February 10, 2003, p. B1.

14. Patricia O'Connell, "The Bank of 7'Eleven," *Business Week Online,* February 6, 2003.

15. Alex Salkever, "Sports Gear Goes Geek," *Business Week Online,* July 16, 2002.

16. Julia Angwin, "E-Mail Goes Postal," *Wall Street Journal,* July 31, 2000, pp. B1, B6.

17. Alec Klein, "The Techies Grumbled, but Polaroid's Pocket Turned Into a Huge Hit," *Wall Street Journal,* May 2, 2000, pp. A1, A10.

18. Norihiko Shirouzu, "High-Tech Hotbed for Car Makers: Lowly Mirror," *New York Times,* August 24, 2000, pp. B1, B4.

19. Gentex Corporation, **http://www.gentex.com**

20. Andrew Kohut, "America the Connected," *New York Times,* June 23, 2000, p. A25.

21. Dean Takahashi, "Antitrend," *Red Herring,* December 4, 2000, p. 170.

22. *Wall Street Journal,* May 4, 2000, p. 1.

23. Heather Green, Steve Rosenbush, "Wi-Fi Means Business," Special Report, *Business Week,* April 28, 2003.

24. Moon Ihlwan, "Half the World's Hot Spots," *Business Week,* April 28, 2003, **http://www.businessweekonline.com**

25. Heather Green, Steve Rosenbush, "Wi-Fi Means Business," Special Report, *Business Week,* April 28, 2003, **http://www.businessweekonline.com**

26. Jane Black, "The Battle to Streamline Business Software," *Business Week Online,* December 4, 2002.

27. Mark Jarvis, "At Oracle, Simplicity Rules All," *Business Week Online,* December 4, 2002.

28. Robert L. Simison, "Ford Rolls Out New Model of Corporate Culture," *Wall Street Journal,* January 13, 1999, p. B1, B4.

29. Ronald Alsop, "Scandal-Filled Year Takes Toll on Firm's Good Names," *Wall Street Journal Online,* February 12, 2003.

30. W. Mathew Juechter, Caroline Fisher, and Randall J. Alford, "Five Conditions for High-Performance Cultures," *Training and Development Journal,* May 1998, p. 65.

31. John F. Runcie, "By Day I Make the Cars," *Harvard Business Review,* May–June 1980, pp. 107–108.

32. Nancy B. Kurland and Diane E. Bailey, "Telework: The Advantages and Challenges of Working Here, There, Anywhere, and Anytime," *Organizational Dynamics,* Autumn 1999, pp. 62–63.

33. Mark Heinzl, "Inco Moves to Take Miners Out of Mining," *Wall Street Journal,* July 6, 1994, p. B6.

34. Michael Hopkins and Jeffrey L. Seglin, "America @ Work," *Inc.,* special issue, May 20, 1997, pp. 77–85.

35. **http://www.osha.gov,** "National Advisory Committee on Ergonomics—68:794–795, 01/07/2003.

36. Kathleen E. Christensen, "Workplace in Transition," *Advertising Supplement,* 1991.

37. Cheryl Powell, "When Workers Wear Walkmans on the Job," *Wall Street Journal,* July 11, 1994, pp. B1, B8.

38. Robert M. Fulmer, "The Evolving Paradigm of Leadership Development," *Organizational Dynamics,* spring 1997, p. 70.

39. New Release, "Motorola, FedEx Develop Wireless, Pocket PC for Couriers to Enhance Customer Service," November 26, 2002, **http://www.federalexpress.com**

40. See Richard M. Hodgetts and Fred Luthans, *International Management,* 4th ed. (Burr Ridge, IL: Irwin/McGraw, 2000), p. 497.

41. "Motivating People," Toolpack Consulting, LLC, Teaneck, New Jersey.

42. Inc. Staff, "So This is Empowerment?", Inc, July 1, 1994 **http://www.inc.com**

43. George Henderson, *Human Relations Issues in Management* (Westport, CT: Quorum Books, 1996), p. 137.

44. Ibid., p. 141.

45. **http://www.osha-slc.gov/SLTC/ workplaceviolence/index.html**

46. **http://www.osha.gov/SLTC/ workplaceviolence/index.html**

47. **http://www.osha.gov/SLTC/ workplaceviolence/index.html**

48. **http://www.osha.gov**

49. **http://www.osha.gov**

50. For additional profiles, see Romould A. Stone, "Workplace Homicide: A Time for Action," *Business Horizons,* March–April 1995, p. 6.

51. Henderson, op. cit., pp. 147–148.

52. Michael G. Harvey and Richard A. Cosier, "Homicides in the Workplace: Crisis or False Alarm?" *Business Horizons,* March–April 1995, p. 16.

53. Henderson, op. cit., pp. 152–153.

54. National Institute of Occupational Safety and Health, *Stress . . . At Work,* NIOSH Publication No. 99-101, 2000, p. 4. **http://www.cdc.gov**

55. Ibid. p. 15.

56. Ibid., p. 9.

57. Joanne Cole, "De-Stressing the Workplace: Hewlett-Packard Pushes the Envelope," *HR Focus,* October 1999, p. 10.

CHAPTER 7

1. Bradley T. Gale and Robert D. Buzzell, "Market Perceived Quality: Key Strategic Concept," *Planning Review,* March–April 1989, pp. 6–15, 48.

2. Rich Miller, Peter Coy, Rob Hof Peter Burrows, and Robert Berner, "Productivity's Second Wind," *BusinessWeek Online,* February 17, 2003.

3. Christopher Drew, "In the Productivity Push, How Much Is Too Much?" *New York Times,* December 17, 1995, sec. 3, pp. 1, 12.

4. Consumer Reports, "Reliability, New Cars," April 2003, p. 86.

5. Editors, "Bottom Line Personal," Volume 24, Number 6, March 15, 2003, p. 1.

6. Anna Wilde Mathews, "Rollover Rankings Could Shake Auto Makers," *Wall Street Journal,* May 24, 1999, pp. B1, B9.

7. See Dianna L. Stone and Erik R. Eddy, "A Model of Individual and Organizational Factors Affecting Quality-Related Outcomes," *Journal of Quality Management* 1, no. 1, 1996, pp. 21–48.

8. For more on this, see R. S. M. Lau, "Strategic Flexibility: A New Reality for World-Class Manufacturing," *SAM Advanced Management Journal,* spring 1996, pp. 11–15.

9. Marco Iansiti and Jonathan West, "Technology Integration: Turning Great Research into Great Products," *Harvard Business Review,* May–June 1997, pp. 92–93.

10. Jay Hall, "Americans Know How to Be Productive if Managers Will Let Them," *Organizational Dynamics,* winter 1994, pp. 39–44.

11. Richard M. Hodgetts, *Quality Measures in America's Most Successful Firms* (New York: American Management Association, 1998), p. 14.

12. "Hewlett-Packard Company," *Wall Street Journal,* March 7, 2003.

13. Alex Taylor III, "Chrysler: Is the Crossfire Just Another Sexy Sportscar?", *Fortune Online,* March 3, 2003.

14. Ibid., chapter 2.

15. News Release, "Xerox Office Products Receive 14 top Industry Awards, **http://www.xerox.com,** March 4, 2003.

16. John Carey, "Making the Space Program Soar Again, *BusinessWeek Online,* February 7, 2003.

17. "Our Commitment to You," **http://www.eastman.com,** 2003.

18. News Release, "GM, Ford Officially Sign Agreement to Develop All-New Front-Wheel-Drive Transmission, **http://www.gm.com,** February 14, 2002.

19. Motorola's Learning Policy, Public Relations, *Motorola Corporation,* March 5, 2003.

20. Spencer E. Ante, "The New Blue: Cover Story," *Business Week,* March 17, 2003, p. 80–88.

21. Claudia H. Deutsch, "New Economy, Old-School Rigor," *New York Times,* June 12, 2000, pp. C1–2.

22. Keith Bradsher, "The Long, Long Wait for Cars," *New York Times,* May 9, 2000, pp. C1, C29.

23. Also see Robert B. Handfield, Gary L. Ragatz, Kenneth J. Petersen, and Robert M. Monczka, "Involving Suppliers in New Product Development," *California Management Review,* fall 1999, pp. 59–82; and Michael Useed and Joseph Harder, "Leading Laterally in Company Outsourcing," *Sloan Management Review,* winter 2000, pp. 25–36.

24. David Welch, "Rick Wagoner's Game Plan," *BusinessWeek Online,* February 10, 2003.

25. Chester Dawson, "Q&A: From the Nexus of Lexus," *BusinessWeek Online,* September 3, 2001.

26. See D. Keith Denton, "Eat or Be Eaten," *Industrial Management,* May–June 1999, pp. 20–22.

27. Richard M. Hodgetts, *Blueprints for Continuous Improvement: Lessons from the Baldrige Winners* (New York: American Management Association, 1993), p. 102.

28. Jeffrey Pfeffer and Robert I. Sutton, "Knowing 'What' to Do Is Not Enough: Turning Knowledge into Action," *California Management Review,* fall 1999, p. 88.

29. News Release, "FedEx Freight Improves Transit Times; Enhancements Support Fast Cycle Distribution, **http://www.fedex.com,** March 5, 2003.

30. Also see Richard M. Hodgetts, Donald F. Kuratko, and Jeffrey S. Hornsby, "Quality Implementation in Small Business: Perspectives from the Baldrige Award Winners," *SAM Advanced Management Journal,* winter 1999, pp. 37–47.

31. Holly Treat, FedEx Corporation, e-mail correspondence with author, April 22, 2003.

32. Flex Time, "The Workplace Challenge," **http://www.semcog.org** (Southeast Michigan Council of Governments, 2003.

33. Ibid.

34. J. Carroll Swart, "Clerical Workers on Flextime: A Survey of Three Industries," *Personnel,* April 1985, p. 44.

35. **http://www.bls.gov,** *April 18, 2002, News Release*

36. **http://www.bls.gov,** *April 18, 2002, News Release*

37. Robert Webb, "Empowerment History," Motivational Tool Chest, 2000, **http://www.motivation-tools.com.**

38. Ibid.

39. "Customer Empowerment," Trends Report 2000, Trends Shaping the Digital Economy, **http://www.trendsreport.net/2000/customer/4.html**

40. The World Bank Group, "How to Measure Empowerment?" March 6, 2003, DevNews Media Center.

41. Donna Lipari, Xerox Corporation, e-mail correspondence with author, April 10, 2003.

42. Steven C. Brandt, *Entrepreneuring in Established Companies* (Homewood, IL: Dow Jones-Irwin, 1986), p. 54.

43. Donald F. Kuratko and Richard M. Hodgetts, *Entrepreneurship,* 2d ed. (Fort Worth: Dryden Press, 1992), p. 99.

44. Chris Fox, "Some Thoughts on Intrapreneurship," **http://www.ChrisFoxInc.com**

45. **http://intrapreneur.com www.askbc.com.my/A_WhyEntrepreneurship**

46. D.F. Twomey and D.L. Harris, 2000. From Strategy to Corporate Outcomes: Aligning Human Resource Management Systems with Entrepreneurial Intent, *International Journal of Commerce and Management,* Vol. 10, pp. 43–55.

47. Ibid., p. 553.

48. Stephen J. Simurda, "There's a Word for It: Intrapreneurism," *Worldbusiness Magazine,* Nov./Dec. 1996.

49. ChrisFox, op cit.

CHAPTER 8

1. See "Autonomy Is In!" *HR Focus,* October 1993, p. 10.

2. Also see Robert Frey, "Empowerment or Else," *Harvard Business Review,* September–October 1993, pp. 80–94; Richard J. Magjuka, "The 10 Dimensions of Employee Involvement," *Training and Development Journal,* April 1993, pp. 61–67; John H. Dobbs, "The Empowerment Environment," *Training and Development Journal,* February 1993, pp. 55–57; and David E. Bowen and Edward E. Lawler III, "The Empowerment of Service Workers: What, Why, How, and When," *Sloan Management Review,* Spring 1992, pp. 31–39.

3. For more on this, see Robert W. Renn and Robert J. Vandenberg, "The Critical Psychological States: An Underrepresented Component in Job Characteristics Model Research," *Journal of Management* 21, no. 2, 1995, pp. 279–303; Steven P. Brown and Thomas W. Leigh, "A New Look at Psychological Climate and Its Relationship to Job Involvement, Effort, and Performance," *Journal of Applied Psychology,* August 1996, pp. 358–368; and Greg R. Oldham and Anne Cummings, "Employee Creativity: Personal and Contextual Factors at Work," *Academy of Management Journal,* June 1996, pp. 607–634.

4. Thomas A. Stewart, "GE Keeps Those Ideas Coming," *Fortune,* August 12, 1991, pp. 41–49.

5. Ibid., p. 44.

6. Noel M. Tichy, "Revolutionize Your Company," *Fortune,* December 13, 1993, p. 118.

7. General Electric Corporation, 2003. **http://www.ge.com**

8. Anne Bruce, "Southwest: Back to the FUNdamentals," *HR Focus,* March 1997, p. 11.

9. Southwest Airlines, March 11, 2002. **http://www.southwestairlines.com**

10. Joan O'C. Hamilton, Stephen Baker, and Bill Vlasic, "The New Workplace," *Business Week,* April 29, 1996, p. 112.

11. Elizabeth Schatz, "Cranky Consumer: Scan-It-Yourself Checkout Lines," *Wall Street Journal,* March 5, 2003, p. D2.

12. Chuck Salter, "Rethinking Work," *Fast Company,* April 2000, p. 262. Also see Chuck Salter, "Office of the Future," *Fast Company,* April 2000, pp. 273–286.

13. Gary McWilliams and Ann Zimmerman, "Dell Plans to Peddle PCs Inside Sears, Other Large Chains," *Wall Street Journal,* January 30, 2003, p. B1.

14. Steve Hipple, Bureau of Labor Statistics, e-mail correspondence with author, March 17, 2003.

15. Joanne H. Pratt, "Telework and the New Workplace of the 21st Century," 2000, Dallas, TX, **http://www.dol.gov**

16. Bernie Kelly and Bruce McGraw, *Successful Management in the Virtual Office,* May 10, 1995, Internet publication, p. 5.

17. Costa, op. cit., pp. 63F–64F.

18. Eleena de Lisser, "Two UPS Part-Timers, Two Different Worlds," *Wall Street Journal,* August 14, 1997, p. B1.

19. Steven Greenhouse, "U.P.S. Says Fears of Bigger Losses Made It Cut Deal," *New York Times,* August 20, 1997, pp. A1, A14.

20. Steve Hipple, Bureau of Labor Statistics, e-mail correspondence with author, March 17, 2003.

21. For more on this, see Shari Caudron, "Building Better Bosses," *Workforce,* May 2000, pp. 32–39.

22. Minda Zetlin, "Nurturing Nonconformists," *Management Review,* October 1999, p. 32.

23. John F. Middlebrook, "Avoiding Brain Drain: How to Lock in Talent," *HR Focus,* March 1999, pp. 9–10.

24. David Woodruff, "Europe's Companies Coddle Employees," *Wall Street Journal,* August 4, 2000, pp. A7, A9.

25. "Fortune Magazine Names Stew Leonard's Among the 100 Best Companies to Work for America," Norwalk, Conn., January 7, 2003, **http://www.stewleonards.com**

26. Linda Davidson, "The Power of Personal Recognition," *Workforce,* July 1999, p. 49.

27. Amy Zipkin, "The Wisdom of Thoughtfulness," *New York Times,* May 31, 2000, pp. C1, C10.

28. Also see Melinda Ligos, "The Nicest Man on Wall St." *New York Times,* May 31, 2000, p. C10.

29. Also see "The Challenges Facing Workers in the Future," *HR Focus,* August 1999, p. 6.

CHAPTER 9

1. Also see Ronald A. Heifetz and Donald L. Laurie, "The Work of Leadership," *Harvard Business Review,* January–February 1997, pp. 124–134.

2. Ralph Stogdill, *Handbook of Leadership* (New York: Free Press, 1974), p. 81.

3. Bernard M. Bass, *Bass & Stogdill's Handbook of Leadership* (New York: Free Press, 1990), pp. 64–65.

4. Stogdill, op. cit., pp. 80–81.

5. For more of these, see Robert M. Fulmer and Stacey Wagner, "Leadership: Lessons from the Best," *Training and Development Journal,* March 1999, p. 31.

6. Keith H. Hammonds, "The Secret Life of the CEO: Do They Even Know Right From Wrong?" *Fast Company Magazine,* October 2002, **http://www.fastcompany.com**

7. Oren Harari, "Leadership vs. Autocracy: They Just Don't Get It!" *Management Review,* August 1996, pp. 42–45.

8. Douglas McGregor, *The Human Side of Enterprise* (New York: McGraw-Hill, 1960).

9. Ibid., pp. 33–34.

10. Ibid., pp. 47–48.

11. Edmund L. Andrews, "No Apologies from Stuttgart," *New York Times,* December 2, 2000, pp. B1–2.

12. See "The Superior CEO: A Profile," *Fortune,* June 21, 1999, p. 78.

13. Ron Zemke, "Can You Manage Trust?" *Training,* February 2000, pp. 80–82.

14. Fred E. Fiedler, *A Theory of Leadership Effectiveness* (New York: McGraw-Hill, 1967).

15. Fred Fiedler, "Style or Circumstance: The Leadership Enigma," *Psychology Today,* March 1969, p. 42.

16. R. R. Blake and J. S. Mouton, *The Managerial Grid* (Houston: Gulf, 1964).

17. Patricia Sellers, "What Exactly Is Charisma?" *Fortune,* January 15, 1996, pp. 70–71.

18. Gary McWilliams, "Dell Looks for Ways to Rekindle the Fire It Had as an Upstart," *Wall Street Journal,* August 31, 2000, pp. A1, A8.

19. Bernard M. Bass, *Bass and Stogdill's Handbook of Leadership,* 3d ed. (New York: Free Press, 1992), p. 221.

20. Bernard M. Bass, "Is There Universality in the Full Range Model of Leadership?" *International Journal of Public Administration* 19, no. 6, 1996, p. 742.

21. Book Excerpts, *Business Week Online,* June 13, 2002, Patrick J. McKenna and David H. Maister. *First Among Equals,* Chapter 4, "Dare to be Inspiring", The Free Press, 2002.

22. Bob Nelson, "1001 Ways to Reward Employees," **http://www.fed.org**

23. Robert Hertzberg, "When IT Success Taps Team Spirit, *Baseline Magazine,* September 9, 2002, **http://www.baselinemag.com/print_article/0,3668,a=30838,00.asp**

24. "Virtual Company Advice, *Inc Magazine,* October 21, 1999, **http://www.inc.com**

25. Alison Overholt, "The Art of Multitasking," *Fast Company,* October 2002, p. 118, **http://www.fastcompany.com/online/63/multitasking.html**

26. "Global Leader of the Future," *Management Review,* October 1999, p. 9.

27. Scott Thurm, "How to Drive an Express Train," *Wall Street Journal,* June 1, 2000, pp. B1, B4.

28. John C. Maxwell, *The 21 Irrefutable Laws of Leadership* (Nashville: Thomas Nelson, 1998), p. 208.

29. James Waldroop and Timothy Butler, "Managing Away Bad Habits," *Harvard Business Review,* September–October 2000, pp. 91–98.

30. Ibid., p. 96.

31. For additional insights regarding how leaders must act, see Nancy S. Ahlrichs, *Competing for Talent* (Palo Alto: Davies-Black, 2000), pp. 173–175.

CHAPTER 10

1. "Three Ways to Build Recruiter Relationships," *Workforce,* July 2002, pp. 74–77, **http://www.workforce.com**

2. "Women Roar", Tom Peters Times! March 18, 2003, **http://www.tompeters.com**

3. "A Recruiter Explores the Intangibles," *Workforce* July 2002, pp. 74–77 **http://www.workforce.com**

4. "Spending on HR and Recruiting," *Workforce Week,* Vol. 3, Issue 13, March 31–April 5, 2003.

5. Samuel Greengard, "Are You Well Armed to Screen Applicants?" *Personnel Journal,* December 1995, pp. 84–85.

6. "200 Questions Job Candidates May Ask Your Company: Questions for Hiring Managers" Reprinted from 201 Best Questions to Ask on Your Interview by John Kador, 2002, McGraw-Hill Companies, Inc., *Workforce,* **http://www. workforce.com**

7. Diann R. Newman and Richard M. Hodgetts, *Human Resource Management: A Customer-Oriented Approach* (Upper Saddle River, NJ: Prentice Hall, 1998), pp. 166–167.

8. Peter Carbonara, "Hire for Attitude, Train for Skill," *Fast Company,* August 1996, **http://www.fastcompany. com/online/04/hiring.html**

9. **http://www.southwestairlines.com**

10. Jeffrey A. Mello, "Personality Tests and Privacy Rights," *HR Focus,* March 1996, pp. 22–23.

11. Staff, "How It Can Pay to Teach," *BusinessWeek Online,* June 6, 2000.

12. Sarah Fister Gale, "Making E-Learning More Than 'Pixie Dust,'" *Workforce,* March, 2003, pp. 58–62.

13. Sarah Fister Gale, "Blended Formats Engage All Learners," *Workforce,* March, 2003, p. 60.

14. Patrick J. Kiger, "Cisco's Homegrown Gamble," *Workforce,* March, 2003, p. 34, **http://www.workforce.com**

15. Sarah Fister Gale, "Tracking Learning Impact," *Workforce,* March, 2003, pp. 60–62, **http://www.workforce.com**

16. "Honeywell's Director: Constant Challenges Thrown in Front of Us," *Workforce Week,* February 9–15, 2003, **http://www.workforce.com**

17. Jennifer Weyrauch, Motorola, Inc., e-mail correspondence with the author, April 25, 2003.

18. Brien N. Smith, Jeffrey S. Hornsby, and Roslyn Shirmeyer, "Current Trends in Performance Appraisal: An Explanation of Managerial Practices," *SAM Advanced Management Journal,* summer 1996, pp. 10–15.

19. Mark R. Edwards and Ann J. Ewen, *360° Feedback* (New York: American Management Association, 1996).

20. Francis J. Yammarino and Leanne E. Atwater, "Do Managers See Themselves as Others See Them? Implication of Self–Other Rating Agreement for Human Resources Management," *Organizational Dynamics,* spring 1997, p. 36.

21. Richard Lepsinger and Anntoinette D. Lucia, *The Art and Science of 360° Feedback* (San Francisco: Jossey-Bass, 1997), p. 6.

22. For more on this see, Richard M. Hodgetts, *Measures of Quality and High Performance: Simple Tools and Lessons from America's Most Successful Companies* (New York: American Management Association, 1998), chapter 6; Keith E. Morical, "A Product Review: 360° Assessments," *Training and Development Journal,* April 1999, pp. 43–47; Kenneth M. Nowack, Jeanne Hartley, and William Bradley, "How to Evaluate Your 360° Feedback Efforts," *Training and Development Journal,* April 1999, pp. 48–53; and Adrian Furnham and Paul Stringfield, "Congruence in Job-Performance Ratings: A Study of 360° Feedback Examining Self, Manager, Peers, and Consultant Ratings," *Human Relations,* April 1998, pp. 517–530.

23. Sharon Davis, "Minority Execs Want an Even Break," *Workforce,* April 2000, p. 52.

24. Amelia J. Prewett-Livingston, John G. Veres III, Hubert S. Field, and Philip M. Lewis, "Effects of Race on Interview Ratings in a Situational Panel Interview," *Journal of Applied Psychology,* April 1996, pp. 178–186.

25. Cynthia M. Marlowe, Sandra L. Schneider, and Carnot E. Nelson, "Gender and Attractiveness Biases in Hiring Decisions: Are More Experienced Managers Less Biased?" *Journal of Applied Psychology,* February 1996, pp. 11–21.

26. Juan I. Sanchez and Phillip De La Torre, "A Second Look at the Relationship Between Rating and Behavioral Accuracy in Performance Appraisal," *Journal of Applied Psychology,* February 1996, pp. 3–10.

27. Neal P. Mero and Stephan J. Motowidlo, "Effects of Rater Accountability on the Accuracy and the Favorability of Performance Ratings," *Journal of Applied Psychology,* August 1995, pp. 517–524.

28. Steven L. Thomas and Robert D. Bretz Jr., "Research and Practice in Performance Appraisal: Evaluating Employee Performance in America's Largest Companies," *SAM Advanced Management Journal,* spring 1994, pp. 33–34.

29. "Money Isn't Everything" *Workforce,* March 6, 2003, Source: August Vlak, principal at Katzenbach Partners LLC, New York, NY. January 20, 2003.

30. See Louise O'Brien and Charles Jones, "Do Rewards Really Create Loyalty?" *Harvard Business Review,* May–June 1995, pp. 75–82.

31. "Latest Data on Alternative Pay," *HR Focus,* July 2000, pp. 11–15.

32. See, for example, "Why Gainsharing Works Even Better Today Than in the Past," *HR Focus,* April 2000, pp. 3–5.

33. Larry Reynolds, "Successfully Administering Flex Plans," *HR Focus,* April 1995, pp. 7–8.

34. See, for example, "Do Incentive Awards Work?" *HR Focus,* October 2000, pp. 1, 14–15.

35. "What Distinguishes High Performing Company Pay Practices from the Pack?" *HR Focus,* May 2000, p. 4.

36. Shari Caudron, "Master the Compensation Maze," *Personnel Journal,* June 1993, p. 64C.

37. Interview with Jessie Torres, District Manager, Taco Bell, March 31, 2003.

38. Lewis Braham, "A Perk for the Rank and File, Too," *Business Week Online,* March 10, 2003, **http://www. businessweek.com**

39. Reported in Newman and Hodgetts, op. cit., p. 229.

40. "Perks Job Seekers Are Looking for from Their New Employer" *Workforce Week,* February 9–15, 2003 **http://www.workforce.com**

41. Everett T. Suters, "The Toughest Job Around," *Inc.,* November 1986, pp. 138, 140.

42. Bureau of Labor Statistics, **http://www.bls.gov**

43. For more on this, see Susan Gardner, Glenn M. Gomes, and James F. Morgan, "Wrongful Termination and the Expanding Public Policy Exception: Implications and Advice," *SAM Advanced Management Journal,* winter 2000, pp. 38–44.

44. See Sara Siwolop, "Recourse or Retribution?" *New York Times,* June 7, 2000, pp. C1, C10.

45. Dawn Anfuso, "Coors Taps Employee Judgment," *Personnel Journal,* February 1994, pp. 50–59.

CHAPTER 11

1. D. Clark, "Managing the Mountain," *Wall Street Journal,* June 21, 1999, p. R4.

2. R. L. Daft and R. H. Lengel, "Information Richness: A New Approach to Managerial Behavior and Organizational Design," in *Research in Organizational Behavior,* edited by B. M. Staw and L. L. Cummings (Greenwich, CT: JAI Press, 1984), p. 196.

3. Ibid., p. 197.

4. R. E. Rice and D. E. Shook, "Relationships of Job Categories and Organizational Levels to Use of Communication Channels, Including Electronic Mail: A Meta-Analysis and Extension," *Journal of Management Studies,* March 1990, pp. 195–229.

5. Sue Shellenberger and Carol Hymowitz, "As Population Ages, Older Workers Clash with Younger Bosses," *Wall Street Journal,* June 13, 1994, pp. A1, A5.

6. Crystal L. Owen and William D. Todor, "Attitudes Toward Women as Managers: Still the Same," *Business Horizons,* March–April 1993, pp. 12–16; and Robert A. Snyder, "The Glass Ceiling for Women: Things That Don't Cause It and Things That Won't Break It," *Human Resource Development Quarterly,* spring 1993, pp. 97–106.

7. Dan R. Dalton and Idalene F. Kesner, "Cracks in the Glass: The Silent Competence of Women," *Business Horizons,* March–April 1993, pp. 6–11.

8. Patricia Schiff Estess, "Open-Book Policy," *Entrepreneur,* March 2000, pp. 130–131.

9. K. Denise Bane, "Gaining Control By Losing It? The Dilemma of Entrepreneurial Information," *Academy of Management Executive,* May 1997, pp. 80–82.

10. Raymond S. Nickerson, "How We Know—And Sometimes Misjudge—What Others Know: Imputing One's Own Knowledge to Others," *Psychological Bulletin* 125, no. 6, 1999, pp. 737–759.

11. Jerry E. Bishop, "Why Vacuum Cleaners Are Louder and Other Acoustic Mysteries," *Wall Street Journal,* August 30, 1994, pp. B1, B5.

12. Daniel Benjamin and Tony Horwitz, "German View: You Americans Work Too Hard—and for What?" *Wall Street Journal,* August 14, 1994, pp. B1, B6.

13. Jenny C. McCune, "The Birth of Tech Terms," *Management Review,* February 1999, p. 11.

14. Lin Grensing-Pophal, "Talk to Me," *HR Magazine,* March 2000, p. 70.

15. Also see Paul Sandwith, "Building Quality into Communications," *Training and Development Journal,* January 1994, pp. 55–59.

16. See Howard E. Butz Jr. and Leonard D. Goodstein, "Measuring Customer Value: Gaining the Strategic Advantage," *Organizational Dynamics,* winter 1996, p. 72.

17. Larry L. Barker, *Communication* (Englewood Cliffs, NJ: Prentice Hall, 1978), p. 151.

18. "Speaking to the Boss," *Training,* February 2000, p. 28.

19. Albert Mehrabian, *Nonverbal Communication* (Chicago: Aldine-Atherton, 1972), pp. 25–30.

20. Roger E. Axtell, *Gestures: The DO's and TABOO's of Body Language Around the World,* 2nd edition, 1991, pp. 42–45.

21. "In Brief: Employee Satisfaction," *Workforce Week,* Vol. 3 Issue 15, April 13–19, 2003 **http://www.workforce.com**

22. For more on this topic, see "Listening Is a 10-Part Skill," *Nation's Business,* September 1987, p. 40.

23. "Fogen's First Law," *Across the Board,* January 2000, p. 78.

24. Annette C. Easton, Nancy S. Eickelmann, and Marie E. Flatley, "Effects of an Electronic Meeting System Group Writing Tool on the Quality of Written Documents," *Journal of Business Communication,* January 1994, pp. 27–40.

25. See, for example, Reid Buckley, "When You Have to Put It to Them," *Across the Board,* October 1999, pp. 44–47; and Curtis Sittenfild, "How to WOW an Audience—Every Time," *Fast Company,* September 1999, p. 86.

26. Richard M. Hodgetts and Jane Whitney Gibson, "Building Effective Oral Presentations: The PLAN Approach," *1986 IEEE International Professional Communication Conference Proceedings,* pp. 67–69.

27. J. C. Tingley, *Genderflex: Men & Women Speaking Each Other's Language at Work* (New York: American Management Association, 1994).

28. Deborah Tannen, "The Power of Talk: Who Gets Heard and Why," *Harvard Business Review,* September–October 1995, p. 139.

29. For more on this, see A. H. Eagly and W. Wood, "The Origins of Sex Differences in Human Behavior," *American Psychologist,* June 1999, pp. 408–423.

30. Deborah Tannen, "The Power of Talk: Who Gets Heard and Why," in R. J. Lewicki and D. M. Saunders, eds., *Negotiation: Readings, Exercises, and Cases,* 3d ed. (Boston, MA: Irwin/McGraw-Hill, 1999), pp. 160–173; and Deborah Tannen, *You Just Don't Understand: Women and Men in Conversation* (New York: Ballantine Books, 1990).

31. See, for example, K. Hawkins and C. B. Power, "Gender Differences in Questions Asked During Small Decision-Making Group Discussions," *Small Group Research,* April 1999, pp. 235–256; and K. C. Gordon, D. H. Baucom, N. Epstein, C. K. Burnett, and L. A. Rankin, "The Interaction Between Marital Standards and Communication Patterns: How Does It Contribute to Marital Adjustment," *Journal of Marital Family Therapy,* April 1999, pp. 211–223.

32. June Kronholz, "How 23 E-Mails Sent by a 9th-Grade Girl Got 160,478 Replies," *Wall Street Journal,* February 13, 2003, p. A1.

33. For more information read: Christine Nuzum, "U.S. Wireless Market Sees Surprising Growth," *Wall Street Journal Online,* August 15, 2003. **http://www.online.wsj.com**

34. Nanette Byrnes, "The Boss in the Web Age," *Business Week,* August 28, 2000.

35. Frances Hesselbein, "Managing in a World That is Round," *Leader to Leader Institute,* No. 2 Fall 1996, pp. 6–8.

36. Philip Ball, "E-mail Reveal Real Leaders," Nature Science Update, March 20, 2003, *Nature News Service,* Macmillan Magazines Ltd, 2003.

37. Reference: Adapted from Debra L. Nelson and James Campbell Quick, *Organizational Behavior,* "How Do Communication Technologies Affect Behavior?" South-Western Publishers, 4th edition, 2003, pp. 277–278.

CHAPTER 12

1. Stephanie N. Mehta, "What Minority Employees Really Want," *Fortune,* July 10, 2000, pp. 181–186.

2. Edmund L. Andrews, "Daimler Says Chrysler's Problems Are Worsening," *New York Times,* December 19, 2000, p. W1; and Jeffrey Ball, "DaimlerChrysler Official Expects Restructuring, Change Next Year," *Wall Street Journal,* December 20, 2000, p. A4.

3. David de Long and Patricia Seemann, "Confronting Conceptual Confusion and Conflict in Knowledge Management," *Organizational Dynamics,* summer 2000, p. 37.

4. **http://www.samhsa.gov/oas/work.htm** updated March 20, 2003.

5. Donald A. Phillips and Harry J. Older, "Alcoholic Employees Beget Troubled Supervisors," *Supervisory Management,* September 1981, p. 5.

6. Mark R. Edwards and J. Ruth Sproull, "Confronting Alcoholism Through Team Evaluation," *Business Horizons,* May–June 1986, p. 82.

7. Becky Vance, "Drug Use and Abuse Remains a Serious Workplace Problem," *Houston Business Journal,* July 21, 2000, p. 49.

8. U. S. Department of Health **http://www. drugtestcenter.com/content1/employers/sub_ab use_facts_figs.htm**

9. Bill Oliver, "Ten Steps to a Near-Drug-Free Workplace," *HR Focus,* December 1993, p. 9.

10. Erica Gordon Sorohan, "Making Decisions About Drug Testing," *Training and Development Journal,* May 1994, p. 112.

11. "Drug Testing in the Workplace," *ACLU Briefing Paper,* no. 5, July 26, 1997.

12. For more on EAPs, see Peggy Stuart, "Investments in EAPs Pay Off," *Personnel Journal,* February 1993, pp. 43–54.

13. **http://www.samhsa.gov/oas/work.htm,** updated March 19, 2003.

14. **http://www.samhsa.gov/oas/work.htm,** updated March 10, 2002.

15. James A. Wall Jr. and Ronda Roberts Callister, "Conflict and Its Management," *Journal of Management,* Fall 1995, p. 395.

16. Also see Willem F. G. Mastenbroek, "Organizational Innovation in Historical Perspective: Change as Duality Management," *Business Horizons,* July–August 1996, pp. 5–14.

17. Seth Godin, "Survival Is Not Enough," *FastCompany,* January 2002, issue 54, p. 90.

18. Robert B. Reich, "Your Job Is Change," *Fast Company,* October 2000, p. 143.

19. Pierre Mornell, "Nothing Endures But Change," *Inc.,* July 20, 2000, pp. 131–132.

20. Eric Abrahamson, "Change Without Pain," *Harvard Business Review,* July–August 2000, p. 74.

21. See Kenneth P. De Meuse and Kevin K. McDaris, "An Exercise in Managing Change," *Training and Development Journal,* February 1994, pp. 55–57.

22. Alan M. Webber, "Will Companies Ever Learn?" *Fast Company,* October 2000, pp. 275–282.

23. For more on this topic, see Daniel C. Feldman and Carrie R. Leana, "A Study of Reemployment Challenges After Downsizing," *Organizational Dynamics,* summer 2000, pp. 64–74.

24. Research, "26+ Reasons Why Employees Resist Changes," *Anderson Consulting,* Philadelphia, PA, 1988-1999, **http://www.andersonconsulting.com**

25. Shari Caudron, "What Skills Are Needed by Today's Managers?" *Workforce,* May 2000, p. 36.

26. Curt M. Thompson, "Preparation Is Key to Successful Change," *HR Focus,* April 1994, pp. 17–18.

27. Alan L. Frohman, "Igniting Organizational Change: The Power of Personal Initiative," *Organizational Dynamics,* winter 1997, pp. 39–53.

28. "How Does Change Management Need to Change?" *Harvard Management Update,* January 2001, **http://www. hbsp.harvard.edu**

29. Mary Buchel, "Accelerating Change," *Training and Development Journal,* April 1996, pp. 48–51.

30. Paul Strebel, "Choosing the Right Change Path," *California Management Review,* winter 1994, p. 46.

31. John H. Zimmerman, "The Principles of Managing," *HR Focus,* February 1995, pp. 15–16.

32. Shikha Sharma, "Organizational Change," "Structural Interventions," *Organizational Design,* 1995, Faculty of Information Studies, University of Toronto.

33. "How Organizational Development Works: Conceptual View," *Toolpack Consulting,* LLC, Teaneck , New Jersey.

34. Wendell L. French and Cecil H. Bell Jr., *Organizational Development,* 2d ed. (Englewood Cliffs, NJ: Prentice Hall, 1978), p. 137.

35. A White Paper, "Employee Surveys: A Tool for Change," *Toolpack Consulting,* October 2001, Version 1.1b.

36. David G. Bowers, "OD Techniques and Their Results in 23 Organizations: The Michigan ICL Study," *Journal of Applied Behavioral Science,* January–February 1973, pp. 21–43.

37. For a complete account of the program, see Alfred J. Marrow, David G. Bowers, and Stanley E. Seashore, *Management by Participation* (New York: Harper & Row, 1967).

CHAPTER 13

1. Alan M. Rugman and Richard M. Hodgetts, *International Business,* 2d ed. (London: Pearson Education, 2000), p. 5.

2. For a look at the entire list that evaluates companies in 27 industries, see Nicholas Stein, "The World's Most Admired Companies," *Fortune,* October 2, 2000, pp. 182–196.

3. Craig S. Smith, "The Race Begins to Build a Small Car for China," *New York Times,* October 24, 2000, p. W1.

4. Peter Wonacott, "Wal-Mart Finds Market Footing in China," *Wall Street Journal,* July 17, 2000, p. A31.

5. William Boston and Ann Zimmerman, "Wal-Mart Plans Major Expansion in Germany," *Wall Street Journal,* July 20, 2000, p. A21.

6. Jon E. Hilsenrath, "Ford Builds a Car to Suit India's Tastes," *Wall Street Journal,* August 8, 2000, p. A17, A19.

7. The EU consists of Austria, Belgium, Denmark, Finland, France, Germany, Greece, Ireland, Italy, Luxembourg, the Netherlands, Portugal, Spain, Sweden, and the United Kingdom.

8. Richard M. Hodgetts and Fred Luthans, *International Management,* 4th ed. (Burr Ridge, IL: Irwin/McGraw, 2000), p. 108.

9. Esmond D. Smith Jr. and Cuong Pham, "Doing Business in Vietnam: A Cultural Guide," *Business Horizons,* May–June 1996, pp. 47–51; and Arvind V. Phatak and Mohammed M. Habib, "The Dynamics of International Business Negotiations," *Business Horizons,* May–June 1996, pp. 30–38.

10. "Now Solutions," *Workforce,* February 27, 2003, **http://www.workforce.com/archieve/article/23/33/40.php**

11. Carolena Lyons Lawrence, "Teaching Students How Gestures Communicate Across Cultures," *Business Education Forum,* February 2003, pp. 38–40.

12. Geert Hofstede, *Culture's Consequences: Differences in Work-Related Values* (Beverly Hills, CA: Sage, 1980), p. 420.

13. Simcha Ronen and Allen I. Kraut, "Similarities Among Countries Based on Employee Work Values and Attitudes," *Columbia Journal of World Business,* summer 1977, p. 90.

14. Simcha Ronen and Oded Shenkar, "Clustering Countries on Attitudinal Dimensions: A Review and Synthesis," *Academy of Management Journal,* September 1985, pp. 435–454.

15. Dominic Rushe, "UK Bosses Top World Stress Poll," *Sunday Times,* July 23, 2000, p. 2G.

16. Hodgetts and Luthans, op. cit., p. 389.

17. Sebastian Moffett, "Going Gray: For Ailing Japan, Longevity Begins to Take Its Toll," *Wall Street Journal,* February 11, 2003, p. A1.

18. Suzanne Daley, "Spain Rudely Awakened to Workaday World," *New York Times,* December 26, 1999, pp. 1, 6.

19. Richard M. Hodgetts, "A Conversation with Geert Hofstede," *Organizational Dynamics,* spring 1994, pp. 53–54.

20. Pete Engardio, Aaron Bernstein, and Manjeet Kripalani, "The New Global Job Shift," *Business Week Online,* February 3, 2003.

21. Ibid.

22. John Varoli, "It's a Free Market, but Who's Fit to Manage?" *New York Times,* December 26, 1999, pp. 1, 6.

23. Phred Dvorak, Robert A. Guth, Peter Landers, and Todd Zaun, "Distress, Deregulation and Diplomacy Breach Walls of Fortress Japan," *Wall Street Journal,* December 28, 2000, p. A4.

24. Margaret Linehan and James S. Walsh, "Recruiting and Developing Female Managers for International Assignments," *Journal of Management Development* 18, no. 6, 1999, pp. 521–530.

25. Hodgetts and Luthans, op. cit., p. 433.

26. Suzanne Daley, "A Spy's Advice to French Retailers: Politeness Pays," *New York Times,* December 26, 2000, p. A4.

27. For more on culture and negotiations, see Philip R. Harris and Robert T. Moran, *Managing Cultural Differences,* 5th ed. (Houston: Gulf, 2000); and Richard D. Lewis, *When Cultures Collide* (London: Nicholas Brealey, 1999).

28. Sheida Hodge, *Global Smarts: The Art of Communicating and Deal Making Anywhere in the World* (New York: John Wiley & Sons, 2000), pp. 152–153.

29. Andrew Ross Sorkin, "The Year That European Corporate Acquirers Invaded America," *New York Times,* December 18, 2000, p. C14.

30. Jenny C. McCune, "Exporting Corporate Culture," *Management Review,* December 1999, p. 55.

31. Andrew Rosenbaum, "Testing Cultural Waters," *Management Review,* July–August 1999, pp. 41–43.

32. Gail Dutton, "Building a Global Brain," *Management Review,* May 1999, p. 34.

33. Yoshio Tateishi, Representative Director and CEO, "Meeting the Challenges of the 21st Century," *GD2010,* May 28, 2003, **http://www.omron.com**

34. Gail Dutton, op. cit., p. 36.

35. Larraine Segil, *Intelligent Business Alliances* (New York: Random House, 1996).

36. McCune, op. cit., p. 56.

37. Cyrus F. Freidheim Jr., "The Battle of the Alliances," *Management Review,* September 1999, p. 47.

CHAPTER 14

1. For more on entrepreneurial myths, see Donald F. Kuratko and Richard M. Hodgetts, *Entrepreneurship: A Contemporary Approach,* 5th ed. (Orlando: Harcourt, 2001), pp. 71–72.

2. Tom Peters, *Thriving on Chaos* (New York: Knopf, 1987), p. 229.

3. Kathryn Martell and Stephen J. Carroll, "Which Executive Human Resource Management Practices for the Top Management Team Are Associated with Higher Firm Performance?" *Human Resource Management* 34, no. 4, 1995, pp. 497–512.

4. Philip M. Mirvis, "Human Resource Management: Leaders, Laggards, and Followers," *Academy of Management Executive,* May 1997, p. 49.

5. Ibid., p. 55.

6. Michael Hammer and James Champy, *Reengineering the Corporation* (New York: HarperCollins, 1993), p. 32.

7. Spencer E. Ante, New York, "Savings Tip: Don't Do It Yourself," *Business Week Online,* June 23, 2003.

8. Press Release from Wipro Limited, April 24, 2003, **http://www.nervewire.com** and **http://www. wipro.com**

9. Check Free Corporation, 2003, **http://www.checkfree.com**

10. Jane Shealy, "Playing for Keeps," *Success,* December–January 2001, p. 63.

11. Be Free, 2003, **http://www.befree.com**

12. Ibid. opcit Jane Shealy.

13. **http://www.CNSNews.com** Christine Hall, Staff Writer, "Employee Perks Hit by Weak Economy, But Some Survive," December 2, 2002.

14. Robert Levering and Milton Moskowitz, "How Companies Satisfy Workers," *Fortune,* January 7, 2003.

15. Anne Robertson, "Employee Perks and Comforts Keep Creative Juices Flowing" *The Business Journal,* Phoenix, February 17, 2003.

16. Ibid. opcit Jane Shealy.

17. See Robert Levering and Milton Moskowitz, "The 100 Best Companies to Work For," *Fortune,* January 8, 2001, pp. 148–168.

18. Katharine Q. Seelye, "Future U.S.: Grayer and More Hispanic," *New York Times,* March 27, 1997, p. A18.

19. Table: "Median Weekly earnings of full-time wage and salary workers by selected characteristics," *Household Data Annual Averages,* Bureau of Labor Statistics, 2002.

20. Susanne Craig, "Smith Barney Gender Case to be Heard," *Wall Street Journal,* July 14, 2003, page C1.

21. Patrick McGeehan, "Morgan Stanley Is Cited for Discrimination Against Women," *New York Times,* June 6, 2000, pp. C1–2.

22. Steven Greenhouse, "Plastics Company Is to Pay $782,000 to Settle Charges of Sex Discrimination," *New York Times,* December 7, 2000, p. C17.

23. "Jury finds Outback Steakhouse guilty of sex discrimination and illegal retaliation; awards victim $2.2 million," September 19, 2001, **http://www.eeoc.gov**

24. "Court gives final approval to $47 million settlement in sex discrimination suits against Rent-A-Center by EEOC and private plaintiffs," October 4, 2002, **http://www.eeoc.gov**

25. "Labor department signs settlement agreement with Jimmy Dean Foods that will benefit 48 female job applicants," April, 10, 2003, **http://www.dol.gov**

26. "Labor department signs settlement agreement with Swissport USA, Inc., to remedy hiring discrimination," May 5, 2003, **http://www.dol.gov**

27. "Coke Settles Racial Suit for Record $192 Million," *Miami Herald,* November 17, 2000, pp. 1A, 2A; Ann Harrington, "Prevention Is the Best Defense," *Fortune,* July 10, 2000, p. 188; Constance L. Hays, "Group of Black Employees Calls for Boycott of Coca-Cola Products," *New York Times,* April 20, 2000, pp. C1–2; Nikhil Deogun, "Coke Was Told in '95 of Need for Diversity," *Wall Street Journal,* May 20, 1999, p. A3; and Nikhil Deogun, "A Race-Bias Suit Tests Coke," *Wall Street Journal,* May 18, 1999, pp. B1, B4.

28. Seth Schiesel, "Workers Plan Bias Lawsuits Against Nextel," *New York Times,* June 20, 2000, pp. C1, C6.

29. Carey Goldberg, "Fat People Say an Intolerant World Condemns Them on First Sight," *New York Times,* November 5, 2000, p. 30y.

30. American Obesity Association, downloaded July 14, 2003, **http://www.aoa.org**

31. Leslie M. Dawson, "Women and Men, Morality and Ethics," *Business Horizons,* July–August 1995, p. 68.

32. Shari Caudron, "Learning to Understand Each Other by 'Genderflexing,'" *Personnel Journal,* May 1995, p. 54.

33. "Diversity Training," **http://www.NCRVE.org**

34. Linda Gravett, Ph.D., SPHR, "Why Diversity Training Fails," **http://www.e-Hresources.com**

35. See Diane C. Harris, "Grease the Gears of Equality," *Personnel Journal,* September 1995, pp. 120–127.

36. The information in this section can be found in Fred Luthans, Richard M. Hodgetts, and Sang M. Lee, "New Paradigm Organizations: From Total Quality to Learning to World-Class," *Organizational Dynamics,* winter 1994, pp. 5–19.

37. Laura Saunders Egodigwe, John C. Long, and Nima Warfield, "A Year of Scandals and Sorrow," *Wall Street Journal,* January 2, 2003, Section R.

38. "Fast Forward: 25 Trends That Will Change the Way You Do Business," *Workforce,* June 2003, pp. 43–56.

39. Passwords Without Pain: The Compelling Value of Integrated Identity Management," *NerveWire,* Inc. 2003, **http://www.nervwire.com**

40. Ray A. Smith, "New Warehouses Take on a Luxe Look," *Wall Street Journal,* June 18, 2003.

41. Dennis K. Berman, "Will Camera-Phones BE Used to Humiliate Us Ordinary People?" *Wall Street Journal,* June 2, 2003, p. B1.

42. Carlos Tejada and Gary McWilliams, "New Recipe for Cost Savings: Replace Expensive Workers," *Wall Street Journal,* June 11, 2003, p. A1.

43. "In Age of SARS, Wal-Mart Adjusts Global Buying Machine," *Wall Street Journal,* May 28, 2003, p. B1.

44. Carol Hymowitz, "Baby Boomers Seek New Ways to Escape Career Claustrophobia," *Wall Street Journal,* June 24, 2003, p. B1.

45. Jane Spencer, "Shirk Ethic: How to Fake a Hard Day at the Office," *Wall Street Journal,* May 15, 2003, p. D1.

46. Kortney Stringer, "How to Have a Pleasant Trip: Eliminate Human Contact," *Wall Street Journal,* October 31, 2002.

47. "DBM Survey Finds Companies Have Not Prepared Younger Workers for Senior Leadership Roles," *Drake Beam Morin,* July 14, 2003, **http://www.dbm.com**

CHAPTER 15

1. Louisa Wah, "The Generation 2001 Workforce," *Management Review,* April 1999, p. 8.

2. For some examples, see "Sanity Tool Box" in Pamela Kruger, "Jobs for Life," *Fast Company,* May 2000, p. 250;

and Jean-Marie Hiltrop, "The Quest for the Best: Human Resource Practices to Attract and Retain Talent," *European Management Journal* 17, no. 4, 1999, pp. 422–430.

3. James E. Challenger, "Brief Resume May Shortchange Employment Chances," *Miami Herald,* section L, November 20, 1994.

4. Kemba J. Dunham, "Wacky Resumes Get Attention—But a Job, Too?" *Wall Street Journal,* December 19, 2000, p. B16.

5. Joann S. Lublin, "College Students Make Job-Hunting Tougher With Weak Resumes," *Wall Street Journal,* April 29, 2003, p. B1.

6. Michelle Conlin, "The Resume Doctor Is In," *Business Week,* July 14, 2003, pp. 116–117.

7. Joann S. Lublin, "Job Hunters With Gaps in Their Resumes Need to Write Around Them." *Wall Street Journal,* May 6, 2003, p. B1.

8. Cynthia Crossen, "Classified Ads Tell Tales of Social Change: Sober Need Not Apply," *Wall Street Journal,* April 16, 2003, p. B1.

9. Victor Godinez, "Recruiters Often Prefer Getting Resumes by E-mail," *Miami Herald,* Monday business section, December 25, 2000, p. 40.

10. Kris Maher, "Online Job Hunting is Tough. Just Ask Vinnie." *Wall Street Journal,* June 24, 2003, p. B1.

11. George Anders, "Talent Bank," *Fast Company,* November 2000, p. 96.

12. Samuel Greengard, "Gimme Attitude," *Workforce,* July 2003, pp. 56–60 **http://www.workforce.com**

13. Greengard.

14. Greengard.

15. Tod Balf, "Don't Conduct an Interview," *Fast Company,* September 2000, p. 86; and Cynthia Key Stevens and Amy L. Kristof, "Making the Right Impression: A Field Study of Applicant Impression Management During Job Interviews," *Journal of Applied Psychology* 80, no. 5, 1995, pp. 587–606.

16. Bill Radin, "Seven Keys to Interview Preparation," **http://www.shaytannas.com**

17. Jack Thomas, "Hiring in Times of Anger and Fear," *Career Journal of the Wall Street Journal,* **http://www.careerjournal.com/columnists/perspective/20030512-des**

18. Carol Hymowitz, "Managers Face Battle to Keep Salaries Fair in a Tight Job Market," *Wall Street Journal,* March 21, 2000, p. B1.

19. Robyn D. Clarke, "The Way to Work," *Black Enterprise,* August 2000, p. 135.

20. Bill Radin, "Seven Keys to Interview Preparation," **http://www.shaytannas.com**

21. Anne Fischer, "Ways to Rise," *Fortune,* January 13, 1997, p. 47.

22. Thomas A. Stewart, "Looking Out for Number 1: A Complete Guide to Your Career," *Fortune,* January 15, 1996, pp. 33–48.

23. Brent B. Allred, Charles C. Snow, and Raymond E. Miles, "Characteristics of Managerial Careers in the 21st Century," *Academy of Management Executive* 10, no. 4, 1996, pp. 17–27.

24. "Knowledge and Livelihood: The Global Forces Reshaping Work," Trend: Power, *4Work Food for Thought,* **http://www.4work.com**

25. Kemba J. Dunham, "Executives Seek Career Boost From Writing, Speaking Stints," *Wall Street Journal,* August 22, 2000, p. B12.

26. Adele Scheele, "When You've Been Passed Over," *Working Woman,* April 1994, pp. 64–66, 90.

27. Pepi Sappal, "Should I Stay or Should I Go?" *Wall Street Journal,* April 18, 2000, p. B15.

28. "Hot jobs for the 21st Century," Facts on Working Women, Women's Bureau, *Department of Labor,* May 2003, **http://www.dol/gov/wb**

29. Donna J. Abernathy, "A Get-Real Guide to Time Management," *Training and Development Journal,* June 1999, pp. 22–26.

30. "Extreme Job Stress: Survivors' Tales," *Wall Street Journal,* January 17, 2001, pp. B1, B4; and Carol Hymowitz and Rachel Emma Silverman, "Can Workplace Stress Get Worse?" *Wall Street Journal,* January 16, 2001, pp. B1, B4.

31. Michael Copeland, "Me & My Mentor," *Red Herring,* August 2000, pp. 172–186; and Susan Caminiti, "Straight Talk," *Working Woman,* September 1999, pp. 66–69.

32. Margaret Hennig and Anne Jardim, *The Managerial Woman* (New York: Anaheim Press/Doubleday, 1977.

33. Murray H. Reich, "The Mentoring Connection," *Personnel,* February 1986, p. 52.

34. Justin Martin, "Job Surfing: Move On to Move On," *Fortune,* January 13, 1997, pp. 50–54; and Ronald Henkoff, "So You Want to Change Your Job," *Fortune,* January 15, 1996, pp. 52–56.

35. New Analysis, "Hiring Outlook '03, Part One," *BusinessWeek Online,* January 2, 2003, **http://www.businessweek.com**

Glossary

The following glossary contains definitions of many of the concepts and terms used in this book. For the most part, the terms correspond to those given in the text and represent words the reader is most likely to encounter in the business world. In addition, a few extra definitions not included in the book have been added to provide the most comprehensive and useful glossary possible.

1,1 Managerial Style (*See* Managerial Style.)
1,9 Managerial Style (*See* Managerial Style.)
5,5 Managerial Style (*See* Managerial Style.)
9,1 Managerial Style (*See* Managerial Style.)
9,9 Managerial Style (*See* Managerial Style.)

Acceptance The third step in the communication process that involves getting the receiver to agree to comply or accept the directive. The term also refers to willingness to go along with a change because one sees more to be gained than lost from the new conditions.

Achievement The desire to accomplish things. High achievers tend to want not only to get things done but also to receive concrete feedback on their performance so they can learn how well they have done (*see* High Achiever).

Action The last step in the communication process that involves a duty on the part of both the receiver and the sender to follow up and do what was expected or see that it is done.

Advice Network An informal network that shows who depends on whom.

Aesthetic Value A principle characterized by interest in form and harmony. Artists have high aesthetic values.

Affective Component The emotional feeling attached to an attitude.

Assertiveness Training teaches people how to assert themselves in work and social situations.

Attention The first step in the communication process that involves screening out all disturbances or other distractions that can interrupt one's concentration.

Attitude Questionnaire A survey instrument that measures a person's feelings, opinions, and other intervening variables that make up attitudes.

Attitudes A person's feelings about objects, activities, events, and people.

Authenticity Seekers Individuals who are interested in self-expression and are best represented by the cliché, "I gotta be me."

Authoritarian Leadership A leadership style that tends to be heavily work-centered, with major emphasis given to task accomplishment and little to the human element.

Authority The right to command.

Automated Technology Technology in which assembly-line machines are linked together and integrated in such a fashion that many functions are performed automatically without human intervention.

Autonomy The degree to which a job provides freedom, independence, and discretion in scheduling the work and determining how to carry it out.

Behavioral Component The tendency to act in a particular way toward a person, an object, or an event.

Behavioral Scientist An individual highly skilled in one of the behavioral sciences (psychology, sociology, anthropology) who applies such training to the study of human behavior in organizations.

Benchmarking An ongoing process of measuring products, services, and practices against those of competitors and industry leaders.

Brainstorming Technique of calling out as many ideas as possible to stimulate creative thinking.

Broadbanding A process of replacing the number of salary grades with fewer, wider bands.

Careerists Individuals who want to get ahead and are prepared to make the necessary sacrifices to do so.

Cause-and-Effect Diagram A diagram that often is used as a follow-up to Pareto analysis, its objective being to help identify reasons for the problem under investigation.

Central Tendency A problem generated by the evaluator in which everyone receives an average rating, regardless of effectiveness.

Change Any alteration of the status quo.

Charismatic Leader An individual who leads by the force of his or her personal abilities.

Cluster Chain A grapevine network in which people selectively pass information to other members of the informal organization. In this process, some people are given information and others are deliberately bypassed. This is the most common grapevine network.

Code of Conduct A guide summarizing the ethical principles and standards for individual behavior.

Cognitive Component   The beliefs a person has about an object or event.

Cohesiveness   The closeness of interpersonal attractions that exist among group members.

Collaboration   A conflict resolution approach in which all parties try to iron out their differences, realizing that without full cooperation all of them will fail.

Collectivism   The tendency of people to belong to groups in which the members look after one another in exchange for loyalty.

Collegiality Seekers   Individuals who like to work with others, are very social in orientation, and are excellent team players.

Communication   The process of transmitting meanings from sender to receiver.

Communication Network   An informal network that shows who communicates with whom.

Competence   Control over environmental factors, often revealed in the form of a desire for job mastery and professional growth.

Compressed Workweek   A workweek arrangement that allows the individual to work a shorter week, such as four 10-hour days rather than five 8-hour days.

Compromise   A conflict resolution approach that involves each party giving something such that no one of them is the clear winner.

Conceptual Skills   Abilities that help a manager to understand how all parts of an organization or department fit together. These skills are very important for top managers, who must be able to operate the enterprise as an integrated unit.

Conflict   The result of individuals or groups in the organization clashing over some issue that, at least to them, is important. Sometimes this occurs on an interpersonal basis and, at other times, it takes place between groups.

Conformity   Willingness to comply with the norms or sanctions of other individuals. Conformity, within bounds, is required if one hopes to remain a member of the informal organization.

Confrontation   Problem solving on a face-to-face basis.

Consultative Selling   The process of finding out what the customer wants before trying to sell anything to the individual.

Control Group   A group that is not subjected to any change. Its purpose is to serve as a comparison to the test group (*see* Test Group).

Core Job Dimensions   Characteristics that job-enrichment experts attempt to design into the work to increase worker motivation. The five most important are skill variety, task identity, task significance, autonomy, and feedback.

Counseling   The discussion of an emotional problem with an employee with the purpose of eliminating or reducing it.

Covert Resistance   Resistance that is not readily observable because it is conducted under the guise of working as usual.

Illustrations include "forgetting" to file reports or providing more information than is required in the hopes of swamping the reader and slowing up his or her progress.

Cross-Functional Group   A group composed of individuals from two or more different functional areas.

Cultural Assimilator   A programmed learning technique designed to expose members of one culture to the values, customs, and beliefs of another culture.

Cultural Match   The similarity of individual and organizational culture.

Culture   The acquired knowledge that people use to interpret experience and to generate social behavior.

Customer Value Added   The provision of products and services that offer greater value than those of the competition.

Cybernated Technology   Technology in which machines run and control other machines.

Decoding   Interpreting the message that one has received from a sender (*see* Encoding).

Dialectic Inquiry   The use of structured discussion and debate in arriving at a final decision.

Dimensions of Change   Characteristics of a change in policy or procedure. They are (1) the logical dimension, based on technological and scientific reasons for the change; (2) the psychological dimension, the logic of the change in terms of the individuals affected; and (3) the sociological dimension, the logic of the change in terms of the work group.

Discharge   The ultimate discipline penalty that calls for a separation of the individual from the organization.

Disciplinary Layoff   A severe form of discipline that calls for the individual to leave the organization for a period and to forfeit the pay for these days.

Economic Value   A principle characterized by interest in what is useful. This value is important to the average American businessperson.

Elaboration   Taking part of a message or story that is received through the informal organization and building it up to fit one's own point of view.

Emergent Conflict   Conflict that arises from personal and social causes.

Emotional Intelligence   The capacity for recognizing one's own feelings and those of others, for motivating oneself, and for managing emotions well in both oneself and one's relationships.

Empathy   Putting oneself, figuratively speaking, into another person's shoes. In so doing, one begins to understand the other person's point of view.

Empowerment   A process by which workers are given the authority and the resources for performing the work correctly.

Encoding   Translating a message into a code (words, facial expressions, gestures) that will be intelligible to the receiver (*see* Decoding).

Equity   Fairness in the distribution of rewards for work. Equity plays a key role in expectancy theory. In particular, expectancy theorists like to point out that rewards must be commensurate with contribution, but also the individual must feel that what is given to him or her is fair or equitable.

Equity Theory   A theory holding that people will compare their work-reward ratio to that of others in determining whether they are being properly rewarded.

Ergonomics   A field that is concerned with redesigning the physical environment to meet the needs of the personnel.

Esteem Needs   The need to feel important and to have self-respect. These needs often are satisfied by attaining prestige or power.

Ethics   The study of standards and moral judgment.

Ethnocentrism   The belief that one's way of doing things is superior to that of others.

Expectancy   A person's perception of the probability that a specific outcome will follow from a specific act.

Expectancy Theory   A motivation theory that holds that motivation is a force equal to the product of valence and expectancy (see Valence, Expectancy).

Expert Power   Power held by a leader because of knowledge and expertise. Leaders who have demonstrated competence acquire expert power.

Extinction   A learning strategy in which the individual is not reinforced for a specific behavior, thereby reducing the likelihood that he or she will perform the same act again in the future.

Extrinsic Rewards   Rewards that are external to the work itself. Common examples are money, increased fringe benefits, and a company car.

Feedback   The degree to which the work required by a job results in the individual receiving direct, clear information about his or her performance effectiveness.

Femininity   The degree to which the dominant values of a society are caring for others and for the quality of life.

Fiedler's Contingency Model   The best-known contingency model of leader effectiveness, which holds that the best leadership style will be the result of three situational variables: leader-member relations, the task structure, and the leader's position power.

First Law of Service   Satisfaction equals perception minus expectation.

First Principle of TQM   Do it right the first time.

Flextime   A flexible work arrangement that allows the worker some control over when he or she starts and finishes the workday.

Flowchart   A pictorial representation of the steps in a work process.

Follower   An individual who goes along with whatever the opinion leader or the group at large wants done.

Forming Stage   The first stage of group development, characterized by efforts to determine the group's initial direction.

Fringe Group   Those who are seeking admission to the informal organization.

Frustration   The thwarting or blocking of an attempt at need satisfaction.

Functional Group   A group composed of workers all performing the same basic tasks. In a manufacturing firm, for example, it is common to find major functional groups or departments such as marketing, production, and finance.

Future Shock   The effect of enduring too much change in too short a time.

Gatekeeper   This person regulates the flow of information to other members of the group.

Glass Ceiling   An artificial barrier preventing women from being promoted.

Goal Conflict   Conflict that occurs whenever someone is asked to pursue two goals that are not in harmony. The term also refers to a power struggle that takes place between groups, in which one or more may win only at the expense of the others.

Gossip Chain   A grapevine network in which one person passes information to all the others in the informal organization. This is one of the less frequently used grapevine networks.

Grapevine   The name given to the communication network used to carry information among members of the informal organization.

Graphic Rating Scales   The most widely used of all performance appraisal tools, it is a list of factors and degrees of each factor on which an individual will be rated. The evaluator reads every factor and then checks the degree of each that applies to the person being evaluated.

Group   A social unit consisting of two or more interdependent, interactive individuals who are striving to attain common goals.

Halo Effect   A performance evaluation error caused by the rater's giving the ratee the same rating on all traits, regardless of actual performances.

Handicraft Era   The first phase of technological development, during which people made things by hand.

Hawthorne Effect   The novelty or interest in a new situation that leads, at least initially, to positive results.

Hawthorne Studies   Important behavioral studies that provided the impetus for the human relations movement.

High Achiever   An individual who tends to like situations in which he or she can take personal responsibility for finding solutions to problems, is a moderate risk taker, and likes concrete feedback on performance to evaluate how well he or she is doing.

Human Relations   A process by which management brings workers into contact with the organization in such a way that the objectives of both groups are achieved.

Human Resources Model A descriptive model that presents the worker as an ambitious individual who has self-direction, self-control, and creativity and who, if managed properly, will contribute to the extent of his or her talents.

Human Skills Abilities that help an individual to interact with other people. These skills are very important for middle-level managers, who must lead other managers.

Hygiene Factors Identified by Frederick Herzberg in his two-factor theory of motivation, factors that will not motivate people by their presence but will cause dissatisfaction by their absence. Some Herzberg identified include money, security, and working conditions.

Illumination The third stage of creative thinking, characterized by the group's realization of the best decision to make.

Incentive Payment Plans Wage incentive schemes designed to reward increased efficiency by individuals, groups, or the organization at large.

Incubation The second stage of creative thinking, which involves sitting back and letting the subconscious mind work on the problem.

Independent Thinkers Employees who are very entrepreneurial in their approach and want to be free to choose what they are going to do and how they are going to do it.

Individual Culture The norms, attitudes, values, and beliefs that a person brings to the job.

Individualism The tendency of people to look after themselves and their immediate family only.

Industrial Democracy A formal, usually legally sanctioned arrangement of worker representation in the form of committees, councils, and boards at various levels of decision making in the organization.

Inference An assumption made by the receiver of a message. Inferences are most commonly made about messages that are very long and involve a very large number of facts.

Information Richness The potential information-carrying capacity of data.

Institutionalized Conflict Conflict that results from organizational attempts to structure work assignments.

Instrumental Value A value that reflects the means for achieving desired goals.

Interest-Friendship Group A group formed on the basis of common beliefs, concerns, or activities. These groups sometimes are found within departments and, in other instances, cut across departmental lines.

Interpersonal Conflict Conflict that results from disagreement between personnel.

Intervening Variable A variable that is influenced by a causal variable and that affects an end-result variable.

Intrapreneur An entrepreneur who works within the confines of an enterprise.

Intrinsic Rewards Rewards that are experienced internally by the worker. Common examples are a feeling of accomplishment, increased responsibility, and the opportunity to achieve.

Isolate A person who generally is ignored by the group and receives very little communication.

Isolation A psychological condition that results when individuals become detached from society. Technology is causing this state in some people, who are fleeing the big city and trying to raise their families in the relaxed, slower-paced environment of rural areas.

Job Enlargement A job redesign technique that involves giving the worker more to do and, if possible, increasing his or her job motivation.

Job Enrichment A job redesign technique that attempts to build psychological motivators into the job. In particular, it is common to find the worker being given more authority in planning the work and in controlling the pace and procedures.

Job Profile Chart A device used to measure the degree of each core job dimension possessed by a particular job.

Job Redesign Any activities that involve work change, the purpose of which is to increase the quality of the worker's job experience or improve his or her productivity.

Job Rotation Moving a worker from one job to another for the purpose of reducing boredom.

Knowledge-Based Organization An organization in which information sharing, teamwork, trust, and empowerment are used to help employees pursue predetermined goals.

Laissez-faire Leadership A leadership style characterized by a lack of concern for either the people or the work.

Leader-Member Relations The relationships that exist between the leader and the subordinates.

Leader Position Power The authority vested in the leader's position.

Leadership The process of influencing people to direct their efforts toward the achievement of some particular goal(s).

Leadership Characteristics Characteristics possessed by effective leaders. The most commonly cited include drive, originality, persistence, and the tolerance of stress.

Leadership Dimensions Dimensions or concerns central to the process of influencing people to direct their efforts toward the achievement of some particular goal(s). There are two—concern for work and concern for people—and they are independent dimensions. A person can score low on one without scoring high on the other.

Least Preferred Coworker Scale A questionnaire that asks the leader to describe the person with whom he or she can work least well. The instrument is used by Fiedler in his contingency model.

Left-Brain People Individuals who are logical, rational, detailed, active, and objectives-oriented.

Legitimate Power Power vested in the manager's position in the organization hierarchy. For example, a vice-president has greater legitimate power than a district manager, who in turn has greater power than a unit manager.

Leniency A rater-generated problem in performance evaluation in which the manager gives all the people the highest possible rating.

Liaison The contact person who communicates with the other groups and gets information from them.

Lifestylers Individuals who are most interested in their quality of life and for whom the job is but a means to an end.

Linguistic Style A person's speaking pattern, which includes such things as pacing, pausing, word choice, directness, and the use of figures of speech, stories, and questions.

Logical Dimension The dimension of changes that is based on scientific reasons.

Management The process of achieving organizational objectives through the effective use of resources.

Management by Objectives (MBO) An overall performance appraisal system used at all levels of the employment hierarchy entailing six steps: (1) identifying the goals of the unit or department; (2) sketching out the duties and responsibilities of each individual; (3) meeting with the subordinate and mutually setting goals for him or her; (4) employing an annual goal-setting worksheet to push the subordinate toward the objective; (5) periodically reviewing the goals and revising them where necessary; and (6) at the end of the assigned period, evaluating the results and starting the cycle again.

Managerial Grid A two-dimensional leadership model that permits simultaneous consideration of concern for production and concern for people.

Managerial Style
1,1 A managerial style in which the manager tends to put people in jobs and then leave them alone. The manager does not check up on their work or try to interact with them by offering praise or encouraging them to keep up the good work. There is low concern for both work and people.
1,9 A managerial style in which the manager tends to have a high concern for people's feelings, comfort, and needs and a low concern for getting the work out.
5,5 Often called a *middle-of-the-road management philosophy,* which assumes that there is an inherent conflict between the concerns for production and people. Such a manager tries to compromise and balance these two dimensions.
9,1 A managerial style in which the manager has a high concern for production and a low concern for people. The manager plans the work and pushes to get it out. Little interest is shown in the workers. If they cannot keep up, they are replaced by others who can.
9,9 A managerial style known as *team management,* regarded by many as the ideal management style. The manager has high concern for work and high concern for people.

Masculinity The degree to which the dominant values of a society are success, money, and material things.

Meaninglessness A condition occurring when employees are unable to determine what they are doing or why they are doing it.

Mechanistic Technology Technological era during which interchangeable parts and job simplification were introduced on a wide scale.

Mechanization Era A phase of technological development characterized by machine labor replacing human labor.

Mentor A person who coaches, counsels, teaches, or sponsors others.

Motivating Potential Score (MPS) An approach for identifying the motivating potential of a particular job that encompasses the five core job dimensions. The formula is:

$$\left(\frac{\text{Skill variety} + \text{Task identity} + \text{Task significance}}{3} \right) \times \text{Autonomy} \times \text{Feedback}$$

Motivation A psychological drive or force that directs someone toward an objective.

Motivational Force A mathematically computed motivational drive equal to the product of valence and expectancy (*see* Valence, Expectancy).

Motivators Identified by Frederick Herzberg in his two-factor theory of motivation, factors that will build high levels of motivation and job satisfaction. Some Herzberg identified are recognition, advancement, and achievement.

Motive A "why" of behavior, consisting of needs, drives, wants, and impulses within the individual.

Multinational Enterprise A company that is headquartered in one country but has operations in two or more countries.

Mutual Problem Solving Problem solving that involves bringing together all the parties to a conflict and discussing the issues face-to-face.

Need Mix A term that refers to the fact that people tend to be partially satisfied and partially dissatisfied at all levels of the hierarchy simultaneously. It is never an all-or-nothing situation.

Networking The process of socializing, politicking, and interacting with people throughout the enterprise.

Normative Reality Interpretive reality, in which there is no right answer. Examples are matters of opinion related to personal taste, politics, religion, and other areas in which there is no one correct answer.

Norming Stage The third stage of group development, characterized by cooperation and teamwork.

Norms Rules of conduct that are adopted by group members.

Nucleus Group Those who are full-fledged members of the informal organization.

OD Change Agent The individual who introduces the intervention, gets personnel involved, and leads the intervention.

OD Intervention A catchall term used to describe the behavioral science techniques used to intervene in a situation for the purpose of improving it.

Opinion Leader An individual who often is the informal leader of the group. This person receives more communiqués than anyone else in the group and is most responsible for determining group goals and actions.

Oral Warning   Usually the first step in the disciplinary process, which involves orally pointing out that repetition of a particular act will result in discipline.

Organizational Climate   The overall favorability of member attitudes and perceptions with reference to specific activities and features of an organization. The climate may be highly favorable for, say, good communication but relatively unfavorable for rapid change or tough-minded decision making.

Organizational Culture   The environment in which a person works.

Organizational Development (OD)   An effort to improve an organization's effectiveness by dealing with individual, group, and overall organizational problems from both a technical and human standpoint.

Organizational Iceberg   The formal and informal aspects of the organization. The formal consist of structural considerations that can be readily observed, including job definitions, job descriptions, and forms of departmentalization. The informal are social-psychological processes and behavioral considerations that cannot be seen, including power, influence, interpersonal relations, and employee satisfaction.

Orientation   The process of introducing new employees to their jobs.

Outer Group   Those who have been rejected for membership in the informal organization.

Overt Resistance   Resistance that is observable. Illustrations include worker slowdown, setting low informal production norms, and outright sabotage.

Paired Comparison Method   A performance evaluation method that involves comparing each individual who is being rated against every other individual on a number of different bases, including work quality and work quantity.

Pareto Chart   A vertical bar graph that helps to identify problems and the order in which they should be solved.

Participative Leadership   A leadership style characterized by high concerns for both people and work.

Participative-Leaders   have high concern for people and work.

Participative Management   An informal style of face-to-face leadership in which management and the workers share decision making in the workplace. It is an example of shop-floor democracy.

Paternalistic Leadership   A leadership style that tends to be heavily work-centered but has some consideration for the personnel as well.

Perception   A person's view of reality.

Performance Appraisal Cycle   A four-step process used in appraising individuals, consisting of (1) establishing performance standards, (2) determining individual performance, (3) comparing performance against standards, and (4) evaluating individual performance.

Performing Stage   The stage of group development that is characterized by openness and collaboration among group members.

Personal Characteristics   Personal attributes often possessed by effective leaders. The most commonly cited include superior mental ability, emotional maturity, and problem-solving skills.

Personal Developers   Individuals who are interested in jobs that give them the opportunity to continue learning and becoming more and more proficient.

Personality   A relatively stable set of characteristics and tendencies that determines similarities and differences between one person and another.

Physiological Needs   Basic requirements, such as food, clothing, and shelter.

Political Value   A principle characterized by an interest in power. Politicians have high political values.

Postindustrial Society   A society characterized by a service-oriented workforce, dynamic increase of workers in professional and technical jobs, an increase in the importance of theoretical knowledge, and an interest in planning and controlling technological growth.

Power   The ability to influence, persuade, or move another to one's own point of view.

Power Distance   The degree to which less powerful members of the society accept the fact that power is not distributed equally.

Powerlessness   A psychological condition that occurs when workers feel that they are at the mercy of technology. Workers on assembly lines, for example, report feelings of powerlessness because they are forced to keep up with the speed of the line; the technology controls them.

Preparation   The first stage of creative thinking, which requires that participants prepare mentally to make a decision.

Prestige   The respect, status, and influence an individual has among other people.

Probability Chain   A grapevine network in which people randomly pass information to other members of the informal organization.

Product Departmentalization   An organizational arrangement in which people are grouped on the basis of product line. General Motors, Ford Motor, and RCA all use product departmentalization.

Productivity   Output/input.

Project Group   A group consisting of individuals from many different areas or backgrounds, the purpose of which is to attain its objective within predetermined time, cost, and quality limits. The group is disbanded when the goal is attained, and everyone goes back to his or her original department.

Proxemics   The study of the way in which people use physical space to communicate.

Psychological Dimension   The dimension of change that is based on how the individual will be affected.

Quality Council   A group of individuals who oversee an organization's quality initiative and make decisions regarding the projects to be undertaken and the funding to be provided.

"Red-Hot-Stove" Rule A system of employing discipline that holds that all disciplinary practices should (1) be immediate, (2) offer advance warning, (3) be consistent from person to person, and (4) be impersonal.

Reengineering The fundamental redesign of business processes to achieve dramatic results.

Referent Power Power based on the followers' identification with the leader.

Regression Behavior characterized by a reversion to childlike behavior, as when a manager throws a temper tantrum when annoyed at a worker who asks too many questions.

Rejection Refusal to accommodate some condition or change because it is perceived as potentially destructive.

Reliability A measurement quality of a performance evaluation technique that refers to whether the instrument measures the same factor repeatedly.

Religious Value A principle characterized by an interest in unity. Members of the clergy have high religious values.

Resource-Based Organization An organization in which management provides the necessary tools, equipment, and direction and employees use these resources to pursue predetermined goals.

Résumé A summary of one's education, work experience, training, and references. This form is used when applying for a job.

Reward Power Power held by leaders who can give extrinsic satisfiers to subordinates who do their jobs well.

Right-Brain People Individuals who are spontaneous, emotional, holistic, nonverbal, and visual in their approach to things.

Risky-Shift Phenomenon The tendency to take greater risks in a group than when acting alone.

Role An expected behavior.

Role Ambiguity A role-related condition that occurs when job duties are unclear and a person is unsure of what to do.

Role Conflict A condition that occurs when an individual faces a situation in which he or she must assume two roles and the performance of the first precludes the performance of the second.

Role Playing A common form of training used in organizational development consisting of the spontaneous acting out of a realistic situation involving two or more people. The purpose of the training is to acquaint one or more of the participants with the proper way of handling a given situation.

Rumor The unverified or untrue messages of the grapevine. It is considered the most undesirable feature of the informal organization and often is defined as "interest × ambiguity."

Safety Needs Needs such as those of survival and security.

Satisficing Behavior Behavior in which individuals accept results or payoffs that are adequate, in contrast to choices that would maximize outcomes.

Scientific Management A system of management, popularized by Frederick W. Taylor and others in the early twentieth century, that sought to develop (1) ways of increasing productivity by making work easier to perform and (2) methods for motivating workers to take advantage of these labor-saving devices and techniques.

Scientific Method An objective approach for identifying a problem, gathering information on it, analyzing the data, arriving at a tentative resolution, and testing it.

Screening The process of eliminating applicants who are unlikely to be successful on the job.

Second Law of Service First impressions are the most important.

Selecting The process of determining those applicants who will be offered jobs.

Selective Filtering The screening of rumors so that part of the story is maintained and the rest is discarded.

Self-Actualization Need The urge to maximize one's potential, often satisfied through attainment of competence and a feeling of achievement.

Self-Estrangement A condition that occurs when an individual can no longer find intrinsic satisfaction in what he or she is doing. The work becomes a mere means to earn a living and, if the individual could go elsewhere and make more money, he or she would do so.

Sensory Reality Physical reality as characterized by objects such as an automobile, a house, or a car.

Shift Work Work that is assigned based on time shifts, such as 8 A.M. to 5 P.M. or 5 P.M. to 1 A.M.

Single Strand An informal grapevine network in which each person receives information from one individual and passes it to another; the flow of information moves down a line. This is the least frequently employed grapevine network.

Skill Variety The degree to which a job requires the completion of different activities, all of which involve varying talents and capabilities.

Smoothing The downplaying of differences between individuals and groups while emphasizing their common interests.

Social Need The urge for interaction with others for the purpose of meaningful relationships.

Social Network Informal structures created by people in the workplace and used for interaction and social exchange on the job.

Social Responsibility The obligations a business has to society.

Social Value A value characterized by love of people. Social workers have high social values.

Sociogram A schematic drawing that shows the social relationships existing among members of a group. It provides information regarding informal group behavior.

Sociological Dimension The dimension of change that is based on how the change will affect the group.

Status The relative ranking of an individual in an organization or group.

Status Discrepancy Conflict that occurs when people do things that do not fit with their status in the group. Union representatives can negatively affect their status by becoming too friendly with company supervisors, as can managers who eat lunch with their subordinates.

Status Incongruence A discrepancy between a person's supposed status and the way he or she is treated.

Stereotyping Generalizing a particular trait or behavior to all members of a given group.

Storming Stage The second stage of group development, characterized by confrontation, questioning, and resistance by the members.

Strategic Intent A company's vision.

Stress A condition characterized by emotional strain or physical discomfort (or both) which, if it goes unrelieved, can impair one's ability to cope with the environment.

Structured Interview An interview in which specific questions are asked in a predetermined manner.

Survey Feedback An overall or comprehensive OD intervention that entails three distinct steps: (1) a systematic collection of data on the current state of the organization, usually obtained through questionnaires or interviews; (2) feedback of the findings to the organizational personnel; and (3) the development of an action plan for dealing with the problems that have been identified.

System 1 An exploitative-autocratic management style, in which management has little confidence in the subordinates and makes wide use of threats and punishment in getting things done.

System 2 A benevolent-autocratic leadership style, in which management acts in a condescending manner toward the subordinates and has little trust in them.

System 3 A consultative-democratic leadership style, in which management has quite a bit of confidence and trust in the subordinates, decision making tends to be delegated to some degree, and some confidence and trust exist between superiors and subordinates.

System 4 A participative-democratic leadership style, in which management has complete confidence and trust in the subordinates, decision making is highly decentralized, communication flows up and down the hierarchy, and the formal and informal organizations often are the same.

Task Identity The degree to which a job requires completion of a whole or identifiable piece of work.

Task Significance The degree to which a job has a substantial impact on the lives and work of other people.

Task Structure The degree to which the leader's job is programmed or specified in step-by-step fashion.

Team Building A popular OD intervention that consists of working with intact, permanent work teams in an effort to improve the relationships that exist among them.

Technical Skills Abilities that help an individual determine how things work. These are very important for lower-level managers, such as supervisors.

Terminal Value A value that is expressed in terms of a desired goal or end.

Test Group People who are subjected to some behavioral change and then studied to determine the effect of this change (*see* Control Group).

Theoretical Value A principle characterized by interest in truth, system, and the ordering of knowledge.

Theory X A set of assumptions that holds that people (1) dislike work, (2) have little ambition, (3) want security above all else, and (4) must be coerced, controlled, and threatened with punishment to attain organizational objectives.

Theory Y A set of assumptions that holds that (1) if the conditions are favorable, people will not only accept responsibility but will seek it; (2) if people are committed to organizational objectives, they will exercise self-direction and self-control; and (3) commitment is a function of the rewards associated with goal attainment.

Third Law of Service Service attitude alone will not assure good service.

Tolerance Putting up with change. This usually occurs because the workers have no particular positive or negative feelings toward the change; they are basically neutral about it.

Total Quality Management (TQM) A people-focused management system that aims at continual increases in customer service at continually lower costs.

Traditional Model A descriptive model that presents the worker as an individual who is lazy, works only for money, and needs to be supervised and controlled, and that holds that if the work is simple enough and the people are closely controlled, they will produce up to standard.

Trait Theory The study of leadership characteristics.

Transactional Leader An individual who leads others by giving rewards in return for effort and performance.

Transformational Leader A visionary leader with a sense of mission who can motivate followers to accept new goals and ways of doing things.

Trust Network An information network that shows who shares delicate political information with whom.

Type A Person An individual aggressively involved in a chronic, incessant struggle to achieve more and more in less and less time.

Type B Person An individual who is evenly paced and does not have an overwhelming need to get more and more done in less and less time.

Uncertainty Avoidance   The extent to which people feel threatened by ambiguous situations and have created institutions for minimizing or avoiding these uncertainties.

Understanding   The second step in the communication process, which involves getting the receiver to comprehend the meaning of the transmission.

Unstructured Interview   An interview in which the interviewer may have a general direction or objective but the questions are not predetermined and the interview is allowed to develop spontaneously.

Valence   A person's preference for a particular outcome.

Validity   A measurement quality of a performance evaluation technique that refers to whether the instrument is measuring what it is intended to measure.

Value   Something that has worth or importance to an individual.

Verification   The fourth stage of creative thinking, which involves the group modifying or making final changes in the solution.

Vertical Loading   A job-enrichment principle that involves closing the gap between the "doing" and "controlling" aspects of the job.

Virtual Group   A task-focused group that meets without all the members being present in the same locale or at the same time.

Workplace Violence   Any physical assault, threatening behavior, or verbal abuse occurring in the work setting.

World-Class Organization   An enterprise that can compete effectively on a global basis.

Written Warning   A form of discipline that involves placing a warning in the employee's file that can be cited as evidence if it is decided to terminate his or her employment in the future.

Name Index

Stevens, John F., 212
Stewart, Martha, 22
Stone, Barry, 22
Stoess, Edward, 244
Sulloway, Frank, 15–16
Swanson, Celia, 337
Syfrett, Shannon, 354–355

Tavelo, Jill, 246
Tess, Janna, 227
Thompson, Leigh, 142
Tow, L., 57

Tumlinson, Rick N., 198
Twomey, Daniel F., 218

Vroom, Victor, 52-53

Wagoner, Rick, 25-26, 202
Wallace, John, 212
Walters, Brian, 193–194
Watkins, Sherron, 22
Weber, Lisa, 58
Weill, S. I., 57
Welch, Jack, 238, 257

Wendt, Gary, 38
White, M. D., 57
Whitman, Meg, 19, 337
Williams, Bob, 231
Williams, Roberta, 140
Wilson, Maureen, 312
Winfrey, Oprah, 19, 275
Woertz, Pat, 19
Wright, Steve, 331-332

Zechella, Dena, 439

Subject Index

dependency, behavioral control, 142–143
drawbacks of, 149–150
influencing direction of, 151–152
informal leadership for, 135–142
initial appraisal of, 134
interpersonal relations and, 134–135
nature of, 134–142
networking value in, 140–142
politics in, 138–140
Information
feedback of, 390
grapevine, 151–152
lack of, 384
richness, 335–336
security, 356
volume of, 357
Innovation, 204–205, 218, 227
creativity and, 429–433, 445–446
of individuals, 114
of teams, 101–102
Insecurity, 145
Inspection, 120
Institutionalized conflict, 371
Instrumental values, 72
Integrated-based diversity training, 443–444
Intelligence, 88–89, 259, 278
Interest-friendship group, 103–104
Intergroup behavior, 118–119
International culture, 246. *See also* World-class
organization
achievement motivation and, 414–415
attitudinal dimensions and, 409–413
collectivism, 408, 410
country cluster's synthesis of, 412–413
dimensions of, 406–413
ethnocentrism, 404
femininity, 408–409, 412
human relations problem from, 401
individualism, 408, 409, 410
integrating, 409–413
masculinity, 408, 412
multinational enterprises in, 402–404
nature of, 405–409
power distance, 407–408, 409, 410
time, future and, 415–416
uncertainty avoidance, 408, 409, 412
values' comparison of, 407
work impact of, 413–416
world's largest companies and, 404
world's most admired companies and, 403
International human resources
challenges of, 416–419
cultural assimilators and, 417–418
cultural challenges for, 28–29
global perspective, 419–421
importance of, 27–28
language training and, 417, 419
personnel selection of, 416–419
personnel training of, 416–419
Internet
commerce, 27, 212, 228, 460
résumé, job hunt and, 469–470

Interpersonal behavior
assertive training and, 90–93
gender differences and, 89–90
motivational profiles and, 92–93
Interpersonal conflict, 369–371
Interpersonal relations, 134–135
Interpretative reality, 79–80
Intervening variable, 84, 86
Interviews, 463
acing of, 473
process of, 470–472
structured, 15, 205
unstructured, 15, 295
Intragroup behavior, 110–119
Intrapreneurship
characteristics of, 214, 215–217
climate of, 217
defined, 214
development of attitudes of, 214–217
foundations of, 218
strategies developed for, 218–219
Intrinsic rewards, 311–312
IQ, 88–89, 259
Isolate, 110
Isolation, 171–172

Job. *See also* Alternative work schedules;
Career; Performance
bored, 228
employees feeling about, 172–174
fastest growing, in new economy, 479
finding, 464–471
knowing, 475
modification, 433
obsolescence of, skills, 383
quality desired from, 53
replacement trained for, 478
requirements vs. abilities, 429
satisfaction, 147–148, 173, 209
sharing, 423
stress, 182–183
successful, hunt, 470–475
wages of, 213, 313, 323, 337
Job design, 240
contract workers, 244–245
managing hard-to-keep employees in, 245
new workplace designs in, 240–242
telework, 227, 242–244, 448
Job enlargement, 230
Job enrichment
in action/implementation, 237–240
combining tasks for, 236
core job dimensions and, 230–232, 235
defined, 230
formation of natural work units and, 235
at General Electric, 237–239
opening feedback channels for, 236
principles, 234–236
at Southwest Airlines, 239–240
vertical loading and, 236
worker–client relationships for, 235–236
Job profile charts, 233–234

Job redesign, 431–432
autonomy and, 232
core job dimensions and, 230–232
current challenges in, 240–247
defined, 228
feedback and, 232
motivating potential score and, 232–233
nature of, 228–229
skill variety and, 231
task identity and, 231
task significance and, 231–232
techniques of, 229–230
Job rotation, 229–230
Job title, 107
Judgment, 475–477

Karoshi, 414
Knowledge
acquisition, 4, 28
risk function of, 113
theoretical, increased, 167
Knowledge-based organizations, 176–179
Knowledge Perspective Web site, 27
Knowledge workers
examples of, 16–17
hiring of, 17–18
knowledge-sharing culture for, 17, 27,
213, 420
management of, 16–18

Laissez-faire leadership, 265
Language
bilingual, 476
communication with, 339–340, 344–349
training, 417, 419
Law, 320–321
Layoffs, 318, 332, 433–434, 484
Leader(s)
emerging challenges of, 281
-member relations, 272
New Business, 368
new, emerging, 257
opinion, 110
position power, 271, 272
profile of, 261
self, 265–266
-subordinate interactions, 266
time management for effective, 480
in twenty-first century, 279–281
Leadership
in action, 273
authoritarian, 264, 383–384
authority, power and, 136–138
autocratic to participative, 383–384
behavior, 263–266
characteristics of, 258–261
charismatic, 275–277
contingency, 269–279
contingent reward (CR) behaviors and,
278–279
defined, 258
dimensions, 266–270

Wages, 213, 313, 323, 337
Wellness performance, 449
Wide banding, 428
Wi-Fi (Wireless Fidelity), 166
Women, 3
    communication, gender differences and, 352–354, 405
    conforming of, 106
    cultural diversity, leadership and, 266–267, 316, 405, 408–409, 412
    discrimination against, 3, 19–20, 26–27, 28–29, 316, 320, 439–440
    family responsibility of, 20, 439
    gender differences and, 89–90, 352–354, 405, 408–409, 412
    glass ceiling for, 19–20, 316
    hiring of, 3, 21, 316, 449, 479
    international management and, 316, 405
    mentors and, 482
    moral reasoning of, 441–442
    retaining of, 317
    sexual harassment of, 19–20, 26–27, 370, 439–440

single vs. married, 245
top, in business, 19, 139–140, 257, 266–267
Work
    in America, 228
    attitudes, 414
    changing nature of, 433–439
    in Europe, 448
    flowcharting and, 433–435
    international culture and, 413–416
    reengineering and, 433–434, 445
    service, 435–438
    24/7, 448
Work units, natural, 235
Worker-client relationships, 235–236
Work-out sessions, 428
Workplace designs, 240–242, 448
Workplace violence
    dealing with, 181–183
    defined, 179
    examples of, 180
    homicide rates in, 179
    individual's behavior of, 181

prevention program for, 180–181
simmering of, 448
stress and, 182–183
World market, 402–403
World-class organization (WCO). *See also* Multinational enterprises
    continuous improvement for, 445–446
    customer-based focus for, 445
    defined, 444
    egalitarian climate of, 446
    human resources and, 446
    technological support of, 447
    virtual organizations and, 446
Writing skills, 352
Written warning, 318
Wrongful discharge, 321

Company Index

Abbott Laboratories, 57, 163
Adecco, 460
Adelphia, 22
Advantica, 20
Aetna Life & Casualty, 10, 240, 321
Alcoa, 57, 307
Alliance Data System, 165
Allianz, 404
Altru Health Systems, 438
American Century Investment, 438
American Express, 57, 415, 447
American Management Systems, 438
American Telephone & Telephone (AT&T), 3, 71, 161, 205, 206, 230, 445, 481
AmeriTax, 447
Ameritech, 313
Ames Rubber, 197, 203
Amoco, 78
Analog Devices, 57
Andersen Windows, 161
A&P, 242
Apple Computer, 57, 242
Applied Creative, Inc., 438
Applied Micro Circuits, 57
Autodesk, 316
Avon Products, 19–21, 268, 337

Babies R Us, 26
Bain & Company, 245–246
bakosgroup.com, 470
Bank of America, 307
Bank One, 57
BDO Seidman, 23
BeFree! Inc., 437

Bed, Bath & Beyond, 57
Bell Labs, 481
BellSouth, 20
Berkshire Hathaway, 403
Best Buy, 57
Bestfoods, 419
BETA Systems Software Inc., 420
Black & Decker, 57
Boeing, 115, 166, 267
Born Information Services, 438
BP (British Petroleum), 404
Brink's, Inc., 26
British Airways, 101–102
Broadcom, 57
Buckman Laboratories International, 17
Burger King, 402

CalPERS, 60
Campbell Soup, 230
Career Architects, 468
careerbuilder.com, 469
careercity.com, 469
careermart.com, 469
careersite.com, 470
CCH, Inc., 62
Cendant, 57
Charles Schwab, 403
CheckFree, 437
ChevronTexaco, 16, 19, 404, 441
Chi Chi's, 315
Chrysler, 149, 197, 264, 321, 368, 369–371, 419
Circuit City, 298
Cisco Systems, Inc., 281, 298, 315, 403, 438

Citigroup, 57, 403, 404, 439
Citizen Communications, 57
Coach, 268
Coca-Cola, 24, 57, 71–72, 403, 440
Cognex, 437–438
Colgate-Palmolive, 20, 57
Cometa Networks, 166
ComPsych, 83
Conseco, Inc., 22, 38
Consolidated Edison, 20
Coors, 321
Corning, Inc., 101
Costco, 419

DaimlerChrysler, 149, 161, 197, 264, 368, 369–371, 404, 419, 446
Dell Computer, 15, 16, 58, 202, 242, 277, 403, 415
Deutsche Telekom, 421
DiversityInc.com, 3
Dow Chemical, 24
Dress for Success, 268
Drucker Foundation, 355
Duke Power, 22
Dun & Bradstreet, 445
DuPont Corporation, 10

Eastman Chemical, 197, 199
Eastman Kodak, 415
eBay, 19, 337
Eddie Bauer, Inc., 240
Edge International, 279
Electronic Data Systems (EDS), 57
Enron, 22, 404, 447